Spices of the World Cookbook by McCormick

Revised Edition

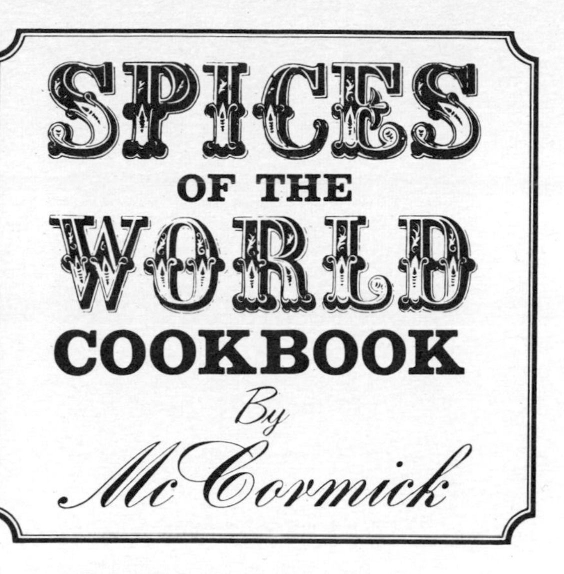

Revised Edition

Prepared and Tested
in the Kitchens of McCormick

McGraw-Hill Book Company

New York St. Louis San Francisco Auckland Bogotá Guatemala Hamburg
Johannesburg Lisbon London Madrid Mexico Montreal New Delhi Panama
Paris San Juan São Paulo Singapore Sydney Tokyo Toronto

Spices of the World Cookbook by McCormick

123456789 SEM SEM 87654

ISBN 0-07-044872-8

First McGraw-Hill Paperback Edition, 1984

Library of Congress Cataloging in Publication Data

McCormick and Company, Baltimore.
Spices of the World Cookbook.
1964 ed. prepared by Mary Collins and published
under title: The McCormick Spices of the World Cookbook.
Includes indexes.
1. Cookery. 2. Spices. I. Collins, Mary, pseud.
The McCormick spices of the world cookbook. II. Title.
TX715.M133 1979 641.6'3'83 79-14255
ISBN 0-07-044871-X
0-07-044872-8 (PBK)

Preface

Designed for all who appreciate fine food, this volume adds new dimensions to an ancient art.

For generations, McCormick & Company, Inc., has provided a variety of seasonings and flavorings to cooks at home and in many countries of the world. We take pleasure in sharing with you a wealth of knowledge in the art and science of food preparation. *The Spices of the World Cookbook by McCormick* will be equally at home in your library or kitchen.

In this revised edition we have retained the carefully developed content of the original book while adding many new recipes—all created and tested by the staff of our Corporate Test Kitchens.

We wish you the joys of creativity as you explore the world of cooking with spices and herbs.

Corporate Test Kitchens
McCormick & Co., Inc.
Hunt Valley, Maryland 21031

Contents

Brief History of Spices 1

How to Use Spices 7

General Cooking Information 47

Appetizers 61

Soups 81

Salads, Salad Dressings 95

Meats 113

Poultry 139

Sea Food 167

Casseroles, Special Dishes, 183

Vegetables 205

Special Appliance Cooking 225

Outdoor Cooking 237

Breads 253

Desserts 269

Cakes, Frostings 287

Pies 303

Cookies, Confections 321

Beverages 343

Sauces 357

Canning 377

Spice Index 395

General Index 415

Spices of the World Cookbook by McCormick

Revised Edition

Brief History of Spices

Today we take spices for granted. There they are, always handy on the spice shelf, as ordinary as our daily newspaper; and if we run out, they are as near as the neighborhood grocery or supermarket. We can scarcely imagine a time when spices weren't commonplace and familiar. Yet the fact is that in nearly all of recorded history, man's fate has been closely bound up with his hunger for these marvelous spices.

A trace of this urgency lingers in our subconscious memories. To most of us the word spices still conveys an impression of vague and wonderful adventure; and when we speak of the "spice of life," we mean something more than piquancy—we mean romance.

The first known reference to spices occurs in the scriptures of the ancient Assyrians. According to their version of the creation, which they chiseled into stone tablets 5,000 years ago, the gods who made the earth were so impressed by the difficulty of the task that they held a sort of celestial committee meeting before they began their work. And while they discussed the problems of the creation, they drank sesame seed wine.

Long before the Assyrians, men were well acquainted with spices. Archaeologists believe that the knowledge of seasoning extends back at least 50,000 years. Very likely the first experience with seasoning came when primitive men wrapped meat in leaves before cooking it on hot coals. Their purpose was to protect the meat from dirt and ashes; however, they soon learned that certain leaves imparted a pleasant new flavor to the meat.

Of course it was not only a pleasant flavor that made spices important. Primitive men often had to eat foods that were strong-tasting or even spoiled; and later on civilized men, too, suffered greatly from unpalatable diets. In the days before modern methods of preserving and refrigerating foodstuffs, spices made it possible to eat foods which otherwise would have been inedible.

In time it was discovered that certain spices also had medicinal properties, and many of the treatises written by the doctors of ancient Greece and Rome tell how to prepare herbs and spices for use as drugs. Wine mulled

with spices and honey was thought to be particularly effective in the treatment of many illnesses. Indeed, spices became important in all departments of life, even in religion. Today the ceremonial meaning of spicery remains in the incense used in many churches. Incense is only spices and other aromatics that have been prepared for burning.

For tens of thousands of years men relied on the aromatic plants they could find in their own regions; and fortunately, there are few parts of the earth which do not grow at least one or two native spices or herbs. The primitive tribes which inhabited the great forests of Europe could find dill, marjoram, parsley, thyme and several other herbs growing in their area. Generally speaking, the most important spices come from the East, specifically from India, Ceylon and the Spice Islands, which include Sumatra, Java, Bali, the Moluccas and neighboring territories. Pepper, which has always been and still is the most widely used spice, is the dried berry (called a peppercorn) of a vine that is native to Sumatra.

By the time the great civilizations of ancient Greece and Asia Minor had developed, in the centuries before the birth of Christ, a flourishing spice trade had sprung up between the East and the main cities of the Mediterranean region. The spices were brought from their source to various ports in India, where they were loaded on caravans for the long overland journey to Syria. Cities along the route—Persepolis, Susa, Palmyra, Damascus —became legendary outposts of romance for the boys and girls of ancient

Athens and Rome. The Bible gives numerous references to the importance of the spice trade. When the Queen of Sheba visited King Solomon, her principal gifts of state were "camels that bare spices"; and when Joseph was betrayed by his brothers, he was sold to the spice traders of a passing caravan.

As the Greek and Roman colonizers spread their civilizations throughout Europe, they took their knowledge of spices with them. It is on record, for example, that the first mustard seed were brought to England by Roman soldiers in 50 B.C. Very quickly the fierce tribes of Gaul and the Celtic outlanders learned the value of these "new" spices; and when Alaric the Visigoth subjugated Rome in 410 A.D., he demanded 3,000 pounds of peppercorns as part of his price for sparing the lives of the inhabitants.

When the great civilizations of the ancient world declined, the connection between Europe and the Orient was broken; and it was not until several centuries later that the spice trade was resumed. This time the Arabs, who were expanding aggressively eastward and westward from their base on the shores of the Red Sea, controlled traffic with the Far East. In fact, the Prophet Mohammed himself had married a widow whose wealth came

from the spice trade; and hence from the very beginning the Islamic Empire derived its strength from both religious and commercial considerations. For several hundred years the Moslems enjoyed a complete monopoly of the spice trade. They brought spices to such European ports as Venice and Seville, where they sold them for enormous profit. They either would not tell the Europeans where the spices came from or they invented elaborate and frightening tales of the dangers surrounding their origin. This only added, of course, to the mystery and romance already associated with the spice trade.

The value of spices to Europeans in the late Middle Ages can hardly be imagined today. A handful of cardamom was worth as much as a poor man's yearly wages, and many a slave was bought and sold for a few handfuls of peppercorns.

At last, however, the Europeans rediscovered the sources of the spice trade. Beginning with Marco Polo, more and more travelers ventured eastward and found where the centers of spice-growing and spice-trading were located. European traders organized new overland routes to the East, bringing new names—Kabul, Samarkand, Trebizond, Baghdad—into the mythology of Oriental adventure. And soon the intrepid sea explorers, men like Vasco da Gama, Columbus and Magellan, discovered practical sea routes to the lands of spice, and every major European port became a center of the spice trade. For years the dockworkers of London had their pockets sewed up to prevent them from pilfering peppercorns from the cargoes they unloaded. The first pure food law in history was an English ordinance passed in 1447 preventing the adulteration of spices and so checking fraud.

With the discovery of Central America and the islands of the Caribbean, new spices were added to the world's cuisine, notably paprika, cayenne and allspice. Some of these, such as paprika, became extremely popular in Europe, and then, centuries later, were reintroduced in America by emigrants from Central Europe.

The popularity of spices during the entire period of European expansion, from the fifteenth to the eighteenth century, cannot be exaggerated. Spice cookery reached extremes of complexity, especially in puddings and meat dishes; and the combinations of spices used might seem strange to modern palates. Hot spices, such as pepper, ginger and cloves from the Orient, were frequently mixed with native herbs like fennel and coriander. Sweet seasonings, such as anise, nutmeg and mint, were often added for good measure. These were the staple seasonings of the Renaissance diet, and these same seasonings and combinations of these seasonings have survived and are widely used in spice cookery today.

As the Arab monopoly of the spice trade declined, the great colonizing nations of Europe fought for supremacy. At first the Portuguese and Spanish, whose sea captains and navigators were supreme among early voyagers, enjoyed virtual dominion, and their sphere of influence extended from India and Burma to the Philippines. In 1493 Pope Alexander VI divided the New World between Spain and Portugal. In the 1500's Spain was dominant; then England and Holland successfully challenged her.

In the late seventeenth century America benefited indirectly from the spice trade. Boston-born Elihu Yale grew up in England where he worked as a clerk for the British East India Company, which held a monopoly on all trade with India and whose ships brought the first cargo of cinnamon from the Moluccas. He eventually became governor of Madras, India, and his fortune later endowed Yale University. In the late eighteenth and early nineteenth century Americans became directly involved in the spice trade as the clipper ships of New England began to dominate world trade. Indeed, so many pepper voyages from New England to Sumatra were undertaken that in 1843 the price of pepper dropped to less than three cents a pound, a disastrous slump which affected many aspects of American business. Later the New England spice trade fell off sharply when piracy in the Java and China Seas made the long pepper voyages too dangerous. Meanwhile the spice business, like the rest of the country, was moving west. In 1835 American settlers in Texas developed chili powder by combining various ground peppers from Mexico, thus uncovering an entire new dimension of American taste. Later in California, once the gold rush had subsided, mustard seed and some herbs were grown.

America was settled by people from many nations who, in their native lands, enjoyed dishes which were distinctively spiced. The move to America often separated them from their source of flavoring materials. Here, a different, better or more varied food supply removed one of the previous incentives for spicing. And many times the newer generation—to its own loss—consciously tried to depart from the traditional dishes of the old country. Only in recent times has the increase in international travel created a vogue for foods seasoned with spices from everywhere in the

world. World War II provided an especially keen incitement; hundreds of thousands of American soldiers brought home from the war a taste for Oriental and Mediterranean foods. For example, between 1948 and 1956 the sale of oregano in the United States increased 5200 per cent. This was primarily the effect of an extraordinary new demand for pizza and other Italian specialties. Similarly, monosodium glutamate, which in cruder form had been used for centuries in Japan, was eagerly accepted by American consumers during the 1950's.

Today modern methods of growing, curing, grinding, mixing and packaging have made available a wide variety of spices, and at a cost which permits everyone to maintain a well-stocked spice shelf. Many spices, such as basil, marjoram and tarragon, are well-known and widely enjoyed; others, such as turmeric and fenugreek, are still, for the most part, known only to commercial users. But the interest in experimenting in spice cookery prevails throughout the country, and the appetite for new dishes from foreign lands is virtually insatiable. The result is that Americans today enjoy more interesting, more varied and more satisfying food than any nation has ever known before.

HOW TO USE SPICES

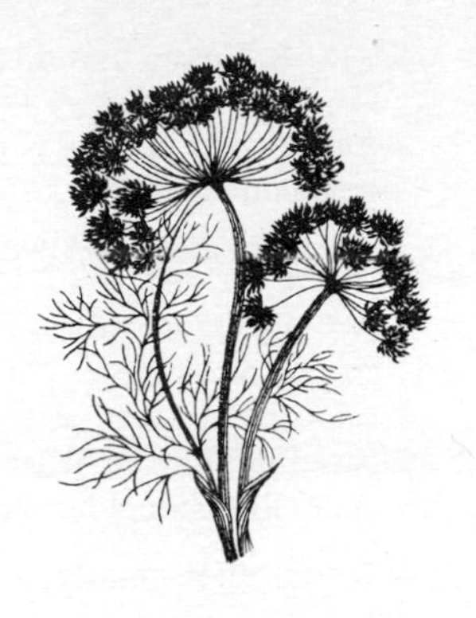

The term "spice" or "spices" is often used in a general sense to mean any aromatic flavoring material of vegetable origin, and is often used in a more specific sense, together with the terms "herb," "seed" and "condiment" as defined below.

Spices: Aromatic natural products which are the dried seeds, buds, fruit or flower parts, bark or roots of plants, usually of tropical origin.
Herbs: Aromatic leaves and sometimes the flowers of plants, usually of temperate origin.
Seeds: Aromatic, dried, small, whole fruits or seeds, usually of temperate origin.
Blend: A mixture of spices, herbs, seeds or other flavoring materials either ground or whole.
Condiment: Any spice, herb or seed; but more frequently a pungent, prepared mixture of seasonings sometimes in liquid form. Condiments in many forms may be served as an accompaniment to foods.

Tastes differ greatly; therefore, it is very difficult to give exacting and precise directions for seasoning. What may be the ultimate to one person may be objectionable to another. The seasoning of food must vary to suit the tastes of those whom you are serving. One important rule to remember is that seasonings should be used in small quantities, particularly if it is a new flavor, as one may always add more if desired, but it is impossible to correct or remove seasoning if too much has been used initially.

Seasonings of all kinds, as well as spices and herbs, should enhance the natural flavor of food, never overpower it. Of course, there will always be a few exceptions to any rule as is the case in dishes such as curry or chili.

Spices and herbs make it possible for you to serve food which has variety and is more appetizing in aroma, more appealing in color and tastier. Spice and herb cookery need not be complicated nor time-consuming nor expensive. It doesn't necessarily mean preparing and serving fancy, hot, exotic dishes; although, you might find these to be fun to prepare occasionally.

Well seasoned food, very simply, is food that has been made to taste especially good without any predominating flavor. It is food that has been given a bit of flavor variety—through the correct use of spices and herbs.

GUIDE TO CREATIVE SEASONING

The simplest cooking methods can be employed along with imaginative use of herbs and spices for an endless variety of delicious flavors in everyday foods. It is best to start with small amounts of spice and taste to correct seasoning.

MEATS may be seasoned before, during, or after cooking. Steaks and chops may be seasoned before cooking, marinated, or seasoned after cooking. Stews develop the best flavor when spices and herbs are added during cooking. The surface of a roast should be rubbed with seasonings before cooking. Salt and pepper are basic. Season-All® or Bon Appétit may be used in place of salt. A blend of two or three herbs, crushed in the palm of the hand, then mixed with the salt and pepper, adds subtle flavor. Such a blend can be rubbed on roasts, steaks and chops; added to melted butter or sauce used for basting chicken or fish during cooking; mixed with ground meat; or sprinkled over meat patties before cooking. Use a small quantity of one or more of the suggested seasonings.

FOR BEEF

Garlic
Onion
Marjoram
Rosemary
Basil
Tarragon
Thyme
Oregano
Chili Powder
Curry Powder
Bay Leaves

FOR PORK

Allspice
Anise Seed
Basil
Bay Leaves
Caraway Seed
Cloves
Curry Powder
Dill Weed
Garlic
Ginger
Lemon Peel
Orange Peel
Marjoram
Mustard
Nutmeg
Onion
Oregano
Poultry Seasoning
Rosemary
Sage
Savory
Tarragon
Thyme

FOR CHICKEN OR VEAL

Celery Salt
Bay Leaves
Dill Weed
Fennel Seed
Garlic
Mustard
Onion
Paprika
Oregano
Parsley
Poultry Seasoning
Rosemary
Saffron
Sage
Savory
Sesame Seed
Tarragon
Thyme

FOR LAMB

Garlic
Dill Weed
Mustard
Rosemary
Thyme
Tarragon
Basil
Curry Powder
Onion
Marjoram
Mint
Savory
Oregano

SEAFOOD Scallops, shrimp, crabmeat and fish—broiled, baked, fried, poached or steamed. Seasoning may be used in melted butter for basting, in stuffings for whole baked fish, in batter or breading for fried seafood, added to water for poaching and steaming or used in sauces and casseroles.

Bay Leaves
Curry Powder
Garlic
Lemon Peel
Marjoram
Anise Seed
Basil
Celery Seed or Salt
Dill Weed
Fennel Seed
Mustard
Onion
Oregano
Parsley
Red Pepper
Poultry Seasoning
Rosemary
Saffron
Sage
Savory
Sesame Seed
Tarragon
Thyme

VEGETABLES Herbs and spices enhance the natural flavors of vegetables. Add seasoning to the cooking water or mix herbs with melted butter and sauces. Try one or a combination using small amounts of the suggested seasonings.

GREEN BEANS plain and with mushrooms, onions, water chestnuts or almonds.

Tarragon
Dill
Marjoram
Onion
Basil
Thyme

TOMATOES and combinations with onions, green peppers, mushrooms, celery, corn or zucchini.

Basil
Bay Leaves
Celery Salt
Dill
Garlic
Marjoram
Onion
Oregano
Rosemary
Savory
Tarragon
Thyme
Chili Powder
Curry Powder

CORN

Celery Salt
Chili Powder
Dill
Curry Powder
Marjoram
Onion
Parsley
Savory
Thyme

CARROTS and combinations with cauliflower, onions or celery.

Allspice	Marjoram	Oregano
Bay Leaves	Mint	Parsley
Celery Salt	Mustard	Tarragon
Dill Weed	Onion	Thyme

SPINACH and combinations with mushrooms, onions or tomatoes.

Nutmeg	Basil	Mustard
Mace	Marjoram	Oregano
Onion	Mint	Thyme

PEAS and combinations with mushrooms, onions or carrots.

Basil	Marjoram	Tarragon
Mint	Onion	Dill Weed

EGGPLANT and combinations with tomatoes, onions and mushrooms.

Oregano	Cloves	Sage
Bay Leaves	Garlic	Savory
Basil	Marjoram	Tarragon
Chili Powder	Onion	Thyme
Curry Powder	Rosemary	

ONIONS boiled or creamed.

Cloves	Basil	Sage
Paprika	Bay Leaves	Savory
Parsley	Celery Salt	Tarragon
Nutmeg	Marjoram	Thyme
Dill Weed	Oregano	

POTATOES mashed, in salad, stuffed baked, au gratin or scalloped with onions.

Celery Salt	Marjoram	Parsley
Dill Weed	Onion	Poppy Seed
Coriander Seed	Oregano	Sesame Seed
Celery Seed	Paprika	Thyme

SALAD DRESSINGS In oil and vinegar or mayonnaise based dressings.

TOSSED GREEN OR COOKED VEGETABLE SALADS.

Basil	Garlic	Oregano
Bay Leaves	Marjoram	Tarragon
Dill Weed	Onion	Thyme

POTATO OR MACARONI SALAD

Caraway Seed	Mustard	Poppy Seed
Celery Seed	Onion	Savory
Coriander Seed	Oregano	Sesame Seed
Dill Weed	Paprika	Tarragon
Garlic	Parsley	Thyme
Marjoram		

FRUIT SALADS

Allspice	Cloves	Mint
Anise Seed	Ginger	Nutmeg
Caraway Seed	Lemon Peel	Poppy Seed
Cardamom	Orange Peel	Sesame Seed
Cinnamon	Mace	Vanilla Bean

BREADS Add to dough for white or whole wheat bread, 1½ teaspoons to 2 teaspoons per loaf. Use one herb or a mixture:

Dill Weed	Oregano	Tarragon
Basil	Savory	Thyme
Marjoram		

Mix with melted butter to be brushed on French bread before heating or toasting:

Garlic	Oregano	Basil
Onion	Thyme	Dill Weed

Add to batter for cornbread—½ to 1 teaspoon in batter to fill an 8-inch square pan:

Dill Weed	Marjoram	Tarragon
Caraway Seed	Savory	Thyme

Add to biscuit dough, dumplings or waffle batter—½ to 1 teaspoon to 2 cups flour:

Basil	Marjoram	Savory
Cardamom	Oregano	Thyme
Dill Weed	Parsley	

ALLSPICE *(Pimenta officinalis);* also called Pimento, Jamaica Pepper, or Jamaica Pimento; native to Western Hemisphere and the only major spice produced exclusively in this area: discovered by Columbus in 1494, but not recognized as a spice at that time; introduced in Europe in early 17th century; the nearly ripe fruit of evergreen tree of myrtle family; fruit or berries are sun-dried until dark reddish-brown in color; available both whole and ground; flavor resembles a blend of Cloves, Cinnamon and Nutmeg and intensifies in food on standing.

USES:

Allspice has versatility in its uses. Whole Allspice may be used in soups, stews, pot roasts, sauerbraten, sauces, marinades, beverages, pickled beets, pickles, preserves, stewed fruit and in poaching, boiling or steaming fish or shellfish.

Use ground Allspice in cakes, cookies, candy, frostings, plum pudding, fruit pies, mincemeat, fruit, meat loaf, pot roast, chili sauce, ketchup, tomato sauce, spaghetti sauce, barbecue sauce, French dressing, soups, pickled eggs, sweet potatoes and squash.

SUGGESTED AMOUNTS TO USE IN VARIOUS DISHES:

Ground

¼ teaspoon to 1 teaspoon in angel food cake mix or other cake mixes
⅛ teaspoon to ¼ teaspoon in 2 cups sweet potatoes
1 teaspoon in 1½ to 2 cups graham cracker crumbs for pie crust
¼ teaspoon to ½ teaspoon to 1 pound powdered sugar for frosting
½ teaspoon to 1 cup coconut, toasted
½ teaspoon to 1-inch thick slice ham
2 teaspoons to 2 cups waffle mix or recipe using 2 cups flour
⅛ teaspoon to 1 pound ground beef

Whole

3 in 2 to 3 cups pea soup
4 to 6 for each 2 pounds fish when poaching

ANISE SEED *(Pimpinella anisum);* native to Mediterranean area, also grown in Mexico; one of the commodities taxed by Edward I for revenue to repair London Bridge; green-grey fruit or seed of plant of parsley family; available whole and in extract; unmistakable strong licorice flavor.

USES:

Anise Seed may be used whole or crushed in cookies, cakes, breads, candy, cheese, applesauce, sausage, beverages, fruit pies, pickles, beef stew, fruit salads, salad dressings, appetizers, baked apples, stewed fruits, sauces and in fish and shellfish cookery.

SUGGESTED AMOUNTS TO USE IN VARIOUS DISHES:

¼ teaspoon to ½ teaspoon, crushed, in 8-inch coffee cake recipe or mix
1 tablespoon sprinkled over tops of 2 dozen cup cakes
½ teaspoon to 1 teaspoon, crushed, to 6 apples—baked or stewed
1½ teaspoons to 2 teaspoons in cookie recipe yielding about 5 dozen
¼ teaspoon to ½ teaspoon, crushed, in 2 tablespoons butter for basting 1 pound fish
¼ teaspoon to ½ teaspoon in 8-ounce package cream cheese for spread for canapés

BASIL *(Ocimum basilicum);* also called Sweet Basil; native to India, also comes from North Mediterranean countries; called "Herb of Kings" by ancient Greeks and worshiped in India; leaf of plant of mint family; available as dried leaf; has aromatic clove-like aroma.

USES:

Basil is sometimes called the "tomato herb" and may be used in most tomato recipes. Also widely used when preparing stuffings, noodles, rice, beef stew, venison, pork, hamburger, meat loaf, duck, lobster, shrimp, fish, veal, lamb, pizza, green or vegetable salads, French dressing, soups, eggplant, potatoes, carrots, spinach, peas, eggs, cheese, jelly, barbecue sauce and blends well with other herbs in seasoning foods.

SUGGESTED AMOUNTS TO USE IN VARIOUS DISHES:

¼ teaspoon to ¾ teaspoon in ½ cup butter for spreads on bread
¼ teaspoon to ½ teaspoon in 2½ cups tomato or vegetable soup
¼ teaspoon to ½ teaspoon in 2 cups green vegetables
¾ teaspoon to 1½ teaspoons to 1½ pounds pork chops or roasts
½ teaspoon to ¾ teaspoon to 1 head cauliflower
⅛ teaspoon to ¼ teaspoon in 2 tablespoons butter for basting 1 pound fish or 1½-pound chicken
¼ teaspoon to ½ teaspoon to 6 eggs—scrambled, egg salad or eggs à la goldenrod

BAY LEAVES *(Laurus nobilis);* also called Laurel Leaves; native to Mediterranean area; ancient Greeks gave bay or laurel wreaths to winners of Olympic Games, poets and heroes; aromatic dried green leaf of evergreen tree; has a distinct, strong, pungent flavor, almost bitter; strength of flavor increases with amount used and cooking time; usually removed from food when cooking is completed.

USES:

Bay Leaves are used in soups; chowders; pickling; steaming, boiling or poaching fish and shellfish; tomato juice; custard sauce; French dressing; marinades; water for cooking vegetables; and when preparing aspics, pot roast, sauerbraten, game, variety meats and stews.

BEEF FLAVOR BASE; seasoned extract of beef; add to water for broth; gives flavor to sauces and gravy; decrease salt in recipe when using.

USES:

Beef Flavor Base is an excellent base for soup and gravy. It may also be used in sauces; sour cream and onion dips; casseroles; vegetables; stew; beef pot pie; noodles; certain molded salads; spreads; dumplings; beef hash; hamburgers; meat loaf; meat balls; wild or brown rice; fried rice; liquid for simmering meat balls, Swiss or country fried steak and pot roast; spaghetti sauce and in butter or liquids for stuffings.

BON APPÉTIT®; a blend of seasonings which has a celery note; used to enhance most foods with the exception of sweets; decrease salt in recipe when using. Bon Appétit® is an extremely versatile seasoning.

USES:

Use in all types of meat cookery, chicken and other poultry, soups, some breads, sauces, gravies, vegetables, appetizers, eggs, cheese dishes, fish and sea food, salads, salad dressings, dips, spreads, sandwich fillings, stuffings, tomato juice, cocktail sauce and seasoned butter. May also be used at the table to sprinkle over food to taste, as salt and pepper.

SUGGESTED AMOUNTS TO USE IN VARIOUS DISHES:

1 teaspoon to 1½ teaspoons to 1 pound ground beef
½ teaspoon to 1 teaspoon to 6 eggs—stuffed, scrambled or for omelets
¾ teaspoon to 1½ teaspoons to 2 cups vegetables
¾ teaspoon to 1½ teaspoons to 1½ pounds beef, veal or other meats
1½ teaspoons to 2 teaspoons to 1 pound dried beans or lentils
¼ teaspoon to ½ teaspoon to each 1 cup white sauce
½ teaspoon in 1½ to 2 cups oyster stew
Sprinkle to taste over baked potatoes, French fries, cottage cheese, tossed salads or sliced tomatoes.

CARAWAY SEED *(Carum carvi);* native to Europe; imported chiefly from the Netherlands; recorded in 1552 B.C. in medical papyrus of Thebes; used by ancient Greeks and Romans in cooking; the fruit or seed of plant of parsley family; small, brown, crescent-shaped seed; distinctive pleasant flavor with sweet undertone; use sparingly.

USES:

Caraway Seed gives rye bread its distinctive flavor. Also use in sauerkraut; cabbage; corn bread; biscuits; waffles; rice; cheese dips; cottage cheese; noodles; cheese straws; potatoes; cookies; baked or stewed apples; seasoned butters; cake; beef or lamb stew; marinades for meats; potato, cream of pea and corn soup and chowders; turnips; cauliflower; coleslaw;

marinated cucumbers; beets; green beans; carrots; zucchini; cabbage rolls; and in preparing pork, lamb, spareribs, roast goose and guinea hen.

SUGGESTED AMOUNTS TO USE IN VARIOUS DISHES:

1 teaspoon to 1 tablespoon to 2 cups corn bread, waffle or biscuit mix
1 teaspoon in ¼ cup melted butter for vegetables
½ teaspoon to ¾ teaspoon, crushed, to 1½ pounds pork
¼ teaspoon to 1 teaspoon to 8-ounce package noodles
1 tablespoon to 2 tablespoons to 1½ cups cheese dip
¼ teaspoon to 1 teaspoon for each pound sauerkraut
½ teaspoon to 1 teaspoon in one-crust pastry for cheese, onion, meat or vegetable pies
1 teaspoon to 2 teaspoons to 3 cups potato salad
½ teaspoon to 1 teaspoon mixed in batter of pound cake or spice cake or sprinkled over top before baking
½ teaspoon in vinegar or cream dressings for 2 cups sliced cucumbers

CARDAMOM *(Elletaria cardamomum);* native to India; also comes from Guatemala and Ceylon; grown in the garden of King of Babylon in 721 B.C.; used in perfumes in ancient Greece and Rome and in cosmetic industry today; fruit or seed of plant of ginger family; small three-sided, creamy white, pithy pod, having no flavor and containing aromatic dark brown seed; available both whole and ground (decorticated —pod removed); aromatic, pungent, sweet flavor; use with discretion and is good to freshen breath.

USES:

Cardamom is a principal spice in Danish pastry. Also use in coffee cake, sweet breads, fruit salad dressings, fruit salads, curry powder, fruit pies, cookies, cakes, pickles, pickling spice, gingerbread, punch, grape jelly, custards, puddings, sweet potatoes, squash, fruit soups, hot spiced wines, barbecue sauce, rice pudding and honey.

SUGGESTED AMOUNTS TO USE IN VARIOUS DISHES:

Ground

Dash to ¼ teaspoon in blueberry muffin mix or recipe making 12 muffins
Dash to ⅛ teaspoon in 4 cups crushed strawberries, peaches or raspberries
⅛ teaspoon to ½ teaspoon to 8 egg whites for meringue shells or floating island meringues
⅛ teaspoon to ¼ teaspoon in 2-layer cake recipe or cake mix
Dash in 2 cups baked beans
Dash in 1 cup coconut, toasted
⅛ teaspoon to ¼ teaspoon to 2 cups sweet potatoes

Whole

2 to 4 to a 4-pound roast for sauerbraten
2 to 3 in 1 quart mulled wine

4 to 6 in 6 cups Glögg
4 to 6 in frozen fruit ring (1- to 1½-quart mold) for punch
6 to 8 in 2 gallons fruit punch
2 to 4 in 2½ cups fruit for compote
4 to 6 in 2 cups scalded milk for custards

Ten whole Cardamom, pods removed and brown seeds crushed, equals ½ teaspoon ground Cardamom.

CELERY SEED, SALT AND FLAKES *(Apium graveolens);* native to Mediterranean area and Central Asia; history says very little about use of Celery Seed in cooking; Celery Seed is imported from India and France; is the dried fruit or seed of celery plant; aromatic with slight bitterness; aroma characteristic of celery; Celery Salt is a blend of ground celery seed and salt; Celery Flakes are dried leaves and some stalk of the American celery plant.

USES:

Celery Seed is widely used in pickling. Also use in canapés, dips, bread and rolls, pastries, tomato juice, tomato sauce, egg dishes, meat loaf and hamburger, stews, soups and chowders, salad dressings, tuna or salmon salad, stewed tomatoes, coleslaw, potato salad, tomato aspic, fruit salad, sandwich spreads, vegetables, croquettes, sauerkraut, clam juice, relishes, stuffings and butters. Celery Salt may also be used in any of the above dishes; however, since it contains salt, reduce the salt in the recipe.

Celery Flakes may be used in soups, stews, tomato juice cocktail, sauces, pot pie, stuffings; or in preparing pot roast, roast duck or goose.

SUGGESTED AMOUNTS TO USE IN VARIOUS DISHES:

Celery Seed

⅛ teaspoon to ¼ teaspoon in 4 cups potato salad
1 teaspoon to 2 teaspoons in 2 tablespoons butter for brushing over hot bread and rolls
½ teaspoon to 2 teaspoons in 1 cup coleslaw dressing
½ teaspoon to 2 teaspoons to each pint pickles or relish
1 teaspoon in 1½ cups salad dressing for fruits or vegetables

Celery Salt

1 to 1¼ teaspoons to 1 pound liver
½ teaspoon to 1 teaspoon to 6 eggs—stuffed, creamed or in salad
Dash to ¼ teaspoon in 1 cup spread for sandwiches—deviled ham, tuna or American, Cheddar or cream cheese

Celery Flakes

2 tablespoons to ¼ cup in 2 cups white sauce for cream of celery soup
1 tablespoon to 3 tablespoons in 4 cups tomato juice for making aspic
1 tablespoon to 2 tablespoons to 3 pounds meat for stew or pot roast or 3 pounds chicken for stewing
2 tablespoons to 3 tablespoons in 4 cups vegetable soup

CHICKEN FLAVOR BASE; gives richer flavor to foods; serves as a base for chicken soup or stock; decrease salt in recipe when using; is a very versatile seasoning.

USES:

Chicken Flavor Base may be used in preparing certain molded salads, dips, spreads, vegetables, soups, pilaf, poultry dishes, stuffed eggs, rice, noodles, creamed dishes, biscuits, dumplings, gravy, sauces, poached eggs and fish, curries, chicken pie, skillet dishes, casseroles, in butter or liquid for stuffings and in water for boiling corn.

CHILI POWDER; blend of spices; Aztecs used similar blend but Chili Powder is truly from United States; Hot Mexican-Style Chili Powder is available in some sections; flavor earthy and slightly sweet; flavor usually intended to dominate food rather than enhance.

USES:

Chili Powder is a major ingredient in many Mexican or Mexican-style dishes such as chili con carne, tamale pie, enchiladas and tamales. It may also be used in cocktail, cream, tomato and barbecue sauces; dips; egg dishes; gravy; stews; hamburgers and meat loaf; salad dressings; venison dishes; corn and corn meal dishes; some skillet dishes; chicken dishes; cheese dishes; marinades for meats and poultry; seasoned, toasted bread slices; guacamole; bean casseroles; eggplant and Spanish rice.

SUGGESTED AMOUNTS TO USE IN VARIOUS DISHES:

¼ teaspoon to ½ teaspoon in 2 cups cream-style corn
⅛ teaspoon to ½ teaspoon to 1 large avocado when making guacamole
1 tablespoon to 2 tablespoons for ground beef, noodle or rice skillet dishes (about 8 cups)
2 tablespoons to 3 tablespoons in 6 cups chili con carne
¼ teaspoon in 1½ cups French dressing
1 tablespoon to 2 tablespoons to 4-pound pot roast

CINNAMON *[Cinnamomum zeylanicum (C. loureirii) (C. cassia)];* term "cinnamon" refers to several *Cinnamomum* species grown in Southeast Asia and Indonesia, sometimes called cassia, and to another *Cinnamomum* species grown in Ceylon which is mild in flavor, rarely sold in this country, and is always called cinnamon; in 1500 B.C. Egyptian Queen Hatshepsut used Cinnamon in perfumes; Moses told by God to use Cinnamon in preparing holy anointing oil; was one of the principal spices monopolized by the Dutch in 17th century; is the dried, inner bark of evergreen tree of laurel family; reddish-brown in color; the bark is peeled from young shoots of tree biannually; available whole (called sticks or quills), ground and as Cinnamon Sugar which is ground cinnamon mixed with sugar; is the most important baking spice; distinctively sweet, mildly pungent and spicy.

USES:

Cinnamon is one of the best known and most versatile of all spices. Whole Cinnamon is used in pickling and preserving; beverages; certain apple dishes; stewed prunes, apricots and other dried fruits; cooking some vegetables; hot chocolate; mulled wine; fruit compotes and as stirrers for beverages.

Ground Cinnamon is used in preparing cinnamon toast, sweet breads, fruit soup, some vegetable and meat soups, hot chocolate, fruit punches, plum pudding, fruit cake, spice cake, apple pie, apple dumplings, applesauce, apple butter, baked apples, fruit salads, puddings, custards, sweet potatoes, squash, pumpkin pie, cookies, ice cream, French toast, doughnuts, cinnamon rolls, jams, preserves, ham glaze, ham, pork, lamb roast, lamb or beef stews, creamed chicken, spiced nuts, chocolate fudge and dessert sauces. Sprinkle over cakes; cookies; hot cereals; eggnog; milk shakes; custards; broiled grapefruit and rice, bread or tapioca puddings.

AMOUNTS TO USE IN VARIOUS DISHES:

Ground

1 teaspoon to 4 teaspoons in 2-layer chocolate cake recipe or mix
½ teaspoon to 1 teaspoon in chocolate pudding recipe or mix using about 2 cups milk
⅛ teaspoon to ¾ teaspoon in vanilla pudding recipe or mix using about 2 cups milk
1 teaspoon in 1 quart vanilla ice cream
1 teaspoon in 2½ to 3 cups apples for pie, apple crisp or stewed apples
¼ teaspoon to 1 teaspoon in 2 cups sweet potatoes
Dash to ⅛ teaspoon in 1 quart chicken, tomato or fruit soup

Whole

1 3-inch piece to 4 cups rhubarb
1 to 2 3-inch pieces to 3 cups stewed fruit or fruit compotes
1 to 2 3-inch pieces in 1 quart hot beverage such as cider, tea or coffee
1 to 2 3-inch pieces to 1 quart cranberries for pie, sauce, relish or salad
1 3-inch piece in making 2 cups custard sauce
1 3-inch piece in each quart spiced peaches

CLOVES *(Eugenia caryophyllata);* name comes from "clou" (French) meaning nail; native to Molucca Islands, also from Zanzibar and the Malagasy Republic; courtiers required to hold Cloves in mouth when addressing emperor during Chinese Han Dynasty 206 B.C. to 220 A.D.; Constantine presented Cloves to Bishop of Rome; seed of the clove tree were stolen from the Dutch in 18th century in an attempt to break Dutch monopoly on spice trade; is the dried, unopened bud of evergreen tree of myrtle family; available whole and ground; whole Cloves resemble nails; reddish-brown in color; flavor is penetrating, sweet and pungent—almost hot; use cautiously; flavor intensifies upon standing.

USES:

Whole Cloves are used widely for garnishes as well as flavor. Use to stud ham, fruit, fruit peels, onions or glazed pork or beef. Use in beverages, pot roast, marinades, sauces, pickling, soups, tomato juice, spiced tongue and in making pomander balls.

Ground Cloves is used in spice cakes, fruit cakes, gingerbread, plum pudding, cookies, some breads, fruit salads, chili sauce, ketchup, pickling, frostings, cooked fruits, beef stew, pot roast, tomatoes, sweet potatoes, squash, green vegetables, spiced nuts, meringues, glazes, mincemeat, fruit pies, beverages, soups and in combination with other spices.

SUGGESTED AMOUNTS TO USE IN VARIOUS DISHES:

Ground

⅛ teaspoon to ¼ teaspoon in 4 cups rhubarb
¾ teaspoon to 6-pound pork roast
Dash to ¼ teaspoon in mincemeat or fruit pies
⅛ teaspoon in 2 cups green vegetables, squash, carrots or sweet potatoes
¼ teaspoon to ½ teaspoon in 8 cups blueberry, cherry or grape jam or jelly
½ teaspoon in cookie recipe yielding about 7 dozen cookies
½ teaspoon to 1 teaspoon in recipe yielding 12 to 14 pounds fruit cake

Whole

4 to 12 when cooking 1 cup rice
1 to 2 for each cup hot or iced tea or mulled wine
2 to 3 for each peach in making spiced pickled peaches
6 to 8 in marinade for 4 pounds meat
1 in each Kaurabiedes (Greek Easter cookie)
½ teaspoon to 1 teaspoon in 2 cups spiced cherries

CORIANDER *(Coriandrum sativum);* native to Southern Europe and Mediterranean region; recorded in 1552 B.C. in medical papyrus of Thebes; Moses compared color of manna with Coriander Seed; ancient Greeks and Romans used it in love potions; is the dried fruit or seed of plant belonging to parsley family and has slight lemon flavor.

USES:

Use the whole Coriander Seed in punch, sweet pickles, after-dinner coffee and wassail bowl. The crushed seed are used in preparing candies; cookies; gingerbread; Danish pastry; poaching, broiling or baking fish; chicken; curry sauces; sausage; meat loaf and hamburgers; bean, pea, lentil and vegetable-beef soups and Scotch broth; apple pie; coffee cake; sweet buns; muffins; waffles; rice pudding; bread pudding; tapioca; custards; cream cheese (especially good for filling for date bread); applesauce; stewed fruits; fruit sauces; beef or lamb stew; roast pork; pork chops; ham; stuffing for poultry and game and meat sauces.

SUGGESTED AMOUNTS TO USE IN VARIOUS DISHES:

2 teaspoons, crushed, to 3-pound chicken
¾ teaspoon, crushed, in 9- or 10-inch apple pie
½ teaspoon to 1 teaspoon, crushed, to 1 pound fish
¼ teaspoon, crushed, in 2 cups biscuit mix or recipe making 12 biscuits or muffins
1 teaspoon, crushed, to 2 pounds ground beef
¼ teaspoon, crushed, in 1 quart vegetable-beef soup
¼ teaspoon, crushed, in ¼ cup butter for 2 cups vegetables
1 whole seed in each cup demitasse coffee
6 to 10 whole seeds in marinade for 2 pounds meat

CUMIN *(Cuminum cyminum);* also Comino and Cummin; native to Mediterranean region; imported from Iran and Morocco; Babylonian and Assyrian doctors used it in drugs; used as food preservative by early Greeks and Romans; is the dried, yellowish-brown fruit or seed of plant of parsley family; available whole and ground; has an earthy and strong flavor; use sparingly.

USES:

Cumin is used commercially as a principal ingredient in both Chili Powder and Curry Powder. Cumin Seed are sometimes substituted for Caraway Seed. May be used either whole or ground in cheese and cheese dishes, rice, chili con carne, tamales, tamale pie, eggs, meat loaf and hamburgers, soup, stew, salad dressings, tomato sauce, barbecue sauce, sauerkraut, cookies, bread, marinades for shish kebab, potatoes, lentils, cabbage, dried beans of all kinds and in cooking game, wild fowl and spareribs.

SUGGESTED AMOUNTS TO USE IN VARIOUS DISHES:

⅛ teaspoon to ¼ teaspoon in cooking 1 cup rice
Dash to ¼ teaspoon to 6 eggs—stuffed or baked Mexican style
¼ teaspoon to ½ teaspoon in marinade for 1½ pounds lamb or beef
Dash to ⅛ teaspoon in 1 cup salad dressing or mayonnaise
Dash to ⅛ teaspoon in 4 cups chowders, bisques and lentil, bean, pea or chicken soup
Dash to ½ teaspoon to 3 pounds beef for pot roast or stew

Ground Cumin and Cumin Seed, whole or crushed, may be used interchangeably in many recipes.

CURRY POWDER; not a single spice but a blend of many spices which will vary according to the type Curry Powder as well as to the manufacturer; basic ingredient for all curried dishes; available as Indian Curry Powder, mild, and Madras Curry Powder, hot; is golden yellow to yellow-brown in color; use sparingly at first; may be used to enhance the flavor of food as well as to dominate; has an exotic aroma; is one of the oldest spice blends; originated in India where the Indians mixed their own spices to taste, and probably varied from time to time or meal to meal. Curry in India is usually very hot.

USES:

Both Indian and Madras Curry Powder are used to make curried beef, lamb, fish, shrimp, lobster, rice, chicken, meat pastries, meat balls, eggs, fruit, pork, veal, duck, sauce, soup, casseroles, dips and as a seasoning in salad dressings, some vegetables, dried beans, breads and marinades.

SUGGESTED AMOUNTS TO USE IN VARIOUS DISHES:

1 tablespoon to 3 tablespoons to 1 pound cubed lamb
½ teaspoon to 1 teaspoon in corn bread recipe or mix making 12 muffins
1 tablespoon to 2 tablespoons in 6 cups mixed fruit for compote
¼ teaspoon to ½ teaspoon for 6 stuffed eggs
1 teaspoon to 3 teaspoons for 2 cups creamy curry sauce
1 teaspoon in 1 cup mayonnaise, cream cheese, dairy sour cream or a combination of these for a dip
½ teaspoon to 1 teaspoon in 2 cups sea food salad

DILL *(Anethum graveolens);* native to Europe; Dill Seed imported from India; Dill Weed grown in California; was used in drugs by Babylonian and Assyrian doctors; the dried fruit or seed and leaves of plant of parsley family; is available as seed and weed (leaves); Dill Seed are flat, oval and light brown; Dill Weed is bright green; the flavor of Dill Weed is delicate, more subtle than Dill Seed and imparts a pleasing flavor to mild or bland foods; Dill Seed have a pungent, aromatic and characteristic flavor.

USES:

Dill Seed are used in dill pickles, Kosher dill pickles, salads, sauerkraut, green beans, egg dishes, tomato juice, soups, sauces, cottage and cream cheese, stews, pickled beets, salad dressings, breads, butters and in preparing fish, shellfish and chicken.

Dill Weed is used in salads, sauces, egg dishes, tomato juice, vegetables, breads, fish and shellfish recipes, cottage or cream cheese, salad dressings, noodles, rice and may be used as a garnish; 1 to 2 teaspooons in each pint may be used in combination with Dill Seed for pickling cucumbers or green beans.

SUGGESTED AMOUNTS TO USE IN VARIOUS DISHES:

Dill Seed

¼ teaspoon to 1 teaspoon to 1 head cauliflower
⅛ teaspoon to ½ teaspoon in 2 cups green vegetables
½ teaspoon to ¾ teaspoon, crushed, to 1 pound ground beef
3 tablespoons to 5 tablespoons in each quart dill pickles
¼ teaspoon to ½ teaspoon, crushed, in 2 tablespoons butter for seasoning fish, vegetables or bread

Dill Weed

⅛ teaspoon to 1 teaspoon in 1½ cups cottage cheese
¼ teaspoon to ½ teaspoon in 1 cup white sauce
¼ teaspoon to ½ teaspoon to 6 stuffed eggs

¼ teaspoon to ¾ teaspoon in 2 cups green vegetables
½ teaspoon to 1 teaspoon in 8-ounce package noodles
¼ teaspoon to ½ teaspoon to 3-pound chicken
½ teaspoon in 1 cup dairy sour cream

FENNEL SEED *(Foeniculum vulgare);* native to Mediterranean region; imported from India; was used in drugs by Babylonian and Assyrian doctors; grew in gardens of Charlemagne; Puritans nibbled the seed in church and called it "meetin' seed"; is the aromatic dried fruit or seed of plant of parsley family; oval and yellowish-brown; and has slight flavor of licorice.

USES:

Fennel Seed are used in egg dishes, fish cookery, stews, breads, seafood salads, salad dressings, vegetables, cheese dishes, baked or stewed apples, pickles, soups, sauerkraut, spaghetti sauce, marinades, sautéed mushrooms, boiling shellfish, cakes, cookies and oyster dishes.

SUGGESTED AMOUNTS TO USE IN VARIOUS DISHES:

1 teaspoon to 2 teaspoons, crushed, to 1 pound fish
A few seed to ⅛ teaspoon in water when cooking artichokes, broccoli, Brussels sprouts, cauliflower, beans and lentils
¼ teaspoon to ¾ teaspoon for 4-pound pork roast
⅛ teaspoon, crushed, in 3 cups potato salad
5 to 10 seeds in ½ cup sautéed mushrooms
⅛ teaspoon to ½ teaspoon in water when boiling 1 pound shrimp

GARLIC *(Allium sativum);* probably native to Southern Europe or Central Asia; grown world over; famous in history and various parts of the world since earliest recorded days; prized as a food by ancient Greeks and Romans; was an important food in the diet of Egyptian slaves who built the Pyramids and among the legions of ancient Rome; was considered valuable as a remedy; Hippocrates warned that it was bad for the eyes but good for the body; the ancients thought the smell of garlic drove away serpents and scorpions; is a bulbous annual of the lily family; edible part is the bulbous root made of small sections called "cloves" covered by a thin white skin; is available in a number of convenient forms—Garlic Powder, Garlic Salt, Instant Minced Garlic and Garlic Juice—which eliminate peeling and mincing of fresh garlic; dehydrated products release flavor only after they are moistened; flavor is strong and pungent; one of the most popular seasonings; a favorite seasoning in many French and Italian foods. Garlic Powder and Instant Minced Garlic may be used in any recipe calling for fresh garlic. Decrease the amount of salt called for in recipe when using Garlic Salt.

EQUIVALENTS:

⅛ teaspoon Garlic Powder or Instant Minced Garlic is equivalent to 1 average-size clove of fresh garlic

½ teaspoon Garlic Salt is equivalent to 1 average-size clove fresh garlic

USES:

Any of the garlic products may be increased or decreased to suit individual taste.

Garlic products are excellent in tomato dishes; soups; dips; sauces; butters; gravies; salads; salad dressings; dill pickles; some vegetables; meat, poultry or fish cookery; some cheese dishes; stews; marinades and for making garlic bread. Garlic may be used in combination with onion.

SUGGESTED AMOUNTS TO USE IN VARIOUS DISHES:

Garlic Powder

⅛ teaspoon to ¼ teaspoon to 2 pounds pork, beef, lamb or other meats

⅛ teaspoon to ½ teaspoon in ½ cup butter for bread, vegetables and grilled meats

⅛ teaspoon to ¼ teaspoon in 3 cups tomato, barbecue or other sauces

Dash to ⅛ teaspoon in 3 cups tomato or meat stock soups

When using Garlic Powder in a recipe with a high acid content, a more distinctive garlic flavor may be obtained by moistening the Garlic Powder in water before adding. Use 2 parts water to 1 part Garlic Powder.

Garlic Salt

1 teaspoon to 1¼ teaspoons to 1 pound ground beef or lamb

Dash to ½ teaspoon to 6 eggs, stuffed or for omelets

May be sprinkled to taste on broiled foods such as chicken, chops, fish, steaks and tomatoes.

Instant Minced Garlic

1½ teaspoons in 1 cup vinegar-oil salad dressing

Dash to ⅛ teaspoon in making 2 pints chutney or relish

⅛ teaspoon to ¼ teaspoon in each quart Kosher dill pickles or in each pint dilled green beans

Garlic Juice

Use Garlic Juice when a mild flavor of garlic is desired. It combines well with other ingredients, giving an even over-all hint of garlic.

½ teaspoon to 1 teaspoon in 2 cups tomato, pizza or spaghetti sauce
1 teaspoon to 2 teaspoons in ½ cup butter for garlic butter
½ teaspoon to 1 teaspoon combined with 1 tablespoon oil or melted butter for basting broiled fish, chops, chicken or steak

GINGER *(Zingiber officinale);* native to Southeast Asia; also comes from Jamaica; one of the first Oriental spices known in Europe; Marco Polo wrote of finding Ginger in China; is the dried and peeled rhizomes (roots) of ginger plant; available whole and ground; is light buff in color and has a hot, spicy, sweet flavor; Crystallized Ginger is fresh root cooked in syrup and is used as a confection or condiment, not a spice.

USES:

Whole Ginger is used in pickling, syrups, beverages, marinades, stewed fruit, teriyaki sauce, preserves, tea and ginger beer.

Some recipes refer to "bruised" Ginger. To bruise Ginger, pound to break skin but not root.

Ground Ginger is one of the most versatile of all spices. Use in preparing cakes; cookies; gingerbread; ginger toast; bread; rice, bread, fruit or steamed puddings; custards; whipped cream; sauces; soups; appetizers; Oriental dishes; lamb; pork; beef; veal; venison; nearly all vegetables, particularly good in sweet potatoes and carrots; pickles; chutney; preserves; conserves; baked or stewed fruits; fruit pies and salads; salad dressings; punch; chicken and other poultry; and ice cream. It is excellent in combination with other spices.

SUGGESTED AMOUNTS TO USE IN VARIOUS DISHES:

¼ teaspoon to 2 teaspoons for 1½ pounds pork
Dash to ¼ teaspoon to 2 cups sliced carrots
¼ teaspoon to 3 cups mixed fruit
¼ teaspoon to 1 cup coconut, toasted
¼ teaspoon to 1 teaspoon in 2 cups sweet potatoes
Dash to ¼ teaspoon in bread puddings and rice puddings yielding 4 to 6 servings
1 teaspoon to 1½ teaspoons in cookie recipe (2 cups flour)
⅛ teaspoon to ¼ teaspoon to 2 egg whites for meringues

Ground Ginger may be used in many recipes in place of whole Ginger—1 teaspoon ground Ginger may be substituted for 10 to 12 pieces whole Ginger about the size of shelled peanuts.

HERB SEASONING; a unique blend of a number of herbs and spices in proportions that impart a well-rounded, smooth flavor to foods; designed primarily as an all-purpose seasoning; for those who desire a warm, full-bodied flavor without an onion or garlic note.

USES:

Herb Seasoning is a convenient seasoning to use in the preparation of meats, vegetables, breads, gravies, poultry, game, meat spreads, croutons, cheese spreads, fish, sauces, stuffings and herb butters.

SUGGESTED AMOUNTS TO USE IN VARIOUS DISHES:

¼ teaspoon to ¾ teaspoon in 2 cups tomatoes

½ teaspoon to 1 teaspoon in 2 cups biscuit mix or recipe making 12 biscuits

¼ teaspoon to 1¼ teaspoons in 2 cups green vegetables

¾ teaspoon to 1½ teaspoons for 1½ pounds beef

1 teaspoon in 2 cups waffle mix or recipe using 2 cups flour

Dash to ¼ teaspoon to 1 cup bread cubes for herb croutons

½ teaspoon to 1½ teaspoons in corn bread mix or recipe making 12 muffins or corn sticks

LEMON PEEL *(Citrus limon)* and ORANGE PEEL *(Citrus sinenis);* lemon tree probably native to Northern India; today is grown in subtropics and tropics for commercial purpose; toward the end of the 1st century lemon trees were grown in Mediterranean region. Orange tree probably native to Southern China and Burma; the sweet orange is grown in every subtropical region of the world; was apparently unknown to Europeans prior to the 15th century; there are many familiar varieties of the sweet orange. Both Lemon and Orange Peel are the dried natural rind of the fresh fruits used for juice extraction; dried rinds are processed by milling; small particles are sifted out; flavor of oil is restored to peel since some oil is lost in processing; the flavor of the dehydrated peels is very similar to that of the grated fresh peel.

EQUIVALENTS:

It is difficult to give exact equivalents in relation to the fresh peel. This is due to the great variance in fresh lemons and oranges as to type of fruit, source, size, ripeness, peel thickness, how grated, size of grate used and how measured (loosely or packed down). Use slightly less or equal amounts of Lemon Peel and Orange Peel to grated fresh peel as called for in recipes.

USES:

Lemon Peel and Orange Peel may be used in the preparation of bread or rice puddings, breads, meringue shells and tortes, short cakes, cakes, cookies, frostings, fillings, custards, dessert soufflés, fruit pies, pastry, pork, chicken, duckling, glazes for ham, dessert and meat sauces, stuffings and most vegetables.

SUGGESTED AMOUNTS TO USE IN VARIOUS DISHES:

Lemon Peel or Orange Peel

1 teaspoon to 3 teaspoons to 2 cups dried prunes or other fruits

4 teaspoons in 2 cups waffle mix or recipe using 2 cups flour
½ teaspoon to 1 teaspoon Lemon Peel to 1 pound fish
¼ teaspoon to 1½ teaspoons in vanilla pudding recipe or mix using 2 cups milk
1½ teaspoons to 3 teaspoons in 2-layer cake or 8-inch coffee cake
½ teaspoon to 1½ teaspoons in 2 cups peas or carrots
1 teaspoon to 2 teaspoons for 3 pounds pork, ham, chicken or duckling

MACE *(Myristica fragrans);* native to Molucca Islands; imported from Indonesia and West Indies; at end of 12th century Mace was mentioned in Denmark and Europe and may have been used earlier but historians are not sure; the Dutch tried to destroy half the nutmeg trees in the Moluccas but birds carried seed to other islands; a part of the fruit of the evergreen nutmeg tree; is the bright red aril or skin covering the shell of the Nutmeg and turns brownish-orange when dried; whole Mace is called blades of Mace; available ground; flavor similar to Nutmeg but more delicate; Mace and Nutmeg are the only two spices found naturally on same plant.

USES:

Mace has a variety of uses and can be substituted for Nutmeg in recipes. Use Mace in preparing pound cake; spice cake; devil's food cake; gingerbread; frostings; hot chocolate; puddings; custards; fruit, chiffon, custard or refrigerator pies; breads; soups; punches; pork; beef; lamb; chicken; fish; apple dishes; sauces; creamed dishes; waffles; pancakes; doughnuts; coffee cakes; Danish pastries; glazes; muffins; vegetables; fruit salads; fruit salad dressings; cream cheese spreads for fruit and nut breads and candy.

SUGGESTED AMOUNTS TO USE IN VARIOUS DISHES:

Dash to ½ teaspoon in recipe or mix making 12 muffins
⅛ teaspoon to ¼ teaspoon in chocolate pudding mix or recipe using about 2 cups milk or in 2-layer chocolate cake recipe or mix
¼ teaspoon in stewing 2 cups dried apricots
⅛ teaspoon to ¼ teaspoon in 8-inch coffee cake recipe or mix
1 teaspoon in 2 cups waffle mix or recipe using 2 cups flour
Dash in 1 package frozen spinach or about 1 cup cooked, fresh spinach
Dash to ⅛ teaspoon in 4 cups creamed chicken or tuna
Dash to ⅛ teaspoon in 2 cups white sauce
⅛ teaspoon to ¼ teaspoon in 2 cups powdered sugar for glaze
⅛ teaspoon to ¼ teaspoon in a pound cake recipe or mix

MARJORAM *(Majorana hortensis);* native to Mediterranean region; probably used by ancient Egyptians; used as medicine by Hippocrates; symbol of happiness in ancient Greece; was used in medicines in Middle Ages; is the dried, grey-green leaves of plant of mint family; available as dried leaves and ground; has a distinctively aromatic and pleasant flavor with bitter undertone; use sparingly at first and increase to taste.

USES:

Marjoram may be used in almost any dish except sweet foods. Use it in the preparation of lamb; pork; beef; veal; venison and other game; chicken; broiled or baked fish; shellfish; practically all tomato dishes; other vegetables such as carrots, cauliflower, peas, spinach, squash, mushrooms, beans, broccoli and Brussels sprouts; pizza; spaghetti and brown sauces; stuffings; egg dishes; breads; tossed green salads; salad dressings; soups such as onion, turtle, vegetable, spinach, Scotch broth and minestrone; oyster and clam chowder; and jelly.

SUGGESTED AMOUNTS TO USE IN VARIOUS DISHES:

½ teaspoon to 1 teaspoon in 2 cups green vegetables
¼ teaspoon to ½ teaspoon to 3-pound chicken
⅛ teaspoon to ½ teaspoon for 1½ pounds pork
¼ teaspoon to ½ teaspoon for 1 pound beef or veal
Dash to ¼ teaspoon to 4 eggs—scrambled, stuffed or for omelets
½ teaspoon in 2 cups carrots
Dash to ¼ teaspoon in 2 cups tomato sauce
¼ teaspoon for each 3 cups bread cubes for stuffing
½ teaspoon in 2 cups biscuit, waffle or corn bread mix

MINT *(Mentha spicata);* also called Spearmint; native to Europe and Asia; was used by ancient Assyrians in rituals to the Fire-God; mentioned in New Testament; named by Greeks after mythical character Minthe; is the dried leaf of spearmint plant; available as flakes or in extract form; has an aromatic, sweet flavor with cool aftertaste.

USES:

Use in punches, tea, sauces for desserts, sauces for lamb, mint jelly, syrups, fruit compotes, fruit soup, split pea soup, devil's food cake, frostings, ice cream and sherbet, chocolate desserts, custards, candies, hot chocolate, vegetables, lamb stew and on lamb roast.

SUGGESTED AMOUNTS TO USE IN VARIOUS DISHES:

Mint Flakes

¼ teaspoon to ½ teaspoon, crushed, in chocolate pudding mix or recipe using about 2 cups milk
¼ teaspoon to 1 teaspoon, crushed, in 2-layer white cake recipe or mix
½ teaspoon to 1½ teaspoons, crushed, in 2-layer chocolate cake recipe or mix
¼ teaspoon to 1 teaspoon, crushed, in 2 cups peas
¼ teaspoon in lamb stew (1 to 1½ pounds meat)
¼ teaspoon to 1 teaspoon in 3 to 4 cups fruit
½ teaspoon in 1 quart tea or fruit beverages

MUSTARD (*Brassica hirta*—Yellow or White; *Brassica juncea*—Brown or Black); native to Europe and Southwestern Asia; grown in temperate regions, especially California and Montana; well known since days of ancient Greece as a condiment and for medicinal uses; frequently referred to in the New Testament and in Greek and Roman writings; is an annual herb plant bearing small seed; two varieties are utilized, yellow seed and brown seed; the yellow often referred to as white and the brown as black; dry Mustard is a mixture of the two varieties. The yellow variety is used for the whole Mustard Seed; both varieties are pungent in flavor; is available as Mustard Seed and dry Mustard, often referred to as mustard flour.

USES:

Mustard Seed are used in preparing cucumber pickles, vegetable relishes, corned beef, boiled beef, coleslaw, potato salad, boiled cabbage and sauerkraut. Dry Mustard adds zip to egg and cheese dishes, salad dressings, appetizers, meats, poultry, sauces and vegetables.

SUGGESTED AMOUNTS TO USE IN VARIOUS DISHES:

Dry Mustard

¼ teaspoon to ½ teaspoon in 6 eggs—stuffed, scrambled or for omelets

¼ teaspoon to ½ teaspoon in 1 pound ground beef

¼ teaspoon to ¾ teaspoon to 1 pound ham

½ teaspoon to 1 teaspoon in 1 teaspoon vinegar and dash Turmeric to make about 2 teaspoons mustard sauce (hotter than commercial prepared mustard)

Mustard Seed

2 tablespoons for 8 pints bread and butter pickles

¼ cup to ⅔ cup for 6 pints tomato or vegetable relish

NUTMEG *(Myristica fragrans);* native to Molucca Islands; now grown in hot moist climates of the tropics (Indonesia or West Indies); reached Europe by 12th century; the Portuguese, and then the Dutch, monopolized nutmeg trade for centuries; Yankee traders, making and selling wooden Nutmegs for real Nutmegs, caused Connecticut to be known as "The Nutmeg State"; is the oval-shaped, dried seed of an apricot-like fruit of an evergreen tree which bears for more than fifty years; scarlet aril covering the shell of the Nutmeg is Mace; after separation both are dried; Nutmeg is available whole and ground; flavor sweet, warm and highly spicy; commercially used to season sausage and luncheon meats.

USES:

Nutmeg is not only appetizing in sweet foods but enhances flavor of meats and vegetables. Ground Nutmeg or the freshly grated whole Nutmeg may be sprinkled over hot and cold milk drinks, eggnog, fruits, puddings, soups and used to season meats, poultry, sea food, vegetables and sauces. Use in making cakes, cookies, doughnuts, pies, pastries, muffins, waffles and coffee cake.

SUGGESTED AMOUNTS TO USE IN VARIOUS DISHES:

¼ teaspoon to ½ teaspoon in 2-layer white or yellow cake recipe or mix
½ teaspoon to 1 teaspoon for two-crust pastry
Dash to ¼ teaspoon in 2 cups spinach, mixed vegetables, sliced carrots and most other vegetables
⅛ teaspoon to ¾ teaspoon in vanilla pudding mix or recipe using about 2 cups milk
¼ teaspoon in about 2 cups batter for muffins, coffee cakes and waffles
½ teaspoon in chocolate frosting for 2 cake layers
⅛ teaspoon to ¼ teaspoon in 1 cup heavy cream, whipped, or 1 cup powdered sugar for a glaze
Dash to ⅛ teaspoon in 4 cups creamed chicken or tuna
⅛ teaspoon for 1 pound beef
¼ teaspoon to ½ teaspoon in a pound cake recipe or mix

One whole Nutmeg, grated, equals 2 to 3 teaspoons ground Nutmeg.

ONION *(Allium cepa);* native to Western Asia; known to history for more than 4,000 years; was cultivated by ancient Babylonians; also part of diet of slaves who built the Pyramids in Egypt; available as Onion Powder, Onion Salt, Instant Minced Onion, Onion Flakes, Chopped Instant Onions and Onion Juice; the bulb of onion plant which is member of lily family; bottled Onion Juice is processed from juice squeezed from fresh onion; all other products are obtained from dehydrated onion bulb; Onion Salt, a mixture of salt and onion powder—decrease salt in recipe when using; Instant Minced Onion, Onion Flakes and Chopped Instant Onions differ only in size of particle.

Onion is probably one of the most universal seasonings. All onion products are interchangeable as far as flavor is concerned. Use Onion Powder, Onion Salt or Onion Juice for flavor only; or for both flavor and texture, use Instant Minced Onion, Chopped Instant Onions or Onion Flakes.

USES:

Onion products may be used in the preparation of appetizers and dips, soups and chowders, stews, all meats, game, fish, shellfish, poultry, salads and salad dressings, sauces, vegetables, gravies, stuffings, cheese dishes, egg dishes, breads, casseroles, croquettes and rice dishes.

EQUIVALENTS:

1 tablespoon Onion Powder equals 1 medium-size fresh onion
1 tablespoon Instant Minced Onion equals ¼ cup minced raw onion
1 tablespoon Onion Flakes equals ¼ cup chopped raw onion
¼ cup Chopped Instant Onions equals 1 cup chopped raw onion

SUGGESTED AMOUNTS TO USE IN VARIOUS DISHES:

Onion Powder

¼ teaspoon to 1 teaspoon in 2 cups green, yellow or white vegetables
1 teaspoon to 1 pound cooked meat for spreads

When using Onion Powder in a recipe with an extremely high acid content, a more distinctive onion flavor may be obtained by moistening Onion Powder in water before adding to the recipe; use 2 parts water to 1 part Onion Powder.

Onion Salt

1 teaspoon to 2 teaspoons in 2 cups green, yellow or white vegetables
¼ teaspoon to 1 teaspoon to 1 pound chicken, stew meat, ground meat, veal, variety meats, game, roasts, steaks or chops

Instant Minced Onion

½ teaspoon to 1½ teaspoons in 1 cup vinegar-oil salad dressing
1 tablespoon to 2 tablespoons for 1 pound dried beans
1 teaspoon to 2 teaspoons in 2 cups green, yellow or white vegetables
2 teaspoons to 3 teaspoons to 1 pound ground beef, lamb or veal
1 teaspoon to 3 teaspoons to a 7-ounce can tuna for salad or spreads

Onion Flakes

1 tablespoon to 2 tablespoons in 4 cups soup
1 tablespoon to 2 tablespoons in 2 cups barbecued beef
2 teaspoons to 2 tablespoons in 2 cups sauces and gravies

Chopped Instant Onions

1 tablespoon to 3 tablespoons, plain or toasted, in 1 cup dairy sour cream for dip
¼ cup in 6 cups chowder or chicken or vegetable soup

Particularly good as sautéed onions for French onion soup or with liver or hamburgers. Reconstitute in ice water for use in salads.

Onion Juice

Use Onion Juice when a mild flavor of onion is desired. It combines well with other ingredients giving an even over-all hint of onion.

1 teaspoon to 2 teaspoons in ½ cup dairy sour cream to use as dip or topping for vegetables and soup

1 teaspoon in 1½ cups oil-vinegar salad dressing

OREGANO (Species of *Lippia, Origanum* and sometimes other genera); native to Mediterranean region; another strain of Oregano is common to Mexico; has been used since early days of ancient Rome; the dried leaves of a perennial plant; available as leaves and ground; flavor strong and aromatic with pleasant bitter undertone; sometimes referred to as "Wild Marjoram"; flavor similar to sweet Marjoram but stronger; an essential ingredient of Chili Powder; practically unknown in the United States until after World War II; the increased popularity of pizza has stimulated the use of Oregano.

USES:

Oregano goes well with tomatoes and is a natural seasoning with any tomato dish. Use to season pasta sauces, tomato juice, pizza, chili con carne, barbecue sauce and vegetable soup. It is excellent in egg and cheese dishes, onions, sea food salads, stuffings for meat or poultry, sauce for fish, and on pork, lamb, chicken and fish.

SUGGESTED AMOUNTS TO USE IN VARIOUS DISHES:

Ground

¼ teaspoon to ¾ teaspoon in 1 pound ground beef

¼ teaspoon to ½ teaspoon for 1 pound pork

Leaves

¼ teaspoon to ¾ teaspoon to 4 eggs for egg salad

¼ teaspoon to ½ teaspoon in ½ cup butter for baked potatoes, bread or basting fish

¼ teaspoon to ½ teaspoon in 2 cups spinach, green beans or 3 cups tomatoes

1 teaspoon to 3 cups flour in making yeast bread

1 teaspoon sprinkled over top of 12- to 14-inch pizza

⅛ teaspoon to ¼ teaspoon in 2 cups tomato, spaghetti or barbecue sauce (ground Oregano may also be used)

PAPRIKA *(Capsicum annuum);* native to Central America; early Spanish explorers took plants back to Europe; most is imported from Spain and Central Europe, but the plant is grown commercially in California as well; Hungarian scientist won Nobel Prize for research in vitamin content of Paprika; a richer source of Vitamin C than citrus fruits; valuable vitamins in Paprika, principally C and A; the dried, stemless pod of a sweet red pepper; available ground; most Paprika consumed in the United States is mild and slightly sweet in flavor; agreeably aromatic and bright red in color; another type, pungent and of lighter color, is Hungarian Paprika.

USES:

Paprika is one of the three most popular seasonings. Use as a colorful garnish for any light colored food. Sprinkle on fish, meats, canapés, soups, potatoes, eggs and sauces. Used in generous quantities, Paprika is the principal seasoning in such dishes as Hungarian goulash and chicken or veal paprika and is often used in making French dressing.

SUGGESTED AMOUNTS TO USE IN VARIOUS DISHES:

½ teaspoon to 2 tablespoons in flour for dredging 3 pounds chicken or meat
¼ teaspoon to ¾ teaspoon in 1 cup vinegar-oil for French dressing
½ teaspoon in ¼ cup butter for sautéing potatoes or to season white vegetables
½ teaspoon to 1 teaspoon in 1 cup Welsh rabbit
1 teaspoon to 1 tablespoon to 3 pounds beef in Hungarian goulash
1 teaspoon to 1 tablespoon to 2 pounds veal in veal paprika

PARSLEY *(Petroselinum crispum);* native to rocky shores of the Mediterranean; the curly leaf variety, chiefly grown in California, is the main source of dehydrated Parsley Flakes; plain leaf parsley is naturalized both in the United States and several European countries; used generously to flavor and garnish foods as early as the 3rd century B.C.; the colonists introduced it to America; the dried leaves of a biennial plant; available as dehydrated flakes; excellent source of Vitamin C and several minerals; pleasant mild odor and agreeable taste; blends well with all other herbs; is used both for eye and taste appeal in most food except sweets.

USES:

This mild flavored herb is often used both in and on food. Garnish and flavor canapés, soups, tossed green salads, coleslaw, breads, herb sauces and butters, tomato and meat sauces, stuffings for fish and meats, broiled or fried fish, meats and poultry.

SUGGESTED AMOUNTS TO USE IN VARIOUS DISHES:

2 teaspoons to 4 teaspoons in 8-ounce package noodles or 3 cups cooked rice
1 teaspoon to 2 teaspoons in 2 cups waffle mix or recipe using 2 cups flour
1 teaspoon to 2 teaspoons in 2 to 3 cups tomato sauce
1 teaspoon to 2 teaspoons to 1 pound crab meat for crab cakes; 1 pint oysters for scalloped oysters; or 2 cups tuna, salmon or chicken for croquettes
½ teaspoon to 1 teaspoon in ½ cup butter for vegetables, fish or meats
¼ teaspoon to 1 teaspoon to 2 eggs—scrambled or for omelets

PEPPER *(Piper nigrum);* native to East Indies; imported from India, Indonesia, Borneo and Malaysia; is the world's most popular spice; ancient Greeks and Romans used both White and Black Pepper for cooking; in early 5th century, 3,000 pounds pepper was demanded for ransom of Rome; in 1179 A.D. Guild of Pepperers was founded in London; Marco Polo wrote of great quantities of pepper used in China; the dried fruit or berry of climbing vine which grows on spikes like currants; available as whole Black Pepper (Peppercorns), ground White Pepper, ground Black Pepper, Coarse Grind Black Pepper and Cracked Black Pepper; to obtain Black Pepper, berries are picked before fully ripe and they turn black and shrivel when dried; to obtain White Pepper, berries are allowed to ripen before harvesting and the outer shell is removed, leaving greyish-white kernel; has a hot, biting and very pungent taste; White Pepper is milder in flavor than Black Pepper; has slight musty flavor.

USES:

Peppercorns or whole Black Peppers are used in pepper mills. Grind the pepper over foods at the table or when food is being prepared. Peppercorns are also used in some salad dressings, marinades, pickling, poaching fish, soups, sauces and stews.

Ground White Pepper is especially popular in white or light colored foods where the dark specks of Black Pepper do not add to the aesthetic appearance. White Pepper may be substituted for Black Pepper in any recipe.

Black Pepper comes in three different grinds—fine, coarse and cracked. Black Pepper may be used in any dish except sweets. However, it is sometimes used in cake and is a characteristic ingredient in the German Christmas cookie, pfeffernüsse.

SUGGESTED AMOUNTS TO USE IN VARIOUS DISHES:

Peppercorns

10 to 12 in marinade for sauerbraten, 4 pounds beef
4 to 6 in liquid for poaching 1 to 2 pounds fish
8 to 10 in liquid when boiling chicken, shrimp, pot roast and variety meats such as tongue

Ground Black Pepper

⅛ teaspoon to ½ teaspoon in spice cake mix
⅛ teaspoon to ½ teaspoon to a 7-ounce can tuna for salad
¼ teaspoon to ½ teaspoon in pfeffernüsse recipe making 6 dozen cookies

Coarse Grind Black Pepper

¼ teaspoon to ½ teaspoon in 1½ cups French or other salad dressings
⅛ teaspoon to ½ teaspoon to 4 cups bread cubes for stuffings
⅛ teaspoon to ¼ teaspoon sprinkled over 1 pound steak, chops, fish, chicken or liver before broiling

Cracked Black Pepper

1 teaspoon to 2 teaspoons to 1 pound steak for peppered steak
½ teaspoon to 1 teaspoon in 2 cups marinade for meats
⅛ teaspoon to each individual salad bowl of chef's or tossed salad

Ground White Pepper

Dash to ⅛ teaspoon to 6 eggs—stuffed, scrambled, creamed or for omelets

⅛ teaspoon to ¼ teaspoon in 2 cups mashed potatoes

¼ teaspoon in 2 cups white or light-colored sauce

⅛ teaspoon to ¼ teaspoon in 2 cups vichyssoise or other light-colored soups

⅛ teaspoon to ¼ teaspoon for 1 pound fish

⅛ teaspoon to ¼ teaspoon for 1 head cauliflower

PEPPER, RED *[Capsicum frutescens (C. annuum)];* native to tropical America and West Indies; known in pre-Inca days; Columbus found hot red peppers in Cuba and introduced them to Europe; fruit of pepper plant; has no relation to Black and White Pepper; available crushed and ground; ground Red Pepper is available as a blend; orange-red to deep red in color; has a hot, pungent flavor; use with caution; in some sections of the United States whole red pepper may be purchased as Chili Tepines.

USES:

Red Pepper is widely used in Mexican and Italian dishes. Use to season meats, sea food, deviled eggs, appetizers, soups and chowders, tomato aspic, cottage and cream cheese, cheese dishes, sauces, gravy, salad dressing, pickles, poultry, game, vegetables, spaghetti sauce, tamales, curried dishes, creamed dishes, ceviche, cheese straws or wafers, dips, spreads for canapés, sauces for sea food appetizers, tomato juice cocktail, Bloody Marys, omelets, soufflés, croquettes, tamale pie, guacamole, barbecued beef and pork.

Crushed Red Pepper is particularly important in pickling, chowders, gumbos, spaghetti sauce, pizza sauce and in making sausage.

SUGGESTED AMOUNTS TO USE IN VARIOUS DISHES:

Ground Red Pepper

Dash to ¼ teaspoon to 1 pound shrimp

Dash to ⅛ teaspoon to 6 eggs—stuffed, scrambled or for omelets

Dash to ⅛ teaspoon in ½ cup butter for basting chicken or fish or to use over vegetables

Crushed Red Pepper

⅛ teaspoon to 1 teaspoon to 1 pound ground beef

⅛ teaspoon to ¼ teaspoon in 2 cups pizza or spaghetti sauce

1 teaspoon to 2 teaspoons to 4 pints tomato relish, mixed pickles or dilled green beans

A good rule to follow is to use a dash to ⅛ teaspoon in most recipes for 4 servings unless extremely hot food is desired. Increase to suit individual taste.

PICKLING SPICE; blend of whole and broken spices, herbs and seeds; designed primarily for use in pickling but may be used in other food preparation; tie Pickling Spice in a cheesecloth bag for easy removal when used in such dishes as pot roast, spiced fruits and vegetables.

USES:

Pickling Spice may be used in pickles, stewed prunes, pickled beets, pickled eggs, marinades, sauerbraten, spiced fruits, boiled shrimp, pot roast and game cookery.

SUGGESTED AMOUNTS TO USE IN VARIOUS RECIPES:

1 teaspoon to 2 teaspoons to 2 cups prunes for stewing
1 teaspoon to 1 tablespoon to 2 cups whole beets
1 tablespoon in 4 cups mixed fruits or fruit cocktail
2 tablespoons to 4 tablespoons in 1 quart water for boiling 1 to 2 pounds shrimp
1 tablespoon to 2 tablespoons to 4-pound pot roast of beef or venison

POPPY SEED *(Papaver somniferum);* native to Southwestern Asia; imported mainly from the Netherlands, Poland and Iran; was cultivated as a source of cooking oil by Egyptians as early as 1500 B.C.; seed come from the opium poppy but contain no narcotic properties; the Dutch cultivate the best quality seed; is a uniform slate-blue color; seed come from the pod of an annual plant which belongs to the poppy family; appears round to the eye but is actually kidney-shaped; the tiny dried seed have a pleasant, crunchy, nut-like flavor and add eye appeal and texture as well as flavor to foods; is of culinary importance especially in Slavic and Hungarian baked goods.

USES:

Poppy Seed may be used as an ingredient in a recipe, sprinkled over the top of food before cooking or as a garnish. Use in cottage cheese, cream cheese, scrambled eggs, pie crust, cheese sticks, fruit compotes, fruit salad dressings, cookies, cakes, breads and noodles. Sprinkle over top of fruit salads, vegetables, breads, cookies, cakes and casseroles.

SUGGESTED AMOUNTS TO USE IN VARIOUS DISHES:

1 teaspoon to 3 teaspoons in recipe or mix making 12 corn bread or plain muffins
2 teaspoons to 4 teaspoons in a two-crust pastry
½ teaspoon to 1 teaspoon in ½ cup butter and stir into 8-ounce package noodles, cooked
2 teaspoons in 8-ounce package cream cheese
1 teaspoon in 1 cup fruit salad dressing
¼ cup to ⅓ cup in 2-layer white cake recipe or mix
2 tablespoons to 4 tablespoons in cookie recipe using about 3 cups flour

POULTRY SEASONING; a blend of herbs; was created primarily for seasoning stuffings but may be used in many other dishes.

USES:

Poultry Seasoning may be used in stuffings; roasting, broiling or frying chicken; roasting turkey; veal dishes; waffles; biscuits; meat loaf and hamburgers; gravy; creamed chicken; chicken, turkey or salmon croquettes; sautéed chicken livers; liver pâté; chicken soups; chicken and dumplings; chicken pot pie and pastry for meat pies.

SUGGESTED AMOUNTS TO USE IN VARIOUS DISHES:

¼ teaspoon to ¾ teaspoon for 3-pound frying chicken
½ teaspoon in about 4 cups creamed chicken or turkey
½ teaspoon to 2 teaspoons to 4 cups bread cubes for stuffing
⅛ teaspoon to ¼ teaspoon for 1 pound veal

PUMPKIN PIE SPICE; a blend of Cinnamon, Ginger, Allspice, Nutmeg and Cloves; a certain percentage of each is blended to bring out the finest flavor of each spice; the whole spices are placed on high speed mills and ground together; this welding of the spice particles assures a permanent smoothness of flavor not possible by merely mixing after grinding; as with all blends of spices, manufacturers have their own secret formulas.

USES:

Pumpkin Pie Spice is a mouth-watering blend with just the right flavor note for seasoning pumpkin pie. Excellent used in gingerbread, cookies, fruits, squash, sweet potatoes, applesauce and other apple dishes, sweet rolls, frostings, waffles, muffins, whipped cream, glazes, cakes, puddings, dessert sauces and for making toast.

SUGGESTED AMOUNTS TO USE IN VARIOUS DISHES:

¼ teaspoon to 1 teaspoon in pound cake recipe or mix
¼ teaspoon to 1 teaspoon in 1 cup flake or shredded coconut, toasted
2 teaspoons to 3 teaspoons in 1½ cups mashed pumpkin for pie
½ teaspoon to ½ cup uncooked rice for rice pudding
½ teaspoon to 1 teaspoon for 2 cups sweet potatoes, mashed or candied
½ teaspoon to 1 teaspoon for 2 cups apricots for stewing, tarts or pie

ROSEMARY *(Rosmarinus officinalis);* native to the Mediterranean area; present sources are Yugoslavia, France, Spain, Portugal and, to an extent, the moist climates of North Carolina, Virginia and California; an herb used extensively as early as 500 B.C.; prominent in folklore; one legend says that Rosemary will grow only in the gardens of the righteous; in *Hamlet*, Ophelia said, "There's rosemary, that's for remembrance"; even today in England Rosemary is placed on graves of English heroes; used by the colonists to scent soap; is the dried leaves from small perennial evergreen shrub of the mint family; the slender, slightly curved leaves are greyish-green in color, resembling miniature curved pine needles; distinctive, fresh, sweet pinewoods flavor; is used to great extent in perfumery.

USES:

Rosemary, a sweet, fragrant herb, is excellent in lamb dishes, soups, stews, marinades, poached or boiled fish or sea food, Italian tomato sauce for fish, liver pâté, boiled potatoes, cauliflower, spinach, mushrooms, turnips, fruits, fruit juices, breads; and is used in preparing poultry, veal, beef, pork, wild fowl and venison. Sprinkle Rosemary over coals when barbecuing meats.

SUGGESTED AMOUNTS TO USE IN VARIOUS DISHES:

½ teaspoon to 1 teaspoon, crushed, in 1 package corn bread mix, 2 cups biscuit mix or recipe making 12 muffins or biscuits
¼ teaspoon to 1 tablespoon for a 3-pound chicken
¼ teaspoon in 4 cups mixed fruit or 2 cups fruit juice
¼ teaspoon to ½ teaspoon in 2 cups potatoes, cauliflower or tomatoes
¼ teaspoon to 1 tablespoon in 6 cups barbecue sauce
½ teaspoon, crushed, for 3- to 4-pound lamb roast or use in combination with Thyme and Sage

SAFFRON *(Crocus sativus);* native to Mediterranean area; imported primarily from Spain; ancient Assyrians used Saffron for medicinal purposes; listed in medical papyrus of Thebes (1552 B.C.); Constantine presented gift of spices, including Saffron, to the Bishop of Rome; is the dried stigmas of the saffron crocus; most expensive spice in the world; requires 75,000 blossoms or 225,000 stigmas to make 1 pound; available whole; is orange-yellow in color; used as much in cooking for color as for flavor; has a pleasantly bitter flavor; use sparingly—a little goes a long way.

USES:

Saffron is widely used in French, Spanish and South American dishes. An essential ingredient in arroz con pollo, bouillabaisse, paella and risotto. May also be used in yeast breads, rice, chicken dishes, soups, cakes, sauces and sea food dishes. The individual pieces of Saffron may be used in recipes; however, it is usually crushed before using.

SUGGESTED AMOUNTS TO USE IN VARIOUS DISHES:

Dash to ¼ teaspoon, crushed, for 1 cup uncooked rice
Dash to ⅛ teaspoon, crushed, for 3-pound chicken
8 to 10 individual pieces, crushed, in 8- or 9-inch layer cake
⅛ teaspoon to 1 teaspoon in 4-cup flour recipe for bread or buns or in a package hot roll mix
Dash to ⅛ teaspoon, crushed, for 2 pounds veal

SAGE *(Salvia officinalis);* native to Mediterranean area; imported primarily from Dalmatian region of Yugoslavia; do not confuse with sagebrush of American West; was used for medicinal purposes during Middle Ages; the dried leaf of a plant of mint family; is grey-green in color; available as dried leaves and rubbed; very aromatic and slightly bitter; use sparingly.

USES:

Sage is well known for its use in stuffings for poultry, fish, game and other meats. Thousands of pounds go into the commercial making of sausage each year. Sage may also be used in soups, chowders, waffles, biscuits, lima beans, saltimbocca, onions, eggplant, sauces, tomatoes, cheese, marinades, potatoes and in preparing poultry, fish, beef, pork and veal.

SUGGESTED AMOUNTS TO USE IN VARIOUS DISHES:

¼ teaspoon to ½ teaspoon in 2 cups green vegetables
¼ teaspoon to ¾ teaspoon to 1 quart bread cubes for stuffing for poultry, fish, pork chops, breast of veal and crown roasts
¼ teaspoon to 1 tablespoon in 6 cups barbecue sauce in combination with Rosemary and Thyme
2 teaspoons in 2 cups waffle mix or recipe using 2 cups flour
½ teaspoon to 3 pounds pork, veal, lamb, beef and other meats
¼ teaspoon to ½ teaspoon in 1 pound ground lamb
Dash to ¼ teaspoon in 3 cups soup—cream, chowder, vegetable, tomato or sea food
½ teaspoon to ¼ cup flour for dredging meats
Dash to ¼ teaspoon in ¼ cup butter for basting 1 pound fish when baking or broiling
Dash to ¼ teaspoon in 3 cups tomatoes

SAVORY *(Satureja hortensis);* sometimes called Summer Savory; native to Mediterranean countries; Hippocrates speaks of its medicinal properties; used for seasoning cakes, pies and puddings in Middle Ages; is the dried, brownish-green leaves of plant of mint family; has aromatic, piquant flavor; available ground.

USES:

Savory blends well with other herbs. It may be used alone or in combination with other herbs in stuffings for meat, fish or poultry; egg dishes; sauces; soups; meat loaf and hamburgers; stews; beans; cabbage; peas and tomato juice.

SUGGESTED AMOUNTS TO USE IN VARIOUS DISHES:

¼ teaspoon to ½ teaspoon in 2 cups green beans, Brussels sprouts, lima beans, peas or other green vegetables
¼ teaspoon to ½ teaspoon in 1 pound ground beef

Dash to ¼ teaspoon in 3 cups consommé, fish chowder or bean, split pea, tomato or vegetable soup
¼ teaspoon to 3 cups bread cubes for stuffing
⅛ teaspoon to 6 stuffed eggs
¼ teaspoon to ½ teaspoon for 3-pound chicken
¼ teaspoon for 1 pound of fish
Dash to ¼ teaspoon in 1½ cups brown sauce or gravy

SEASON-ALL®; blend of seasonings; an extremely versatile seasoning used to enhance flavor of most food except sweets; adds color to light-colored foods; reduce salt in recipe when using Season-All®; may also be used as a garnish or at the table as one would use salt and pepper.

USES:

Use Season-All in preparing vegetables; cheese dishes such as cheese soufflés, Welsh rabbit, cheese sauce and grilled cheese sandwiches; tomato, mushroom, barbecue and cream sauces; soups; beef; lamb; veal; variety meats; pork; poultry; game; fish; sea foods; seasoned butter; salad dressings; coleslaw and potato, chicken, tuna, salmon, shrimp, crab and macaroni salads. Sprinkle over broiled or fresh sliced tomatoes; cottage cheese; fried potatoes; corn on the cob; cheese cubes for appetizers; dips; canapés; spreads; omelets; scrambled, fried, poached, stuffed or creamed eggs and on raw vegetables such as celery, carrot sticks, cauliflower and radishes.

SUGGESTED AMOUNTS TO USE IN VARIOUS DISHES:

2 teaspoons in ½ cup butter for breads and vegetables or to brush over fish or meat when broiling
1 tablespoon for 3-pound pork or beef roast
½ teaspoon to 1 teaspoon to 1½ cups cottage cheese
1 teaspoon to 1½ teaspoons in 1 pound ground beef
¾ teaspoon to 1 teaspoon in 2 cups fresh, frozen or canned vegetables
2 teaspoons to 1 tablespoon for 3-pound chicken
½ teaspoon to 1 teaspoon for 6 eggs—scrambled, stuffed or for omelets

SESAME SEED *(Sesamum indicum);* also known as "Benne Seed"; native to Asia; cultivated extensively in China, India and Central America; a food of the ancient Egyptians and Persians; regarded highly by Orientals as a staple food, as valuable as the soy bean; Sesame Seed signifies immortality to Brahmins; Negro slaves brought Sesame Seed to America; early Assyrians, several thousand years before Christ, believed their gods drank Sesame Wine at their conference prior to creating the earth; Sesame Seed is the dried, hulled fruit of a tropical annual herb; creamy white, smooth and slippery oval-shaped seed; rich nut-like flavor; tons of seed are utilized every year to make a rich Middle Eastern candy, Halvah; the seed is a source of a fine cooking oil and paste.

USES:

Sesame Seed is one of the most versatile seeds. The flavor of toasted Sesame Seed resembles that of toasted almonds. Use, toasted or untoasted, in many of the same ways nuts are used. Sprinkle canapés, breads, cookies, casseroles, salads, noodles, soups and vegetables with Sesame Seed. Add to pie crust, pie fillings, candy, cakes, cookies, dumplings, cheese spreads and dips and stuffings. When recipe calls for "toasted" seed—toast Sesame Seed in 350°F. oven 15 minutes or until lightly browned before using.

SUGGESTED AMOUNTS TO USE IN VARIOUS DISHES:

1 teaspoon to 2 teaspoons, toasted, in 1½ cups flour for dumplings
1 tablespoon to 4 tablespoons, toasted, in 1 pound ground beef
1 teaspoon to 1 tablespoon, toasted, in 2 tablespoons melted butter for vegetables
2 tablespoons to 4 tablespoons, toasted, for two-crust pastry
⅓ cup, toasted, to 3 cups stuffing for poultry or pork chops
¼ cup, toasted, in pecan pie filling
Sprinkle over waffles, biscuits, muffins and rolls before baking.

TARRAGON *(Artemisia dracunculus);* native to Western and Southern Asia; is cultivated in Southern Europe, especially France, and the temperate zones of the United States; one of the most aromatic herbs and a favorite of connoisseurs for its intriguing flavor; a festive herb, often used as garnish by the French on aspic-coated meats; slender dark green leaves of a shrub-like perennial; available as dried leaves; has a somewhat astringent flavor, reminiscent of Anise; best known as the flavoring for tarragon vinegar; the flavor of Tarragon, being very aromatic, stands alone well and should be used sparingly.

USES:

Tarragon is the distinctive flavor in Béarnaise sauce. May be used in mayonnaise; tartar, mustard and sour cream sauces; pickles; turtle soup; tuna salads and casseroles; marinades; ragouts and pot roasts. Use in preparing veal, lamb, venison and other game, chicken, duck, Cornish hens, squab, pheasant, fish, shellfish and egg dishes. Excellent sprinkled over salad greens.

SUGGESTED AMOUNTS TO USE IN VARIOUS DISHES:

¼ teaspoon to ½ teaspoon in 2 cups peas or spinach
¼ teaspoon in 2 cups soup—turtle, tomato, mushroom or fish chowders
½ teaspoon to 1 teaspoon in ½ cup butter for sautéing shellfish or as a sauce for fish
¼ teaspoon to ½ teaspoon for 2 pounds veal
¼ teaspoon to ½ teaspoon in 2 cups white sauce for creamed eggs or fish dishes
¼ teaspoon for 1 pound broiled or baked fish
1 tablespoon in 3 cups mayonnaise for green goddess salad dressing

1 teaspoon for 3-pound chicken
1½ teaspoons in Béarnaise sauce recipe using 3 egg yolks
½ teaspoon to 1 teaspoon in ½ cup butter for topping steaks and chops
1 tablespoon in 1 pint white wine vinegar to make tarragon vinegar (let stand before using)

THYME *(Thymus vulgaris);* native to the Mediterranean area; cultivated in Southern Europe and United States; France is the leading producer of Thyme; French Thyme and Lemon Thyme are the two varieties that are commercially important; Assyrian doctors and chemists recognized the medicinal properties of Thyme; used as a fumigant, as well as to flavor cheese and liquor by the ancient Greeks and Romans; is still used to flavor certain Scandinavian cheeses; in ancient times it was thought that Thyme would not grow well unless grown within the range of sea breezes; has a pale lavender blossom which is a favorite of the honey bee; is the greyish-green leaves of a perennial plant of the mint family; available as dried leaves and ground; has a distinctively warm, aromatic and slightly pungent flavor; commercially used to flavor Bénédictine liqueur.

USES:

Thyme, one of the most popular herbs, is used to season meat, poultry and fish. Combine Thyme with melted butter and serve over vegetables or broiled sea food or use in stuffing for fish and meats. Add to dishes made with tomato or cheese. Seasoning clam chowder with Thyme is a must. Thyme is one of the popular herbs used in making a bouquet garni.

SUGGESTED AMOUNTS TO USE IN VARIOUS DISHES:

Ground

¼ teaspoon to ½ teaspoon in flour for dredging 3-pound chicken
Dash to ½ teaspoon in 3 cups clam chowder
½ teaspoon to 1¼ teaspoons to 4-pound leg of lamb—use alone or in combination with Sage and Rosemary
¼ teaspoon to ½ teaspoon in biscuit mix or recipe making 12 biscuits
¼ teaspoon to 1 tablespoon in 6 cups barbecue sauce

Leaves

¼ teaspoon to ½ teaspoon for 1 pound liver
Dash to ¼ teaspoon in 2 cups Brussels sprouts or green beans
¼ teaspoon to ½ teaspoon for 1½ pounds round steak
¼ teaspoon to ½ teaspoon for 5-pound stewing chicken

TURMERIC *(Curcuma longa);* native to Cochin China; imported from India, Haiti, Jamaica and Peru; Turmeric is mentioned in writings of Greek physician Dioscorides (ca. A.D. 40–90); was used as a dye; today used to color butter, cheese and pickles; extensively used in East Indian cookery; rhizome or root of plant of ginger family; is washed, cleaned and sun-dried; available ground; golden yellow color; musky odor and slightly bitter flavor; small amount adds color to foods; a major ingredient in Curry Powder and prepared mustard.

USES:

Turmeric is used in egg dishes, pickles, chow-chow, rice dishes, cream sauces, salad dressings, breads, relish, mayonnaise, soups, noodles and in preparing chicken and fish.

SUGGESTED AMOUNTS TO USE IN VARIOUS DISHES:

Dash to ⅛ teaspoon in 6 stuffed or scrambled eggs

Dash to ¼ teaspoon for 1 cup uncooked rice or 8-ounce package noodles

Dash to ¼ teaspoon in 2 cups white sauce or cheese sauce

⅛ teaspoon to ¼ teaspoon in ½ cup butter for basting chicken and sea food when broiling or baking

¼ teaspoon to ½ teaspoon in 1 cup mayonnaise or dairy sour cream for dressing or dunk for shrimp, lobster and other sea food

VANILLA *(Vanilla planifolia);* is native to Central America and Mexico. Mexico monopolized the profitable Vanilla trade for three centuries. It is now produced mainly in the Malagasy Republic (Madagascar) and neighboring islands of Réunion and Comores. Lesser amounts come from Java, Tahiti and Mexico. Long before Columbus discovered America, the Aztecs enjoyed a drink called "Xoco-Latl" made from cocoa and vanilla beans. This was discovered by Cortez, and Vanilla was taken back to Spain from where its use soon spread to other parts of Europe. Vanilla is the fruit of an orchid plant; each hand-pollinated flower becomes a long slender pod or bean which is picked while still green. It undergoes a curing and drying process during which aroma and flavor are developed.

Pure Vanilla Extract, a delicate, subtle flavoring, is a complex mixture of natural ingredients, many of which are unknown. Imitation vanilla extract is a mixture of color and synthetic flavors, mainly vanillin. Pure Vanilla has a pleasant "bouquet" and a full, well-rounded flavor that is not present in an imitation vanilla extract. For the protection of consumers, Federal standards have now been issued to define the name Vanilla Extract and provide that no imitation flavors may be used in making pure Vanilla Extract.

USES:

Use Vanilla to flavor most sweet foods such as eggnog, milk shakes, hot chocolate and other milk beverages; ice cream; rice, bread and other puddings; cakes; cookies; dessert or fruit sauces; custards; stewed fruits; fruit compotes; candies; glazes; frostings; whipped cream; pies; coffee;

tortes; meringue shells; cheesecake; dessert soufflés; sundae toppings; cream puff and pastry fillings; muffins; coffee cakes and cream cheese filling for fruit bread.

SUGGESTED AMOUNTS TO USE IN VARIOUS DISHES:

1 teaspoon to 2 teaspoons in 2-layer cake recipe or mix
¼ teaspoon to ½ teaspoon in 1 cup heavy cream, whipped
1 teaspoon to 1½ teaspoons in 2 cups custard sauce
1 teaspoon to 1½ teaspoons in frostings for 2 cake layers
2 teaspoons to 3 teaspoons in cookie recipe making about 5 dozen
½ teaspoon to 1 teaspoon in candy recipe using 2 cups sugar
2 teaspoons in about 4 cups custard for making ice cream

The items previously discussed are merely a sampling of the many, many spices, herbs and blends available to you. After reading this section and trying the suggestions it contains, we hope you will be encouraged by the evident ease of spice and herb cookery to experiment with the many other seasonings, equally popular and useful in food preparation, which have not been mentioned here because of space limitations. Some of these are: Hickory Smoked Salt, Italian Seasoning, Meat Tenderizer, Seasoned Meat Tenderizer, Salad Herbs, Seafood Seasoning, Bell Pepper Flakes, Vegetable Flakes, Barbecue Spice, Chives, Apple Pie Spice and Arrowroot.

To add even greater variety in flavor, color and eye appeal, you will wish to make use of the wide variety of extracts, food colors and attractive and colorful décors.

USE OF SPICES AND HERBS IN RESTRICTED DIETS:

Spices and herbs can help make restricted diets more interesting and palatable with a great variety of flavor combinations. Always consult your doctor before adding any food to a prescribed diet.

Most spices and herbs are low in sodium and can be used for good flavor when salt consumption is restricted.

Add a pinch of herbs, one or a mixture, to the water used for cooking vegetables . . . or sprinkle on after cooking.

Lean meats, fish and poultry may be seasoned before or after cooking, with herbs such as Rosemary, Thyme, Savory, Oregano, Basil, Marjoram, Dill Weed or Tarragon, used singly or in combinations of two or three for more subtle flavor.

Dress salads with lemon juice or vinegar and your choice of herbs or blended seasonings.

For more suggestions see pages 9–12.

The following recipes can be used to help reduce caloric intake. Use smaller servings of meat dishes. Omit any optional sauces and stuffings. Omit butter in the vegetable recipes.

Beverages
- Tomato Juice Cocktail, page 68
- Zippy Tomato Juice, page 354

Fish
- Ceviche, page 71
- Spiced Shrimp, page 78
- Scallops and Mushrooms en Brochette, page 179
- Fish Fillets in a Package, page 243
- Scampi on a Skewer, page 243

Meat • Use smaller servings.
- Beef Teriyaki, page 71
- Roast Whole Tenderloin, page 123
- Rolled Rib Roast Royale, page 123
- Roast Leg of Lamb, page 124
- Herb-Roasted Rack of Lamb, page 124
- Spiced Tongue, page 135
- Broiled Chicken, page 145
- Roast Turkey Supreme, page 160
- Rolled Rump Roast, page 240
- Shish Kebabs, page 245
- Grilled Chuck Steak, page 250
- Peppered Steak, page 250
- Rolled Rib Roast, page 251

Vegetables—Omit butter and any sauces suggested.
Marinated Mushrooms, page 78
Celery Victor, page 79
Chef's Salad Bowl, page 98
Piquant Tomato Aspic, page 101
Sweet-Sour Cucumbers with Onions, page 106
Sauerkraut Caraway, page 210
Carrots Vichy, page 218
Herb Seasoned Broccoli, page 220
Green Beans with Dill, page 220

Fruit
Fresh Fruit Medley, page 104

These recipes are indicated in text by use of *L.C.* before the recipe title, and in the index by l.c. *before* the page reference.

GENERAL COOKING INFORMATION

GENERAL

Always measure correctly. Measure liquids in a measuring cup especially designed for this purpose. These cups have head space above the one cup marking to prevent liquid from spilling over. Measure dry ingredients in nested measuring cups which do not have head space, so ingredients may be leveled with a spatula for more accurate measurement.

To measure ⅛ teaspoon of a dry ingredient, first measure a level ¼ teaspoon. Remove half of the measured ingredient.

To measure honey or molasses, first very lightly grease or oil the cup or spoon; otherwise, the measurement will be inaccurate because much of the honey or molasses will adhere to the utensil.

If a recipe calls for 1 cup chopped nuts, the nuts are chopped before measuring. In a recipe calling for 1 cup nuts, chopped, the nuts are first measured, then chopped.

When measuring brown sugar, always pack firmly into the cup.

To prevent brown sugar from hardening, store in a covered container. Insert a damp paper towel or napkin in the lid. If brown sugar has hardened, the same treatment will soften it.

When creaming butter and sugar for a cake, continue the creaming process until the mixture is light and fluffy and slightly resembles whipped cream.

When adding flour to cake batter, do not overmix.

When adding flour alternately with liquid, always start and end with the flour.

When using a glass cake pan, decrease the oven temperature 25°F.

To test for doneness insert a cake tester, skewer or toothpick in the center of the cake; when it comes out clean, the cake is done. Another test is to gently touch the center of the cake with finger. When no imprint remains, cake is done.

Arrowroot is ideal for thickening pie fillings since it becomes very clear upon thickening and does not cover any natural flavor.

After fluting the edge of pastry, press or crimp under rim in several places to prevent shrinkage.

Use 1½ to 2 cups crushed graham crackers, zwieback, gingersnaps, vanilla or chocolate wafers for an 8- or 9-inch pie.

The secret in making a perfect meringue that does not shrink nor weep:

(1) Have egg whites at room temperature.
(2) Add ¼ teaspoon Cream of Tartar to 2 to 3 whites.

(3) Beat until peaks form.

(4) Beat in sugar, adding 1 to 2 tablespoons at a time; then continue beating until sugar is dissolved and meringue forms stiff peaks.

(5) When spreading meringue over pie filling, be sure to seal meringue by spreading to crust.

(6) Bake in 400° to 425°F. oven until lightly browned.

(7) Cool in warm place free from draft.

When sauces are made in a double boiler, never allow the water in the bottom boiler to touch the bottom of the top boiler.

If Hollandaise sauce, Béarnaise sauce or any rich butter-egg sauce separates while preparing, add 1 to 2 teaspoons boiling water, stirring briskly while adding.

To steam a pudding use a large covered kettle. Place the pudding molds on a rack. Add enough boiling water to come two thirds up the side of the mold. Be sure the top of the mold is tightly covered. Cover kettle and always keep the water boiling.

Overcooking causes custards, rice pudding and custard-type bread puddings to become watery.

Freeze carbonated drinks, fruit juices or a small amount of a punch mixture to make an ice block or ice ring to float in punch to prevent diluting.

Tie whole spices in a bag for easy removal.

Tea may tend to cloud if refrigerated. Even though the cloudiness does not affect tea flavor, it can be cleared up by adding a small amount of boiling water.

Always stir rice with a fork—helps to prevent gummy rice.

Use low heat when cooking eggs or cheese.

To hard cook eggs, cover with cold water, bring to a boil, cover and let stand, off heat, 20 to 25 minutes.

A baking dish, as referred to in this book, is shallow and usually uncovered; whereas, a casserole dish is deep and has a cover.

Vegetables will retain their original color if cooked quickly in a small amount of water and in a saucepan with a tight-fitting cover.

Strong-flavored vegetables require more seasoning than mild-flavored vegetables.

To remove a gelatine salad or dessert from a mold follow these steps:

(1) First of all, lightly oil the mold before filling.

(2) Be sure the gelatine is thoroughly set before attempting to remove. Remember, large molds require more time to set than small ones.

(3) Loosen around top edge with a thin spatula.

(4) Dip the mold in warm, not hot, water for a few seconds.

(5) Gently pull the molded product away from the mold on one side to let air in.

(6) Quickly turn out, upside-down, on plate.

Serve hot foods hot and cold foods cold.

OUTDOOR COOKING

Start the fire early enough to have a good bed of coals before cooking begins.

A grey ash on briquets indicates they are burning.

The amount of heat depends on the number of briquets used and their distance apart. Cooking temperature may also be varied by raising or lowering the grill over the coals.

Cooking times vary due to thickness of food, heat of coals, distance from coals, outside temperature and amount of wind.

Barbecuing is not limited to expensive cuts of meat. Use Meat Tenderizer on less tender cuts for economy and variety of menu.

You will find a meat thermometer is helpful when cooking large pieces of meat on a spit. Caution should be taken when inserting the meat thermometer so the end is as near the center as possible but does not rest against the spit, the locking tines or bone.

COOKIES

Allow room for cookies to spread on baking sheet.

Remove from baking sheet as soon as removed from oven unless otherwise directed.

Remove cookies with a flat, flexible spatula.

Cool cookies on rack.

The yield will vary depending upon size of cutter used, thickness to which dough is rolled or sliced or amount of batter dropped from spoon.

The cooking time may vary from that given in recipe due to size or thickness of cookie.

If dough is to be chilled, Chill Well. You will find it easier to work with.

When making rolled cookies, cut as many as possible on first rolling of dough. Each time the dough is rolled more flour will be worked in and the cookies will become dryer and harder.

Store crisp cookies and moist cookies in separate containers.

To mail cookies, wrap each cookie separately or use dividers between layers and rows. Fill all the empty holes and spaces and around the edges of the box with popped corn.

CANDY

Test for Candy Making:

Soft Ball—232° to 240° for fudge, panocha and fondant. Syrup makes ball in cold water which can be picked up with fingers but will not hold its shape.

Firm Ball—242° to 248° for caramels and caramel corn. Syrup makes ball in cold water which holds its shape when picked up.

Hard Ball—250° to 268° for divinity and taffy. Syrup makes ball in cold water which feels hard to the touch but is still plastic.

Soft Crack—270° to 290° for toffee and butterscotch. Syrup makes hard but not brittle threads rather than a ball in cold water.

Hard Crack—300° to 310° for brittles, lollypops and taffy apples. Syrup makes brittle threads in cold water.

A good candy thermometer is well worth its price, for it takes the "guesswork" out of candy making.

Subtract 1° for each 500 feet elevation above sea level when testing candy with a thermometer.

Use a deep, fairly heavy saucepan with straight sides rather than a shallow skillet. (Liquid evaporates too fast in a skillet.)

Cook candy at a slow, but constant, boil unless directed otherwise.

Wash down sides of pan to help prevent crystal formation and graininess. Use any of the following methods:

(1) Wrap fork in a damp cloth and wash around sides of pan.

(2) Brush sides of pan with a pastry brush, with natural bristles, dipped in water.

(3) Cover the pan for 2 to 3 minutes after it begins to boil, being careful not to let it cook over.

To insure creaminess, cool fudge to 110° or lukewarm before stirring.

On rainy or humid days, cook candy 1° to 2° higher temperature or to a slightly firmer stage than recipe directs.

Do not worry if candy curdles while cooking. Beating will remedy this.

FISH AND SEA FOOD

Cook fish briefly. Fish is done when it flakes easily with a fork.

As a rule, do not turn fish when broiling or baking.

Baste fish and shellfish when baking or broiling.

For moist, tender shrimp, cook in well-seasoned, boiling water 7 minutes or until shells turn pink.

Spiced steamed shrimp, popular in many sections of the country, requires 10 to 15 minutes cooking time. Place shrimp on rack in kettle, add small amount of water and sprinkle generously with spices and herbs. Cover and steam. Shrimp is firmer and less moist which is characteristic of this cooking method.

Boil frozen rock lobster tails (it is not necessary to thaw) in boiling, salted water to cover. Allow 3 minutes longer than the ounce weight of largest lobster tail, such as 10 minutes for 7-ounce lobster tail.

CANNING

Examine jars for chips; wash well. Just before filling sterilize by boiling 10 minutes.

Spoons, funnels and other equipment used in canning and filling should also be sterilized.

Use fruits and vegetables of top quality. Be sure fresh fruits and vegetables are not overripe.

Use stone, glass or enamel container when soaking fruits or vegetables in a salt, alum or slaked lime solution.

When soaking vegetables or fruits in a solution, a plate or pie plate should be placed on top of the food and weighted down to insure the food being covered by the solution at all times . . . referred to as weighting.

Use a pure refined pickling, dairy, Kosher or rock salt. Table salt may be used; however, the brine may become cloudy.

When soaking cucumbers in a brine solution, scum will form on the top. It should be removed daily.

When whole spices are sealed in the jar with fruit or pickles, you may expect a very slightly darker product upon standing.

For best results when making jelly and preserves, work with small amounts of fruit.

Jellying stage refers to a degree of doneness in cooking jelly when two drops of the liquid will run together and flake or sheet off a spoon. When using a candy thermometer, cook jelly to about 8°F. above the boiling point of water in your locality.

Head space is the amount of space left between the top of the food and the lid.

Process refers to placing sealed jars on a rack in a large covered container with enough boiling water to come 1 to 2 inches above top of jars. Cover. Begin the timing after water has come back to a rolling boil.

The yield of a recipe will vary with the size of the vegetables or fruit being used and how compactly they are packed in the jar.

Follow manufacturer's directions for closing and sealing canning jars.

MEAT AND POULTRY

The most accurate way to judge the doneness of meat or poultry is with a meat thermometer. *For meat,* insert the thermometer into the thickest part, being sure the bulb does not rest on fat or bone. *For poultry,* insert thermometer so that the bulb is in the center of the inside thigh muscle or the thickest part of the breast meat. If meat thermometer is not used, test bird for doneness by moving drumstick from side to side. When it moves easily, bird is done.

Meat Roasting Chart

Meat	*Oven Temperature*	*Internal Temperature Indicated on Meat Thermometer*		*Approximate Time per Pound*	
				Weight of Meat	*Cooking Time*
Beef	300° to 325°F.	Rare	140°F.	6 to 8 pounds	18 to 20 min.
		Medium	160°F.		22 to 25 min.
		Well Done	170°F.		27 to 30 min.
Pork, Fresh	350°F.	185°F.		3 to 7 pounds	35 to 40 min.
Ham, Pre-cooked	300° to 325°F.	130°F.		10 to 12 pounds	12 to 15 min.
Ham, Smoked (uncooked)	300° to 325°F.	160°F.		10 to 14 pounds	18 to 20 min.
Lamb	300° to 325°F.	170° to 185°F.		3 to 5 pounds	30 to 35 min.
Veal	300°F.	170°F.		5 to 8 pounds	25 to 30 min.

Poultry Roasting Chart

Poultry	*Oven Temperature*	*Internal Temperature Indicated on Meat Thermometer*	*Approximate Time per Pound*	
			Ready-to-Cook Weight	*Cooking Time*
Turkey	325°F.	190°F.	10 to 14 pounds	4 to 5 hours
Chicken	375°F.	190°F.	4 to 6 pounds	2½ to 3½ hours
Duckling	325° to 350°F.	190°F.	4 to 5 pounds	2 to 3 hours
Capon	325° to 350°F.	190°F.	6 to 8 pounds	2½ to 3½ hours
Goose	325°F.	190°F.	10 to 12 pounds	4 to 5 hours

When bird is stuffed, cooking time is increased slightly.

SUBSTITUTIONS

It is best to use the ingredients recommended in the recipe, but the following suggestions are made if there must be substitutions.

For	*Use*
1 tbsp. arrowroot	2 tbsp. flour 1 tbsp. cornstarch
1 cup butter	1 cup margarine ⅞ cup lard plus ½ tsp. salt ⅞ to 1 cup hydrogenated shortening plus ½ tsp. salt

For	*Use*
1 sq. unsweetened chocolate (1 oz.)	3 tbsp. cocoa plus 1 tbsp. fat
1 whole egg	2 egg yolks, as in custards 2 egg yolks plus 1 tbsp. water, as in cookies
1 cup cake flour	⅞ cup all-purpose flour
1 cup honey	1¼ cups sugar plus ¼ cup liquid
1 cup fresh whole milk	½ cup evaporated milk plus ½ cup water 1 cup sour milk or buttermilk plus ½ tsp. soda. In recipes such as pancakes, biscuits and some cakes which call for baking powder omit 2 tsp. of the baking powder.
1 cup sour milk or buttermilk	1 tbsp. lemon juice or vinegar plus enough fresh whole milk to make 1 cup
1 cup sugar	¾ cup honey and omit 3 tbsp. plus 1 tsp. of the liquid. In baked products it is best to substitute honey for only one half of the sugar called for in the recipe.
1 cup canned tomatoes	About 1⅓ cups cut-up fresh tomatoes simmered 10 minutes
1 package active dry yeast	1 cake compressed yeast

COMMON FOOD EQUIVALENTS

	Unit or Weight	*Measure*
Apples	1 lb.	3 medium (3 cups sliced)
Butter and other fats	1 lb.	2 cups
Butter	¼ stick	2 tbsp.
	½ stick (⅛ lb.)	¼ cup
	1 stick (¼ lb.)	½ cup
	2 sticks (½ lb.)	1 cup
	4 sticks (1 lb.)	2 cups
Cheese, Cream	3-oz. package	6 tbsp.
Cheese, grated	1 lb.	4½ cups
Chocolate, unsweetened	1 oz.	1 square
Coconut, shredded	1 lb.	5 cups
Cranberries	1 lb.	4 cups
Cream, heavy	½ pt. (1 cup)	2 cups whipped cream
Currants	1 lb.	3 cups
Dates, pitted	1 lb.	2½ cups
Eggs, whole	3 (medium)	Approx. ½ cup
Egg, whites	4 (medium)	½ cup
Egg, yolks	3 (medium)	Approx. ¼ cup
Flour, All-purpose	1 lb.	4 cups (sifted)
Flour, Cake	1 lb.	4½ cups (sifted)
Flour, Whole Wheat	1 lb.	3½ cups

COMMON FOOD EQUIVALENTS (Cont.)

	Unit or Weight	Measure
Flour, Rye	1 lb.	4½ to 5 cups
Fruits & Peels, candied	1 lb.	3 cups (cut-up)
Gelatine, unflavored	1 envelope	1 tbsp.
Lemon, juice of	1	Will vary—2 to 3 tbsp.
Lemon Rind, grated	1	1½ tsp.
Macaroni	1 cup (uncooked)	2 to 2½ cups cooked
Noodles or Spaghetti	1 cup (uncooked)	1¾ to 2 cups cooked
Nuts, whole (shelled)		
almonds	1 lb.	3½ cups
pecans	1 lb.	4 cups
peanuts	1 lb.	3 cups
walnuts	1 lb.	4 cups
Orange, juice of	1	Approx. ½ cup
Orange Rind, grated	1	1 tbsp. (lightly grating only the outer part of rind)
Raisins	1 lb.	3¼ cups
Rice	1 lb.	2 cups
	1 cup (uncooked)	3 cups cooked
	1½ cups packaged pre-cooked	3 cups cooked
Sugar		
superfine	1 lb.	2 cups
granulated	1 lb.	2 cups
brown	1 lb.	2¼ cups firmly packed
Powdered or Confectioners'	1 lb.	3 cups to 5 cups; varies according to fineness of grind and way in which it is measured

EQUIVALENT MEASURES

Dash (used frequently in spice and herb cookery) = less than ⅛ teaspoon
3 teaspoons = 1 tablespoon
16 tablespoons = 1 cup
1 cup = ½ pint
2 cups = 1 pint
2 pints (4 cups) = 1 quart
4 quarts (liquid) = 1 gallon
8 quarts (solid) = 1 peck
4 pecks = 1 bushel
16 ounces = 1 pound

TABLESPOON MEASUREMENTS

1 tbsp. = ½ fl. ounce
2 tbsp. = 1 fl. ounce
4 tbsp. = ¼ cup
5 tbsp. + 1 tsp. = ⅓ cup
8 tbsp. = ½ cup
10 tbsp. + 2 tsp. = ⅔ cup
12 tbsp. = ¾ cup
14 tbsp. = ⅞ cup
16 tbsp. = 1 cup

COMMONLY USED ABBREVIATIONS

tsp. = teaspoon
tbsp. = tablespoon
pt. = pint
qt. = quart
pk. = peck
bu. = bushel
oz. = ounce or ounces
lb. = pound or pounds
sq. = square
min. = minute or minutes
hr. = hour or hours
mod. = moderate or moderately
doz. = dozen

GLOSSARY OF FOOD AND COOKING TERMS

bake: To cook by dry heat in oven; called roasting when applied to meats.

baste: To moisten food while it is cooking by spooning or brushing on liquid or fat.

beat: To stir thoroughly and vigorously.

blanch: To plunge into boiling water and then, in some cases, into cold water. Fruits and nuts are blanched to remove skin easily.

blend: To mix thoroughly.

boiling point, to the: The boiling point is reached when bubbles rise continuously and break at the surface. "To the boiling point" refers to the temperature reached just before bubbles begin to break surface.

bouquet garni: A combination of herbs tied together in thin cloth, used to season foods such as soups and stews; usually removed before serving.

braise: To brown in small amount of hot fat then cook slowly in covered utensil, adding a small amount of liquid.

bread: To coat with flour or crumbs and egg or liquid prior to cooking.

bread crumbs: *Soft bread crumbs*—fresh bread pulled into small pieces.
Fine dry bread crumbs—dried stale bread rolled into crumbs; may also be purchased ready-to-use.
Buttered bread crumbs—fine bread crumbs sautéed in butter.

bread cubes, soft: Day-old bread cut into ½- to 1-inch cubes.

brew: To steep or let stand in hot water to extract the flavor, as in tea.

broil: To cook directly under heat or over an open fire.

brown: To cook in a small amount of fat until brown.

canapés: Small pieces of fried or toasted bread with seasoned toppings.

caramelize: To melt granulated sugar in skillet over medium heat, stirring constantly, until it becomes a golden brown syrup.

champignons: Mushrooms.
chill: To cool in refrigerator but not freeze.
chopped: Cut into small pieces with chopper or sharp knife—do not use a food grinder.
coat: To cover with a thin layer of flour, sugar, nuts, crumbs, Sesame or Poppy Seed, Cinnamon Sugar or a few of the ground spices.
coats a spoon: Refers to a degree of thickness obtained when mixture is thick enough to form a definite film on a metal spoon, as in sauces and soft custards.
coddle: To cook slowly and gently just below the simmering point, as eggs and fruits.
cognac: Brandy from the Cognac region of France.
compote: Fruits cooked slowly in syrup (may be spiced), during which time they retain their shape. Also refers to a stemmed dish.
coquille: Shell or shell dish for baking and serving foods.
cream: To make soft, smooth and creamy by rubbing with back of spoon or by beating with mixer; usually applied to fat and sugar.
crêpe: A very thin pancake of French origin.
crisp-tender: Cooked until just tender, but not soft nor limp.
croquette: Finely chopped meat or fish combined with thick white sauce, frequently cone-shaped, coated with egg and crumbs and fried until crisp.
croutons: Small toasted or fried cubes of bread—excellent when seasoned.
cube: To cut into small pieces with 6 equal sides.
custard: A cooked or baked sweetened mixture of milk and eggs.
dairy sour cream: Cultured, dairy soured cream.
deep fat fry: To fry food in enough fat to cover. Keep at least 3 inches between surface of fat and top of kettle. Never cover utensil while heating or frying.
dice: To cut into very small cubes.
dredge: To coat with a dry ingredient, such as flour or sugar.
drippings: The fat and juices obtained when cooking meats.
drizzle: To pour in a fine thread-like stream over a surface.
dust: To sprinkle or coat lightly with flour or sugar.
filet mignon: A slice of steak cut from the tenderloin of beef.
filet or fillet: A boneless strip of meat or fish.
fines herbes: Mixed herbs, such as Parsley, Chervil, Tarragon and Chives.
flake: To break into small pieces.
fold in: A gentle and careful combining of a light or delicate mixture with a heavier mixture.
Grand Marnier: Orange-flavored liqueur.
grate: To cut into minute particles by rubbing over grater.
hors d'oeuvres: Savory dainty foods served as appetizer; made from different combinations of delicacies and tidbits and served hot or cold.
knead: To work dough using heel of hand with a pressing motion while stretching and folding the dough.

marinade: A seasoned sauce, usually an oil and acid mixture, in which meats or other foods are soaked.

marinate: To let food stand in a marinade to season and tenderize.

meunière: Fish dipped in flour and sautéed in butter.

mince: To chop into very small bits.

mix: To combine ingredients by stirring.

mousse: A frozen dessert of sweetened and flavored whipped cream or light cream and gelatine; frozen without stirring.

pan-fry: To cook, uncovered, in small amount of hot fat not deep enough to cover food.

parboil: To cook partially in boiling salted water or other liquid.

pare: To cut away outside covering.

pâté: A paste of meat or sea food used as a spread for toast or crackers.

peel: To strip away outside covering.

pilaf, pilaff, pilau or pilaw: A dish of rice or cracked wheat, sometimes in combination with vermicelli.

plump: To soak in liquid or moisten thoroughly and heat in 350°F. oven until full and round.

poach: To simmer gently in enough hot liquid to cover, using care to retain shape of food.

powdered sugar: The terminology "powdered sugar" as used in the United States is referred to in many places as "confectioners' sugar" and in Canada and England as "icing sugar."

purée: A smooth paste, usually of vegetables or fruits, made by putting foods through a sieve, food mill or beating in a blender.

ragout: A well seasoned meat stew.

ramekins: Small oval or round individual baking dishes.

reconstitute: To put moisture back into dehydrated foods by soaking in liquid.

reduce: To boil liquid until part of the water is evaporated.

rice: To force vegetables through "ricer" or fine colander to break into small particles.

roast: To cook, uncovered, in oven or to cook outdoors on spit.

sauté: To cook or brown in small amount of hot fat.

scald: To heat to just under boiling point. Used frequently in reference to heating milk.

scaloppine: Thin slices of meat, usually veal.

score: To mark food with cuts, notches or lines to prevent curling or to make food more attractive.

sear: To brown surface quickly over high heat in hot skillet or similar utensil or over grill.

shred: To cut or tear into small, usually long, narrow pieces.

simmer: To cook slowly on top of range just below boiling point. Small bubbles form but liquid is practically motionless.

skewer: A long pin of wood or metal on which food or meat is held while cooking; or to position food on "skewer."
slivered: Sliced into long, thin pieces, usually in reference to nuts.
spätzle: Dough forced through a coarse colander to form noodles, usually used with goulash and stews.
steep: To soak in a liquid below boiling point to extract flavor.
stud: To adorn with; for example, baked ham studded with whole Cloves.
suet: White fat of beef or mutton.
thicken: To make a thin, smooth paste by mixing together Arrowroot, cornstarch or flour with an equal amount cold water. Stir into hot liquid and cook, stirring, until thickened.
tortilla: A thin unleavened pancake prepared from coarse corn meal.
toss: To gently mix ingredients with two forks or fork and spoon.
truffle: An edible fungus grown underground, highly prized as a delicacy, and used as a seasoning or garnish.
whip: To beat rapidly to incorporate air and produce expansion.

APPETIZERS

Pâtés, Spreads and Dips

Bon Appétit Dip aux Herbes 70
Cheese Dip Caraway 77
Chili Cheese Roll 68
Crab Meat Dunk 65
Curry Dip 80
Dilly of a Dip 70
Guacamole 65
Herb Roquefort Dip 66
Liver Pâté Bon Appétit 73
Mephisto Ham Dip 66
Pâté de Foie en Aspic 67
Sesame Cheese Ball 68
Sour Cream Dip for Fresh Fruit 63
Toasted Onion Dip 75

Snacks and Cold Hors d'Oeuvres

Barbecued Nibblers 69
  Curried Nibblers 69
Best Ever Stuffed Eggs 69
  Dill Stuffed Eggs 69
  Curry Stuffed Eggs 69
  Chicken or Bacon Stuffed Eggs 69
Bologna Pinwheels 75
Ceviche 71
Cheese and Caviar Croutelettes 67
Salted Spiced Walnuts 72
Spiced Shrimp 78
  Oriental Spiced Shrimp 78
  Spiced Shrimp Maison 78

Hot Hors d'Oeuvres

Beef Teriyaki 71
Chinese Stuffed Mushrooms 73
Cocktail Meatballs in Red Wine 64
Crab-Stuffed Mushrooms 80
Curried Chicken Balls 72
Curry Puffs 75
Hot Canapés 72
Marjoram Meat Balls 70
Quiche Lorraine 66
Rumaki 77
Sauerbraten Nibblers 63
Savory Onion Rounds 65
Surprise Cheese Puffs 74

Vegetable and Fruit Relishes

Marinated Artichoke Hearts 74
Marinated Mushrooms 78
Stuffed Celery Sticks 79
Tinted-Minted Pineapple 74

First Course Hors d'Oeuvres

Broiled Clams 77
Celery Victor 79
Coquille Saint-Jacques 76
Oysters Rockefeller 76

Juices

Pineapple-Grapefruit Delight 79
  Pineapple-Grapefruit Refresher 79
Spiced Cranberry Juice Cocktail 64
Tomato Juice Cocktail 68

Sour Cream Dip for Fresh Fruit

1/8 teaspoon Cinnamon
1/8 teaspoon Nutmeg
Dash Allspice
Dash salt
2 tablespoons sugar
1 cup dairy sour cream
1/2 teaspoon pure Vanilla Extract
1/8 teaspoon Rum Extract

Mix cinnamon, nutmeg, allspice and salt with sugar. Stir into sour cream. Add extracts and mix well. Chill 2 hours to allow flavors to blend. Serve with fresh fruit—strawberries, bing cherries, green grapes, apples and bananas.

Makes 1 cup.

Sauerbraten Nibblers

2 pounds round or sirloin steak, cut 3/4 inch thick
3/4 cup red wine vinegar
1 cup water
2 tablespoons dark molasses
2 tablespoons Instant Minced Onion
3 Bay Leaves
12 Peppercorns
6 whole Cloves
1/2 teaspoon Thyme Leaves
1 tablespoon flour
2 tablespoons salad oil
1 tablespoon cornstarch
1 teaspoon Ginger
1/8 teaspoon Allspice
1/4 teaspoon Garlic Salt
1 teaspoon salt

Cut steak into bite-size cubes. Combine with vinegar, water, 1 tablespoon of the molasses, onion, bay leaves, peppercorns, cloves and thyme leaves. Cover and refrigerate 24 to 48 hours. Drain, reserving marinade. Remove whole spices. Sprinkle meat with flour. Lightly brown meat, 1/2 at a time, in oil in large skillet over medium-high heat. Return all the meat to skillet. Combine cornstarch, ginger, allspice, garlic salt and salt. Stir in 1/3 cup of the reserved marinade. Add to meat in skillet, along with remaining 1 tablespoon molasses. Cook over medium-high heat, stirring constantly just until sauce thickens.

Makes 1 quart.

Cocktail Meatballs in Red Wine

1 pound ground beef
1 egg
1 teaspoon Instant Minced Onion
1 teaspoon Season-All
¼ teaspoon Black Pepper
¼ teaspoon Garlic Salt
¼ teaspoon dry Mustard
1½ cups crushed shredded wheat (coarse crumbs)
1 cup red wine

Lightly mix ground beef with next 6 ingredients and ½ cup of the shredded wheat crumbs. Shape into 1-inch meatballs. Roll in remaining shredded wheat crumbs. Place in single layer in an 11¾ x 7½ x 1¾-inch baking dish. Pour wine around meatballs. Bake in 350° F. oven 30 minutes. Serve hot.

Makes 36 meatballs.

Spiced Cranberry Juice Cocktail

6 whole Cloves
4 whole Allspice
4 Peppercorns
1 small piece Ginger Root, bruised
2 whole Cardamom seeds, bruised
1 3-inch piece stick Cinnamon
¼ cup sugar
1 cup water
1 48-ounce bottle cranberry juice cocktail

In saucepan combine all ingredients except cranberry juice. Bring to boil, reduce heat to low, cover and simmer 10 minutes.

FOR HOT COCKTAIL: Add cranberry juice to spiced liquid, heat to steaming, do not boil. Strain before serving.

FOR CHILLED COCKTAIL: Remove spices from liquid. Add liquid to cranberry juice. Chill.

Makes 1¾ quarts.

Crab Meat Dunk

1 cup crab meat
¼ cup lime or lemon juice
1 3-ounce package cream cheese
¼ cup heavy cream
2 tablespoons mayonnaise
1 teaspoon Instant Minced Onion
⅛ teaspoon Garlic Powder
2 dashes ground Red Pepper
1 teaspoon Worcestershire sauce
½ teaspoon salt
⅛ teaspoon MSG

Marinate crab meat in lime or lemon juice 30 minutes. Beat together cream cheese, cream, mayonnaise and seasonings until smooth and creamy. Fold in marinated crab meat. For a really attractive service, serve in a deep shell or shell-shaped bowl nested in crushed ice with an interesting arrangement of bite-size pieces of Chinese cabbage, celery, sliced cauliflowerettes, green peppers and thin, wide slices of carrot. Do not forget a basket of crackers or chips. *Makes about 1½ cups.*

Savory Onion Rounds

¼ teaspoon Season-All
¼ teaspoon Savory
¼ teaspoon dry Mustard
Dash MSG
¼ cup mayonnaise
12 thin slices onion
12 crackers

Combine seasonings and mayonnaise. Put onion slices on crackers and spread with mayonnaise mixture. Broil until bubbly and brown. Serve hot. *Makes 12.*

Guacamole

This avocado dip, a favorite in Mexico, is colorful, tart and delicious!

1 large ripe avocado
½ ripe tomato, peeled and finely chopped
½ green pepper, seeded and finely chopped
1 teaspoon Onion Salt
½ teaspoon Chili Powder
½ teaspoon salt
¼ teaspoon Black Pepper
½ teaspoon olive oil
1 teaspoon lime juice
½ cup mayonnaise

Mash avocado with a fork. Blend in remaining ingredients except mayonnaise. Spread mayonnaise over top of dip to keep it from darkening. When ready to serve, blend in mayonnaise. Serve with corn chips or use as topping for cherry tomatoes. *Makes about 2 cups.*

Herb Roquefort Dip

1 8-ounce package cream cheese
1 3-ounce package Roquefort cheese
1 teaspoon Beef Flavor Base
1 tablespoon hot water
½ teaspoon dry Mustard
½ teaspoon Herb Seasoning
Dash Nutmeg or Mace
5 tablespoons dairy sour cream or milk

Have cheese at room temperature. Dissolve beef flavor base in hot water. Combine all ingredients, mixing thoroughly. Serve with crackers, chips, celery or carrot sticks. *Makes about 1½ cups.*

Quiche Lorraine

Pastry for 10-inch pie shell
4 thin slices Smithfield ham
1 cup grated Swiss cheese
5 eggs
1¼ cups milk
1¼ cups light cream
¼ teaspoon salt
⅛ teaspoon ground Red Pepper
½ teaspoon Season-All or Bon Appétit
Dash Nutmeg
Dash MSG

Line a 10-inch pie plate with pastry. Cut ham into small pieces (should have about ¾ cup) and heat in frying pan for a few minutes; sprinkle over pastry. (Twelve slices bacon may be substituted for ham. Cook bacon until crisp, then crumble into small pieces.) Sprinkle cheese over ham. Beat eggs; add remaining ingredients and mix well. Pour over cheese and ham. Bake in 375°F. oven 40 minutes. You can cut Quiche Lorraine into wedges and serve as a first course or for a light luncheon. Or, cut into small squares for appetizers. *Serves 8 to 10 when cut into wedges or many more when cut into squares, depending upon size.*

Mephisto Ham Dip

A mixture zesty enough to please the devil himself.

1 8-ounce package cream cheese
1 2¼-ounce can deviled ham or Smithfield ham spread
2 teaspoons Instant Minced Onion
2 teaspoons Parsley Flakes
4 teaspoons milk
1 teaspoon prepared horseradish
Dash Garlic Salt
Dash Celery Salt
Dash Black Pepper

Have cheese at room temperature. Add remaining ingredients and mix until thoroughly blended. Serve with potato chips, crisp fresh vegetables or spread on crackers and toasted bread rounds. Excellent for sandwiches too. If any dip is leftover, you may freeze it for future use.

Makes 1½ cups.

Cheese and Caviar Croutelettes

A different and easy-to-make appetizer—cream cheese and caviar in small pastry shells.

1 8-ounce package cream cheese
¼ teaspoon Onion Salt
⅛ teaspoon White Pepper
¼ teaspoon dry Mustard
¼ teaspoon Lemon Peel
Dash MSG
1 teaspoon lemon juice
2 tablespoons milk
4 drops Red Food Color
1 carton croutelettes (30 to 36)
2 tablespoons caviar

Have cheese at room temperature. Add onion salt, pepper, dry mustard, lemon peel, MSG, lemon juice, milk and food color. Mix until smooth and creamy. Fill croutelettes. You can make attractive shapes by using a pastry bag with tube. Top each with about ⅛ teaspoon caviar. *Makes 30 to 36.*

Pâté de Foie en Aspic

A smooth, subtly seasoned pâté for your most elegant party.

1 pound chicken livers
1 tablespoon Instant Minced Onion
1 stalk celery, chopped
1 Bay Leaf
1 teaspoon Parsley Flakes
⅛ teaspoon Thyme Leaves
⅛ teaspoon Rosemary Leaves, crushed
1 tablespoon Chicken Flavor Base
1 cup hot water
¾ cup dry white wine or tomato juice
2 envelopes unflavored gelatine
¼ cup cold water
1 3-ounce package cream cheese
¾ teaspoon Celery Salt
½ teaspoon dry Mustard
1 teaspoon prepared horseradish

Combine first nine ingredients and ½ cup of the wine or tomato juice in a saucepan. Bring to a boil; simmer 20 minutes or until livers are tender. Remove livers; strain and reserve liquid. If necessary, add water to make 1½ cups liquid; heat and mix with gelatine which has been softened in the cold water. Stir to melt. Cover bottom of 1-quart mold with a thin layer of the gelatine mixture and chill until firm. Set aside remaining gelatine mixture. Put chicken livers through fine blade of food chopper or purée in a blender. Combine with remaining wine or tomato juice, cream cheese, celery salt, dry mustard and horseradish. Mix well. Thoroughly blend chicken liver mixture with remaining gelatine mixture; pour into mold. Chill until firm. Remove from mold; serve with crackers or Melba toast.

Makes 1 quart, serving about 12 to 15 people.

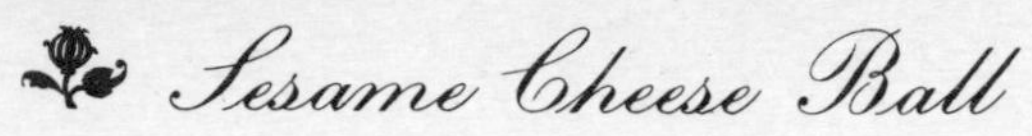

Sesame Cheese Ball

¼ cup Sesame Seed
2 tablespoons Instant Minced Onion
1 teaspoon Beef Flavor Base
2 tablespoons lemon juice
½ pound medium sharp cheese
2 tablespoons mayonnaise
1 tablespoon ketchup
1 teaspoon Worcestershire sauce
1 teaspoon dry Mustard

Toast sesame seed in 350°F. oven 15 minutes or until lightly browned. Soak onion and beef flavor base in lemon juice. Grate cheese. Mix all ingredients, except sesame seed, until well blended. Shape into ball. Spread toasted sesame seed on waxed paper; roll cheese ball in seed until outside is coated. Chill. For a festive party idea serve on a tray with a cheese knife. Surround with assorted crackers and Melba toast. Excellent when spread on toast rounds and broiled until cheese melts. Makes good sandwiches.

Makes 1 cup.

Chili Cheese Roll

Crunchy pecans in a cheese roll coated with spicy Chili Powder.

1 8-ounce package American cheese, grated
1 3-ounce package cream cheese
⅛ teaspoon Garlic Powder
¼ cup chopped pecans
2 tablespoons Chili Powder

Have cheese at room temperature; mix both until well blended. Stir in garlic powder and pecans. Form into a roll about 10 inches long. Spread the chili powder on waxed paper and coat the outside of cheese with the chili powder by rolling over the waxed paper. Chill. Slice and serve with crackers or Melba toast.

Makes forty ¼-inch thick slices.

L.C. Tomato Juice Cocktail

6 cups tomato juice or 1 46-ounce can
6 whole Cloves
2 whole Allspice
1 Bay Leaf
1 tablespoon Instant Minced Onion
⅛ teaspoon Black Pepper
1 teaspoon Bon Appétit
1 tablespoon sugar
Dash MSG
3 tablespoons vinegar

Combine all ingredients except vinegar. Bring to a boil, then simmer 15 minutes. Strain. Add vinegar. Chill several hours. Serve cold.

Makes about 6 cups or 10 to 12 servings.

NOTE:

It's fun to experiment with tomato juice. Why don't you try other combinations of spices from your spice rack?

Barbecued Nibblers

½ cup butter
1 tablespoon Barbecue Spice
2 teaspoons Bon Appétit
¼ teaspoon Garlic Powder
2 tablespoons Sesame Seed, toasted
2 cups rice cereal, bite size
2 cups corn cereal, bite size
1 cup wheat cereal, bite size
1 cup thin pretzel sticks
2 cups mixed nuts

Melt butter in small saucepan; stir in seasonings and toasted sesame seed. (Toast sesame seed in 350°F. oven 15 minutes or until golden brown.) Pour hot seasoned butter over dry cereals, pretzel sticks and nuts. Mix thoroughly until all pieces are coated. Spread evenly in a 15½ x 10½ x 1-inch baking pan and bake in 250°F. oven 1 hour, stirring occasionally.

Makes 2 quarts.

VARIATION:

Curried Nibblers—Substitute ½ teaspoon Curry Powder, ½ teaspoon Cinnamon, 2 teaspoons Onion Salt and dash ground Red Pepper for the above seasonings.

Subtle spices give a new and savory twist to old favorites.

6 eggs, hard cooked
¼ cup mayonnaise
2 teaspoons lemon juice or vinegar
½ teaspoon Chicken Flavor Base
⅛ teaspoon Onion Powder
⅛ teaspoon White Pepper
½ teaspoon Bon Appétit
⅛ teaspoon Savory or Turmeric
"Little tidbits" for toppings: Parsley Flakes, Paprika, capers, anchovies, olive slices or pimiento

Carefully cut hard-cooked eggs in half. You can vary the shape by cutting the eggs crosswise instead of lengthwise. Remove yolks and mash or force through a sieve. Add mayonnaise, lemon juice, flavor base, onion powder, pepper, Bon Appétit and savory or turmeric. Mix thoroughly. Refill the whites, piling the yolk mixture high. Top with parsley flakes, a dash paprika or one of the other "tidbits."

Makes 12 halves.

VARIATIONS:

Dill Stuffed Eggs—In place of Bon Appétit and savory or turmeric use ½ to 1 teaspoon Dill Weed, ¾ teaspoon Celery Salt and dash ground Red Pepper.

Curry Stuffed Eggs—Add ½ to 1 teaspoon Curry Powder to above recipe.

Chicken or Bacon Stuffed Eggs—To any of the above recipes stir in ½ cup finely minced, cooked or canned chicken or 3 slices bacon which has been crisp-cooked and crumbled.

Marjoram Meat Balls

½ cup fine dry bread crumbs
¼ cup milk
1 pound ground beef
1 teaspoon Season-All
½ teaspoon Onion Powder
½ teaspoon ground Marjoram
¼ teaspoon ground Thyme
¼ teaspoon Black Pepper
⅛ teaspoon MSG
Dash Mace
3 tablespoons oil
1 teaspoon Beef Flavor Base
¼ cup hot water

Soak crumbs in milk, then combine with ground beef, Season-All, onion powder, marjoram, thyme, pepper, MSG and mace. Shape into 30 to 36 small balls, using a rounded teaspoonful for each. Brown on all sides in hot oil. Dissolve beef flavor base in hot water; pour over meat balls. Cover and simmer 20 minutes. For extra zest, add ½ cup wine to these miniature meat balls before simmering. Serve plain or with your favorite sauce.

Makes 3 dozen.

Bon Appétit Dip aux Herbes

Flavoring so subtle no one will be sure quite what's in it—and everyone will want to know!

1 8-ounce package cream cheese
6 tablespoons milk or cream
1 teaspoon Chicken Flavor Base
1 tablespoon hot water
1 tablespoon Instant Minced Onion
½ teaspoon Bon Appétit
½ teaspoon Marjoram Leaves
½ teaspoon Tarragon Leaves
½ cup finely minced, cooked chicken, shrimp, clams or crab meat

Have cheese at room temperature. Beat until creamy. Gradually stir in milk or cream and flavor base which has been dissolved in hot water. Add remaining ingredients, mixing well. Serve with an assortment of crisp crackers or chips. For an interesting idea use as a filling for marinated mushrooms or bite-size tart shells.

Makes about 1 cup.

Dilly of a Dip

1 cup commercial sour cream
1 teaspoon Dill Weed
⅛ teaspoon Onion Powder
1 teaspoon Bon Appétit
Dash MSG

Thoroughly mix together all ingredients. Refrigerate at least 1½ hours to blend flavors. Excellent served with crackers, chips or crisp raw vegetables. You will also find this delicious served on hot baked potatoes.

Makes 1 cup.

L.C. Ceviche

Spicy and exotic lime-marinated fish bits from Mexico.

1 pound firm, white, fish fillets
Lime juice to cover
3 Bay Leaves
¼ teaspoon White Pepper
1 teaspoon Bon Appétit
⅛ teaspoon Instant Minced Garlic
⅓ cup Chopped Instant Onions
1 teaspoon Crushed Red Pepper
1 teaspoon salt
¼ cup sliced, stuffed olives
¼ cup juice from olives
1 tablespoon oil
¼ cup catchup
2 tomatoes, finely chopped
1 hot chili pepper, chopped

Remove tissue-like skin from fish. Cut fish into very thin strips 1 inch long or into small cubes. Put in glass jar and cover with lime juice. (It will take about 1½ cups juice or 1 dozen limes, depending on size and amount of juice in limes.) Refrigerate overnight or for several hours. Drain. Combine fish with remaining ingredients. Store in refrigerator at least one hour, preferably longer. Will keep well in refrigerator for several days. When ready to serve, remove bay leaves and serve in individual dishes with a garnish of lettuce. *Serves 6 to 8.*

L.C. Beef Teriyaki

1 pound tenderloin or sirloin beef, cut 1 inch thick
¾ cup soy sauce
¼ cup dark brown sugar, packed
¼ teaspoon Garlic Powder
½ teaspoon Onion Salt
2 tablespoons lemon juice
1 teaspoon ground Ginger or 10 to 12 pieces whole Ginger, about the size of a shelled peanut

Cut meat into bite-size cubes. Combine remaining ingredients; pour over beef cubes and let stand at room temperature one hour or in the refrigerator several hours. Thread cubes of meat onto a skewer. (Pineapple chunks may be alternated with the beef cubes.) Broil about 3 inches from heat 10 to 12 minutes, turning once, or cook over grill or hibachi. Serve hot as an appetizer or with rice as a main course. *Makes appetizers for 10 to 12.*

Salted Spiced Walnuts

2 teaspoons Ginger
½ teaspoon Allspice
5 cups water
1 pound walnut halves
4 tablespoons melted butter
½ teaspoon Garlic Salt or Season-All

Add ginger and allspice to water; bring to boil. Drop in walnuts and boil about 3 minutes. Drain well. Spread in a shallow pan and bake in 350°F. oven 15 minutes or until lightly browned. Remove from oven and toss with melted butter and garlic salt or Season-All.

Hot Canapés

1 pound ground beef
½ teaspoon MSG
½ teaspoon dry Mustard
¾ teaspoon salt
¼ teaspoon Black Pepper
⅛ teaspoon Nutmeg
1 tablespoon Instant Minced Onion
12 slices bread

Mix ground beef with MSG, dry mustard, salt, pepper, nutmeg and onion, blending well. Cut bread into 2-inch squares or into circles 1½ to 2 inches in diameter. Arrange on baking sheet and toast on one side until golden brown. Turn bread over and spread the untoasted side of each with about 1 tablespoon of the seasoned meat. (Preparation up to this point may be done in advance. Cover and refrigerate until ready to broil and serve.) Broil 3 inches from heat 1 to 2 minutes. Serve immediately. *Makes about 48.*

Curried Chicken Balls

Unusual and distinctively different are the words your guests will use to describe these delicious hors d'oeuvres.

2 pounds ground, raw chicken or turkey
1 teaspoon Onion Powder
1 tablespoon Curry Powder
1 teaspoon Season-All
¼ teaspoon MSG
1 egg, lightly beaten
2 teaspoons salt
2 teaspoons lemon juice
2 tablespoons fine bread crumbs
¼ cup flour
¼ cup butter

Combine all ingredients except flour and butter; mix well. Form into small, bite-size balls. Roll lightly in flour and sauté in butter 15 minutes or until golden brown on all sides. Serve in a chafing dish or candle-warmed casserole in Creamy Curry Sauce (see recipe page 341). Be sure to have plenty of toothpicks handy. *Makes about 90.*

Chinese Stuffed Mushrooms

The nutty flavor of toasted Sesame Seed adds elegance to these mushrooms.

1 pound mushrooms
1 tablespoon butter
2 tablespoons water
½ teaspoon Chicken Flavor Base or Beef Flavor Base
½ pound ground, cooked pork (2 to 2½ cups)
¼ teaspoon Ginger
2 teaspoons Instant Minced Onion
¼ teaspoon MSG
Dash ground Red Pepper
¼ cup minced water chestnuts
2 teaspoons soy sauce
2 tablespoons melted butter
¼ cup Sesame Seed

Select uniform-size mushrooms about 1¼ inches in diameter. Wash and remove stems. In a saucepan, combine 1 tablespoon butter, water and flavor base. Heat to boiling. Add mushrooms; cover and simmer 3 minutes. Remove from heat; carefully lift out mushroom caps and save liquid. Let mushrooms cool while you prepare the filling. Combine remaining ingredients except sesame seed; mix well. If mixture seems dry, add 2 to 4 tablespoons water or broth. Stuff mushroom caps and dip tops in sesame seed. (Preparation up to this point may be done in advance. Cover and refrigerate until ready to bake and serve.) Place in shallow baking pan, and add liquid in which mushrooms were cooked. Bake in 375°F. oven 25 minutes or until sesame seed are lightly browned. Serve hot. *Makes about 30.*

Liver Pâté Bon Appétit

1 pound chicken livers
½ cup dry white wine
½ cup water
1 teaspoon Chicken Flavor Base
1 teaspoon Parsley Flakes
1 tablespoon Instant Minced Onion
¼ teaspoon Ginger
¼ teaspoon MSG
1 tablespoon soy sauce
½ cup soft butter
1 teaspoon Bon Appétit
¼ teaspoon dry Mustard
Dash Nutmeg
1 tablespoon brandy

Combine the first nine ingredients; bring to a boil. Reduce heat and simmer 20 minutes. Cool livers in liquid; drain. Put livers through fine blade of food grinder or purée in blender. Add remaining ingredients. Beat hard until well mixed and smooth. If mixture seems too thick, add small amount of the cooking liquid. Store in refrigerator in covered container at least 24 hours to blend flavors. Serve on crisp, shredded lettuce as an appetizer or with crackers and toast as a cocktail spread. *Makes about 1¾ cups.*

Surprise Cheese Puffs

Bite into these golden hot puffs and find a heart of stuffed olive.

½ cup butter
2 cups grated sharp cheese
½ teaspoon salt
1 teaspoon Paprika
Dash ground Red Pepper
1 cup sifted all-purpose flour
50 small stuffed green olives

Allow butter to soften; blend with cheese, salt, paprika and red pepper. Stir in flour, mixing well. Mold 1 teaspoon of this mixture around each olive, covering it completely. Arrange on a baking sheet and chill until firm. Bake in 400°F. oven 15 minutes. Serve hot. *Makes 50 puffs.*

NOTE: These little puffs are so easy to serve at parties as they may be made in advance, frozen on a baking sheet to keep round and stored in a plastic bag in the freezer. Bake as needed.

Marinated Artichoke Hearts

1 9-ounce package frozen artichoke hearts
2 tablespoons lemon juice
2 tablespoons olive oil
¼ teaspoon Oregano Leaves
¼ teaspoon Tarragon Leaves
¼ teaspoon Garlic Salt

Cook artichoke hearts following directions on package. Drain and put in small bowl. Combine remaining ingredients and pour over artichoke hearts. Chill at least 2 hours. You will find marinated artichoke hearts excellent served with egg, sea food or tossed green salad. *Serves 4.*

Tinted-Minted Pineapple

1 20-ounce can (2½ cups) pineapple chunks
½ cup vinegar
1 cup sugar
2 tablespoons Mint Flakes
Red Food Color or Green Food Color

Drain syrup from pineapple chunks. To the syrup add vinegar, sugar and mint flakes. Stir to dissolve sugar and bring to a boil. Cover and simmer 10 minutes. Remove from heat; keep covered and set aside to cool. Strain to remove mint flakes. To the liquid add ¼ teaspoon (about 25 drops) red or green food color; stir. Add pineapple chunks. Store in a covered dish or jar in refrigerator. You will also find this a tasty and attractive garnish for meats, especially lamb.

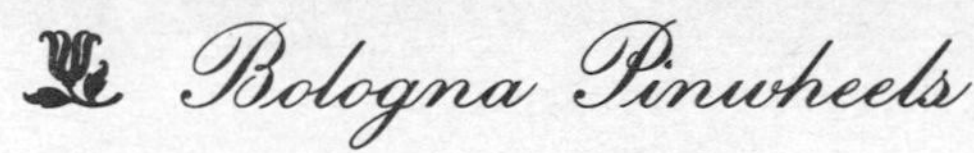

Bologna Pinwheels

1 3-ounce package cream cheese
1 tablespoon milk
¼ cup finely chopped green olives
½ teaspoon Season-All
Dash MSG
Dash White Pepper
¼ pound sliced bologna

Have cheese at room temperature; blend with milk. Stir in olives, Season-All, MSG and pepper. Spread cheese mixture over bologna slices; roll tightly. Wrap in waxed paper and chill. Before serving, cut each roll into slices. *Makes about ½ cup cheese mixture or about 30 delicious bite-size pieces.*

Toasted Onion Dip

The secret of this crunchy nutty flavor is Chopped Instant Onions *delicately* toasted.

1 cup dairy sour cream
2 teaspoons Beef Flavor Base
1 teaspoon Bon Appétit
2 tablespoons Chopped Instant Onions

Combine sour cream, beef flavor base and Bon Appétit. Mix well and set aside. Toast onions in 350°F. oven 1 minute or until lightly browned. Add to sour cream mixture. Allow mixture to stand at least 20 minutes before serving. Serve with assorted crackers or chips. *Makes 1 cup.*

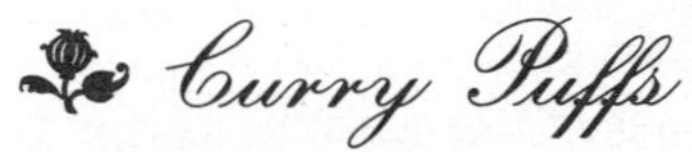

Curry Puffs

Crisp little bite-size pastries filled with an exotic curry-meat stuffing, called *Samosas* in India.

1 recipe for two-crust pastry
2 cups finely chopped cooked lamb
1 tablespoon Curry Powder
1 tablespoon syrup from chutney
1 teaspoon Season-All
¼ cup condensed cream of mushroom soup, undiluted
Fat for deep fat frying

Make pastry using your favorite recipe or package mix; roll thin. Cut out circles using a round cookie cutter 3 inches in diameter. Mix together remaining ingredients. Place 1 heaping teaspoon of the mixture on each circle of dough. Fold over to make a semicircle; thoroughly seal edges by pressing with the tines of a fork. Fry in deep fat, 375°F., 4 minutes or until golden brown. You may make these ahead of time and heat in oven when ready to serve. *Makes about 3 dozen.*

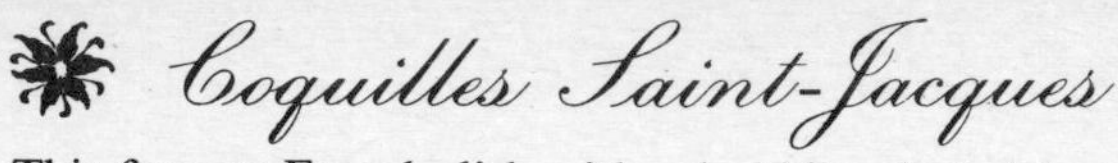

Coquilles Saint-Jacques

This famous French dish with a bubbling-hot, delectable sauce makes an elegant first course.

6 tablespoons butter
3 tablespoons flour
¼ teaspoon dry Mustard
½ teaspoon Lemon Peel
½ teaspoon Bon Appétit
½ teaspoon prepared horseradish
2 cups light cream
½ cup sliced mushrooms
2 teaspoons Instant Minced Onion
½ pound scallops
½ pound cleaned, cooked shrimp
¼ pound crab meat
2 tablespoons dry sherry
Bread crumbs

Melt 4 tablespoons of the butter in saucepan. Add flour, dry mustard, lemon peel, Bon Appétit and horseradish, then stir until well blended. Add cream. Cook, stirring, until thickened. Sauté mushrooms and onion in the remaining 2 tablespoons butter. Remove from pan with slotted spoon. To butter in pan add scallops, which have been cut into bite-size pieces, and sauté 3 minutes. Cut shrimp into small pieces. Combine sauce, mushrooms, scallops, shrimp, crab meat and sherry. Spoon into shells or ramekins; top with bread crumbs. Bake in 400°F. oven 10 minutes then broil a few minutes until lightly browned. *Serves 8 to 10.*

Oysters Rockefeller

A version of the famous recipe created in 1889 by Antoine's Restaurant in New Orleans and named for its rich sauce.

6 tablespoons butter
6 tablespoons thawed, frozen chopped spinach
1½ teaspoons Instant Minced Onion
1 tablespoon Parsley Flakes
1 tablespoon Celery Flakes
1½ teaspoons Bon Appétit
3 Fennel Seeds, crushed
⅛ teaspoon Tarragon Leaves
Dash ground Red Pepper
Dash Garlic Powder
¼ cup bread crumbs
Rock salt
24 oysters on the half shell

Combine butter, spinach and seasonings. Simmer 15 minutes. Put through food mill or purée in blender. Add bread crumbs. Spread layer of rock salt in shallow baking pan. Arrange oysters on salt and spread 1 teaspoon of the spinach mixture over each oyster. Preheat broiler and broil 4 to 5 inches from heat 8 minutes or until lightly browned. *Serves 4.*

Rumaki

The delightful seasoning and crisp texture are reminiscent of the South Seas.

1 pound chicken livers
1 teaspoon Season-All
¼ teaspoon Black Pepper
⅛ teaspoon Ginger
2 5-ounce cans water chestnuts
1 pound or about 15 slices bacon
Fat for deep fat frying

Cut livers into sections. Mix Season-All, pepper and ginger and sprinkle over livers. Pierce livers 2 or 3 times with fork to prevent excess popping. Slice the large chestnuts in half and cut slices of bacon in half. Wrap one section of liver and one slice of water chestnut with a strip of bacon and fasten with a toothpick. Fry in deep fat, 340°F., until golden brown, or broil if you prefer. Serve piping hot and you will want to have a bowl of Hot Chinese Mustard (see recipe page 340) close by to use as a dip.

Makes about 30.

Broiled Clams

4 tablespoons butter
¼ teaspoon Onion Powder
½ teaspoon Bon Appétit
½ teaspoon Lemon Peel
½ teaspoon Instant Minced Onion
Dash dry Mustard
Small dash Mace
Rock salt
24 clams on the half shell
2 slices bacon

Melt butter and add seasonings. Spread layer of rock salt in shallow baking pan. Arrange clams on salt. Pour ½ teaspoon of the butter mixture over each clam. Cut bacon into 24 pieces and place one piece on top of each clam. Preheat broiler and broil 4 to 5 inches from heat 4 minutes or until lightly browned and bacon is crisp.

Serves 4.

NOTE: If fresh clams are not available, you may acquire a set of shells and use whole canned clams. You could even arrange clams in a shallow baking dish, omitting rock salt, and not use shells.

Cheese Dip Caraway

1 8-ounce package cream cheese
½ cup dairy sour cream
2 tablespoons Caraway Seed
2 teaspoons Instant Minced Onion
1 teaspoon Season-All
1½ teaspoons Worcestershire sauce

Have cheese at room temperature; add sour cream and beat until smooth and creamy. Stir in caraway seed, onion, Season-All and Worcestershire sauce. Blend thoroughly.

Makes about 1¼ cups.

S.C. Marinated Mushrooms

2 tablespoons vinegar
2 tablespoons olive oil
½ teaspoon Basil Leaves
½ teaspoon Marjoram Leaves
½ teaspoon Mustard Seed
¼ teaspoon Onion Salt
1 4-ounce can mushroom crowns, drained

Combine vinegar, olive oil and seasonings. Pour over mushrooms. Chill several hours before serving. You may use the same marinade for 1 pint sliced, raw mushrooms but leave them in the marinade 24 hours.

Serves 6 to 8, allowing 4 to 5 per person.

S.C. Spiced Shrimp

3 tablespoons Pickling Spice
2 tablespoons Season-All
1 teaspoon Crushed Red Pepper
1 teaspoon salt
¼ cup vinegar
1 quart water
1 pound fresh or frozen shrimp

Add spices, salt and vinegar to water. Let boil 10 minutes, then add shrimp. (If you use frozen shrimp, thaw before cooking.) Boil 5 to 7 minutes or until shrimp turn pink. (Shrimp become tough when boiled too long.) Remove from heat; let stand 20 minutes, then drain. Cool, shell, devein and chill. For a buffet arrange on a tray, on a platter of cracked ice or place around a bowl of cocktail sauce. Serve as individual cocktails, or use in preparation of other dishes. *Serves 4 to 5.*

VARIATIONS:

Oriental Spiced Shrimp—For above spices substitute 6 Peppercorns, ½ teaspoon Onion Powder, ⅛ teaspoon Garlic Powder, ½ teaspoon Celery Seed, 2 teaspoons Parsley Flakes, 2 Bay Leaves, 1 teaspoon Curry Powder and 1 teaspoon Oregano Leaves.

Spiced Shrimp Maison—For even more variety, why don't you mix your own spices using a combination of any of the following: Allspice, Bon Appétit, Ginger, dry Mustard, Tarragon Leaves, Thyme Leaves, Basil Leaves, Rosemary Leaves, Coriander Seed, whole Cardamom or Fennel Seed?

L.C. Celery Victor

2 bunches celery
2 cups water
½ cup wine vinegar
¾ cup oil
2 tablespoons lemon juice
1 tablespoon Chicken Flavor Base
4 Peppercorns
1 teaspoon Instant Minced Onion
1 teaspoon Parsley Flakes
2 teaspoons Season-All
2 whole Cloves
½ teaspoon salt
8 anchovy fillets, washed
8 strips pimiento

Cut hearts of celery and tender stalks into 3-inch sections. Place in rows in a baking dish or skillet. Combine remaining ingredients except anchovy and pimiento. Pour over celery. Simmer 15 minutes or until celery is crisp-tender. Remove from heat; let celery cool in liquid and chill. When ready to serve, remove celery from liquid and place several pieces on shredded lettuce. Top with anchovy fillets and thin strips of pimiento. *Serves 4.*

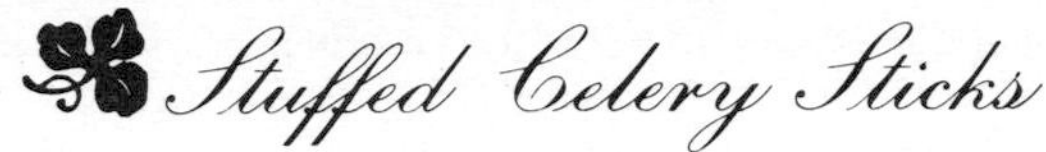

Stuffed Celery Sticks

8 4-inch pieces celery
1 3-ounce package cream cheese
⅛ teaspoon dry Mustard
¼ teaspoon Paprika
¼ teaspoon Bon Appétit
1 tablespoon finely chopped olives

Cut tender stalks of crisp celery into 4-inch pieces. Have cheese at room temperature; add dry mustard, paprika and Bon Appétit. Mix until smooth and creamy. Stir in olives. Fill celery sticks. Serve as an appetizer, on a relish tray or with soup. *Makes about ½ cup filling.*

Pineapple-Grapefruit Delight

2½ cups canned pineapple-grapefruit juice
2 whole Cardamom
4 whole Cloves
1 3-inch piece Cinnamon

Pour juice in a saucepan; add spices. Cover and simmer 30 minutes. Remove spices and chill juice. For a stronger spice note, chill juice before removing spices. Serve in small glasses before any meal, or you will find this ideal to serve over ice cubes for a summer cooler. *Makes 2¼ cups.*

VARIATION:

Pineapple-Grapefruit Refresher—In the above recipe use ¼ teaspoon Mint Flakes and 5 Coriander Seeds, crushed, instead of whole cinnamon, cardamom and cloves.

Crab-Stuffed Mushrooms

Piping hot and spicy, these will make a hit at any party.

2 dozen large, firm mushrooms
1 tablespoon Instant Minced Onion
2 tablespoons butter or margarine
Dash ground Red Pepper
1 tablespoon prepared English mustard
1½ teaspoons Bon Appétit
3 tablespoons lemon juice
1 tablespoon Worcestershire sauce
1 pound crab meat
¼ cup sherry
2 tablespoons flour
¼ cup cream

Rinse mushrooms; remove stems. Cook caps in salted boiling water (1 tablespoon salt to 1 quart water) 2 to 3 minutes. Drain. Thinly slice tender part of stems; sauté with minced onion in butter but do not brown. Add remaining ingredients, mixing thoroughly. Cook over low heat about 5 minutes. Pile the caps high with this mixture. (Tops may be brushed with a mixture of mayonnaise and cream, using about 2 tablespoons each.) Place in a buttered baking dish and bake in 450°F. oven 15 minutes or until tops are delicately browned. *Makes 24.*

½ cup mayonnaise
½ cup dairy sour cream
1 teaspoon Curry Powder
1 teaspoon lemon juice
Dash ground Red Pepper
Dash MSG

Combine all ingredients, blending well. Use as a dip for shrimp, lobster and other sea food. May also be combined with flaked tuna for an interesting dip to serve with crackers. *Makes 1 cup.*

SOUPS

Soups from Around the World

Bouillabaisse 90

French Onion Soup 84

Lentil Soup 84

Lobster Bisque Elégante 88

Minestrone 87

Mulligatawny 87

Scotch Broth 93

Swedish Fruit Soup 86

Vichyssoise 89

Uniquely American

Chicken Corn Soup 92

Chicken or Turkey Soup 85

Corn Chowder 83

Manhattan Clam Chowder 89

Uniquely American (Cont.)

New England Clam Chowder 90

New Orleans Shrimp Gumbo 86

Oyster Stew 84

Vegetable Soups

Cream of Zucchini Soup 88

Golden Cream of Carrot Soup 91

Old-Fashioned Vegetable Soup 92

Spinach Soup 83

Tomato-Vegetable Soup 91

Quick-and-Easy Soups

Consommé Royale 92

Egg Drop Soup 91

Quick Curry Soup Indienne 85

Tomato Soup Oregano 85

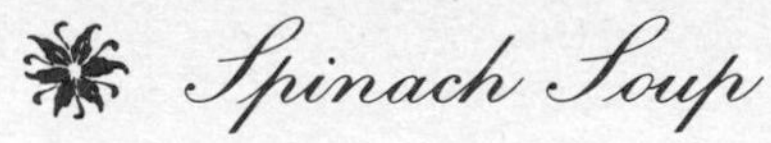

Spinach Soup

1 10-ounce package fresh spinach or 10-ounce package frozen spinach
3 cups milk
¼ cup butter
¼ cup flour
¾ teaspoon salt
¼ teaspoon Nutmeg
½ teaspoon White Pepper
½ pint plain yogurt
1 tablespoon Instant Minced Onion
1 teaspoon Chicken Flavor Base

Wash and drain spinach, or thaw frozen spinach. Put 1 cup of the milk in blender jar, add spinach, a little at a time, blending until smooth after each addition. In saucepan, melt butter. Stir in flour, salt, nutmeg and pepper. Cook over medium-low heat until bubbly. Stir in spinach mixture. Add remaining milk, yogurt, onion and chicken flavor base. Cook, stirring constantly, over medium heat, until mixture begins to boil. Reduce heat and simmer, stirring, 2 minutes.

Makes 5½ cups.

Corn Chowder

3 slices bacon
1 stalk celery, chopped
2 tablespoons flour
3 cups milk
1 17-ounce can cream-style corn
1 12-ounce can vacuum-packed corn
2 tablespoons Instant Chopped Onion
1 teaspoon Season-All
⅛ teaspoon White Pepper
⅛ teaspoon Basil Leaves

Cook bacon in large saucepan over medium-low heat until crisp. Drain on absorbent paper. Sauté celery in remaining bacon fat 3 minutes. Remove from heat. Add flour, stir until well blended. Gradually stir in milk. Add remaining ingredients. Cook over medium heat, stirring frequently until mixture comes to a boil. Cook 1 minute longer. Serve topped with crumbled bacon.

Makes 1½ quarts.

Lentil Soup

1½ cups lentils
7 cups water
1 tablespoon salt
½ teaspoon Coarse Grind Black Pepper
1 tablespoon Celery Flakes
1 teaspoon Basil Leaves
¼ cup Chopped Instant Onions
1 teaspoon Marjoram Leaves
2 carrots, sliced thin
½ pound ham hock
6 frankfurters
Sherry, optional

Rinse lentils. Place in a large kettle with water, seasonings, carrots and ham hock. Cover and boil gently 2 hours. Cut frankfurters into ¼-inch slices; add to soup and cook 10 minutes longer. Lentil soup traditionally is a thick, hearty potage, a meal in itself. However, you may personally prefer a thinner soup; if so, thin with water to your taste. Serve steaming hot. For a real gourmet touch let each person add sherry to taste.

Makes 3 quarts.

6 oysters with liquor
2 tablespoons butter
⅛ teaspoon MSG
½ teaspoon Bon Appétit
¼ teaspoon Paprika
¼ teaspoon salt
Dash White or Black Pepper
¼ teaspoon Worcestershire sauce
1 cup milk (use part cream if desired)

Shuck oysters if in shell. Check for bits of shell. Heat butter until it sizzles, but do not let it brown. Add oysters with liquor, seasonings and Worcestershire sauce. Heat until edges of oysters curl slightly. Add milk. Heat thoroughly, but do not boil. Serve hot topped with a dash of paprika.

Serves 1.

Make your own savory onion soup in just 20 minutes using Chopped Instant Onions.

½ cup Chopped Instant Onions
4 tablespoons butter
4 cups hot water
2 tablespoons Beef Flavor Base
½ Bay Leaf
¼ teaspoon Black Pepper
¼ teaspoon ground Marjoram
Herb Croutons
Grated Parmesan cheese

Brown onions in melted butter over low heat to prevent burning. Add hot water, beef flavor base, bay leaf, pepper and marjoram. Simmer 20 minutes. Serve piping hot topped with Herb Croutons (see recipe page 258) and grated Parmesan cheese.

Serves 4.

Chicken or Turkey Soup

Chicken or turkey carcass
Meat from carcass (about 1 cup)
3 tablespoons Vegetable Flakes
¼ cup Chopped Instant Onions
6 Peppercorns
5 whole Cloves
Dash Nutmeg or Mace
1 Bay Leaf
Water
1 tablespoon Chicken Flavor Base
1 cup long grain rice

Remove meat from carcass. For full flavor, you should have about 1 cup meat, but the more, the better. Crack bones, and put in a large saucepan along with any remaining skin. Add vegetable flakes, onions, peppercorns, cloves, nutmeg or mace, bay leaf and enough water to cover bones. Bring to boil. Reduce heat and simmer, covered, 2 hours. Cool slightly and strain. Spoon off excess fat if you wish. To the broth add flavor base, the chicken or turkey meat and rice. Add salt if needed. Simmer 20 to 25 minutes. Serve hot.

Makes 6 to 8 servings.

Tomato Soup Oregano

1 10½-ounce can condensed cream of tomato soup
2½ cups canned tomatoes
½ teaspoon Bon Appétit
¼ teaspoon ground Oregano
¼ teaspoon Onion Powder
½ teaspoon sugar
4 tablespoons dairy sour cream

Combine all ingredients, except sour cream, in saucepan. Cut tomatoes into small pieces. Simmer 20 minutes. Top with sour cream just before serving. Good served with stuffed celery. *Serves 4.*

Quick Curry Soup Indienne

½ teaspoon Indian or Madras Curry Powder
1 10½-ounce can cream of chicken or cream of mushroom soup

Add curry powder to soup; prepare following directions on can. For added interest and flavor, you may like to serve a tray of condiments with curry soup—a few suggestions:

Crumbled crisp bacon
Herb seasoned croutons
Finely chopped fresh onions
Slivered toasted almonds
Parmesan cheese
Thinly sliced water chestnuts

Makes four 5-ounce servings.

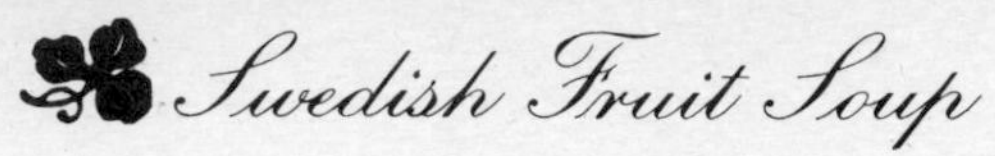

Swedish Fruit Soup

You will find this chilled blend of puréed fruits topped with cream a refreshing summer favorite.

- *2 cups mixed dried fruit (peaches, apricots, pears)*
- *1 cup dried apples*
- *1 cup pitted prunes*
- *1 16-ounce can (2 cups) red tart pitted cherries*
- *¼ cup raisins or currants*
- *2 quarts water*
- *½ cup sugar*
- *1 3-inch piece Cinnamon*
- *1 teaspoon Lemon Peel*
- *¼ teaspoon Mace*
- *⅛ teaspoon Cardamom*
- *⅛ teaspoon Allspice*
- *⅛ teaspoon Nutmeg*
- *Whipped cream or dairy sour cream*

Combine all ingredients, except whipped cream or sour cream, in large saucepan. Bring to a boil; reduce heat and simmer, covered, 1 hour or until fruit is tender. Remove cinnamon; rub cooked fruit with liquid through a fine sieve or purée in blender. Chill. Serve cold topped with whipped cream or sour cream. *Makes 2½ quarts.*

New Orleans Shrimp Gumbo

- *2 pounds shrimp*
- *4 tablespoons butter*
- *4 teaspoons Instant Minced Onion*
- *1½ cups chopped celery*
- *1 tablespoon Bell Pepper Flakes*
- *¼ teaspoon Instant Minced Garlic*
- *¼ teaspoon ground Black Pepper*
- *4 cups fresh or frozen sliced okra (two 10-ounce packages)*
- *2 tablespoons flour*
- *4 teaspoons Chicken Flavor Base*
- *4 cups water*
- *3½ cups tomatoes (28-ounce can)*
- *½ pound cubed, cooked ham*
- *1 Bay Leaf*
- *1 teaspoon Thyme Leaves*
- *2 teaspoons Arrowroot mixed with 2 teaspoons cold water*
- *Hot steamed rice, optional*

Cook and clean shrimp; cut into bite-size pieces. Heat butter (you may use bacon drippings if you like) in large kettle or Dutch oven. Add onion, celery, pepper flakes, garlic and pepper; sauté lightly. Dredge okra with flour. If you are using frozen okra, thaw it first. Add okra to kettle; continue to sauté for a few minutes. Add flavor base, water, tomatoes, ham, bay leaf and thyme leaves. Lower heat; cover and simmer 1 hour. Add shrimp and cook 15 minutes longer. Remove from heat. Stir in arrowroot and cook, stirring until slightly thickened. Serve in soup bowls. In New Orleans a spoonful of hot cooked rice is always placed in the center of each serving.

Makes 3 quarts.

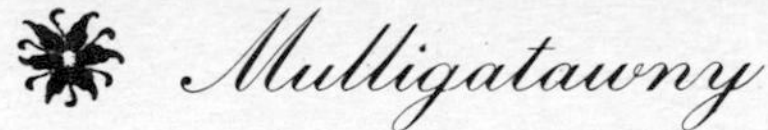

The most famous soup of India, spicy-hot, tantalizingly good.

¼ cup butter
1 3-pound chicken, cut in pieces
1 tablespoon Instant Minced Onion
3 quarts boiling water
1 tablespoon Vegetable Flakes
1 tablespoon Curry Powder
¼ teaspoon MSG
1 teaspoon Turmeric
¼ cup Chicken Flavor Base
⅛ teaspoon Mace
½ teaspoon Parsley Flakes
¼ teaspoon Black Pepper
6 tablespoons flour

Melt butter in large saucepan or Dutch oven. Add chicken pieces and onion; cover and simmer over low heat 20 minutes. Add remaining ingredients except flour. Simmer 40 minutes or until chicken is tender. Remove chicken and strain stock. Return stock to saucepan. Remove chicken from bones; chop meat and add to stock. Simmer 15 minutes. Make a thin, smooth paste by mixing together the flour with an equal amount of water. Then stir into the soup; continue cooking until thickened. Remove excess fat, if you wish. Serve piping hot. *Makes 3 quarts.*

Minestrone

1 cup dried marrow beans or garbanzos or lima beans
7 cups water
¼ cup Chopped Instant Onions
1 tablespoon Parsley Flakes
3 tablespoons Celery Flakes
⅛ teaspoon Instant Minced Garlic
2 tablespoons Bell Pepper Flakes
¼ cup olive oil
¼ teaspoon Crushed Red Pepper
½ pound fresh spinach
2 teaspoons Beef Flavor Base
⅛ teaspoon rubbed Sage
¼ teaspoon Italian Seasoning
1 teaspoon ground Thyme
2 teaspoons salt
¼ teaspoon Coarse Grind Black Pepper
1 cup diced potatoes
2 cups canned tomatoes
1 cup chopped cabbage
1 small zucchini, thinly sliced
1 cup elbow macaroni
Grated Parmesan cheese

Soak beans overnight in enough water to cover. Drain. Add the 7 cups water; cover and simmer 3 hours or until tender. Sauté onions, parsley flakes, celery flakes, garlic and pepper flakes in oil until well coated and hot but do not allow to brown. Add to beans with remaining seasonings, vegetables and macaroni. Cook over low heat 30 minutes longer. This is a thick soup; if you prefer a thinner consistency, add a little water. Serve hot with Parmesan cheese sprinkled over top of each serving.

Makes about 3 quarts.

Lobster Bisque Elégante

An epicurean delight, delicately spiced.

- *4 frozen rock lobster tails, weighing about 8 ounces each*
- *3 cups water*
- *1 tablespoon Chicken Flavor Base*
- *1 tablespoon Onion Flakes*
- *6 Coriander Seeds*
- *1 Bay Leaf*
- *1 tablespoon Vegetable Flakes*
- *3 Peppercorns*
- *5 tablespoons butter*
- *5 tablespoons flour*
- *1 teaspoon Bon Appétit*
- *1 teaspoon salt*
- *3 cups milk*
- *1 cup light cream*

Bring enough water to a boil to cover lobster tails; add 1 teaspoon salt to each 1 quart of water. Drop frozen lobster tails into water and boil 11 minutes (or 3 minutes plus the weight of the largest lobster tail). Remove meat from lobster shells and dice; set aside. Crush shells and put in saucepan. Add the 3 cups water, flavor base, onion flakes, coriander seed, bay leaf, vegetable flakes and peppercorns. Simmer 30 minutes; strain. Melt butter; stir in flour, Bon Appétit and salt. Cook until bubbly. Remove from heat and add milk. Simmer over low heat, stirring constantly, until thickened. Stir in lobster stock, lobster meat and cream. Do not allow it to boil. Serve piping hot.

Makes 7 to 8 cups.

A soup as delicately green and fresh as springtime.

- *3 cups sliced zucchini (4 small zucchini or 1 pound)*
- *½ cup water*
- *1 tablespoon Instant Minced Onion*
- *1 teaspoon Season-All*
- *½ teaspoon Parsley Flakes*
- *2 teaspoons Chicken Flavor Base*
- *2 tablespoons butter*
- *2 tablespoons flour*
- *⅛ teaspoon White Pepper*
- *⅛ teaspoon MSG*
- *¼ teaspoon Bon Appétit*
- *1 cup milk*
- *½ cup light cream*
- *Dairy sour cream*
- *Paprika*

Combine zucchini, water, onion, Season-All, parsley flakes and 1 teaspoon of the flavor base. Cook until zucchini is tender and only a small amount of water is left. Mash, put through sieve or purée in blender. In a saucepan melt butter; add flour, the remaining flavor base, pepper, MSG and Bon Appétit. Blend well. Add milk and cream; simmer, stirring until thickened. Stir in zucchini, mixing well. If soup is thicker than you like, add additional milk. Serve topped with a spoon of sour cream garnished with paprika.

Makes about 4 cups.

Vichyssoise

One of the top-ranking favorites of all summer soups. Serve chilled with a sprinkling of Chives.

3 cups sliced potatoes
3 cups water
2½ teaspoons Chicken Flavor Base
1 teaspoon Onion Powder
3 tablespoons butter
1 cup light cream
1 cup milk
¼ teaspoon Celery Salt
¼ teaspoon White Pepper
¼ teaspoon Bon Appétit
Chives

Wash, peel and slice potatoes (takes about 2 large potatoes). Add water and flavor base. Bring to boil and cook until potatoes are very tender. Force through a fine sieve or purée in a blender, including the liquid. Combine with remaining ingredients except chives. Heat 10 minutes, but do not allow to boil. Chill. Serve in bowls placed in crushed ice. Top each serving with chives.

Makes 6 cups.

Manhattan Clam Chowder

2 slices bacon
2 tablespoons Chopped Instant Onions
1 tablespoon Bell Pepper Flakes
2 tablespoons Celery Flakes
5 cups boiling water
3 whole Cloves
1 whole Cardamom
1 Bay Leaf
⅛ teaspoon Garlic Powder
1 tablespoon Season-All
½ teaspoon Thyme Leaves
¼ teaspoon Coarse Grind Black Pepper
¼ teaspoon MSG
1 cup finely diced carrots
2 cups diced potatoes
1 cup canned tomatoes
2 cups minced clams
2 tablespoons butter
2 tablespoons flour

Cut bacon into ½-inch pieces; fry in large saucepan or kettle until brown and crisp. Add onions, pepper flakes and celery flakes; continue cooking until onions brown lightly. Add water. Tie cloves, cardamom and bay leaf in cheesecloth bag; drop into soup. Add garlic powder, Season-All, thyme leaves, pepper, MSG, carrots, potatoes, tomatoes and the liquid drained from clams. Simmer 40 minutes. Sauté clams in butter but do not brown. Add to soup and simmer 10 minutes. Make a thin, smooth paste by mixing together the flour with an equal amount of water. Then stir into chowder; continue cooking until thickened. Remove bag of spices. Serve hot.

Makes 9 cups.

New England Clam Chowder

3 slices bacon
2 cups diced potatoes
2 tablespoons Instant Minced Onion
2 teaspoons Bon Appétit
¼ teaspoon White Pepper
1 teaspoon salt
2 cups water
1 quart milk
1 7½-ounce can minced clams
4 tablespoons flour

Cut bacon into ½-inch pieces; fry over low heat until crisp. Add potatoes, onion, Bon Appétit, pepper, salt and water. Bring to a boil; reduce heat and simmer 10 minutes. Stir in milk; heat but do not allow to boil. Add clams, including liquid. Make a thin, smooth paste by mixing together the flour with an equal amount of water. Then stir into chowder; continue cooking over low heat until thickened. Remember, do not let it boil. Serve piping hot. *Serves 6 to 8.*

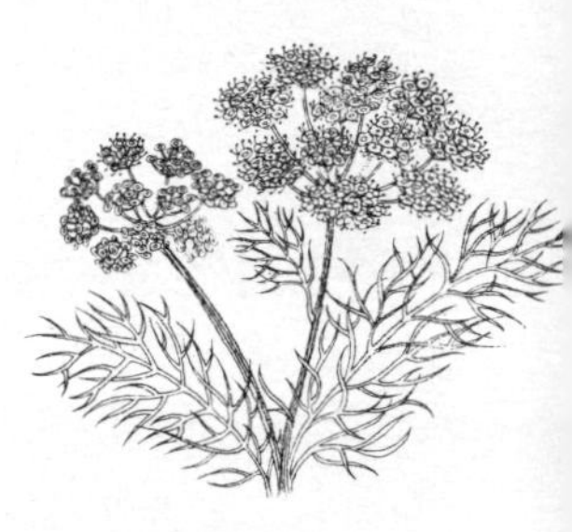

Bouillabaisse

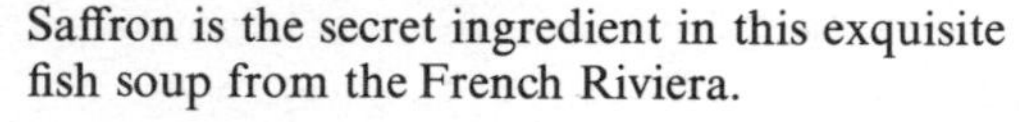

Saffron is the secret ingredient in this exquisite fish soup from the French Riviera.

1 carrot
1 pound tomatoes
4 7-to 8-ounce rock lobster tails
1 pound each perch, cod, rock, sole, red snapper
½ cup Chopped Instant Onions
¼ teaspoon Instant Minced Garlic
2 teaspoons Parsley Flakes
24 individual pieces Saffron
1 Bay Leaf
¼ teaspoon Thyme Leaves
⅛ teaspoon Fennel Seed
1 teaspoon Orange Peel
5 teaspoons Bon Appétit
¼ teaspoon Black Pepper
⅓ cup olive oil
1 8-ounce bottle clam juice
1 tablespoon lemon juice
French bread
Water

Peel and cut carrot into small cubes; peel, seed and chop tomatoes. Cut lobster tails into large pieces. Cut fish into 2-inch pieces. Put all ingredients except perch, cod and French bread in a large saucepan or kettle. Cover with water; boil hard 8 minutes. Add perch and cod and boil 8 minutes longer. Remove fish to large bowl or platter. Cut French bread into ¼-inch slices and put in bottom of soup tureen. Pour broth over bread. Serve the soup in soup plates and the fish on side plates. *Serves 8 to 10.*

Golden Cream of Carrot Soup

2 cups thinly sliced carrots (4 to 5 large carrots)
½ cup water
1 teaspoon Bon Appétit
3 teaspoons Chicken Flavor Base
1 tablespoon lemon juice
4 tablespoons butter
2 tablespoons flour
¼ teaspoon Ginger
⅛ teaspoon Onion Powder
2 cups milk

Combine carrots, water, ½ teaspoon of the Bon Appétit, 1 teaspoon of the flavor base and the lemon juice. Cook until carrots are tender and liquid is reduced to about 1 tablespoon. Melt butter; add flour and the remaining seasonings, stirring until smooth. Add milk and simmer, stirring until thickened. Mash carrots, put through sieve or purée in blender. Add to milk mixture and stir until well blended. Add additional milk or cream to get the consistency you like. Serve hot. *Makes about 4 cups.*

Tomato-Vegetable Soup

½ cup Vegetable Flakes
2½ cups canned tomatoes
2 cups water
1 tablespoon Beef Flavor Base
½ teaspoon Black Pepper
¼ teaspoon dry Mustard
1 Bay Leaf
¼ teaspoon Thyme Leaves
1 teaspoon Season-All
1 teaspoon sugar
½ teaspoon Dill Seed, crushed
½ teaspoon Oregano Leaves

Combine all ingredients and simmer 30 minutes or longer. Remove bay leaf. This is a quick 'n' easy soup to make. *Makes 4 cups.*

Egg Drop Soup

1 egg
⅓ cup flour
1 tablespoon water
7 teaspoons Chicken Flavor Base
6 cups boiling water

Beat egg with fork; add flour and the 1 tablespoon water and continue beating until smooth. Dissolve flavor base in the boiling water. Drop the egg mixture, in a thin stream, from a spoon into the boiling broth. Move spoon slowly back and forth for even distribution. Do not stir soup until egg is cooked. For a change, use Beef Flavor Base in place of Chicken Flavor Base.
Makes six 1-cup servings.

Old-Fashioned Vegetable Soup

3 pounds soup bones
2 quarts water
1 Bay Leaf
2 cups canned tomatoes
1 cup sliced carrots
½ cup chopped celery
2 cups diced potatoes
2 cups sliced okra
2 cups whole kernel corn
¼ cup Chopped Instant Onions
2 tablespoons Season-All
1 teaspoon Celery Salt
½ teaspoon Black Pepper
¼ teaspoon Thyme Leaves
½ teaspoon Savory
¼ teaspoon MSG
1 tablespoon Beef Flavor Base

Put soup bones in a large saucepan or Dutch oven; add water and bay leaf. Bring to a boil and simmer 45 minutes, then add remaining ingredients and simmer, covered, 3 hours. Remove bones. Serve piping hot. Extra soup may be frozen and reheated as needed. *Makes 3 quarts.*

Consommé Royale

2 10½-ounce cans consommé
2 Bay Leaves
6 whole Cloves
4 Peppercorns
3 whole Allspice
⅛ teaspoon Lemon Peel
Thin slices of avocado or fresh mushrooms

Combine consommé, bay leaves, cloves, peppercorns, allspice and lemon peel. Heat just to the boiling point. Remove the whole spices. For an elegant touch float very thin slices of avocado or mushroom on each serving. Serve with herb seasoned bread sticks. *Serves 4 to 6.*

Chicken Corn Soup

1 3- to 4-pound chicken
6 cups water
3 teaspoons Chicken Flavor Base
1 teaspoon salt
10 individual pieces Saffron
2 cups noodles
2 cups whole kernel corn
½ teaspoon Parsley Flakes
1 teaspoon Instant Minced Onion
¼ teaspoon Black Pepper
⅛ teaspoon Celery Salt
Dash MSG
2 hard-cooked eggs

Cut chicken in pieces. Cook in water with flavor base, salt and saffron about 1½ hours or until tender. Remove chicken from stock; take meat off the bones and cut into bite-size pieces. (Save the breast for other uses if desired.) Return cut-up chicken to stock and bring to a boil. Add noodles, corn, parsley flakes, onion, pepper, celery salt and MSG. Simmer 15 minutes. Chop eggs and add to soup. *Makes 2½ quarts.*

Scotch Broth

Here is a delicious recipe you will find in very few cookbooks, and one you will want to add to your collection.

STOCK:

4 pounds lamb, meat and bones
9 cups water
2 teaspoons salt
1 tablespoon Season-All
2 tablespoons Celery Flakes
½ teaspoon Thyme Leaves
12 Peppercorns
2 whole Cardamom
1 Bay Leaf

Combine all ingredients and simmer slowly 3 to 4 hours. Strain.

Should make 2 quarts stock.

SOUP:

¼ cup butter
2 tablespoons Instant Minced Onion
1 large carrot, diced small
½ cup finely diced celery
Dash Garlic Powder
½ cup barley
3 tablespoons flour
2 quarts lamb stock
1 cup cream

Melt butter in 3- to 4-quart saucepan. Add onion, carrot, celery and garlic powder. Sauté 5 minutes. Do not allow to brown. Add barley and flour. Cook 2 minutes longer. Add hot lamb stock; mix well and simmer slowly 1½ hours. Stir in cream and simmer 10 minutes more before serving.

Makes 5 bowls or 10 cups.

Salads, Salad Dressings

First Course or Luncheon Salads

Buffet Turkey Loaf 98

Chef's Salad Bowl 98

Chicken Salad 102

Crab Salad 99

Curried Sea Food Salad 99

Egg Salad 102

Fiesta Egg Salad 102

Shrimp Salad 98

Tarragon Tuna Salad 99

Tuna and Tomato Mold 107

Go-With Salads

Beet Surprise Salad 100

Caesar Salad 101

Country Kitchen Potato Salad 107

Potato-Fennel Salad 107

Creamy Coleslaw 104

Coleslaw Bon Appétit 104

Cucumbers in Sour Cream 102

Dill Macaroni Salad 103

Garden Vegetable Salad 100

Green Bean Salad 97

Piquant Tomato Aspic 101

Sweet-Sour Cucumbers with Onions 106

Fruit Salads

Champagne Salad 103

Fresh Fruit Medley 104

Frozen Bing Cherry Salad 105

Layered Orange-Cranberry Mold 105

Party Pink Fruit Salad 106

Waldorf Salad 106

Salad Dressings

Cardamom Cream Dressing 108

Celery Seed Dressing 108

Creamy Roquefort Dressing 108

French Dressing 110

American French Dressing 110

Herb French Dressing 110

South-of-the-Border Dressing 110

Ginger Cream Dressing 110

Green Goddess Dressing 109

Honey Spice Dressing 110

Italian Dressing 111

Lamaze Dressing 109

Poppy Seed Dressing 109

Ranch-Style Salad Dressing 97

Roquefort Dressing 111

Green Bean Salad

2 9-ounce packages frozen French-style green beans
1 8½-ounce can water chestnuts, thinly sliced
¼ cup salad oil
2 tablespoons vinegar
1 teaspoon sugar
1 teaspoon Bon Appétit
¼ teaspoon Tarragon Leaves
¼ teaspoon Basil Leaves
⅛ teaspoon dry Mustard
⅛ teaspoon coarse grind Black Pepper
1 tablespoon Onion Flakes
Cherry tomatoes

Cook beans. Drain. Toss with water chestnuts. In small jar with screw cap, mix next 9 ingredients and shake to mix well. Pour over beans. Toss to mix well. Chill. Serve with cherry tomatoes. *Makes 4 cups.*

Ranch-Style Salad Dressing

1 cup mayonnaise
1 cup buttermilk
½ teaspoon Onion Salt
¼ teaspoon Garlic Salt
¼ teaspoon MSG
⅛ teaspoon Celery Salt
¼ teaspoon Black Pepper
¼ teaspoon Marjoram Leaves
⅛ teaspoon Savory
½ teaspoon Parsley Flakes

Combine all ingredients. Mix well. Refrigerate 30 minutes before serving. *Makes 2 cups.*

Buffet Turkey Loaf

2 envelopes unflavored gelatine
1 cup water
1 teaspoon Chicken Flavor Base
3 cups chopped, cooked turkey
½ cup chopped celery
¼ cup sliced stuffed olives
1 cup dairy sour cream
½ cup white wine
¼ cup mayonnaise
1 teaspoon lemon juice
½ teaspoon Season-All
⅛ teaspoon Onion Powder
½ teaspoon salt
Dash Paprika

In a small saucepan soften gelatine in water. Add flavor base and heat until gelatine melts. Cool. Then combine with remaining ingredients. Pour into a 1½-quart mold. Chill until firm; then remove from mold. This loaf is particularly good garnished with slices of olive and surrounded with asparagus topped with pimiento strips. *Serves 6.*

L.C. Chef's Salad Bowl

½ head lettuce or romaine
1 bunch endive or escarole
2 carrots
1 cucumber, sliced
1 Italian onion, sliced and separated
1 avocado, sliced
2 tomatoes, cut into wedges
8 radishes, sliced
Salad Herbs
Cracked Black Pepper

Tear salad greens into bite-size pieces. Make carrot curls. Put salad greens, carrot curls, cucumber, onion, avocado, tomatoes and radishes in salad bowl. Sprinkle generously with salad herbs, and cracked black pepper or freshly ground black pepper from pepper mill. Toss lightly with Roquefort, Italian, French or your own special herb-blended salad dressing. Serve immediately. *Serves 6 to 8.*

Shrimp Salad

1 pound cooked, cleaned shrimp
½ cup chopped celery
2 hard-cooked eggs, chopped
⅔ cup mayonnaise
1 teaspoon Bon Appétit
⅛ teaspoon Tarragon Leaves
¼ teaspoon White Pepper
Dash ground Red Pepper

Reserve about 6 shrimp for garnish and cut remaining shrimp into bite-size pieces. Add celery and eggs. Combine remaining ingredients; spoon over shrimp. Mix gently. Chill. Garnish with whole shrimp and lemon slices. *Serves 4 to 6.*

Crab Salad

1 teaspoon Bon Appétit
¼ teaspoon White Pepper
⅛ teaspoon dry Mustard
Dash MSG
Dash ground Red Pepper
Dash Ginger
2 teaspoons lemon juice
½ cup mayonnaise
1 pound crab meat
1 cup chopped celery
½ cup chopped stuffed olives
Paprika

Blend together Bon Appétit, pepper, dry mustard, MSG, red pepper, ginger, lemon juice and mayonnaise. Pick over crab meat to remove bits of shell. Combine mayonnaise mixture, crab meat, celery and olives. Chill. Serve on crisp lettuce; sprinkle top with paprika. Serve with side dish of mayonnaise if desired. *Serves 4 to 6.*

Curried Sea Food Salad

1 cup flaked tuna (7-ounce can)
1 cup chopped, cooked shrimp
½ cup chopped celery
¼ cup sliced ripe olives
½ cup mayonnaise
2 tablespoons lemon juice
½ teaspoon Curry Powder
½ teaspoon Bon Appétit
¼ cup Parsley Flakes
2 tablespoons water
3 cups cold, cooked rice
2 tablespoons French dressing

Chill tuna and shrimp. Add celery and olives. Blend together mayonnaise, lemon juice, curry powder and Bon Appétit; add to tuna mixture and toss lightly. Soak parsley flakes in the water about 5 minutes, then toss with rice and French dressing. Transfer to serving plate. Spoon tuna-shrimp mixture over rice. You may garnish with water cress or radish roses.
Serves 4 to 6.

Tarragon Tuna Salad

2 7-ounce cans tuna
1 cup diced celery
¼ cup India or sweet relish
½ teaspoon Season-All
¼ teaspoon White Pepper
½ teaspoon dry Mustard
¼ teaspoon Tarragon Leaves
1 teaspoon Parsley Flakes
1 tablespoon Instant Minced Onion
1 tablespoon lemon juice
1 cup mayonnaise

Drain and flake tuna; add celery and relish. Combine remaining ingredients; mix well. Add to tuna; mix thoroughly. Serve on crisp lettuce. Garnish with sliced hard-cooked eggs, tomato wedges or thin slices of avocado. May also be used as filling for sandwiches. *Serves 4 to 6.*

Beet Surprise Salad

Who would think of adding cinnamon and cloves to beet salad? Yet it's this little touch that gives this salad mold excitement.

1 3-ounce package lemon gelatine
2 cups diced or julienne canned beets
1 tablespoon brown sugar
1 tablespoon prepared Horseradish
¼ teaspoon salt
6 whole Cloves
12 whole Allspice
1 3-inch piece Cinnamon
⅓ cup wine vinegar
⅔ cup dry white wine or water

Put gelatine in large bowl. Drain liquid from beets into measuring cup; add enough water to make 1 cup. Pour into saucepan; add brown sugar, horseradish, salt and spices. Heat to boiling; reduce heat and simmer 1 minute. Strain into gelatine and stir until gelatine dissolves. Add vinegar, wine and drained beets. Pour into 1½-quart ring mold or 6 individual molds. Chill until firm, then remove from mold. Serve on shredded greens. *Serves 6.*

Garden Vegetable Salad

1 10-ounce package frozen lima beans
1 10-ounce package frozen peas
4 medium-size carrots
2 medium-size potatoes
1 cup cooked, diced beets
1 cup chopped celery
½ cup salad oil
¼ cup white vinegar
Dash Garlic Powder
Dash MSG
1 tablespoon Bon Appétit
1 teaspoon Instant Minced Onion
¼ teaspoon White Pepper
½ teaspoon dry Mustard
⅔ cup mayonnaise

Cook lima beans and peas as directed on package; drain. Slice carrots and cook in salted water until tender; drain. Cook potatoes in salted water; peel and dice. Put all vegetables in bowl and toss gently. Combine remaining ingredients except mayonnaise; mix well. Pour over vegetables and toss until vegetables are coated. Chill several hours. Stir in mayonnaise. Serve in crisp lettuce cups. *Serves 6 to 8.*

L.C. Piquant Tomato Aspic

An attractive and delicious tomato aspic.

- 2 *envelopes unflavored gelatine*
- ¼ *cup cold water*
- 4 *cups tomato juice*
- 3 *tablespoons Celery Flakes*
- 4 *tablespoons Onion Flakes*
- 3 *Bay Leaves*
- 3 *whole Cloves*
- 6 *Peppercorns*
- 4 *whole Allspice*
- ½ *teaspoon Basil Leaves*
- 2 *tablespoons brown sugar*
- 1 *teaspoon Season-All*
- 3 *tablespoons lemon juice*

Add gelatine to the cold water; set aside to soften. In a saucepan combine tomato juice, celery flakes, onion flakes, bay leaves, cloves, peppercorns, allspice, basil leaves, brown sugar and Season-All. Bring to a boil, then simmer 15 minutes. Strain; add softened gelatine and lemon juice, stirring until gelatine melts. Pour into a 1½-quart mold. Chill until firm. Remove from mold; garnish with salad greens and cottage cheese. *Serves 6 to 8.*

Caesar Salad

A man's salad—superb with steak.

- 2 *small heads romaine lettuce, thoroughly chilled*
- *Herb Croutons*
- ½ *teaspoon Season-All*
- ⅛ *teaspoon MSG*
- ¼ *teaspoon dry Mustard*
- *Freshly ground Black Pepper*
- *Dash Garlic Powder*
- 1 *tablespoon lemon juice*
- ½ *teaspoon Worcestershire sauce*
- ⅛ *teaspoon sugar*
- 6 *tablespoons olive oil*
- 2 *tablespoons wine vinegar*
- 1 *2-ounce can anchovy fillets*
- 1 *egg, coddled (see below)*
- ¼ *cup grated Parmesan cheese*

Wash romaine; remove outside leaves. Break the tender leaves crosswise into pieces about 1 inch wide. Store in plastic bag in refrigerator until ready to use. Make Herb Croutons (see recipe page 258). When ready to serve, place romaine in large wooden salad bowl. In a small mixing bowl combine seasonings, lemon juice, Worcestershire sauce, sugar, oil, vinegar and 3 anchovy fillets which have been mashed or minced. Mix thoroughly. Break coddled egg over greens, then pour salad dressing over all and toss lightly. Sprinkle with cheese and croutons and toss again lightly. Serve immediately on chilled salad plates. Top each serving with 2 anchovy fillets. Excellent with roast beef as well as steak. *Serves 4 to 6.*

NOTE:
To coddle egg, cook whole egg in hot but not boiling water 2 minutes.

Chicken Salad

It's the seasoning that makes this chicken salad memorable.

2 cups cubed, cooked chicken
1 cup chopped celery
¼ cup chopped pickle
1 hard-cooked egg, chopped
½ cup mayonnaise
1 tablespoon lemon juice
½ teaspoon Season-All
½ teaspoon dry Mustard
⅛ teaspoon MSG
Dash Nutmeg
⅛ teaspoon White Pepper
¼ teaspoon salt
Paprika
Capers, optional

Toss chicken with celery, pickle and egg. Mix together mayonnaise, lemon juice and seasonings except paprika. Add to chicken. Mix well. Serve on crisp lettuce, or use to fill tomato or avocado halves. Garnish each serving with paprika and three or four capers. May be used for sandwiches.

Makes 4 to 6 servings.

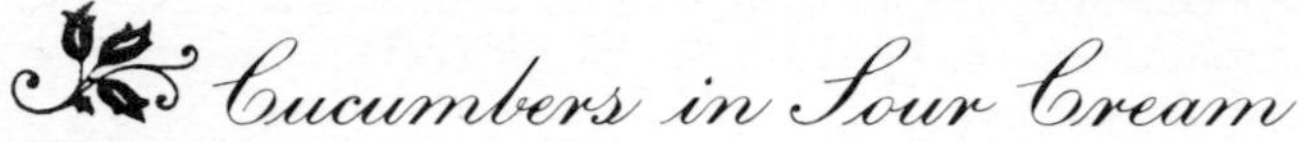

Cucumbers in Sour Cream

Cool and refreshing.

2 cups thinly sliced, pared cucumbers
½ teaspoon salt
½ cup dairy sour cream
2 teaspoons vinegar
½ teaspoon sugar
2 teaspoons Instant Minced Onion
½ teaspoon Dill Weed
Dash ground Red Pepper or Chili Powder
Cracked Black Pepper

Place cucumber slices in a bowl; sprinkle with salt and cover with cold water. Refrigerate 30 minutes; drain well. Combine sour cream, vinegar, sugar, onion, dill weed and red pepper. Add cucumber slices to sour cream and toss lightly. Chill at least 1 hour before serving. Sprinkle with cracked black pepper.

Serves 4.

Egg Salad

6 hard-cooked eggs
¼ cup finely chopped celery
¼ cup finely chopped pickle
¼ cup mayonnaise
1 teaspoon vinegar
¼ teaspoon dry Mustard
1 teaspoon Season-All
⅛ teaspoon White Pepper
Dash Onion Powder
Dash MSG

Chop eggs; add celery and pickle. Combine remaining ingredients, mixing well. Add to eggs and mix carefully. Serve as a salad on crisp lettuce or as a filling for sandwiches.

Makes 2 cups.

VARIATION:

Fiesta Egg Salad—To the above recipe, add ⅛ teaspoon ground Cumin or crushed Cumin Seed.

Dill Macaroni Salad

1 8-ounce package elbow macaroni or salad macaroni
1 cup chopped celery
½ cup thinly sliced green pepper
¼ cup thinly sliced carrots
2 tablespoons chopped pimiento
½ cup mayonnaise
1 tablespoon vinegar
1 tablespoon sugar
2 tablespoons Instant Minced Onion
1 teaspoon Dill Weed
2 teaspoons Season-All
¼ teaspoon dry Mustard
⅛ teaspoon White Pepper
Dash ground Red Pepper

Cook macaroni as directed on the package. Drain and cool. Add celery, green pepper, carrots and pimiento. Mix remaining ingredients; spoon over macaroni and toss to mix thoroughly. Chill. Serve in bowl or on salad plates in crisp lettuce cups. *Serves 6 to 8.*

Champagne Salad

CHAMPAGNE LAYER:

1 envelope unflavored gelatine
2 tablespoons water
1 cup champagne
¾ cup water
3 drops Red Food Color
1 pint fresh strawberries

Soften gelatine in the 2 tablespoons water, then set over hot water to melt. Combine champagne, the ¾ cup water and food color. Stir in melted gelatine. Pour into 2-quart mold and chill until almost set. Carefully push about one half of the strawberries, pointed end first, into gelatine mixture. Chill until firm, then add Spiced Cheese Layer.

SPICED CHEESE LAYER:

1 8-ounce package cream cheese
1 teaspoon Lemon Peel
½ teaspoon Ginger
Dash Mace
Dash Cardamom
1 8½-ounce can crushed pineapple, drained
¾ cup reconstituted frozen limeade
3 drops Green Food Color
¼ cup toasted slivered almonds
1 envelope unflavored gelatine
2 tablespoons water

Have cheese at room temperature. Add lemon peel, ginger, mace and cardamom and beat until fluffy. Add pineapple, limeade, food color and almonds. Mix well. Soften gelatine in water; set over hot water to melt. Add gelatine to cream cheese mixture, mixing well. Spread over Champagne Layer. Chill until firm. Remove from mold. Garnish with crisp lettuce and the remaining fresh strawberries. *Serves 8.*

Creamy Coleslaw

½ cup dairy sour cream
1 tablespoon vinegar
1 teaspoon Season-All
1½ tablespoons sugar
½ teaspoon dry Mustard
¼ teaspoon Ginger
½ teaspoon Celery Seed
Dash White Pepper
4 cups finely shredded cabbage
¼ cup minced green pepper
Paprika

Combine sour cream with the next seven ingredients. Refrigerate 20 minutes, allowing seasonings to blend. Spoon over cabbage and green pepper, tossing lightly. Sprinkle with paprika. *Serves 4 to 6.*

VARIATION:

Coleslaw Bon Appétit—Use ½ cup mayonnaise, 1 tablespoon vinegar, 1 tablespoon cream, ½ teaspoon Bon Appétit, ⅛ teaspoon Onion Salt, ½ teaspoon sugar, ¼ teaspoon dry Mustard, dash ground Red Pepper and ½ teaspoon Celery Seed in place of the first eight ingredients in the above recipe. Proceed as above.

L.C. Fresh Fruit Medley

1 grapefruit
2 oranges
1 pint fresh strawberries
1 cantaloupe or other melon
1 fresh pineapple
2 pears
2 apples
2 bananas
¼ cup lemon juice
½ teaspoon Ginger
Dash Mace
Dash Cardamom

Peel and section grapefruit and oranges. Remove caps from strawberries. Cut melon in half; remove seed. With ball cutter, cut balls from the melon. Peel pineapple, remove core and cut into bite-size pieces. Peel and slice pears, apples and bananas and dip in a mixture of lemon juice, ginger, mace and cardamom. Combine all of the fruit and mix gently. Pour remaining lemon juice mixture over all. You may serve plain, or with a dressing, such as Poppy Seed Dressing, Celery Seed Dressing or a whipped cream dressing. *Serves 6 to 8.*

Layered Orange-Cranberry Mold

A two-tiered mold pretty enough to grace any party table, and exquisitely flavored.

CRANBERRY LAYER:

2 envelopes unflavored gelatine
¼ cup cold water
1 1-pound can whole cranberry sauce
2 tablespoons lemon juice
¼ teaspoon Allspice
⅛ teaspoon Mace or Nutmeg
1 cup ginger ale
1 cup orange sections

Soften gelatine in cold water; melt over hot water. Combine remaining ingredients, then stir in melted gelatine. Pour into 2-quart mold. Chill until firm.

CHEESE-NUT LAYER:

1 envelope unflavored gelatine
2 tablespoons cold water
1 cup orange juice
1 3-ounce package cream cheese
½ teaspoon Ginger
½ cup pecan pieces
½ cup heavy cream
½ cup dairy sour cream

Soften gelatine in cold water; melt over hot water. Gradually mix orange juice into cream cheese. Add ginger and nuts; mix well. Stir in gelatine. Combine heavy cream and sour cream and whip until stiff; fold into gelatine mixture. Pour over cranberry layer. Chill until firm. Remove from mold; garnish with crisp greens and orange sections.

Makes 8 to 10 servings.

Frozen Bing Cherry Salad

1 16½-ounce can (2½ cups) pitted Bing cherries
1 8-ounce can pineapple tidbits
4 ounces cream cheese
½ cup dairy sour cream
2 tablespoons sugar
⅛ teaspoon salt
1 teaspoon Lemon Peel
½ teaspoon Ginger
⅛ teaspoon Mace
1 teaspoon pure Vanilla Extract
4 drops Red Food Color
1 cup miniature marshmallows

Drain cherries and pineapple. Have cream cheese at room temperature, then beat until fluffy. Add sour cream, sugar, salt, lemon peel, ginger, mace, vanilla and food color; mix well. Carefully stir in cherries, pineapple and marshmallows. Pour into ice cube tray or a 1-quart mold. Freeze. Remove from mold; slice and serve on crisp lettuce.

Makes 6 servings.

Party Pink Fruit Salad

A cool, refreshing summer salad.

1 8-ounce package cream cheese
½ cup mayonnaise
½ teaspoon Allspice
½ teaspoon Orange Peel
¼ teaspoon Cloves
Dash Nutmeg
Few drops Red Food Color
1 17-ounce can fruit cocktail (2 cups)
1 orange
¼ cup maraschino cherries
½ cup chopped pecans or walnuts
1 cup miniature marshmallows
1 cup heavy cream

Have cheese at room temperature; add mayonnaise, spices and food color, mixing thoroughly. Drain fruit cocktail; peel and section orange and cut cherries into halves. Add fruits, nuts and marshmallows to cheese mixture. Mix carefully. Whip cream; fold into fruit mixture. Spoon into freezer trays or 1½-quart mold. Freeze. Remove from mold; slice and serve on crisp lettuce. *Serves 8 to 10.*

Waldorf Salad

3 cups diced apples
½ cup chopped celery
½ cup chopped walnuts or pecans
¼ cup raisins
½ teaspoon Lemon Peel
¼ teaspoon dry Mustard
¼ teaspoon Ginger
⅛ teaspoon Mace
Dash Cardamom
2 teaspoons lemon juice
½ cup mayonnaise
1 tablespoon light cream

Put diced apples, celery, nuts and raisins in bowl. Combine remaining ingredients; toss with apple mixture. Serve in lettuce cups. *Serves 6 to 8.*

L.C. Sweet-Sour Cucumbers with Onions

2 cups thinly sliced, pared cucumbers
½ teaspoon salt
1 cup thinly sliced onions
¼ cup vinegar
1 tablespoon water
1 tablespoon sugar
½ teaspoon Dill Weed
¼ teaspoon Cracked Black Pepper
Dash ground Red Pepper

Place cucumber slices in a bowl. Sprinkle with salt and cover with cold water. Refrigerate 30 minutes; drain well. Add onions, Combine vinegar, the 1 tablespoon water, sugar, dill weed, cracked black pepper and red pepper. Pour over cucumbers and onions; toss lightly. Chill 1 hour or longer, tossing occasionally, before serving. *Serves 4.*

Country Kitchen Potato Salad

No picnic table is complete without this summertime favorite.

4 cups diced, cooked potatoes
2 hard-cooked eggs, chopped
½ cup chopped celery
¼ cup chopped pickle
⅔ cup mayonnaise
1 tablespoon vinegar
1 tablespoon Instant Minced Onion
2 teaspoons Bon Appétit
⅛ teaspoon MSG
¼ teaspoon White Pepper
1 teaspoon dry Mustard

Put potatoes, eggs, celery and pickles in bowl. Blend together remaining ingredients and gently mix with potato mixture. Chill. *Serves 6.*

VARIATION:
Potato-Fennel Salad—To the above recipe, add ¼ teaspoon crushed Fennel Seed.

Tuna and Tomato Mold

This is an impressive and delicious salad for a buffet supper or luncheon.

2 envelopes unflavored gelatine
1½ teaspoons Beef Flavor Base
1¾ cups tomato juice
1 teaspoon sugar
¼ teaspoon ground Oregano
½ teaspoon dry Mustard
1 tablespoon lemon juice
¼ cup water
¼ cup mayonnaise
½ cup dairy sour cream
½ teaspoon Lemon Peel
½ teaspoon Instant Minced Onion
¼ cup chopped stuffed olives
¼ cup chopped celery
1 7-ounce can tuna, flaked

Mix 1 envelope of the gelatine with beef flavor base and ¾ cup of the tomato juice. Heat, stirring, until gelatine melts. Remove from heat; add remaining tomato juice, sugar, oregano, dry mustard and lemon juice. Mix well, then pour into a 1-quart mold. Chill until firm. Meantime, soften the remaining envelope of gelatine in the ¼ cup water; melt over boiling water. Remove from heat. Stir in mayonnaise and sour cream, blending thoroughly. Gently stir in remaining ingredients. Spoon this mixture over top of tomato layer and return to refrigerator. Chill until firm. Remove from mold and garnish with salad greens. *Serves 5 to 6.*

Creamy Roquefort Dressing

½ pound Roquefort cheese
½ cup mayonnaise
½ cup light cream
or dairy sour cream
2 teaspoons lemon juice
¼ teaspoon dry Mustard
Dash MSG
Dash White Pepper
Dash Garlic Salt

Crumble cheese; add remaining ingredients and mix thoroughly. If a thinner dressing is desired, add additional cream or milk.

Makes about 1 pint.

Cardamom Cream Dressing

Cardamom makes a wonderful difference in this creamy dressing for fruit salad.

4 egg yolks
¼ cup vinegar
1 tablespoon sugar
1 tablespoon butter
¼ teaspoon dry Mustard
⅛ teaspoon ground Cardamom
¼ teaspoon salt
Dash White Pepper
½ pint heavy cream
1 cup miniature marshmallows
½ cup chopped pecans

Beat egg yolks lightly; add vinegar, sugar, butter and seasonings. Mix well. Cook over low heat or in double boiler, stirring constantly, until thick, about 3 minutes. Remove from heat; cool. When ready to serve, whip cream. Fold whipped cream, marshmallows and nuts into the cooled mixture. Serve with fruit salads. *Makes about 2½ cups.*

Celery Seed Dressing

1 teaspoon Celery Seed
½ cup sugar
1 teaspoon Onion Salt
1 teaspoon Paprika
1 teaspoon dry Mustard
¼ cup vinegar
1 cup salad oil

Put celery seed, sugar, onion salt, paprika and dry mustard in small mixing bowl. Add alternately 1 tablespoon vinegar and ¼ cup oil until vinegar and oil are used up, beating hard after each addition. Continue beating for 5 minutes or until dressing thickens. Serve on fruit salad, avocado salad, sliced tomatoes or use on head lettuce. *Makes about 1½ cups.*

Lamaze Dressing

1 cup mayonnaise
1 cup chili sauce
¼ cup India relish
1 hard-cooked egg, chopped
½ pimiento, chopped
¼ green pepper, finely chopped
2 tablespoons finely chopped celery
1 teaspoon vinegar
1 teaspoon dry Mustard
½ teaspoon Instant Minced Onion
⅛ teaspoon Paprika
¼ teaspoon Black Pepper
½ teaspoon Season-All
⅛ teaspoon Turmeric
1 teaspoon A-1 sauce

Combine all ingredients, mixing well. Chill before using. If full recipe is not used at once, keep in refrigerator in tightly covered jar. This dressing is especially good with shrimp, crab or lobster, and may be used on tossed salad and some sandwiches. *Makes about 3 cups.*

Green Goddess Dressing

1 2-ounce can anchovy fillets
Dash Garlic Powder
⅛ teaspoon Onion Powder
1 tablespoon Instant Minced Onion
1 tablespoon Parsley Flakes
1 tablespoon Tarragon Leaves
1 tablespoon Chives
3 cups mayonnaise
¼ cup white wine vinegar
Dash MSG

Mash anchovies. Add remaining ingredients, blending well. Let stand 30 minutes or longer for flavors to blend. Serve with salad greens. You may toss chicken, shrimp or crab meat with the greens. *Makes about 3½ cups.*

Poppy Seed Dressing

½ cup sugar
1 teaspoon salt
1 teaspoon dry Mustard
½ teaspoon Onion Powder
⅓ cup cider vinegar
1 tablespoon lemon juice
1 cup salad oil
1½ tablespoons Poppy Seed

Combine sugar, salt, dry mustard, onion powder, vinegar and lemon juice. Stir until sugar dissolves. Add oil slowly, beating well. Dressing thickens as oil is added. Stir in poppy seed. Store in refrigerator. Just before serving, shake to mix well. Especially delicious with fruit or avocado salad. *Makes about 1⅔ cups.*

Ginger Cream Dressing

½ teaspoon Ginger
½ pint heavy cream
¼ cup chopped dates
¼ cup chopped nuts

Add ginger to cream; whip until stiff. Fold in dates and nuts. Serve with fruit salads. *Makes about 2 cups.*

Honey Spice Dressing

½ cup French dressing
1 tablespoon honey
½ teaspoon Cinnamon
¼ teaspoon ground Cloves
⅛ teaspoon Ginger

Combine all ingredients and mix well. Excellent on fruit salads.
Makes about ½ cup.

French Dressing

½ cup vinegar (wine, cider or malt)
¾ teaspoon salt
Dash MSG
¼ teaspoon White Pepper
½ teaspoon dry Mustard
1½ cups olive or salad oil

Combine all ingredients in jar; cover and shake vigorously. Set aside or chill 30 minutes or longer to allow flavors to blend. Shake well when ready to use. *Makes about 2 cups.*

VARIATIONS:

American French Dressing—To the above recipe add 2 teaspoons sugar, 1 teaspoon Paprika and ¼ teaspoon Garlic Powder.

South-of-the-Border Dressing—To above recipe for French Dressing add 2 teaspoons sugar, 1 teaspoon Paprika, ¼ teaspoon Chili Powder, ¼ teaspoon Dill Seed, 1 teaspoon Celery Salt and 6 Coriander Seeds, crushed.

Herb French Dressing—Be creative. To the above recipe add one or a combination of the following: Curry Powder, Basil Leaves, Tarragon Leaves, Marjoram Leaves, Parsley Flakes, Oregano Leaves, Dill Weed, Italian Seasoning or Salad Herbs.

NOTE: Reduce oil to 1 cup for a lighter bodied or less oily dressing.

Italian Dressing

¼ teaspoon Oregano Leaves
⅛ teaspoon Garlic Powder
⅛ teaspoon White Pepper
¼ teaspoon dry Mustard
½ teaspoon Chives
½ teaspoon Parsley Flakes
1 teaspoon Season-All
1 teaspoon Instant Minced Onion
Dash ground Red Pepper
½ teaspoon sugar
½ cup wine vinegar
1 cup olive oil

Combine all ingredients in jar; cover and shake vigorously. Chill 1 hour for flavors to blend. Shake well when ready to serve. *Makes 1½ cups.*

Roquefort Dressing

¼ pound Roquefort cheese
1 teaspoon Worcestershire sauce
1½ teaspoons Bon Appétit
½ teaspoon Black Pepper
½ teaspoon Paprika
½ teaspoon dry Mustard
⅛ teaspoon MSG
Dash ground Red Pepper
¼ cup vinegar
1 cup salad oil

Crumble cheese, then mix together all ingredients in a pint jar. Shake well. Keep in covered jar in refrigerator. Shake again before using.
Makes about 1½ cups.

MEATS

Beef

Beef Stew 116

Beef Stroganoff 116

Glazed Boiled Beef 117

Hamburger De Luxe 117

Herb Steak 117

Herbed Minute Steaks 118

Hungarian Goulash 118

Meat Loaf Baked in Sauce 119

Meat Loaf with Mushrooms 122

Old-Fashioned Sauerbraten 120

Oven Braised Short Ribs 122

Peppered Tenderloin 119

Pot Roast aux Herbes 120

Roast Whole Tenderloin 123

Rolled Rib Roast Royale 123

Sauerbraten with Potato Dumplings 121

Sesame Steaks 123

Swedish Meat Balls 122

Swiss Steak 124

Lamb

Crown Roast of Lamb 126

Gingered Crown Roast 126

Herbed Crown Roast 126

East Indian Lamb Curry 126

Herb-Roasted Rack of Lamb 124

Lamb in Gingered Cranberry Sauce 125

Lamb Kebabs 125

Lamb Shanks Divine 127

Ragout of Lamb Rosemary 127

Roast Leg of Lamb 124

Pork

Clove-Studded Broiled Ham 128

Golden Clove Glazed Ham 131

Curry Glazed Ham 131

Honey Glazed Ham 131

Orange Glazed Ham 131

Honey-Glazed Pork Shoulder 130

Indonesian Spareribs 129

Pork Chops à l'Orange 129

Pork Mandarin 128

Spiced Baked Ham Slice 128

Stuffed Pork Chops 129

Sweet-Sour Pork 130

Veal

Osso Bucco 134

Saltimbocca 133

Stuffed Breast of Veal 133

Veal Birds 132

Veal Cutlets Viennese 132

Veal Marsala 115

Veal Orloff 115

Veal Paprika 134

Veal Parmigiana 131

Veal Scaloppine 135

Wiener Schnitzel 135

Specialty Meats and Game

Country Style Venison Steak 136

Kidneys in Sherry Sauce 137

Ris de Veau à la Crème 136

Spiced Tongue 135

Zesty Stuffed Frankfurters 137

Veal Marsala

1½ pounds veal cutlets, cut ¼ inch thick
2 tablespoons flour
½ teaspoon Garlic Salt
⅛ teaspoon Black Pepper
1 slice bacon, chopped
2 tablespoons butter
¼ cup cold water
1 teaspoon cornstarch
⅓ cup dry Marsala wine
½ teaspoon Marjoram Leaves
¼ teaspoon Basil Leaves
¼ teaspoon Onion Salt

Cut veal into 12 serving-size pieces. Combine flour, garlic salt and pepper. In large skillet, fry bacon over low heat until cooked but not crisp, add 1 tablespoon of the butter. Dust veal with flour mixture and sauté, a few pieces at a time, over medium heat 2 minutes on each side. Add the remaining butter to skillet when needed. Place veal on warm serving platter while preparing the sauce. Slowly stir water into cornstarch, add wine and remaining ingredients. Pour into skillet and cook, stirring, over low heat until mixture begins to boil. Pour over veal. *Makes 6 servings, 2 pieces each.*

Veal Orloff

1 10-ounce package frozen chopped spinach
1 teaspoon butter
½ teaspoon Instant Minced Onion
¼ teaspoon Bon Appétit

Cook spinach and drain. Stir in butter, onion and Bon Appétit. Spread in bottom of 11 x 7 x 2-inch baking dish.

3 tablespoons flour
½ teaspoon salt
⅛ teaspoon Black Pepper
1½ pounds veal cutlets (6 pieces 4 × 2½ × ½ inches)
2 tablespoons butter

Mix flour, salt and pepper. Dredge veal pieces. Melt butter in large skillet. Brown veal on both sides. Arrange veal over spinach.

2 tablespoons butter
1 tablespoon flour
½ teaspoon Bon Appétit
⅛ teaspoon White Pepper
Dash Nutmeg
2 egg yolks, beaten
1 cup milk
3 cups shredded Swiss cheese

In 1-quart saucepan, melt butter over very low heat, stir in next 4 ingredients. Cook, stirring until bubbly. Remove from heat. Quickly stir in egg yolks. Immediately begin adding milk in small amounts, stirring after each addition. Cook, stirring until slightly thickened. Add cheese and stir until melted. Pour over veal. Bake in 350° F. oven 20 minutes. Place under broiler, *top* of dish about 6 inches from heat, 5 to 10 minutes or until lightly browned.

Beef Stew

2 pounds chuck, cut into 1-inch cubes
¼ cup shortening
1 Bay Leaf
1 teaspoon salt
1 tablespoon Season-All
¼ teaspoon Black Pepper
½ teaspoon Marjoram Leaves
⅛ teaspoon Tarragon Leaves
½ teaspoon Parsley Flakes
2 teaspoons Beef Flavor Base
2 cups water
4 carrots
4 potatoes
4 small onions
¼ cup flour

Brown meat in hot shortening. Add seasonings and water. Cover and simmer 1½ hours or until meat is almost tender. Peel carrots and cut into 1-inch pieces. Peel and quarter potatoes. Peel onions. Add vegetables to stew and continue cooking 30 minutes or until vegetables are tender. Make a thin, smooth paste by mixing together the flour and an equal amount of water; stir into stew and cook, stirring occasionally, until thickened.

Serves 4 to 6.

Beef Stroganoff

2 pounds beef, sirloin or tenderloin
2 tablespoons butter or margarine
1 tablespoon Instant Minced Onion
1 teaspoon Season-All
½ teaspoon salt
Dash Nutmeg
¼ cup sherry
1 cup dairy sour cream

Cut beef into bite-size strips; sauté in butter. Add onion, Season-All, salt, nutmeg and sherry. Cover and simmer about 20 minutes. Remove from heat and allow to cool. Have sour cream at room temperature. Stir into the cooled beef mixture and heat over very low heat or in double boiler until hot, being careful not to allow it to boil. (Boiling will cause a sour cream mixture to separate, resulting in a curdled appearance.) For parties or buffets or even table service, you may want to heat and serve in a chafing dish or a candle warmer type dish. Serve with white or wild rice or buttered noodles.

Serves 4.

Glazed Boiled Beef

1 4-pound beef brisket
2 teaspoons Meat Tenderizer
2 tablespoons Celery Flakes
¼ teaspoon Coarse Grind Black Pepper
1 teaspoon Season-All
20 whole Cloves
Water
½ cup brown sugar, packed

Pierce meat deeply with long-tined fork. Sprinkle meat tenderizer on all surfaces. Let stand 30 minutes at room temperature. Put in deep kettle; add celery flakes, pepper, Season-All and 6 to 8 whole cloves. Cover with water. Cover kettle and simmer very slowly 2 hours or until meat is tender. (Do not boil.) Remove meat from broth and place in shallow roasting pan. Score fat in diamond shapes. Sprinkle lightly with brown sugar and stud with remaining whole cloves. Bake in 400°F. oven 20 minutes. Slice and serve hot with a horseradish or mustard sauce. *Serves 6 to 8.*

2 pounds ground round steak
1 egg
1 tablespoon Worcestershire sauce
1 tablespoon soy sauce
1 teaspoon Bon Appétit
½ teaspoon dry Mustard
Dash Nutmeg
¼ teaspoon Black Pepper
½ teaspoon Onion Powder
1 teaspoon Beef Flavor Base
½ cup hot water
Fat for searing

Mix meat, egg and seasonings thoroughly. Dissolve beef flavor base in water and gradually mix into beef. Do not overmix. Shape into 4 to 8 patties. Sear quickly on both sides in a little fat in hot skillet; finish cooking to desired degree of doneness over low heat. Serve thin patties on split and toasted hamburger buns and thick patties as a dinner entrée.
Makes 8 hamburgers or 4 hamburger steaks.

1 pound round steak
2 tablespoons flour
1 teaspoon Season-All
2 tablespoons salad oil
1 10½-ounce can condensed cream of mushroom soup
¾ cup water
1 tablespoon Herb Seasoning

Cut steak into serving-size pieces. Combine flour and Season-All; pound into steak. Brown meat on both sides in hot oil in heavy skillet. Add remaining ingredients. Cover; simmer 45 minutes, or bake in 350°F. oven 1 hour. Excellent served with hot Buttered Noodles with Dill or with Poppy Seed (see recipe page 197). *Serves 3 to 4.*

Herbed Minute Steaks

Marinating in a wine and herb sauce before grilling does wonders for minute steaks.

1 cup salad oil
½ cup red wine (Burgundy or Bordeaux) or ¼ cup wine vinegar
½ teaspoon Garlic Powder
½ teaspoon Onion Powder
½ teaspoon Bon Appétit
Dash Nutmeg
¼ teaspoon MSG
¼ teaspoon Black Pepper
½ teaspoon salt
½ teaspoon Oregano Leaves
½ teaspoon Basil Leaves
6 minute or cube steaks
½ cup dairy sour cream
Paprika

Combine all ingredients, except steaks, sour cream and paprika, in glass or enameled flat pan; mix well. Add steaks and marinate 1 hour, turning steaks several times. Remove from marinade; pan fry in hot skillet, or broil just until browned on each side. Top each steak with a spoon of sour cream and sprinkle with paprika. *Serves 6.*

Hungarian Goulash

Paprika, lots of it, gives this Hungarian stew its distinctive flavor.

¼ cup Chopped Instant Onions
3 tablespoons shortening
3 pounds beef shoulder (cut into 1½-inch cubes)
1 tablespoon Paprika
½ teaspoon Coarse Grind Black Pepper
2 teaspoons Season-All
6 Anise Seeds
Dash ground Red Pepper
1 green pepper
2 tomatoes
4 tablespoons tomato purée
1 cup water
3 slices bacon

Brown onions in hot shortening; remove. Add beef and brown on all sides. Combine paprika, pepper, Season-All, anise seed and red pepper; sprinkle over meat. Add browned onions. Chop green pepper into medium-size pieces. Peel and cut tomatoes into wedges. Add green pepper, tomatoes, tomato purée and water to meat; stir. Lay bacon strips over top. Cover and simmer 2 hours or until meat is tender. Add more water if necessary. Serve over noodles or spätzle. *Serves 4 to 6.*

Meat Loaf Baked in Sauce

2 pounds ground beef
1 medium-size potato
2 eggs, lightly beaten
¼ cup melted butter
1 teaspoon prepared horseradish
2 tablespoons Instant Minced Onion
⅛ teaspoon Garlic Powder
¼ teaspoon Black Pepper
¼ teaspoon MSG
1 tablespoon Season-All
3 tablespoons ketchup
¼ cup milk or water

For a good meat loaf, have fresh-ground beef. Scrub uncooked potato and grate, peel and all. (You should have about 1 cup after grating.) Mix all ingredients well, being careful not to overmix. Shape into a loaf in a shallow baking pan. Spoon sauce, recipe below, over loaf. Bake in 350°F. oven 1 hour and 15 minutes. *Serves 6 to 8.*

ZESTY TOMATO SAUCE:

2 teaspoons Beef Flavor Base
1 cup hot water
1 6-ounce can tomato paste
½ cup chili sauce
2 teaspoons Instant Minced Onion
¼ teaspoon ground Oregano
⅛ teaspoon ground Marjoram
Dash Nutmeg
¼ teaspoon Black Pepper
1 teaspoon sugar

Dissolve beef flavor base in hot water. Add to remaining ingredients and mix well. You will find this makes a thick sauce; and if you prefer a thinner sauce, add ¼ to ½ cup additional water.

Peppered Tenderloin

A gourmet steak, peppery, pungent, with a zesty sauce.

6 slices beef tenderloin (cut 1 inch thick)
½ teaspoon salt
⅛ teaspoon Garlic Salt
¼ teaspoon MSG
Coarse Grind Black Pepper
3 tablespoons butter
1 teaspoon flour
½ teaspoon Beef Flavor Base
¼ cup hot water
2 tablespoons sauterne

Trim off most of the outside fat. Slash remaining fat, about 1 inch apart, to prevent curling. Season steak with a mixture of salt, garlic salt and MSG. Sprinkle coarse grind black pepper generously over each side and press down with knife. Sauté in butter about 4 minutes on each side. Remove meat to heated serving platter. To essence in skillet add flour and beef flavor base, stirring to mix well; then add hot water and sauterne. Bring to a boil and spoon sauce over steak. Serve immediately. You will find these steaks excellent served with wild rice and sautéed mushrooms. *Serves 6.*

Old-Fashioned Sauerbraten

An old, old recipe—well worth the time it takes to prepare.

1 4-pound chuck roast
2 teaspoons salt
¼ teaspoon Black Pepper
½ teaspoon MSG
2 cups water
2 cups cider or wine vinegar
½ cup Chopped Instant Onions
3 Bay Leaves
12 Peppercorns
6 whole Cloves
2 tablespoons Celery Flakes
¼ teaspoon Thyme Leaves
1 teaspoon Mustard Seed
1 large carrot, sliced
¼ cup sugar
Flour
2 tablespoons oil
¼ cup seedless raisins, plumped
18 dark, old-fashioned gingersnaps, crushed

Rub beef with salt, pepper and MSG; place in large bowl or crock with water, vinegar, onions, bay leaves, peppercorns, cloves, celery flakes, thyme leaves, mustard seed, carrot and sugar. (One half cup dry red wine may be added to marinade if desired.) Cover and marinate in refrigerator 3 days. Turn several times. When ready to cook, remove meat from marinade, dry and dust with flour; brown on all sides in hot oil. Add marinade. Cover and simmer slowly 3 hours or until tender. Lift meat onto hot platter. Keep hot in warm oven. Strain the stock. Add raisins and gingersnaps; cook, stirring, until thick. Pour part of the gravy over the meat and serve the remaining gravy in a side dish. Serve with Potato Dumplings (see recipe for Potato Dumplings page 121). *Serves 4 to 6.*

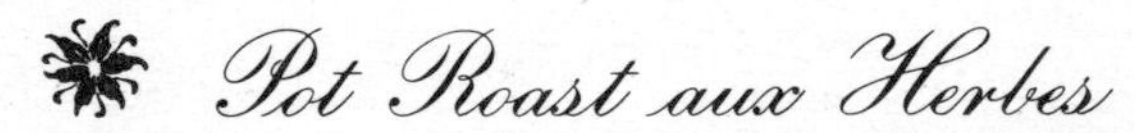

Pot roast simmered in an aromatic blend of herbs and spices.

1 4-pound boneless chuck or rump roast of beef
2 tablespoons flour
5 teaspoons Bon Appétit
1 teaspoon Cracked Black Pepper
½ teaspoon dry Mustard
2 tablespoons shortening
1 piece whole Ginger
1 teaspoon Oregano Leaves
½ teaspoon Marjoram Leaves
2 Bay Leaves
3 whole Allspice
¼ teaspoon MSG
2 teaspoons Beef Flavor Base
1 cup water

Dredge roast with mixture of flour, Bon Appétit, pepper and dry mustard. Brown on all sides in hot shortening in large skillet or Dutch oven. Add remaining ingredients. Cover and simmer 2½ hours or until tender. If desired, add small whole white onions, potatoes, celery and carrots during the last 45 minutes of cooking. *Serves 6 to 8.*

Sauerbraten with Potato Dumplings

A shortened version of the German classic, some think just as good.

- *2 cups wine vinegar*
- *2 cups water*
- *1 teaspoon salt*
- *¼ teaspoon Black Pepper*
- *3 tablespoons Chopped Instant Onions*
- *2 teaspoons Celery Flakes*
- *2 teaspoons Pickling Spice*
- *1 5-pound chuck roast*
- *½ cup sugar*
- *18 dark, old-fashioned gingersnaps, crushed*

Combine vinegar, water, salt, pepper, onions, celery flakes and pickling spice to make marinade. Place meat in this mixture, making sure it is covered with liquid. Cover; let stand 2 hours. Add sugar. Place over heat and simmer, covered, 3 hours or until tender. Remove meat to platter. Keep hot. Strain liquid to remove spices. Return liquid to cooking pan; stir in gingersnap crumbs to thicken gravy and simmer 20 minutes. Serve with Potato Dumplings, recipe below. *Serves 6 to 8.*

POTATO DUMPLINGS:

- *2 cups riced potatoes (about 3 medium-size potatoes)*
- *1 egg, beaten*
- *½ cup dry bread crumbs, not toasted*
- *⅛ teaspoon Onion Salt*
- *¼ teaspoon White Pepper*
- *¼ teaspoon MSG*
- *½ teaspoon salt*
- *Flour*
- *Herb Croutons*

After potatoes are boiled, peel and put through ricer or coarse sieve. Add egg, bread crumbs, onion salt, pepper, MSG and salt, mixing well. Add 3 to 4 tablespoons flour to potato mixture until the consistency is that of dough but not too sticky. Roll into 1½-inch balls, putting an Herb Crouton (see recipe page 258) in center of each. Gently drop into rapidly boiling, salted water. Cook 8 minutes or until dumplings change in appearance and begin to look fluffy. *Makes 16 to 18 dumplings.*

Swedish Meat Balls

½ cup dry bread crumbs
¼ cup cream
 or evaporated milk
1 pound ground beef
1 egg
2 teaspoons Instant Minced
 Onion
⅛ teaspoon Allspice
1 teaspoon Season-All
¼ teaspoon Black Pepper
¼ teaspoon Garlic Salt
¼ cup shortening or oil
½ teaspoon Beef Flavor Base
¼ cup hot water

Soak crumbs in cream, then combine with beef, egg and seasonings. Shape into balls 1½ inches in diameter. Brown on all sides in hot shortening; pour off excess fat. Dissolve beef flavor base in hot water; add to meat balls. Cover and simmer 20 minutes. *Serves 6.*

Oven Braised Short Ribs

5 pounds short ribs of beef
3 tablespoons shortening
1 tablespoon Instant Minced
 Onion
⅛ teaspoon Garlic Powder
1 tablespoon Bon Appétit
1 teaspoon Herb Seasoning
¼ teaspoon ground Thyme
1 Bay Leaf
½ teaspoon Black Pepper
1 teaspoon Beef Flavor Base
1 cup hot water
6 medium-size potatoes, peeled
6 medium-size carrots, peeled

Brown short ribs on all sides in hot shortening. Add seasonings and beef flavor base dissolved in the hot water. Cover. Bake in 350°F. oven 2½ hours or until tender. Drain off excess fat. Add potatoes and carrots; cover and bake 45 minutes to 1 hour longer. Thicken liquid for gravy if desired. *Serves 4.*

Meat Loaf with Mushrooms

1 pound ground beef
½ pound ground pork
½ pound ground veal
2 eggs, beaten
2 tablespoons Instant Minced
 Onion
1 teaspoon prepared horseradish
2 teaspoons salt
½ teaspoon dry Mustard
1 teaspoon Season-All
½ cup soft bread crumbs
½ cup chopped celery
1 4-ounce can mushroom crowns
¼ cup mushroom liquid or water

Mix together all ingredients until blended, being careful not to overmix. Shape into loaf in shallow baking pan, or put in 9¼ x 5¼ x 2¾-inch loaf pan. Bake in 375°F. oven 1½ hours. *Serves 6 to 8.*

L.C. Roast Whole Tenderloin

Pungently flavored tenderloin, roasted to a crusty brown outside, delicate pink inside and marvelously juicy.

1 4-pound beef tenderloin
¼ cup lemon juice
¼ cup oil
1 teaspoon Coarse Grind Black Pepper
1 teaspoon Herb Seasoning
2 teaspoons Bon Appétit
¼ teaspoon Mace
⅛ teaspoon Garlic Powder

Marinate tenderloin in mixture of lemon juice and oil 30 minutes to 1 hour, turning once or twice. Remove meat from marinade. Combine seasonings and rub over meat. Roast in 450°F. oven 45 minutes for rare, or until meat thermometer registers desired degree of doneness. (See Meat Roasting Chart.) *Serves 6 to 8.*

L.C. Rolled Rib Roast Royale

1 4- to 5-pound rolled rib or rib eye beef roast
3 teaspoons Bon Appétit
⅛ teaspoon Garlic Powder
¼ teaspoon Onion Salt
½ teaspoon Black Pepper
¼ teaspoon dry Mustard
1 teaspoon salt

Wipe roast with damp cloth. Combine seasonings and rub thoroughly into meat. Place on rack in pan. Insert a meat thermometer into the center of the thickest part. Roast in 325°F. oven 2 hours for rare, or until meat thermometer registers desired degree of doneness. Serve on platter garnished with parsley and spiced crab apples. *Serves 8 to 10.*

Sesame Steaks

Add the nutty flavor of sesame seed and a delicious oriental marinade—and steak becomes exotic.

1 pound sirloin steak, cut ½ inch thick
1 teaspoon lemon juice
1 tablespoon salad oil
¼ cup soy sauce
1 tablespoon brown sugar
1 teaspoon Onion Powder
¼ teaspoon Black Pepper
¼ teaspoon Garlic Salt
¼ teaspoon Ginger
1 tablespoon Sesame Seed
Dash MSG

Cut steak into 3 or 4 serving-size pieces; place in flat baking dish. Combine remaining ingredients; pour over steak, being sure to coat all sides. Let stand 1 hour or longer, turning once or twice. Broil 3 inches from heat a few minutes on each side to desired degree of doneness. Serve with rice. *Serves 2 to 3.*

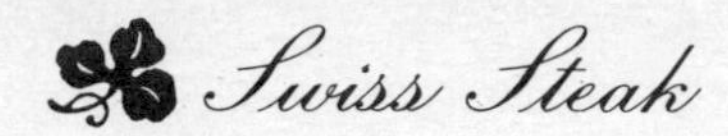

Swiss Steak

½ teaspoon salt
2 teaspoons Season-All
Dash Garlic Powder
¼ teaspoon dry Mustard
½ teaspoon Black Pepper
½ cup flour
3 pounds round steak, cut ¾ inch thick
¼ cup shortening
3 tablespoons Instant Minced Onion
1 green pepper, sliced
½ teaspoon Basil Leaves
⅛ teaspoon MSG
2 cups canned tomatoes

Mix salt, Season-All, garlic powder, dry mustard, pepper and flour; pound well into steak. Cut meat into serving pieces. Brown on both sides in hot shortening. Add onion, green pepper, basil leaves, MSG and tomatoes. Cover. Bring to boil; reduce heat and cook slowly 1½ hours or until tender. If you would like a variation in flavor, substitute ½ teaspoon Italian Seasoning for basil leaves. *Serves 5 to 6.*

L.C. Roast Leg of Lamb

1 6-pound leg of lamb
2 teaspoons Season-All
¼ teaspoon Black Pepper
⅛ teaspoon Nutmeg
1 teaspoon ground Thyme
¼ teaspoon Onion Powder
Dash Garlic Powder
2 teaspoons salt

Wipe lamb with a damp cloth. Combine remaining ingredients and rub over entire surface of meat. Place, fat side up, on rack in a shallow baking pan. Insert a meat thermometer into the center of the roast. Roast in 300°F. oven 30 to 35 minutes per pound or until meat thermometer indicates desired degree of doneness. Remove lamb to a hot platter. Gravy may be made from drippings in pan. Serve very hot with any of the following accompaniments: mint jelly or sauce, currant jelly, minted pear halves or pineapple slices, chutney or peach halves filled with mint jelly. *Serves 8.*

L.C. Herb-Roasted Rack of Lamb

¼ teaspoon ground Thyme
¼ teaspoon Black Pepper
⅛ teaspoon Onion Powder
¼ teaspoon MSG
½ teaspoon Season-All
½ teaspoon salt
1 8-rib rack of lamb (about 2½ pounds)

Combine seasonings and rub on lamb. Place on rack in shallow pan, fat side up. Bake in 325°F. oven 30 minutes per pound or to desired degree of doneness. Serve hot. Excellent with Wheat Pilaf (see recipe page 195) and mint jelly. *Serves 4.*

Lamb Kebabs

- 2 pounds lean lamb
- 2 teaspoons Season-All
- ½ teaspoon Coarse Grind Black Pepper
- ½ teaspoon Oregano Leaves
- 1 teaspoon Instant Minced Onion
- ⅛ teaspoon MSG
- ⅛ teaspoon Thyme Leaves
- Dash Allspice
- 2 tablespoons lemon juice
- ¼ cup oil
- 3 medium-size tomatoes
- 1 large green pepper
- 12 small onions
- 2 tablespoons melted butter

Cut meat into 2-inch cubes. Combine seasonings, lemon juice and oil; pour over meat. Cover and marinate in refrigerator 1 hour, turning meat several times. Quarter tomatoes, cut green pepper into 1-inch squares and remove outer skin of onions. Brush vegetables with melted butter. Thread the meat, tomatoes, green pepper and onions onto skewers alternating meat with vegetables. Broil 4 inches from heat 8 minutes, turn and continue broiling 6 minutes longer or until meat is nicely browned. Brush with marinade several times while broiling. Serve with rice or Wheat Pilaf (see recipe page 195). *Serves 4.*

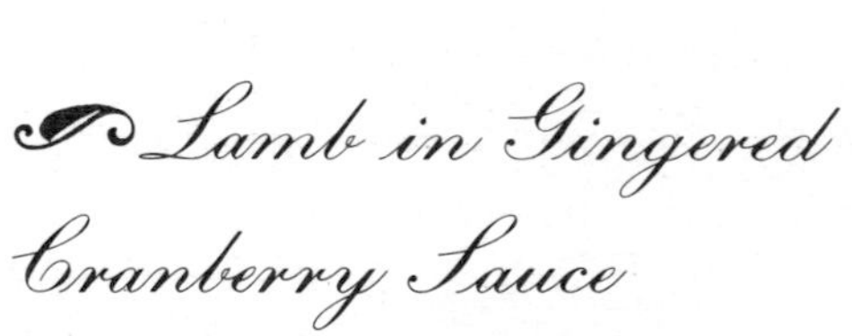

Lamb in Gingered Cranberry Sauce

Tart, spicy and luscious sauce—and it becomes even better with reheating.

- 2 pounds lean lamb, cubed
- 2 teaspoons Season-All
- ¼ teaspoon Black Pepper
- ⅓ cup Chopped Instant Onions
- Dash MSG
- ⅛ teaspoon Garlic Powder
- 1 6-ounce can tomato paste
- 1 cup red Burgundy
- 1½ cups water
- ¾ cup whole cranberry sauce
- ¼ teaspoon Ginger
- ¼ teaspoon ground Oregano

Trim off small pieces of fat from lamb and fry a few minutes to grease skillet. Add lamb cubes and brown on all sides; pour off excess fat. Add Season-All, pepper, onions, MSG, garlic powder, tomato paste, wine and water. Cover and simmer 45 minutes. Add cranberry sauce, ginger and oregano and simmer 45 minutes longer or until meat is tender. Add additional water if sauce becomes too thick. Serve hot over rice. *Serves 4 to 6.*

Crown Roast of Lamb

Festive and very special for grand occasions; a succulent crown of lamb delicately spiced with Cardamom and Orange Peel.

¼ teaspoon dry Mustard
⅛ teaspoon Cardamom
½ teaspoon Orange Peel
1 teaspoon Bon Appétit
½ teaspoon ground Marjoram
¼ teaspoon Black Pepper
¼ teaspoon MSG
1 teaspoon salt
1 14-rib crown roast of lamb (about 3 pounds)
Stuffing

Combine seasonings and rub over roast. Place on rack in shallow roasting pan. Fill center with Basic Bread Stuffing (see recipe page 162). Roast in 325°F. oven 2 hours (about 35 minutes per pound), or until meat thermometer registers 170°F. to 185°F., depending upon desired degree of doneness. You may roast the crown roast of lamb without the stuffing and when ready to serve, fill center with cooked minted peas or a combination of cooked carrots and potato balls. *Serves 6 to 7.*

VARIATIONS:

Herbed Crown Roast—Instead of marjoram in above recipe, use ½ teaspoon of one of the following: Thyme, Rosemary or Herb Seasoning. Substitute Season-All for Bon Appétit.

Gingered Crown Roast—Add 1 teaspoon Ginger to seasonings suggested in above recipes.

East Indian Lamb Curry

The true flavor of the East is captured in this famous curry.

2 pounds lean lamb, cubed
¼ cup flour
3 tablespoons shortening
¼ cup Chopped Instant Onions
2 teaspoons salt
¼ teaspoon MSG
¼ teaspoon dry Mustard
4 tablespoons Indian or Madras Curry Powder
1 teaspoon sugar
1 cup water
2 tablespoons lemon juice
1 tart apple, peeled and diced
2 tablespoons grated or flake coconut
2 tablespoons seedless raisins or currants
Dash Nutmeg

Dredge meat in flour and brown on all sides in hot shortening. Add onions to skillet; sauté a few minutes but do not brown. Add remaining ingredients; mix well. For a mild curry, decrease amount of curry powder used; for hot curry, increase the amount. Cover. Simmer 45 minutes or until meat is tender. Serve with rice and an assortment of condiments. *Serves 4.*

Lamb Shanks Divine

4 *lamb shanks*	½ *teaspoon Garlic Salt*
2 *tablespoons flour*	½ *teaspoon Sage Leaves, crumbled*
1½ *teaspoons Season-All*	½ *teaspoon Oregano Leaves*
½ *teaspoon Black Pepper*	½ *teaspoon Celery Salt*
¼ *teaspoon MSG*	2 *tablespoons lemon juice*
2 *tablespoons shortening*	1 *8-ounce can tomato sauce*
½ *cup Instant Minced Onion*	½ *cup water*

Roll lamb shanks in flour seasoned with Season-All, pepper and MSG; brown in hot shortening. Combine remaining ingredients; pour over meat. Cover and simmer gently 1½ hours or until tender. *Serves 4.*

Ragout of Lamb Rosemary

2 *pounds lean lamb, cubed*	1 *teaspoon Beef Flavor Base*
1 *tablespoon oil*	½ *teaspoon sugar*
¼ *teaspoon Rosemary Leaves*	1 *Bay Leaf*
½ *teaspoon Mint Flakes*	*Dash MSG*
¼ *teaspoon Instant Minced Garlic*	2 *cups water*
¼ *cup Chopped Instant Onions*	3 *potatoes*
1 *teaspoon Season-All*	3 *carrots*
1 *teaspoon Celery Salt*	2 *tablespoons butter*
	2 *tablespoons flour*

Slowly brown lamb on all sides in oil. Add seasonings and water; gently simmer 1½ hours or until lamb is almost tender. Peel potatoes and carrots. Cut potatoes into quarters and carrots into 2-inch pieces; add to stew. Simmer 40 minutes or until vegetables are tender. In a separate pan, melt butter; add flour and cook until flour is brown, stirring constantly. Stir into stew and cook a few minutes longer to thicken gravy slightly. You might like to serve with noodles, dumplings or hot biscuits. *Serves 4 to 6.*

Clove-Studded Broiled Ham

1 center cut ham slice (1½ inches thick)
Whole Cloves
2 tablespoons lemon juice
2 teaspoons brown sugar
1 teaspoon Lemon Peel
½ teaspoon prepared horseradish

Slash outside fat about 1 inch apart to prevent curling. Broil 3 to 4 inches from heat about 7 minutes. Turn. Stud edge of ham slice with whole cloves. Brush with mixture of lemon juice, brown sugar, lemon peel and horseradish. Broil 7 minutes or until ham is lightly browned. For added color, garnish with tinted pineapple cubes. *Serves 4 to 6.*

Spiced Baked Ham Slice

1 ham slice (1 inch thick)
2 teaspoons whole Cloves
1 teaspoon dry Mustard
½ teaspoon Allspice
⅓ cup brown sugar, packed
¼ cup vinegar

Slash outside fat about 1 inch apart to prevent curling. Stick whole cloves around edge of ham. Mix remaining ingredients; pour over ham slice in shallow pan or baking dish. Bake in 350°F. oven 1 hour. Serve with green peas and broiled grapefruit slices, bananas or peach halves sprinkled with Cinnamon or Nutmeg. *Serves 4 to 5.*

Pork Mandarin

Orange, honey and spices give distinctive flavor.

2 teaspoons salt
¼ teaspoon MSG
¼ teaspoon ground Thyme
1 teaspoon Bon Appétit
1 teaspoon Orange Peel
½ teaspoon dry Mustard
½ teaspoon Ginger
1 5-pound pork loin roast
½ cup orange juice
½ cup honey
Orange slices
Whole Cloves
1 11-ounce can Mandarin orange sections, drained

Combine seasonings and rub over meat. Place on rack in roasting pan; bake in 325°F. oven 2½ hours (30 minutes per pound) or until meat thermometer registers 185°F. After 40 minutes, baste 2 or 3 times with orange juice, using about one half of it. During the last 45 minutes, combine remaining orange juice with honey and baste several times with this mixture. After removing meat to platter, surround the glazed roast with orange slices studded with whole cloves and lettuce cups filled with Mandarin orange sections. *Serves 6 to 8.*

Indonesian Spareribs

3 pounds spareribs
¾ teaspoon Hickory Smoked Salt
¼ teaspoon Black Pepper
1 tablespoon Coriander Seed, crushed
1 tablespoon Cumin Seed, crushed
1 tablespoon Instant Minced Onion
1 teaspoon MSG
½ teaspoon Ginger
¼ cup salad oil
1 tablespoon brown sugar
¼ cup soy sauce
¼ cup lime or lemon juice

Cut spareribs into serving-size pieces. Place on rack in shallow pan. Combine remaining ingredients, mixing well. Spoon or brush sauce over ribs to coat all sides. Bake in 325°F. oven 1½ hours or until ribs are tender and browned, basting with sauce several times. *Serves 4 to 6.*

Pork Chops à l'Orange

4 loin or rib pork chops (1½ inches thick)
¼ teaspoon Black Pepper
½ teaspoon Paprika
2 teaspoons Season-All
Dash MSG
¾ cup orange juice
1 tablespoon sugar
¼ teaspoon Curry Powder
10 whole Cloves
½ teaspoon Orange Peel
Flour to thicken

Rub pork chops with mixture of pepper, paprika, Season-All and MSG. Brown chops on both sides in heavy skillet, no fat added. Combine orange juice, sugar, curry powder, cloves and orange peel; pour over chops. Cover; reduce heat and simmer 1 hour or until tender. Remove chops to warm platter. Thicken remaining liquid with flour. Spoon sauce over chops or serve in a small bowl. *Serves 4.*

Stuffed Pork Chops

6 double-rib pork chops
3 cups bread cubes
1 teaspoon Poultry Seasoning
1 teaspoon Bon Appétit
¼ teaspoon Black Pepper
1 tablespoon Instant Minced Onion
½ cup finely diced celery
⅓ cup melted butter
⅛ teaspoon Black Pepper
¾ teaspoon Season-All
¼ teaspoon Ginger
¼ teaspoon dry Mustard
2 tablespoons shortening
¼ cup water

Have pocket cut in each chop. Toss together bread cubes, poultry seasoning, Bon Appétit, the ¼ teaspoon pepper, onion, celery and butter. Fill each pocket with ½ cup of the stuffing; close opening with toothpicks. Combine the remaining seasonings and rub well over chops. Brown both sides in hot shortening in skillet. Add water. Cover skillet or transfer to covered casserole, and bake in 350°F. oven 1 hour or until tender. *Serves 6.*

Sweet-Sour Pork

2 *pounds lean pork*
1 *cup water*
6 *whole Cloves*
¼ *cup butter or margarine*
1 *cup brown sugar, packed*
¼ *cup Arrowroot*
¼ *cup soy sauce*
¼ *cup vinegar*
1½ *cups pineapple juice*
½ *teaspoon **Onion Powder***
½ *teaspoon Ginger*
1 *green pepper*
1 *carrot*
¼ *cup onion slices*
2 *tablespoons butter or margarine*
2 *tablespoons soy sauce*
2 *tablespoons cornstarch*
½ *cup shortening*

Cut pork into pieces about ¾ inch thick and 2 inches long. Place in pan with water and cloves and bring to a boil. Reduce heat and cook 25 minutes or until tender. Pour off any remaining water. Cool meat. While meat is cooking combine the next 8 ingredients; cook over low heat until thickened, stirring constantly. (These two steps may be completed in advance; store meat and sauce in refrigerator until needed.) Cut green pepper into large pieces and the carrot into thin slices; sauté along with onion in the 2 tablespoons butter 1 to 2 minutes, stirring once or twice. Remove from skillet. Mix the 2 tablespoons soy sauce and cornstarch until smooth. Pour over the cooled pork; toss to coat pieces of pork. Heat shortening in skillet and fry pork until crisp and brown. Combine meat, vegetables and sauce (if sauce was made ahead of time, heat before using). Serve piping hot with rice as a side dish.

Serves 4 to 6.

Honey-Glazed Pork Shoulder

1 *4- to 5-pound fresh pork shoulder*
2 *teaspoons salt*
1 *tablespoon Season-All*
⅛ *teaspoon Garlic Powder*
¼ *teaspoon Black Pepper*
¼ *teaspoon MSG*
2 *tablespoons honey*
½ *teaspoon Ginger*
½ *teaspoon prepared horseradish*

Thoroughly rub pork shoulder with mixture of salt, Season-All, garlic powder, pepper and MSG. Place, fat side up, on rack in shallow pan. Roast in 325°F. oven 40 minutes per pound or until meat thermometer registers 185°F. Carefully remove skin and score fat in diamond pattern. Pour mixture of honey, ginger and horseradish over scored fat and return meat to oven. Roast 20 minutes longer or until well glazed.

Serves 4 to 6.

Golden Clove Glazed Ham

½ ready-to-eat ham (about 8 pounds)
½ cup brown sugar, packed
⅛ teaspoon ground Cloves
Whole Cloves

Place ham, fat side up, on rack in roasting pan. Bake in 325°F. oven 1½ hours. Carefully remove skin. Score fat by cutting into diamond shapes. Combine brown sugar and ground cloves. Spread this mixture over scored fat and stud each diamond with a whole clove. Increase temperature to 375°F. and bake ham 30 minutes longer or until well glazed.

Serves 10 to 12.

VARIATIONS:

Curry Glazed Ham—In above recipe, increase brown sugar to 1 cup, use 2 teaspoons Curry Powder in place of ground cloves and combine with ¼ cup pineapple juice.

Orange Glazed Ham—In above recipe, use 1 tablespoon Orange Peel in place of ground cloves.

Honey Glazed Ham—Instead of brown sugar and ground cloves in above recipe, combine ¼ cup honey, 1 teaspoon dry Mustard and ½ teaspoon Lemon Peel; spoon over scored fat side of ham as above.

Veal Parmigiana

1 6-ounce can tomato paste
1 can water
½ teaspoon Italian Seasoning
¼ teaspoon Oregano Leaves
⅛ teaspoon Garlic Powder
1 teaspoon Season-All
⅛ teaspoon MSG
1 tablespoon brown sugar
1 teaspoon Worcestershire sauce
1 tablespoon butter

Mix all ingredients together. Cook until thickened, stirring constantly. Set aside.

2 pounds veal cutlets
2 teaspoons Season-All
¼ teaspoon Black Pepper
2 eggs
1 cup fine dry bread crumbs
½ cup olive oil
¼ cup grated Parmesan cheese
½ pound Mozzarella cheese

Have cutlets sliced ½ inch thick and cut into serving-size pieces or leave whole. Add Season-All and pepper to eggs; beat lightly. Dip cutlets into egg mixture, then into bread crumbs. Brown on both sides in hot oil. Place cutlets in 8 x 13 x 1¾-inch baking dish. Pour sauce over meat and sprinkle with Parmesan cheese. Cover, using aluminum foil if necessary, and bake in 350°F. oven 30 minutes or until tender. Remove cover and top with slices of Mozzarella cheese. Continue baking until cheese melts.

Serves 4 to 6.

Veal Birds

1½ pounds veal steak, cut about ¼ inch thick
2 teaspoons Bon Appétit
½ teaspoon salt
Dash MSG
¼ teaspoon dry Mustard
Bread Stuffing
2 tablespoons butter
1 cup water
2 tablespoons flour
1 cup light cream

Cut veal steak into 3 x 5-inch pieces; pound to flatten slightly. Season with a mixture of Bon Appétit, salt, MSG and dry mustard. Spread each piece with Bread Stuffing; roll up and fasten with toothpick. Brown on all sides in hot butter. Transfer to a 2-quart baking dish. Add water to the skillet and scrape brown particles from bottom of skillet as it simmers. Pour over meat and bake, uncovered, in 350°F. oven 30 minutes. Blend flour with cream until smooth, then pour over meat. Bake 30 minutes longer. Remove toothpicks before serving. *Serves 4 to 5.*

BREAD STUFFING:

1½ cups soft bread crumbs
1 tablespoon Instant Minced Onion
1 tablespoon Parsley Flakes
⅛ teaspoon rubbed Sage
⅛ teaspoon Poultry Seasoning
¼ teaspoon Black Pepper
½ teaspoon Beef Flavor Base
¼ cup hot water
1 tablespoon melted butter

Combine bread crumbs and seasonings. Dissolve beef flavor base in hot water. Pour over bread crumbs along with melted butter, tossing well.

Veal Cutlets Viennese

2 pounds veal cutlets
2 tablespoons butter or margarine
1 tablespoon Season-All
¼ teaspoon MSG
¼ teaspoon Onion Powder
½ teaspoon Black Pepper
¼ cup white wine or water
1 cup dairy sour cream
Grated Parmesan cheese

Sauté cutlets in butter until well browned on each side. Combine seasonings; sprinkle over both sides of meat. Place in a baking dish. Mix wine with drippings in the frying pan; pour over meat. Cover dish (use foil if it does not have its own cover) and bake in 350°F. oven 45 minutes. Remove cover, spoon sour cream over meat; sprinkle with Parmesan cheese. Continue baking, uncovered, 15 to 20 minutes longer. Serve from the baking dish with sauce spooned over meat. Excellent with noodles which have been tossed with butter and any of the following: Poppy Seed, Dill Weed, Caraway Seed or toasted Sesame Seed. *Serves 4.*

Stuffed Breast of Veal

1 4- to 5-pound breast of veal
1 tablespoon Season-All
1½ teaspoons salt
3 cups soft bread cubes
½ cup seedless raisins
1½ cups chopped tart apples, peeled
1 teaspoon Orange Peel
2 teaspoons Instant Minced Onion
¾ teaspoon Celery Seed
1 teaspoon Marjoram Leaves
3 tablespoons butter, melted
1 teaspoon Beef Flavor Base
3 cups hot water
3 tablespoons flour

Have pocket cut in breast of veal. Wipe meat with damp cloth. Combine Season-All and 1 teaspoon of the salt; lightly rub inside of meat with one half this mixture. Toss together the remaining ½ teaspoon salt, bread cubes, raisins, apples, orange peel, onion, celery seed, marjoram leaves and butter. Fill pocket with stuffing. Close opening with skewers then lace shut. Place meat on rack in roasting pan. Combine the remaining Season-All and salt mixture, beef flavor base and 1 cup of the water and pour over meat. Cover and roast in 350°F. oven 2 hours, basting occasionally. Uncover and continue roasting 30 minutes longer or until tender. Remove meat to warm serving platter. Stir flour into drippings in pan and cook about 1 minute. Add the remaining 2 cups water; cook over medium heat, stirring, until gravy thickens. *Serves 5 to 6.*

Saltimbocca

A Roman delight, zesty with sage.

2 pounds veal cutlet, very thinly sliced
2 teaspoons Bon Appétit
¼ teaspoon Black Pepper
½ teaspoon rubbed Sage
⅛ teaspoon MSG
½ pound prosciutto (Italian ham), sliced thin
6 tablespoons sweet butter
½ teaspoon Beef Flavor Base
¼ cup hot water
2 tablespoons dry white wine

Cut veal into serving-size pieces. Sprinkle with mixture of Bon Appétit, pepper, sage and MSG. Place a slice of prosciutto on each piece of veal; fasten with a toothpick or small skewer. Melt 4 tablespoons of the butter in large skillet. Sauté meat 2 to 3 minutes on each side, ending with the prosciutto side up. Remove to hot platter. To the drippings in skillet add beef flavor base, water and the remaining butter, stirring to mix well. Heat until butter is melted, then add wine and simmer 2 to 3 minutes. Spoon sauce over meat. Serve immediately with sautéed mushrooms and zucchini. You will find this recipe good for the chafing dish. *Makes 6 servings.*

Veal Paprika

2 pounds cubed veal
¼ cup butter
¼ cup Chopped Instant Onions
1 teaspoon Season-All
½ teaspoon salt
1 tablespoon Paprika
¼ teaspoon Black Pepper
1 tablespoon Parsley Flakes
1½ cups water
½ pound mushrooms, sliced
2 tablespoons butter
1 cup dairy sour cream

Brown veal in the ¼ cup butter. Add onions, Season-All, salt, paprika, pepper, parsley flakes and water. Cover and simmer 1 hour or until meat is tender. Sauté mushrooms in the 2 tablespoons butter and add to veal during the last 15 minutes of cooking time. Remove from heat; stir in sour cream. Reheat, but do not allow it to boil. If you prefer a thicker sauce, make a thin, smooth paste using 2 tablespoons water and 2 tablespoons flour or 1 tablespoon Arrowroot. Stir in and continue heating very carefully until thickened. Serve over buttered noodles or rice. *Serves 4 to 5.*

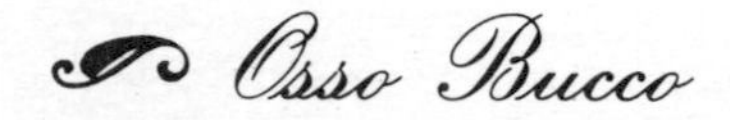

Osso Bucco

Braised veal shanks—a speciality of Milan.

6 tablespoons butter or margarine
4 veal shanks, cut about 3 inches in length
1 tablespoon Season-All
½ teaspoon Coarse Grind Black Pepper
3 tablespoons flour
1 teaspoon Italian Seasoning
¼ teaspoon Garlic Powder
1 tablespoon Parsley Flakes
1 tablespoon Celery Flakes
2 small carrots, diced
½ teaspoon Lemon Peel
3 tablespoons tomato paste or 1 cup canned tomatoes
1 cup hot water
1 teaspoon Beef Flavor Base
Parmesan cheese

Melt butter in deep skillet. Rub veal shanks with Season-All and pepper; dredge with flour. Brown slowly in butter; add remaining ingredients except cheese. Cover. Bring to a boil; reduce heat and simmer 1½ hours or until meat is very tender but not falling from the bone. Turn shanks over while cooking and add small amount of water if necessary. Remove cover; if sauce is still quite thin, cook uncovered to reduce liquid, or thicken with flour, by stirring in a smooth, thin paste made by mixing together equal amounts of flour and water, using 1 to 2 tablespoons of each. Serve hot over Buttered Noodles with Poppy Seed (see recipe page 197). Grated Parmesan cheese and extra sauce may be passed at the table.
Serves 4.

- 1 pound veal, cut for scaloppine
- 2 tablespoons flour
- 2 tablespoons salad oil
- 1½ teaspoons Season-All
- ½ teaspoon Garlic Powder
- ¼ teaspoon Black Pepper
- ¼ teaspoon Nutmeg
- 1 tablespoon Instant Minced Onion
- 1 4-ounce can sliced mushrooms
- 2 tablespoons chopped green pepper
- 1 tablespoon lemon juice
- ¾ cup water

Dredge veal with flour. Sauté on both sides in hot oil until well browned. Add remaining ingredients, including liquid from mushrooms. (If a more piquant scaloppine is desired, you may increase lemon juice to 2 tablespoons.) Cover and simmer 10 minutes. Serve from platter attractively garnished with tomato wedges, potato cakes or parsley or Paprika rimmed slices of lemon. *Serves 2 to 4.*

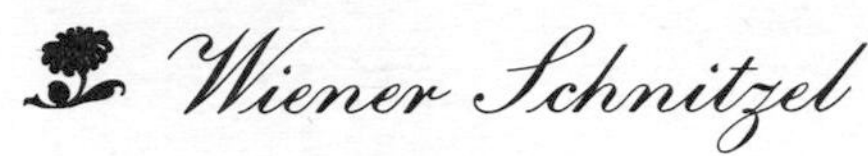

- 6 5-ounce veal cutlets
- ⅓ cup flour
- 1 teaspoon Season-All
- ¼ teaspoon Black Pepper
- ½ teaspoon Nutmeg
- 2 eggs, beaten
- 2 tablespoons water
- 1 cup fine dry bread crumbs
- ½ cup butter
- 1 tablespoon Parsley Flakes
- 2 tablespoons lemon juice
- 2 tablespoons butter

Pound veal until ¼ inch thick. Dredge with mixture of flour, Season-All, pepper and nutmeg. Dip in mixture of egg and water, then in bread crumbs. Let dry 30 minutes. Brown veal on both sides in the ½ cup butter, cooking about 15 minutes. Remove veal to hot platter. To skillet add parsley flakes, lemon juice and the 2 tablespoons butter, stirring to blend with pan drippings. Pour sauce over veal. *Serves 6.*

L.C. Spiced Tongue

- 1 3- to 4-pound beef tongue
- 1 tablespoon Celery Flakes
- 2 tablespoons Chopped Instant Onions
- ½ teaspoon MSG
- ¼ teaspoon Crushed Red Pepper
- 2 tablespoons salt
- 2 Bay Leaves
- 8 whole Cloves
- 10 whole Allspice
- 10 Peppercorns

Cover tongue with water; add seasonings. Cover and simmer until tongue is tender, allowing 1 hour per pound. Cool slightly; remove from liquid. Cut off bones and gristle from large end of tongue; split skin lengthwise on underside and peel off. Slice tongue at a slant. You may serve either hot or cold, but you will find it especially good served cold for buffet or picnic dinner. *Serves 8 to 12.*

Country Style Venison Steak

2 tablespoons flour
2 teaspoons Season-All
¼ teaspoon Black Pepper
⅛ teaspoon MSG
Dash Nutmeg
2 pounds venison round steak, cut ½ inch thick
3 tablespoons oil
2 tablespoons Chopped Instant Onions
2 carrots, sliced
1 teaspoon Beef Flavor Base
1½ cups hot water

Combine flour, Season-All, pepper, MSG and nutmeg. Pound this seasoned flour into both sides of steak. Brown on both sides in hot oil in a heavy skillet. Add onions, carrots and beef flavor base which has been dissolved in water. If you like to cook with wine, replace about one half of the water with red wine. Cover and simmer 1½ hours or until tender.

Serves 4.

Ris de Veau à la Crème

Sweetbreads in a delicate cream sauce enriched with sherry.

2 pair sweetbreads
2 tablespoons lemon juice
1½ teaspoons salt
4 tablespoons butter
⅛ teaspoon White Pepper
¼ teaspoon MSG
⅛ teaspoon Onion Powder
½ cup sherry
¾ cup light cream or half and half
1 tablespoon flour

Soak sweetbreads in ice water 1 hour. (If using frozen sweetbreads, thaw just before cooking.) Drain and cover with fresh cold water. Add lemon juice and 1 teaspoon of the salt and bring slowly to a boil. Simmer 10 minutes, then quickly plunge them into ice cold water to cool. Remove tubes and connecting tissues. Cut slices diagonally about 1 inch thick. Sauté in butter 4 minutes or until sweetbreads just begin to brown. Turn and sauté other side. Sprinkle with the remaining ½ teaspoon salt, pepper, MSG and onion powder. Add sherry; cover and simmer 5 minutes. Add cream and simmer 15 minutes longer. Make a thin, smooth paste by mixing together the flour and an equal amount of water. Stir into sweetbreads and continue cooking, stirring, until thickened. Serve hot on toast.

Makes 4 servings.

Zesty Stuffed Frankfurters

1 pound frankfurters
¼ pound grated sharp cheese
½ teaspoon prepared horseradish
½ teaspoon dry Mustard
1 teaspoon Worcestershire sauce
Dash Onion Powder
1 8-ounce can tomato sauce
½ teaspoon sugar
1 teaspoon Instant Minced Onion
1 teaspoon Chili Powder

Make a slit lengthwise in each frankfurter. Mix together cheese, horseradish, dry mustard. Worcestershire sauce and onion powder. Stuff frankfurters with cheese mixture; place in shallow baking dish. Combine remaining ingredients and pour over top. Bake in 350°F. oven 30 minutes. *Serves 4 to 5.*

Kidneys in Sherry Sauce

12 lamb kidneys
4 slices bacon
1 tablespoon Instant Minced Onion
3 tablespoons flour
Dash MSG
1 teaspoon Bon Appétit
⅛ teaspoon Black Pepper
2 teaspoons Beef Flavor Base
2 cups water
1 tablespoon Sherry Extract

Scald kidneys 3 minutes; rinse in cold water. Skin, quarter and remove white portion from kidneys. Cut bacon slices into four or five pieces; fry until golden brown. Add onion and kidneys to bacon and brown lightly, about 2 minutes. Stir in flour, MSG, Bon Appétit and pepper. Add beef flavor base and water, stirring to dissolve beef base. Cover and simmer 25 minutes or until kidneys are tender. Just before serving, stir in the sherry extract. Serve on fluffy rice or hot buttered toast. *Serves 4.*

POULTRY

Chicken

Arroz con Pollo 144
Baked Chicken Oriental 146
Broiled Chicken 145
Chili Broiled Chicken 145
Coriander Broiled Chicken 145
Herb Broiled Chicken 145
Smoky Chicken 145
Chicken Cacciatore 145
Chicken Cantonese 150
Chicken Curry in Papaya 147
Chicken Curry in Avocado 147
Chicken en Casserole 144
Chicken Italienne 146
Chicken Kiev 148
Chicken Paprika 150
Chicken Rosemary 148
Chicken Tarragon 146
Coq au Vin 149
Country Captain 141
Creamed Chicken Supreme 149
Fried Chicken Curry 152
Herb Chicken 147
Old-Fashioned Chicken and Dumplings 151
Herb Dumplings 151
Rolled Dumplings 151
Oven Fried Chicken 153
Sautéed Chicken Livers 152
Sautéed Chicken Livers Rosé 152
Stuffed Roast Capon 153
Truffled Chicken Breasts Elégante 154

Turkey

Curried Turkey Amandine 154
Roast Turkey Supreme 160
Savory Turkey Croquettes 155
Turkey Creole 160
Turkey Pot Pie 161
Turkey Pot Pie with Vegetables 141
Turkey Rolls Delicious 155

Duck and Game

Apricot Duckling 142
Canard au Grand Marnier 158
Cornish Hens Stuffed with Wild Rice 15
Cornish Hens with Fruited Rice Stuffing 143
Country Inn Pheasant 157
Duckling à l'Orange 157
Roast Goose Superb 159
Roast Pheasant 156

Stuffings

Basic Bread Stuffing 162
Chestnut Stuffing 162
Herb Stuffing 162
Oyster Stuffing 162
Holiday Stuffing 164
Mushroom-Rice Stuffing 162
Old South Corn Bread Stuffing 163
Quick 'n' Easy Stuffing 161
Sausage Stuffing 164
Savory Stuffing 163
Sesame Stuffing 165
Spiced Chestnut Stuffing 165
Wild Rice Stuffing 163

Country Captain

1 2½-to 3-pound chicken, cut up
¼ cup flour
1 teaspoon Bon Appétit
¼ teaspoon Black Pepper
¼ cup butter
2 teaspoons Madras Curry Powder
1 teaspoon Thyme Leaves
½ teaspoon Garlic Salt
2 tablespoons Onion Flakes
¼ teaspoon Black Pepper
1 28-ounce can whole Italian plum tomatoes
¼ cup dried currants
¼ cup slivered almonds

Wash and dry chicken. Mix flour, Bon Appétit and pepper. Dredge chicken pieces in flour mixture. Melt butter in large skillet. Brown chicken on all sides. Put chicken pieces in 4-quart casserole or Dutch oven with a lid. Mix next 5 ingredients with a small amount of the tomato liquid. Pour over chicken. Add tomatoes. Cover and bake in 350°F. oven 40 minutes. Remove cover. Sprinkle currants and almonds over chicken. Bake, uncovered, 15 minutes. Serve over rice. *Serves 4.*

Turkey Pot Pie with Vegetables

FILLING:

2 carrots, thinly sliced
1 stalk celery, sliced
1¾ cups water
2 teaspoons Chicken Flavor Base
1 10-ounce package frozen peas
2½ to 3 cups cooked turkey, cut in bite-size pieces
3 tablespoons butter
¼ cup flour
½ teaspoon Onion Salt
¼ teaspoon Basil Leaves
¼ teaspoon Sage
¼ teaspoon Black Pepper
Dash Nutmeg

Combine carrots, celery, water and chicken flavor base. Bring to a boil, reduce heat, cover and simmer 3 minutes. Add frozen peas, remove from heat and let stand until peas are separated. Drain, reserving liquid. Mix vegetables and turkey pieces in 1½-quart casserole. In saucepan, melt butter, stir in flour and seasonings. Gradually stir in reserved liquid from vegetables. Cook, stirring until thickened. Pour over turkey mixture in casserole.

CRUST:

1 cup flour
¾ teaspoon Season-All
⅛ teaspoon Sage
2 tablespoons butter
3 tablespoons vegetable shortening
1 to 1½ tablespoons cold water

Combine flour, Season-All and sage. With 2 knives or pastry blender, cut in butter and shortening until mixture resembles coarse cornmeal. Sprinkle with water, toss with fork just until moistened. Press into a ball. Roll out on floured wax paper to fit casserole. Place over filling. Trim edges, if necessary. Cut 6 small vents in crust with tip of knife. Bake in 350°F. oven 45 minutes. *Makes six 1-cup servings.*

Apricot Duckling

2 4-pound ducklings
2 tablespoons Poultry Seasoning
2 stalks celery, with leaves
1 onion, cut in half
¾ cup honey
½ cup Grand Marnier
¼ cup butter
½ teaspoon Chicken Flavor Base
½ teaspoon Season-All
1 teaspoon Herb Seasoning
1 Bay Leaf
⅛ teaspoon Nutmeg
⅛ teaspoon Cinnamon
⅛ teaspoon Mace
⅛ teaspoon rubbed Sage
⅛ teaspoon White Pepper
¼ teaspoon salt
1 12-ounce can apricot nectar
1 tablespoon grated lemon peel
1 tablespoon Arrowroot
1 17-ounce can apricot halves, drained

Wash and dry ducklings. Rub 1 tablespoon poultry seasoning inside each duckling and put 1 stalk celery and 1 onion half in each. Tie legs together securely. Prick skin with a fork every half inch all over both ducklings. Place on rack in roasting pan and cook in 325°F. oven 2½ hours. Increase heat to 400°F. and cook 30 minutes longer, brushing every 10 minutes with a mixture of ½ cup honey and ¼ cup Grand Marnier. While ducklings are cooking, melt butter and stir in next 12 ingredients and the remaining ¼ cup honey. Heat to boiling and simmer 5 minutes. Hold over very low heat until ducklings are cooked. Remove bay leaf. Mix arrowroot with equal amount of cold water. Stir into sauce and cook, stirring constantly, until mixture thickens. Add remaining ¼ cup Grand Marnier and apricot halves. Cut ducklings into quarters and serve with sauce.

Makes 8 servings. (3 cups sauce).

Cornish Hens with Fruited Rice Stuffing

STUFFING:

1 cup brown rice (4 cups after cooking)
1 can (17 ounces) apricot halves
1 can (13¼ ounces) pineapple tidbits
½ cup butter
1 teaspoon Ginger
½ teaspoon Allspice
3 tablespoons Parsley Flakes
¼ teaspoon Savory
1 teaspoon salt

Cook rice following package directions. Drain apricot halves and pineapple tidbits, reserving syrup for glaze. Cut apricot halves into quarters. Melt butter in large skillet. Stir in remaining ingredients. Add fruit and rice, toss lightly to mix.

HENS:

8 Cornish game hens 1 to 1½ pounds each
2 tablespoons salt
2 teaspoons Season-All
½ teaspoon Poultry Seasoning
1 teaspoon MSG
½ teaspoon Ginger

Rinse hens and wipe dry. Combine seasonings and rub each hen with about 1 teaspoon of spice mixture. Fill body cavity of hens with stuffing. Tie legs together. Place on rack in roasting pan and cook in 350°F. oven 1 hour and 15 minutes, brushing with glaze every 20 minutes.

GLAZE:

1½ cups syrup drained from apricots and pineapple
½ teaspoon Ginger
¼ teaspoon Allspice
¼ teaspoon salt
2 tablespoons butter
2 tablespoons lemon juice

Combine all ingredients in a saucepan and heat to boiling.

Makes 8 generous servings.

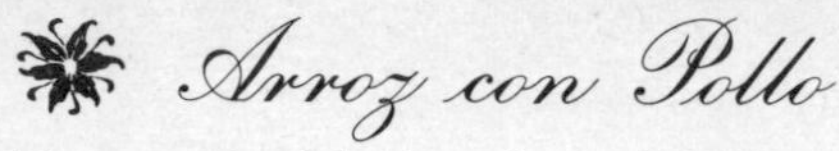

Arroz con Pollo

The renowned Saffron rice and chicken dish which is a meal in itself.

1 3-pound chicken
1 tablespoon Season-All
¼ teaspoon Black Pepper
¼ cup flour
½ cup olive oil
1 medium-size green pepper
½ cup Chopped Instant Onions
2 cups tomatoes (16-oz. can)
1 4-ounce can sliced mushrooms
2 cups rice, washed and drained
4 cups water
1 tablespoon chopped pimiento
⅛ teaspoon Instant Minced Garlic
1 Bay Leaf
5 teaspoons Chicken Flavor Base
⅛ teaspoon ground Red Pepper
¼ teaspoon Coarse Grind Black Pepper
⅛ teaspoon crushed Saffron
½ cup sherry or water
1 10-ounce can green peas
Parsley Flakes

Cut chicken in pieces; dredge with mixture of Season-All, pepper and flour. Brown in hot olive oil in skillet. Place browned chicken in a 4-quart casserole. Chop green pepper and sauté with onions in remaining hot oil until onions are lightly browned. Add tomatoes, mushrooms including liquid, rice, water, pimiento, seasonings and sherry. Mix thoroughly and pour over chicken. Cover and bake in 375°F. oven 40 minutes. Add drained peas and continue baking, covered, 15 to 20 minutes longer. Garnish with parsley flakes. Serve hot. *Serves 6.*

Chicken en Casserole

1 3-pound chicken, cut in pieces
⅓ cup flour
2 teaspoons Bon Appétit
¼ teaspoon Black Pepper
½ teaspoon salt
½ cup butter or margarine
1 tablespoon Celery Flakes
Dash MSG
2 tablespoons Instant Minced Onion
1 tablespoon Bell Pepper Flakes
¼ teaspoon Nutmeg
1 4-ounce can mushrooms with liquid
1 8-ounce can tomato sauce
1 cup water

Dredge chicken in mixture of flour, Bon Appétit, pepper and salt. Brown in butter. Transfer the chicken to a baking dish. To butter in skillet stir in 2 tablespoons of the flour mixture and the remaining ingredients; mix well. Simmer 5 minutes. Pour over chicken; cover and bake in 350°F. oven 45 minutes or until tender. *Serves 4.*

Chicken Cacciatore

A famous Italian dish with a rich, hearty taste.

1 3-pound frying chicken
¼ cup flour
½ cup olive oil
2 tablespoons Instant Minced Onion
2 tablespoons Bell Pepper Flakes
⅛ teaspoon Instant Minced Garlic
⅛ teaspoon Allspice
1 tablespoon Season-All
¼ teaspoon Black Pepper
1 teaspoon Italian Seasoning
¼ teaspoon Crushed Red Pepper
3½ cups tomatoes (28-oz. can)
½ cup white wine or water

Cut chicken in pieces. Dredge with flour; brown in oil until golden on all sides. Drain off oil. Add seasonings, tomatoes and wine or water; cover and simmer slowly 45 minutes or until chicken is tender. Makes a superb meal when served with hot toasted Italian bread and crisp tossed salad.
Serves 4.

S.C. Broiled Chicken

Here the herbs put new zest into an old stand-by.

2 2-pound broiling chickens, cut in half lengthwise
½ cup melted butter
1 teaspoon salt
1 tablespoon Season-All
¼ teaspoon MSG
½ teaspoon Onion Powder

Break wing, thigh and leg joints so chicken will remain flat while broiling. Put, skin side down, on broiler rack. Combine remaining ingredients and brush over chicken. Broil 5 to 7 inches from heat 15 minutes. Turn chicken and brush with seasoned butter; broil 15 minutes longer. Continue turning and basting chicken every 15 minutes until drumstick is tender and shows no pink when cut. Total cooking time is about 45 minutes. *Serves 4.*

VARIATIONS:

Herb Broiled Chicken—Substitute 2 teaspoons Italian Seasoning, 2 teaspoons salt, 1 tablespoon Bon Appétit and ½ teaspoon Paprika for above seasonings.

Chili Broiled Chicken—Substitute 2 teaspoons salt, 1 tablespoon Chili Powder and ¼ teaspoon MSG for above seasonings.

Smoky Chicken—Substitute 1½ teaspoons salt, 2 teaspoons Hickory Smoked Salt and ½ teaspoon Paprika for above seasonings.

Coriander Broiled Chicken—Crush 2 teaspoons Coriander Seed and add to seasonings in Broiled Chicken recipe.

Chicken Italienne

1 3-pound frying chicken
¼ cup butter or margarine
1 teaspoon Italian Seasoning
2 teaspoons Season-All
½ teaspoon salt
⅛ teaspoon Garlic Powder
¼ teaspoon Black Pepper
1 cup milk
1 cup canned tomatoes or tomato juice
1 tablespoon flour
2 tablespoons water

Cut chicken in pieces. Brown on all sides in butter. Combine seasonings, milk and tomatoes; pour over chicken. Cover and simmer 45 minutes or until chicken is tender. Remove chicken to serving dish. Blend flour and water together; add to liquid in skillet. Simmer over low heat, stirring, until sauce thickens. Pour over chicken. *Serves 4.*

Baked Chicken Oriental

1 3-pound chicken
¼ cup flour
2 teaspoons Season-All
¼ teaspoon Black Pepper
¼ cup melted butter
2 tablespoons pineapple juice
2 teaspoons soy sauce
1 teaspoon Chicken Flavor Base
2 teaspoons Instant Minced Onion
¼ teaspoon Ginger
¼ teaspoon MSG
Dash Cardamom

Cut chicken in pieces; dredge with mixture of flour, Season-All and pepper. Place in greased 2-quart shallow baking dish. Combine remaining ingredients; pour over chicken. Cover and bake in 375°F. oven 1 hour. Remove cover and bake 30 minutes longer, basting several times. *Serves 4.*

Chicken Tarragon

1 3-pound chicken
¼ cup flour
1 tablespoon Season-All
¼ teaspoon MSG
¼ teaspoon Black Pepper
¼ teaspoon Paprika
¼ cup butter or margarine
1 teaspoon Brandy Extract
2 teaspoons Instant Minced Onion
1 teaspoon Tarragon Leaves
½ cup dry white wine or water

Cut chicken in pieces; dredge with mixture of flour, Season-All, MSG, pepper and paprika. Brown in hot butter. Sprinkle browned chicken with brandy extract, onion and tarragon leaves; add wine or water. Cover and simmer 45 minutes or until tender. *Serves 4.*

Herb Chicken

1 3-pound chicken
¼ cup flour
1 tablespoon Season-All
¼ teaspoon Black Pepper
½ teaspoon Paprika
½ teaspoon Herb Seasoning
¼ cup butter or margarine
2 teaspoons Instant Minced Onion
1 teaspoon Parsley Flakes
½ teaspoon Thyme Leaves
½ cup dry white wine or water

Cut chicken in pieces; dredge with mixture of flour, Season-All, pepper, paprika and Herb Seasoning. Brown in hot butter. Sprinkle onion, parsley flakes and thyme leaves over chicken; add wine or water. Cover and simmer 45 minutes or until chicken is tender. *Serves 4.*

Chicken Curry in Papaya

Exotic, delectable and different.

⅓ cup butter or margarine
2 tablespoons Instant Minced Onion
1 stalk celery, chopped
1 tart apple, peeled and diced
5 tablespoons flour
1 tablespoon Curry Powder
¼ teaspoon Garlic Powder
½ teaspoon dry Mustard
2 teaspoons Season-All
1 Bay Leaf
3 whole Cloves
4 teaspoons Chicken Flavor Base
2½ cups hot water
4 cups cooked chicken, cut into bite-size pieces
¼ cup cream or milk
2 tablespoons chopped chutney
3 papayas

In a 3-quart saucepan melt butter; add onion, celery and apple and cook about 10 minutes, stirring occasionally. Mix together flour, curry powder, garlic powder, dry mustard and Season-All; stir into apple mixture along with bay leaf and cloves. Dissolve flavor base in water and stir into apple mixture; cook, stirring, until sauce thickens. Reduce heat and simmer 30 minutes. Add chicken, cream and chutney and cook 5 minutes longer. Cut 3 papayas in half. Carefully remove seed, being sure not to leave one. Fill papaya halves with curried chicken. Arrange in baking dish and bake in 350°F. oven 25 minutes. Serve with rice and chutney.

Serves 6.

VARIATION:

Chicken Curry in Avocado—Instead of papaya halves, use 4 large firm but ripe avocados. *Serves 8.*

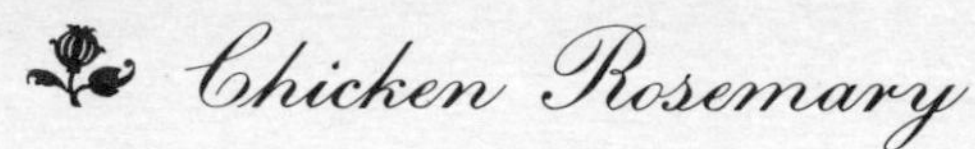

Chicken Rosemary

The delicate taste of Rosemary gives this dish its distinction.

1 3-pound chicken
1 tablespoon flour
5 tablespoons oil
1 teaspoon Garlic Salt
1 tablespoon Season-All
1 tablespoon Rosemary Leaves
¼ teaspoon Black Pepper
1 tablespoon vinegar

Cut chicken in pieces and dredge with flour. Heat 2 tablespoons of the oil in a skillet; brown chicken on all sides. Remove chicken from skillet. Brush 1 tablespoon of the oil over bottom of a shallow baking dish and place pieces of browned chicken close together in dish, skin side down. Combine garlic salt, Season-All, rosemary leaves, pepper and the remaining oil; brush over chicken. Drizzle with vinegar; cover and marinate in refrigerator several hours before baking. Bake, covered, in 350°F. oven 45 minutes. Remove cover and turn chicken skin side up, then continue baking 20 minutes or until tender. *Serves 4.*

Chicken Kiev

3 chicken breasts, boned
2 teaspoons Season-All
¼ teaspoon Black Pepper
⅛ teaspoon Onion Powder
½ teaspoon Savory
6 tablespoons chilled butter
¾ cup flour
2 eggs, beaten
½ cup milk
1½ cups toasted bread crumbs
Fat for frying

Cut boned chicken breasts in half lengthwise and pound to flatten. Sprinkle with mixture of Season-All, pepper, onion powder and savory. Place 1 tablespoon of the chilled butter in center of each piece of breast; fold edges over butter, envelope fashion. Carefully seal the edges with toothpicks. Flour the stuffed breasts; dip in egg beaten with milk and roll in bread crumbs. Again flour, dip in egg and roll in bread crumbs. Fry in 3 to 4 inches of fat, 375°F., 12 minutes or until golden brown. Remove toothpicks and serve hot. *Serves 6.*

Creamed Chicken Supreme

1 8-ounce can water chestnuts
¼ cup butter or margarine
¼ cup flour
1 teaspoon Chicken Flavor Base
1 teaspoon Season-All
⅛ teaspoon Nutmeg
Dash Mace
Dash Poultry Seasoning
Dash White Pepper
2½ cups milk
2 cups cubed cooked chicken
1 tablespoon chopped pimiento
2 tablespoons thinly sliced green pepper

Drain water chestnuts; slice thin. Melt butter in saucepan; blend in flour, flavor base and other seasonings. Cook over low heat until mixture is smooth and bubbly. Remove from heat and stir in milk. Bring to a boil and cook 1 minute, stirring constantly. Add chicken, water chestnuts, pimiento and green pepper. Reduce heat to low. Continue cooking 10 to 15 minutes, stirring occasionally. Serve hot in patty shells or over waffles, toast or rice.
Serves 4 to 6.

Coq au Vin

This French dish, chicken with wine, is famous the world over.

2 1½- to 2-pound chickens
¼ cup flour
1 tablespoon Season-All
½ teaspoon Paprika
¼ teaspoon Black Pepper
⅛ teaspoon Nutmeg
½ cup butter
¼ cup cognac or other brandy
12 small white onions
12 small whole mushrooms or 8-ounce can mushrooms
½ teaspoon Rosemary Leaves
¼ teaspoon Thyme Leaves
⅛ teaspoon Garlic Powder
1 teaspoon Parsley Flakes
1 cup dry red wine

Cut chicken in pieces; dredge with mixture of flour, Season-All, paprika, pepper and nutmeg. Brown slowly in hot butter. Without removing from heat, pour cognac over chicken; light immediately and flame. Add whole onions, mushrooms, remaining seasonings and wine. Cover and simmer 1 hour or until chicken is tender. May be cooked ahead of time and reheated. May also be frozen and reheated. *Serves 6 to 8.*

Chicken Cantonese

1 8-oz. can pineapple tidbits
1 cup sliced celery
1 cup thinly sliced raw carrots
¼ cup Chopped Instant Onions
¼ cup toasted slivered almonds
¼ cup butter or margarine
1 tablespoon Arrowroot
¼ teaspoon Ginger
⅛ teaspoon Nutmeg
¾ cup water
1 tablespoon soy sauce
1 teaspoon lemon juice
1 teaspoon Chicken Flavor Base
1½ cups chopped, cooked chicken
1 5-ounce can water chestnuts, drained and sliced thin
Chow mein noodles or rice

Drain pineapple; reserve juice. Cut celery into 1-inch diagonal slices. Sauté celery, carrots, onions and almonds in butter in large skillet until onions are golden brown. Combine arrowroot, ginger, nutmeg, pineapple juice, water, soy sauce, lemon juice and flavor base, mixing until well blended. Add to sautéed vegetables and cook until mixture thickens, stirring constantly. Stir in pineapple tidbits, chicken and water chestnuts. Cover and simmer 10 to 15 minutes. Serve over chow mein noodles or rice.

Serves 4.

Chicken Paprika

1 3-pound chicken
¼ cup flour
2 teaspoons Season-All
1½ tablespoons Paprika
¼ teaspoon Black Pepper
¼ teaspoon Ginger
⅛ teaspoon Garlic Powder
¼ teaspoon Basil Leaves
Dash Nutmeg
2 tablespoons butter or margarine
2 tablespoons shortening
¼ cup sherry or water
2 teaspoons Worcestershire sauce
1 teaspoon Chicken Flavor Base
1 4-ounce can mushrooms
1 cup dairy sour cream

Cut chicken in pieces; coat with mixture of flour, Season-All, paprika, pepper, ginger, garlic powder, basil leaves and nutmeg. Heat butter and shortening in heavy skillet. Brown chicken slowly. Combine sherry, Worcestershire sauce and flavor base; pour over browned chicken. Add mushrooms. Cover and simmer 45 minutes or until tender. Remove chicken to serving platter. Blend sour cream with drippings in skillet; stir 2 to 3 minutes until sour cream is heated but do not allow it to boil. Pour sauce over the chicken; sprinkle with additional paprika. Chicken Paprika is excellent with hot buttered noodles.

Serves 4.

Old-Fashioned Chicken and Dumplings

1 4-pound stewing chicken
1 teaspoon Celery Flakes
½ teaspoon Onion Flakes
⅛ teaspoon MSG
1 tablespoon salt
1 teaspoon Season-All
¼ teaspoon Black Pepper
1 medium-size carrot, sliced
Dumplings
Flour

Cut chicken in pieces; put in kettle with just enough water to cover. Add seasonings and sliced carrot; cover and bring to a boil. Reduce heat and simmer until tender, about 2 hours. Let cool in broth, then remove meat from bones in as large pieces as possible. Return meat to broth; bring to a boil. Add dumplings and cook (see recipe below). Remove dumplings and thicken broth with a flour-water paste, using equal amounts of each.

Serves 6.

ROLLED DUMPLINGS:

2 cups all-purpose flour
3 teaspoons baking powder
2 teaspoons Season-All
2 teaspoons Instant Minced Onion
¼ cup shortening
¾ cup milk

Sift flour, measure and sift again with baking powder and Season-All. Stir in onion. With pastry blender or two knives cut shortening into flour mixture until it resembles corn meal. Add milk and stir until dough forms ball and leaves side of bowl. Turn out on lightly floured board. Roll dough to ¼-inch thickness. Cut into ½ x 4-inch strips and drop onto chicken in boiling broth. Cover and cook 15 to 20 minutes.

HERB DUMPLINGS:

1½ cups all-purpose flour
2 teaspoons baking powder
2 teaspoons Bon Appétit
1 tablespoon shortening
1 teaspoon Chives
¼ teaspoon Coarse Grind Black Pepper
1 teaspoon Instant Minced Onion
¾ cup milk

Sift flour, measure and sift again with baking powder and Bon Appétit. With pastry blender or two knives cut shortening into flour until it resembles corn meal. Stir in chives, pepper and onion. Add milk and stir only enough to mix well. Drop by tablespoonfuls onto chicken in boiling broth. Cover and cook 10 minutes. Remove cover; cook 10 minutes longer.

Fried Chicken Curry

A golden, crisp-fried chicken, with a creamy sauce pungent with curry.

1 3-pound frying chicken, cut in pieces
2 teaspoons salt
⅓ cup flour
¼ teaspoon Black Pepper
¼ teaspoon Onion Powder
Dash MSG
2 tablespoons Curry Powder
3 cups shortening
2 cups milk

Wash chicken and wipe dry. Sprinkle with salt. Combine flour and seasonings, mixing well. Flour chicken in the seasoned flour and set aside that flour not used. Fry chicken, covered, in hot shortening in a heavy skillet or chicken fryer 15 minutes or until golden brown. Turn with tongs and fry until second side is deep golden brown. Never turn chicken more than once. Remove cover and continue cooking about 5 minutes to crisp chicken. Remove chicken to a heated platter. Pour off fat, leaving about 2 tablespoons. Stir in 2 to 3 tablespoons of the curry-seasoned flour. If you like a very hot sauce, add more curry powder. Cook 1 minute. Remove from heat; stir in milk and cook several minutes to thicken. Serve the crisp golden chicken with hot steamed rice and pass the curry sauce. *Serves 4.*

Sautéed Chicken Livers

1 pound chicken livers
3 tablespoons butter
½ teaspoon Onion Powder
2 teaspoons Chicken Flavor Base
⅛ teaspoon Nutmeg
¼ teaspoon Paprika
⅛ teaspoon Black Pepper
¼ teaspoon Garlic Salt
⅛ teaspoon Thyme Leaves
⅛ teaspoon Marjoram Leaves

Cut chicken livers in half; pierce with tines of fork to prevent popping. Melt butter in skillet; stir in seasonings. Sauté livers in seasoned butter 5 minutes or until browned on all sides. Serve on triangles of buttered toast, in patty shells or over rice. *Serves 2 to 3.*

VARIATION:

Sautéed Chicken Livers Rosé—Use 1 teaspoon Chicken Flavor Base, 1 teaspoon Season-All, ¼ teaspoon Ginger, ¼ teaspoon dry Mustard and dash Mace in place of the above seasonings. Add ¼ cup rosé to the sautéed livers; cover and simmer 5 minutes.

Stuffed Roast Capon

1 6-pound capon
1 teaspoon Poultry Seasoning
1 teaspoon salt
2 teaspoons Season-All
¼ teaspoon Black Pepper
¼ teaspoon Ginger
  or Nutmeg
  Savory Stuffing
2 tablespoons melted butter
  or margarine

Clean capon. Mix together poultry seasoning, salt, Season-All, pepper and ginger; rub inside the cavity and on outside of bird. Stuff neck cavity lightly with Savory Stuffing (see recipe page 163); skewer neck skin to back. Fold wing tips back and under, in toward the body. Stuff body cavity lightly with the remaining stuffing. Fasten opening with skewer; lace shut with cord. Tie legs together and fasten to tail. Brush bird lightly with melted butter. Place on a rack, breast side up, in an open roasting pan. Roast in 325°F. oven 2½ hours or 25 minutes per pound. If you use a meat thermometer, insert it so the bulb is in the center of the inside thigh muscle or thickest part of the breast, making sure the bulb does not touch bone. Thermometer should register 190°F. when bird is done. Baste several times with drippings.

Serves 4 to 5.

1 3-pound chicken,
  cut in pieces
½ cup melted butter
1 teaspoon salt
¼ teaspoon Black Pepper
1 teaspoon Season-All
⅛ teaspoon Onion Powder
½ teaspoon Dill Weed
¼ teaspoon Paprika
  Flour

Clean and dry chicken. Dip in mixture of melted butter, salt, pepper, Season-All, onion powder, dill weed and paprika. Dredge in flour and place, skin side down, in shallow baking pan. Spoon any remaining seasoned butter over chicken. Cook in 425°F. oven 30 minutes. Turn chicken and continue cooking 15 minutes or until tender and brown.

Serves 3 to 4.

Truffled Chicken Breasts Elégante

4 whole chicken breasts
4 truffles, thinly sliced
¼ teaspoon Ginger
¼ teaspoon MSG
Dash Nutmeg
¼ teaspoon Poultry Seasoning
¼ teaspoon Black Pepper
¼ teaspoon dry Mustard
¼ teaspoon Bon Appétit
1½ teaspoons salt
3 tablespoons flour
½ cup sweet butter
½ cup dry white wine
½ cup hot water

Wash and dry chicken breasts. With a sharp knife, loosen the skin from breast in 3 or 4 places on each side and insert thin slices of truffle. Wrap in aluminum foil or put in covered dish; refrigerate several hours. When ready to cook, combine spices and salt; rub into chicken, covering all sides carefully. Flour, using only enough to coat lightly. Brown slowly in hot butter in heavy skillet, turning to brown evenly. Transfer the browned chicken breasts to a baking dish. Drizzle ¼ cup of the wine over chicken. Stir 1 tablespoon flour into drippings in skillet; brown lightly, then add hot water. Mix well and pour over chicken. Cover. Bake in 325°F. oven 1 hour or until tender, basting with the remaining wine. Remove cover during the last 15 minutes to crisp chicken. Serve with wild rice, white rice or buttered noodles. Excellent with broiled bananas. *Serves 4.*

NOTE: Even without the truffles and wine this is a superb dish, real epicurean fare.

Curried Turkey Amandine

½ cup slivered almonds
¼ cup butter or margarine
2 tablespoons flour
½ teaspoon Season-All
1 teaspoon Curry Powder
¼ teaspoon Black Pepper
1 tablespoon Instant Minced Onion
¾ cup milk
¾ cup light cream
¼ cup dry white wine
1 8-ounce can sliced mushrooms
6 thin slices cooked turkey

Slowly brown almonds in butter. Remove almonds with slotted spoon and drain on absorbent paper. To butter add flour, Season-All, curry powder, pepper and onion; stir until well blended and smooth. Gradually stir in milk and cream. Cook over low heat, stirring constantly, until mixture thickens. Add wine, mushrooms which have been drained and turkey. Simmer about 10 minutes. Serve over hot buttered rice and top each serving with almonds. *Serves 6.*

Savory Turkey Croquettes

¼ cup butter or margarine
¼ cup flour
1 teaspoon Chicken Flavor Base
½ teaspoon Celery Salt
¼ teaspoon Black Pepper
¼ teaspoon rubbed Sage
1 cup milk
2 teaspoons Instant Minced Onion
2 cups ground cooked turkey
2 teaspoons Parsley Flakes
½ cup fine dry bread crumbs
1 egg, lightly beaten
2 tablespoons water
Cooking oil or shortening

Melt butter in saucepan. Blend in flour and add the next four ingredients; cook over low heat until mixture is smooth and bubbly. Remove from heat; stir in milk and onion. Bring just to a boil; reduce heat and cook 1 minute, stirring constantly. Add turkey and parsley flakes. Spread mixture out on plate. Chill. Divide chilled mixture into 8 portions; shape into cones or cylinders. Roll in bread crumbs; dip into mixture of egg and water; roll again in bread crumbs. Fry in deep fat, 375°F., 2 minutes or until golden brown. Drain on absorbent paper. Serve hot. Cream or mustard sauce goes well with croquettes. And, you will also want to serve a relish such as: Corn Relish, Dixie Relish, Pickle Relish or Chow-Chow. *Makes 8 croquettes.*

¼ cup butter
¼ cup flour
⅛ teaspoon Onion Salt
⅛ teaspoon Mace
⅛ teaspoon ground Red Pepper
¼ teaspoon Poultry Seasoning
1½ teaspoons Chicken Flavor Base
1½ cups hot water
2 cups cubed cooked turkey
1 4-ounce can mushrooms, drained and chopped
5 cups soft bread crumbs
2 eggs, beaten
8 slices bacon

Melt butter; stir in flour, onion salt, mace, red pepper and poultry seasoning; cook until bubbly. Dissolve flavor base in hot water; stir into flour mixture. Cook over low heat, stirring constantly, until thickened. Stir in turkey and mushrooms. Remove from heat; cool to room temperature, then chill. Shape into eight 3 x 1½-inch rolls. Roll in bread crumbs, dip in egg and, again, roll in bread crumbs. Wrap each roll with a slice of bacon; fasten with a toothpick. Bake in 375°F. oven 30 minutes or until brown. Serve piping hot. *Makes 8 rolls.*

Cornish Hens Stuffed with Wild Rice

4 1-pound Cornish hens
¾ cup wild rice
2¼ cups water
2 teaspoons Chicken Flavor Base
½ cup melted butter
½ teaspoon Basil Leaves
¼ teaspoon Cinnamon
2 teaspoons Parsley Flakes
3½ teaspoons Bon Appétit
1 tablespoon Instant Minced Onion
¼ teaspoon Coarse Grind Black Pepper
½ teaspoon salt

Wash and pat dry the Cornish hens; set aside. Wash rice; add water and flavor base; cover and cook until tender and all water is absorbed, about 50 minutes. Add ¼ cup of the butter, basil leaves, cinnamon, parsley flakes, 2 teaspoons of the Bon Appétit, onion, pepper and salt; mix well. Fill cavities of Cornish hens with stuffing. Cover exposed stuffing with aluminum foil during the first 30 minutes of cooking time to prevent drying. Brush hens with a mixture of the remaining ¼ cup butter and 1½ teaspoons Bon Appétit. Roast in 450°F. oven 20 minutes; reduce temperature to 350°F. and roast 45 minutes longer or until drumstick twists easily and birds are nicely browned. Baste several times with seasoned butter. Serve garnished with lettuce and pineapple slices topped with cream cheese-filled prunes. *Serves 4.*

Roast Pheasant

1 2- to 3-pound pheasant
2½ teaspoons Season-All
¼ teaspoon Black Pepper
⅛ teaspoon Mace
Dash Cloves
2 slices onion
1 Bay Leaf
1 slice lemon
2 tablespoons chopped celery leaves
4 slices bacon
¼ cup melted butter

Clean pheasant. Combine Season-All, pepper, mace and cloves; rub inside cavity and over outside of bird. Place onion, bay leaf, lemon and celery leaves inside cavity. Close opening with skewers; lace shut. Fold wings back and under body and tie legs together. Place pheasant, breast side up, on rack in an open roasting pan; cover breast with bacon slices. Roast in 350°F. oven until tender, about 30 minutes per pound, basting frequently with melted butter and pan drippings. *Serves 2 to 3.*

Duckling à l'Orange

1 3- to 4-pound duckling
1 teaspoon salt
¼ teaspoon Black Pepper
2 tablespoons orange juice
¾ cup brown sugar, packed
4 teaspoons Orange Peel
½ teaspoon dry Mustard
¼ teaspoon Allspice
⅛ teaspoon Ginger
2 tablespoons flour
2 cups orange juice

Clean duckling. Rub inside cavity and outside of duckling with mixture of salt and pepper. Remove wing tips to first joint. Fasten neck skin and wings to back of duckling with skewers. Close the cavity opening with skewers and tie legs together. Place on rack in roasting pan, breast side down. Roast in 450°F. oven 30 minutes. Reduce temperature to 350°F. and turn duckling so breast side is up. Continue roasting, allowing 30 minutes per pound. The last 30 minutes of cooking time begin basting with mixture of the 2 tablespoons orange juice, brown sugar, 3 teaspoons of the orange peel, dry mustard, allspice and ginger. Continue basting with drippings from pan until duckling is tender and skin is crisp and brown. Remove to platter and keep hot. Pour off grease, leaving only brown drippings. Stir flour and the remaining 1 teaspoon orange peel into pan drippings. Add the 2 cups orange juice and cook over low heat until thickened, stirring constantly. Strain into sauce dish and serve with hot duckling.

Serves 2 to 3.

Country Inn Pheasant

1 2- to 3-pound pheasant, quartered
2 tablespoons flour
1½ teaspoons Season-All
1 teaspoon Paprika
4 tablespoons butter
2 tablespoons shortening
2 teaspoons Chicken Flavor Base
½ cup water
¼ cup sauterne or Chablis
1 tablespoon lemon juice
2 tablespoons Onion Flakes or Chopped Instant Onions
¼ teaspoon Nutmeg
1 cup sliced fresh mushrooms or 6-ounce can mushrooms
½ cup heavy cream

Dredge pheasant with mixture of flour, Season-All and paprika. Heat 1 tablespoon of the butter with shortening in heavy skillet. Add pheasant and brown slowly to a rich golden color on all sides. Combine flavor base, water, sauterne, lemon juice, onion flakes and nutmeg; pour over pheasant. Cover and simmer 45 minutes or until tender. Remove pheasant to heated platter. To the skillet add the remaining 3 tablespoons butter; when it is melted, add mushrooms and cook 5 minutes or until tender. Remove skillet from heat, then stir in cream. Pour sauce over pheasant. Serve hot with rice.

Serves 3 to 4.

Canard au Grand Marnier

1 4- to 5-pound duck
1½ teaspoons Bon Appétit
1 teaspoon Orange Peel
⅛ teaspoon rubbed Sage
¼ teaspoon ground Thyme
¼ teaspoon Onion Powder
¼ teaspoon Black Pepper
3 tablespoons Grand Marnier

Thoroughly clean and dry duck. Remove giblets, neck and wing tips to first joint; reserve for sauce. Combine all seasonings, except Grand Marnier, and rub inside cavity and outside of duck. Tie legs together and fasten wings to body of bird. Place on rack in pan, breast side up, and roast in 450°F. oven 30 minutes. Reduce temperature to 350°F. and turn duck on its side. Roast 30 minutes; turn duck on other side and roast 30 minutes. Turn duck breast side up. During the last 30 minutes of cooking time, baste with Grand Marnier. Total cooking time is 2 hours or about 30 minutes per pound. Garnish with orange sections. *Serves 4.*

SAUCE:

Wing tips, neck and giblets
4 tablespoons butter
2 tablespoons Chopped Instant Onions
1 tablespoon Vegetable Flakes
3 teaspoons Chicken Flavor Base
1 teaspoon Parsley Flakes
1 Bay Leaf
3 cups water
3 tablespoons sugar
¼ cup vinegar
1 teaspoon Orange Peel
½ teaspoon Bon Appétit
2 tablespoons cornstarch
¾ cup port wine
3 tablespoons Grand Marnier

While duck is roasting, brown wing tips, neck and giblets in 2 tablespoons of the butter. Add onions and vegetable flakes; cook until lightly browned. Add flavor base, parsley flakes, bay leaf and water; simmer 1 hour. Strain and reduce to 2 cups of stock by boiling over high heat. Combine sugar and vinegar and cook until sugar caramelizes to dark brown. Add stock, orange peel and Bon Appétit. Combine cornstarch and ¼ cup of the wine; stir into sauce and cook, stirring, until slightly thickened. Set aside. Pour off fat from roasting pan, leaving the browned particles and rich juices from duck. Add the ½ cup wine to roasting pan and cook until about 3 tablespoons liquid remains, scraping bottom of pan to remove browned particles. Add to sauce. Stir in Grand Marnier and the remaining 2 tablespoons butter. Serve hot over slices of duck.

Roast Goose Superb

1 10-pound goose
1 teaspoon Black Pepper
2 teaspoons Bon Appétit
2 teaspoons Season-All
¼ teaspoon MSG
½ teaspoon Onion Powder
¼ teaspoon dry Mustard
⅛ teaspoon Nutmeg
1 tablespoon salt
Water or dry white wine for basting
¼ teaspoon Marjoram Leaves
1 tablespoon Celery Flakes
1 teaspoon Parsley Flakes
1 teaspoon Bon Appétit
⅓ cup dry white wine
1 Bay Leaf
2 cups water
Flour

Rinse goose inside and outside and pat dry. Combine pepper, the 2 teaspoons Bon Appétit, Season-All, MSG, onion powder, dry mustard, nutmeg and salt; rub inside cavity and over outside of goose. Turn the skin of the neck backward and fasten with skewer. (If desired, stuff cavity with 16 dried prunes and 4 tart apples which have been peeled, cored and quartered. Sew up the vent.) Tie the legs together loosely. Prick well all over with a 2-tined fork. Place on a rack in a roasting pan. Roast in 400°F. oven 20 minutes; reduce heat to 325°F. and continue to roast, allowing 30 minutes per pound. Baste several times with small amount of water or wine. If goose browns too rapidly, cover breast and drumsticks with cheesecloth, moistened with goose fat. Remove cheesecloth during the last hour of roasting to crisp skin. Pour off most of the fat as it accumulates in the pan. (Save every drop of the goose fat. It is a real treasure in cooking!) While goose is roasting, place the giblets and neck in a saucepan; add marjoram leaves, celery flakes, parsley flakes, Bon Appétit, wine, bay leaf and water. Bring to boil and simmer 2½ to 3 hours. Strain the broth; reserve for gravy. Chop giblets. When goose is done, remove to heated platter. Pour off fat, leaving the browned bits in roasting pan; stir in 1 to 2 tablespoons flour, cooking until bubbly and lightly browned. Gradually add the broth, stirring and scraping the bottom of pan to remove all the brown bits. Add the chopped giblets and simmer about 5 minutes. Serve gravy in sauceboat. Serve goose with stewed apples and prunes or the fruit used for stuffing. Well worth the time it takes to prepare. *Serves 8.*

L.C. Roast Turkey Supreme

1 12-pound turkey
2 tablespoons salt
1 teaspoon Season-All
¼ teaspoon MSG
½ teaspoon Poultry Seasoning
⅛ teaspoon Nutmeg
½ teaspoon dry Mustard
Butter or oil

Clean and rinse cavity and outside of turkey; wipe dry. Combine seasonings and rub inside and outside of turkey. (If desired, lightly fill neck and body cavities with stuffing. You will find a variety of stuffing recipes in this chapter.) Skewer neck skin to back. Fold wing tips back and under, in toward the body, or skewer to the body. Fasten body cavity with skewers and lace shut. Tie drumsticks to tail or push under bridge of skin. Place turkey on rack in shallow open pan. Rub butter or oil over entire surface of bird. If a meat thermometer is used, insert so the bulb is in the center of the inside thigh muscle or the thickest part of the breast meat. Cover top and sides with butter-moistened cheesecloth or aluminum foil. (If cheesecloth dries during cooking, moisten it with pan drippings.) Roast in 325°F. oven 5 hours or until meat thermometer registers 190°F. The bird is also sufficiently cooked when the drumsticks move easily from side to side.

Serves 8.

NOTE: For variety, other seasonings may be used instead of the ones listed above. Some suggested seasonings are: Bon Appétit, ground Thyme, Curry Powder, rubbed Sage, Savory, Onion Powder, White Pepper, Paprika and Ginger.

Turkey Creole

¼ cup shortening
¼ cup flour
½ cup chopped celery
½ cup chopped green pepper
⅛ teaspoon Instant Minced Garlic
1 teaspoon Instant Minced Onion
1 teaspoon Season-All
1 teaspoon salt
¼ teaspoon Coarse Grind Black Pepper
½ teaspoon ground Marjoram
⅛ teaspoon ground Red Pepper
2 cups tomatoes (16-oz. can)
1 cup tomato juice
2 cups cubed cooked turkey

Heat shortening in large skillet. Add flour, stirring constantly until smooth and lightly browned. Add celery and green pepper; sauté 5 minutes, stirring constantly. Add remaining ingredients except turkey; simmer 15 minutes, stirring frequently. Add turkey and simmer 20 minutes longer. Serve hot over rice.

Serves 6.

Turkey Pot Pie

A delightful dish, with an unusual crust.

- *2 cups cooked turkey, cut into medium-size pieces*
- *2 tablespoons Chopped Instant Onions*
- *4 tablespoons butter*
- *6 tablespoons flour*
- *½ teaspoon Poultry Seasoning*
- *1 teaspoon Bon Appétit*
- *¼ teaspoon Coarse Grind Black Pepper*
- *2 teaspoons Chicken Flavor Base*
- *2 cups hot water*
- *Caraway Biscuit Crust*

Put turkey and onions in a buttered 8-inch square baking dish. Melt butter; stir in flour, poultry seasoning, Bon Appétit and pepper. Cook until bubbly and remove from heat. Dissolve flavor base in hot water; stir into flour mixture and cook over low heat until thickened. Pour over turkey. Place Caraway Biscuit Crust over turkey mixture, pressing down firmly around the edges. Bake in 425°F. oven 20 to 25 minutes. *Serves 4 to 6.*

CARAWAY BISCUIT CRUST:

- *1 cup all-purpose flour*
- *1½ teaspoons baking powder*
- *½ teaspoon salt*
- *½ teaspoon dry Mustard*
- *¼ cup shortening*
- *1 teaspoon Caraway Seed*
- *⅓ cup milk*

Sift flour, measure and sift again with baking powder, salt and dry mustard. Cut in shortening with pastry blender or two knives until mixture resembles coarse corn meal. Add caraway seed and milk. Mix until dough can be shaped into a ball. Roll out on floured board to a 9-inch square. Prick pastry with tines of fork to allow steam to escape. Carefully place over turkey mixture.

Quick 'n' Easy Stuffing

- *¾ cup Chopped Instant Onions*
- *2 cups melted butter*
- *5 quarts soft bread cubes (¼-inch square)*
- *1 teaspoon salt*
- *½ teaspoon Black Pepper*
- *½ teaspoon ground Thyme*
- *1 teaspoon Poultry Seasoning*
- *2 tablespoons Parsley Flakes*

Sauté onions in butter until lightly brown. Add remaining ingredients; mix well, tossing gently. *Makes about 3 quarts, enough stuffing for a 12- to 14-pound bird.*

Basic Bread Stuffing

- ½ cup Chopped Instant Onions
- 1½ cups chopped celery
- 1 cup melted butter or margarine
- 12 cups bread cubes, white and whole wheat bread
- 2 tablespoons Parsley Flakes
- 1½ teaspoons Poultry Seasoning
- 1 tablespoon Bon Appétit
- ½ teaspoon Black Pepper
- 1 teaspoon Chicken Flavor Base
- ½ cup hot water

Sauté onions and celery in butter in a large skillet or Dutch oven. Toss together bread cubes, parsley flakes, poultry seasoning, Bon Appétit and pepper; add to sautéed mixture and toss while lightly browning bread cubes. Dissolve flavor base in water; sprinkle over stuffing, stirring lightly. Stuff loosely into neck and breast cavities of bird. *Makes about 8 cups.*

VARIATIONS:

Herb Stuffing—To the above recipe add one of the following: 2 teaspoons rubbed Sage, 2 teaspoons ground Thyme or 2 teaspoons ground Marjoram.

Chestnut Stuffing—Wash ½ pound chestnuts; cut slits on both sides of shells. Bake in 500°F. oven 15 minutes. Shell and skin nuts, then put in salted water; cover and boil 20 minutes. Drain and chop fine. (Or, if preferred, use canned chestnuts which are ready for use.) Toss with bread cubes in above recipe.

Oyster Stuffing—Cook ½ to 1 pint small or medium-size oysters in the oyster liquor until the edges curl. Drain and chop, or leave whole as preferred. Toss with bread cubes in above recipe.

Mushroom-Rice Stuffing

So good! Serve as a dish by itself or as a stuffing for meat or poultry.

- ½ cup butter or margarine
- 3 cups cooked rice
- 3 tablespoons Instant Minced Onion
- 2 cups diced celery
- 2 teaspoons Parsley Flakes
- ½ teaspoon ground Marjoram
- 1 4-ounce can mushrooms, drained
- ½ teaspoon salt
- ⅛ teaspoon Black Pepper
- ⅛ teaspoon ground Thyme
- 1 teaspoon Chicken Flavor Base
- ⅔ cup chopped pecans

Melt butter in large skillet; add remaining ingredients except pecans. Sauté, stirring until lightly browned. Remove from heat and add pecans; toss gently. Use to stuff a 5- to 6-pound bird. When serving this as a side dish for meat or fowl, bake in a covered casserole in 325°F. oven 30 minutes. *Makes 6 cups.*

Old South Corn Bread Stuffing

4 cups crumbled corn bread
3 cups crumbled biscuits
1½ cups cooked rice
¼ cup Chopped Instant Onions
½ cup water
1½ cups chopped celery
1 teaspoon Black Pepper
1 teaspoon Parsley Flakes
¼ teaspoon Poultry Seasoning
1 teaspoon Season-All
5 teaspoons Chicken Flavor Base
1½ cups hot water
1 egg
½ cup milk
½ cup butter, melted

Combine corn bread, biscuits and rice. Soak onions in the ½ cup water about 10 minutes. Add to bread mixture along with celery, pepper, parsley flakes, poultry seasoning and Season-All. Dissolve flavor base in hot water. Beat egg; stir in milk. Add liquids and butter to bread mixture. Mix well. Add additional liquid if stuffing seems too dry. Spoon into a buttered shallow 3-quart baking dish and bake in 375°F. oven 40 minutes or until golden brown. *Serves about 10.*

Wild Rice Stuffing

1 cup wild rice
1½ teaspoons Chicken Flavor Base
1 cup chopped celery
¼ cup Chopped Instant Onions
½ cup melted butter
½ teaspoon Marjoram Leaves
¼ teaspoon Oregano Leaves
¼ teaspoon Black Pepper
1 teaspoon Season-All
¼ teaspoon Thyme Leaves
½ teaspoon salt
1 4-ounce can mushroom crowns
2 tablespoons mushroom liquid

Cook wild rice as directed on package, adding flavor base to the water. Sauté celery and onions in butter. Then combine all ingredients and mix well.
Makes about 6 cups, enough to stuff a 10-pound bird.

Savory Stuffing

1 tablespoon Chopped Instant Onions
¼ cup diced celery
½ cup butter or margarine
4 cups dry bread cubes
½ teaspoon salt
1½ teaspoons Poultry Seasoning
¼ teaspoon rubbed Sage
¼ teaspoon Black Pepper

Sauté onions and celery in butter until lightly browned. Add remaining ingredients; mix well, tossing gently. This stuffing is excellent for turkey, Cornish hens, whole fish, pork chops or a crown roast of lamb.
Makes about 4 cups.

Sausage Stuffing

An excellent stuffing to bring out the succulence of any turkey.

6 cups coarse bread crumbs
1 teaspoon Garlic Salt
1 teaspoon Season-All
1 pound bulk pork sausage
2 cups tomatoes (16-oz. can)
2 cups cooked rice
½ cup seedless raisins
¼ cup Instant Minced Onion
2 teaspoons Poultry Seasoning
½ teaspoon Black Pepper
2 eggs, lightly beaten

Combine bread crumbs, garlic salt and Season-All. Toast in 300°F. oven, stirring occasionally, until lightly browned and crisp. Fry sausage until brown, breaking it into small pieces with a fork as it cooks. Pour off excess fat. Drain tomatoes; chop pulp very fine. (Do not use juice; save for use in other recipes.) Thoroughly mix crumbs, sausage, tomatoes, rice, raisins, onion, poultry seasoning, pepper and eggs. *Makes about 8 cups, enough to stuff a 12- to 15-pound bird.*

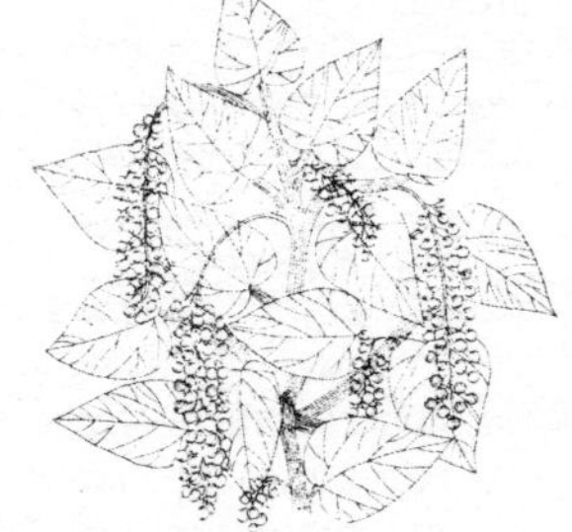

Holiday Stuffing

3½ cups chopped celery
5 tablespoons Instant Minced Onion
1½ cups melted butter
1 tablespoon Poultry Seasoning
2 teaspoons Season-All
½ teaspoon salt
½ teaspoon Black Pepper
8 cups white bread cubes
4 cups whole wheat bread cubes
4 cups corn bread cubes
2 eggs, lightly beaten
⅔ cup slivered toasted almonds
2 teaspoons Chicken Flavor Base
1½ cups hot water

Sauté celery and onion in butter until tender but not brown. Sprinkle poultry seasoning, Season-All, salt and pepper over bread cubes. Add celery and onion mixture, eggs and almonds. Toss. Dissolve flavor base in water; pour over bread mixture. Toss lightly until well blended. Stuff bird. Put remaining stuffing in casserole; cover and bake in 300°F. oven 40 minutes, then remove cover and allow to brown.

Makes about 10 cups, enough to stuff a 10- to 12-pound bird plus an extra amount for a casserole.

Sesame Stuffing

2 teaspoons Beef Flavor Base
½ cup hot water
2 tablespoons Celery Flakes
1 tablespoon Chopped Instant Onions
½ cup butter or margarine
⅓ cup Sesame Seed
3 cups toasted bread cubes
2 teaspoons Poultry Seasoning
¼ teaspoon Black Pepper
¼ teaspoon Ginger
1 egg, lightly beaten

Dissolve beef flavor base in hot water. Cook celery flakes and onions in butter 5 minutes. Toast sesame seed in 350°F. oven 15 minutes or until golden brown. Combine all ingredients, tossing lightly until thoroughly mixed. You will find this stuffing excellent for chicken, turkey, Cornish hens, pork chops or crown roast of pork or lamb. *Makes about 3 cups.*

Spiced Chestnut Stuffing

½ cup chopped celery
2 tablespoons Instant Minced Onion
1 cup melted butter
2 cups boiled or canned chestnuts, sliced (2-pound can)
8 cups dry bread cubes
2 teaspoons salt
1 teaspoon Black Pepper
2 tablespoons Parsley Flakes
½ teaspoon rubbed Sage
½ teaspoon Rosemary Leaves
⅛ teaspoon Nutmeg
1 teaspoon Chicken Flavor Base
¾ cup hot water

Sauté celery and onion in butter until tender. Add chestnuts and cook 5 minutes. Mix together bread cubes, salt, pepper, parsley flakes, sage, rosemary leaves and nutmeg. Dissolve flavor base in water and add to bread mixture along with chestnut mixture. Toss well.

Makes 8 cups, enough to stuff a 12- to 15-pound bird.

SEA FOOD

Fish Dishes and Frogs' Legs

Baked Fish with Herb Stuffing 174

Broiled Fish Amandine 174

Broiled Salmon Tarragon 171

Broiled Salmon with Dill 171

Fillet de Sole Véronique 171

Fillet Neapolitan 172

Fish Poached in Court Bouillon 181

Pan-Fried Fish 177

Sautéed Frogs' Legs 173

Frogs' Legs aux Fines Herbes 173

Frogs' Legs Provençale 173

Sole Epicurean 173

Sole Meunière 172

Shellfish

Crab Cakes 177

Crab Imperial 170

Shellfish (Cont.)

Crab Newburg 169

Deviled Crab 176

Deviled Lobster Tails 170

Lobster Cantonese 178

Scallops and Mushrooms en Brochette 179

Scallops and Mushrooms in Sherry Sauce 169

Sea Food Crêpes 175

Shrimp and Lobster with Sauce Caviar 180

Shrimp Creole 176

Shrimp Sautéed in Herb Butter 177

Superb Scalloped Oysters 178

Quick Supper Dishes

Creamed Clams 172

Savory Salmon Loaf 180

Tuna Croquettes 179

Crab Newburg

12 ounces crabmeat, fresh or frozen
½ cup butter
½ teaspoon Instant Minced Onion
¼ cup Sherry
Dash ground Red Pepper
¼ teaspoon Bon Appétit
¼ teaspoon White Pepper
3 egg yolks
1 cup light cream

Heat crabmeat in saucepan over very low heat while preparing sauce. Melt butter in top of double boiler over boiling water. Add onion, sherry, red pepper, Bon Appétit and white pepper. Beat egg yolks. Add cream and mix well. Stir into butter mixture and cook, stirring constantly until slightly thickened. Stir in warm crabmeat. Serve immediately on toast or rice.

Makes 3 cups.

Scallops and Mushrooms in Sherry Sauce

1½ pounds sea scallops
¼ cup dry sherry
¼ cup water
⅛ teaspoon Black Pepper
2 Bay Leaves
¼ teaspoon Thyme Leaves
½ pound fresh mushrooms or 1 4-ounce can mushroom caps
2 tablespoons butter
1 teaspoon lemon juice
1 tablespoon cornstarch
2 teaspoons Instant Minced Onion
1 teaspoon Parsley Flakes

Rinse and drain scallops. Combine sherry, water, pepper, bay leaves and thyme in skillet. Bring to a boil, add scallops, return to boil, reduce heat and simmer 3 to 4 minutes. Drain, reserving liquid. Discard bay leaves. Wash, trim and halve fresh mushrooms, or drain canned mushrooms. Melt butter in skillet. Add mushrooms and cook over medium heat, stirring frequently about 3 minutes. Stir lemon juice and a little of the reserved scallop cooking liquid into cornstarch. Add remaining cooking liquid. Return scallops to skillet along with cornstarch mixture, onion and parsley flakes. Cook, stirring, until sauce thickens. Serve over rice or noodles.

Makes 4 servings, ¾ cup each.

Deviled Lobster Tails

4 *frozen rock lobster tails*
1 *tablespoon Instant Minced Onion*
2 *teaspoons Season-All*
¼ *teaspoon White Pepper*
½ *teaspoon Lemon Peel*
½ *teaspoon dry Mustard*
Dash ground Red Pepper
½ *cup dry bread crumbs*
¾ *cup mayonnaise*
4 *tablespoons butter, melted*
Paprika

Select lobster tails weighing about 6 ounces each. Boil 9 minutes in salted water (1 teaspoon salt to each quart of water). Remove from water and drain. With scissors, cut away thin undershell and remove meat, being careful not to break shells. Cut lobster meat into bite-size pieces. Combine lobster with onion, Season-All, pepper, lemon peel, dry mustard, red pepper, bread crumbs, mayonnaise and 2 tablespoons of the melted butter. Mix well. Refill shells with the lobster mixture. Brush with remaining butter and sprinkle with paprika. Broil 5 to 6 inches from heat 10 minutes or until lightly browned. *Serves 4.*

Crab Imperial

1 *cup milk*
1 *tablespoon butter*
2 *tablespoons flour*
1 *egg, well beaten*
1 *teaspoon dry Mustard*
¼ *teaspoon ground Red Pepper*
1 *teaspoon Season-All*
½ *teaspoon Celery Salt*
1 *teaspoon salt*
¼ *teaspoon Black Pepper*
1 *tablespoon lemon juice*
½ *teaspoon Worcestershire sauce*
4 *tablespoons mayonnaise*
2 *pounds crab meat*
2 *tablespoons milk*
Paprika

Heat the 1 cup milk to boiling point. Melt butter; stir in flour. Pour heated milk into flour and butter mixture, beating until smooth and creamy. Cool. Add egg, seasonings, lemon juice, Worcestershire sauce and 2 tablespoons of the mayonnaise; blend well. Add crab meat and mix well, but gently. Fill shells, ramekins or heatproof small dishes. Now mix the remaining 2 tablespoons mayonnaise with the 2 tablespoons milk and brush over tops. Sprinkle with paprika. Bake in 400°F. oven 8 minutes or until piping hot and lightly browned. You will find a slice of pimiento and a slice of green pepper make an attractive garnish. *Makes 8 servings.*

Broiled Salmon Tarragon

½ cup butter, melted
2 teaspoons lemon juice
2 teaspoons Season-All
½ teaspoon ground Marjoram
1 teaspoon Tarragon Leaves
¼ teaspoon Garlic Powder
½ teaspoon Lemon Peel
Dash ground Red Pepper
2 pounds salmon steaks

Combine melted butter and lemon juice with seasonings. Arrange salmon steaks on greased broiler rack and brush with one half of the seasoned butter. Broil 2 inches from heat 5 to 10 minutes. Carefully turn and brush with remaining butter mixture. Broil steaks 7 minutes longer or until they can be flaked easily with a fork. Serve hot, garnished with stuffed olives, lemon wedges and sprigs of parsley. *Serves 4 to 6.*

VARIATION:

Broiled Salmon with Dill—Combine ½ cup melted butter, 2 teaspoons lemon juice, 2 teaspoons Bon Appétit, 1 teaspoon Dill Weed, ¼ teaspoon Onion Powder, ½ teaspoon Lemon Peel, ⅛ teaspoon White Pepper and dash each Oregano and Paprika. Brush mixture over salmon and cook following directions in above recipe.

Fillet de Sole Véronique

6 fillets of sole
1 teaspoon salt
¼ teaspoon White Pepper
¼ teaspoon Onion Powder
1 teaspoon Chicken Flavor Base
1 cup hot water
½ cup dry white wine
2 Bay Leaves
4 whole Allspice
1 cup seedless white grapes
2 tablespoons butter
½ cup cream
1 tablespoon flour

Press fillets out flat; sprinkle with a mixture of the salt, pepper and onion powder, then fold in half. Place the folded fillets in a buttered, deep skillet. Dissolve flavor base in hot water, then pour over fish along with wine. Drop in bay leaves and allspice. Cover. Cook gently 10 minutes or until the fish is tender and flakes easily with a fork. Carefully remove the fillets to a heated platter and garnish with grapes. Keep hot in warm oven. Reduce liquid in skillet over high heat to about ½ cup. Remove bay leaves and allspice. Stir in butter and cream. Make a thin, smooth paste by mixing together the flour with an equal amount of water. Then stir into liquid in skillet and cook, continuing to stir until sauce thickens slightly. Pour over fillets and grapes. Broil a few minutes to glaze sauce, but do not allow to brown. For an especially attractive dish sprinkle top of fillets with paprika and garnish around sides with parsley and spiced crab apples. *Serves 6.*

Fillet Neapolitan

¼ cup flour
2 teaspoons Bon Appétit
½ teaspoon salt
¼ teaspoon Black Pepper
2 pounds fish fillets (sole, flounder, perch or halibut)
¼ cup olive oil
¼ cup Chopped Instant Onions
1 6-ounce can tomato paste
1 8-ounce can tomato sauce
½ teaspoon sugar
⅛ teaspoon Garlic Powder
2 teaspoons Parsley Flakes
½ teaspoon Italian Seasoning
¼ cup water

Combine flour, Bon Appétit, salt and pepper. Dip fish fillets in seasoned flour, then sauté in hot oil until lightly browned on both sides. Remove. Brown onions, then add remaining ingredients. Mix well and simmer 10 minutes. Place fish in sauce and simmer 5 minutes longer or until fish is heated through. Serve with lemon wedges. *Serves 4 to 6.*

Sole Meunière

⅓ cup flour
1 teaspoon Season-All
Dash Onion Salt
Dash dry Mustard
Dash White Pepper
2 pounds fillet of sole
½ cup butter or margarine
⅓ cup lemon juice
¼ teaspoon Dill Weed
Paprika

Combine flour, Season-All, onion salt, dry mustard and pepper. Dip fillets in seasoned flour; sauté in butter over medium heat until lightly browned. Remove fillets to heated platter. Add lemon juice and dill weed to butter in skillet; heat and pour over fish. Sprinkle with paprika. *Serves 4.*

Creamed Clams

2 7½-ounce cans minced clams
2 tablespoons butter
¼ teaspoon dry Mustard
⅛ teaspoon Ginger
¾ teaspoon Onion Salt
Dash ground Red Pepper
1 tablespoon lemon juice
2 tablespoons Arrowroot
1 cup light cream
1 5-ounce can water chestnuts, sliced
1 teaspoon Instant Minced Onion
1 tablespoon sherry

Simmer clams and butter 5 minutes. Stir in dry mustard, ginger, onion salt, red pepper and lemon juice; mix well. Combine arrowroot and cream. Add to clams and cook over medium heat, stirring constantly, until thickened. Add water chestnuts; just before serving add onion and sherry. Serve in patty shells or over toast. *Serves 6.*

Sautéed Frogs' Legs

4 pair frogs' legs (about 1½ pounds)
Milk to cover
1½ teaspoons Season-All or Bon Appétit
½ teaspoon Onion Powder
¼ teaspoon White Pepper
Flour
6 tablespoons butter

Soak frogs' legs in milk 1 hour. Remove from milk and sprinkle with Season-All or Bon Appétit, onion powder and pepper. Coat lightly with flour. Melt butter; as soon as it sizzles, add frogs' legs and sauté 7 minutes on each side or until golden brown. Remove to heated platter. Spoon butter from skillet over frogs' legs. *Serves 2.*

VARIATIONS:

Frogs' Legs Provençale—Prepare frogs' legs following directions in above recipe. Remove to heated platter. To butter in skillet add ½ teaspoon Garlic Powder, 1 tablespoon lemon juice and 1 teaspoon Parsley Flakes. Stir to mix well and pour over frogs' legs.

Frogs' Legs aux Fines Herbes—Prepare frogs' legs following directions in above recipe. Remove to heated platter. To butter in skillet add ¼ teaspoon Tarragon Leaves, ½ teaspoon Parsley Flakes, ½ teaspoon Chives and 2 tablespoons dry white wine. Stir well and pour over frogs' legs.

Sole Epicurean

Broiled in a delectable sauce until golden, this is food for gourmets.

2 pounds fillet of sole
1½ teaspoons Season-All
¼ teaspoon White Pepper
⅛ teaspoon Paprika
½ cup butter
3 tablespoons lemon juice
8 Coriander Seeds, crushed
½ teaspoon Tarragon Leaves

Place fillets with the thin tissue-like skin side down in broiler pan. Sprinkle with mixture of Season-All, pepper and paprika. Melt butter, carefully skimming off the white milk solids. Combine lemon juice, crushed coriander seed and tarragon leaves. Boil quickly to reduce to 1 tablespoon. Simmer the clarified butter (the clear yellow portion) over medium heat until golden brown, then slowly add lemon juice mixture. As soon as bubbling stops, the sauce is ready to use. Brush about half of it over the fillets and keep the remainder warm over hot water. Broil fillets 4 inches from heat 10 minutes or until easily flaked with a fork. Serve at once with side dish of the remaining sauce. *Serves 4.*

Baked Fish with Herb Stuffing

- 1 4- to 5-pound whole fish (cod, red snapper, haddock, rock, halibut, bass or whitefish)
- 2 tablespoons Instant Minced Onion
- ½ cup diced celery
- ½ cup butter or margarine
- ¼ teaspoon Marjoram Leaves
- ½ teaspoon rubbed Sage
- 1 teaspoon Parsley Flakes
- ¼ teaspoon Tarragon Leaves
- ¼ teaspoon Dill Weed
- 1 teaspoon Bon Appétit
- ¼ teaspoon Lemon Peel
- ¼ teaspoon Savory
- 1 egg, beaten
- 3 cups soft bread crumbs, packed
- ¼ cup butter, melted
- ½ teaspoon dry Mustard
- ¼ teaspoon MSG
- ½ teaspoon Fennel Seed, crushed
- 1 tablespoon Bon Appétit
- 1 tablespoon lemon juice

Clean and wash fish. Sauté onion and celery in the ½ cup butter until onion is lightly browned. Blend in the next eight ingredients. Remove from heat; add to egg and bread crumbs, tossing lightly. Loosely fill cavity of fish with stuffing; close cavity with toothpicks or skewers, drawing edges together by lacing with string. Place fish on a piece of oiled, heavy paper or aluminum foil to prevent sticking and put in a shallow baking pan. Combine remaining ingredients and brush fish thoroughly with part of this mixture. Bake in 400°F. oven, basting occasionally with the remaining seasoned butter, until fish flakes easily with a fork, allowing 12 to 15 minutes per pound. Serve on a fish platter garnished with parsley, tomato wedges and slices of lemon centered with whole Clove. *Serves 6 to 8.*

Broiled Fish Amandine

The crunchy topping of golden almonds makes this a favorite recipe.

- 2 12-ounce packages frozen perch or trout, or 2 pounds any fresh fish fillets
- 4 tablespoons melted butter
- 1 teaspoon Bon Appétit
- ¼ teaspoon salt
- Dash Onion Powder
- ⅛ teaspoon Black Pepper
- Dash Nutmeg
- Dash Paprika
- 2 tablespoons slivered blanched almonds
- 2 tablespoons lemon juice
- 1 tablespoon Parsley Flakes

If using frozen fillets, thaw just enough to separate. Brush with 2 tablespoons of the melted butter. Combine seasonings and sprinkle over fish. Place fish with the tissue-like skin side down in a well greased broiler pan. Broil 4 to 5 inches from heat 10 minutes or until fish is easily flaked with fork. Sauté almonds in the remaining butter until golden brown, then stir in lemon juice. Spoon the almonds and the lemon-butter mixture over fish. Sprinkle with parsley flakes. Serve immediately. *Serves 5 to 6.*

Sea Food Crêpes

CRÊPES:

¾ cup sifted all-purpose flour
1 tablespoon sugar
Dash salt
Dash Nutmeg
Dash Black Pepper
2 eggs, beaten
1 cup milk
1 tablespoon cognac
1 tablespoon melted butter
Sea Food Filling

Sift together flour, sugar, salt, nutmeg and pepper. Combine eggs, milk and cognac and add to flour mixture. Beat until smooth. Stir in butter; cover and let batter stand 2 hours. Prepare Sea Food Filling, following recipe below. To cook crêpes, pour 3 tablespoons of the batter into a lightly buttered, hot, 7-inch skillet. Tilt pan to spread batter evenly. Brown crêpe on one side; turn and brown second side. Remove from pan and keep warm. Continue until all batter is used. Place Sea Food Filling across center of each crêpe; fold sides over to form roll. Place filled crêpes in shallow baking dish or heatproof platter. Spoon remaining sauce that was not used in filling over top of crêpes. (If sauce seems a little thick, add 2 to 3 tablespoons cream or milk.) Bake in 375°F. oven 15 minutes or until heated through, then broil a few seconds to brown top lightly. *Makes 12 crêpes.*

SEA FOOD FILLING:

¼ cup butter
3 tablespoons Arrowroot
3 teaspoons Chicken Flavor Base
½ teaspoon dry Mustard
¼ teaspoon White Pepper
4 Fennel Seeds, crushed
¼ teaspoon Onion Powder
1 teaspoon Bon Appétit
Dash ground Red Pepper
Dash MSG
2 cups milk
1 egg yolk, beaten
¼ cup dry white wine
¼ cup mayonnaise
1 cup crab meat
1 cup finely chopped, cooked shrimp
1 cup finely chopped, cooked lobster

Melt butter; stir in arrowroot and seasonings. Remove from heat and add milk. Cook over low heat until thickened, stirring constantly. Remove from heat. Add some of the hot mixture to egg yolk while stirring briskly, then stir egg yolk mixture into hot sauce. Add wine and mayonnaise, blending well. Combine crab meat, shrimp and lobster. Mix 1 cup of the sauce into the sea food mixture. Use to fill crêpes. Reserve the remaining sauce.

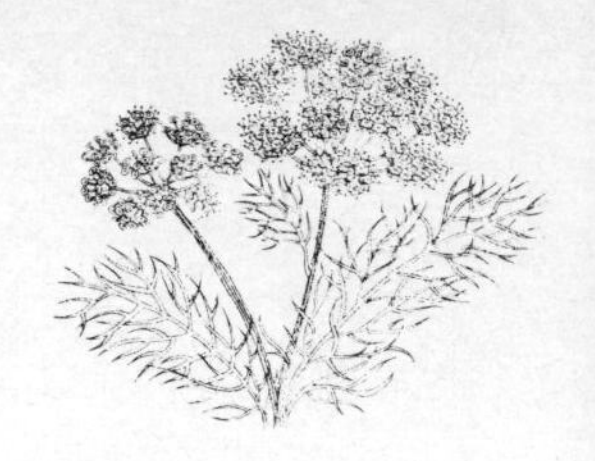

Deviled Crab

¼ cup flour
2 teaspoons Instant Minced Onion
⅛ teaspoon ground Red Pepper
1 teaspoon dry Mustard
1 teaspoon salt
¼ cup melted butter
1 cup milk
2 egg yolks, beaten
2 teaspoons lemon juice
1 teaspoon Worcestershire sauce
2 cups crab meat
2 tablespoons melted butter
1 cup soft bread crumbs

Combine flour, onion, red pepper, dry mustard and salt; stir into the ¼ cup melted butter in a saucepan. Cook until bubbly, then remove from heat. Add milk and cook over medium heat until thickened, stirring constantly. Add small amount of the hot sauce to egg yolks while stirring briskly, then combine egg mixture with the remaining sauce. Cook over low heat 2 minutes, stirring. Remove from heat; add lemon juice, Worcestershire sauce and crab meat. Mix well. Place crab mixture in individual ramekins, custard cups or cleaned crab shells. Combine the 2 tablespoons melted butter and bread crumbs; sprinkle over crab mixture. Bake in 400°F. oven 20 minutes or until crumbs are delicately browned. *Serves 5 to 6.*

Shrimp Creole

¼ cup butter or margarine
2 tablespoons Instant Minced Onion
1 cup chopped celery
½ cup chopped green pepper
2 tablespoons flour
1 tablespoon Season-All
⅛ teaspoon ground Red Pepper
1 Bay Leaf
2 teaspoons Parsley Flakes
3½ cups tomatoes (28-oz. can)
½ cup water
1 pound cooked, cleaned shrimp

Melt butter in large skillet. Sauté onion, celery and green pepper in butter until onion is lightly browned. Blend in flour. Add remaining ingredients except shrimp; mix well. Cover and simmer 30 minutes. Stir in shrimp and continue simmering just until shrimp is heated through. Serve over hot steamed rice. *Serves 4.*

Pan-Fried Fish

4 whole fish for frying (trout, perch, bass) or 1½ pounds fillet of sole
2 teaspoons Bon Appétit
½ teaspoon Black Pepper
1½ teaspoons Paprika
¼ teaspoon Onion Powder
¼ teaspoon dry Mustard
Dash Nutmeg
¼ cup corn meal
Shortening for frying

When using whole fish, clean and remove heads. Combine seasonings and rub over fish. Roll in corn meal. Fry fish in hot shortening, about ¼ inch deep in a heavy skillet, until crisp and brown on both sides. It should take about 8 minutes. Serve piping hot with Tartar Sauce (see recipe page 371) and slices of lime or lemon. *Serves 4.*

Crab Cakes

2 slices bread
1 egg, lightly beaten
1 tablespoon mayonnaise
1 teaspoon Parsley Flakes
1½ teaspoons Celery Salt
¼ teaspoon dry Mustard
⅛ teaspoon Ginger
⅛ teaspoon Black Pepper
1 tablespoon Worcestershire sauce
⅛ teaspoon ground Red Pepper
1 tablespoon baking powder
Dash Cloves
1 pound crab meat
Shortening

Break bread into fine crumbs and mix with beaten egg. Add mayonnaise, parsley flakes, celery salt, dry mustard, ginger, pepper, Worcestershire sauce, red pepper, baking powder and cloves. Mix thoroughly, then combine with crab meat. Shape into 8 cakes. Fry in hot shortening or deep fat at 375°F. 4 minutes or until golden brown. *Serves 4.*

Shrimp Sautéed in Herb Butter

These sautéed shrimp make an excellent supper.

1 pound raw shrimp
¼ cup butter
2 tablespoons lemon juice
1 teaspoon Parsley Flakes
1 teaspoon Chives
½ teaspoon Tarragon Leaves
½ teaspoon dry Mustard
¾ teaspoon Season-All
⅛ teaspoon ground Red Pepper
⅛ teaspoon Garlic Powder

Shell and devein shrimp. Melt butter in chafing dish or skillet; add lemon juice and seasonings. Sauté shrimp in hot herb butter over medium heat 8 minutes or until pink, turning once. Serve hot. You will find this excellent when served on a bed of rice. *Makes 2 to 3 servings.*

Lobster Cantonese

6 rock lobster tails (6 to 8 ounces each)
¾ pound lean pork, coarsely ground
2 teaspoons Instant Minced Onion
1½ teaspoons salt
½ teaspoon Black Pepper
½ teaspoon Bon Appétit
¾ cup thinly sliced celery
¼ cup salad oil
½ cup thinly sliced water chestnuts
½ pound Chinese snow peas (fresh or frozen)
1½ teaspoons Chicken Flavor Base
1½ cups hot water
3 tablespoons Arrowroot
1 tablespoon soy sauce
⅓ cup water
2 eggs, well beaten

Thaw lobster, if frozen, and remove meat from shells. Cut into 1½-inch pieces. Combine ground pork, onion, salt, pepper and Bon Appétit. Sauté pork mixture and celery 1 minute in hot oil, stirring constantly. Add lobster, water chestnuts, snow peas, flavor base and hot water. Cover and simmer 8 minutes, stirring once. Combine arrowroot, soy sauce and the ⅓ cup water. Stir into lobster mixture; cook 2 minutes. Add beaten eggs, stirring well, and cook 1 minute longer. Serve immediately with rice. *Serves 6.*

Superb Scalloped Oysters

Subtle seasoning makes the difference in this luscious version of an old favorite.

1 quart oysters
½ cup butter or margarine
2 cups coarse cracker crumbs
½ teaspoon Season-All
¼ teaspoon Celery Salt
Dash Onion Powder
¼ teaspoon Coarse Grind Black Pepper
¾ cup cream
¼ cup oyster liquor
1 teaspoon Worcestershire sauce
1 teaspoon Parsley Flakes

Drain oysters and save liquor. Melt butter and combine with cracker crumbs, Season-All, celery salt, onion powder and pepper. Spread ⅓ of this mixture in buttered 2-quart shallow baking dish. Cover with ½ of the oysters. Make a second layer of each. Combine cream, oyster liquor and Worcestershire sauce; pour over oysters. Add parsley flakes to remaining crumbs and sprinkle over top of oysters. Bake in 350°F. oven 30 minutes or until oysters are heated through and crumbs are golden brown.

Serves 4.

L.C. Scallops and Mushrooms en Brochette

2 pounds fresh scallops
½ cup olive oil
2 tablespoons lemon juice
¼ teaspoon Black Pepper
1 Bay Leaf
⅛ teaspoon Garlic Salt
8 Coriander Seeds
2 teaspoons Season-All
Dash MSG
1 8-ounce can mushroom crowns

Wash and drain scallops, and put in flat baking dish. Combine remaining ingredients, except mushrooms, and pour over scallops, turning them to coat all sides. Marinate in refrigerator several hours. Thread scallops onto skewers alternately with mushroom crowns, which have been drained. Place on broiler rack and broil 3 to 4 inches from heat 8 to 10 minutes. Turn and broil 8 to 10 minutes longer. Brush several times with marinade during broiling. Serve with Tartar Sauce. *Serves 6 to 8.*

Tuna Croquettes

2 tablespoons butter
6 tablespoons flour
¼ teaspoon dry Mustard
¼ teaspoon Black Pepper
1½ teaspoons Onion Salt
Dash ground Red Pepper
1½ teaspoons lemon juice
¾ cup milk
2 7-ounce cans tuna
2 teaspoons minced pimiento
1 teaspoon Instant Minced Onion
½ cup cracker meal
1 egg, lightly beaten
Fat for deep fat frying

Melt butter in saucepan. Remove from heat; blend in flour, dry mustard, pepper, onion salt, red pepper and lemon juice. Add milk. Cook over low heat, stirring, until mixture thickens and is very smooth. Drain and flake tuna. Add tuna, pimiento and onion to sauce, mixing well. Spread mixture out on plate; chill. Divide chilled mixture into 8 to 10 portions; shape into cones or cylinders. Roll in cracker meal, then in egg and again in cracker meal. Chill again. Fry in deep fat, 375°F., 4 minutes or until golden brown. Drain on absorbent paper. Serve piping hot. For variety you may serve with one of the following: Tasty Cream Sauce, Sour Cream Mustard Sauce, Sweet-Sour Mustard Sauce, Mushroom Sauce or Tomato Sauce. These recipes may be found in the sauce section. *Makes 8 to 10 croquettes.*

Shrimp and Lobster with Sauce Caviar

Excitingly different, superbly seasoned.

1 pound raw shrimp
4 rock lobster tails
½ cup butter
¼ teaspoon Paprika
1 teaspoon Bon Appétit
¼ teaspoon Onion Salt
3 tablespoons lemon juice
Dash Nutmeg
9 Fennel Seeds, crushed
¼ teaspoon Black Pepper
Sauce Caviar

Cook and clean shrimp and lobster tails; cut lobster into cubes. Thread shrimp and lobster onto skewers. Melt butter and add remaining ingredients. Brush shrimp and lobster thoroughly with this butter sauce. Broil 4 inches from heat 3 minutes. Turn; brush again and broil until delicately browned. Serve hot with Sauce Caviar. You will need, of course, to increase the amount of shrimp or lobster if you prefer to use only one of these instead of the combination. *Serves 4 to 6.*

SAUCE CAVIAR:

½ cup mayonnaise
½ cup dairy sour cream
½ teaspoon dry Mustard
⅛ teaspoon MSG
Dash White Pepper
⅛ teaspoon salt
2 tablespoons lemon juice
¼ teaspoon Onion Salt
2 tablespoons black caviar (giant grain)
1 tablespoon cognac

Combine all ingredients, mixing thoroughly but gently. Let stand at least 1 hour for flavors to blend. You may make this sauce ahead of time and keep in refrigerator. *Makes about 1¼ cups.*

Savory Salmon Loaf

1 1-pound can salmon
1 cup soft bread crumbs
¾ cup milk
2 eggs, well beaten
2 tablespoons Instant Minced Onion
¼ cup sliced stuffed olives
1 teaspoon lemon juice
2 tablespoons melted butter
¾ teaspoon Celery Salt
½ teaspoon Parsley Flakes
¼ teaspoon Basil Leaves
¼ teaspoon dry Mustard
¼ teaspoon Black Pepper
1 teaspoon Lemon Peel

Drain and flake salmon; add remaining ingredients. Mix well. Pour into a greased 1½-quart loaf pan. Bake in 350°F. oven 1 hour or until top is delicately golden and loaf is firm yet moist and tender. *Serves 6.*

Fish Poached in Court Bouillon

Elegant and exquisitely seasoned, a superb fish dish.

6 fish fillets (about 2 pounds)
2 teaspoons Season-All
¼ teaspoon Garlic Powder
¼ teaspoon Celery Salt
¼ teaspoon White Pepper
1¼ cups hot water
1 teaspoon Chicken Flavor Base
4 whole Allspice
3 whole Cloves
6 Coriander Seeds
1 Bay Leaf
1 piece whole Ginger, broken
⅓ cup lemon juice
1 4-ounce can mushrooms, drained
2 tablespoons chopped olives
¼ cup melted butter
1 tablespoon Arrowroot
2 teaspoons Instant Minced Onion
½ cup cream or milk
Paprika

Cut fillets lengthwise into strips 1½ inches wide. Combine Season-All, garlic powder, celery salt and pepper; sprinkle over fillet strips. Roll each strip, fasten with toothpick and place in skillet. Combine hot water and flavor base; pour over fillets. Add allspice, cloves, coriander seed, bay leaf, ginger and lemon juice. Cover and simmer gently 10 minutes or just until fish is tender and flakes easily with a fork. Carefully remove rolled fillets to heated baking dish or platter; top with mushrooms and chopped olives. Drizzle with melted butter. Keep hot in warm oven. Reduce liquid in skillet to 1 cup by boiling over high heat. Remove whole spices. Combine arrowroot, onion and cream; stir into hot liquid. Cook, stirring, over low heat until thickened. Spoon over fish. Sprinkle generously with paprika and serve at once.

Serves 6.

CASSEROLES
SPECIAL DISHES

Party Casseroles and Other Specialities

Brunswick Stew 186
Cannelloni 187
Chinese Chicken Casserole 190
Eggplant Florentine with Beef 188
Mock Enchilada Casserole 188
Paella 189
Party Beef Casserole 191
Sausage and Wild Rice Casserole 189
Veal and Wild Rice in Casserole 192

Pastas

Italian Spaghetti Sauce 185
Lasagne 194
Macaroni and Cheese 199
Spaghetti with Superb Meat Sauce 197

Family Favorites–Easy to Prepare

Beef and Noodle Casserole 192
Busy Day Casserole 203
Cabbage Rolls 190
Chili con Carne 190
Italian Pizza 201
  Herb Pizza 201
Lima-Sausage Casserole 191
Mexican Skillet Dinner 193
Savory Stuffed Peppers 193
Texas Barbecued Beef 195

Family Favorites (Cont.)

Tuna Casserole with Batter Topping 198

Elegant Side Dishes

Buttered Noodles with Dill 197
  Buttered Noodles with Poppy Seed 197
Fried Rice 201
Indian Rice 194
Noodles Romanoff 193
Rice Gourmet 195
Saffron Rice 196
Spanish Rice 196
Viennese Noodles au Gratin 198
Wheat Pilaf 195
  Rice Pilaf 195

Cheese and Egg

Baked Eggs Florentine 185
Cheese Omelet aux Herbes 196
Cheese Soufflé 202
Easter Egg Casserole 202
Eggs à la Goldenrod 186
Herb-Broiled Sandwiches 200
Princess Omelet 200
Salmon Luncheon Pie 199
Snappy Cheese-wiches 200
Welsh Rabbit 203

Italian Spaghetti Sauce

1 pound ground beef
1½ teaspoons Season-All
1 teaspoon Basil Leaves
1 teaspoon Thyme Leaves
1 teaspoon Oregano Leaves
½ teaspoon Garlic Powder
½ teaspoon Black Pepper
1 Bay Leaf
1 28-ounce can tomato puree
1 6-ounce can tomato paste
3 cans water
1 4-ounce can sliced mushrooms with liquid

In Dutch oven, brown ground beef. Add next 7 ingredients. Mix well. Stir in remaining ingredients. Bring to boil, reduce heat and simmer over very low heat 3 hours, stirring occasionally. *Makes 5 cups.*

Baked Eggs Florentine

1 10-ounce package frozen chopped spinach
1 tablespoon Instant Minced Onion
⅛ teaspoon Black Pepper
¼ teaspoon salt
2 ounces coarsely chopped cooked ham
4 teaspoons melted butter
8 eggs

Cook spinach following package directions. Drain. Combine spinach, onion, pepper, salt and ham. Pour 1 teaspoon butter into each of 4 individual (10-ounce) ovenproof dishes. Divide spinach mixture among dishes. Top each spinach portion with 2 eggs. Bake in 400°F. oven 6 minutes.

SAUCE:

2 tablespoons butter
1 tablespoon flour
½ cup milk
½ cup coarsely shredded Monterey Jack or Muenster cheese
½ teaspoon Parsley Flakes
¼ teaspoon Garlic Salt
Dash dry Mustard
Dash White Pepper

In saucepan, melt butter, stir in flour and cook until bubbly. Gradually stir in milk and cook, stirring, until thickened. Add remaining ingredients. Cook just until cheese is melted. Pour over spinach and eggs and bake 4 to 6 minutes longer, or until desired degree of doneness is reached.

Makes 4 servings.

Brunswick Stew

1 4- to 5-pound stewing chicken
3 teaspoons salt
1 teaspoon Celery Salt
1 Bay Leaf
½ cup Chopped Instant Onions
1 tablespoon Bell Pepper Flakes
¼ cup butter
2 cups tomatoes (16-oz. can)
1 tablespoon Parsley Flakes
½ teaspoon ground Red Pepper
⅛ teaspoon Ginger
⅛ teaspoon Cumin
½ teaspoon Lemon Peel
¼ teaspoon Black Pepper
1 tablespoon Season-All
1 tablespoon Worcestershire sauce
1 teaspoon sugar
1 17-oz. can whole kernel corn
2 cups fresh, frozen or canned lima beans
⅓ cup flour
½ cup water

Cover chicken with water; add 2 teaspoons of the salt, celery salt and bay leaf. Simmer until chicken is tender. Remove chicken, reserving 3 cups of the stock. Remove chicken from bone and cut into bite-size pieces. In large saucepan or Dutch oven sauté onions and pepper flakes in butter. Add tomatoes, the remaining salt, seasonings, sugar and the 3 cups stock; simmer 30 minutes. Add corn, lima beans and chicken and simmer 2 hours longer. Mix flour and water to a smooth paste and stir into stew. Continue cooking until thickened. *Makes about 3 quarts.*

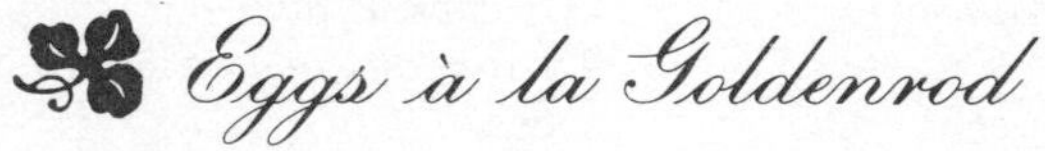

A luncheon or supper dish . . . ideal during Lent.

6 hard-cooked eggs
3 tablespoons butter
½ teaspoon dry Mustard
¼ teaspoon White Pepper
Dash Nutmeg
Dash ground Red Pepper
½ teaspoon Tarragon Leaves
2 teaspoons Chicken Flavor Base
4 teaspoons Arrowroot
2 cups milk
1 teaspoon vinegar
6 slices bread
Paprika

Cut eggs in half; remove yolks. Press yolks through coarse sieve and chop whites. Melt butter in saucepan; stir in dry mustard, pepper, nutmeg, red pepper, tarragon leaves, flavor base and arrowroot. Add milk; cook over medium heat, stirring, until sauce thickens. Add vinegar and chopped egg whites, blending well. Toast bread; butter if desired. Arrange toast on heated platter and pour sauce over toast. Top with sieved yolks; sprinkle with paprika. Arrange slices of Canadian bacon and tomato wedges around platter for a meal-in-one. *Serves 4 to 6.*

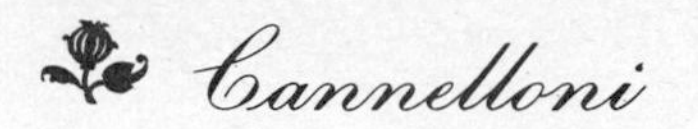

Cannelloni

PANCAKES:

1 cup all-purpose flour
1 tablespoon corn meal
½ teaspoon Bon Appétit
2 eggs
½ cup dairy sour cream
1 cup water
2 tablespoons oil

Combine dry ingredients. Beat eggs; add sour cream and water and mix well. Stir in flour mixture and oil. Cook pancakes on a lightly greased hot griddle, using about 3 tablespoons of the batter for each. *Makes about 12.*

FILLING:

1 pound raw chicken meat
½ pound veal
½ pound pork
4 slices prosciutto ham
2 tablespoons olive oil
2 tablespoons Instant Minced Onion
¼ teaspoon MSG
½ teaspoon salt
⅛ teaspoon Garlic Powder
¼ teaspoon Rosemary Leaves
¼ teaspoon Basil Leaves
¼ teaspoon Oregano Leaves
¼ teaspoon Thyme Leaves
2 teaspoons Season-All
¼ teaspoon Black Pepper
½ cup sherry
½ pound ricotta cheese
½ cup cream
Monterey Jack or Muenster cheese
Grated Parmesan cheese

Cut meat into pieces. Sauté in hot oil about 2 minutes, stirring to turn meat. Add seasonings; cover and simmer slowly 45 minutes or until tender. Add sherry and cook 10 minutes longer. Remove from heat; stir in ricotta cheese. Cool, then grind in food mill twice. Add the broth from skillet (there should be about ½ cup) and the cream, mixing well. Add additional broth or cream if necessary to make a very moist, but not runny, filling. Fill pancakes with mixture, folding sides over to make a long roll. Place in buttered baking dish; when ready to serve, heat in 350°F. oven about 20 minutes. Top with a slice of Monterey Jack or Muenster cheese. Continue baking until cheese melts. Serve with Parmesan cheese and sauce. *Serves 6.*

SAUCE:

1 cup chili sauce
1 8-ounce can tomato sauce
2 tablespoons lemon juice
2 teaspoons Instant Minced Onion
⅛ teaspoon Garlic Powder
⅛ teaspoon ground Oregano
Dash or two ground Red Pepper
⅛ teaspoon MSG
2 tablespoons butter

Combine all ingredients and simmer slowly about 20 minutes.

Eggplant Florentine with Beef

Rich, wonderful Mediterranean flavor.

1 medium-size eggplant
¼ cup butter or margarine
1 pound ground beef
1 tablespoon Instant Minced Onion
1 teaspoon Bon Appétit
⅛ teaspoon Black Pepper
1 teaspoon sugar
¼ teaspoon MSG
¼ teaspoon Basil Leaves
¼ teaspoon ground Oregano
1 8-ounce can tomato sauce
¼ cup grated Parmesan cheese
½ pound Mozzarella cheese

Wash, but do not peel eggplant; cut into ½-inch slices. Melt butter over low heat in skillet; add eggplant and brown lightly on both sides, adding extra butter if needed. Put in shallow 2-quart baking dish. To drippings in skillet, add ground beef, onion, Bon Appétit, pepper, sugar, MSG, basil leaves and oregano; mix well and cook until meat is lightly browned. Spoon meat mixture over eggplant; add tomato sauce and Parmesan cheese. Bake, uncovered, in 350°F. oven 20 minutes. Slice Mozzarella cheese and place over top of casserole. Bake 10 minutes longer or until cheese is melted. Serve hot. *Serves 6.*

Mock Enchilada Casserole

2 tablespoons butter or margarine
2 tablespoons Instant Minced Onion
1 8-ounce can tomato sauce
1 4-ounce can green chili peppers, chopped
1 teaspoon Italian Seasoning
½ teaspoon Celery Salt
¼ teaspoon White or Black Pepper
2 eggs
1 cup light cream
6 tortillas, torn into pieces or 6-ounce package corn chips
½ pound Monterey Jack or Muenster cheese, cubed
½ pint dairy sour cream
½ cup grated Cheddar cheese
Paprika

Melt butter in skillet; add onion and sauté but do not brown. Add tomato sauce, chili peppers, Italian Seasoning, celery salt and pepper. Simmer 5 minutes. Lightly beat eggs; add cream, mixing well. Remove tomato mixture from heat; quickly stir in egg mixture. Cover the bottom of a 2-quart casserole with ⅓ of the tortillas; cover with ⅓ of the sauce and ⅓ of the cubed cheese. Repeat layers until all tortillas, sauce and cubed cheese have been used. Top with sour cream; sprinkle with grated Cheddar cheese and paprika. Bake in 350°F. oven 25 minutes or until bubbly hot. Serve immediately with a crisp tossed salad. *Makes 4 to 6 servings.*

Paella

Saffron gives this most famous of Spanish rice dishes its special goodness.

½ pound raw shrimp
1 3- to 4-pound chicken
¼ cup olive oil
¼ pound pepperoni, sliced
2 tomatoes
¼ cup Chopped Instant Onions
⅛ teaspoon Garlic Powder
1 teaspoon Paprika
1 tablespoon Parsley Flakes
1 teaspoon Season-All
10 individual pieces Saffron
1 teaspoon salt
¼ teaspoon Black Pepper
2 teaspoons Chicken Flavor Base
1½ cups rice
3 cups water
1 9-ounce package frozen artichokes, cooked
1 pimiento, sliced
12 whole clams or about 1 cup canned minced clams
1 cup lobster pieces
1 8-ounce can peas, drained

Remove shell from the raw shrimp; set aside. Cut chicken in pieces. In large skillet, brown chicken on all sides in oil; remove. Then add pepperoni and brown. Peel and cut tomatoes into sections, then add to skillet with onions; cook until onions are lightly browned. Return chicken to pan, add shrimp and the remaining ingredients except peas. Cover and simmer 30 minutes. Add peas and cook, uncovered, 5 minutes longer. All you need to serve with Paella is plenty of salad. *Serves 6 to 8.*

Sausage and Wild Rice Casserole

A wonderful party casserole.

¾ pound bulk pork sausage
1 tablespoon Bell Pepper Flakes
½ cup chopped celery
1 4-ounce can pimiento
1 cup wild rice
2 teaspoons Chicken Flavor Base
1½ cups hot water
1 10½-ounce can condensed cream of mushroom soup
1 2-ounce can mushrooms
1 tablespoon Instant Minced Onion
½ teaspoon Marjoram Leaves
½ teaspoon Thyme Leaves
1 cup grated American cheese

Crumble sausage and brown in a large skillet. Add pepper flakes and celery and continue cooking until celery is soft. Drain off excess fat. Drain and chop pimiento; add to sausage mixture along with remaining ingredients, mixing well. Pour into a 3-quart casserole. Cover. Bake in 325°F. oven 1½ hours or until rice is tender and dry. Rich, tasty and filling! Serve with a crisp green salad and dessert. *Serves 6 to 8.*

Chinese Chicken Casserole

½ teaspoon Chicken Flavor Base
⅓ cup hot water
1 10½-ounce can condensed cream of mushroom soup
1 cup chopped cooked chicken
1 tablespoon Instant Minced Onion
½ cup whole cashew nuts
Chow mein noodles

Dissolve flavor base in water. Combine with soup, chicken, onion, nuts and half of the noodles. Put in buttered 1½-quart casserole; top with the remaining noodles. Bake in 375°F. oven 30 minutes. *Serves 4.*

Cabbage Rolls

8 large cabbage leaves
½ cup long grain rice
1 cup water
½ teaspoon salt
1 pound ground beef
1 tablespoon Instant Minced Onion
2½ teaspoons Season-All
¼ teaspoon Black Pepper
¼ teaspoon Basil Leaves
3½ cups tomatoes (28-oz. can)
1 tablespoon flour
¼ cup dairy sour cream

Steam cabbage leaves 8 minutes or until slightly tender. Combine rice, water and salt and cook 20 minutes or until tender. Mix together rice, beef, onion, 1½ teaspoons of the Season-All, pepper and basil leaves. Place ⅓ cup of the meat mixture in each cabbage leaf. Fold leaf over meat, tucking in ends, and fasten with toothpick. Place rolls, overlapped side down, in frying pan. Pour tomatoes over rolls and simmer 1½ hours. Remove rolls. Combine flour, sour cream and the remaining Season-All; stir into liquid in frying pan. Simmer very gently until slightly thickened but do not allow to boil. Serve cabbage rolls, steaming hot, with sauce. *Makes 8 rolls.*

Chili con Carne

1 pound ground beef
2 tablespoons shortening
1 teaspoon salt
3 tablespoons Chili Powder
⅓ cup Onion Flakes
1 8-ounce can tomato sauce
1 17-oz. can red kidney beans
2 tablespoons vinegar
Dash Garlic Powder
Dash MSG

Crumble beef; brown in hot shortening, stirring until meat loses its pink color. Add remaining ingredients; mix well. Cover. Simmer 45 minutes, stirring occasionally. *Serves 4 to 6.*

Party Beef Casserole

Savory beef in a red wine sauce, topped with a "crust" of mashed potato.

2 pounds beef round
(cut into 1-inch cubes)
3 tablespoons flour
1 teaspoon Season-All
⅛ teaspoon Black Pepper
3 tablespoons bacon drippings
or salad oil
1 cup water
1 teaspoon Beef Flavor Base
⅓ cup Chopped Instant Onions
½ teaspoon Garlic Powder
1 teaspoon Bon Appétit
½ teaspoon Marjoram Leaves
½ teaspoon Thyme Leaves
1 cup red wine, Burgundy
or Bordeaux
2 cups fresh, frozen
or canned peas
3 cups hot, stiff, mashed
potatoes
1 tablespoon melted butter
Paprika

Dredge meat with mixture of flour, Season-All and pepper; brown on all sides in hot fat. Transfer browned meat to a 2-quart casserole. Add water to skillet and stir to loosen all the browned bits. Add beef flavor base, onions, garlic powder, Bon Appétit, marjoram leaves and thyme leaves. Simmer about 5 minutes, then add wine and mix well. Pour sauce over meat in casserole. Cover and bake in 350°F. oven 1½ hours or until meat is tender. Cook peas; drain. (Reserve several pieces of the meat and ¼ cup of the peas to use for garnishing the top if desired.) Sprinkle peas over meat. Spoon potatoes completely over top; brush with butter. Sprinkle generously with paprika. Bake 15 minutes longer or until potatoes are lightly browned. A favorite with the men. *Serves 5 to 6.*

Lima-Sausage Casserole

1 pound bulk pork sausage
1 tablespoon Instant Minced
Onion
⅛ teaspoon Garlic Powder
⅛ teaspoon MSG
¼ teaspoon Rosemary Leaves
¼ teaspoon Thyme Leaves
1 8-ounce can tomato sauce
2 16-oz. cans lima beans
¼ cup butter
1 cup dry bread crumbs
1 tablespoon Parsley Flakes

Crumble sausage; add onion, garlic powder and MSG. Cook until sausage is browned, stirring and breaking it up with a fork while cooking. Crush rosemary leaves and add to sausage along with thyme leaves and tomato sauce. Simmer 15 minutes. Drain limas; add to sausage mixture. Stir to mix well. Transfer to a 1½-quart casserole. Melt butter; stir into bread crumbs and parsley flakes, tossing lightly. Spoon over top of bean mixture. Bake in 350°F. oven 1 hour or until crumbs are golden. *Serves 4 to 6.*

Veal and Wild Rice in Casserole

1 cup wild rice
3 cups water
1 teaspoon Chicken Flavor Base
2 pounds veal cutlet, thinly sliced
6 tablespoons butter
2 teaspoons Instant Minced Onion
¼ teaspoon ground Thyme
¼ teaspoon Savory
½ teaspoon Season-All
½ cup white wine
1 4-ounce can mushrooms
1 cup dairy sour cream
Paprika

Wash rice. Add water and flavor base and cook, covered, until rice is fluffy and water absorbed, 45 minutes to 1 hour. Cut veal into 3- to 4-inch pieces. Brown in butter; add onion, thyme, savory, Season-All and wine. Remove from heat. Stir mushrooms, including liquid, into rice; transfer to a 2-quart baking dish. Place pieces of veal over top of rice. Add sour cream to wine-herb mixture in skillet, stirring until thoroughly blended. Pour over top of veal; sprinkle with paprika. Bake in 325°F. oven 20 minutes.

Serves 4 to 5.

Beef and Noodle Casserole

2 cups (½ pound) noodles
1 tablespoon oil
¼ cup Instant Minced Onion
1 pound ground beef
1½ teaspoons Season-All
½ teaspoon Thyme Leaves
¼ teaspoon MSG
¼ teaspoon Black Pepper
1 10½-ounce can condensed cream of celery soup
½ cup water
½ cup evaporated milk
1 cup grated sharp cheese
2 eggs, beaten

Cook noodles as directed on package; drain and rinse. Put oil, onion, beef, Season-All, thyme leaves, MSG and pepper in large skillet and cook until meat loses its red color but is not brown. Combine soup, water and milk. In 2-quart casserole put ⅓ of the noodles, ½ of the meat mixture and ½ of the soup mixture. Repeat. Put remaining noodles on top. Sprinkle grated cheese over noodles and pour beaten eggs over cheese. Bake, uncovered, in 350°F. oven 1 hour or until thoroughly heated and bubbly and top is very crisp.

Serves 6.

Noodles Romanoff

2½ cups noodles
1 cup cottage cheese
1 cup dairy sour cream
1 teaspoon Instant Minced Onion
⅛ teaspoon Instant Minced Garlic
1 teaspoon Worcestershire sauce
1½ teaspoons Season-All
Dash ground Red Pepper
⅓ cup grated Cheddar cheese

Cook noodles as directed on package; drain. Combine noodles with remaining ingredients except grated cheese. Put in buttered 1½-quart casserole; sprinkle top with grated cheese. Bake in 350°F. oven 30 minutes or until heated through and bubbly and cheese has melted. *Serves 6.*

Savory Stuffed Peppers

Topped with bubbly cheese to make them extra special.

6 medium-size green peppers
1 pound ground beef
1 tablespoon oil
¼ cup Chopped Instant Onions
¼ cup ketchup
1 cup soft bread crumbs
½ teaspoon Basil Leaves
2 teaspoons Season-All
½ teaspoon salt
¼ teaspoon rubbed Sage
½ teaspoon Beef Flavor Base
¼ cup hot water
6 slices Muenster cheese
Paprika

Wash peppers, cut off tops and remove seed, leaving peppers whole. Steam 5 minutes. Brown beef in hot oil; add onions, ketchup, bread crumbs, basil leaves, Season-All, salt and sage. Fill peppers with meat mixture and place in a baking dish. Dissolve beef flavor base in hot water and add to dish with peppers. Cover and bake in 350°F. oven 40 minutes. Place slice of cheese on top of each pepper; sprinkle with paprika and bake, uncovered, 10 minutes longer. *Serves 6.*

Mexican Skillet Dinner

A spicy, hearty budget dish, so easy to put together.

1 pound bulk pork sausage
¼ cup Chopped Instant Onions
1 cup diced green pepper
1 8-ounce package elbow macaroni
2 cups tomatoes (16-oz. can)
1 cup buttermilk or dairy sour cream
2 tablespoons sugar
2 tablespoons Chili Powder
2 teaspoons Season-All

Brown sausage in deep heavy skillet; add onions and green pepper. Cook until onions are golden brown. Pour off excess fat. Add remaining ingredients; stir to moisten macaroni. Cover; bring to a boil, then reduce heat and cook 30 minutes. *Serves 4.*

Lasagne

Rich, hearty and delicious.

- *1 pound ground beef*
- *2 tablespoons olive oil*
- *3½ cups tomatoes (28-oz. can)*
- *2 8-ounce cans tomato sauce*
- *2 tablespoons Instant Minced Onion*
- *⅛ teaspoon Garlic Powder*
- *1½ teaspoons Oregano Leaves*
- *¼ teaspoon Basil Leaves*
- *¼ teaspoon Rosemary Leaves*
- *½ teaspoon MSG*
- *2 teaspoons salt*
- *1 teaspoon sugar*
- *1 3-ounce can sliced mushrooms*
- *½ pound lasagne noodles*
- *1 pound ricotta cheese*
- *½ pound Mozzarella cheese*
- *½ cup grated Parmesan cheese*

Sauté ground beef in hot oil until meat loses its pink color. Add tomatoes, tomato sauce, seasonings and mushrooms. Mix well; cook slowly about 2 hours or until sauce is thickened. Cook noodles following directions on package; drain, rinse in cold water and separate. In a buttered 3-quart baking dish make two layers of the noodles, meat sauce, ricotta, slices of Mozzarella cheese and Parmesan cheese, in this order, using about half of each for each layer. Bake in 350°F. oven 30 minutes or until bubbly.

Serves 6 to 7.

NOTE: Pepperoni may be added to meat sauce if desired. You may double the recipe for sauce; use half in making the lasagne, as above, and serve the remainder, cooked down until quite thick, in a sauceboat along with the lasagne.

Indian Rice

- *½ cup butter*
- *1 cup rice*
- *2 tablespoons Instant Minced Onion*
- *4 whole Cardamom*
- *1 Bay Leaf*
- *¼ teaspoon Saffron pieces*
- *Dash Cinnamon*
- *¼ teaspoon Coarse Grind Black Pepper*
- *¼ cup currants or raisins*
- *¼ cup slivered almonds*
- *2 tablespoons Chicken Flavor Base*
- *2 cups hot water*

Melt half the butter; add rice and onion and sauté until brown. Remove the little black seed from the whole cardamom pod and crush, discarding the outer pod. Crumble the bay leaf and saffron. Then add the spices to rice along with remaining butter and other ingredients. Cover. Cook over low heat 25 to 30 minutes. Though Indian Rice may be served with any kind of meat, it is especially good with pork or chicken. *Serves 4 to 6.*

Texas Barbecued Beef

1 pound ground beef
3 tablespoons shortening or oil
2 tablespoons Chopped Instant Onions
1 tablespoon flour
¾ cup hot water
¾ cup chili sauce
1 teaspoon Barbecue Spice
1 teaspoon dry Mustard
¼ teaspoon MSG

Crumble beef and sauté in hot shortening until meat loses its pink color and is lightly browned. Stir in onions and flour. Add hot water and cook 5 minutes, stirring constantly. Add remaining ingredients and simmer 15 minutes. Serve piping hot over hamburger buns which have been split and toasted, or you may prefer to serve over rice or noodles. *Serves 6.*

Wheat Pilaf

½ cup vermicelli
5 tablespoons butter
1 cup cracked wheat
1 tablespoon Instant Minced Onion
1 teaspoon Bon Appétit
5 teaspoons Chicken Flavor Base
2 cups hot water

Break vermicelli into ½-inch pieces; then measure. Melt butter over medium heat; add vermicelli and sauté until it begins to turn in color. Add wheat and onion and continue to cook, stirring constantly, until vermicelli is golden brown. Add Bon Appétit. Dissolve flavor base in hot water and pour over wheat. Cover and cook 25 minutes or until liquid is absorbed. Stir with a fork to fluff. Cook, uncovered, a few minutes to dry out. Serve immediately or cover to keep hot until ready to serve. *Serves 6.*

VARIATION:
Rice Pilaf—Substitute 1 cup rice for wheat in above recipe.

Rice Gourmet

1 4-ounce can mushrooms, stems and pieces
¼ cup butter or margarine
½ cup sherry
1 teaspoon Parsley Flakes
1½ teaspoons Season-All
2 teaspoons Instant Minced Onion
⅛ teaspoon Black or White Pepper
1 cup rice
2 cups water

Drain mushrooms, reserving liquid. Sauté mushrooms in butter 2 to 3 minutes. Add sherry and seasonings and simmer slowly 5 minutes. Pour rice over mushrooms; add reserved mushroom liquid and water. Cover and cook slowly 25 to 30 minutes. *Serves 6.*

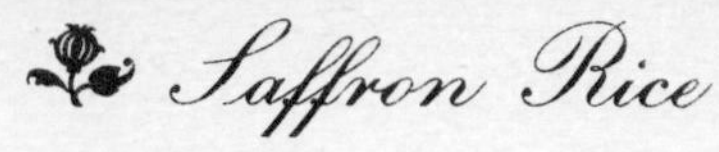

Saffron Rice

¼ cup butter
½ cup slivered almonds
1 cup rice
1 cup chopped green pepper
1 4-ounce can mushrooms, stems and pieces
¼ teaspoon Saffron pieces
¼ teaspoon Black Pepper
1 tablespoon Instant Minced Onion
1½ teaspoons salt
2½ cups water

Melt butter in skillet; add almonds and rice. Cook over low heat, stirring, until rice is delicately browned. Add remaining ingredients. Cover skillet. Bring to a boil; reduce heat and simmer about 25 minutes. Remove from heat; keep covered until ready to serve. You will find Saffron Rice excellent with chicken; but you can use it, of course, as you would plain white rice.

Serves 6.

Cheese Omelet aux Herbes

4 eggs
2 tablespoons milk
1 teaspoon Season-All
1 teaspoon Parsley Flakes
¼ teaspoon Black Pepper
½ cup grated Cheddar cheese
1 tablespoon butter

Beat together eggs, milk, Season-All, parsley flakes and pepper. Stir in cheese. Melt butter in 7- to 8-inch skillet until hot but not allowing it to brown. Tilt skillet in all directions to butter sides. Pour egg mixture into skillet; as mixture sets, lift edges with spatula or fork, allowing uncooked portion to run under cooked portion of omelet. When bottom of omelet is lightly browned and top is soft and creamy, fold in half. Immediately slip out onto plate. Especially nice with ham and Sautéed Mushrooms (see recipe page 216).

Serves 2.

Spanish Rice

1 cup long grain rice
½ cup Chopped Instant Onions
¼ cup butter or margarine
2 teaspoons Chicken Flavor Base
2 teaspoons Season-All
¼ teaspoon Black Pepper
Dash Garlic Powder
1 tablespoon Bell Pepper Flakes
⅛ teaspoon MSG
½ teaspoon sugar
1 tablespoon chopped pimiento
1 teaspoon Worcestershire sauce
1 cup water
3 cups tomatoes (28-oz. can)

Sauté rice and onions in butter, stirring, until onions are lightly browned. Add remaining ingredients, cutting whole tomatoes into pieces. Cover and simmer 30 minutes.

Serves 6.

Spaghetti with Superb Meat Sauce

Long, slow simmering of meat and herbs produces the base for this incomparable sauce.

1 3-pound beef roast (round, chuck or rump)
3 teaspoons salt
¼ cup flour
¼ cup olive oil
2 cups hot water
¼ teaspoon Garlic Powder
1 teaspoon Onion Powder
2 Bay Leaves
1 teaspoon Celery Salt
1 teaspoon Black Pepper
2 teaspoons sugar
½ teaspoon Crushed Red Pepper
1 tablespoon Season-All
¼ teaspoon MSG
½ teaspoon Oregano Leaves
½ teaspoon Basil Leaves
½ teaspoon Parsley Flakes
½ teaspoon Rosemary Leaves, crushed
⅛ teaspoon Nutmeg
4 6-ounce cans tomato paste
1 quart water
1 cup red wine, optional
½ cup sliced ripe olives
½ cup sliced stuffed olives
2 4-ounce cans mushrooms
8 anchovy fillets, mashed
Spaghetti
Grated Parmesan cheese

Season roast with salt; dredge with flour. In Dutch oven brown slowly on all sides in hot olive oil. Add hot water; cover and cook slowly 3 hours or until meat almost falls apart. Tear into small pieces with fork. Add remaining ingredients except spaghetti and cheese. Cover tightly and simmer 2 hours longer, stirring occasionally. Remove cover and continue cooking until sauce thickens to desired consistency. Cook spaghetti following directions on package, allowing 1 pound for 4 servings. Ladle sauce over spaghetti. Top with cheese.

Makes about 3½ quarts sauce, enough for 4 pounds spaghetti.

NOTE: Since you may not need such a large quantity of spaghetti, freeze extra sauce in half-pint, pint or quart freezer jars and use as needed.

Buttered Noodles with Dill

1 8-ounce package noodles
½ cup melted butter
2 teaspoons Dill Weed

Cook noodles as directed on package; drain. Toss lightly with melted butter and dill weed.

Serves 6 to 8.

VARIATION:

Buttered Noodles with Poppy Seed—In the above recipe use 2 teaspoons Poppy Seed in place of dill weed.

Viennese Noodles au Gratin

½ pound noodles
1 tablespoon Poppy Seed
½ pound Cheddar cheese, grated
1 pint dairy sour cream
Paprika

Cook noodles in boiling salted water following directions on package. Drain well. Toss gently with poppy seed and cheese until well mixed. Alternate layers of noodle mixture and sour cream in a buttered 2-quart casserole, ending with sour cream on top. Sprinkle with paprika. Bake in 350°F. oven 20 minutes or until bubbly hot. *Serves 6 to 8.*

Tuna Casserole with Batter Topping

¼ cup butter
¼ cup flour
1 teaspoon Chicken Flavor Base
1 teaspoon Bon Appétit
⅛ teaspoon White Pepper
½ teaspoon Lemon Peel
¼ teaspoon Tarragon Leaves
1 cup hot water
1 cup cream or milk
1 teaspoon lemon juice
2 7-ounce cans tuna, drained
Batter Topping

Melt butter; add flour, flavor base, Bon Appétit, pepper, lemon peel and tarragon leaves. Cook until bubbly. Remove from heat; add water and cream or milk. Cook over low heat, stirring, until thickened. Add lemon juice and tuna, mixing well. Spoon into a 2-quart shallow baking dish. Cover with Batter Topping and bake in 425°F. oven 15 minutes or until golden brown. (The tuna mixture may be prepared ahead of time and refrigerated. Add Batter Topping when ready to bake and serve.) Serve piping hot.

Serves 6.

BATTER TOPPING:

¾ cup all-purpose flour
½ teaspoon Bon Appétit
2 teaspoons baking powder
1 teaspoon Instant Minced Onion
2 eggs, separated
½ cup milk
1 tablespoon butter, melted

Sift flour, measure and sift again with Bon Appétit and baking powder. Add onion. Beat egg yolks until light; add milk and butter. Add to dry ingredients and mix lightly. Beat egg whites until stiff but not dry. Fold into batter. Pour over top of tuna mixture and bake as directed above.

Macaroni and Cheese

½ pound sharp Cheddar cheese
4 tablespoons butter
4 tablespoons flour
1 teaspoon Chicken Flavor Base
½ teaspoon Onion Powder
¼ teaspoon White Pepper
1½ teaspoons Season-All
¼ teaspoon dry Mustard
Dash ground Red Pepper
Dash Nutmeg
2 cups milk
1 8-ounce package macaroni
Paprika

Cut cheese into ½-inch cubes. Melt butter; blend in flour, flavor base and seasonings. Cook over low heat, stirring, until mixture is smooth and bubbly. Do not allow to brown. Remove from heat and stir in milk. Bring to a boil, stirring, and cook until sauce thickens. Add 1 cup of the cheese and stir until melted. Cook macaroni following directions on package; drain. Place half the macaroni in a buttered 11½ x 7½ x 1½-inch baking dish; sprinkle ½ cup cheese cubes over macaroni. Top with second layer of macaroni and cheese. Pour cheese sauce over all. Sprinkle with paprika. Bake in 350°F. oven 30 to 40 minutes. Serve hot from baking dish. *Serves 6 to 8.*

Salmon Luncheon Pie

1 unbaked 10-inch pastry shell
1 1-pound can salmon
1 tablespoon lemon juice
¼ cup Chopped Instant Onions
1 tablespoon Parsley Flakes
2 tablespoons butter
6 eggs, lightly beaten
1½ cups milk
1 teaspoon Season-All
¼ teaspoon White or Black Pepper

Prick pastry shell with tines of a fork; bake in 450°F. oven 5 minutes. Drain salmon, reserving liquid. Remove bones and skin. Flake salmon and place in bottom of pastry shell. Sprinkle with lemon juice. Sauté onions and parsley flakes in butter; sprinkle over salmon. Mix liquid from salmon with eggs, milk, Season-All and pepper. Pour over salmon. Bake in 350°F. oven 50 minutes or until firm. Serve hot. *Serves 6.*

Princess Omelet

4 eggs
¼ cup dairy sour cream
2 teaspoons Instant Minced Onion
¼ teaspoon Crushed Red Pepper
½ teaspoon salt
1 3-ounce package cream cheese
1 tablespoon butter
8 asparagus spears, canned or cooked

Beat together eggs, sour cream, onion, pepper and salt. Cut cheese into ¼-inch cubes; stir into egg mixture. Melt butter in 7- to 8-inch skillet until hot but not allowing it to brown. Tilt skillet in all directions to butter sides. Pour egg mixture into skillet; as mixture sets, lift edges with spatula or fork, allowing uncooked portion to run under cooked portion of omelet. When bottom of omelet is lightly browned and top is soft and creamy, arrange asparagus spears across the center with stem ends together and spears toward outside edge. Fold sides over asparagus and slide from skillet onto plate. Serve garnished with crisp bacon, tomato wedges and water cress. *Serves 2.*

Snappy Cheese-wiches

4 English muffins, split
½ pound grated sharp cheese
½ teaspoon Onion Salt
⅛ teaspoon Nutmeg
⅛ teaspoon Allspice
⅛ teaspoon ground Red Pepper
2 teaspoons prepared mustard
1 teaspoon Worcestershire sauce
1 teaspoon prepared horseradish
1 teaspoon lemon juice
¼ cup mayonnaise or salad dressing

Toast split sides of muffins under broiler until lightly browned. Combine remaining ingredients, mixing well; spread mixture over toasted side of muffins. Broil 4 inches from heat 5 minutes or until cheese is bubbly and lightly browned. *Makes 8 open-faced sandwiches.*

Herb-Broiled Sandwiches

6 slices bacon
6 slices bread
Butter or margarine
Herb Seasoning
6 slices cheese
6 slices tomato

Partially broil or fry bacon. Toast slices of bread on one side. Spread the untoasted side with butter; sprinkle with Herb Seasoning. Top each with a slice of cheese, tomato and bacon. Broil until bacon is crisp and cheese begins to melt. *Makes 6 open-faced sandwiches.*

Italian Pizza

SAUCE:

3½ cups tomatoes (28-oz. can)
1 6-ounce can tomato paste
½ teaspoon Oregano Leaves
¼ teaspoon Basil Leaves
1 teaspoon Garlic Salt
¼ teaspoon crushed Rosemary Leaves
¼ teaspoon Crushed Red Pepper
½ teaspoon Coarse Grind Black Pepper

Press tomatoes, including juice, through a sieve, then combine with remaining ingredients in saucepan. Cook over medium heat, stirring occasionally, until mixture is reduced to one half the original volume, leaving about 2 cups sauce.

CRUST:

1 package hot roll mix
½ teaspoon ground Oregano
½ teaspoon Onion Powder
⅛ teaspoon Garlic Powder
2 tablespoons oil
1 8-ounce package sliced Mozzarella cheese
Toppings: anchovies, pepperoni, mushrooms or sliced olives

Prepare pizza dough as directed on package of hot roll mix, adding oregano, onion powder and garlic powder to the yeast-water mixture. Divide dough in half; roll each half to fit a 14-inch pizza pan and arrange dough in pans. Brush with oil, spread with sauce and top with cheese and one or more of the toppings. Bake in 450°F. oven 15 to 20 minutes.

Serves 4 to 6 as a luncheon or supper dish.

VARIATION:

Herb Pizza—Make pizza as in recipe above. Before baking sprinkle top with any one or a combination of the following herbs: Basil Leaves, Oregano Leaves, Marjoram Leaves, Thyme Leaves or Italian Seasoning.

¼ cup Instant Minced Onion
¼ cup oil or butter
3 cups cold, cooked rice
2 eggs, lightly beaten
¼ teaspoon Black Pepper
2 teaspoons Beef Flavor Base
2 tablespoons soy sauce
1 cup chopped, cooked meat (chicken, pork, beef, shrimp, lobster, sausage or bacon)

Sauté onion in hot oil until golden brown. Add rice; heat thoroughly, stirring often. Stir in beaten eggs, pepper, beef flavor base and soy sauce. Sauté 3 minutes, continuing to stir. Add meat and continue heating until mixture is steaming hot.

Serves 6.

Easter Egg Casserole

Here is how those pretty Easter eggs may be used to make a gay supper dish for Easter Monday.

1 cup rice
2 cups water
1 teaspoon salt
8 individual pieces Saffron
2 cups medium White Sauce Supreme
1 cup diced ham
8 small slices ham
Stuffed Eggs

Combine rice, water, salt and saffron; bring to a boil. Cover; reduce heat and simmer 20 minutes or until rice absorbs all the water. Make White Sauce Supreme (see recipe page 360). Mix rice with diced ham and 1 cup of the white sauce; spoon into a buttered shallow 2-quart baking dish. Pour the remaining white sauce over rice. Arrange ham slices on top and place a stuffed egg on each slice. Bake in 325°F. oven 30 minutes. You might like to serve with green peas tossed with toasted slivered almonds and a relish tray to round out the meal.

Serves 4 to 8.

STUFFED EGGS:

4 hard-cooked eggs
¼ cup mayonnaise
1 teaspoon vinegar
2 teaspoons Instant Minced Onion
¼ teaspoon dry Mustard
½ teaspoon salt
Dash Black Pepper
Paprika

Slice eggs lengthwise. Remove yolks; mash and mix with remaining ingredients except paprika. Stuff whites. Sprinkle tops with paprika.

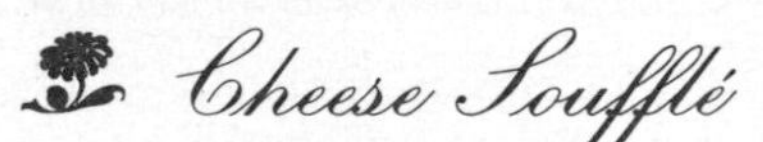

Cheese Soufflé

3 tablespoons butter or margarine
3 tablespoons flour
2 teaspoons Bon Appétit
Dash MSG
½ teaspoon dry Mustard
⅛ teaspoon ground Red Pepper
1¼ cups milk
½ pound Cheddar cheese, grated
5 eggs, separated

Melt butter; stir in flour, Bon Appétit, MSG, dry mustard and red pepper. Cook until bubbly but do not allow to brown. Remove from heat; stir in milk. Cook over low heat, stirring until thickened. Add cheese and stir until melted. Beat egg yolks; add a little of the cheese sauce to beaten yolks, then stir egg yolk mixture into remaining cheese sauce. Beat egg whites until stiff but not dry. Slowly pour cheese sauce into egg whites, carefully folding until evenly combined. Pour into 2-quart ungreased casserole. Bake in 300°F. oven 45 minutes or until set. Serve immediately. Excellent with crisp bacon and Herb Broiled Tomatoes (see recipe page 220).

Serves 5 to 6.

Welsh Rabbit

1 teaspoon Worcestershire sauce
⅛ teaspoon Paprika
½ teaspoon dry Mustard
Dash MSG
Dash ground Red Pepper
Dash Onion Powder
½ cup flat beer or light cream
1 pound sharp Cheddar cheese, crumbled

Combine Worcestershire sauce, paprika, dry mustard, MSG, red pepper and onion powder; mix to smooth paste. Combine with beer or cream in top pan of chafing dish over hot water. (May be made in double boiler.) Adjust flame to keep water hot but not boiling. Heat until beer or cream is hot. Add cheese and stir constantly until cheese melts. Serve hot over toast or waffles. Garnish with bacon if desired. *Serves 4.*

Busy Day Casserole

1 pound ground beef
½ cup chopped green pepper
3 tablespoons oil
2 tablespoons Instant Minced Onion
2 cups tomatoes (16-oz. can)
½ cup rice
1 teaspoon Chili Powder
1 teaspoon Season-All
2 teaspoons salt
¼ teaspoon Black Pepper
⅛ teaspoon ground Thyme

Cook ground beef and green pepper in oil until beef has lost its pink color and is crumbly. Add remaining ingredients, mixing well. Pour into greased 2-quart casserole; cover and bake in 350°F. oven 45 minutes.

Serves 4 to 5.

VEGETABLES

Vegetable Entrées

Baked Stuffed Eggplant 214
Broccoli Soufflé 214
Corn and Pepper Stroganoff 215
Corn Pudding 215
Eggplant Parmigiana 209
Old-Fashioned Baked Beans 209
Barbecued Baked Beans 209

Special Enough for Company

Asparagus Oriental 213
Asparagus Parmesan 222
Broiled Bananas 213
Brussels Sprouts with Chestnuts 211
Candied Sweet Potatoes 218
Candied Sweet Potatoes and Apples 218
Cauliflower with Creamy Cheese Sauce 208
Celery and Carrots in Parsley Cream 222
Clove-Studded Onions 213
Creamed Spinach 211
Delectable Green Beans 221
Ginger Glazed Carrots 208
Green Beans with Water Chestnuts 207
Italian Style Peas 212
Potatoes au Gratin 223
Sautéed Cabbage and Apples 216
Sautéed Mushrooms 216

Special Enough for Company (Cont.)

Sweet Potato Pudding 216
Sweet Potatoes—Pineapple Rings 21
Zucchini Parmesan 207

Old Favorites with New Appeal

Apple Cider Squash 217
Baked Acorn Squash 217
Carrots Vichy 218
Country-Good Baked Squash 217
Creamed Onions 219
Fresh Corn Sauté 219
Green Beans with Dill 220
Harvard Beets 219
Herb Broiled Tomatoes 220
Herb Seasoned Broccoli 220
Lima Bean Casserole 212
Minted Peas 221
Okra Southern Style 211
Parsley Buttered Potatoes 210
Dill Buttered Potatoes 210
Sauerkraut Caraway 210
Scalloped Potatoes with Cheese 207
Stewed Tomatoes with Oregano 210
Sweet-Sour Red Cabbage 221
Zucchini Sauté 212

Scalloped Potatoes with Cheese

6 baking potatoes, peeled and very thinly sliced
2 medium onions, peeled and thinly sliced
1½ cups shredded Cheddar cheese

In an 11¾ x 7½ x 1¾-inch baking dish, arrange ⅓ of the potatoes, ⅓ of the onion slices and ½ cup cheese. Sprinkle this layer with:

½ teaspoon Bon Appétit
⅛ teaspoon White Pepper
⅛ teaspoon Marjoram Leaves
⅛ teaspoon Thyme Leaves

Repeat these layers twice. Pour 3 cups milk between and around potatoes. Bake in 350°F. oven 1½ to 2 hours or until potatoes are tender. *Serves 6.*

Green Beans with Water Chestnuts

2 9-ounce packages frozen French-style green beans
1 8½-ounce can water chestnuts
¼ cup butter
½ teaspoon salt
¼ teaspoon Pepper
½ teaspoon Marjoram Leaves
½ teaspoon Tarragon Leaves
2 teaspoons lemon juice

Cook beans following package directions. Drain water chestnuts, cut in very thin slices. Melt butter and stir in remaining ingredients. Add water chestnuts and seasoned butter to beans. Toss to mix well. Heat to steaming and serve immediately. *Makes 3½ cups.*

Zucchini Parmesan

1½ pounds zucchini
2 teaspoons Chicken Flavor Base
1 tablespoon Instant Minced Onion
¼ teaspoon Ginger
1 teaspoon Season-All
2 tomatoes
¼ cup water
2 tablespoons butter
Parmesan cheese

Wash zucchini but do not peel. Slice in rounds about ¼ inch thick. Mix together chicken flavor base, onion, ginger and Season-All; sprinkle over zucchini and toss until seasoning is well distributed. Slice tomatoes into wedges and put on top of zucchini. Add water; bring to a boil and simmer slowly about 20 minutes. Drain. Add butter and toss gently. Sprinkle generously with Parmesan cheese. *Serves 4.*

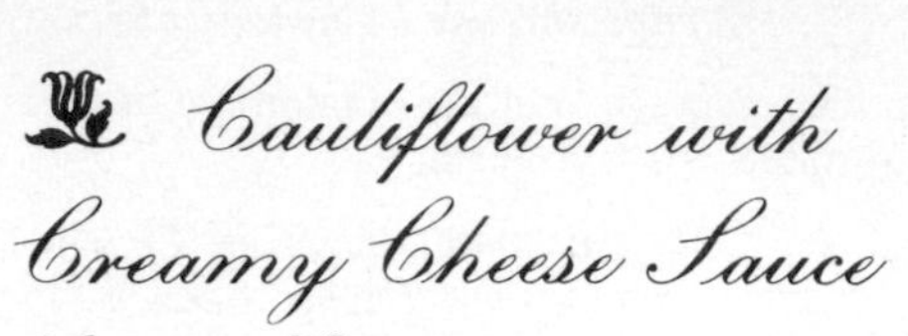

Cauliflower with Creamy Cheese Sauce

1 large cauliflower
2 teaspoons Chicken Flavor Base
1 cup warm water
2 tablespoons butter
1 tablespoon Arrowroot
¼ teaspoon salt
¼ teaspoon White Pepper
½ teaspoon dry Mustard
½ teaspoon Onion Powder
1 cup milk or light cream
¾ cup grated sharp cheese

Wash cauliflower and cut off heavy stalks and leaves. Put in saucepan. Combine 1 teaspoon of the flavor base with water; pour over cauliflower. Cover and bring to boil then simmer 25 minutes or until tender. Drain. Melt butter; stir in the remaining 1 teaspoon flavor base, arrowroot, salt, pepper, dry mustard and onion powder. Add milk and cook over low heat, stirring constantly, until sauce thickens. Stir in cheese and continue cooking until cheese melts. Pour over cauliflower in serving dish. Garnish with radish roses, or you may prefer to sprinkle with paprika or toasted slivered almonds.

Serves 4.

Ginger Glazed Carrots

The spiciest carrots you can imagine, marvelous with pork.

1 bunch carrots
1 teaspoon Chicken Flavor Base
1 teaspoon Bon Appétit
1 teaspoon sugar
¾ cup water
4 tablespoons butter
1 tablespoon lemon juice
3 tablespoons honey
½ teaspoon Ginger
¼ teaspoon Nutmeg
Parsley Flakes

Clean carrots and cut into rounds. Put in skillet with flavor base, Bon Appétit, sugar, water and 1 tablespoon of the butter. Cover; cook 12 minutes; drain. Add the remaining butter, lemon juice, honey, ginger and nutmeg to carrots. Cook, uncovered, over medium heat 2 to 3 minutes, tossing frequently to thoroughly glaze carrots. Sprinkle with parsley flakes just before serving.

Serves 4.

Eggplant Parmigiana

- 1 large or 2 medium eggplant
- Oil for frying
- 2 cups tomatoes (16-oz. can)
- 1 6-ounce can tomato paste
- ¼ teaspoon Garlic Powder
- 1½ teaspoons Season-All
- ⅛ teaspoon Black Pepper
- 1 tablespoon Parsley Flakes
- 1 Bay Leaf
- ½ cup grated Parmesan cheese
- 2 cups soft bread crumbs
- ½ pound Mozzarella cheese, sliced

Cut eggplant into ½-inch slices and peel. Sauté in oil 5 minutes or until tender and lightly browned. Remove and keep warm. In skillet combine tomatoes, tomato paste, garlic powder, Season-All, pepper, parsley flakes and bay leaf. Cover and simmer 15 minutes. Remove bay leaf; add Parmesan cheese and bread crumbs, mixing well. Place a layer of eggplant in buttered, shallow 2-quart baking dish. Cover with half the tomato sauce then with half the Mozzarella cheese. Repeat layers. Bake in 350°F. oven 20 minutes or until cheese melts and is lightly browned. Serve at once. You will find this dish excellent for Lent. *Serves 5 to 6.*

Old-Fashioned Baked Beans

- 1 pound dried marrow, navy or pea beans
- ½ teaspoon baking soda
- 2 cups dark brown sugar, packed
- 4 cups tomato juice
- 2 teaspoons Bon Appétit
- ¼ teaspoon Cloves
- ⅛ teaspoon Cardamom
- 2 tablespoons Instant Minced Onion
- ½ teaspoon dry Mustard
- 1 teaspoon prepared horseradish
- ⅛ teaspoon Black Pepper
- 8 slices bacon

Wash beans; cover with cold water and soak overnight. Drain; cover with fresh water and add soda. Bring to a boil and cook 35 minutes or until beans are tender. Drain and rinse with cold water. Combine brown sugar, tomato juice and seasonings; pour over beans. Cut bacon into 1- to 2-inch pieces; add to beans and mix thoroughly. Put beans in a 3-quart bean pot or casserole. Cover. Bake in 300°F. oven 5 hours or until tender. Add hot water if beans become dry during baking. Remove cover during last 30 minutes of baking. This is a favorite patio food that is excellent to serve with baked ham or broiled chicken. *Makes about 2 quarts.*

VARIATION:

Barbecued Baked Beans—Add 1 tablespoon Barbecue Spice to the above recipe and proceed as directed.

Parsley Buttered Potatoes

1½ pounds small whole potatoes
½ cup water
1 teaspoon Chicken Flavor Base
¼ cup butter
1 teaspoon Parsley Flakes
1 teaspoon Season-All

Wash and peel potatoes. Put in saucepan with water and flavor base. Bring to a boil; reduce heat and cook until tender, 20 to 25 minutes. Drain. Melt butter; add seasonings. Pour over potatoes. Serve hot. *Serves 4 to 6.*

VARIATION:

Dill Buttered Potatoes—Substitute ½ teaspoon Dill Weed for parsley flakes in above recipe.

Stewed Tomatoes with Oregano

1 quart tomatoes (2 16-oz. cans)
½ teaspoon Oregano Leaves
¼ teaspoon Basil Leaves
2 tablespoons Chopped Instant Onions
1 teaspoon salt
Dash Black Pepper
1 tablespoon sugar
1 tablespoon butter
1 tablespoon Arrowroot
1 tablespoon cold water
1 slice bread, optional

Cut whole tomatoes into pieces; add oregano leaves, basil leaves, onions, salt, pepper and sugar. Bring to a boil, reduce heat and simmer, uncovered, 15 minutes. Add butter. Mix together arrowroot and cold water and stir into tomatoes. Continue cooking to thicken. If a still thicker consistency is desired, remove crust from bread; cut bread into small cubes and add to tomatoes just before serving. This is a wonderful vegetable to serve with any starchy food, such as potatoes au gratin, macaroni and cheese, rice or noodles, as well as many fish dishes. *Serves 5 to 6.*

L.C. Sauerkraut Caraway

1 27-oz. can sauerkraut
½ cup port wine
2 teaspoons Caraway Seed
½ teaspoon dry Mustard
1 teaspoon Instant Minced Onion
1 tablespoon sugar

Combine all ingredients in a saucepan; cover. Simmer 2 hours. A favorite with sausage, frankfurters, spareribs and roast pork. In a few sections of the country this is a traditional dish served with the Thanksgiving turkey. *Serves 4.*

Brussels Sprouts with Chestnuts

Rich and wonderful for holiday dinners.

1½ cups canned chestnuts
or ½ pound chestnuts
2 tablespoons melted butter
½ teaspoon Season-All
⅛ teaspoon Savory
¼ teaspoon Basil Leaves
Dash Nutmeg
½ cup water
1½ teaspoons Chicken Flavor Base
¼ teaspoon Black Pepper
1 pint fresh Brussels sprouts or 1 package frozen Brussels sprouts

Drain chestnuts and put in shallow pan; cover with mixture of butter, Season-All, savory, basil leaves and nutmeg. (When fresh chestnuts are used, make a slit in skin. Cover with water and boil 25 minutes; cool and peel before using.) Bake in 325°F. oven 20 minutes, stirring once. Add water, flavor base and pepper to Brussels sprouts. Cook 10 minutes or until tender; drain. Carefully toss together chestnuts and Brussels sprouts; serve hot. *Serves 4.*

Okra Southern Style

1 10-ounce package frozen okra
or 2 cups sliced, fresh okra
¼ cup corn meal
1 teaspoon Season-All
¼ teaspoon Onion Powder
¼ teaspoon Black Pepper
Dash MSG
¼ teaspoon Celery Salt
½ cup salad oil

Trim ends off okra. Cut into ¼-inch slices. Dredge in mixture of corn meal and seasonings. Fry in hot oil 15 minutes or until crisp and brown. Drain on absorbent paper. If preferred, you may leave okra in whole pods and fry exactly as above. *Serves 4.*

Creamed Spinach

1 10-ounce package frozen chopped spinach
¼ teaspoon Onion Salt
½ teaspoon Bon Appétit
Dash MSG
Dash Mace
½ cup dairy sour cream

Place spinach in saucepan. Do not add water. Cover and bring to boil; separate with fork. Simmer until just tender, about 2 minutes. Drain thoroughly. Combine with seasonings and sour cream and purée in a blender. If you do not have a blender, you may put spinach through a coarse sieve, food mill or food grinder, then combine with seasonings and sour cream. This dish will be liked by those who think they don't like spinach. Excellent with steaks and chops. *Serves 3 to 4.*

Italian Style Peas

1 tablespoon Instant Minced Onion
1 teaspoon Parsley Flakes
¼ teaspoon Basil Leaves
2 slices boiled ham, shredded (about ½ cup)
1 tablespoon olive oil
1 teaspoon Chicken Flavor Base
½ cup water
⅛ teaspoon Black Pepper
1 10-ounce package frozen peas or 2 cups fresh or canned peas
1 tablespoon butter

Sauté onion, parsley flakes, basil leaves and shredded ham in olive oil over low to medium heat about 5 minutes, stirring frequently. Add flavor base, water and pepper; stir. (Tap the package of peas on edge of cabinet to break peas apart.) Add peas and butter. Cover. Bring to a boil and simmer slowly 25 minutes or until peas are tender. An excellent and different way to serve peas. Especially good with chicken, veal, beef or omelets. *Serves 4.*

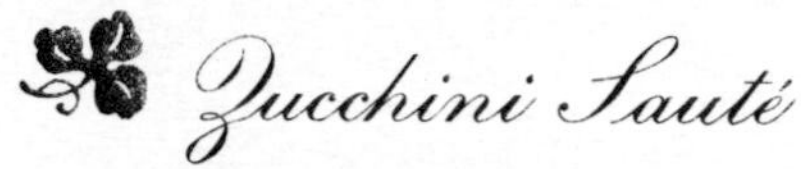

Zucchini Sauté

4 medium-size zucchini
¼ teaspoon White Pepper or Black Pepper
2 teaspoons Season-All
Dash Garlic Powder
2 teaspoons Parsley Flakes
½ teaspoon ground Oregano
1 teaspoon Instant Minced Onion
¼ cup olive oil

Wash zucchini but do not peel. Slice in rounds about ¼ inch thick. Mix together remaining ingredients except olive oil. Sprinkle over zucchini and toss until seasoning is well distributed. Heat oil in skillet; add zucchini and sauté until browned on both sides, about 10 minutes. Drain on absorbent paper. This is a quick and tasty way to cook zucchini and it goes well with any meat. *Serves 4.*

Lima Bean Casserole

1 10-ounce package frozen lima beans
¼ cup water
1 tablespoon Instant Minced Onion
½ teaspoon Lemon Peel
1 teaspoon Bon Appétit
¼ teaspoon Black Pepper
1 10½-ounce can condensed cream of mushroom soup

Cook beans in water 15 minutes or until just tender. Drain. Put beans in 1-quart casserole and sprinkle with onion, lemon peel, Bon Appétit and pepper. Spoon undiluted soup over top. Cover. Bake in 350°F. oven 45 minutes. Excellent with most meats. *Serves 4.*

Clove-Studded Onions

1 16-oz. can whole onions (2 cups)
Whole Cloves
1 teaspoon Season-All
½ teaspoon Chicken Flavor Base
1 tablespoon butter

Empty can of onions with liquid into small saucepan. Stud each onion with a whole clove. Add Season-All and flavor base. Bring to a boil; lower heat and simmer about 15 minutes. Drain. Toss with butter. For added color you may sprinkle with paprika. *Serves 4.*

Broiled Bananas

A new way to serve bananas.

6 bananas
¼ cup lemon or lime juice
¼ cup melted butter
1 tablespoon sugar
½ teaspoon Cinnamon
⅛ teaspoon Mace
¼ teaspoon Allspice

Peel bananas; brush entire surface with lemon juice and place in a shallow baking pan or in the bottom of a broiler pan. Brush with butter. Combine sugar and spices; spoon on top of bananas. Drizzle with butter. Broil 4 to 5 inches from heat 10 minutes or until nicely browned. Baste with juices in pan once while broiling. Serve with ham, chicken, veal, pork, lamb or curried dishes. *Serves 6.*

Asparagus Oriental

1½ pounds fresh asparagus or 1 10-ounce package frozen asparagus spears
3 tablespoons butter
1 teaspoon Chicken Flavor Base
1 teaspoon Season-All
⅛ teaspoon Celery Salt
⅛ teaspoon Ginger
Dash White Pepper
Dash MSG
1 teaspoon soy sauce

When using fresh asparagus, wash and break off stalks as far down as they snap easily. Slice either fresh or the frozen spears at an extreme angle to make diagonal slices about ¼ inch thick. Melt butter in skillet; add flavor base, Season-All, celery salt, ginger, pepper and MSG, mixing well. Add asparagus; toss gently. Cover and cook over high heat 2 minutes or until crisp-tender, stirring two or three times. Add soy sauce and mix well. Serve piping hot. *Serves 4 to 5.*

Baked Stuffed Eggplant

1 large eggplant
3 tablespoons Chopped Instant Onions
1 green pepper, finely minced
1 large tomato, finely chopped
3 tablespoons butter
1 teaspoon Chicken Flavor Base
¼ cup water
½ teaspoon salt
¼ teaspoon Black Pepper
¼ teaspoon MSG
¼ teaspoon Herb Seasoning
1½ cups finely minced or ground ham or any other leftover meat
¾ cup grated sharp cheese
½ cup bread crumbs
1 tablespoon melted butter

Cut eggplant in half lengthwise; remove inside pulp leaving a firm shell about ¼ inch thick. Cover shells with salted water and set aside while preparing filling. Dice eggplant pulp and put in skillet along with onions, green pepper, tomato, the 3 tablespoons butter, flavor base and water. Mix well. Cover and cook 15 minutes or until tender. Remove cover and continue cooking until all liquid is gone. Add salt, seasonings, ham and ½ cup of the cheese; mix well. Drain shells; fill with ham mixture. Bake in 350°F. oven 30 minutes. Remove from oven; sprinkle top with the remaining ¼ cup grated cheese. Toss bread crumbs with the 1 tablespoon melted butter; sprinkle over top. Continue baking 15 minutes longer or until crumbs are lightly browned.

Serves 4 to 6.

Broccoli Soufflé

3 tablespoons butter
3 tablespoons flour
2 teaspoons Instant Minced Onion
1 teaspoon salt
⅛ teaspoon Black Pepper
⅛ teaspoon Nutmeg
Dash ground Red Pepper
1 cup milk
1 cup minced, cooked broccoli
1 tablespoon lemon juice
4 eggs, separated
¼ teaspoon Cream of Tartar

Melt butter; stir in flour, onion, salt, pepper, nutmeg and red pepper. Cook until bubbly then remove from heat. Stir in milk and cook over low heat until thickened, stirring constantly. Remove from heat; add broccoli and lemon juice. Beat egg yolks until thick and add to broccoli mixture, stirring quickly. Cool slightly. Beat egg whites with cream of tartar until stiff but not dry. Fold into broccoli mixture; pour into buttered 1½-quart casserole. Bake in pan of hot water in 350°F. oven 40 minutes or until silver knife inserted in center comes out clean. You will find this good with any meal but especially ideal to serve with ham, chicken, turkey, beef or veal.

Makes 6 servings.

Corn Pudding

So good you can make a meal of it.

1 12-ounce can corn niblets
2 17-oz. cans cream style corn (4 cups)
5 eggs, lightly beaten
½ cup sugar
3 tablespoons Arrowroot
1½ teaspoons Season-All
½ teaspoon dry Mustard
1 teaspoon Instant Minced Onion
Dash ground Red or White Pepper
½ cup milk
½ cup melted butter

If the vacuum packed niblets are not available, whole kernel corn, drained, may be used. Mix together corn and eggs. Combine sugar, arrowroot, Season-All, dry mustard, onion and red pepper, stir into corn mixture. Add milk and butter, mixing well. Pour into a buttered 2½- to 3-quart casserole. Bake, uncovered, in 400°F. oven 1 hour or until silver knife comes out clean when inserted near center. Stir once after 30 minutes cooking. Serve immediately from the casserole in which it was cooked. *Serves 8.*

Corn and Pepper Stroganoff

Deliciously different. An excellent side dish—good with sandwiches too.

4 ounces sausage (about 3 links or 3 patties)
1 17-oz. can whole kernel corn, drained
2 tablespoons Bell Pepper Flakes
¼ teaspoon MSG
½ teaspoon Bon Appétit
1 8-ounce can tomato sauce
1 cup dairy sour cream

Cut sausage into small pieces; fry until browned. Pour off grease. Add drained corn, pepper flakes, MSG, Bon Appétit and tomato sauce; mix well. Cover and simmer 15 minutes. Cool a few minutes then stir in sour cream. Place over low heat 15 minutes, but do not let it boil. *Serves 4.*

NOTE: The first steps may be prepared well in advance, setting aside until time to serve, then add sour cream and heat very slowly, never allowing mixture to come to a boil.

Sautéed Cabbage and Apples

2 large tart apples
⅓ cup butter
8 cups coarsely shredded cabbage
¼ cup Chopped Instant Onions
1 teaspoon Season-All
½ teaspoon Nutmeg
3 tablespoons cider vinegar
2 teaspoons sugar
Dash ground Red Pepper
¼ cup chopped pecans or walnuts, optional

Peel, core and chop apples. Melt butter (bacon drippings may be used if you prefer); add apples, cabbage, onions, Season-All and nutmeg. Mix well. Cover and cook over low heat 20 minutes, stirring frequently. Combine vinegar, sugar and red pepper, add to cabbage. Cook 5 minutes longer. Stir in nuts or serve with nuts sprinkled over top. This is one of those dishes you will find even better when reheated. Excellent served with pork, duckling, goose and game.

Serves 4 to 5.

½ pound fresh mushrooms
2 teaspoons lemon juice
2 tablespoons butter or margarine
¼ teaspoon salt
¼ teaspoon Season-All
⅛ teaspoon Black Pepper
⅛ teaspoon MSG

Wash, dry and slice mushrooms. Sprinkle with lemon juice. Melt butter and stir in seasonings. Add mushrooms and sauté about 7 minutes until delicately browned, stirring frequently. You may serve as a main vegetable or as an accompaniment to steaks, chops, sautéed chicken livers, roast beef or omelets.

Serves 2 to 4, depending on how used.

An old-time favorite, spicy and good.

¼ cup butter or margarine
¾ cup sugar
2 eggs
½ teaspoon Pumpkin Pie Spice
¼ teaspoon salt
1½ cups milk (use part cream for richer flavor)
2½ cups grated, raw sweet potatoes

Cream butter and sugar. Mix in eggs, pumpkin pie spice, salt and milk. Fold in grated sweet potatoes. Pour into a buttered, shallow 2-quart baking dish and bake in 400°F. oven 1 hour. You will want to take the pudding right from the oven to table and serve with pork roast, baked ham or chicken.

Serves 4 to 6.

Country-Good Baked Squash

2 pounds small yellow squash
3 tablespoons Instant Minced Onion
¼ cup water
¼ cup butter, melted
½ cup milk
2 eggs, beaten
½ teaspoon salt
¼ teaspoon Black Pepper
1 teaspoon Parsley Flakes
½ teaspoon Tarragon Leaves
2 tablespoons butter, melted
½ cup cracker crumbs

Wash, but do not peel, squash and cut into small pieces. Add onion and water. Cook about 10 minutes or until just tender, taking care not to overcook. Drain squash and transfer to 1½-quart baking dish. Pour the ¼ cup melted butter over squash. Combine milk, eggs and seasonings and pour over all. Combine the 2 tablespoons melted butter and cracker crumbs; sprinkle over top. Bake in 450°F. oven 20 minutes. *Serves 6 to 8.*

Baked Acorn Squash

2 acorn squash
½ cup water
¼ cup brown sugar, packed
¼ cup butter
¼ teaspoon Black Pepper
½ teaspoon Season-All
¼ teaspoon Basil Leaves, crumbled

Wash squash and cut in half; remove seed. Place cut side down in shallow baking dish containing water. Bake in 350°F. oven 45 minutes. Turn cut side up. Put 1 tablespoon brown sugar and 1 tablespoon butter in each half. Sprinkle with pepper, Season-All and basil leaves. Return to oven and bake 15 minutes longer. *Serves 4.*

Apple Cider Squash

The seasonings make frozen squash extra special.

1 package frozen cooked squash (1¼ cups)
2 tablespoons butter
½ teaspoon salt
⅛ teaspoon Mace
⅛ teaspoon Cinnamon
Dash Black Pepper
⅓ cup apple cider

Place frozen squash in buttered 1½-quart casserole. Add butter, salt, mace, cinnamon and pepper. Pour cider over squash. Cover and bake in 350°F. oven 45 minutes, stirring once during baking period. *Serves 4.*

Sweet Potatoes—Pineapple Rings

2 cups cooked, mashed sweet potatoes
⅔ cup brown sugar, packed
¼ cup butter, melted
½ cup orange juice
1 teaspoon Pumpkin Pie Spice
1 teaspoon Orange Peel
¼ cup chopped pecans
½ cup raisins
1 16-oz. can sliced pineapple
Miniature marshmallows

Combine sweet potatoes, brown sugar, butter, orange juice, pumpkin pie spice, orange peel, pecans and raisins, mixing well. Drain pineapple slices and place in baking dish. Mound ⅓ cup of the sweet potato mixture on top of each pineapple slice. Bake in 375°F. oven 20 minutes. Top with marshmallows and bake 5 minutes longer. *Makes 10 servings.*

2 pounds sweet potatoes
½ cup brown sugar, packed
1 cup orange juice
1 tablespoon Orange Peel
1 teaspoon Pumpkin Pie Spice
⅓ cup sherry
2 tablespoons butter

Boil potatoes in salted water 30 minutes or until almost tender. Drain; peel and cut into serving-size pieces. (Or dry-packed canned sweet potatoes may be used if preferred.) Place potatoes in shallow 1½-quart baking dish. Combine remaining ingredients and bring to a boil, stirring; boil 3 minutes. Pour over potatoes. Bake in 350°F. oven 1 hour, basting often to glaze well. *Serves 4.*

VARIATION:

Candied Sweet Potatoes and Apples—Peel, core and quarter 2 medium-size cooking apples. Place along with sweet potatoes in baking dish and continue as in above recipe.

L.C. Carrots Vichy

6 medium-size carrots
½ cup water
1 teaspoon Chicken Flavor Base
Dash Onion Powder
Dash MSG
2 tablespoons lemon juice
2 tablespoons butter
1 teaspoon Parsley Flakes

Scrape carrots and cut into thin slices. Add water, flavor base, onion powder and MSG. Cook 15 minutes or until tender; drain. Add remaining ingredients and toss gently. *Serves 4 to 5.*

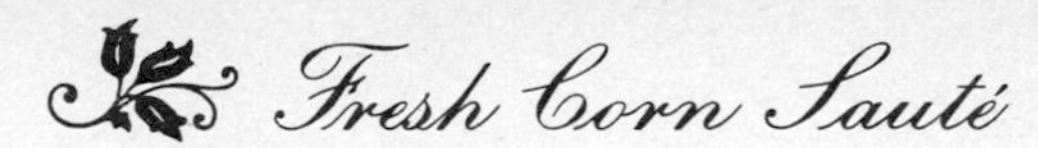

Fresh Corn Sauté

A summertime treat.

4 cups fresh corn (5 to 6 ears)
2 tablespoons butter
1 teaspoon Instant Minced Onion
2 teaspoons Arrowroot
¼ teaspoon White Pepper
1½ teaspoons Bon Appétit
½ teaspoon salt
1 teaspoon sugar
¾ cup milk

Cut corn from cob and measure. Melt butter; add onion and corn. Cook 1 minute, stirring. Mix in arrowroot, pepper, Bon Appétit, salt and sugar. Pour milk into corn mixture. Simmer 20 minutes, stirring frequently to prevent corn from sticking. Garnish with strips of pimiento if desired.

Serves 4 to 5.

Creamed Onions

This is a favorite holiday dish.

2 tablespoons butter
2 tablespoons flour
1 teaspoon salt
⅛ teaspoon White Pepper
1 teaspoon Bon Appétit
¼ teaspoon dry Mustard
Dash MSG
1 cup milk
1 16-oz. can whole white onions, drained

Melt butter in saucepan; stir in flour and seasonings. Cook over low heat, allowing to bubble 1 minute. Remove from heat and add milk. Return to heat and cook, stirring, until thickened. Add onions and continue cooking until onions are heated through.

Serves 4.

Harvard Beets

1 16-oz. can sliced or whole beets
¼ cup cider vinegar
¼ cup sugar
4 teaspoons Arrowroot
½ teaspoon Orange Peel
⅛ teaspoon Cloves
1 tablespoon butter

Drain beets, reserving the juice. Combine beet juice, vinegar, sugar, arrowroot, orange peel and cloves in small saucepan. Cook over medium heat, stirring constantly, until sauce thickens. Stir in beets and butter; simmer 5 minutes or until beets are thoroughly heated. This sweet-sour vegetable adds sparkle to any meal.

Serves 4.

Herb Broiled Tomatoes

4 tomatoes
¼ cup butter, melted
1 teaspoon Season-All
½ teaspoon Herb Seasoning
¼ teaspoon Oregano Leaves
¼ teaspoon MSG
½ teaspoon sugar
½ cup soft bread crumbs

Wash tomatoes; slice in half and place in broiler pan, cut side up. Brush with 1 tablespoon of the butter. Combine Season-All, Herb Seasoning, oregano leaves, MSG and sugar. Sprinkle over tomatoes. Broil 4 inches from heat 5 to 7 minutes. Pour remaining butter over bread crumbs and toss well. Spoon bread crumbs evenly over top of tomatoes and continue to broil 5 minutes or until bread crumbs are toasted. Excellent served with steaks or chops.

Serves 8.

L.C. Herb Seasoned Broccoli

1 10-ounce package frozen or 2 pounds fresh broccoli spears
½ cup hot water
1 teaspoon Chicken Flavor Base
½ teaspoon Marjoram Leaves
½ teaspoon Basil Leaves
¼ teaspoon Onion Powder
Dash Nutmeg
1 tablespoon butter

Place broccoli in saucepan. Combine water and flavor base; pour over broccoli, then sprinkle with the seasonings. Cover and bring to a boil; separate broccoli spears with fork. Simmer 6 minutes or until tender; drain. Add butter. Serve with Creamy Lemon-Butter Sauce (see recipe page 370).

Serves 3 to 4.

L.C. Green Beans with Dill

1 9-ounce package frozen green beans
¼ cup water
1 teaspoon Dill Weed or Dill Seed
1 teaspoon Beef Flavor Base
¼ teaspoon salt
2 tablespoons butter or margarine

Place frozen beans in saucepan with water, dill weed or seed, beef flavor base and salt. Cover; bring to a boil. Separate beans with fork, reduce heat and simmer 10 minutes or until tender. Drain. Toss lightly with butter.

Serves 3 to 4.

NOTE: In place of the frozen beans, you may use 2 cups fresh or canned green beans.

Minted Peas

1 10-ounce package frozen peas
¼ cup water
1 3½-ounce bottle cocktail onions, drained
1 tablespoon butter
½ teaspoon Mint Flakes, crushed
¼ teaspoon MSG
1½ teaspoons Chicken Flavor Base

Combine all ingredients in saucepan. Cover. Bring to a boil then reduce heat to low and cook 5 to 7 minutes. Minted Peas go well with any meat, but are especially good with lamb chops and leg of lamb. *Serves 4.*

NOTE: In place of the frozen peas, you may use 2 cups fresh or canned peas.

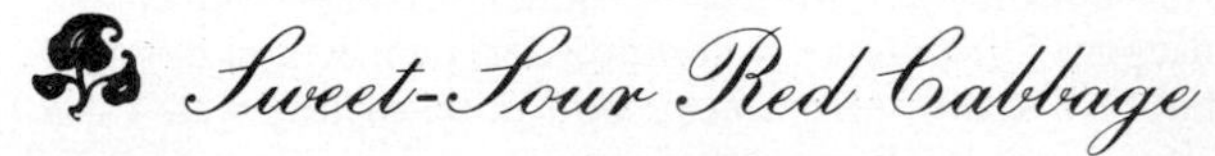

Sweet-Sour Red Cabbage

The German favorite, perfect with roast goose or fresh ham.

½ cup butter
2 tablespoons Chopped Instant Onions
¼ cup brown sugar, packed
1 teaspoon salt
½ teaspoon Black Pepper
1 teaspoon Allspice
¼ teaspoon Cloves
1 2-pound red cabbage, finely shredded
½ cup boiling water
½ cup wine vinegar

Melt butter in skillet; sauté onions until golden brown. Add sugar, seasonings and shredded cabbage; mix lightly. Add water, cover and simmer 1 hour. Add vinegar and simmer 10 minutes longer. This is pleasantly tart; should you prefer it milder, use only ¼ cup vinegar. Serve hot. *Serves 8.*

Delectable Green Beans

1 9-ounce package frozen French style green beans
¼ cup water
¼ teaspoon Instant Minced Onion
2 tablespoons butter
2 tablespoons flour
1¼ teaspoons Bon Appétit
¼ teaspoon Savory
⅛ teaspoon Black Pepper
½ cup dairy sour cream
¼ cup shredded Swiss cheese

Place beans, water and onion in saucepan. Cover. Simmer 8 minutes or until just tender; drain. Melt butter; blend in flour, Bon Appétit, savory and pepper. Add sour cream and cook until thickened, stirring constantly. Do not allow to boil. Fold in beans. Pour into lightly buttered 1-quart casserole and sprinkle cheese over top. Broil 4 inches from heat 4 minutes or until cheese melts. *Serves 3 to 4.*

Asparagus Parmesan

½ cup water
3½ teaspoons Season-All
2 pounds fresh asparagus or
  2 10-ounce packages frozen asparagus spears
1 cup coarse cracker crumbs
3 tablespoons butter
3 tablespoons flour
⅛ teaspoon Onion Powder
¼ teaspoon Black Pepper
¼ teaspoon dry Mustard
1½ cups milk
1 4-ounce can mushroom crowns
Parmesan cheese

Add water and 1½ teaspoons of the Season-All to asparagus. (When you use fresh asparagus, break stalks off as far down as they snap easily; wash well.) Cook about 10 minutes or until tender. Drain. Sprinkle cracker crumbs evenly over bottom of buttered 1½-quart shallow baking dish. Melt butter in saucepan. Stir in flour, onion powder, pepper and dry mustard; cook until bubbly. Remove from heat; add milk, mixing well. Cook over low heat, stirring, until thickened. Stir in mushrooms including liquid and pour over asparagus. Sprinkle with Parmesan cheese. Bake in 350°F. oven 30 minutes. This dish lends itself to entertaining. Can be made ahead, refrigerated and cooked just before serving. *Serves 6 to 8.*

Celery and Carrots in Parsley Cream

2 cups tender celery stalks, cut in 2-inch lengths
1 carrot, thinly sliced
½ teaspoon Rosemary Leaves, crushed
2 teaspoons Chicken Flavor Base
½ cup hot water
2 tablespoons butter
1½ teaspoons Arrowroot
¼ teaspoon salt
Dash Black Pepper
1 tablespoon Chopped Instant Onions
1 cup milk
½ teaspoon Parsley Flakes

Put celery, carrot and crushed rosemary in saucepan. Combine flavor base and water; pour over vegetables. Cover; bring to a boil then simmer 10 minutes or until tender. Drain vegetables and keep warm. Melt butter; stir in arrowroot, salt, pepper, onions and milk. Cook over medium heat, stirring, until sauce thickens. Stir in parsley flakes then pour over vegetables, mixing gently. *Serves 3 to 4.*

Potatoes au Gratin

1 teaspoon Chicken Flavor Base
1 cup hot water
4 large potatoes, peeled
3 tablespoons butter
2 tablespoons Arrowroot or ¼ cup flour
¼ teaspoon salt
¼ teaspoon White Pepper
1 teaspoon Season-All
¼ teaspoon dry Mustard
⅛ teaspoon Nutmeg
2 cups milk
1½ cups grated sharp cheese
1 cup soft bread crumbs
2 tablespoons melted butter
Paprika

Dissolve flavor base in water and pour over potatoes which have been quartered. Bring to a boil then simmer 20 minutes or until tender. Drain; cut into cubes and place in a buttered 1½-quart baking dish. Melt the 3 tablespoons butter in saucepan; stir in arrowroot, salt, pepper, Season-All, dry mustard and nutmeg. Add milk and cook over medium heat, stirring constantly, until smooth and thickened. Stir in 1 cup of the cheese and continue cooking until cheese melts. Pour over potatoes. Toss bread crumbs with the 2 tablespoons melted butter; spoon evenly over all. Top with the remaining cheese and sprinkle generously with paprika. Bake in 350°F. oven 20 minutes. You will find this a favorite of the men in your family.

Serves 4 to 6.

SPECIAL APPLIANCE COOKING

Food Processor

Chicken Liver Spread 228

Cold Cucumber Soup 228

Cranberry Nut Bread 229

Extra-Special Waffles 227

Gazpacho 227

Hot Cheese Snacks 227

Pottery-Lined Slow Cooker

Beef Stew 229

Chicken-Vegetable Soup 231

Chunky Chili 231

Crock Pot Beans 230

Pot Roast with Vegetables 230

Savory Fresh Ham 230

Toaster Oven

Baked Stuffed Tomatoes 232

Herbed Garlic and Cheese Bread 231

Hot Bleu Cheese Canapes 233

Special Turkey Sandwich on Waffles 232

Microwave Oven

Carrot and Cauliflower Casserole 235

Cinnamon Baked Apples 235

Hot Turkey Salad 234

Individual Chili Meatloaves 234

Manicotti 233

Trout with Seasoned Butter 234

Appliances can perform many different food preparation tasks. The microwave oven helps to conserve energy and reduce the time spent on cooking. The toaster oven, especially one designed for broiling, is versatile and convenient in one- or two-person households and busy families when mealtimes vary. The pottery-lined slow cooker brings out flavor in any dish requiring long, slow cooking. The food processor can be a wonderful time-saver. It can chop, grind, slice, shred and mix a great variety of foods.

Always read and follow the manufacturer's directions when using a new appliance. This is important for safety, and the instruction booklet contains many helpful ideas for full use of the appliance. Design features, functions and directions for operation vary.

Hot Cheese Snacks

1 10-ounce package sharp Cheddar cheese
8 slices uncooked bacon
1 large onion
1 teaspoon dry Mustard
1 tablespoon mayonnaise
1 teaspoon Freeze-Dried Chopped Chives
Party rye bread

Cut cheese, bacon and onion in pieces to fit the feed tube of food processor. Using metal blade, grind cheese, bacon and onion together. Add remaining ingredients and mix until smooth, scraping down bowl occasionally, if necessary. Chill. Divide into three portions on wax paper. Shape each into a log about 2 inches in diameter and 6 inches long. Wrap and freeze. Slice, while frozen, in ⅛ inch thick slices. Place each on a slice of party rye bread (2 x 2½ inches). Broil until bubbly and lightly browned.

Gazpacho

1 tablespoon Instant Minced Onion
½ teaspoon Garlic Salt
⅛ teaspoon Marjoram Leaves
¼ teaspon Parsley Flakes
1 teaspoon Freeze-Dried Chopped Chives
1 tablespoon red wine vinegar
1 tablespoon lemon juice
1 tablespoon olive oil
2 cups tomato juice
1 cucumber, peeled and cut up
1 ripe tomato, seeded and cut up
1 green pepper, seeded and cut up
1 cup croutons

Combine first 9 ingredients. In food processor, using metal blade, combine ¾ of the cucumber, the tomato and ½ of the green pepper. Process 10 seconds, scrape down, process 5 seconds longer. Add to tomato juice mixture. Coarsely chop remaining cucumber and green pepper and use to garnish gazpacho along with croutons. *Makes 4 cups.*

Extra-Special Waffles

½ cup butter
1 tablespoon sugar
3 eggs
2 teaspoons pure Vanilla Extract
2 cups sifted flour
3 teaspoons baking powder
½ teaspoon salt
¼ teaspoon Nutmeg
½ teaspoon Cinnamon
1½ cups milk

Process butter and sugar 20 seconds, scrape down, process 10 seconds longer. Add eggs and vanilla, process 5 seconds, scrape down, process 2 seconds longer. Mix together flour, baking powder, salt, nutmeg and cinnamon. Add to butter mixture. Process 3 to 4 times, 2 seconds each. Add milk, process 5 seconds. Bake in waffle iron. *Makes twelve 4 x 4-inch waffles.*

Chicken Liver Spread

1 pound chicken livers
1 teaspoon Chicken Flavor Base
1 cup water
1 Bay Leaf
¼ teaspoon Black Pepper
⅛ teaspoon Celery Seed
¼ teaspoon Marjoram Leaves
1 tablespoon Instant Minced Onion
Dash ground Red Pepper
3 hard-cooked eggs
2 tablespoons butter
½ teaspoon Bon Appétit
1 tablespoon brandy

In saucepan, combine chicken livers with next 8 ingredients. Bring to boil, reduce heat and simmer 15 minutes. Drain. Remove bay leaf. Grind livers in food processor, using chopping blade. Add eggs and butter. Process until smooth. Spoon into small bowl. Stir in Bon Appétit and brandy. Chill.

Makes 2 cups.

Cold Cucumber Soup

3 large cucumbers, peeled
2 teaspoons Instant Minced Onion
⅛ teaspoon Instant Minced Garlic
2 teaspoons Chicken Flavor Base
2 cups boiling water
1 tablespoon white vinegar
1 teaspoon Bon Appétit
1 pint dairy sour cream
Radishes

Cut cucumbers in 1¼-inch pieces. Start food processor, using metal blade, and drop cucumber pieces through feed tube. Add onion and garlic. Process until smooth. Pour into large bowl. Dissolve chicken flavor base in boiling water. Add to cucumber mixture. Stir in vinegar and Bon Appétit. Cool. Stir in sour cream and chill one hour before serving. Garnish with thinly sliced radishes.

Makes 6 cups.

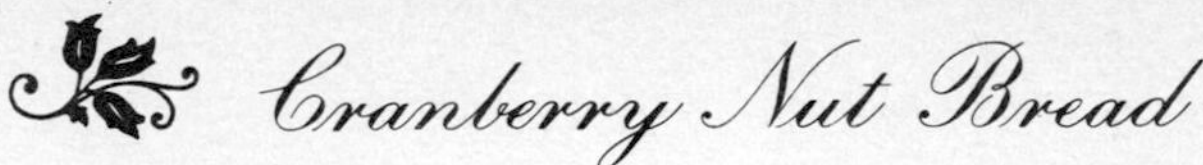

Cranberry Nut Bread

1 cup pecans
1⅓ cups whole cranberries
⅓ cup butter
⅔ cup sugar
3 eggs
1½ cups sifted flour
¼ teaspoon salt
1 teaspoon baking powder
½ teaspoon baking soda
½ teaspoon Cinnamon
½ teaspoon Orange Peel
¼ teaspoon Allspice

Coarsely chop pecans, using metal blade, 5 to 10 seconds. Pour into a large bowl. Process cranberries 10 to 15 seconds, or until finely chopped but not pureed. Add to nuts. Cream butter with sugar by processing 20 seconds, scrape down, process 10 seconds longer. Add eggs, process 2 to 3 times, 2 seconds each, or until blended. Mix flour with remaining six ingredients. Add to egg mixture and process 3 to 4 times, 2 seconds each, or until mixed. Add batter to cranberries and nuts. Stir just until mixed. Pour into greased and floured 8½ x 4½ x 3-inch loaf pan. Bake in 350°F. oven 50 minutes, or until bread tests done. *Makes one 8 x 4 x 2½-inch loaf.*

POTTERY-LINED SLOW COOKER

Beef Stew

2 pounds beef cubes for stew
⅓ cup flour
1½ teaspoons Season-All
¼ teaspoon ground Black Pepper
3 tablespoons salad oil
½ cup water
1 8-ounce can tomato sauce
1 Bay Leaf
1 tablespoon Instant Minced Onion
¼ teaspoon Thyme Leaves
¼ teaspoon Marjoram Leaves
¼ teaspoon Celery Seed
½ teaspoon Season-All
Dash crushed Red Pepper
2 stalks celery, cut in bite-size pieces
3 medium carrots, peeled and cut in bite-size pieces

Dredge meat in flour mixed with Season-All and pepper. In large skillet, brown meat in hot oil. Put meat in pottery-lined slow cooker. Add remaining ingredients except celery and carrots. Stir to mix well. Cook at high setting 1 to 1½ hours. Add celery and carrots. Cook 1 hour longer, or until vegetables are tender. *Makes 5 cups.*

Pot Roast with Vegetables

3 carrots, peeled
3 stalks celery
3 potatoes, peeled
1 tablespoon Beef Flavor Base
¼ teaspoon Oregano Leaves
¼ teaspoon Basil Leaves
⅛ teaspoon Thyme
2 tablespoons Instant Chopped Onion
1 8-ounce can stewed tomatoes
4 pounds bottom round roast
1½ teaspoons Season-All

Quarter carrots, celery and potatoes. Put in pottery-lined slow cooker. Add beef flavor base, oregano, basil, thyme, onion and tomatoes. Trim any excess fat from meat. Sprinkle with Season-All. Put meat on vegetables, cover and cook on high heat 4½ hours, or until meat is tender. Thicken cooking liquid for gravy if desired.

Makes 6 servings, 6 vegetable pieces and 9 ounces of meat each.

1 4 to 5-pound boned and rolled fresh ham
1 8-ounce can tomato sauce
1 tablespoon Beef Flavor Base
1 Bay Leaf
¼ teaspoon Ginger
½ teaspoon Thyme Leaves
½ teaspoon Tarragon Leaves
1 tablespoon Instant Minced Onion
½ teaspoon ground Black Pepper
2 cups water

Cut ham in half, if necessary, and put in pottery-lined slow cooker. Add remaining ingredients. Cover and cook at high setting 3 to 3½ hours, or until meat is tender. Remove meat and slice for serving. Skim fat off liquid. Serve juice over meat or thicken for gravy. There will be approximately 5 cups of juice. Save the excess for soup stock.

Serves 6 to 8.

Crock Pot Beans

1 pound navy beans
6 cups water
½ cup molasses
2 teaspoons dry Mustard
2 tablespoons Instant Minced Onion
¼ teaspoon Black Pepper
¼ teaspoon ground Thyme
1 teaspoon Ginger
2 teaspoons salt
2 slices bacon, diced

Rinse beans and combine with water in pottery-lined slow cooker. Cook at high setting 3 hours. Add remaining ingredients. Cook at high setting 4 hours, stirring occasionally.

Makes 7 cups.

Chicken-Vegetable Soup

5 cups water
2 tablespoons Chicken Flavor Base
2 cups cubed, cooked chicken
1 cup sliced celery
1 cup sliced carrots
1 10-ounce package frozen peas
½ cup long-grain rice, uncooked
1 tablespoon Instant Minced Onion
¼ teaspoon ground Black Pepper
Dash Thyme Leaves

Combine all ingredients in pottery-lined slow cooker. Cook at high setting 1½ hours, or until carrots are tender. *Makes 8 cups.*

Chunky Chili

1 pound stewing beef
3 16-ounce cans kidney beans, drained
1 16-ounce can tomatoes, drained
¼ cup Instant Chopped Onion
2 tablespoons Chili Powder
1 teaspoon Garlic Salt
1 teaspoon Season-All
½ teaspoon Oregano Leaves
1 tablespoon vinegar

Trim off excess fat and cut beef into ½-inch pieces. Put in pottery-lined slow cooker. Add remaining ingredients. Stir. Cook on high setting 3 hours, or until beef is tender. *Makes 7 cups.*

TOASTER OVEN

Herbed Garlic and Cheese Bread

1 20-inch loaf French bread (3 to 4-inch diameter)
½ cup (1 stick) butter
1 teaspoon Instant Minced Onion
1 teaspoon Oregano Leaves
½ teaspoon Garlic Powder
½ teaspoon Celery Seed
¼ teaspoon dry Mustard
1½ cups shredded Cheddar cheese

Cut bread in 1-inch slices. Place on toaster oven pan, a few at a time, or on cookie sheet. Preheat oven to 400°F. Melt butter and stir in next 5 ingredients. Brush over bread slices. Top with cheese. Bake in 400°F. oven or toaster oven 15 minutes, or until cheese is bubbly. Serve hot. *Makes 18 slices.*

Baked Stuffed Tomatoes

4 medium-large tomatoes
1 4-ounce can sliced mushrooms, drained
1 tablespoon Instant Minced Onion
¼ teaspoon Season-All
¼ teaspoon Garlic Salt
Dash Black Pepper
1 teaspoon Parsley Flakes

Wash and cut tops from tomatoes. Scoop out insides. Discard seeds; coarsely chop tomato pulp. Combine with mushrooms and next 5 ingredients. Divide equally among tomato shells.

TOPPING:
¼ cup fine dry bread crumbs
¼ teaspoon Season-All
⅛ teaspoon Basil Leaves
4 teaspoons butter
4 tablespoons shredded cheese

Combine bread crumbs, Season-All and basil leaves. Top each tomato with about 1 tablespoon of this mixture. Place a pat of butter on top of bread crumbs. Bake on baking tray at 350°F., 15 minutes. Top each tomato with 1 tablespoon of shredded cheese and bake 5 minutes longer.

Makes 4 servings, 1 tomato each.

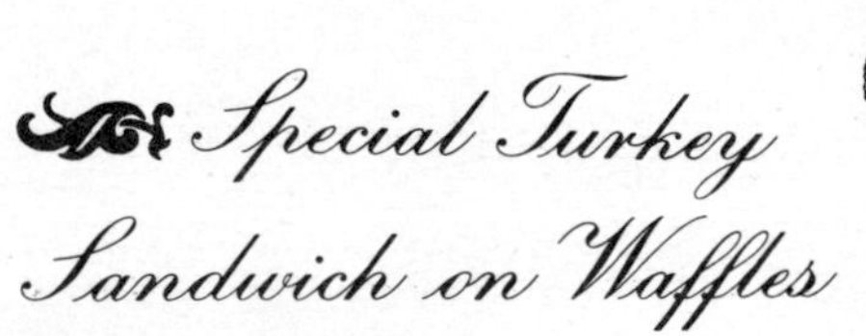

Special Turkey Sandwich on Waffles

4 square toaster waffles
4 slices turkey
4 slices ham
6 slices cooked bacon
1 tablespoon butter
1 tablespoon flour
⅛ teaspoon Season-All
⅛ teaspoon dry Mustard
⅛ teaspoon Onion Powder
⅓ cup milk
½ cup shredded Cheddar cheese

Toast waffles lightly. Place 1 slice each of turkey and ham and 1½ slices bacon on each waffle. In small saucepan, melt butter over medium-low heat; stir in flour, Season-All, mustard and onion powder. Cook until bubbly. Stir in milk and cook, stirring constantly, until mixture thickens. Reduce heat, add cheese and continue to cook, stirring, until smooth. Spoon sauce over sandwiches. Place on baking tray and top-brown 2 minutes, or until sauce begins to brown.

Makes 4 sandwiches.

Hot Bleu Cheese Canapes

3 ounces cream cheese
2 ounces bleu cheese
2 teaspoons butter
¼ teaspoon Poppy Seed
⅛ teaspoon Bon Appétit
Dash Black Pepper
⅛ teaspoon Marjoram Leaves

Bring cheeses and butter to room temperature. Add remaining ingredients. Mix well. Spread on crackers. Place on baking tray and top-brown 1 minute, or until cheese begins to melt. *Makes ⅔ cup spread.*

MICROWAVE OVEN

Manicotti

FILLING:

½ 8-ounce package manicotti noodles
½ pound Italian sausage
1 pound ricotta cheese
1 egg, beaten
1 teaspoon Parsley Flakes
½ teaspoon Garlic Salt
⅛ teaspoon Black Pepper
¼ teaspoon Basil Leaves

Cook manicotti, following package directions. Crumble, cook and drain sausage. Combine with remaining ingredients. Carefully fill each manicotti noodle. Arrange in a single layer in 11 x 7 x 1½-inch baking dish.

SAUCE:

1 16-ounce can tomato sauce
1 tablespoon Instant Minced Onion
½ teaspoon Celery Salt
¼ teaspoon Italian Seasoning
⅛ teaspoon Black Pepper
4 ounces grated Mozzarella cheese

Combine all ingredients except cheese. Micro-cook 3 minutes at full power. Pour over filled manicotti noodles. Micro-cook, covered, 8 minutes. Remove cover. Sprinkle with Mozzarella cheese and micro-cook 7 minutes longer. *Makes 7 manicotti.*

Hot Turkey Salad

1 cup cooked elbow macaroni
2 cups cubed, cooked turkey
½ cup sliced celery
¼ cup slivered green pepper
1 teaspoon Instant Minced Onion

½ cup mayonnaise
¾ teaspoon Season-All
⅛ teaspoon ground Black Pepper
⅛ teaspoon Dill Weed
¼ teaspoon Basil Leaves
Dash crushed Red Pepper

In 2-quart glass casserole, toss together macaroni, turkey, celery, green pepper and onion. Mix remaining ingredients. Add to turkey mixture and toss to mix well. Micro-cook at full power setting 8 to 10 minutes, stirring twice during cooking time. Serve hot. *Makes 3½ cups.*

Individual Chili Meatloaves

2 pounds ground beef
1 teaspoon Season-All
½ teaspoon ground Black Pepper
2 teaspoons Instant Minced Onion
⅛ teaspoon Nutmeg
1 egg

1 8-ounce can tomato sauce
½ teaspoon Season-All
⅛ teaspoon ground Black Pepper
½ teaspoon Instant Minced Onion
1 teaspoon Chili Powder

Lightly but thoroughly mix ground beef with next 5 ingredients. Shape into 6 individual meatloaves. Place in glass baking dish. Micro-cook at full power setting 10 to 12 minutes, turning dish twice during cooking time. Drain off excess fat, if desired. Mix remaining ingredients. Spoon over meatloaves and cook 5 to 7 minutes longer, turning dish twice during cooking. Let stand 5 minutes before serving. *Makes 6 servings, 1 meatloaf each.*

Trout with Seasoned Butter

2 12-inch trout
¼ cup butter, melted
½ teaspoon lemon juice
½ teaspoon Marjoram Leaves

½ teaspoon Bon Appétit
¼ teaspoon Paprika
1½ teaspoon Sesame Seeds
⅛ teaspoon White Pepper

Clean, scale and remove heads from trout. Place in glass baking dish. Combine remaining ingredients. Brush fish inside and out with part of butter mixture. Micro-cook 3 minutes at full power. Brush with additional butter mixture, turn fish and micro-cook 3 minutes longer. Serve whole.

Makes 2 servings, 1 fish each.

Carrot and Cauliflower Casserole

1 pound carrots
¼ cup butter
⅓ cup water
½ teaspoon Season-All
½ teaspoon Onion Powder
¾ teaspoon Basil Leaves
⅛ teaspoon black Pepper
1 small head cauliflower

Peel and cut carrots into 1-inch sticks, about ¼-inch thick. Put in shallow, 2-quart glass baking dish. Melt butter in water and stir in next 4 ingredients. Pour over carrots. Micro-cook at full power setting, covered, 5 minutes. Cut cauliflower into small flowerets. Add to carrots. Stir, cover and cook 5 minutes, turn dish, cook 5 to 7 minutes longer. Carefully remove cover, stir vegetables.

TOPPING:

½ cup fine, dry bread crumbs
½ cup shredded sharp Cheddar cheese
½ teaspoon Season-All
1 teaspoon Parsley Flakes

Combine all topping ingredients. Sprinkle over vegetables. Cook, uncovered, 4 minutes.

Makes 6 cups.

Cinnamon Baked Apples

6 cooking apples
½ cup brown sugar
1 tablespoon flour
1½ teaspoons Cinnamon
¼ teaspoon Allspice
⅛ teaspoon Ginger
1 tablespoon melted butter
¼ cup raisins

Wash and core apples. Mix together brown sugar, flour, cinnamon, allspice and ginger. Stir in melted butter and raisins. Place apples in shallow glass baking dish, fill with sugar-raisin mixture and sprinkle remaining mixture around apples. Micro-cook at full power setting, covered, 4 minutes. Turn dish and cook 4 to 5 minutes longer or until tender. Spoon juice over apples.

Makes 6 baked apples.

OUTDOOR COOKING

Steaks and Burgers

- Charcoal Grilled Steak 247
- Flank Steak Western Style 251
- Grilled Chuck Steak 250
- Hamburgers 249
  - Chili-Cheese Burgers 249
  - Dill Burgers 249
  - Herb Burgers 249
  - Hot 'n' Tangy Burgers 249
  - Oriental Burgers 249
  - Pepper Burgers 249
  - Red Hot Burgers 249
  - Savory Burgers 249
  - Sesame Burgers 249
  - Spice Burgers 249
- Marinated Veal Steak 239
- Outdoor Chefs' Grillburgers 249
- Peppered Steak 250
- Steak Teriyaki 239

Specials for the Spit

- Barbecued Bologna Roll 250
- Canadian Bacon on a Spit 246
- Rolled Rib Roast 251
  - Rosemary Roast 251
  - Thyme Roast 251
- Rolled Rump Roast 240

Sauces Make These Superb

- Barbecued Chicken 246
- Chicken Legs Waikiki 241
- Chinese Style Spareribs 241
- Chuck Wagon Franks 240
- Curried Lamb Chops Bengal 242
- Ham Slice Delicious 241
- Pork Chops Luau 242
- Shish Kebabs 245

Fish and Sea Food Barbecues

- Fish Fillets in a Package 243
  - Dilled Fish Fillets 243
  - Herbed Fish Fillets 243
- Grilled Fish Fennel 244
  - Dill Grilled Fish 244
  - Grilled Fish with Thyme 244
  - Grilled Tarragon Fish 244
- Scampi on a Skewer 243

Vegetables and Breads

- Baked Beans Bar-B-Q 242
- Bonfire Green Beans 246
  - Camper's Green Beans 246
- Celery Seed Rolls 244
  - Dill Rolls 244
  - Oregano Rolls 244
- Grilled Bananas 245
- Grilled Garlic Bread 243
- Grilled Tomatoes 248
- Onion Rounds Delicious 251
- Patio Potatoes 247
  - Dill Flavored Potatoes 247
  - Herbed Potatoes 247
  - Hickory Smoked Potatoes 247
  - Potatoes with Marjoram 247
- Pineapple-Yam Kebabs 245
- Roasted Dilly Corn 248
  - Roasted Fiesta Corn 248
- Vegetable Kebabs 248

Steak Teriyaki

½ cup soy sauce
3 tablespoons dark brown sugar, firmly packed
1 teaspoon Ginger
½ teaspoon dry Mustard
⅛ teaspoon Garlic Powder
½ teaspoon coarse grind Black Pepper
2 teaspoons lemon juice
1 12-ounce bottle or can beer
2 tablespoons salad oil
3 pounds 1 inch thick round or sirloin steak

Combine first nine ingredients. Pour over steak. Pierce surface deeply with fork. Cover and refrigerate 12 to 24 hours. Grill, 3 to 4 inches from hot coals, basting frequently with marinade about 20 minutes (10 minutes each side) or until desired degree of doneness is reached. Thinly slice steak on the diagonal. *Makes 8 servings, 6 ounces each.*

Marinated Veal Steak

¼ cup salad oil
1 8-ounce can tomato sauce
1 teaspoon Oregano Leaves
½ teaspoon Garlic Salt
¼ teaspoon ground Black Pepper
Dash ground Cloves
¼ cup white wine
2 pounds veal steak, 1 inch thick

Mix salad oil, tomato sauce, seasonings and wine. Pour over veal in glass or enamel baking dish. Refrigerate 24 hours. Turn meat once while marinating. Grill steak 3 to 4 inches from coals, 5 to 8 minutes on each side or to desired degree of doneness. *Serves 4.*

L.C. Rolled Rump Roast

1 6-pound rolled rump roast
2 cups water
2 cups vinegar
¼ cup Instant Minced Onion
1 lemon, thinly sliced
4 whole Allspice
12 whole Cloves
3 Bay Leaves
10 Peppercorns
3 teaspoons Season-All
2 teaspoons Hickory Smoked Salt
¼ teaspoon MSG

Have roast rolled and securely tied. It should be about 5 inches in diameter and 10 to 12 inches long. Combine remaining ingredients; mix well and pour over roast. Marinate in refrigerator 24 hours; turn meat several times. Cook on a spit over hot coals about 2 hours, basting frequently with marinade. Cooking time depends on distance from fire and heat of coals. Carve into thin slices. *Serves 8 to 10.*

NOTE: You will find a meat thermometer is helpful when cooking large pieces of meat on a spit. Caution should be taken when inserting the meat thermometer so the end is as near the center as possible but does not rest against the spit, the locking tines or bone.

Chuck Wagon Franks

1 8-ounce can tomato sauce
1 6-ounce can tomato paste
½ cup ketchup
¼ cup brown sugar, packed
2 tablespoons butter or margarine
3 tablespoons vinegar
2 tablespoons Worcestershire sauce
1 tablespoon Season-All
2 teaspoons Barbecue Spice
1 tablespoon prepared mustard
2 teaspoons Instant Minced Onion
2 teaspoons Celery Flakes
Dash Black Pepper
Dash ground Red Pepper, optional
12 frankfurters

Combine all ingredients, except frankfurters, in a saucepan. Cover and slowly bring to a boil; reduce heat, then simmer 1 hour. If you want a thinner sauce, add 1 cup water. Grill frankfurters 4 inches from coals, turning occasionally, 10 minutes or until nicely browned. Brush often with sauce while cooking. A complete meal when served with lots of baked beans and coleslaw. Adults as well as children enjoy this treat. *Serves 6.*

Chicken Legs Waikiki

½ cup pineapple juice
¼ cup soy sauce
2 tablespoons lemon juice
½ cup salad oil
1 teaspoon Ginger
2 teaspoons Season-All
¼ teaspoon MSG
1 teaspoon Rosemary Leaves, crushed
½ teaspoon Black Pepper
½ teaspoon Onion Powder
¼ teaspoon crushed Mint Flakes
½ cup Chablis, optional
8 chicken legs (drumstick and thigh)

Combine all the ingredients except chicken; mix well. Arrange chicken in a single layer in flat baking dish. Pour sauce over chicken and marinate in refrigerator several hours or overnight, turning several times. Cook on grill, 5 to 6 inches from coals, about 1 hour, turning and basting frequently with sauce. Excellent served with a tossed green salad and hot bread.

Serves 8.

Chinese Style Spareribs

½ cup salad oil
1½ cups brown sugar, packed
½ cup orange juice
½ cup lemon juice
1 teaspoon Ginger
1 teaspoon dry Mustard
¼ teaspoon MSG
¼ teaspoon Cloves
½ teaspoon Onion Powder
⅛ teaspoon Garlic Powder
2 teaspoons salt
¼ cup soy sauce
4 pounds spareribs (loin back ribs)

Combine all ingredients except spareribs. Place spareribs, rounded side up, on grill; sear on both sides. Raise grill to 6 inches from coals. Cook over medium heat 30 minutes or until nicely browned and thickest part of the meat tests well done, turning and basting frequently with sauce. For a longer and slower method, cook ribs over very low coals 1 hour or longer, turning and basting frequently.

Serves 3 to 4.

Ham Slice Delicious

1 ham slice, cut 1½ inches thick
2 tablespoons melted butter
3 tablespoons brown sugar, packed
1 tablespoon dry Mustard
1 teaspoon Orange Peel
Dash Paprika
1 tablespoon lemon juice

Trim most of the outside fat from ham. Adjust grill to about 5 inches from coals and place ham on grill. Brown on one side; turn. Begin basting with mixture of the remaining ingredients. Cook 25 minutes, turning and basting frequently. Pineapple-Yam Kebabs (see recipe page 245) are a must with this ham.

Serves 4 to 6.

Curried Lamb Chops Bengal

½ cup salad oil
2 tablespoons sugar
3 tablespoons lemon juice
1 teaspoon salt
1 teaspoon Instant Minced Onion
1 teaspoon Season-All
½ teaspoon Black Pepper
2 teaspoons Curry Powder
¼ teaspoon Garlic Salt
8 lamb chops, cut 1 inch thick

Combine all ingredients, except lamb chops, in saucepan. Bring to a boil, then simmer 10 minutes. Arrange chops on grill 5 to 6 inches from hot coals. Sear on both sides. Continue cooking, basting frequently with the curry sauce, 30 minutes or until chops are browned and done. *Serves 4.*

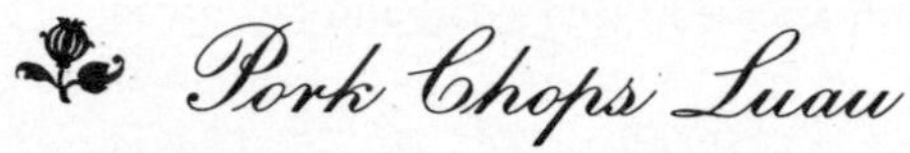

Pork Chops Luau

The Polynesian sauce adds exotic flavor.

½ cup pineapple juice
½ cup salad oil
¼ cup soy sauce
2 tablespoons lemon juice
1 teaspoon dry Mustard
½ teaspoon Ginger
⅛ teaspoon Mace
¼ cup brown sugar, packed
8 pork chops, cut 1 inch thick

Combine all ingredients, except pork chops, and mix well. Marinate pork chops in sauce in a flat baking dish several hours, turning once or twice. Place chops on grill 6 inches from coals; sear on both sides. Cook slowly, basting frequently with sauce, 40 minutes or until well done. May be served with grilled pineapple slices, peach halves or applesauce. *Serves 4.*

Baked Beans Bar-B-Q

4 cups canned baked beans
½ cup ketchup
¼ cup molasses
2 tablespoons brown sugar
2 teaspoons dry Mustard
2 teaspoons Barbecue Spice
½ teaspoon MSG
½ teaspoon Onion Powder
½ teaspoon Ginger
¼ teaspoon Black Pepper
2 teaspoons Sherry Extract
4 slices bacon

Mix together all ingredients, except bacon, in a heavy pot. Cut bacon into 1-inch pieces; place over top of beans. Cover and set on back of grill and cook over a slow fire, stirring occasionally, 45 minutes to 1 hour. If you prefer, you may bake beans in an oven and keep hot on back of grill. *Serves 8 to 10.*

L.C. Fish Fillets in a Package

2 fish fillets (about 1 pound)
½ teaspoon Onion Salt
¾ teaspoon Season-All
Dash Mace
2 tablespoons soft butter
1 tablespoon lemon juice

Place fillets on a piece of heavy duty aluminum foil. Thoroughly blend together onion salt, Season-All, mace, butter and lemon juice. Spread over top of fillets. Fold aluminum foil to make a package; seal edges. Place package on grill about 5 inches from coals. Cook 20 minutes or until fish can be flaked easily with a fork. Turn package over after 10 minutes cooking time. *Serves 2.*

VARIATIONS:

Dilled Fish Fillets—In the above recipe, use ¾ teaspoon salt, ½ teaspoon Dill Weed, ⅛ teaspoon Black Pepper and dash MSG in place of onion salt, Season-All and mace. Proceed as in above recipe.

Herbed Fish Fillets—In the above recipe use ¾ teaspoon salt, ¼ teaspoon crushed Rosemary Leaves, ⅛ teaspoon Tarragon Leaves, ⅛ teaspoon crushed Fennel Seed and dash Black Pepper in place of onion salt, Season-All and mace. Proceed as in above recipe.

L.C. Scampi on a Skewer

A wonderful outdoor appetizer.

1½ pounds fresh or frozen shrimp
½ cup soy sauce
½ cup olive oil
2 tablespoons lemon juice or vinegar
½ teaspoon Ginger
½ teaspoon Garlic Salt
1 teaspoon Italian Seasoning

Wash shrimp thoroughly; do not remove shells. Mix together remaining ingredients to make marinade; pour over shrimp and let stand 1 to 2 hours in refrigerator. Thread shrimp onto skewers. Cook over hot coals about 10 minutes, turning several times. Serve hot from grill. *Serves 4.*

Grilled Garlic Bread

1 loaf French bread
¼ teaspoon Garlic Powder
½ cup butter or margarine, softened

Slice bread but not through the bottom crust. Add garlic powder to butter and blend thoroughly. Spread between slices and over top of bread. Wrap in aluminum foil; seal edges. Heat on back of grill 45 minutes to 1 hour, depending on heat of coals. Serve hot. *Serves 6 to 8.*

Grilled Fish Fennel

Really an outdoor fish feast.

4 *small whole fish*
  (about 2 pounds each)
½ *cup butter*
¼ *cup lemon juice*
4 *teaspoons salt*
2 *teaspoons Fennel Seed*

Clean fish and cut three diagonal slashes on each side. Melt butter; add lemon juice and 2 teaspoons of the salt. Brush part of this mixture over fish. Combine remaining salt and fennel seed; rub inside and over outside of fish. Place fish in a basket grill and cook about 5 inches from coals 30 minutes or until fish flakes easily with fork; cooking time will vary depending on thickness of fish and heat of coals. Baste frequently with remaining butter mixture and turn once or twice during cooking time. Serve hot!

Serves 4.

VARIATIONS:

Dill Grilled Fish—In above recipe use 4 teaspoons Dill Weed in place of fennel seed. Cook as directed.

Grilled Tarragon Fish—In above recipe use 4 teaspoons Tarragon Leaves in place of fennel seed. Cook as directed.

Grilled Fish with Thyme—In above recipe use 2 teaspoons Thyme Leaves in place of fennel seed. Cook as directed.

Celery Seed Rolls

A delicious way of adding new flavor to hot rolls.

¼ *cup soft butter*
½ *teaspoon Celery Seed*
  Dash Season-All
6 *ready-to-serve fan-tan rolls*

Blend together butter, celery seed and Season-All. Break rolls apart from the top and spread butter mixture between sections. Wrap rolls in aluminum foil. Place on grill and heat 10 minutes, turning once or twice.

Serves 3 to 6.

VARIATIONS:

Oregano Rolls—Substitute ½ teaspoon Oregano Leaves, ¼ teaspoon Onion Salt and dash Paprika for seasonings in above recipe.

Dill Rolls—Substitute ½ teaspoon Dill Weed and dash Garlic Powder for seasonings in above recipe.

Pineapple-Yam Kebabs

4 sweet potatoes
Pineapple cubes
4 apples, cut in quarters
½ cup melted butter
2 teaspoons Cinnamon
¼ teaspoon Cloves
¼ teaspoon Nutmeg
2 tablespoons lemon juice

Scrub and cook sweet potatoes in salted water 25 minutes or until just tender. Peel and cut into large pieces. Thread on skewers, alternating potatoes, pineapple and apple quarters. Brush with mixture of remaining ingredients. Grill over hot coals, turning and basting frequently, until lightly browned. You will find these especially good with pork or chicken.

Serves 4 to 6.

L.C. Shish Kebabs

4 pounds lean lamb
1 medium-size onion
2 green peppers
4 tablespoons wine vinegar
½ cup lemon juice
½ cup olive or salad oil
½ teaspoon Garlic Salt
½ teaspoon Onion Salt
1 tablespoon Season-All
½ teaspoon Black Pepper
¼ teaspoon Thyme Leaves
¼ teaspoon Basil Leaves
¼ teaspoon Marjoram Leaves
⅛ teaspoon MSG

Cut lamb into 1½- to 2-inch cubes, removing gristle and most of the fat. Peel onion, separate and cut into large pieces. Cut peppers into pieces. Combine remaining ingredients; mix well. Pour over lamb, onion and pepper; stir to coat with marinade. Cover and let marinate 12 to 24 hours. When ready to cook, thread skewers, alternating lamb, onion and pepper. Cook 5 inches from coals about 25 minutes, turning and basting often with marinade.

Makes 6 large kebabs, serving about 8.

Grilled Bananas

6 whole, unpeeled bananas
¼ cup melted butter
2 tablespoons lemon juice
¼ teaspoon Ginger
⅛ teaspoon Cloves
Cinnamon or Nutmeg

Put the whole, unpeeled bananas on grill 4 inches from heat; cook 4 minutes or until peel turns black. Turn and cook 4 minutes on other side. Combine butter, lemon juice, ginger and cloves. When ready to serve, peel one side of each banana and spoon the spiced butter over top. Sprinkle each with cinnamon or nutmeg. Serve piping hot with grilled chicken, barbecued pork or ham.

Serves 6.

Barbecued Chicken

3 broilers, split in half lengthwise
1 6-ounce can tomato paste
½ cup ketchup
¼ cup unsulphured molasses
½ cup water
1 tablespoon prepared mustard
1 tablespoon vinegar
1 tablespoon Worcestershire sauce
2 tablespoons butter or margarine
1 teaspoon Instant Minced Onion
1 teaspoon Season-All
¼ teaspoon Barbecue Spice
¼ teaspoon Garlic Salt
¼ teaspoon Black Pepper
¼ teaspoon MSG

Clean and dry chicken. Combine remaining ingredients, mixing well; bring to a boil and boil 1 minute. Adjust grill 5 to 6 inches from coals. Place chicken, skin side down, on grill; brown on both sides, then begin basting with sauce. Continue cooking, turning and basting frequently, 45 minutes or until chicken is tender. *Serves 6.*

Canadian Bacon on a Spit

A favorite from 6 to 60!

1 4-pound roll Canadian bacon
¼ cup honey
2 tablespoons wine vinegar
½ teaspoon prepared horseradish
1 teaspoon Hickory Smoked Salt
¼ teaspoon ground Cloves

Tie Canadian bacon in two or three places. Insert spit through center of roll and roast 5 to 6 inches from coals. Combine remaining ingredients and baste Canadian bacon frequently with this mixture. Cook about 30 minutes or until heated through. You will find this is an unusual outdoor treat. May be served either as an appetizer or as the main course. *Serves 6 to 8.*

Bonfire Green Beans

1 9-ounce package frozen French style green beans
2 tablespoons butter
1 teaspoon Onion Salt
1 tablespoon lemon juice

Place green beans, frozen or partially thawed, on piece of aluminum foil. Dot with butter, then sprinkle with onion salt and lemon juice. Seal foil. Place on grill 5 inches from coals. Cook 1 hour or until crisp-tender, turning occasionally. *Serves 3 to 4.*

VARIATION:

Camper's Green Beans—In the above recipe use 1 teaspoon Season-All in place of onion salt and lemon juice. Cook as directed above.

Patio Potatoes

2 medium-size potatoes
¼ cup soft butter
1 teaspoon Barbecue Spice

Parboil potatoes until just tender. Drain and cool. Slice potatoes into ¼-inch rounds; place on a piece of aluminum foil. Dot with butter and sprinkle with barbecue spice. Fold foil to make a package, sealing edges, and place on grill 5 inches from medium coals. Heat 25 minutes or until potatoes are steaming hot. *Serves 2 to 3.*

VARIATIONS:

Hickory Smoked Potatoes—In the above recipe use 1 teaspoon Hickory Smoked Salt and ½ teaspoon Cracked Black Pepper in place of barbecue spice. Cook as directed.

Herbed Potatoes—In the above recipe use ½ teaspoon Herb Seasoning, ¼ teaspoon salt, dash MSG and dash ground Red Pepper in place of barbecue spice. Cook as directed.

Dill Flavored Potatoes—In the above recipe use ½ teaspoon Dill Weed, ½ teaspoon salt and dash Black Pepper in place of barbecue spice. Cook as directed.

Potatoes with Marjoram—In the above recipe use ½ teaspoon Marjoram Leaves, ¾ teaspoon Onion Salt, ¼ teaspoon Paprika and dash Black Pepper in place of barbecue spice. Cook as directed.

Charcoal Grilled Steak

4 club steaks, cut 1 inch thick
½ cup salad oil
2 tablespoons lemon juice
⅛ teaspoon Garlic Powder
1 teaspoon Onion Salt
¼ teaspoon Black Pepper
½ teaspoon Season-All
1 teaspoon Worcestershire sauce

Place steaks in shallow baking dish. Combine remaining ingredients and pour over steaks, being sure to coat all sides. Marinate several hours in refrigerator, turning once. Place on grill and sear on both sides. Raise grill to about 5 inches from coals. Cook 15 minutes, turning once, or until the desired degree of doneness is reached. *Serves 4.*

Vegetable Kebabs

4 small whole onions
4 mushrooms
4 cherry tomatoes
4 pineapple chunks
4 pitted ripe olives
4 jumbo stuffed olives
¼ cup melted butter
2 teaspoons Barbecue Spice
1 teaspoon salt
¼ teaspoon Black Pepper
1 teaspoon Bon Appétit
Dash Nutmeg

Peel and cook onions in boiling salted water 10 minutes or until slightly tender. Thread vegetables, pineapple and olives alternately onto skewers. (Small canned potatoes and pieces of raw green pepper, squash and eggplant may also be used.) Combine remaining ingredients; mix well. Brush vegetables with seasoned butter. Adjust grill 4 to 5 inches from coals. Place skewers on grill. Cook vegetables 10 minutes, turning and basting frequently with seasoned butter. *Serves 4.*

Grilled Tomatoes

4 tomatoes, cut in half
2 tablespoons melted butter
Season-All, Oregano, Thyme, Celery Salt or Herb Seasoning

Brush cut side of tomatoes with butter. Sprinkle with one of the seasonings. Place tomatoes on grill over low coals and cook about 15 minutes or until soft. You will find these tomatoes a perfect accompaniment to any meat, sea food, fish or chicken. *Serves 8.*

Roasted Dilly Corn

6 ears of corn, in husks
½ cup soft butter
1 teaspoon salt
5 Coriander Seeds, crushed
1 teaspoon Dill Weed
Dash MSG
Dash Nutmeg

Loosen husks of corn enough to remove silk. Soak in cold water 30 minutes or longer. When ready to roast, drain well. Combine remaining ingredients and spread generously over corn. Rewrap husks, then wrap in aluminum foil. Place on grill about 5 inches from coals; cook 25 minutes, turning several times. Remove foil and husks. Serve piping hot. *Serves 6.*

VARIATION:

Roasted Fiesta Corn—Use 1 teaspoon Season-All and a dash dry Mustard in place of salt and seasonings in above recipe. Prepare and cook following directions above.

Outdoor Chefs' Grillburgers

2 pounds ground beef
1 tablespoon Instant Minced Onion
¼ teaspoon Garlic Salt
½ teaspoon Barbecue Spice
½ teaspoon dry Mustard
¼ teaspoon Black Pepper
1½ teaspoons Bon Appétit
Hickory Smoked Salt

Combine beef, onion, garlic salt, barbecue spice, dry mustard, pepper and Bon Appétit, being careful not to overmix. Shape into burgers; sprinkle with hickory smoked salt. Grill over coals about 3 minutes on each side for rare or longer, depending on degree of doneness preferred. Serve on buns with your favorite relish and sauce. *Makes 8.*

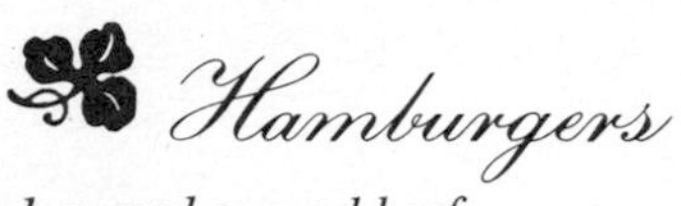

Hamburgers

1 pound ground beef
½ teaspoon salt
¼ teaspoon Black Pepper
1 tablespoon Instant Minced Onion
⅛ teaspoon Garlic Salt

Thoroughly mix together all ingredients but do not overmix. Shape into 4 patties. Place on grill 3 inches from coals. Cook 3 minutes on each side or until desired degree of doneness is reached.

VARIATIONS:

Savory Burgers—Add ¼ teaspoon Savory to above recipe.

Pepper Burgers—Soak 4 teaspoons Bell Pepper Flakes in water 5 minutes. Add to above recipe.

Sesame Burgers—Toast ¼ cup Sesame Seed in 350°F. oven 15 minutes. Add to above recipe.

Red Hot Burgers—Add 1 teaspoon Crushed Red Pepper to above recipe.

Oriental Burgers—Add ¼ teaspoon Ginger, 1 teaspoon Lemon Peel and 1 teaspoon soy sauce to above recipe.

Dill Burgers—Add ½ teaspoon crushed Dill Seed and ¼ cup chopped olives or sweet pickles to above recipe.

Herb Burgers—Add ¼ teaspoon Marjoram, ⅛ teaspoon Thyme, ½ teaspoon Celery Salt and 1 teaspoon Parsley Flakes to above recipe.

Chili-Cheese Burgers—Add 1 cup grated cheese, ¼ cup milk and ½ teaspoon Chili Powder to above recipe.

Hot 'n' Tangy Burgers—Omit salt in above recipe and add 1 teaspoon Season-All and 1 teaspoon Barbecue Spice.

Spice Burgers—Add ½ teaspoon dry Mustard and ¼ teaspoon Nutmeg to above recipe.

S.C. Grilled Chuck Steak

1 4-pound chuck steak, cut 1½ inches thick
2 teaspoons Meat Tenderizer
Season-All
Coarse Grind Black Pepper

Sprinkle steak on both sides with meat tenderizer; pierce surface with tines of a fork. Let stand 1 hour. Place on grill and sear on both sides. Sprinkle each side with Season-All and pepper. Raise grill to about 6 inches from coals and cook 35 minutes, turning once, or until desired degree of doneness is reached. Cut into thin slices and serve. Your whole family will enjoy this juicy and tender steak. *Serves 4 to 6.*

S.C. Peppered Steak

An excellent steak for family and friends! Black Pepper gives the good flavor.

1 T-bone steak, cut 1½ inches thick
2 teaspoons Coarse Grind or Cracked Black Pepper
⅛ teaspoon Garlic Salt
⅛ teaspoon MSG
1 teaspoon salt

Place steak on grill and sear each side. Combine remaining ingredients and sprinkle one half of the pepper mixture over each side of steak, pressing down firmly with spatula. Cook 4 to 5 inches from coals 12 minutes on each side or until desired degree of doneness is reached. For a very rare steak decrease cooking time; increase for well done steak. Cooking time varies with heat of coals and distance from coals. *Serves 2 to 3.*

Barbecued Bologna Roll

1 4-pound bologna roll
Whole Cloves
½ cup chili sauce
2 tablespoons lemon juice
1 teaspoon Barbecue Spice
1 teaspoon prepared horseradish
½ teaspoon dry Mustard

Score bologna roll, cutting diagonal lines ⅛ inch deep, to form a diamond pattern. Stud each diamond with a whole clove. Insert spit through center of roll and cook about 5 inches from coals, basting frequently with sauce made by combining the remaining ingredients. Cook 30 minutes or until heated through. Slice and serve with potato or macaroni salad, baked beans, coleslaw or your favorite relish. *Serves 8 to 10.*

L.C. Rolled Rib Roast

1 rolled rib roast of beef (4 to 5 pounds)
⅛ teaspoon Garlic Powder
½ teaspoon Onion Salt
¼ teaspoon dry Mustard
¼ teaspoon Ginger
2 teaspoons Season-All
1 teaspoon salt
½ teaspoon Coarse Grind Black Pepper

Trim off most of the outside fat from roast. Combine seasonings and rub into all surfaces of the roast. Place on spit, 5 to 6 inches from coals, and cook 1½ hours or until desired degree of doneness is reached. You'll find leftover roast makes excellent sandwiches. *Serves 6 to 8.*

VARIATIONS:

Rosemary Roast—Rub 1 teaspoon Rosemary Leaves into roast along with above seasonings.

Thyme Roast—Rub ½ teaspoon Thyme Leaves into roast along with above seasonings.

NOTE: You will find a meat thermometer is helpful when cooking large pieces of meat on a spit. Caution should be taken when inserting the meat thermometer so the end is as near the center as possible but does not rest against the spit, the locking tines or bone.

Onion Rounds Delicious

3 large onions
¼ cup melted butter
¼ teaspoon Coarse Grind Black Pepper
1 teaspoon Season-All
¼ teaspoon Celery Salt
1 teaspoon Barbecue Spice

Peel and cut onions into ½-inch slices; do not break apart. Grill 6 inches from coals 10 minutes on each side or until tender and brown; brush often with a mixture of the remaining ingredients. *Serves 6 to 8.*

Flank Steak Western Style

1 1½-pound flank steak
½ cup oil
2 tablespoons lemon juice
½ teaspoon Celery Salt
½ teaspoon Coarse Grind or Cracked Black Pepper
½ teaspoon Onion Powder
1 teaspoon Season-All

Put steak in shallow dish. Combine remaining ingredients and pour over steak, coating entire surface. Marinate several hours. Grill 4 inches from coals 15 to 20 minutes, turning once. Baste often with marinade. Carve into thin slices on extreme diagonal against the grain. *Serves 4.*

BREADS

Yeast Breads and Pastries

Cardamom Crescent 261
Cinnamon Raisin Bread 256
Danish Pastry 259
Doughnuts 266
Easy Saffron Bread 267
Holiday Confetti Bread 257
Old-Fashioned Herb Bread 263
Oregano Batter Bread 258
Philadelphia Sticky Buns 255
Whole Wheat Rolls 256
Whole Wheat Salt Sticks 264

Quick Breads

Blueberry Pancakes 268
Muffins 265
  Cinnamon-Streusel Muffins 265
  Mace-Blueberry Muffins 265
  Orange Muffins 265
  Spice Muffins 265
Parsley Biscuits 268
Quick Coffee Cake 263
Spicy Banana Nut Bread 265

Magic with Mixes

Cinnamon-Pineapple Buns 260
Corn Sticks Rosemary 258
Dill Ring 267
Fun with Waffles 264
  Herb Waffles 264
  Mace Waffles 264
  Sage Waffles 264
  Sesame Waffles 264
Hot Cross Buns 257
Rum Buns 260
Sesame Ring 257
Sticky Spice Buns 262

Tricks with Biscuits and Baker's Bread

Cinnamon-Pecan Biscuits 262
Garlic Cheese Bread 262
Herb Croutons 258
Party Biscuits 266
Quick Cinnamon Twists 260
Rye Herb Bread 267

Philadelphia Sticky Buns

DOUGH:

1 cup milk
1 package active dry yeast
¼ cup warm water
4½ cups sifted all-purpose flour
¼ cup butter
1 teaspoon salt
⅓ cup sugar
1 egg, well beaten
¼ teaspoon Nutmeg

FILLING:

¼ cup soft butter
½ cup dark brown sugar
1 tablespoon Cinnamon
⅛ teaspoon Ginger
½ cup raisins

Scald milk; cool to lukewarm. Dissolve yeast in the ¼ cup warm water and combine with milk. Add 1½ cups of the flour, mixing until smooth. Cover and let stand in warm place until top is bubbly. Cream butter, salt, sugar, egg and nutmeg together until smooth; stir into dough. Add the remaining 3 cups flour, mixing until well combined. Place dough in lightly greased bowl; grease top of dough, cover and let rise in warm place until doubled in bulk. Prepare syrup (recipe below) while dough is rising. Roll dough out on lightly floured board to a rectangular shape ¾ inch thick and 12 inches long. Spread with the soft butter. Combine brown sugar, cinnamon and ginger; sprinkle over top of dough. Scatter raisins over dough. Roll up as for jelly roll. Cut into 12 1-inch pieces. Pour ½ syrup into a 13 x 9 x 2-inch baking dish. Place buns, cut side down, in baking dish. Pour remaining syrup over buns. Cover loosely and let rise about 30 minutes. Bake in 350°F. oven 45 minutes or until done.

Makes 1 dozen buns.

SYRUP:

⅓ cup butter
1 cup dark corn syrup
½ cup honey
½ cup dark brown sugar

Heat butter, corn syrup, honey and brown sugar in saucepan until butter is melted and sugar is dissolved. Cool slightly.

NOTE: These buns are very "sticky", which is typical of Philadelphia Sticky Buns.

Cinnamon-Raisin Bread

1 envelope active dry yeast
½ cup warm water
1 egg
¼ cup honey
2 teaspoons salt
½ cup milk
3 to 3½ cups flour
2 tablespoons butter
½ cup sugar
2 teaspoons Cinnamon
1 cup raisins

In large bowl, dissolve yeast in water. Stir in egg, honey, salt and milk. Add 2 cups flour. Beat until smooth. Stir in remaining flour. Mix well. Turn out on floured board and knead until smooth and elastic. Put dough in large greased bowl. Lightly grease top of dough. Cover and let stand in warm place until double in size. Punch down. Divide dough in half. On floured board, roll out each half to form a rectangle 14 x 9 inches. Spread each with 1 tablespoon butter. Sprinkle each with ¼ cup sugar, 1 teaspoon cinnamon and ½ cup raisins. Roll up from short end, jelly roll fashion. Place each loaf, seam side down, in greased 9 x 5 x 3-inch loaf pan. Cover and let rise until nearly double. Bake in 375°F. oven 25 to 30 minutes. Brush crust with melted butter, if desired. *Makes 2 loaves.*

Whole Wheat Rolls

2 envelopes active dry yeast
1½ cups warm water
2 tablespoons molasses
2 tablespoons sugar
1 tablespoon salt
1 egg
2 cups whole wheat flour
1 teaspoon Cinnamon
⅛ teaspoon Mace
¼ teaspoon ground Cardamom
2 cups all-purpose flour

In large bowl dissolve yeast in water. Add molasses, sugar, salt and egg. Mix well. Stir in next 4 ingredients. Beat until smooth. Gradually add all-purpose flour, mixing well. Turn out on floured board. Knead until smooth and elastic. Put in large greased bowl. Lightly grease top of dough. Cover and let stand in warm place until double in size. Punch down. Pinch off balls of dough about 2 inches in diameter. Place in greased 11¾ x 7½ x 1¾-inch baking pan. Cover and let rise until nearly double. Bake in 375°F. oven 20 to 25 minutes. Brush tops with melted butter, if desired. *Makes 24 rolls.*

Hot Cross Buns

1 package hot roll mix
1 teaspoon Cinnamon
¼ teaspoon Allspice
¼ teaspoon ground Cardamom
½ cup seedless white raisins
¾ cup powdered sugar
¾ teaspoon Lemon Extract
3 teaspoons water

To the flour mixture in the hot roll mix add cinnamon, allspice, cardamom and raisins; mix well. Then prepare mix as directed on package. After first rising shape dough into 18 2-inch balls and place on greased baking sheet. Set in warm place and let rise to double in bulk. Bake in 400°F. oven 15 minutes. Cool. Combine sugar, lemon extract and water; drizzle in shape of cross on top of each bun. *Makes 18 buns.*

Sesame Ring

1 package hot roll mix
Sesame Seed

Prepare hot roll mix as directed on package. After first rising, shape dough into 9 balls about 2 inches in diameter. Place balls side by side in well greased 1½-quart ring mold. Set in warm place and let rise to double in bulk. Sprinkle sesame seed on top. Bake in 350°F. oven 30 to 35 minutes. *Makes 1 ring.*

Holiday Confetti Bread

1 cup milk
½ cup sugar
1½ teaspoons salt
6 tablespoons butter
1 teaspoon Lemon Peel
½ teaspoon Allspice
½ teaspoon Ginger
1 package active dry yeast
¼ cup lukewarm water
2 eggs, well beaten
4 cups sifted all-purpose flour
1½ cups mixed candied fruits, cut into small pieces
2 tablespoons flour
½ cup slivered almonds

Scald milk; add sugar, salt, butter and spices. Cool to lukewarm. Dissolve yeast in water. Stir in beaten eggs and milk mixture. Add the 4 cups flour and stir until moistened. Cover and set in warm place and let rise until double in bulk, about 1½ hours. Dredge fruit with the 2 tablespoons flour. Add fruit and almonds to batter; beat 2 minutes (an electric mixer set on low speed may be used). Push into greased 2-quart mold or 9 x 3½-inch tube pan. Set in warm place and let rise until double in bulk, about 1 hour. Bake in 350°F. oven 1 hour. *Makes 1 loaf.*

Corn Sticks Rosemary

1 teaspoon Rosemary Leaves
1 package corn bread mix

Add rosemary leaves to corn bread mix. Prepare according to directions on package. Spoon into well greased corn stick pans filling almost full. Bake in 400°F. oven 15 minutes or until golden brown. You may want to vary shape and use muffin pans instead of corn stick pans.

Makes 14 to 16 corn sticks.

Oregano Batter Bread

1 package active dry yeast
¼ cup warm water
¾ cup milk
1 tablespoon sugar
1½ teaspoons salt
2 teaspoons Oregano Leaves
1 egg
1 tablespoon oil
3 cups all-purpose flour
2 teaspoons Fennel Seed

Dissolve yeast in warm water in large mixing bowl. Scald milk, then cool to lukewarm. Add milk, sugar, salt, oregano leaves, egg, oil and 2 cups of the flour to yeast. Beat on high speed with electric mixer 3 minutes (beat longer if beating by hand). Stir in remaining flour. Set in warm place free from draft and let rise to double in bulk, about 1 hour. Stir well. Put in greased 9¼ x 5¼ x 2¾-inch loaf pan. Push dough so that it fills corners of pan. Brush top lightly with oil and sprinkle with fennel seed. Set in warm place and let rise to double in bulk, about 30 minutes. Bake in 375°F. oven 50 minutes.

Makes 1 loaf.

Herb Croutons

For interesting variations in flavor use different combinations of spices and herbs.

1 cup bread cubes (about ½-inch cubes)
2 tablespoons butter
Dash Herb Seasoning
Dash Season-All
Dash Garlic Salt

Toast bread cubes in 300°F. oven until dry and crisp and golden brown. Sauté in butter seasoned with Herb Seasoning, Season-All and garlic salt. Use in Caesar salad, potato dumplings; spoon on top of soups or use as topping for vegetables and casseroles.

Makes 1 cup.

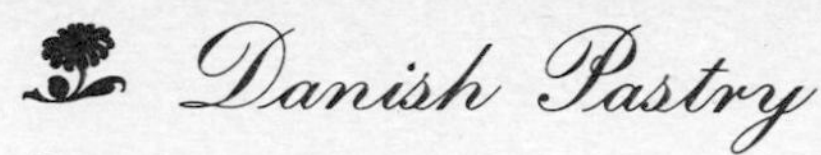

Danish Pastry

2 packages active dry yeast
¼ cup warm water
⅓ cup sugar
Dash ground Cardamom
1 egg, beaten
1 cup milk
3½ cups all-purpose flour
½ pound butter, softened
Filling

Dissolve yeast in water; add sugar, cardamom, egg and milk. Stir in flour to make soft dough. (If dough seems too soft, add extra flour.) Roll out on floured board to 14-inch square. Spread one half of the butter over center third of dough. Fold one side over butter, then fold other side over first side, making three layers. Give dough a quarter turn and roll out to 14-inch square. Spread remaining butter over center and fold once more as directed above. Turn, roll and fold dough again. Chill 1 hour. Again, roll, fold and turn dough three times. Chill 1 hour. Roll dough to ⅛-inch thickness. Cut into 4-inch squares. Put 1 tablespoon filling in center of each. Shape. (For *envelopes*—bring two opposite ends of square to center and overlap; seal edges. For *pockets*—bring all four corners of square to center and overlap; seal edges. For *cockscombs*—cut dough into 5 x 10-inch pieces; put filling on one end of rectangle. Fold other half of dough over filling; seal edges, then cut 4 to 5 deep slashes along one side of pastry.) Chill 2 hours. Bake in 350°F. oven 15 minutes or until golden brown.

Makes about 36 rolls.

RASPBERRY FILLING:

1 10-ounce package frozen raspberries
1 tablespoon sugar
⅛ teaspoon ground Cardamom
¼ teaspoon Almond Extract
2 teaspoons cornstarch

Combine all ingredients. Cook, stirring, until slightly thickened. Cool.

Makes filling for 18 pastries.

APRICOT FILLING:

1 8-ounce package dried apricots, cooked and mashed
3 tablespoons sugar
¼ teaspoon ground Cardamom

Combine all ingredients; mix well.

Makes filling for 18 pastries.

POPPY SEED FILLING:

⅓ cup Poppy Seed
½ cup milk
1 egg yolk
1 teaspoon Orange Peel
¼ cup sugar
¼ cup bread crumbs
1 tablespoon honey

Add poppy seed to milk; bring to a boil. Remove from heat and let stand 1 hour. Drain. Combine poppy seed with remaining ingredients.

Makes filling for 18 pastries.

Quick Cinnamon Twists

1 can refrigerator biscuits
2 tablespoons butter, melted
½ cup finely chopped nuts
2 tablespoons Cinnamon Sugar

Pull each biscuit to about 6 inches in length. Dip in melted butter, then in mixture of nuts and cinnamon sugar. Twist. Place on ungreased baking sheet. Bake in 475°F. oven 8 minutes. Quick to make and wonderful with coffee or tea. *Makes 10.*

1 package hot roll mix
1 1-ounce bottle Rum Extract
2 cups powdered sugar
4 teaspoons water
3 tablespoons soft butter
Cinnamon

Prepare roll mix as directed on package. After first rising, roll dough into a 10 x 12-inch rectangle. Combine rum extract, powdered sugar and water; mix until smooth. Spread soft butter and half of the powdered sugar mixture over dough. Sprinkle with cinnamon. Roll as jelly roll, starting with long side. Cut into 12 1-inch slices. Put into greased muffin cups, cut side down. Set in warm place and allow to rise until double in bulk. Bake in 350°F. oven 25 minutes. Remove from pans. Drizzle remainder of the powdered sugar mixture over buns. *Makes 12.*

Cinnamon-Pineapple Buns

1 8½-ounce can crushed pineapple
½ cup butter, melted
½ cup brown sugar, packed
1 teaspoon Cinnamon
¼ teaspoon Nutmeg
¼ cup chopped pecans
2 cups biscuit mix
4 tablespoons sugar
½ cup milk
⅓ cup melted butter

Drain pineapple. Mix together thoroughly the pineapple, ½ cup melted butter, brown sugar, cinnamon, nutmeg and pecans. Spoon into 12 muffin cups. Combine remaining ingredients and spoon over cinnamon-pineapple mixture. Bake in 425°F. oven 15 to 20 minutes. Immediately turn upside down on rack or tray to remove buns. Serve warm. *Makes 12.*

Cardamom Crescent

½ cup milk, scalded
1 cake compressed yeast
1 egg, beaten
3 tablespoons sugar
1 teaspoon salt
1 teaspoon Lemon Peel
½ teaspoon ground Cardamom
2 cups all-purpose flour
6 tablespoons soft butter
Cardamom Fruit Filling
1 tablespoon melted shortening
Glaze

Cool milk to lukewarm. Crumble in yeast; stir to dissolve. Add egg, sugar, salt and spices. Gradually beat in flour, mixing to a moderately stiff dough. (If dough is too soft, add about ¼ cup more flour.) Turn out on lightly floured board and knead just until smooth. Put in greased bowl; cover and let stand in warm place until double in bulk, about 1½ hours. Turn out on lightly floured board; roll to rectangle about 12 x 15 inches. Spread with 4 tablespoons of the butter. Fold one end to middle and overlap second end to make 3 layers. Roll out again to 12 x 15 inches and spread with remaining butter; fold again as before. Cover and let stand 15 minutes. Roll out dough to 10 x 16 inches. Spread with cooled Cardamom Fruit Filling; roll up as jelly roll, starting from long side. Seal lengthwise seam and ends. Place seam side down on lightly greased baking sheet and shape into crescent. With scissors make cuts ⅔ of way through crescent at about 1-inch intervals. Brush surface of dough with melted shortening. Set in warm place and let rise until double in bulk, 50 to 60 minutes. Bake in 350°F. oven 25 to 30 minutes. Cool on wire rack. Glaze.

Makes 1 large crescent.

CARDAMOM FRUIT FILLING:

¼ cup sugar
¼ teaspoon ground Cardamom
⅛ teaspoon salt
1 cup chopped dates
⅓ cup water or orange juice
1 tablespoon butter or margarine
¼ cup chopped nuts

Combine sugar, cardamom, salt, dates and water. Cook, stirring, over medium heat until mixture becomes thick. Remove from heat; stir in butter and nuts. Cool before using.

GLAZE:

Combine 1 cup sifted powdered sugar and 4 teaspoons milk or water. Drizzle over top of crescent.

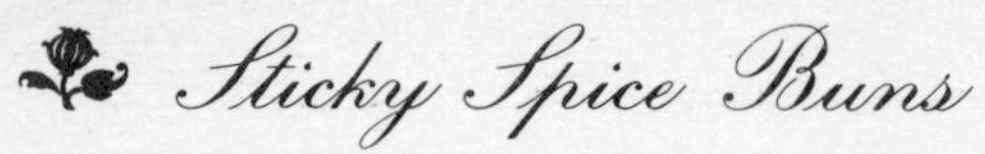

Sticky Spice Buns

Old-fashioned goodness, sweet and mouth-watering.

1 package hot roll mix
½ cup butter
2¼ cups brown sugar, packed
2½ teaspoons Pumpkin Pie Spice
½ cup raisins
1 cup light corn syrup

Prepare hot roll mix as directed on package. After first rising, roll dough to 18 x 20-inch rectangle. With pastry blender or two knives cut ¼ cup of the butter into ¾ cup of the brown sugar and pumpkin pie spice. Add raisins. Sprinkle this mixture evenly over the dough. Roll as jelly roll, starting from long side. Seal edge. Cut into 18 equal pieces. Combine the remaining ¼ cup butter and 1½ cups brown sugar with corn syrup. Cook over low heat until sugar dissolves. Pour syrup into two buttered 9-inch layer pans. Cool slightly. Place nine slices of the dough, cut side down, in each pan. Set in warm place and allow to rise to double in bulk. Bake in 350°F. oven 30 to 35 minutes. Cool 10 minutes. Turn out onto plate. *Makes 18 buns.*

Cinnamon-Pecan Biscuits

Quick and Easy!

2 tablespoons butter
3 tablespoons honey
1 teaspoon Cinnamon
1 teaspoon Orange Peel
½ cup chopped pecans
1 package refrigerator biscuits

Melt butter; add honey, cinnamon and orange peel. Stir until well blended. Add pecans and cook over medium heat until pecans are glazed, stirring constantly. Put biscuits on baking sheet and flatten slightly. Spoon pecan mixture over top of biscuits. Bake as directed on package.

Makes 10 biscuits.

Garlic Cheese Bread

1 loaf French bread
¼ teaspoon Garlic Powder
½ cup butter or margarine
1 cup grated sharp cheese or Parmesan cheese

Cut bread into 1-inch slices. Heat garlic powder and butter slowly until butter is melted. Brush each slice of bread on both sides with garlic butter and place on baking sheet. Sprinkle with cheese and bake in 425°F. oven 10 minutes or until cheese melts. Serve hot. *Serves 6.*

Quick Coffee Cake

CAKE BATTER:

3 tablespoons butter or margarine
⅓ cup sugar
1 egg
1 teaspoon Lemon Peel
1½ cups all-purpose flour
3 teaspoons baking powder
½ teaspoon salt
⅔ cup milk

Cream together butter and sugar; add egg and lemon peel. Sift flour, measure and sift again with baking powder and salt. Add to creamed mixture alternately with milk and mix lightly. Spread in greased and floured 8-inch square pan. Sprinkle Streusel Topping over batter. Bake in 400°F. oven 25 to 30 minutes. *Makes 9 servings.*

STREUSEL TOPPING:

3 tablespoons soft butter or margarine
½ cup sugar
2 teaspoons Pumpkin Pie Spice
2 tablespoons flour
⅛ teaspoon salt
1 teaspoon Lemon Peel
½ cup chopped nuts, optional

Blend together all ingredients and sprinkle over top of cake batter.

Old-Fashioned Herb Bread

1 cup warm water
1 package active dry yeast
1½ teaspoons salt
2 teaspoons sugar
1 tablespoon soft shortening
1 teaspoon Marjoram Leaves
¾ teaspoon Dill Weed
¾ teaspoon Thyme Leaves
½ teaspoon Rosemary Leaves
3 cups sifted all-purpose flour
Poppy Seed

Pour water into bowl; sprinkle yeast on top. Stir until dissolved. Add salt, sugar, shortening and herbs; stir. Add flour to make a soft dough. Turn dough out on lightly floured board and knead until smooth and elastic, 5 to 7 minutes. Put dough in greased bowl; turn to bring greased side up. Cover; set in warm place and allow to rise to double in bulk, about 1½ hours. Shape dough into a roll 18 inches long. Place on greased baking sheet. With sharp knife make ¼-inch deep slashes in top of loaf, about 1½ inches apart. Brush with water. Set in warm place and allow to rise to double in bulk, about 1 hour. Brush again with water. Bake in 425°F. oven 15 minutes. Brush a third time with water and sprinkle poppy seed on top. Bake 15 minutes longer. *Makes 1 loaf.*

Fun with Waffles

2 cups waffle mix
2 tablespoons brown sugar
2 tablespoons melted butter
1 teaspoon pure Vanilla Extract
1 tablespoon Lemon Peel or 1 teaspoon Allspice

Prepare the 2 cups waffle mix as directed on package, adding brown sugar, butter, vanilla and lemon peel or allspice. Bake.

Makes three 9-inch square waffles.

VARIATIONS:

Herb Waffles—Add 2 teaspoons Parsley Flakes and 1 teaspoon Herb Seasoning to 2 cups waffle mix. Prepare as directed on package. Serve with creamed dishes; excellent, too, as a hot bread.

Mace Waffles—Add ½ teaspoon Mace to 2 cups waffle mix. Prepare as directed on package.

Sage Waffles—Add 2 teaspoons rubbed Sage to 2 cups waffle mix. Prepare as directed on package. Excellent with creamed dishes.

Sesame Waffles—Prepare waffle mix as directed. After pouring batter on waffle iron, sprinkle generously with Sesame Seed. Bake.

Whole Wheat Salt Sticks

1 package active dry yeast
¾ cup warm water
¼ cup molasses
1 tablespoon sugar
2 teaspoons salt
1 tablespoon oil
1 teaspoon Anise Seed
1 tablespoon Caraway Seed
1 cup whole wheat flour
1½ cups all-purpose flour
Coarse Salt

Dissolve yeast in warm water. Add molasses, sugar, salt, oil, anise seed and caraway seed; stir well. Stir in whole wheat flour. Sift all-purpose flour, measure and add to dough, mixing well. (If dough seems too soft, add ¼ to ½ cup additional all-purpose flour.) Turn out on lightly floured board and knead until smooth and elastic, about 10 minutes. Shape into a ball and put into greased bowl. Turn dough over to bring greased side up; cover with a cloth. Set in warm place free from draft and allow to rise until double in bulk, about 3 hours. Punch down. Roll on lightly floured board into a circle ¼ inch thick. Cut into 10 pie-shaped pieces. Roll up tightly, beginning at wide end. Seal point firmly. Put on lightly greased baking sheet with point underneath. Set in warm place and allow to rise to double in bulk, 30 to 45 minutes. Brush with water and sprinkle with coarse salt. Bake in 425°F. oven 15 minutes. *Makes 10 rolls.*

Muffins

2 cups all-purpose flour
3 teaspoons baking powder
½ teaspoon salt
3 tablespoons sugar
1 egg
1 cup milk
1 teaspoon pure Vanilla Extract
3 tablespoons shortening, melted

Grease well the bottoms of muffin cups or line with paper baking cups. Sift flour, measure and sift again with dry ingredients. Beat egg lightly; stir in milk, vanilla and melted shortening. Add to dry ingredients. Mix just until dry ingredients are moistened, 10 to 15 strokes. Spoon into muffin cups and bake in 425°F. oven 20 to 25 minutes. Serve hot.

Makes 12 muffins.

VARIATIONS:

Mace-Blueberry Muffins—Add ¼ teaspoon Mace to dry ingredients and substitute 1 cup blueberries for ¼ cup of the milk in above recipe.

Orange Muffins—Add 2 teaspoons Orange Peel to dry ingredients in above recipe and proceed as directed. Mix together ½ cup powdered sugar, ½ teaspoon Orange Peel, ½ teaspoon Orange Extract and 2 teaspoons water. Drizzle over top of hot baked muffins.

Spice Muffins—Add 1 teaspoon Pumpkin Pie Spice to dry ingredients in above recipe. For even greater variety you will find it fun and exciting to vary the flavor of Spice Muffins. Add ¼ teaspoon Cinnamon, Ginger, Nutmeg or ground Cardamom in place of Pumpkin Pie Spice.

Cinnamon-Streusel Muffins—Mix together 1 tablespoon butter and ¼ cup Cinnamon Sugar. Sprinkle over top of muffin batter before baking.

Spicy Banana Nut Bread

⅓ cup shortening
⅔ cup sugar
2 eggs
1 teaspoon pure Vanilla Extract
1¾ cups all-purpose flour
2 teaspoons baking powder
½ teaspoon salt
1 teaspoon Cinnamon
⅛ teaspoon ground Cardamom
⅛ teaspoon Mace
1 cup mashed bananas
½ cup chopped nuts

Cream shortening and sugar until light and fluffy. Add eggs and vanilla and beat well. Sift flour, measure and sift again with baking powder, salt, cinnamon, cardamom and mace. Add alternately with bananas to creamed mixture. Stir in nuts. Grease bottom of 9¼ x 5¼ x 2¾-inch loaf pan. Pour batter into pan. Bake in 350°F. oven 1 hour to 1 hour and 10 minutes. Serve warm or cold at any meal. You will find this especially good with fruit salads, spread with butter or cream cheese for sandwiches and is a school lunch box favorite.

Makes 1 loaf.

Doughnuts

½ cup sugar
1 teaspoon salt
¼ cup butter
¾ cup scalded milk
2 packages active dry yeast
½ cup warm water
1 egg, beaten
2 teaspoons Lemon Peel
4 cups all-purpose flour
½ teaspoon Cinnamon
1 teaspoon Nutmeg
Fat for frying

Add sugar, salt and butter to scalded milk and cool to lukewarm. Dissolve yeast in warm water. Add egg, lemon peel and cooled milk mixture; mix well. Sift flour, measure and sift again with cinnamon and nutmeg. Stir into yeast mixture. Turn out on lightly floured board and knead until smooth and dough no longer sticks to board, about 10 minutes. Put in greased bowl; turn dough over to coat with grease. Cover and set in warm place free from draft and let rise until double in bulk, about 1 hour. Punch down. Roll on lightly floured board to ¼-inch thickness. Cut with doughnut cutter. Spread cloth over baking sheet. Put doughnuts on cloth and set in warm place and let rise to double in bulk, about 1 hour. Fry in deep fat, 375°F., until golden brown. Remove and drain on absorbent paper. Glaze (see recipe page 300). *Makes 3 dozen.*

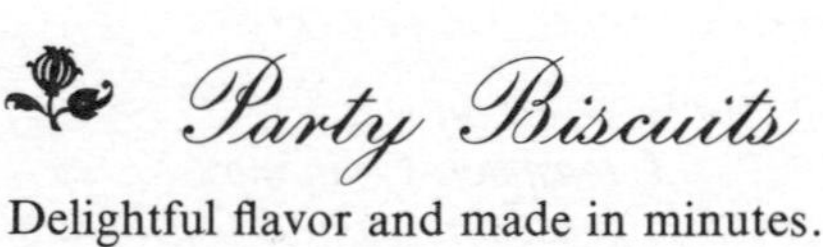

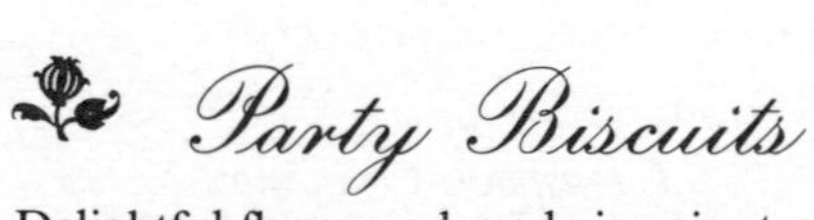

Party Biscuits

Delightful flavor and made in minutes.

1 can refrigerator biscuits
1 teaspoon of one of the following: Barbecue Spice, Curry Powder, Herb Seasoning, Orange Peel or 2 teaspoons Lemon Peel
2 tablespoons butter, melted

Pull each biscuit to about 6 inches in length. Stir one of the spices into melted butter. Dip each length of dough in seasoned butter; twist. Place on ungreased baking sheet. Bake in 475°F. oven 8 minutes. *Makes 10.*

NOTE: For added flavor when using Herb Seasoning, roll dough in Parmesan cheese after dipping in the butter mixture.

1 cup milk
3 tablespoons sugar
2 tablespoons butter or margarine
2 teaspoons Instant Minced Onion
⅛ teaspoon crushed Saffron pieces
2 teaspoons salt
2 packages active dry yeast
1 cup warm water
4½ cups all-purpose flour
Caraway Seed

Scald milk. Stir in sugar, butter, onion, crushed saffron and salt. Cool to lukewarm. Sprinkle yeast over warm water in a large mixing bowl. Stir until dissolved, then add milk mixture. Add flour; stir until well blended. Cover and set in warm place. Let rise to more than double in bulk, about 40 minutes. Stir batter down and beat vigorously ½ minute. Turn into greased 1½-quart round casserole; sprinkle top with caraway seed. Bake in 375°F. oven 1 to 1¼ hours.

Makes 1 loaf.

1 package hot roll mix
¼ cup melted butter
1 teaspoon Dill Weed
Poppy Seed

Prepare roll mix as directed on package. After first rising, roll out dough on lightly floured board to ¼-inch thickness. Cut approximately 30 rounds with a 2-inch biscuit cutter. Dip each round in a mixture of melted butter and dill weed. Arrange the rounds upright (on edge) next to each other in a 9½-inch ring mold. Set in warm place and let rise to double in bulk, about 30 minutes. Sprinkle top with poppy seed. Bake in 375°F. oven 20 minutes.

Makes 1 ring.

Rye Herb Bread

1 tablespoon Parsley Flakes
⅛ teaspoon Garlic Powder
1 teaspoon Bon Appétit
¼ teaspoon Black Pepper
¼ teaspoon dry Mustard
¼ teaspoon Rosemary Leaves
¼ teaspoon rubbed Sage
¼ teaspoon Tarragon Leaves
¼ teaspoon ground Thyme
½ cup butter, creamed
1 loaf light rye bread, sliced

Add seasonings to creamed butter; mix well. Spread mixture generously on each slice of bread and reassemble loaf. Wrap in aluminum foil and heat in 400°F. oven 15 to 20 minutes. You will find this good with almost any dish but is especially good with spaghetti, eggs or cheese dishes.

Serves 8 to 10.

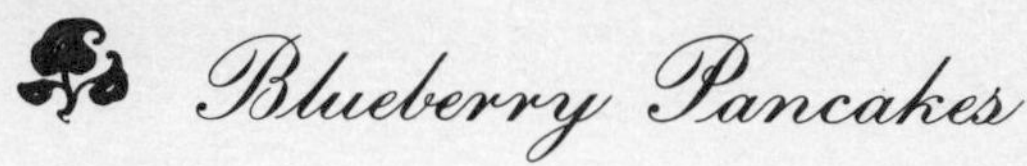

Blueberry Pancakes

1 egg, well beaten
1½ cups buttermilk
1 teaspoon pure Vanilla Extract
1¼ cups sifted all-purpose flour
2 teaspoons sugar
½ teaspoon baking soda
1 teaspoon baking powder
½ teaspoon salt
¼ teaspoon Allspice
2 tablespoons melted shortening
1 cup blueberries (thaw and drain frozen berries)

Combine beaten egg, buttermilk and vanilla; beat until well blended. Sift together flour, sugar, soda, baking powder, salt and allspice. Add to egg mixture along with melted shortening and beat until smooth. Stir in blueberries. Pour small amounts of batter onto heated griddle. Cook until full of bubbles and brown. Turn and brown other side.

Makes 10 to 12 pancakes.

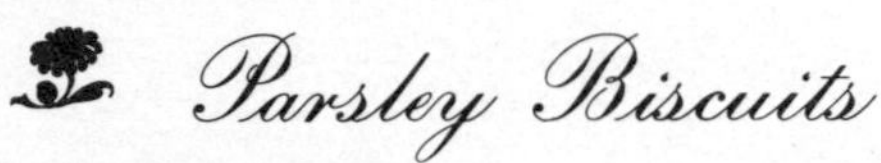

Parsley Biscuits

2 cups all-purpose flour
3 teaspoons baking powder
1 teaspoon salt
2 teaspoons Parsley Flakes
5 tablespoons shortening
¾ cup milk
Sesame Seed, Poppy Seed or Caraway Seed

Sift flour, measure and sift again with baking powder and salt. Add parsley flakes. Using pastry blender or two knives cut shortening into flour until the mixture is consistency of coarse corn meal. Add milk and stir until mixture forms ball and leaves side of bowl. Turn out on lightly floured board. Roll to ¼-inch thickness. Cut with biscuit cutter and put on lightly greased baking sheet. Sprinkle tops with seed and lightly press into biscuits. Bake in 425° F. oven 10 to 12 minutes. *Makes sixteen 2-inch biscuits.*

DESSERTS

Gourmet Desserts

Bananas Flambé 272

Cheesecake Elégante 274

Chocolate Mousse 274

Coffee Torte 275

Cool Lemon Soufflé 273

Crêpes Suzette 277

Ginger Crêpes 277

Curried Fruit Medley 281

Homemade Vanilla Ice Cream 276

Cinnamon-Nut Ice Cream 276

Spiced Coffee Ice Cream 276

Peaches Zanzibar 283

Spiced Bavarian 284

Spiced Soufflé 279

Strawberries Romanoff 271

New Twists on Old Themes

Banana Fritters 280

Choux Glacés à la Crème 278

Cinnamon Ice Cream 279

New Twists on Old Themes (Cont.)

Ginger Dessert Waffles 281

Spicy Meringues 282

Family Favorites

Apple Cobbler 271

Apple Dumplings 282

Baked Apples 280

Floating Island Meringues 280

Heavenly Hash 283

Peach Cobbler Supreme 281

Strawberry-Rhubarb Crisp 283

Colonial Puddings

Apricot Pudding 285

Creamy Rice Pudding 276

Cardamom Rice Pudding 276

English Plum Pudding 284

Orange Bread Custard 285

Spiced Bread Pudding 275

Steamed Date Pudding 278

Apple Cobbler

FILLING:

- 6 *large cooking apples*
- 1 *cup sugar*
- ¼ *cup dark brown sugar, firmly packed*
- 2 *tablespoons flour*
- 1 *teaspoon Cinnamon*
- ¼ *teaspoon Nutmeg*
- ¼ *teaspoon Ginger*
- ⅛ *teaspoon Allspice*
- ½ *teaspoon salt*
- ⅛ *teaspoon Lemon Peel*
- 2 *tablespoons butter*

Peel, core and slice apples. Mix sugar, brown sugar, flour, cinnamon, nutmeg, ginger, allspice, salt and lemon peel. Toss with apples. Spread apple mixture evenly in an 11 x 7 x 2-inch baking dish. Dot with butter.

CRUST:

- 2 *cups flour*
- 1 *teaspoon salt*
- 2½ *teaspoons baking powder*
- ½ *teaspoon Cinnamon*
- ⅛ *teaspoon Nutmeg*
- ⅓ *cup shortening*
- 1 *tablespoon butter*
- 1 *cup milk*

Sift together flour, salt, baking powder, cinnamon and nutmeg. Cut in shortening and butter. Stir in milk. Dough will be moist. Turn out on well-floured board and knead 8 to 10 times. Pat or cut to fit dish and place over apples. Bake in 375°F. oven 40 to 45 minutes. Serve warm with cream or vanilla ice cream. *Serves 6 to 8.*

Strawberries Romanoff

- 1 *quart fresh strawberries*
- ¼ *cup orange juice*
- ½ *teaspoon Mace*
- ¼ *cup Cognac*
- ¼ *cup Cointreau*
- 1 *cup heavy cream*
- ⅛ *teaspoon Mace*
- 4 *tablespoons sugar*
- 1 *quart vanilla ice cream*

Wash and hull berries. Place in a 2-quart bowl. Add orange juice, the ½ teaspoon mace, Cognac and Cointreau. Mix well. Marinate overnight. Whip cream with the ⅛ teaspoon mace and sugar. Soften ice cream at room temperature and beat with electric mixer. Fold in whipped cream. Spoon berries (using a slotted spoon) into cream mixture; mix gently. Pour into serving bowl. Serve immediately, spooning juice over each individual serving. *Makes 6 to 8 servings.*

Bananas Flambé

3 tablespoons butter
3 tablespoons light brown sugar
2 tablespoons water
¼ teaspoon Cinnamon
⅛ teaspoon Nutmeg
3 firm-ripe bananas
1 tablespoon Triple Sec
1 tablespoon light Rum

Melt butter in large skillet or chafing dish over medium heat. Stir in brown sugar, water, cinnamon and nutmeg. Cook 1 minute. Cut bananas in half lengthwise, then cut the pieces in half. Add bananas to mixture in skillet. Turn each piece to coat with sauce. Stir in Triple Sec. Add rum to one side of the skillet, immediately light with a long match. Carefully tip skillet to swirl flaming mixture. Serve over vanilla ice cream.

Makes 6 servings, ½ banana each.

Cool Lemon Soufflé

2 envelopes unflavored gelatine	*¼ teaspoon Mace*
¾ cup cold water	*1 teaspoon Almond Extract*
6 lemons	*2 tablespoons Grand Marnier*
8 eggs	*2 cups heavy cream*
½ teaspoon salt	*½ cup powdered sugar*
2 cups sugar	*Candied Lemon Shreds for garnish, recipe below*
¼ teaspoon Nutmeg	
¼ teaspoon Cinnamon	

To prepare soufflé dish, fold a 30-inch strip of foil in half lengthwise. Tie around outside of a 6-cup soufflé dish to make a collar standing about 5 inches above rim of dish. Soften gelatine in cold water. Cut about ¼ cup long shreds of lemon peel from 1 or 2 lemons. Set aside. Extract enough juice from lemons to make 1 cup. Separate eggs. Combine egg yolks, lemon juice, salt, 1 cup sugar, nutmeg, cinnamon and mace in top of double boiler. Cook over boiling water, stirring constantly, until slightly thickened. Add gelatine and ½ teaspoon almond extract. Stir until gelatine is dissolved. Pour into a large bowl. Cool. Stir in Grand Marnier. Beat egg whites until foamy. Gradually add the remaining 1 cup sugar and beat until stiff peaks form when beaters are lifted. Whip cream with powdered sugar and the remaining ½ teaspoon almond extract. Fold egg whites and cream into gelatine mixture. Pour into prepared soufflé dish. Refrigerate 3 hours. Cut string and carefully remove foil collar. Decorate soufflé with whipped cream, pressed through a pastry bag with a star or fluted tip, and Candied Lemon Shreds.

Makes ten 1-cup servings.

To Make Candied Lemon Shreds—Put ¼ cup thin strips of lemon peel in saucepan with ¼ cup sugar, ¼ cup water, 1 tablespoon Grand Marnier, 1 whole allspice and one 1-inch piece vanilla bean. Bring to a boil and cook until lemon peel is transparent. Remove allspice and vanilla bean. Drain. Use lemon peel to decorate top of soufflé.

To Make Flavorful Whipped Cream—Whip 1 cup heavy cream with 6 tablespoons powdered sugar, 1 teaspoon pure vanilla extract, ⅛ teaspoon each cinnamon, nutmeg and mace. Whip until very stiff. Put in a pastry bag and decorate top of soufflé with cream before sprinkling with lemon peel.

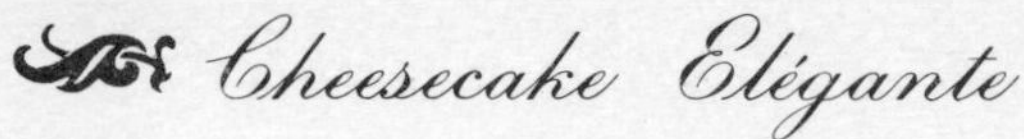

Cheesecake Elégante

CRUST:

1½ cups graham cracker crumbs
¼ cup powdered sugar
1 teaspoon ground Allspice
⅓ cup melted butter

Combine all ingredients. Spread in bottom of a 9-inch spring-form pan, pressing some of the crumbs up the sides to form a rim about 1½ inches high.

CHEESE LAYER:

4 8-ounce packages cream cheese, at room temperature
4 eggs, lightly beaten
1⅓ cups sugar
1 tablespoon pure Vanilla Extract

Beat cheese until soft and creamy. Add eggs, sugar and vanilla, beating until thoroughly creamed and smooth. Pour into crust. Bake in 325°F. oven 1 hour and 15 minutes, then top with sour cream layer.

SOUR CREAM LAYER:

1 pint dairy sour cream
⅓ cup sugar
1 tablespoon pure Vanilla Extract
¼ teaspoon Rum Extract

Combine sour cream, sugar and extracts. Spread over cheese layer. Return to oven; increase temperature to 450°F. and bake 7 minutes. Remove from oven and cool, then chill. *Serves 10 to 12.*

Chocolate Mousse

Rich, smooth, luscious.

1½ teaspoons unflavored gelatine
2 tablespoons cold water
2 1-ounce squares unsweetened chocolate
¾ cup sugar
¼ teaspoon Mace
1 cup milk
2 cups heavy cream
1 teaspoon pure Vanilla Extract

Soften gelatine in cold water. Put chocolate, ½ cup of the sugar, mace and milk in saucepan or in top of double boiler. Heat thoroughly over low heat until chocolate melts. Do not boil. Beat until smooth with rotary beater. Add gelatine; stir until melted. Pour into a bowl and chill until mixture thickens; then beat until light and fluffy. Whip cream, adding remaining sugar and vanilla. Fold into chocolate mixture. Pour into a 2-quart mold. Freeze. Remove from mold onto serving plate.

Serves 6 to 8.

Coffee Torte

An elegant Viennese dessert—impressive, very special.

MERINGUES:

6 egg whites
¼ teaspoon Cream of Tartar
1 cup sugar
1½ cups sifted powdered sugar
1 teaspoon Almond Extract
Dash Allspice
Dash Mace

Beat egg whites until foamy; add cream of tartar. Continue beating until egg whites hold a stiff peak. Slowly add sugar and powdered sugar, one tablespoon at a time, beating well after each addition. Add extract, allspice and mace; beat 2 minutes longer. Cut four 8-inch circles from heavy brown paper. Divide meringue into 4 parts and spread evenly over the circles of paper. Place on baking sheets. Bake in 250°F. oven 1 hour 15 minutes. Remove from oven; cool. Then remove paper from bottom of meringue layers.

FILLING:

6 egg yolks
½ cup sugar
½ cup cold strong coffee
1 tablespoon flour
½ cup soft butter
½ pint heavy cream, whipped

Combine egg yolks, sugar, coffee and flour in top of double boiler. Cook over boiling water, stirring constantly, until mixture thickens. Cool to lukewarm. Add butter; stir until well blended. Spoon and spread filling over top of meringue layers, stacking as a layer cake. Decorate with rosettes of whipped cream. Chill. *Serves 8 to 10.*

Spiced Bread Pudding

2 cups dry bread cubes
4 cups milk, scalded
¾ cup sugar
1 tablespoon butter
¼ teaspoon salt
⅛ teaspoon Nutmeg
½ teaspoon Cinnamon
¼ teaspoon Ginger
4 eggs, lightly beaten
2 teaspoons pure Vanilla Extract
¼ cup raisins

Soak bread in milk 5 minutes. Add sugar, butter, salt, nutmeg, cinnamon and ginger. Pour slowly over eggs. Add vanilla and raisins; mix well. Pour into buttered 1½-quart casserole or baking dish. Bake in pan of hot water in 350°F. oven 1 hour or until silver knife comes out clean when inserted in center. You may serve with lemon or orange sauce or Crème Anglaise (see recipe page 375), if desired. *Makes 8 to 10 servings.*

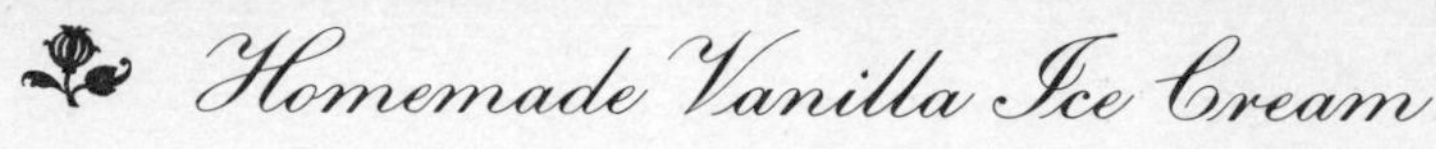

There is no dessert more delicious than old-fashioned homemade ice cream flavored with pure vanilla.

2 cups milk
½ cup sugar
1 tablespoon Arrowroot
¼ teaspoon salt
4 egg yolks
2 teaspoons pure Vanilla Extract
2 cups heavy cream

Scald milk. Combine sugar, arrowroot and salt. Beat egg yolks and gradually add sugar mixture, beating until sugar dissolves. Slowly add milk to egg mixture while beating. Cook in top of double boiler or over lowest heat, stirring constantly, until mixture thickens and coats a metal spoon. Strain and chill. Stir in vanilla and cream. Freeze in 2-quart ice cream freezer. Excellent served with fresh fruits. *Makes about 1½ quarts.*

VARIATIONS:

Spiced Coffee Ice Cream—Blend 2 tablespoons instant coffee (dry), ¼ teaspoon Cinnamon, ⅛ teaspoon Nutmeg and dash Cloves into hot custard before chilling. Proceed as in above recipe.

Cinnamon-Nut Ice Cream—Add 1½ teaspoons Cinnamon with the sugar in recipe for Homemade Vanilla Ice Cream and stir in ½ cup chopped nuts just before freezing.

Nutmeg is essential to give this old-time favorite its special goodness.

½ cup rice
4 cups milk
¼ cup butter
3 eggs
¾ cup sugar
1 teaspoon pure Vanilla Extract
¼ teaspoon salt
½ teaspoon Nutmeg

Combine rice and 2 cups of the milk in top of double boiler; cover and cook over hot water until rice is tender. Add butter. Beat eggs; mix in sugar, vanilla, salt and remaining milk. Add hot rice mixture, mixing well. Pour into a buttered 2-quart baking dish. Sprinkle with nutmeg. Bake in 350°F. oven 50 minutes or until silver knife comes out clean when inserted near center. *Serves 6.*

VARIATION:

Cardamom Rice Pudding—Add ⅛ teaspoon ground Cardamom when adding sugar in the above recipe.

Crêpes Suzette

Make the crêpes ahead, then heat in luscious sauce just before serving with a grand flourish.

CRÊPES:

1 cup milk
2 tablespoons butter
2 eggs, well beaten
½ cup sifted all-purpose flour
¾ teaspoon baking powder
½ teaspoon salt
¼ teaspoon Cinnamon
Dash Mace

Heat milk and butter to just below boiling point. Do not boil. Cool slightly. Combine eggs, flour, baking powder, salt, cinnamon and mace; beat into milk mixture. Pour 2 generous tablespoons batter into lightly buttered 6- to 7-inch fry pan and cook over medium heat 1 minute or until lightly browned on bottom. Turn and brown other side. Remove to plate; set aside until ready to serve. Repeat until batter is used. (These may be made ahead of time.) When ready to serve follow one of the recipes below.

Makes 12 crêpes.

SUZETTE SAUCE:

⅓ cup butter
¼ cup Cointreau
½ cup orange juice
1 teaspoon Orange Peel
¼ cup brandy

Melt butter in chafing dish; add Cointreau, orange juice and orange peel. Heat until mixture comes to a boil. Add crêpes, one at a time, and baste with sauce. Fold crêpes in quarters and move to one side of pan until all are heated. Pour brandy over all and flame. Serve three to each person.

Serves 4.

VARIATION:

Ginger Crêpes—Make crêpes following above recipe. When ready to serve proceed as directed below.

24 small pieces Crystallized Ginger
1 cup Grand Marnier
⅓ cup sweet butter
4 tablespoons sugar
Juice of 1 orange
Few drops lemon juice

Put ginger in ¼ cup of the Grand Marnier and heat a few minutes. Set aside. Melt butter in chafing dish or skillet. Sprinkle sugar into pan; cook until sugar begins to melt and turns golden in color. Add orange juice, lemon juice and ¼ cup of the Grand Marnier. Bring to a boil. Place crêpes in sauce, baste, then carefully turn crêpes over. Put 2 pieces of the ginger in center of each; fold each crêpe in quarters. Push to one side of pan. Continue until all crêpes are folded, then sprinkle with remaining Grand Marnier and flame. Serve with a scoop of vanilla ice cream on one side of the plate.

Serves 4.

Choux Glacés à la Crème

Petite cream puffs with a spicy cream filling, colorfully glazed.

½ cup butter
⅛ teaspoon salt
1 cup boiling water
¼ teaspoon Allspice
1 cup sifted all-purpose flour
4 eggs
Spiced Cream Filling
Gay Tinted Glaze

Add butter and salt to boiling water and stir until mixture boils again. Sift together allspice and flour. Add all at once to boiling mixture and beat vigorously until mixture leaves side of pan. Remove from heat and add eggs, one at a time, beating hard after each addition. Drop by tablespoonfuls on baking sheet. Bake in 450°F. oven 8 minutes; reduce heat to 350°F. and continue baking 10 minutes or until puffs are lightly browned. Remove from baking sheet immediately, cutting small slit in side of each puff. Cool; fill with Spiced Cream Filling and glaze tops using Gay Tinted Glaze (see recipe page 300). If you want to make very crisp puffs, as soon as puffs are removed from oven, cut off tops and pull out soft centers. Bake shells and tops a few minutes longer. *Makes about 40.*

SPICED CREAM FILLING: To one package instant vanilla pudding add one of the following: 1 teaspoon Ginger, ¼ teaspoon Mace, ¼ teaspoon ground Cardamom or 1 teaspoon Lemon Peel. Prepare pudding as directed on package.

Steamed Date Pudding

¼ cup butter
¼ cup shortening
¾ cup sugar
3 eggs
1¼ cups sifted cake flour
1 teaspoon salt
⅛ teaspoon Mace
¾ teaspoon Allspice
1 cup milk
3 cups soft bread crumbs
¾ cup chopped dates
¼ cup chopped walnuts
1 teaspoon Lemon Peel
2 teaspoons Orange Peel

Cream together butter, shortening and sugar until light and fluffy. Add eggs, one at a time, mixing after addition of each. Sift together flour, salt, mace and allspice; add alternately to creamed mixture with milk. Fold in remaining ingredients. Spoon into a 1½-quart mold or eight individual 7-ounce molds, filling ⅔ full. Cover tightly with lid or aluminum foil. Place molds on rack in large kettle. Add enough boiling water to come half way up side of mold. Cover. Steam 1 hour or longer, depending on size mold used. You may use frozen juice cans in place of individual molds.

Makes 16 servings.

Cinnamon Ice Cream

An easy way to create a brand new dessert.

1 quart vanilla ice cream

1 teaspoon Cinnamon

Soften ice cream just enough to stir. Add cinnamon; mix thoroughly. Spoon into freezer tray and immediately refreeze. A delight with apple pie.

Makes 1 quart.

Spiced Soufflé

2 tablespoons butter
1 tablespoon Arrowroot
½ cup milk
5 egg yolks
¼ cup sugar
½ teaspoon Ginger
½ teaspoon Cinnamon
¼ teaspoon Mace
2 teaspoons Lemon Peel
2 teaspoons pure Vanilla Extract
6 egg whites
Dash salt
¼ teaspoon Cream of Tartar
1 tablespoon sugar
Soufflé Sauce Grand Marnier

In small saucepan melt butter; remove from heat. Stir in arrowroot and milk. Cook over medium heat, stirring, until sauce thickens. Beat egg yolks lightly with the ¼ cup sugar, ginger, cinnamon, mace and lemon peel. Gradually add hot sauce to beaten yolks. Stir in vanilla; continue stirring until sugar dissolves. Beat egg whites until foamy; add salt and cream of tartar and continue beating until stiff but not dry. Add the 1 tablespoon sugar during the last minutes of beating; gently fold into cooked mixture. Pour into a 2½-quart soufflé dish or casserole which has been buttered and sugared. Bake in 375°F. oven 30 minutes or until puffy and browned. Dust top with powdered sugar if desired, and serve immediately, with side dish of Soufflé Sauce Grand Marnier.

Serves 4 to 6.

SOUFFLÉ SAUCE GRAND MARNIER:

4 eggs
½ cup sugar
¼ teaspoon salt
1 teaspoon pure Vanilla Extract
1 cup heavy cream
1 cup milk, scalded
3 tablespoons Grand Marnier

Beat eggs until light and fluffy. Gradually beat in sugar. Add salt, vanilla and ½ cup of the cream; mix well. Slowly add scalded milk, beating briskly. Cook over very low heat or in top of double boiler, stirring constantly, until it is thick enough to coat a silver spoon. Chill. Stir in Grand Marnier. Whip remaining cream and fold into sauce. For a real gourmet touch, separate 2 or 3 orange sections by pulling apart the tiny tear-shaped cells which make up each orange section. Stir into sauce. Serve spooned over dessert soufflé.

Makes about 1 quart.

Banana Fritters

1 cup all-purpose flour
2 teaspoons baking powder
1 teaspoon salt
¼ cup sugar
¼ teaspoon Mace
1 egg, well beaten
½ cup milk
1 teaspoon pure Vanilla Extract
2 teaspoons melted shortening
3 firm bananas
Fat for deep fat frying
½ cup heavy cream, whipped
Cinnamon

Sift flour, measure and sift again with baking powder, salt, sugar and mace. Combine egg, milk, vanilla and melted shortening; mix well. Stir into dry ingredients and beat until smooth. Peel bananas and cut each into 3 or 4 pieces. Dip banana pieces into batter. Fry in deep fat, 375°F., until golden brown. Top hot fritters with whipped cream and sprinkle with cinnamon.

Makes 9 to 12 fritters.

Baked Apples

½ cup sugar
1½ cups apple juice
2 teaspoons Lemon Peel
1½ teaspoons Cinnamon
Few drops Red Food Color
6 baking apples

Mix together sugar, apple juice, lemon peel, cinnamon and food color. Bring to a boil, stirring to dissolve sugar. Core apples and remove peel from the top third of apple. Arrange in baking dish and pour syrup over apples. Bake in 350°F. oven about 1 hour. Cook longer if a very soft apple is desired. Baste frequently with syrup. Serve warm or cold and you may serve with cream. Good for breakfast, too! *Serves 6.*

4 egg whites
¼ teaspoon Cream of Tartar
¼ teaspoon salt
¾ cup superfine sugar
1 teaspoon pure Vanilla Extract
Dash Nutmeg

Have egg whites at room temperature. Add cream of tartar and salt; beat until soft peaks form. Beat in sugar, adding 1 tablespoon at a time. Add vanilla and beat 5 minutes. Drop by spoonfuls as "islands" on steaming hot water in a large baking dish or pan. Sprinkle with nutmeg. Bake in 400°F. oven 5 minutes or until delicately browned. Carefully remove with a slotted spoon or two forks. Put in serving bowls or saucers. Pour Crème Anglaise sauce (see recipe page 375) over tops when ready to serve. For variations in flavor, add ⅛ teaspoon ground Cardamom, ¼ teaspoon Mace or 1 teaspoon Lemon Peel to meringue mixture when you add vanilla.

Makes 10 to 12 meringues.

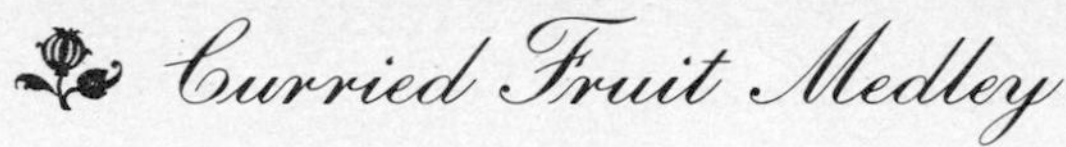

Curried Fruit Medley

Exotically different, a delightful conclusion for a company dinner.

- *1 16 or 20-oz. can each pear halves, peach halves and pineapple slices*
- *½ cup butter or margarine*
- *1 cup brown sugar, packed*
- *1 tablespoon Curry Powder*
- *¼ teaspoon salt*

Drain fruit well; arrange in a 2-quart baking dish. Melt butter; add sugar, curry powder and salt. Heat until sugar is dissolved. Pour over fruit. Bake in 350°F. oven 25 to 30 minutes. Serve hot. You will find sour cream is just right with this fruit. *Serves 8 to 10.*

Peach Cobbler Supreme

A surprise cobbler, batter rises to the top during cooking and forms a golden crust.

- *¼ cup butter*
- *1 cup sifted all-purpose flour*
- *1 cup sugar*
- *⅛ teaspoon salt*
- *1 tablespoon baking powder*
- *⅔ cup milk*
- *1 29-oz. can sliced peaches*
- *¼ teaspoon Nutmeg*
- *¼ teaspoon Cinnamon*
- *½ teaspoon Lemon Peel*

Melt butter in a 7 x 11-inch shallow baking dish. Sift together dry ingredients; add milk and stir well. Pour this mixture into the baking dish. Do not stir. Top with peaches, including juice. Sprinkle nutmeg, cinnamon and lemon peel over peaches, but do not stir. Bake in 350°F. oven 40 minutes or until golden brown. Serve warm with cream. *Serves 6 to 8.*

Ginger Dessert Waffles

- *½ cup butter or margarine*
- *1 cup sugar*
- *2 eggs*
- *1 teaspoon pure Vanilla Extract*
- *1 teaspoon Orange Peel*
- *2½ cups all-purpose flour*
- *1 tablespoon Ginger*
- *1 teaspoon Cinnamon*
- *¼ teaspoon salt*
- *1 teaspoon baking soda*
- *⅔ cup buttermilk*

Cream butter and sugar until light and fluffy. Add eggs, one at a time, beating well after each addition. Add vanilla and orange peel. Sift flour, measure and sift again with ginger, cinnamon, salt and soda. Add flour and buttermilk alternately to butter mixture. Bake in waffle iron. Serve with ice cream, whipped cream or syrup. *Serves 6 to 8.*

Spicy Meringues

8 egg whites
½ teaspoon Cream of Tartar
¼ teaspoon salt
2 cups superfine sugar
1 teaspoon pure Vanilla Extract
¼ teaspoon ground Cardamom

Have egg whites at room temperature. Add cream of tartar and salt to egg whites; beat until soft peaks form. Continue beating, adding sugar one tablespoon at a time, then add vanilla and cardamom. Beat 5 minutes longer. Drop by spoonfuls on brown paper or a piece of lightly greased aluminum foil placed on baking sheet. Shape into circles and with the back of a spoon form a well in center of each. Put in 450°F. oven and immediately turn off heat. Let stand several hours until oven is cold or overnight. Do not open oven door. Remove from paper and place on serving plate. Just before serving fill with ice cream or whipped cream and top with fruit or a tasty sauce. For interesting variations in flavor you may substitute Mace or Allspice for cardamom. Meringues can be made in any desired shapes, such as: puffs, mushrooms, ribbon strips, swans or hollow shells. *Makes 20 large or 40 small meringues.*

Apple Dumplings

Pastry for two-crust pie
¼ teaspoon Nutmeg
1 teaspoon Lemon Peel
4 medium-size cooking apples
4 teaspoons butter
4 teaspoons Cinnamon Sugar
½ cup brown sugar, packed
½ cup light corn syrup
1 teaspoon Cinnamon
¼ teaspoon Nutmeg
⅛ teaspoon Allspice
⅛ teaspoon Cloves
1½ cups water
2 tablespoons butter

Prepare pastry adding ¼ teaspoon nutmeg and the lemon peel. Roll dough about ⅛ inch thick; cut into 4 equal squares. Peel and core apples. Put an apple in center of each pastry square. Fill center of each apple with 1 teaspoon butter and 1 teaspoon cinnamon sugar. Bring opposite ends of pastry over top of apple, overlap and seal edges. Place about 1 inch apart in buttered baking dish. Combine remaining ingredients and bring to a boil. Bake dumplings in 500°F. oven 10 minutes. Reduce heat to 350°F.; bake 45 minutes longer, basting frequently with syrup. Serve warm with cream or ice cream. *Makes 4 dumplings.*

Heavenly Hash

1 11-ounce can Mandarin orange sections
1 8-ounce bottle red maraschino cherries
1 8-ounce bottle green maraschino cherries
2 8-oz. cans pineapple tidbits
1 pound marshmallows
1 pint heavy cream
⅛ teaspoon ground Cardamom
¾ teaspoon Ginger
1 teaspoon Orange Peel

Drain fruit. Cut marshmallows in half. Whip cream; add cardamom, ginger and orange peel. Gently fold all ingredients together. Refrigerate several hours before serving. *Serves 8 to 10.*

Peaches Zanzibar

1 20-oz. can peach halves
2 pieces whole Ginger
2 3-inch pieces Cinnamon
8 whole Allspice
4 whole Cardamom
6 whole Cloves
1 pint vanilla ice cream
½ pint heavy cream, whipped
Red and green cherries

Drain peaches, cut ginger into small pieces and add with other spices to the juice. Simmer 15 minutes. Arrange peaches in baking dish and pour spiced juice over top. Cover and chill several hours or overnight. Put scoop of ice cream in coupe or dessert dish. Place peach half over ice cream and spoon juice over peach. Garnish with whipped cream and pieces of red and green cherries. *Serves 5 to 6.*

Strawberry-Rhubarb Crisp

⅔ cup sugar
2 tablespoons Arrowroot
⅛ teaspoon Cloves
Dash ground Cardamom
1 10-ounce package frozen strawberries, thawed
3 cups diced rhubarb
Red Food Color
⅓ cup soft butter
⅔ cup brown sugar, packed
½ cup all-purpose flour
½ cup quick-cooking rolled oats
1½ teaspoons Lemon Peel
½ teaspoon Nutmeg
2 tablespoons Cinnamon Sugar

Combine sugar, arrowroot, cloves and cardamom; add strawberries, rhubarb and a few drops food color. (If frozen rhubarb is used, thaw, then drain thoroughly and use only ⅓ cup sugar.) Mix well and pour into a buttered 1½-quart baking dish. Mix remaining ingredients with pastry blender or fork until crumbly. Sprinkle over strawberries and rhubarb. Bake in 350°F. oven 40 to 45 minutes. *Serves 6.*

Spiced Bavarian

- *3½ cups milk*
- *2 envelopes unflavored gelatine*
- *6 eggs, separated*
- *¾ cup sugar*
- *¼ teaspoon salt*
- *¼ teaspoon Mace*
- *⅛ teaspoon ground Cardamom*
- *½ teaspoon Ginger*
- *1½ teaspoons pure Vanilla Extract*
- *1 cup heavy cream, whipped*

Scald 3 cups of the milk and soak gelatine in remaining ½ cup milk. Beat together egg yolks, sugar, salt and spices. Slowly add scalded milk to egg yolk mixture. Cook over low heat or in a double boiler, stirring constantly, until custard becomes thick and coats a silver spoon. Add softened gelatine, stirring until gelatine melts. Cool. Add vanilla and chill until slightly thickened. Fold the stiffly beaten egg whites and whipped cream into custard. Spoon into 2½-quart mold. Chill until firm. Remove from mold and garnish with whipped cream and fresh strawberries or any fruit you may desire. *Makes 10 servings.*

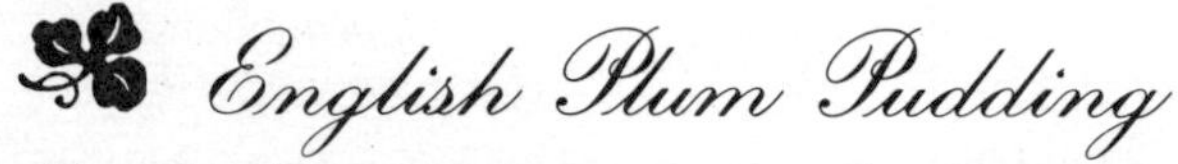

English Plum Pudding

- *1½ cups all-purpose flour*
- *½ teaspoon baking soda*
- *¼ teaspoon salt*
- *½ teaspoon Cinnamon*
- *¼ teaspoon Ginger*
- *¼ teaspoon Nutmeg*
- *¼ teaspoon Allspice*
- *½ cup dry bread crumbs*
- *1 cup brown sugar, packed*
- *1 teaspoon Lemon Peel*
- *1 teaspoon Orange Peel*
- *½ pound suet, ground*
- *1 cup currants, plumped*
- *1 cup raisins, plumped*
- *½ cup chopped candied citron*
- *½ cup chopped candied lemon peel*
- *1 cup chopped apple*
- *½ cup chopped nuts*
- *4 eggs*
- *¾ cup milk*
- *1 teaspoon pure Vanilla Extract*
- *1 tablespoon Rum Extract*

In large bowl sift together flour, soda, salt, cinnamon, ginger, nutmeg and allspice. Add bread crumbs, brown sugar, lemon peel, orange peel, ground suet, fruits and nuts; mix well. Beat eggs; add milk, vanilla and rum extract. Stir into dry ingredients, mixing well. Pour into two well greased 1-quart molds or one 2-quart mold. Fill to about one inch from top. Cover tightly and place on rack in large kettle. Add boiling water to come half way up side of mold. Cover kettle and steam 4½ to 6 hours, depending on size of mold. Remove from mold and serve hot with Spiced Hard Sauce (see recipe page 375). Pudding may be made weeks in advance and stored in a cool place or frozen. To serve, return pudding to mold or wrap in heavy cloth and steam 2 to 3 hours. *Serves 12 to 14.*

Orange Bread Custard

¼ cup sugar
2 tablespoons melted butter
1 egg, lightly beaten
½ teaspoon salt
1 teaspoon pure Vanilla Extract
½ teaspoon Orange Peel
2 cups scalded milk
1 cup bread cubes
½ cup seedless raisins

Mix together sugar, butter, egg, salt, vanilla and orange peel. Gradually add scalded milk, stirring constantly. Add bread cubes and raisins; mix well. Pour into a 1-quart buttered baking dish. Place dish in a pan of warm water. Bake in 350°F. oven 1 hour or until a silver knife comes out clean when inserted in center. *Serves 4.*

Apricot Pudding

1 cup sugar
¼ cup soft butter
1 egg
2 cups chopped apricots, fresh or cooked, dried
1 cup all-purpose flour
1 teaspoon baking soda
1 teaspoon Cinnamon
½ teaspoon Nutmeg
¼ teaspoon salt
½ cup chopped nuts

Gradually add sugar to butter, creaming well. Add egg and beat hard. Mix in apricots. Sift flour, measure and sift again with dry ingredients. Stir into apricot mixture. Add nuts and mix well. Bake in greased 8-inch square pan in 350°F. oven about 45 minutes. Cut into squares. Serve warm with Pudding Sauce (see recipe page 363), hard sauce, custard sauce or whipped cream. Good reheated. This pudding keeps well and it may also be frozen. *Serves 9.*

CAKES FROSTINGS

All-Time Favorites

Applesauce Cake 298
Blackberry Jam Cake 291
Dark Fruit Cake 294
Devil's Food Cake 296
Excellent Prune Cake 292
Gingerbread 299
Old-Fashioned Spice Cake 293
Pound Cake 297
Raisin Spice Cupcakes 296
Spiced Jelly Roll 290

Exciting and Distinctive

Chocolate Carrot Cake 289
Golden Saffron Cake 291
Lane Cake 293
Lemon Angel Food Cake 292
Poppy Seed Cake 295
Spice Chiffon Cake 295
Welsh Pork Cake 298

Tricks with Mixes

Cardamom Ripple Cake 291

Tricks with Mixes (Cont.)

Cinnamon Luncheon Cake 294
Ginger Peach Upside-Down Cake 297
  Pineapple-Upside-Down Cake 297

Frostings and Toppings

Broiled Spiced Topping 302
Cinnamon Frosting 301
Dark Chocolate Frosting 289
Fluffy Snow Peak Frosting 299
Lemon Frosting 301
Lemon Glaze 300
  Allspice Glaze 300
  Cinnamon Glaze 300
  Gay Tinted Glaze 300
  Nutmeg Glaze 300
  Orange Glaze 300
Mint Julep Frosting 299
Sour Cream Frosting 300
  Pink Perfection Frosting 300
Spiced Whipped Cream Topping 301
  Orange Whipped Cream Topping 301
Spicy Chocolate Frosting 302

Chocolate Carrot Cake

2½ cups cake flour
2 cups sugar
3 tablespoons cocoa
1 teaspoon baking powder
1 teaspoon Cinnamon
¼ teaspoon Mace
⅛ teaspoon Nutmeg
1 cup butter, softened
4 eggs
1 tablespoon pure Vanilla Extract
3 cups shredded carrots
4 squares (4 ounces) semisweet chocolate, cut in small pieces
1 cup coarsely chopped walnuts

Sift together first 7 ingredients. Beat butter with eggs. Add vanilla, dry ingredients and carrots. Beat 2 minutes at medium speed. Stir in chocolate and walnuts. Spread in greased and floured 13 x 9 x 2-inch baking pan. Bake in 350°F. oven 40 to 45 minutes. While cake is still hot, spread with Dark Chocolate Frosting.

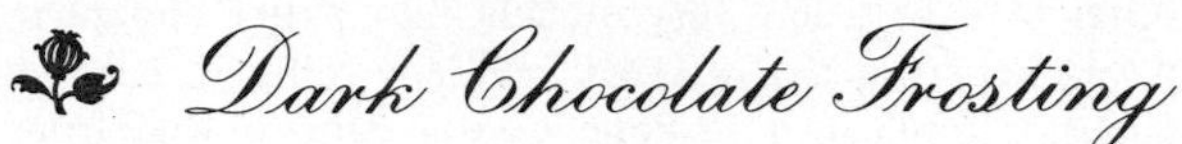

Dark Chocolate Frosting

4 squares (4 ounces) semisweet chocolate
2 tablespoons light corn syrup
1 teaspoon pure Vanilla Extract
⅛ teaspoon Almond Extract
⅛ teaspoon Cinnamon
1 cup powdered sugar
2 tablespoons hot water

Melt chocolate in top of double boiler over hot water. Add corn syrup, vanilla, almond extract and cinnamon. Mix well. Stir in powdered sugar. Gradually add hot water, mixing until smooth. Spread, while still warm, over a 13 x 9 x 2-inch cake. *Makes 1 cup.*

Spiced Jelly Roll

1½ cups sifted cake flour
1½ teaspoons baking powder
¼ teaspoon salt
¼ teaspoon Nutmeg
¼ teaspoon Cinnamon
3 eggs
1¼ cups sugar
2 teaspoons pure Vanilla Extract
¾ cup milk
1½ tablespoons butter

FILLING:

¾ cup currant jelly
¼ teaspoon Cinnamon
¼ teaspoon Ginger

Sift together flour, baking powder, salt, nutmeg and cinnamon. Beat eggs until thick and light, about 5 minutes. Add sugar gradually, beating until thick. Add vanilla. Fold flour mixture into egg mixture about ½ cup at a time. Bring milk and butter to a boil; stir very quickly into batter and pour immediately into a wax paper-lined 15 x 11 x 1-inch jelly roll pan. Bake in 375°F. oven 12 minutes or until cake tests done. Loosen edges of cake from pan; turn onto towel sprinkled with powdered sugar. Trim edges of cake. Roll cake and towel from narrow end immediately; cool thoroughly on rack. Beat filling ingredients together. Carefully unroll cake. Spread inside with filling. Reroll, carefully removing towel. Dust with powdered sugar.

Makes one 10-inch jelly roll.

Blackberry Jam Cake

¾ cup butter
1 cup sugar
3 eggs, separated
1 teaspoon pure Vanilla Extract
2¼ cups sifted cake flour
1 teaspoon baking soda
¼ teaspoon salt
1 teaspoon Cinnamon
1 teaspoon Cloves
1 teaspoon Allspice
½ teaspoon Nutmeg
¼ cup buttermilk
1 cup thick blackberry jam
⅛ teaspoon Cream of Tartar

Cream butter; add sugar and continue to cream until light and fluffy. Add egg yolks, one at a time, beating well after addition of each. Stir in vanilla. Sift together flour, soda, salt and spices. Add alternately with buttermilk and jam to creamed mixture. Add cream of tartar to egg whites and beat until stiff; fold into batter. Pour into two greased and floured 9-inch cake pans. Bake in 375°F. oven 30 minutes or until cake tests done. Frost with Lemon Frosting (see recipe page 301).

Cardamom Ripple Cake

1 package white cake mix
¼ teaspoon ground Cardamom
1 teaspoon pure Vanilla Extract
14 drops Red Food Color

To cake mix add cardamom and vanilla. Prepare cake as directed on package. Pour half the batter into another bowl and tint with food color. Spoon white and pink batters alternately into two greased and floured 8- or 9-inch layer cake pans. Cut through batter with knife several times for rippled effect. Bake as directed on package. Frost with Pink Perfection Frosting (see recipe page 300).

Golden Saffron Cake

½ cup butter or margarine
1 cup sugar
8 individual pieces Saffron
2 eggs
1 teaspoon pure Vanilla Extract
2½ cups sifted cake flour
¼ teaspoon salt
1 tablespoon baking powder
1 cup milk

Cream butter and sugar until light and fluffy. Add saffron which has been finely crushed. Add eggs, one at a time, beating well after each addition. Stir in vanilla. Sift flour, salt and baking powder together; add to butter mixture alternately with milk. If using mixer, set at low speed when mixing in flour. Pour batter into two greased and floured 8-inch cake pans. Bake in 375°F. oven 25 minutes. Remove from pans and when cool frost with Lemon Frosting (see recipe page 301). Decorate with Poppy Seed, Multi-colored Décors or Yellow Crystal Décors for added interest.

Lemon Angel Food Cake

1½ cups sifted cake flour
2 cups superfine sugar
½ teaspoon salt
1½ teaspoons Cream of Tartar
1½ cups (11 or 12) egg whites
2 teaspoons Lemon Peel
1½ teaspoons pure Vanilla Extract
½ teaspoon Almond Extract
½ teaspoon Lemon Extract

Sift flour and 1 cup of the sugar together three times. Set aside. Add salt and cream of tartar to egg whites; beat until stiff but not dry. Add the remaining cup of sugar, 2 tablespoons at a time; if using mixer, set at low speed. Continue beating until meringue holds stiff peaks. Do not use mixer from this point, but fold with wire whip or spatula. Mix in lemon peel and extracts. Fold in the sugar-flour mixture, 2 tablespoons at a time, mixing well but gently. Push batter into ungreased 10-inch tube pan. Cut through batter with knife to remove any large air bubbles. Bake in 375°F. oven 30 minutes or until no imprint remains when lightly touched. Invert pan on funnel or bottle until cake is completely cooled; remove from pan. Drizzle Lemon Glaze (see recipe page 300) over top.

Excellent Prune Cake

1 cup coarsely chopped prunes
½ cup butter
1 cup sugar
1 teaspoon Cinnamon
¼ teaspoon Nutmeg
¼ teaspoon Allspice
2 eggs
2 cups all-purpose flour
3 teaspoons baking powder
¼ teaspoon baking soda
1 teaspoon salt
¼ cup prune juice
½ cup milk
1 cup chopped walnuts

Cook and chop prunes before measuring. Cream butter, sugar and spices until light and fluffy. Add eggs, one at a time, beating well after addition of each. Sift flour, measure and sift again with baking powder, soda and salt. Add dry ingredients alternately with prune juice and milk to creamed mixture. Stir in prunes and walnuts. Pour into two greased and floured 8-inch layer cake pans (lined with paper if desired). Bake in 350°F. oven 30 minutes or until cake tests done. Remove from pan and cool on rack. You may serve plain or frosted. Or serve warm with a tart lemon or orange sauce.

Lane Cake

1 cup butter or margarine
2 cups sugar
2 teaspoons pure Vanilla Extract
3¼ cups sifted cake flour
3½ teaspoons baking powder
½ teaspoon salt
¼ teaspoon Mace
1 cup milk
8 egg whites, stiffly beaten
Lane Filling

Cream butter and sugar together until light and fluffy; add vanilla. Sift together flour, baking powder, salt and mace. Add flour mixture and milk alternately to butter mixture. Fold in stiffly beaten egg whites. Pour into three greased and floured 9-inch layer cake pans. Bake in 375°F. oven 20 minutes or until cake tests done. Turn out on cake racks; cool. Spread Lane Filling between layers and on top of cake. Store in covered container in cool place about 3 days, allowing cake to ripen. Each day spoon filling that has run off back onto cake.

LANE FILLING:

8 egg yolks
1¼ cups sugar
½ cup butter
1 teaspoon Orange Peel
¼ teaspoon Mace
⅛ teaspoon ground Cardamom
¼ teaspoon salt
1 cup chopped pecans
1 cup finely chopped candied pineapple
1 cup finely chopped candied cherries
1 cup shredded coconut
½ cup bourbon

Beat egg yolks lightly; add sugar, butter, orange peel, mace, cardamom and salt. Cook, stirring constantly, 5 minutes or until sugar melts and mixture thickens slightly. Remove from heat and add remaining ingredients. Cool before spreading on cake.

Makes enough for tops of three 9-inch cake layers.

Old-Fashioned Spice Cake

2½ cups sifted cake flour
2 teaspoons baking powder
½ teaspoon baking soda
½ teaspoon salt
¼ teaspoon Cloves
¼ teaspoon Nutmeg or Mace
½ teaspoon Allspice
1 teaspoon Cinnamon
½ cup shortening
1¼ cups brown sugar, packed
3 eggs
1 cup buttermilk

Sift flour, baking powder, soda, salt and spices together. Cream shortening and sugar until light and fluffy. Add eggs, one at a time, beating well after addition of each. Add flour mixture alternately with buttermilk. Pour batter into two greased and floured 9-inch layer cake pans. Bake in 350°F. oven 30 minutes. Remove from pan; cool on racks. Frost with Cinnamon Frosting (see recipe page 301). Decorate with walnut halves.

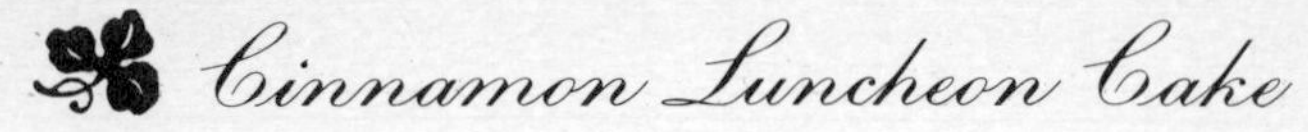

Cinnamon Luncheon Cake

1 package yellow cake mix
2 tablespoons butter or margarine
¼ cup powdered sugar
2 teaspoons Cinnamon

Prepare the cake as directed on package. When removed from pan, brush top of cake with melted butter. Sprinkle with powdered sugar and cinnamon which have been sifted together. Serve warm. It's good cold too! You will find this cake quick and easy. *Makes 16 servings.*

Dark Fruit Cake

A perfect blend of spices makes this an outstanding cake.

1½ pounds seedless raisins
½ pound candied citron
¼ pound candied lemon peel
¼ pound candied orange peel
2 pounds candied cherries
2 pounds candied pineapple
½ pound dates
1 16-oz. can pitted tart red cherries, drained (save juice)
1 pound pecans
5 cups flour
½ pound butter or margarine
2 cups brown sugar, packed
7 eggs, separated
1 12-ounce jar apple jelly
1 tablespoon ground Cinnamon
1 tablespoon ground Allspice
1 teaspoon ground Cloves
1 teaspoon ground Nutmeg
1 teaspoon ground Mace
1 teaspoon baking powder
½ teaspoon baking soda
½ cup cherry juice
1 tablespoon Brandy Extract
2 teaspoons pure Vanilla Extract
½ cup dark syrup or molasses

Plump raisins. (Wash raisins; spread out in a flat pan and cover. Heat in 350°F. oven until they become full and round.) Set aside enough candied fruits and pecans to decorate tops of cakes. Cut remaining fruits and pecans into pieces and dredge in 2 cups of the flour, mixing well. Cream butter; gradually add sugar, beating until fluffy. Add egg yolks, one at a time, beating after each addition. Blend in jelly. Sift remaining flour with spices, baking powder and soda; add to batter alternately with cherry juice, extracts and syrup. Mix well. Beat egg whites until stiff but not dry; fold into batter. Add fruits and pecans; mix carefully. Pour into four 9¼ x 5¼ x 2¾-inch loaf pans which have been greased and lined with paper. Bake in 250°F. oven 3½ to 4 hours. (Cake tests done when a cake tester is inserted and is moist but not doughy when withdrawn.) About ½ hour before cake is removed from oven, brush with additional syrup and decorate with candied fruits reserved for top. You may bake in two 10-inch tube pans, baking 5 to 6 hours. *Makes 12 to 14 pounds fruit cake.*

Spice Chiffon Cake

2¼ cups sifted cake flour
1½ cups sugar
3 teaspoons baking powder
1 teaspoon salt
1 teaspoon Cinnamon
½ teaspoon Nutmeg
½ teaspoon Allspice
½ teaspoon Cloves
½ cup salad oil
5 egg yolks
¾ cup cold water
1 teaspoon Orange Peel
½ teaspoon Cream of Tartar
1 cup egg whites (7 or 8)

Sift flour, sugar, baking powder, salt and spices into a bowl. Make a well and add oil, egg yolks, water and orange peel. Beat with spoon until smooth. Add cream of tartar to egg whites; beat until stiff but not dry. Pour egg yolk mixture slowly over egg whites, folding just until blended. Do not stir. Pour into ungreased 10-inch tube pan. Bake in 325°F. oven 55 minutes, then increase temperature to 350°F. and bake 10 minutes longer. Invert pan on funnel or bottle until cake is completely cooled; remove from pan. Glaze with Lemon Glaze (see recipe page 300) if desired.

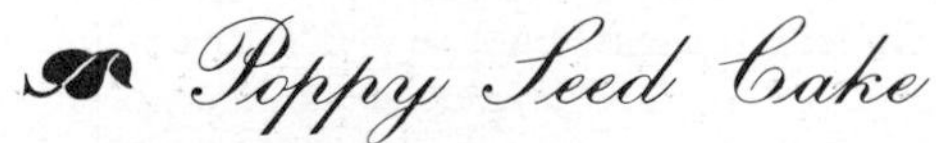

4 eggs, separated
1 cup butter or margarine
1½ cups sugar
⅓ cup Poppy Seed
1 teaspoon baking soda
1 cup dairy sour cream
2 cups sifted cake flour

Have eggs, butter and sour cream at room temperature. Beat egg whites until almost stiff; gradually beat in ½ cup of the sugar. Continue beating until stiff peaks form; set aside. Cream together butter and the remaining sugar until light and fluffy. Add egg yolks, one at a time, beating well after each addition. Stir in poppy seed. Combine soda and sour cream; add to creamed mixture alternately with flour. (Add about ¼ of the flour first, then ⅓ of the cream, and repeat until all is used, mixing just until smooth after each addition.) Gently fold in the stiffly beaten egg whites. Spoon into an ungreased 9-inch tube pan (line bottom with paper if desired). Bake in 350°F. oven 1 hour. Loosen around sides and carefully turn out on rack to cool. Delicious served while still warm.

Raisin Spice Cupcakes

- 1 cup raisins
- ½ cup water
- ½ teaspoon baking soda
- ½ cup butter or shortening
- 1 cup sugar
- 1 teaspoon salt
- ¾ teaspoon Cinnamon
- ⅛ teaspoon Nutmeg
- ⅛ teaspoon Allspice
- 2 eggs
- ½ teaspoon pure Vanilla Extract
- 2 cups all-purpose flour
- ½ teaspoon baking powder
- ½ cup chopped walnuts
- Cinnamon Sugar

Boil raisins in water 5 minutes. Drain, reserving ¼ cup liquid (if necessary add water to make ¼ cup). Cool; then add soda to cooled liquid and set aside. Cream butter, sugar, salt, cinnamon, nutmeg and allspice at low speed until thoroughly creamed. Add eggs and vanilla and beat at high speed until light and fluffy. Sift flour, measure and sift again with baking powder. Add about ¼ flour mixture at a time alternately with small amount of the raisin liquid, mixing just until smooth after each addition. Stir in walnuts and drained raisins. Spoon into muffin cups which have been greased and floured or lined with paper baking cups, filling two thirds full. Sprinkle tops generously with cinnamon sugar. Bake in 350°F. oven 20 to 25 minutes.

Makes about 20 cupcakes.

Devil's Food Cake

- 3 eggs, separated
- 1½ cups sugar
- ½ cup butter
- 1 teaspoon Cinnamon
- ¼ teaspoon Nutmeg
- 2 teaspoons Brandy Extract
- 3 1-ounce squares unsweetened chocolate, melted
- 2 cups sifted cake flour
- 1 teaspoon baking soda
- ½ teaspoon salt
- 1 cup dairy sour cream

Beat egg whites until almost stiff; gradually add ½ cup of the sugar. Continue beating until stiff peaks form; set aside. Cream together butter, the remaining 1 cup sugar and spices until light and fluffy. Add egg yolks, one at a time, beating well after each addition. Stir in extract and melted chocolate. Sift together flour, soda and salt. Add to creamed mixture alternately with sour cream. Gently fold in the stiffly beaten egg whites. Pour into two greased and floured 8-inch square or 9-inch round layer cake pans. Cut through batter with a knife to remove large air bubbles. Bake in 350°F. oven 30 to 35 minutes. Good frosted with Mint Julep Frosting (see recipe page 299). Decorate with Chocolate Décors if desired.

Pound Cake

3½ cups cake flour
1 teaspoon baking powder
½ teaspoon salt
¼ teaspoon Mace
1¾ cups butter (3½ sticks)
2 cups superfine sugar
8 eggs
1 teaspoon pure Vanilla Extract
½ teaspoon Almond Extract
½ teaspoon Lemon Extract

Sift flour, measure and sift twice with baking powder, salt and mace. Cream butter until light and fluffy. Add sugar slowly, beating hard. Continue beating until butter-sugar mixture resembles whipped cream. Add eggs, one at a time, beating well after addition of each. Stir in about half the flour using the lowest position on electric mixer or beat by hand. Add extracts and remaining flour. Pour the batter into two greased and floured 9¼ x 5¼ x 2¾-inch loaf pans or one 10 x 4-inch tube pan. Cut through the thick batter several times with a knife to break air bubbles. Bake in 325°F. oven 1 hour to 1 hour and 10 minutes. Remove from pan immediately and let cool on cake rack. This cake will probably have a characteristic rough crack down the center.

Makes 2 loaf cakes or 1 tube cake.

Ginger Peach Upside-Down Cake

⅓ cup butter
½ cup brown sugar, packed
1 teaspoon Ginger
1 teaspoon Lemon Peel
1 16-oz. can sliced peaches
Maraschino cherries
Pecan halves
½ package yellow cake mix
1 teaspoon pure Vanilla Extract

Melt butter in heavy 10-inch skillet with ovenproof handle or 9-inch square pan. Add brown sugar, ginger and lemon peel; mix well. Spread this mixture evenly over bottom of pan. Drain peaches, saving juice. Arrange peaches, cherries and pecans over sugar mixture in an attractive design. Divide cake mix in half. Prepare cake mix as directed on package being sure to divide all ingredients in half and substituting peach juice for the liquid. Stir in vanilla. Carefully spoon batter over peaches. Bake in 375°F. oven 35 minutes. Turn out on plate. Serve hot or cold and you may top with whipped cream.

Serves 9.

VARIATION:

Pineapple Upside-Down Cake—Make cake following recipe above using 1 teaspoon Cinnamon, ¼ teaspoon Allspice and 1 16-oz. can sliced pineapple, drained, instead of the ginger, lemon peel and peaches.

Welsh Pork Cake

An old, old recipe, seldom found in cookbooks—excellent.

1 pound bulk pork sausage
1 pound seedless raisins
1 pound dates, chopped
1 cup nuts, chopped
4 cups brown sugar, packed
1 tablespoon Orange Peel
3 cups boiling water
6 cups all-purpose flour
1 tablespoon baking soda
2 tablespoons Cinnamon
1 tablespoon ground Cloves
2 teaspoons Nutmeg

Combine sausage, raisins, dates, nuts, sugar, orange peel and boiling water; mix thoroughly. Sift flour, measure and sift again with soda and spices. Add to sausage mixture and mix well. Pour into two 9¼ x 5¼ x 2¾-inch loaf pans which have been greased and lined with paper. Bake in 350°F. oven 1½ hours. Cool; remove from pans. Store in tight containers 3 to 4 weeks. Moisten cakes with brandy at frequent intervals if desired.

Makes 2 cakes.

Applesauce Cake

½ cup butter or margarine
1½ cups sugar
2 eggs, well beaten
2 cups all-purpose flour
1 teaspoon baking powder
½ teaspoon baking soda
¼ teaspoon salt
1 teaspoon Cinnamon
½ teaspoon Nutmeg
½ teaspoon Cloves
1 cup applesauce
1 cup chopped golden seedless raisins
1 tablespoon flour
1 cup pecans, chopped

Cream butter and sugar until light and fluffy. Add eggs, beating well. Sift the 2 cups flour, measure and sift again with baking powder, soda, salt, cinnamon, nutmeg and cloves. Add to butter mixture alternately with applesauce. Dredge raisins in the 1 tablespoon flour. Stir raisins and pecans into batter. Pour into well greased and floured 9¼ x 5¼ x 2¾-inch loaf pan. Bake in 350°F. oven 1 hour. Remove from pan; cool on rack. Serve plain, or you may glaze or frost cake.

Makes 1 loaf cake.

Gingerbread

¼ cup butter
½ cup brown sugar, packed
1 egg
½ cup molasses
1½ cups all-purpose flour
1 teaspoon baking soda
1 teaspoon Ginger
½ teaspoon Cinnamon
⅛ teaspoon ground Cardamom
½ cup buttermilk

Cream butter and sugar until light and fluffy. Add egg, then molasses; beat well. Sift flour, measure and sift again with soda and spices. Add alternately with buttermilk to creamed mixture. Pour into greased 8- or 9-inch square pan. Bake in 350°F. oven 30 minutes. Serve hot or cold with Crème Anglaise (see recipe page 375), lemon sauce or whipped cream.

Serves 6 to 8.

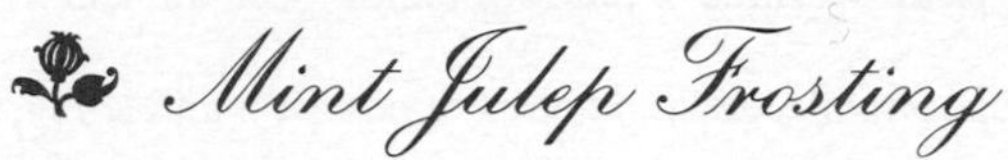

Mint Julep Frosting

2 egg whites
1½ cups sugar
½ teaspoon Cream of Tartar
Dash salt
⅓ cup water
1 teaspoon Mint Extract
or Mint and Peppermint Extract
Green Food Color

Put all ingredients, except extract and food color, in top of double boiler. Beat 1 minute with electric mixer or rotary beater. Cook over boiling water, beating constantly, 7 minutes or until peaks form. Remove from heat; add extract and a few drops food color. Continue beating until spreading consistency is reached. *Makes enough to frost one 10-inch tube cake or tops and sides of two 9-inch cake layers.*

Fluffy Snow Peak Frosting

A divinity type frosting—delicately spiced.

2 cups sugar
2 tablespoons light corn syrup
¾ cup hot water
2 egg whites
⅛ teaspoon ground Cardamom
¼ teaspoon Nutmeg
½ teaspoon pure Vanilla Extract

Combine sugar, corn syrup and hot water. Cook over low heat, stirring, until sugar is dissolved. Wash down sides of pan with water to prevent crystals forming. Cook to 240°F. on candy thermometer (soft ball stage). Beat egg whites until stiff but not dry; beat in spices. Slowly add hot syrup to egg whites, continuing to beat. Add vanilla and continue beating until frosting loses its gloss and holds a stiff peak.

Makes enough to frost tops and sides of two 8- or 9-inch cake layers.

Lemon Glaze

Glazes are easy—festive too!

2 cups sifted powdered sugar
2 teaspoons Lemon Peel
½ teaspoon Lemon Extract
3 tablespoons hot water

Combine all ingredients and mix well. Drizzle over top of cakes, doughnuts, sweet rolls, pastries or cream puffs. *Makes about ¾ cup.*

VARIATIONS:

Cinnamon Glaze—Use ½ teaspoon Cinnamon in place of lemon peel and lemon extract in above recipe.

Nutmeg Glaze—Use ¼ teaspoon Nutmeg in place of lemon peel and lemon extract in above recipe.

Allspice Glaze—Use ⅛ teaspoon Allspice in place of lemon peel and lemon extract in above recipe.

Orange Glaze—Use ½ teaspoon Orange Peel and ¼ teaspoon Orange Extract in place of lemon peel and lemon extract in above recipe.

Gay Tinted Glaze—Add several drops Red, Yellow, Green or Blue Food Color, or a combination of these colors to obtain desired shade or color in Lemon Glaze recipe.

Sour Cream Frosting

An unusually good frosting.

2 pounds powdered sugar
⅛ teaspoon Cream of Tartar
2 egg whites
¼ cup (white) vegetable shortening
¼ cup dairy sour cream
1 teaspoon pure Vanilla Extract

Sift sugar; reserve about 2 cups. Add cream of tartar to egg whites; beat until very stiff. Cream shortening until light and fluffy; add sugar alternately with sour cream and egg whites. Stir in vanilla. Add part or all of the reserved sugar until the desired spreading consistency is reached.

Makes about 3½ cups, enough to frost tops and sides of two 9-inch cake layers or three 8-inch cake layers.

VARIATION:

Pink Perfection Frosting—Make frosting following recipe above, reducing vanilla to ½ teaspoon and adding 2 teaspoons Strawberry or Cherry Extract and about 8 drops Red Food Color. Tint part of the frosting a deeper shade for decorating cake.

Melt-in-your-mouth flavor, superb on lemon or orange cakes.

1 cup heavy cream
1 cup powdered sugar
1 teaspoon pure Vanilla Extract
½ teaspoon Pumpkin Pie Spice

Whip cream until it forms soft peaks. Stir in sugar, vanilla and pumpkin pie spice. Beat until well blended and stiff. Spread on top of an 8- or 9-inch cake layer. Serve immediately, or chill until ready to serve. This topping is excellent when served on chocolate, spice, applesauce, white or yellow cake. You will also find this delicious on waffles, stewed fruits or as a topping for fruit pies. *Makes 1⅔ cups.*

VARIATION:

Orange Whipped Cream Topping—Use 1 teaspoon Orange Peel and omit pumpkin pie spice in above recipe.

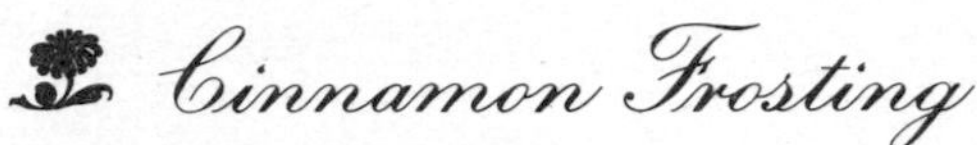

1 pound powdered sugar
1 tablespoon Cinnamon
¼ cup melted butter
1 egg white
Dash salt
3 tablespoons milk

Sift sugar and cinnamon together. Add about one third of it to butter, creaming with mixer or by hand. Beat in egg white and salt. Add the remaining sugar and enough milk to get the desired spreading consistency. Beat hard. Use to frost spice or applesauce cakes.

Makes enough to frost tops and sides of two 8- or 9-inch cake layers.

Lemon Frosting

2 egg whites
1½ cups sugar
½ teaspoon Cream of Tartar
1 teaspoon Lemon Peel
Dash salt
¼ cup water
2 tablespoons lemon juice
1 teaspoon pure Vanilla Extract
Yellow Food Color, optional

Combine egg whites, sugar, cream of tartar, lemon peel, salt and water in top of double boiler. Beat 1 minute with electric mixer or rotary beater. Add lemon juice and cook over boiling water, beating constantly, 7 minutes or until peaks form. Remove from heat; add vanilla and a few drops food color. Beat until spreading consistency is reached.

Makes enough to frost tops and sides of two 9-inch cake layers.

NOTE: For an even creamier frosting, transfer the frosting from the double boiler to a mixing bowl as soon as you remove it from the heat. Add extract and food color and continue as above.

Broiled Spiced Topping

A tasty and quick way to frost a layer of cake.

1/3 cup soft butter
2/3 cup brown sugar, packed
1/4 cup cream
3/4 teaspoon pure Vanilla Extract
1/2 teaspoon Orange Peel
1 teaspoon Cinnamon
1/4 teaspoon Nutmeg
1/8 teaspoon Cloves
1 cup flake coconut

Thoroughly combine all ingredients. Spread evenly over warm cake before removing from pan. Broil 4 inches from heat 3 minutes or until lightly browned. Especially good on a white or yellow cake and is an easy topping to make when using a cake mix.

Makes enough to frost one 9-inch square cake.

Spicy Chocolate Frosting

3 1-ounce squares unsweetened chocolate
1/4 cup melted butter
2 1/2 tablespoons hot water
1 teaspoon pure Vanilla Extract
1 1/2 cups powdered sugar
1/4 teaspoon Mace
1/4 teaspoon Cinnamon
1/8 teaspoon Allspice
3 egg yolks

Melt chocolate in top of double boiler or over lowest heat. Remove from heat; stir in butter, hot water and vanilla. Sift sugar and combine with spices; gradually beat into chocolate mixture alternately with egg yolks. Beat hard. *Makes 1 1/2 cups frosting, enough to frost tops and sides of two 8- or 9-inch cake layers or one 9- or 10-inch tube cake.*

PIES

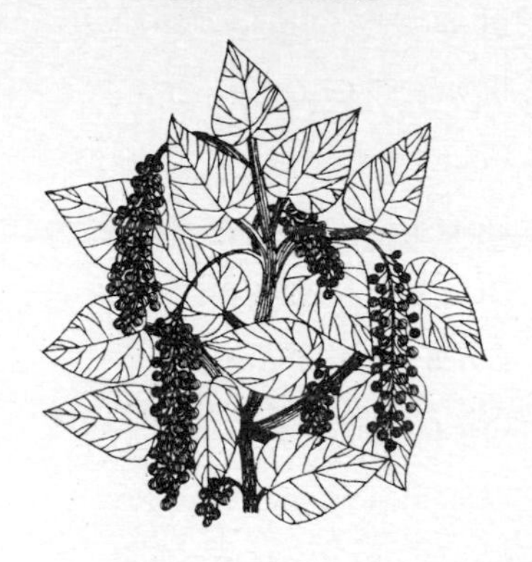

Fruit Pies Superb

Blackberry Cobbler 307
Blueberry Crumble 307
Cherry Pie 311
Deep Dish Apple Pie 308
Deep Dish Peach Pie 310
Dutch Apple Pie 305
Elegant Peach Pie 313
Lemon Meringue Pie 305
Strawberry Patch Pie 309
Wonderful Apple Pie 309

Elegant Chiffon Pies

Black Bottom Pie 311
Cranberry Chiffon Pie 312
Festive Lime Pie 315
Raspberry Cloud Pie 310
Spiced Coconut Chiffon Pie 312
Spicy Lemon Angel Pie 313
Velvety Pumpkin Chiffon Pie 318
  Harvest Pumpkin Chiffon Pie 318

Cream and Custard Pies

Chocolate-Mace Cream Pie 314
Pumpkin Pie 308

Cream and Custard Pies (Cont.)

Rhubarb Custard Pie 320
Sesame Pecan Pie 320
Spicy Custard Pie 315
Spicy Ice Cream Pie 306
Sweet Potato-Pecan Pie 314

Mincemeat and Fruit Tarts

Banbury Tarts 319
Easy Mincemeat Pie 318
Fried Pies 316

Interesting Pastry and Pie Crust

Coconut Crust 317
Ginger Cracker Crust
  (See Festive Lime Pie) 315
Meringue Cracker Crust
  (See Strawberry Patch Pie) 309
Plain Pastry 317
  Lemon Pastry 317
  Poppy Seed Pastry 317
  Sesame Seed Pastry 317
  Spicy Pastry 317
Spiced Graham Cracker Crust 319

Dutch Apple Pie

Pastry for 9-inch pie shell
2½ pounds apples
⅔ cup light brown sugar, firmly packed
⅓ cup granulated sugar
¼ teaspoon salt
¼ teaspoon Cinnamon
½ teaspoon Nutmeg
¼ teaspoon Anise Seed
2 tablespoons lemon juice
1 tablespoon flour
2 tablespoons butter
Topping

Line a 9-inch pie plate with pastry. Flute edges. Peel, core and slice apples in ½-inch slices (about 6 cups.) Put apples in a large bowl. Combine brown sugar, granulated sugar, salt, cinnamon, nutmeg and anise seed. Toss with apples, coating slices evenly. Pile into pie shell. Sprinkle with lemon juice and flour. Dot with butter. Crumble topping over apples. Bake in 350°F. oven 1½ hours. Serve warm. Top with Cheddar cheese or ice cream.

TOPPING:
Combine 1 cup flour, ½ cup butter, ½ cup light brown sugar, firmly packed, 1 teaspoon cinnamon and ¼ teaspoon salt. Mix well with fork or pastry blender.

Makes one 9-inch pie.

Lemon Meringue Pie

1 baked 9-inch pie shell
1 cup sugar
5 tablespoons cornstarch
⅛ teaspoon Lemon Peel
⅛ teaspoon Mace
Dash Ginger
Dash salt
2 cups water
½ cup lemon juice
4 egg yolks, beaten
¼ teaspoon pure Vanilla Extract

In top of double boiler, combine sugar, cornstarch, lemon peel, mace, ginger and salt. Mix well, Stir in water, lemon juice and beaten egg yolks. Cook over boiling water, stirring occasionally, until thickened. Cool. Stir in vanilla and pour into pie shell.

MERINGUE:
Beat 4 egg whites until foamy. Gradually beat in ¾ cup sugar, dash salt and ¼ teaspoon pure Vanilla Extract. Spread over pie filling, sealing to edge. Sprinkle with cinnamon sugar. Bake in 375°F. oven until meringue is lightly browned. Cool out of drafts. Chill 3 to 4 hours.

Makes one 9-inch pie.

Spicy Ice Cream Pie

CRUST:

1½ cups crushed chocolate wafers
¼ cup melted butter
¼ cup sugar
⅛ teaspoon Mace

Thoroughly combine all crust ingredients. Press into 9-inch pie plate. Bake in 350°F. oven 8 minutes. Cool, then freeze.

FILLING:

1 pint vanilla ice cream
1 pint chocolate ice cream
¼ teaspoon Cinnamon
⅛ teaspoon Nutmeg

Soften ice creams in refrigerator 1 to 2 hours. In chilled bowl, mix vanilla ice cream with cinnamon. Spread over bottom of crust. Freeze until firm, about 30 minutes. In a chilled bowl, mix chocolate ice cream with nutmeg. Spread over vanilla ice cream. Freeze until firm. Serve garnished with whipped cream and chopped nuts, if desired. *Makes one 9-inch pie.*

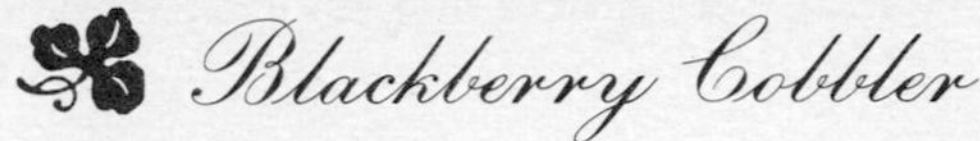

Blackberry Cobbler

1 pastry recipe for two-crust pie
6 cups fresh blackberries
2 teaspoons quick-cooking tapioca
¾ cup sugar
½ teaspoon Cinnamon
1 teaspoon pure Vanilla Extract
2 tablespoons butter
1 tablespoon Arrowroot
1 tablespoon sugar

Prepare pastry; roll out half of it and line 1½-quart shallow baking dish. Cook blackberries just until heated through. Remove 1 cup of the juice and set aside. Combine blackberries and the remaining juice with tapioca, the ¾ cup sugar and cinnamon. Pour into pastry-lined baking dish; sprinkle with vanilla and dot with butter. Make lattice top using 1-inch wide strips of pastry. Bake in 425°F. oven 15 minutes; reduce temperature to 350°F. and bake 30 minutes longer. Combine the 1 cup reserved juice and arrowroot and cook, stirring, over medium heat until thickened. Remove from heat and stir in the 1 tablespoon sugar. Serve cobbler in bowls with sauce spooned over top. You may like to serve with cream, whipped cream or ice cream. *Serves 8.*

Blueberry Crumble

Easier than rolling out pie crust, deliciously good.

2½ cups fresh blueberries or 2 10-ounce packages frozen unsweetened blueberries
½ cup sugar
¼ teaspoon Orange Peel
Dash Mace
⅛ teaspoon ground Cardamom
1 cup pie crust mix
1 tablespoon butter
2 teaspoons lemon juice
½ teaspoon pure Vanilla Extract

Place blueberries in buttered 1¼-quart shallow baking dish. Combine sugar, orange peel, mace and cardamom. Sprinkle sugar mixture and pie crust mix in alternate layers over blueberries. Continue until all is used. Dot with butter. Drizzle lemon juice and vanilla over all. Bake in 350°F. oven 45 minutes. Serve with cream if desired. *Serves 4 to 6.*

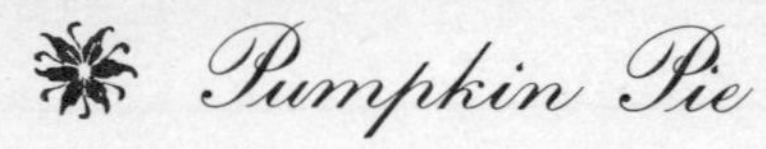

Pumpkin Pie

Pastry for 9-inch pie shell
2 eggs
1½ cups mashed, cooked pumpkin
½ cup brown sugar, packed
1 tablespoon Pumpkin Pie Spice
1½ teaspoons Arrowroot
½ teaspoon salt
1½ cups milk

Line a 9-inch pie plate with pastry. Beat eggs until light and fluffy; stir in pumpkin. Combine sugar, pumpkin pie spice, arrowroot and salt. Add to pumpkin mixture, mixing thoroughly. Gradually stir in milk. Part light cream or half and half makes a richer filling and may be used if desired. Pour into pastry shell. Bake in 450°F. oven 15 minutes. Reduce temperature to 350°F. and continue baking 40 minutes or until silver knife inserted in center comes out clean. Serve plain or topped with whipped cream. *Serves 6 to 8.*

NOTE: If desired, make your own spice blend to use in place of pumpkin pie spice in above recipe. For a spicy pie use 1½ teaspoons Cinnamon, ½ teaspoon Ginger, ½ teaspoon Nutmeg, ¼ teaspoon Cloves and ¼ teaspoon Allspice. For a milder spice note use 1 teaspoon Cinnamon, ¼ teaspoon Ginger, ¼ teaspoon Nutmeg and ⅛ teaspoon Allspice. Of course, you may use other spices in varying amounts as desired.

Deep Dish Apple Pie

1 pastry recipe for one-crust pie
6 cups sliced tart apples
¾ cup sugar
¼ cup flour
1 teaspoon Cinnamon
¼ teaspoon Nutmeg
¼ teaspoon Cloves
2 tablespoons water
1 teaspoon Brandy Extract
2 tablespoons butter
Cinnamon Sugar

Prepare pastry; set aside. Toss together apples, sugar, flour, cinnamon, nutmeg and cloves. In place of the spices listed above, you may use 1½ teaspoons Apple Pie Spice if desired. Put in buttered 1½-quart shallow baking dish. Sprinkle with water and extract; dot with butter. Roll pastry to ⅛-inch thickness. Place on top of baking dish. Trim, leaving ½-inch overhang. Fold the overhang back and under; flute edges. Cut two or three steam vents in top of pastry. Sprinkle top with cinnamon sugar. Bake in 425°F. oven 15 minutes; reduce temperature to 350°F. and bake 30 minutes longer or until top is nicely browned. Serve warm or cold with cream or ice cream. *Serves 8.*

Strawberry Patch Pie

MERINGUE CRACKER CRUST:

3 egg whites
1 cup sugar
⅛ teaspoon Mace
1 teaspoon pure Vanilla Extract
12 soda crackers, crushed
1 teaspoon baking powder
¾ cup chopped nuts

Beat egg whites until stiff. Combine sugar and mace; add, one tablespoon at a time, to egg whites, beating well after each addition. Add vanilla. Combine crushed soda crackers, baking powder and nuts. Fold into egg white mixture. Spoon into a buttered 10-inch pie plate, pushing mixture to conform to shape of pie plate. Bake in 350°F. oven 30 minutes. Cool. You will find this crust excellent for chiffon or ice cream pie.

STRAWBERRY FILLING:

1½ cups crushed fresh strawberries
¼ cup sugar
1 teaspoon Lemon Peel
1 envelope unflavored gelatine
¼ cup cold water
30 whole fresh strawberries

Combine crushed strawberries, sugar and lemon peel. Soften gelatine in cold water, then melt over hot water. Add to crushed berry mixture. Chill until mixture begins to thicken. Spread half of the mixture over bottom of cooled crust. Add enough whole berries, placing them stem end down and close together to fill the pie. Carefully spoon remaining crushed berry mixture around whole berries. Chill until firm. You may serve with whipped cream if desired.

Makes one 10-inch pie.

Wonderful Apple Pie

Pastry for 9- or 10-inch pie shell
1 cup light brown sugar, packed
½ cup all-purpose flour
1 teaspoon Cinnamon
⅛ teaspoon Allspice
⅛ teaspoon Cloves
⅛ teaspoon Nutmeg
½ teaspoon Lemon Peel
½ cup butter
6 medium-size apples

Line pie plate with pastry. Mix sugar, flour, spices and butter with pastry blender until crumbly. You may use 1½ teaspoons Apple Pie Spice in place of above spices if desired. Spread one third of this mixture over bottom of unbaked pastry. Peel apples, core and cut into slices; put in crust. Spoon remaining sugar and spice mixture over apples. Bake in 400°F. oven 50 to 55 minutes.

Serves 6 to 8.

Deep Dish Peach Pie

1 pastry recipe for two-crust pie
6 cups sliced peaches
¾ cup sugar
¼ cup flour
¼ teaspoon Nutmeg
¼ teaspoon Allspice
Dash ground Cardamom
2 tablespoons water
2 tablespoons butter
Cinnamon Sugar

Prepare pastry; roll out half of it and line 1½-quart shallow baking dish. Toss together peaches, sugar, flour, nutmeg, allspice and cardamom. Place in pastry-lined baking dish. Sprinkle with water and dot with butter. Cover with a lattice top and sprinkle with cinnamon sugar. Bake in 425°F. oven 15 minutes; reduce temperature to 350°F. and bake 50 minutes longer. Especially good served with cream. *Serves 8.*

Raspberry Cloud Pie

2 10-ounce packages frozen raspberries, thawed
2 cups vanilla wafer crumbs
¼ cup sugar
1 teaspoon Cinnamon
5 tablespoons melted butter
1 envelope unflavored gelatine
¼ cup cold water
½ teaspoon Lemon Peel
½ pint heavy cream
1 teaspoon pure Vanilla Extract

Drain raspberries, reserving 1 cup of the juice. Combine crumbs, sugar, ½ teaspoon of the cinnamon and the butter; pat into a 10-inch pie plate. Bake in 375°F. oven 8 to 10 minutes; cool. Soften gelatine in water. Mix the reserved raspberry juice, the remaining ½ teaspoon cinnamon and lemon peel and heat to boiling. Remove from heat; add gelatine and stir until melted. Chill until mixture just begins to thicken. Whip cream; add vanilla. Fold raspberries, gelatine mixture and whipped cream together. Pour into pie shell. Chill. You may decorate with additional whipped cream if desired. *Serves 6 to 8.*

Black Bottom Pie

24 small gingersnaps
¼ cup melted butter or margarine
2 teaspoons unflavored gelatine
¼ cup cold water
2 eggs, separated
2 cups milk, scalded
1 cup sugar
1½ tablespoons Arrowroot
⅛ teaspoon salt
2 1-ounce squares unsweetened chocolate, melted
⅛ teaspoon Mace
1 teaspoon pure Vanilla Extract
¼ teaspoon Rum Extract
1 teaspoon Cream of Tartar
1 cup heavy cream
1 tablespoon powdered sugar
1 tablespoon shaved bitter or semi-sweet chocolate

Roll gingersnaps into fine crumbs; you should have about 1½ cups. Blend in butter; press evenly into bottom and around sides of 10-inch pie plate. Bake in 350°F. oven 5 minutes. Cool. Soak gelatine in water. Beat egg yolks; slowly add scalded milk, stirring constantly. Mix together ¾ cup of the sugar, arrowroot and salt; stir into milk-egg yolk mixture. Cook over low heat, stirring constantly, until mixture thickens and coats a metal spoon. Remove from heat. To one cup of the custard mixture add the melted chocolate, mace and vanilla; mix well. Spoon into crust and allow to cool. To the remaining custard mixture add gelatine, stirring until melted. Cool. Stir in rum extract. Add cream of tartar to egg whites and beat until stiff but not dry. Gradually add the remaining ¼ cup sugar, beating constantly. Fold into gelatine-custard mixture; spread over chocolate layer in pie crust. Chill. Before serving whip cream until stiff. Add powdered sugar, mixing well. Spread whipped cream on pie and sprinkle with chocolate shavings. Or, you may want to use Chocolate Décors.

Serves 6 to 8.

Cherry Pie

1 pastry recipe for two-crust pie
2 16-oz. cans red tart pitted cherries
2½ tablespoons quick-cooking tapioca
1 cup sugar
⅛ teaspoon Nutmeg
⅛ teaspoon Allspice
½ teaspoon Lemon Peel
¼ teaspoon salt
½ teaspoon Almond Extract
1 tablespoon butter or margarine

Line 9-inch pie plate with pastry. Drain cherries, saving juice. Combine tapioca with ½ cup of the cherry juice. Add sugar, nutmeg, allspice, lemon peel, salt, and extract. Mix well. Stir in cherries. Fill pie shell. Dot with butter. Make lattice top and a stand-up fluted rim. Bake in 425°F. oven 40 minutes.

Serves 6 to 8.

Spiced Coconut Chiffon Pie

1 baked 9- or 10-inch pastry shell
1½ cups flake coconut
1 teaspoon Cinnamon
¼ teaspoon Ginger
⅛ teaspoon ground Cardamom
1 envelope unflavored gelatine
¼ cup cold water
4 eggs, separated
½ cup sugar
¼ teaspoon salt
1 cup milk, scalded
1 teaspoon pure Vanilla Extract
¼ teaspoon Cream of Tartar
1 pint heavy cream

Bake and cool pastry shell. Combine 1 cup of the coconut with spices. If desired ¾ teaspoon Pumpkin Pie Spice and ⅛ teaspoon Mace may be substituted for the above spices. Spread in a shallow pan. Toast in 350°F. oven 8 minutes or until brown, stirring occasionally. Soften gelatine in water. Beat egg yolks; stir in sugar and salt. Slowly add scalded milk, stirring constantly. Cook over low heat, stirring, until mixture thickens. Add gelatine; stir until melted. Cool. Stir in vanilla and the remaining ½ cup coconut. Add cream of tartar to egg whites and beat until stiff but not dry. Whip ½ pint of the cream until stiff. Fold egg whites and whipped cream into egg yolk mixture. Line bottom of pie shell with half the toasted coconut. Pour filling into shell. Chill. Before serving, whip remaining cream and spoon on top of pie; sprinkle with remaining toasted coconut.

Serves 6 to 8.

Cranberry Chiffon Pie

1 baked 10-inch pastry shell
1 envelope unflavored gelatine
½ cup water
4 eggs, separated
2 tablespoons lemon juice
1 cup sugar
1 teaspoon Orange Peel
¼ teaspoon Cream of Tartar
8 drops Red Food Color
2 cups crushed raw cranberries
½ pint heavy cream
2 tablespoons powdered sugar

Bake and cool pastry shell. Soften gelatine in ¼ cup of the water. Beat egg yolks lightly; mix in the remaining ¼ cup water, lemon juice, ½ cup of the sugar and orange peel. Cook in double boiler, stirring, until thick. Add softened gelatine; stir until melted. Set aside to cool. Add cream of tartar to egg whites and beat until stiff. Gradually beat in the remaining ½ cup sugar. Blend in food color. Fold cooled mixture into egg whites, then fold in crushed cranberries. Pour into pie shell; chill until firm. Whip cream, gradually adding powdered sugar. Spread on top of pie before serving.

Serves 6 to 8.

Spicy Lemon Angel Pie

Spiced Graham Cracker Crust
1 envelope unflavored gelatine
2 tablespoons cold water
1 15-ounce can sweetened condensed milk
3 eggs, separated
½ teaspoon Lemon Peel
¼ teaspoon Ginger
¼ teaspoon Mace
1 cup heavy cream
¾ cup lemon juice

Make Spiced Graham Cracker Crust for a 10-inch pie (see recipe page 319). Soak gelatine in cold water to soften; then set over hot water to melt. Combine milk, egg yolks, lemon peel, ginger and mace. Heat over boiling water or lowest heat on range, beating with a rotary beater until slightly warm. Stir in melted gelatine, mixing well. Beat egg whites in a large bowl until stiff. Whip cream. Add lemon juice to gelatine mixture, beating with rotary beater until thoroughly mixed. Gently fold beaten egg whites, whipped cream and gelatine mixture together. Pile into crust. Chill. Serve plain or you may decorate top with rosettes of whipped cream. *Serves 8.*

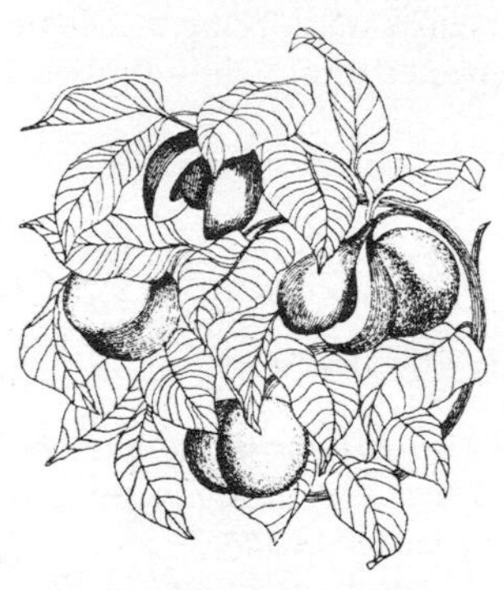

Elegant Peach Pie

Sesame Seed Pastry
¾ cup brown sugar, packed
3 tablespoons quick-cooking tapioca
½ teaspoon Lemon Peel
¾ teaspoon Ginger
4 cups sliced fresh peaches
2 tablespoons butter
¼ teaspoon Almond Extract

Prepare Sesame Seed Pastry (see recipe page 317) and line 9-inch pie plate. Combine brown sugar, tapioca, lemon peel and ginger. Sprinkle half of this mixture over bottom of pastry. Arrange peaches over sugar mixture. Sprinkle remaining sugar mixture over peaches; dot with butter. Drizzle almond extract over all. Cover with a lattice top. Bake in 425°F. oven 10 minutes; reduce temperature to 350°F. and continue baking 30 minutes. For variety serve à la mode. *Serves 6 to 8.*

Chocolate-Mace Cream Pie

1 baked 9-inch pastry shell
1½ cups sugar
½ teaspoon salt
5 tablespoons cornstarch
1 tablespoon flour
¼ teaspoon Mace
3 cups milk
3 1-ounce squares unsweetened chocolate, melted
3 eggs, separated
1 tablespoon butter
1½ teaspoons pure Vanilla Extract
¼ teaspoon Cream of Tartar
6 tablespoons sugar

Bake and cool pastry shell. In a saucepan blend together the 1½ cups sugar, salt, cornstarch, flour and mace. Gradually stir in milk and melted chocolate. Cook over medium heat, stirring constantly, until thickened. Remove from heat. Gradually stir part of this hot mixture into the lightly beaten egg yolks. Blend the two mixtures; add butter. Return to heat and continue cooking until thick, stirring constantly. Remove from heat; cool. Stir in vanilla. Pour into pastry shell. Add cream of tartar to egg whites and beat until peaks form. Add the 6 tablespoons sugar, 1 tablespoon at a time. Beat hard 5 minutes. Spoon meringue over top of chocolate filling, being sure to bring meringue to edge of crust. Bake in 400°F. oven 8 minutes or until lightly browned. Chill several hours before serving.

Serves 6 to 8.

Out of the Old South, a memorable pastry.

Pastry for 9-inch pie shell
1 cup brown sugar, packed
½ teaspoon salt
2 teaspoons Pumpkin Pie Spice
3 eggs, beaten
1½ cups milk
1½ cups cooked mashed sweet potatoes
Pecan Topping

Line 9-inch pie plate with pastry and make a high fluted edge. Mix sugar, salt and pumpkin pie spice; stir in eggs, mixing well. Add milk and sweet potatoes and mix thoroughly. Pour into pie shell. Bake in 425°F. oven 10 minutes; reduce heat to 300°F. and bake 30 minutes. Cover top of pie with Pecan Topping. Bake 30 minutes longer or until silver knife comes out clean when inserted in center.

Serves 6 to 8.

PECAN TOPPING:

2 tablespoons melted butter
¼ cup dark brown sugar, packed
1 cup chopped pecans
1 teaspoon Pumpkin Pie Spice

Combine all ingredients; mix well. Spoon over pie.

Festive Lime Pie

GINGER CRACKER CRUST:

¼ cup finely minced Crystallized Ginger
1½ cups crushed graham crackers
½ cup powdered sugar
¼ cup melted butter or margarine
Dash Nutmeg

Mix the finely minced ginger, cracker crumbs and powdered sugar so that the pieces of ginger will be evenly distributed throughout. Add melted butter; mix well. Press mixture into bottom and around sides of 9-inch pie plate; sprinkle with one or two dashes of nutmeg. Bake in 325°F. oven 10 minutes. Cool.

LIME CHIFFON FILLING:

1 envelope unflavored gelatine
2 tablespoons cold water
4 eggs, separated
1 cup sugar
¼ teaspoon salt
½ cup lime juice
½ teaspoon grated lime rind
Green Food Color

Soften gelatine in cold water. Beat egg yolks in top of double boiler or saucepan. Stir in ½ cup of the sugar, salt and lime juice, mixing well. Cook over boiling water or lowest heat, stirring constantly, until mixture thickens slightly. Remove from heat. Add gelatine and lime rind. Continue stirring until gelatine melts. Set aside to cool. Beat egg whites until soft peaks form. Add the remaining sugar, 1 tablespoon at a time, and 6 to 8 drops green food color. Beat 3 to 4 minutes longer. Fold the cooled gelatine mixture into egg whites, folding gently but thoroughly. You may also fold in one half cup heavy cream, whipped, if desired. Pour into pie shell and chill. Garnish with paper-thin slices of lime. *Serves 6 to 8.*

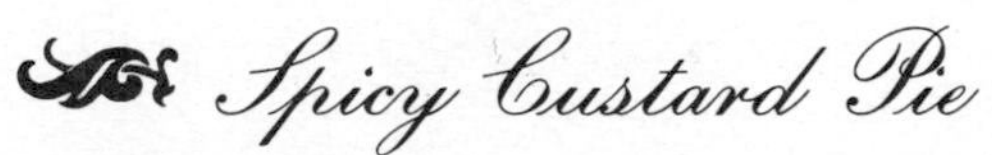

Pastry for 9-inch pie shell
4 eggs
6 tablespoons sugar
¼ teaspoon salt
¼ teaspoon Mace
1 teaspoon pure Vanilla Extract
2¾ cups milk
Dash Nutmeg

Line a 9-inch pie plate with pastry. Break eggs into bowl, removing enough of one egg white to lightly brush the bottom of the pastry shell. Beat eggs lightly; add sugar, salt, mace, vanilla and milk, mixing well. Pour custard into pie shell; sprinkle top with nutmeg. Bake in 450°F. oven 10 minutes. Reduce heat to 300°F. and bake 45 minutes longer or just until silver knife inserted in center of pie comes out clean. Caution: You will find overbaking makes custard watery. *Serves 6 to 8.*

Fried Pies

2 cups all-purpose flour
½ teaspoon Nutmeg
¼ teaspoon Cloves
½ teaspoon salt
½ teaspoon baking soda
½ cup shortening
1 tablespoon vinegar
5 tablespoons cold water
Filling
Fat for frying
Cinnamon Sugar

Sift flour, measure and sift again with nutmeg, cloves, salt and soda. With pastry blender or two knives cut shortening into flour until particles are size of peas. Add vinegar and water and mix until dry ingredients are moist. Chill. Roll out thin and cut into 4-inch squares. Put one tablespoon filling on one half of each pastry square; moisten edges. Fold other half of pastry over filling to form triangle. Seal edges well, pressing with the tines of a fork. Chill. Fry in deep fat, 375°F., until golden brown. Drain on absorbent paper. Sprinkle with cinnamon sugar. *Makes about 16 pies.*

APPLE FILLING:

1 8-ounce package dried apples
½ teaspoon Nutmeg
½ teaspoon Cinnamon
1 teaspoon Lemon Peel
1 tablespoon sugar

Simmer apples in small amount of water until soft. Drain and mash or cut into small pieces. Combine with remaining ingredients. Cool.

Makes filling for 16 pies.

APRICOT FILLING:

1 8-ounce package dried apricots
1 tablespoon sugar
1 teaspoon Orange Peel
¼ teaspoon Coriander Seed, crushed

Simmer apricots in small amount of water until soft. Drain. Cut into small pieces. Combine with remaining ingredients. Cool. This is a tart filling and you may prefer to add more sugar. *Makes filling for 16 pies.*

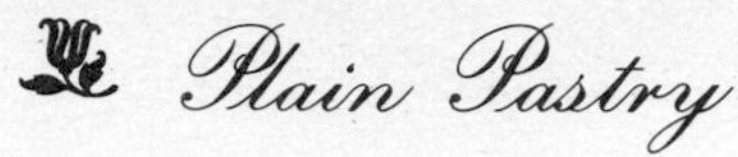

Plain Pastry

ONE-CRUST:

1 cup sifted all-purpose flour
½ teaspoon salt
⅓ cup shortening
2 tablespoons cold water

TWO-CRUST:

2 cups all-purpose flour
1 teaspoon salt
⅔ cup shortening
4 tablespoons cold water

Sift flour and salt into a bowl. Remove about ¼ cup of the mixture; set aside. With pastry blender or two knives cut in shortening until particles are the size of peas. (For a shorter, richer pastry, increase shortening 1 tablespoon for each cup flour.) Make a paste of the ¼ cup flour and water; sprinkle over flour-shortening mixture. Using a fork, quickly blend together until the flour is moistened and can be pressed into a ball; overmixing causes pastry to be tough. Roll out on lightly floured board to ⅛-inch thickness. Line pie plate. For a baked pastry shell, prick thoroughly with tines of a fork. Bake in 475°F. oven 8 minutes or until golden brown.

VARIATIONS:

Sesame Seed Pastry—Toast Sesame Seed in 350°F. oven 15 minutes or until golden; cool. Add 2 tablespoons Sesame Seed to flour-shortening mixture for one-crust pastry and 4 tablespoons for two-crust pastry.

Lemon Pastry—Add ¾ teaspoon Lemon Peel to flour-shortening mixture for one-crust pastry and 1¼ teaspoons Lemon Peel for two-crust pastry.

Poppy Seed Pastry—Add 2 teaspoons Poppy Seed to flour-shortening mixture for one-crust pastry; 4 teaspoons Poppy Seed for two-crust pastry.

Spicy Pastry—Add ⅛ to ¼ teaspoon Nutmeg, Allspice, Mace, Cardamom or Cloves to flour-shortening mixture for one-crust pastry and ¼ to ½ teaspoon of any one of these spices for two-crust pastry.

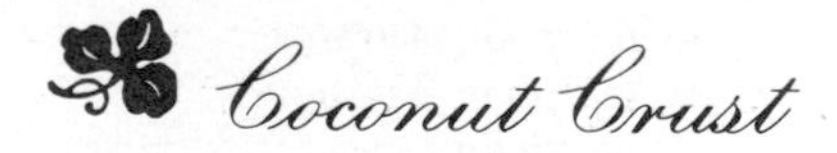

Coconut Crust

1½ cups flake coconut
2 tablespoons melted butter
¼ cup finely crushed graham cracker crumbs
2 tablespoons sugar
¼ cup finely chopped pecans
¼ teaspoon Pumpkin Pie Spice
½ teaspoon Orange Peel

Combine coconut and butter; mix well. Add remaining ingredients, mixing thoroughly. Press firmly over bottom and around sides of 9-inch pie plate. Bake in 375°F. oven 8 minutes or until lightly browned. Chill. Fill with ice cream, chiffon or cream pie filling. *Makes one 9-inch crust.*

Velvety Pumpkin Chiffon Pie

1 baked 10-inch pastry shell
1 envelope unflavored gelatine
¼ cup cold water
3 eggs, separated
¾ cup brown sugar, packed
1⅓ cups mashed, cooked pumpkin
2 teaspoons Pumpkin Pie Spice
½ teaspoon salt
½ cup milk
¼ teaspoon Cream of Tartar
6 tablespoons sugar
1 cup heavy cream, whipped

Bake and cool pastry shell. Soften gelatine in water. Beat egg yolks; add brown sugar, pumpkin, pumpkin pie spice and salt. (You may increase the pumpkin pie spice to 3 teaspoons for a delightful heavy spice note.) Mix well, then stir in milk. Cook over medium heat, stirring, until it begins to boil. Then cook 2 minutes, stirring constantly. Remove from heat. Add softened gelatine, stirring until melted. Cool. Add cream of tartar to egg whites and beat until soft peaks form. Add the 6 tablespoons sugar, 1 tablespoon at a time, beating until stiff but not dry. Beat cooled pumpkin mixture until smooth, then gently fold in egg whites. Spoon into crust. Chill. Top with whipped cream. *Serves 6 to 8.*

VARIATION:

Harvest Pumpkin Chiffon Pie—In the above recipe, after beating the pumpkin mixture until smooth, add ¼ cup slivered almonds, ¼ cup chopped dates and 3 tablespoons thinly sliced Crystallized Ginger, mixing well. Then fold in beaten egg whites and spoon into crust. Chill and top with whipped cream.

Easy Mincemeat Pie

Add your own fresh spices to prepared mincemeat for real homemade flavor.

Pastry for 2-crust 9-inch pie
1 1-pound-12-ounce jar prepared mincemeat
1 medium-size apple, grated
½ teaspoon Cinnamon
⅛ teaspoon Allspice
⅛ teaspoon Nutmeg
⅛ teaspoon Ginger
2 tablespoons Brandy Extract

Line a 9-inch pie plate with pastry. Combine all remaining ingredients and pour into unbaked pastry shell. If mincemeat seems quite moist, bring to boil and cook to reduce moisture before filling pastry. Add top crust or make lattice top if desired. Bake in 425°F. oven 30 to 35 minutes. For a festive dinner, you may like to serve this pie topped with hard sauce or whipped cream. *Serves 6 to 8.*

Spiced Graham Cracker Crust

1½ cups graham cracker crumbs (about 20 squares)
¼ cup soft or melted butter or margarine
¼ cup sugar
⅛ teaspoon Nutmeg

Combine all ingredients in 9- or 10-inch pie plate. Mix thoroughly with fingers. If a fork or pastry blender is used, it is better to mix in a bowl and transfer to pie plate. Press crumbs evenly over bottom and around sides of pie plate. Bake in 350°F. oven 8 minutes. Cool. If you are making an ice cream pie, freeze crust before filling. *Makes 9- or 10-inch pie crust.*

NOTE: For intriguing spice variations, add one of the following in place of nutmeg:

⅛ teaspoon Mace
⅛ teaspoon Cloves
¼ teaspoon Allspice
½ teaspoon Cinnamon
½ teaspoon Ginger
⅛ teaspoon Cardamom

Banbury Tarts

1 pastry recipe for two-crust pie
½ teaspoon Lemon Peel
1 cup raisins
1 cup sugar
3 tablespoons cracker meal
2 egg yolks
1 tablespoon butter, melted
⅛ teaspoon salt
¼ teaspoon Nutmeg
2 teaspoons Lemon Peel
2 tablespoons lemon juice
½ cup chopped nuts

To a plain pastry recipe for a two-crust pie or packaged mix add the ½ teaspoon lemon peel. Soak raisins in warm water 15 minutes; drain. Put raisins through food grinder, or chop fine, and combine with remaining ingredients. Roll pastry thin. Cut 5-inch circles or squares. Put a heaping tablespoon of the filling on one half of each pastry circle or square; moisten edges. Fold other half of pastry over filling and seal edge by pressing with tines of a fork. Prick top of tarts and put on baking sheet. Bake in 400°F. oven 15 minutes or until lightly browned. Serve plain or with lemon sauce for dessert. You will also find these excellent for picnics or lunch box surprises. *Makes about 14 tarts.*

Rhubarb Custard Pie

Pastry for 9-inch pie shell
1½ cups sugar
3 tablespoons flour
¼ teaspoon salt
½ teaspoon Nutmeg
1 teaspoon Orange Peel
¼ teaspoon Allspice
2 eggs, beaten
2 tablespoons cream
3 cups 1-inch pieces rhubarb
2 tablespoons butter or margarine

Line a 9-inch pie plate with pastry. Combine sugar, flour, salt, nutmeg, orange peel and allspice. Add beaten eggs and cream; mix well. Add rhubarb and pour into pastry-lined pie plate. Dot with butter. Pastry strips may be arranged over top in lattice fashion if desired. Bake in 400°F. oven 20 minutes; reduce heat to 350°F. and bake 25 minutes longer or until custard is firm and pastry is golden brown. *Makes one 9-inch pie.*

Pastry for 9-inch pie shell
¼ cup Sesame Seed
3 eggs
¾ cup sugar
¼ teaspoon salt
⅓ cup melted butter
1 cup light corn syrup
1½ teaspoons pure Vanilla Extract
1 cup pecan halves

Line a 9-inch pie plate with pastry. Toast sesame seed in 350°F. oven 15 minutes or until golden brown. Sprinkle evenly over bottom of pastry shell. Beat eggs with rotary beater or electric mixer until light and fluffy. Add sugar, salt, butter, corn syrup and vanilla; continue to beat until well mixed. Gently stir in pecan halves. Pour into pastry. Bake in 350°F. oven 1 hour or until set and pastry is nicely browned. Serve slightly warm or cold. *Serves 6 to 8.*

COOKIES
CONFECTIONS

Rolled

Fancy Decorated Cookies 325
Filled Cookies 325
Filled Fancies 326
  Apricot Filling 326
  Fig Filling 326
  Poppy Seed-Cheese Filling 326
Gingerbread Boys 332
Lebkuchen 333
Old-Fashioned Tea Cakes 327
Sugared Vanilla Wafers 332

Drop

Date Nut Cookies 328
Fruit Cake Cookies 327
Poppy Seed Goodies 334
Rocks 329
Sesame Macaroons 332
Southern Praline Cookies 330
Spicy Oatmeal Cookies 334

Shaped

Cinnamon Sandies 329
Date Sticks 333
Frosted Nutmeg Logs 335
Gingersnaps 328
Orange Butter Gems 331
  Lemon Butter Gems 331
Pecan Cookie Balls 329
Sesame Wafers 339

Refrigerator

Anise Cookies 340
Cardamom Butter Cookies 336
Mincemeat Refrigerator Cookies 335
Pfeffernüsse 331
Refrigerator Spice Cookies 328

Bars

Butterscotch Squares 324
Chocolate Nut Brownies 336
Cinnamon Sledges 336
Czechoslovakian Cookies 330
Date-Filled Squares 323
Holiday Chews 338
Prune-Filled Squares 340
  Apricot Squares 340
Sesame Toffee Bars 341

Confections

Chewy Popcorn Balls 342
  Crunchy Popcorn Balls 342
  Holiday Popcorn Balls 342
Cinnamon Chocolate Fudge 338
Date Roll 337
Filled Benne Lace Cookies 323
Fondant 341
  Fondant Tipped Almonds 341
Sesame Pralines 337
Spiced Divinity 339
Spiced Mixed Nuts 330
Sugared Nuts 339

Date-Filled Squares

1 cup (8 ounces) chopped dates
¼ cup sugar
¼ cup chopped pecans or walnuts
4 teaspoons lemon juice
⅓ cup water
1 teaspoon pure Vanilla Extract
½ cup butter, softened
1 cup brown sugar, packed
3 cups rolled oats
½ teaspoon Cinnamon
¼ teaspoon Allspice

In a saucepan combine dates, sugar, nuts, lemon juice and water. Cook over low heat, stirring frequently, until thick, about 5 minutes. Remove from heat, cool slightly. Stir in vanilla. Cream butter with brown sugar. Stir in oats, cinnamon and allspice until well blended. Press half the oat mixture evenly into a greased and floured 9-inch square pan. Spread with date mixture. Sprinkle with remaining oat mixture. Press lightly. Bake in 375°F. oven 30 minutes or until lightly browned. Cut into squares while warm. Cool before removing from pan.

Makes sixteen 2-inch squares.

Filled Benne Lace Cookies

¼ cup butter
¼ cup light corn syrup
¼ cup light brown sugar
½ cup + 2 tablespoons sifted flour
¼ teaspoon baking powder
¼ teaspoon Cinnamon
⅓ cup Sesame Seed, lightly toasted
2 ounces German's sweet chocolate

Melt butter, corn syrup and brown sugar in top of a double boiler. Sift together flour, baking powder and cinnamon. Stir into butter mixture, along with sesame seeds, until well blended. Drop by ½ teaspoonfuls, 3 inches apart, on greased baking sheet. Bake in 325°F. oven 8 minutes. Cool on baking sheet about 2 minutes, remove with a thin spatula, finish cooling on flat surface. Melt chocolate over hot water. Spread bottom of cookie with thin coating of chocolate. Place another cookie on top.

Makes 2 dozen filled cookies.

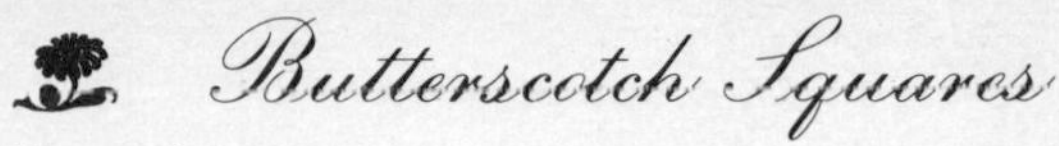

Butterscotch Squares

½ cup butter
2 cups dark brown sugar, packed
2 eggs, lightly beaten
2 teaspoons pure Vanilla Extract
2 cups sifted flour
2 teaspoons baking powder
¼ teaspoon salt
1 teaspoon Cinnamon
1 cup chopped pecans

Cook butter and sugar over low heat, stirring frequently, until it bubbles. Pour into mixing bowl. Cool slightly. Beat in eggs and vanilla. Sift together flour, baking powder, salt and cinnamon. Add to egg mixture, mix until well blended. Stir in pecans. Spread in greased 15½ x 10½ x 1-inch jelly roll pan. Bake in 350°F. oven 25 minutes. Cut into squares and remove from pan while warm. *Makes forty 2-inch squares.*

Fancy Decorated Cookies

½ cup butter
¾ cup sugar
1 egg
1½ teaspoons pure Vanilla Extract
1½ cups all-purpose flour
1 teaspoon baking powder
¼ teaspoon salt
Décors
Food Color
Frosting or glaze
Tinted coconut

Cream butter and sugar until light and fluffy. Add egg and vanilla and beat hard. Sift flour, measure and sift again with baking powder and salt. Stir into creamed mixture. (This makes a soft dough to work with. If you prefer a stiffer dough, add 2 to 4 tablespoons additional flour.) Chill dough 1 hour or longer. Roll out thin on floured cloth or board, working with only part of the dough at a time. Cut with cookie cutters. Place on lightly greased baking sheet. Bake in 350°F. oven 6 to 8 minutes. Remove immediately to cooling racks. Number of cookies depends on size and shape of cookie cutters. *Makes about 7 dozen 2-inch cookies.*

TO DECORATE COOKIES:

Sprinkle with décors, nonpareils and colored crystal sugars before baking.
Tint dough before baking.
Make pinwheels of white and tinted dough.
Frost or glaze cookies, then decorate using frosting in a decorating tube or with décors.
Tint coconut with food color and decorate.

Filled Cookies

½ cup butter
1 cup sugar
2 eggs
1½ teaspoons pure Vanilla Extract
3 cups all-purpose flour
1 teaspoon baking powder
½ teaspoon ground Cardamom
Jam or jelly

Cream butter and sugar until light and fluffy. Add eggs, one at a time, beating after each addition. Stir in vanilla. Sift flour, measure and sift again with baking powder and cardamom; add to butter mixture. Mix well. Chill dough. Roll out on floured board to ⅛-inch thickness. Cut out with 2½-inch cutters. Using center of doughnut cutter or small fancy cutters, cut centers from half the cookies. Put the whole cookies on greased baking sheet and top with cookies which have had centers removed. Fill center of each cookie with jam. Bake in 350°F. oven 12 to 15 minutes.

Makes about 3 dozen.

¾ cup butter
1½ cups sugar
2 eggs
2 teaspoons pure Vanilla Extract
4¾ cups all-purpose flour
½ teaspoon baking soda
¼ teaspoon salt
¾ cup dairy sour cream
Filling

Cream butter and sugar until light and fluffy. Add eggs and vanilla; beat well. Sift flour, measure and sift again with soda and salt. Add dry ingredients to creamed mixture alternately with sour cream. (This makes a soft dough. If you prefer to work with a stiffer dough, add 2 to 4 tablespoons more flour.) Thoroughly chill dough. Roll out on floured cloth or board to ⅛-inch thickness. Cut with 2½-inch cutters of any desired shape. Cut 2 alike for each cookie, putting them together with a spoonful of filling between each. Use one of the fillings below or mincemeat. Press edges together. (For interesting decorative effect, centers may be cut from top pieces with small, fancy cutters.) Bake on lightly greased baking sheet in 400°F. oven 10 to 12 minutes. *Makes about 6 dozen.*

APRICOT FILLING:

1 8-ounce package dried apricots
½ cup sugar
1 cup water
¼ teaspoon Mace
Dash Allspice
¼ teaspoon Almond Extract
¼ cup finely chopped pecans

Combine apricots, sugar, water, mace and allspice in saucepan. Cover and simmer until apricots are soft and mixture is thickened. Cool; stir in almond extract and pecans.

Makes enough filling for about 3 dozen cookies.

FIG FILLING:

2 cups chopped dried figs
¾ cup water
½ cup sugar
¼ teaspoon Ginger
½ teaspoon Cinnamon
2 teaspoons Lemon Peel
2 tablespoons lemon juice
Dash Allspice

Combine all ingredients in saucepan. Cover and cook until figs are tender.
Makes enough filling for about 3 dozen cookies.

POPPY SEED-CHEESE FILLING:

1 8-ounce package cream cheese
2 teaspoons Rum Extract
2 teaspoons Poppy Seed

Have cream cheese at room temperature; thoroughly blend with extract and poppy seed. *Makes enough filling for about 2 dozen cookies.*

Fruit Cake Cookies

½ pound candied pineapple
1 pound candied cherries
1 pound pitted dates
3 tablespoons flour
4 cups pecan pieces
¼ cup butter
½ cup dark brown sugar, packed
2 eggs
1½ cups all-purpose flour
1½ teaspoons baking soda
¼ teaspoon Cloves
¼ teaspoon Allspice
½ teaspoon Cinnamon
¼ teaspoon Nutmeg
1 tablespoon milk
4 tablespoons orange juice

Cut fruit into medium-size pieces. Sprinkle lightly with the 3 tablespoons flour and toss to coat fruit. Add pecans and mix well. Cream butter and sugar until light and fluffy; add eggs, one at a time, beating well after each addition. Sift flour, measure and sift again with soda and spices; add to creamed mixture alternately with milk and orange juice. Stir in fruits and pecans, mixing well. Drop by teaspoonfuls onto greased and floured baking sheet. For more colorful cookies you may want to top with half a red or green cherry. Bake in 350°F. oven 15 minutes.

Makes about 9 dozen cookies.

Old-Fashioned Tea Cakes

½ cup butter
½ cup granulated sugar
½ cup brown sugar, packed
1 egg
½ teaspoon pure Vanilla Extract
3 cups all-purpose flour
½ teaspoon baking powder
¼ teaspoon baking soda
¼ teaspoon Nutmeg
¼ cup buttermilk

Cream butter, granulated sugar and brown sugar until light and fluffy. Add egg and vanilla. Sift flour, measure and sift again with baking powder, soda and nutmeg. Add dry ingredients and buttermilk alternately to creamed mixture. Chill dough. Roll out to ⅛-inch thickness on lightly floured board. Cut with cookie cutters. Bake on lightly greased baking sheet in 400°F. oven 8 minutes. *Makes about 6 dozen 2-inch cookies.*

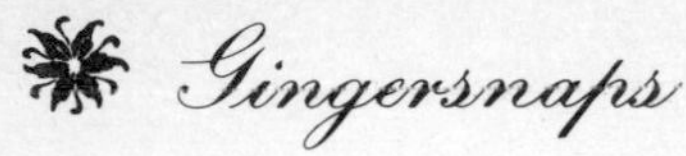

- ¾ cup butter
- 1 cup sugar
- ¼ cup molasses
- 1 egg
- 2 cups all-purpose flour
- ¼ teaspoon salt
- 2 teaspoons baking soda
- 1 teaspoon Cinnamon
- 1 teaspoon Cloves
- 1 teaspoon Ginger

Cream shortening and sugar together. Add molasses and egg; beat well. Sift flour, measure and sift again with remaining ingredients. Add to butter mixture and mix thoroughly. Roll into small balls and dip into additional granulated sugar or leave plain. Place two inches apart on greased baking sheet. Bake in 375°F. oven 10 to 12 minutes. *Makes 6 to 7 dozen.*

Date Nut Cookies

- 2 cups all-purpose flour
- 2 cups pitted dates
- ½ teaspoon salt
- ½ teaspoon baking soda
- 1 teaspoon Pumpkin Pie Spice
- ½ cup butter or margarine
- 1 cup brown sugar, packed
- 1 egg
- 1 teaspoon pure Vanilla Extract
- ½ cup buttermilk
- ½ cup chopped pecans

Sift and measure flour. Slice dates; dredge with 2 tablespoons of the flour. Sift remaining flour with salt, soda and pumpkin pie spice. Cream butter and sugar thoroughly. Add egg and vanilla; beat hard. Add flour mixture alternately with milk. Stir in dates and pecans. Drop by teaspoonfuls onto greased baking sheets. Bake in 375°F. oven 8 to 10 minutes. These cookies should be soft and not too brown. *Makes about 5 dozen.*

Refrigerator Spice Cookies

- ½ cup butter
- 1 cup dark brown sugar, packed
- 1 egg
- 1 teaspoon pure Vanilla Extract
- 2¼ cups all-purpose flour
- ½ teaspoon baking soda
- ¼ teaspoon salt
- 1 teaspoon Cinnamon
- ½ teaspoon Nutmeg
- 1 cup nuts, finely chopped

Cream butter and sugar until light and fluffy. Beat in egg and vanilla. Sift flour, measure and sift again with soda, salt, cinnamon and nutmeg. Stir into butter-sugar mixture. Add nuts, mixing well. Shape into roll; wrap in wax paper and chill. Cut into thin slices and bake on lightly greased baking sheet in 350°F. oven 8 to 10 minutes.

Makes 6 to 7 dozen cookies.

Rocks

1 cup butter or margarine
1½ cups brown sugar, packed
3 eggs
3 cups all-purpose flour
1 teaspoon baking soda
¼ teaspoon Cloves
¼ teaspoon Allspice
1 teaspoon Cinnamon
Dash Nutmeg
2 cups seedless raisins
1½ cups chopped walnuts

Cream butter and sugar until light and fluffy. Add eggs, one at a time, beating well after each addition. Sift and measure flour; reserve 2 tablespoons. Sift remaining flour with soda and spices and stir into creamed mixture. Dredge raisins in the 2 tablespoons flour, then stir into batter along with walnuts. Drop by tablespoonfuls onto lightly greased baking sheet. Bake in 375°F. oven 8 to 10 minutes. *Makes about 6 dozen.*

Cinnamon Sandies

1 cup butter or margarine
1½ cups powdered sugar
2 teaspoons pure Vanilla Extract
1 tablespoon water
2 cups sifted all-purpose flour
1 cup finely chopped nuts
2 teaspoons Cinnamon

Cream butter and ½ cup of the sugar; stir in vanilla and water. Add flour, mixing well. Stir in nuts. Shape small pieces of dough into crescents. Bake on an ungreased baking sheet in 300°F. oven 20 minutes or until very lightly browned. Sift the remaining 1 cup powdered sugar and cinnamon together. Roll hot cookies in this mixture. Allow cookies to cool, then roll again in the sugar-spice mixture. *Makes about 5 dozen.*

Pecan Cookie Balls

1 cup butter or margarine
2½ cups sifted powdered sugar
⅛ teaspoon salt
½ teaspoon Nutmeg
2 teaspoons pure Vanilla Extract
2 cups sifted all-purpose flour
2 cups finely chopped pecans

Cream butter until soft; add ½ cup of the powdered sugar, salt, nutmeg and vanilla; continue creaming until thoroughly mixed. Stir in flour and pecans. Shape dough into small balls. Place on baking sheet and bake in 350°F. oven 15 minutes. Remove from baking sheet and quickly roll the hot cookies in the remaining 2 cups powdered sugar. Cool; roll again in powdered sugar. Store in tight container.

Makes 4 to 5 dozen cookies about 1 inch in diameter.

Southern Praline Cookies

1 cup brown sugar, packed
1 egg white, stiffly beaten
½ teaspoon pure Vanilla Extract
¼ teaspoon salt
¼ teaspoon Cinnamon
2 cups pecan halves

Stir brown sugar into stiffly beaten egg white. Add remaining ingredients, mixing well. Drop from a teaspoon onto a greased baking sheet, allowing 2 or 3 pecans to each cookie. Bake in 250°F. oven 30 minutes. Remove to rack or paper immediately. *Makes 3 to 4 dozen cookies.*

Spiced Mixed Nuts

1½ cups walnut halves
2 cups boiling water
2 cups superfine sugar
1 teaspoon salt
1 teaspoon Nutmeg
2 tablespoons Cinnamon
2 teaspoons Ginger
½ teaspoon Cloves
1 teaspoon Allspice
2 teaspoons Orange Peel
2 egg whites
2 tablespoons water
1 cup pecan halves
½ cup blanched almonds

Drop walnuts into boiling water and simmer 10 minutes. Drain. Sift sugar, salt and spices together 2 or 3 times to blend well. Beat egg whites until frothy; add the 2 tablespoons water and mix well. Add walnuts, pecans and almonds; stir to coat well with egg white mixture. Drain in colander. Make a shallow layer of the spiced sugar, using about half of it, in a 15½ x 10½ x 1-inch jelly roll pan. Add nuts to the remaining sugar mixture and mix well. Separate nuts and spread in a single layer over sugar in pan. Bake in 200°F. oven 2½ to 3 hours. Be sure the oven is not over 200°F. Remove from oven and while warm break into small pieces, allowing 2 to 3 nuts to each piece. *Makes about 4 cups.*

Czechoslovakian Cookies

1 cup butter or margarine
1 cup sugar
2 egg yolks
1 teaspoon pure Vanilla Extract
⅛ teaspoon ground Cardamom
¼ teaspoon Allspice
2 cups sifted all-purpose flour
1 cup chopped walnuts or pecans
½ cup strawberry jam

Cream butter until soft. Add sugar gradually, beating until light and fluffy. Add egg yolks and vanilla; beat hard. Sift cardamom and allspice with flour; gradually add to butter mixture, mixing thoroughly. Stir in chopped nuts. Spoon half of the dough into a greased 8-inch square cake pan; spread evenly. Top with strawberry jam. Cover with remaining dough. Bake in 325°F. oven 1 hour or until lightly browned. Cool. Cut into about 1½-inch squares. *Makes about 2 dozen.*

Orange Butter Gems

1 cup butter
1 cup powdered sugar
2½ cups all-purpose flour
¼ teaspoon Mace
¼ teaspoon salt
1 egg
2 teaspoons Orange Peel
2 teaspoons Orange Extract

Cream butter and sugar until light and fluffy. Sift flour, measure and sift again with mace and salt. Add 1 cup of the flour mixture to the butter-sugar mixture. Beat in egg, orange peel and orange extract. Add remaining flour mixture. Put dough into cookie press and form cookies on ungreased baking sheet. Bake in 375°F. oven 10 minutes or until lightly browned. Decorate with tinted frosting if desired. *Makes about 6 dozen.*

VARIATION:

Lemon Butter Gems—Substitute 2 teaspoons Lemon Peel and 2 teaspoons Lemon Extract for orange peel and orange extract in the above recipe.

Pfeffernüsse

German Christmas cookie meaning Peppernuts.

2 eggs
1 cup brown sugar, packed
2 teaspoons Lemon Peel
½ cup finely chopped citron
2 cups sifted all-purpose flour
1 teaspoon baking powder
½ teaspoon salt
1 teaspoon Cinnamon
⅛ teaspoon Nutmeg
⅛ teaspoon Cloves
⅛ teaspoon Mace
¼ teaspoon Black Pepper
⅛ teaspoon ground Cardamom
½ cup chopped nuts
Brandy Extract
or Rum Extract

Beat eggs until thick; add brown sugar and lemon peel. Continue beating until well blended. Stir in citron. Sift flour with baking powder, salt and spices and add to egg mixture. Stir in nuts. Shape into roll 1 inch in diameter. Chill. Cut into ½-inch slices and place on baking sheet; allow to dry overnight. Turn cookies over and put 1 to 2 drops extract in center of each cookie. Bake in 375°F. oven 12 to 15 minutes. Store in tightly covered container several days to mellow. *Makes about 6 dozen.*

Sugared Vanilla Wafers

1 cup butter or margarine
1½ cups sugar
2 eggs
3 teaspoons pure Vanilla Extract
3 cups sifted all-purpose flour
2 teaspoons baking powder
2 tablespoons milk
Sugar for sprinkling
Cinnamon Sugar, optional

Cream butter and the 1½ cups sugar thoroughly; add eggs and vanilla and beat well. Sift together flour and baking powder; add to creamed mixture. Stir in milk and chill several hours. Lightly flour a board and sprinkle with 1 tablespoon sugar. Roll out chilled dough very thin and cut with cookie cutters. Place on lightly greased baking sheet. Sprinkle with sugar or cinnamon sugar. Bake in 400°F. oven 6 to 8 minutes.

Makes about 5 dozen 2-inch cookies.

½ cup shortening
½ cup sugar
1 cup molasses
1 egg, beaten
3½ cups all-purpose flour
1 teaspoon baking soda
1½ teaspoons Cinnamon
1½ teaspoons Ginger
¼ teaspoon salt
Raisins

Heat shortening, sugar and molasses until shortening is melted, stirring constantly. Cool; add egg and mix well. Sift flour, measure and sift again with soda, spices and salt. Stir into molasses mixture. Chill well. Roll out dough on lightly floured board to ¼-inch thickness; and cut with 3- to 4-inch gingerbread-boy cutter. Carefully place on lightly greased baking sheet. Decorate with raisins. Bake in 350°F. oven 10 minutes. Carefully remove and cool on rack. *Makes about 24 gingerbread boys.*

½ cup Sesame Seed
¼ teaspoon Cream of Tartar
¼ cup egg whites (about 2)
¼ cup sugar
½ teaspoon Almond Extract

Toast sesame seed in 350°F. oven 15 minutes or until golden brown. Pulverize in blender or with mortar and pestle. Add cream of tartar to egg whites; beat until stiff. Gradually add sugar, beating well after each addition. Fold in sesame seed and almond extract. Drop by teaspoonfuls onto lightly greased baking sheet. Bake in 250°F. oven 30 minutes. Remove at once from baking sheet. *Makes about 3 dozen.*

Lebkuchen

German Christmas Honey Cakes.

- ½ cup honey
- ½ cup molasses
- 1 cup sugar
- ⅓ cup butter
- 2 teaspoons lemon juice
- 1 egg
- 2 teaspoons Lemon Peel
- 1 teaspoon Orange Peel
- 3¼ cups all-purpose flour
- ¾ teaspoon baking soda
- ¼ teaspoon salt
- 1 teaspoon Cinnamon
- 1 teaspoon Allspice
- 1 teaspoon Cloves
- ¾ teaspoon Mace
- ¼ teaspoon ground Cardamom
- ½ cup chopped mixed candied fruits
- ½ cup slivered blanched almonds
- 3 cups powdered sugar
- ¼ cup boiling water
- ½ teaspoon Almond Extract

Combine honey, molasses and sugar in saucepan; bring to a boil. Remove from heat; add butter, then cool. Beat in lemon juice, egg, lemon peel and orange peel. Sift flour, measure and sift again with soda, salt and spices. Add to honey-molasses mixture, mixing well. Stir in candied fruits and almonds. Chill dough overnight. Roll out on floured board to ¼-inch thickness, using one fourth of the dough at a time. Cut into rectangles, 1½ x 2½ inches. Place on greased baking sheet and bake in 400°F. oven 10 minutes or until brown. To make glaze, thoroughly blend powdered sugar, boiling water and extract. Brush glaze over cookies as soon as they are removed from oven. Immediately remove from baking sheet. Store in tight container a few days to mellow. You may add a sliced apple or orange for added moisture.

Makes about 5 dozen cookies.

Date Sticks

- ½ cup butter
- 1 cup sugar
- 1 egg
- 1 teaspoon pure Vanilla Extract
- 1 teaspoon Lemon Peel
- 2 cups all-purpose flour
- ½ teaspoon baking powder
- ¼ teaspoon baking soda
- 1 teaspoon Cinnamon
- ⅛ teaspoon Nutmeg
- ¼ teaspoon salt
- 1 cup chopped dates

Cream butter; gradually add sugar, beating until light and fluffy. Add egg, vanilla and lemon peel, beating well. Sift flour, measure and sift again with baking powder, soda, cinnamon, nutmeg and salt. Slowly add the dry ingredients to creamed mixture. Stir in dates. Shape cookies into thin sticks about 1½ inches long. Place on a greased baking sheet; bake in 350°F. oven 15 to 20 minutes.

Makes about 6 dozen.

Spicy Oatmeal Cookies

1 cup raisins or currants
⅔ cup shortening
1½ cups sugar
2 eggs, lightly beaten
½ cup milk
1 teaspoon pure Vanilla Extract
2 cups sifted all-purpose flour
½ teaspoon baking soda
1 teaspoon salt
1 teaspoon baking powder
½ teaspoon Cinnamon
¼ teaspoon Nutmeg
¼ teaspoon Allspice
2½ cups quick-cooking rolled oats

Rinse and drain raisins. Cream together shortening and sugar until fluffy. Stir in eggs, milk, vanilla and raisins. Sift together flour, soda, salt, baking powder and spices; combine with rolled oats. Stir into creamed mixture, mixing well. Drop by teaspoonfuls onto greased baking sheet. Bake in 350°F. oven 15 minutes or until lightly browned.

Makes 5 to 6 dozen cookies, depending on size.

Poppy Seed Goodies

½ cup butter
½ cup brown sugar, packed
¼ cup honey
1 egg
1 teaspoon pure Vanilla Extract
1 cup all-purpose flour
½ teaspoon baking soda
¼ teaspoon salt
¼ teaspoon Mace
2 tablespoons Poppy Seed
1½ cups quick-cooking rolled oats

Cream butter, brown sugar and honey until light and fluffy. Add egg and vanilla; beat well. Sift flour, measure and sift again with soda, salt and mace. Add to creamed mixture along with poppy seed and rolled oats, mixing well. Drop by teaspoonfuls onto greased baking sheet. Bake in 400°F. oven 10 minutes or until lightly browned. Cool slightly before removing from baking sheet. *Makes about 4½ dozen.*

Mincemeat Refrigerator Cookies

¾ cup shortening
1 cup sugar
1 egg
1 teaspoon Lemon Peel
¼ teaspoon crushed Coriander Seed
½ teaspoon pure Vanilla Extract
2½ cups all-purpose flour
½ teaspoon baking soda
½ teaspoon salt
1 teaspoon Cinnamon
Dash Nutmeg
¼ teaspoon Cloves
¼ teaspoon Ginger
½ cup mincemeat
½ cup chopped nuts

Cream shortening and sugar until fluffy. Add egg; beat well. Stir in lemon peel, crushed coriander seed and vanilla. Sift flour, measure and sift again with soda, salt, cinnamon, nutmeg, cloves and ginger. Add to creamed mixture, mixing thoroughly. Stir in mincemeat and nuts. Shape into rolls 1½ inches in diameter and wrap in wax paper. Chill. Cut thin slices and place on baking sheet. Bake in 375°F. oven 9 to 10 minutes.

Makes 8 to 9 dozen.

Frosted Nutmeg Logs

1 cup butter or margarine
¾ cup sugar
1¼ teaspoons Nutmeg
1 egg
2 teaspoons Rum Extract
2 teaspoons pure Vanilla Extract
3 cups all-purpose flour
Vanilla-Rum Frosting

Cream butter and sugar. Add nutmeg, egg and extracts, mixing thoroughly. Sift flour and measure; stir into creamed mixture. Shape into rolls ½ inch in diameter and 3 inches long. Place, about 2 inches apart, on ungreased baking sheet. Bake in 350°F. oven 15 minutes or until lightly browned. Cool. Frost with Vanilla-Rum Frosting. *Makes 3 to 4 dozen.*

VANILLA-RUM FROSTING:

¼ cup soft butter
3 cups powdered sugar
1 teaspoon pure Vanilla Extract
1 teaspoon Rum Extract
1 to 2 tablespoons cream
Nutmeg

Cream butter until soft and fluffy. Add part of the sugar and extracts, mixing well. Add remaining sugar and enough of the cream to obtain the desired spreading consistency. Frost cookies and run the tines of a fork down frosting. Sprinkle with nutmeg. *Makes 1⅓ cups frosting.*

Cinnamon Sledges

2 cups all-purpose flour
3 teaspoons Cinnamon
1 cup butter
1 cup sugar
1 egg, separated
½ cup chopped pecans

Sift flour, measure and sift again with cinnamon. Cream butter and sugar until light and fluffy. Add egg yolk; beat well. Add flour and cinnamon, mixing until well blended. Spread this stiff mixture to about ¼-inch thickness on a 12 x 15-inch baking sheet, leaving a border about 1½ inches around the edge to allow for spreading. Beat egg white until foamy and brush over top of dough. Sprinkle with nuts and press in lightly. Bake in 300°F. oven 45 to 50 minutes. Cut into bars while still hot and remove from baking sheet. *Makes 3 to 4 dozen, depending on size.*

Chocolate Nut Brownies

4 1-ounce squares unsweetened chocolate
¾ cup butter
4 eggs
2 cups sugar
¼ teaspoon salt
¼ teaspoon Mace
1 teaspoon pure Vanilla Extract
1 cup sifted all-purpose flour
1 cup pecan or walnut pieces

Melt chocolate over hot water; add butter. Beat eggs until light and fluffy; gradually add sugar, salt and mace. Stir in vanilla; beat until light. Stir in chocolate mixture, then flour, beating until smooth. Add nuts and mix well. Pour into a greased and floured 15½ x 10½ x 1-inch jelly roll pan. Bake in 350°F. oven 30 minutes. When cool cut into oblong pieces or squares. Makes a moist brownie. *Makes 32 to 40.*

Cardamom Butter Cookies

1 cup butter
1¼ cups sugar
2 eggs
1 teaspoon pure Vanilla Extract
3 cups sifted all-purpose flour
1 teaspoon baking powder
½ teaspoon salt
1 teaspoon ground Cardamom
½ teaspoon Cinnamon
¼ teaspoon Allspice

Cream butter and sugar until light and fluffy. Add eggs and vanilla and beat well. Sift together remaining ingredients; stir into creamed mixture and mix well. Chill dough, roll and cut with cookie cutters. Or, if you prefer, shape dough into two rolls and wrap in wax paper. Chill. Cut into thin slices. Bake in 350°F. oven 8 to 10 minutes, depending on thickness of cookies. *Makes 8 dozen thin cookies.*

Sesame Pralines

A delightfully different version of the famous New Orleans confection.

¼ cup Sesame Seed
1 cup dark brown sugar, packed
1 cup granulated sugar
1 cup cream
2 tablespoons butter or margarine
2 cups pecan halves

Toast sesame seed in 350°F. oven 15 minutes or until golden brown. In a 3-quart saucepan combine both sugars and cream. Cook over medium heat, stirring until sugar dissolves. Wash crystals from side of pan. Cook to 230°F. on candy thermometer. Add butter, pecans and sesame seed; continue cooking, stirring occasionally, to 238°F. (soft ball stage). Remove from heat. Cool 2 to 3 minutes, then stir 2 minutes or until slightly thickened. Drop from spoon, working fast, onto buttered wax paper, aluminum foil or marble slab. *Makes about 15, depending on size.*

Date Roll

3 cups sugar
1 tablespoon light corn syrup
½ teaspoon salt
1 cup milk
1 teaspoon Orange Peel
½ teaspoon Cinnamon
¼ teaspoon Nutmeg
⅛ teaspoon Allspice
1 8-ounce package dates, cut into pieces
2 tablespoons butter
1 teaspoon pure Vanilla Extract
1 cup chopped pecans or walnuts

Combine sugar, corn syrup, salt and milk. Cook over low heat, stirring until sugar dissolves. Wash down sides of pan to prevent crystals forming. Continue cooking to 236°F. on candy thermometer (soft ball stage). Add orange peel, spices and dates and continue cooking to 238°F. Remove from heat and add butter. Do not stir. Let cool to 110°F. or lukewarm. Add vanilla and beat until mixture just begins to thicken. Add nuts and continue beating until it begins to hold its shape. Turn out onto damp cheesecloth and shape into a roll 2 inches in diameter. Set aside and when firm cut into thin slices as needed. *Makes about 2 pounds.*

Cinnamon Chocolate Fudge

Everyone likes chocolate fudge—and this one is extra special.

4 1-ounce squares unsweetened chocolate
3 cups sugar
2 teaspoons Cinnamon
2 tablespoons light corn syrup
1¼ cups milk
4 tablespoons butter or margarine
1 teaspoon pure Vanilla Extract
2 cups pecans or walnuts, broken

Melt chocolate in 3-quart saucepan on lowest heat or over hot water. Stir in sugar, cinnamon, corn syrup and milk. Increase heat to medium and cook, stirring until sugar dissolves. Wash crystals from side of pan. Cook to 238°F. on candy thermometer (soft ball stage). Remove from heat; add butter and, without stirring, let cool to 110°F. or lukewarm. Add vanilla and beat until mixture begins to thicken. Stir in nuts and continue beating until candy holds its shape. Drop from spoon onto buttered wax paper or pour into buttered pan. When cool, cut into squares. *Makes about 3 pounds.*

Holiday Chews

Double-decker cookie bars the children will adore.

½ cup butter or margarine
½ cup brown sugar, packed
1 cup sifted all-purpose flour
½ teaspoon Pumpkin Pie Spice
½ teaspoon Ginger
1 cup brown sugar, packed
2 eggs
2 tablespoons flour
1 teaspoon Orange Peel
¼ teaspoon salt
1 teaspoon pure Vanilla Extract
1 cup chopped nuts
1½ cups shredded coconut
½ teaspoon baking powder
¼ teaspoon Mace

With a pastry blender or two knives thoroughly blend together butter, the ½ cup brown sugar, the 1 cup flour, pumpkin pie spice and ginger. Pat into a greased, shallow 8 x 12-inch pan. Bake in 375°F. oven 20 minutes or until crisp. Remove from oven and reduce temperature to 350°F. Thoroughly mix remaining ingredients and spoon over baked mixture. Return to oven and bake 25 minutes longer or until topping is brown and bubbly. Cool and cut into 1 x 1½-inch bars. *Makes 32.*

Sugared Nuts

1 cup sugar
1 teaspoon Cinnamon
1 teaspoon Orange Peel
⅛ teaspoon Mace
½ cup milk
1 teaspoon butter
1 teaspoon pure Vanilla Extract
2 cups walnut halves

Combine sugar, cinnamon, orange peel and mace. Stir in milk; cook to 238°F. on candy thermometer (soft ball stage). Remove from heat; add butter. Let stand 2 to 3 minutes, then add vanilla and nuts. Stir mixture until thick and begins to hold its shape. Immediately turn out on wax paper and, working quickly, separate the nuts. *Makes about 70 halves.*

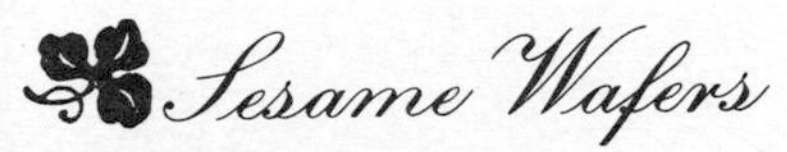

Sesame Wafers

½ cup Sesame Seed
1 cup butter
⅔ cup sugar
¼ teaspoon salt
1 tablespoon milk
½ teaspoon Almond Extract
1⅔ cups sifted all-purpose flour

Toast sesame seed in 350°F. oven 15 minutes or until golden brown. Cream butter, sugar and salt until light and fluffy. Add remaining ingredients, mixing well. Chill. Shape into small balls. Place on ungreased baking sheet 2 to 3 inches apart. Bake in 350°F. oven 15 minutes or until lightly browned. Cool slightly before removing from pan. *Makes 4 dozen.*

Spiced Divinity

A new treat in Divinity!

2 cups superfine sugar
½ cup light corn syrup
½ cup water
⅛ teaspoon Cream of Tartar
2 egg whites
¼ teaspoon Mace
⅛ teaspoon Allspice
1 teaspoon pure Vanilla Extract
1½ cups chopped nuts

Combine sugar, corn syrup and water. Bring to a boil, stirring until sugar dissolves. Cook to 252°F. on candy thermometer (hard ball stage), washing down sides of saucepan to prevent crystals forming. Add cream of tartar to egg whites; beat until stiff. Pour the hot syrup in a thin stream over egg whites, beating vigorously. Continue beating until the mixture just begins to thicken, then add mace, allspice and vanilla. Continue beating until it begins to hold its shape and loses its high gloss. Stir in nuts. Drop quickly from tip of spoon in individual pieces onto wax paper; or spread in a buttered pan and cut into squares when firm.

Makes 3 to 4 dozen pieces, depending on size.

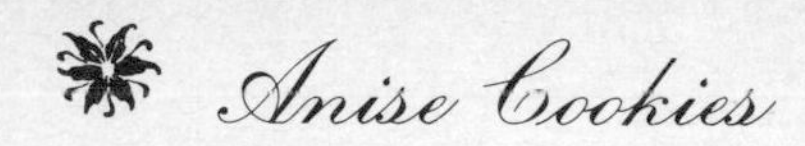

Anise Cookies

½ cup butter
1 cup sugar
1 egg
½ teaspoon pure Vanilla Extract
1¾ cups sifted all-purpose flour
½ teaspoon salt
1½ teaspoons baking powder
1½ teaspoons Anise Seed

Cream butter; add sugar and continue beating until light and smooth. Add egg and vanilla, mixing well. Sift together flour, salt and baking powder. Gradually add dry ingredients and anise seed, beating hard after each addition. Shape dough into a roll. Wrap in wax paper and chill. Cut into thin slices. Place on a lightly greased baking sheet and bake in 400°F. oven 8 minutes or until golden brown. *Makes about 5 dozen.*

Prune-Filled Squares

PRUNE FILLING:

1½ cups chopped, cooked prunes
2 tablespoons liquid from prunes
2 tablespoons lemon juice
1 teaspoon Orange Peel
3 tablespoons sugar
⅛ teaspoon Cloves
¼ teaspoon Ginger
Dash Nutmeg
Dash salt

Combine all ingredients. Cook over low heat, stirring occasionally, 8 minutes or until thickened. Cool to room temperature. Prepare crumb layer.

CRUMB LAYER:

1¼ cups all-purpose flour
½ teaspoon Cinnamon
½ teaspoon salt
¾ cup brown sugar, packed
1 cup quick-cooking rolled oats
1 tablespoon Poppy Seed
½ cup butter or margarine

Sift flour, then measure. Add cinnamon and salt and sift again into a large bowl. Stir in brown sugar, rolled oats and poppy seed. Using a pastry blender or 2 knives, cut in butter until mixture resembles coarse meal. Spread half this mixture evenly over the bottom of a well greased 8-inch square pan. Press down firmly. Cover with prune filling, spreading it evenly to edges and into corners. Sprinkle remaining crumb mixture over filling. Carefully press down crumbs to make smooth top. Bake in 400°F. oven 30 minutes or until top is browned. Cool in pan on cake rack. Cut into squares. Store in tightly covered container. These cookies keep well. *Makes about 16.*

VARIATION:

Apricot Squares—Use 1½ cups chopped, cooked, dried apricots in place of prunes. Proceed as in recipe above.

Fondant

2½ cups sugar
1½ cups water
⅛ teaspoon Cream of Tartar
Extract, any flavor
Food Color

Combine sugar, water and cream of tartar. Cook over medium heat, stirring until sugar dissolves. Wash down side of pan. Cook to 238°F. on candy thermometer. (This is near the highest degree for soft ball stage. A little syrup when dropped in cold water forms a ball which will just hold its shape when picked up.) Immediately pour onto platter or marble slab. Do not scrape syrup from pan. When mixture has cooled to lukewarm, begin working with wide spatula, scraping fondant from outside edge toward center. Continue working, using a wooden spoon if necessary, until the fondant is white, creamy and firm; then knead well, until smooth but not flaky. Put in a bowl; cover and set aside 12 to 24 hours to ripen. To all or part of fondant add few drops of any desired extract to taste, using about 1 teaspoon per pound. Tint with a few drops of food color if desired. *Makes about 1 pound.*

VARIATION:

Fondant Tipped Almonds—Toast 2 cups whole blanched almonds. After Fondant, recipe above, has ripened, put it in top of double boiler and melt over hot water. Stir in 1 teaspoon Mint Extract or Mint and Peppermint Extract and tint using Red, Green, Yellow or Blue Food Color. For an assortment of colors, divide fondant into small amounts, tinting each a different shade or color. Dip large end of almond into melted fondant and place on wax paper to dry.
Makes about 1½ pounds.

Sesame Toffee Bars

¼ cup Sesame Seed
1 cup butter or margarine
1 cup dark brown sugar, packed
1 egg
1 teaspoon pure Vanilla Extract
2 cups sifted all-purpose flour
¼ teaspoon Cinnamon
¼ teaspoon Allspice
⅛ teaspoon Nutmeg
½ cup finely chopped or ground nuts
2 6-ounce packages semi-sweet chocolate pieces

Toast sesame seed in 350°F. oven 15 minutes or until golden brown. Cream butter and sugar. Add egg and vanilla and mix well. Sift flour with spices. Add to creamed mixture and mix well. Stir in nuts. Spread ¼ inch thick into a 13 x 15-inch rectangle on a baking sheet. Bake in 350°F. oven 20 minutes. While baking, melt chocolate pieces over hot water or on lowest heat. Spread chocolate over cookies while hot. Sprinkle top with sesame seed and cut into bars while warm. *Makes about 4 dozen.*

Chewy Popcorn Balls

A sure way to delight the younger generation. These are fine to offer for trick-or-treats, too.

- 1 cup sugar
- 1 cup light corn syrup
- ½ teaspoon salt
- ½ teaspoon Cinnamon
- ¼ teaspoon Ginger
- ⅛ teaspoon Mace
- 2 tablespoons butter
- ½ cup water
- 1 teaspoon pure Vanilla Extract
- ½ teaspoon Almond Extract
- 3 quarts crisp salted popped corn
- 1½ cups chopped mixed nuts

Combine sugar, corn syrup, salt, spices, butter and water in saucepan. Cook over low heat, stirring until sugar dissolves. Wash crystals from side of pan. Cook over medium heat to 245°F. on candy thermometer (firm ball stage). Remove from heat; stir in extracts. Pour slowly over mixture of popped corn and nuts, stirring to mix well. Shape, with buttered hands, into balls. *Makes about 2 dozen balls, 2 inches in diameter.*

VARIATIONS:

Holiday Popcorn Balls—In the above recipe, add ½ cup minced candied cherries (mixture of red and green) to popped corn and nuts. Pour hot syrup over this mixture and proceed as directed.

Crunchy Popcorn Balls—In recipe for Chewy Popcorn Balls use only 2 quarts popped corn instead of 3 quarts; make syrup following directions, cooking to 290°F. on candy thermometer (hard crack stage). Pour over popped corn and nuts. Shape into balls if desired, or spread in thin layer on aluminum foil. When cool, break into small pieces.

BEVERAGES

Party Punches

Island Fruit Punch 349

Party Punch 346

Spice-Fruit Ring 346

Spiced Grape Punch 347

Tropical Delight 347

Special for the Holidays

Cranberry Wassail Bowl 348

Eggnog 350

Glögg 348

Holiday Cranberry Punch 355

Hot Cranberry Punch 350

Traditional Wassail Bowl 354

Hot or Cold—Good Both Ways

Autumn Spiced Cider 349

Hot 'n' Spicy Punch 355

Minted Mocha Float 351

Tea House Punch 348

Steaming Hot and Heart-Warming

Café Diable 347

Cocoa with a Hint of Spice 351

French Hot Chocolate 352

French Mint Chocolate 352

Mexican Chocolate with Marshmallows 351

Mulled Wine 352

Spiced Tea 349

Summer Refreshers, Tall and Frosty

Apple Blossom Cooler 350

Banana Frost 352

Cinnamon-Vanilla Milk Shake 354

Ginger Peach Freeze 353

Iced Viennese Coffee 353

Lime-Mint Cooler 353

Mint Tea Hawaiian 350

Spiced Sangria 345

Zippy Tomato Juice 354

Spiced Sangria

1 orange
1 lemon
½ apple
½ cup apple juice
1 3-inch piece stick Cinnamon
8 whole Allspice
1 tablespoon sugar
¼ cup dry vermouth
1 fifth (⁴⁄₅ quart) dry red wine
1 10-ounce bottle chilled soda water

Cut orange in half crosswise. Squeeze one half, reserving juice. Thinly slice remaining half. Do the same to the lemon. Core, quarter and slice apple. Combine juice of the orange and lemon and pieces of orange, lemon and apple in a 2-quart pitcher. In a small saucepan combine apple juice, cinnamon and allspice. Heat to boiling, reduce heat and simmer, covered 5 minutes. Stir in sugar until dissolved. Pour over fruit in pitcher. Add vermouth and red wine. Refrigerate ½ hour before serving. Add soda water. Serve over ice. *Makes about 1½ quarts.*

Party Punch

For extra sparkle add champagne.

1 46-ounce can pineapple-grapefruit juice
1 quart apple juice
3 6-ounce cans frozen orange juice concentrate
1 can frozen lemon juice (5¾-ounce can)
24 whole Cloves
4 3-inch pieces Cinnamon
½ teaspoon Ginger
½ teaspoon ground Allspice
½ teaspoon Mace
6 whole Cardamom
½ cup sugar
4 quarts ginger ale (13 or 14 7-ounce bottles)

Combine fruit juices. Tie whole cloves in cheesecloth bag and add to juice with other spices and sugar; mix well to dissolve sugar. Let stand several hours. When ready to serve, remove spice bag; stir well. Pour into punch bowl over ice; add ginger ale. (If you want to mix small amount at a time, use 1 cup fruit juice mixture to 1 cup or 1 7-ounce bottle ginger ale.) Float a Spice-Fruit Ring (see recipe below) in punch bowl.

Makes 2 gallons, or about 64 4-ounce servings.

Spice-Fruit Ring

An attractive way to chill punch without diluting the flavor.

Pineapple spears
Pineapple slices
Red maraschino cherries with stems
Green maraschino cherries
Lemon slices, cut ¼ inch thick
Orange slices, cut ¼ inch thick
Whole Cloves
Whole Cardamom
1 quart ginger ale
Whole Ginger
Cinnamon Sticks
Whole Allspice

Drain pineapple; rinse cherries. Stud outer edges of lemon and orange slices with whole cloves and place whole cardamom in center. Pour enough ginger ale into ring mold or interestingly shaped mold to cover bottom; freeze. Arrange fruits and whole spices in an attractive design over frozen ginger ale and pour enough ginger ale over fruits and spices to just cover. Freeze. Pour remaining ginger ale into ring mold and freeze until solid. When ready to serve, remove from mold and float in punch bowl.

Makes 1 ring.

Spiced Grape Punch

A subtle blending of fruit juice and spices.

1½ cups reconstituted frozen limeade
½ teaspoon ground Allspice
½ teaspoon ground Cinnamon
½ teaspoon ground Nutmeg
3 6-ounce cans frozen grape juice concentrate
6 12-ounce bottles ginger ale

Combine limeade and spices in saucepan. Boil 3 minutes. Add limeade-spice mixture to grape juice concentrate and ginger ale. Chill.

Makes 25 4-ounce servings.

Tropical Delight

1 46-ounce can grapefruit juice, unsweetened
1 12-ounce can apricot juice
1 12-ounce can papaya juice
1 12-ounce can guava nectar
1 12-ounce can pear nectar
1 cup water
½ cup sugar
4 whole Cardamom
1 3-inch piece Cinnamon
⅛ teaspoon Mace
4 7-ounce bottles ginger ale

Combine juices. Bring water, sugar, cardamom, cinnamon and mace to a boil; reduce heat and simmer 10 minutes. Cool and strain into juices. Add ginger ale and serve over ice.

Makes about 1 gallon, or 32 4-ounce servings.

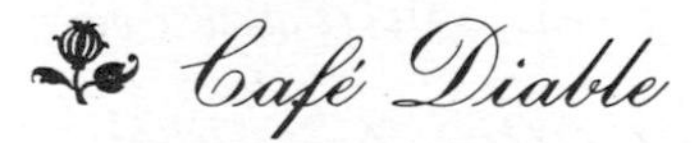

Café Diable

1 orange
Whole Cloves
4 tablespoons sugar
2 3-inch pieces Cinnamon, broken in half
1 thin slice lemon
1½ cups rum or cognac
2 cups strong coffee

Peel orange, being careful to keep peeling in one long piece. Stud peel with whole cloves, putting them about 1 inch apart down the full length of orange peel. Put sugar, 2 whole cloves and cinnamon in café diable dish or chafing dish (remove the water pan when using chafing dish). Heat until sugar melts and just begins to turn golden. Drop in lemon slice and orange peel; pour in rum. Dip up a ladleful of the hot rum; set afire and lower the flaming ladle into the dish. Slowly pour in the coffee. With a long-handled fork or pair of tongs hold the orange peel up by one end; ladle the flaming rum mixture over peel until flame dies. Serve in café diable or demitasse cups. When flaming, turn lights down.

Serves 6.

Glögg

The traditional Swedish Christmas drink.

6 whole Cardamom
1 3-inch piece Cinnamon
1 piece whole Ginger, broken
5 whole Cloves
1 tablespoon Orange Peel
2 cups port wine
2 cups dry red wine
1 cup water
½ cup seedless raisins
½ cup blanched almonds
½ cup sugar
1 cup brandy

Open white cardamom pods and remove the little black seed. Tie seed in a bag along with cinnamon, ginger, cloves and orange peel. Combine all ingredients except brandy. Heat to just under boiling point and hold at this temperature for 15 minutes. Remove spice bag. Carefully pour brandy into mixture. Light and flame. Serve in cups or mugs. *Makes about 6 cups.*

Tea House Punch

½ cup sugar
¼ teaspoon Nutmeg
¼ teaspoon Allspice
¼ teaspoon Cinnamon
2 cups hot water
3 Tea Bags
¼ cup orange juice
¼ cup lemon juice
2 cups cold water

Combine sugar, spices and hot water in saucepan; boil 1 minute and pour while boiling hot over tea bags. Steep 5 minutes. Strain; mix with fruit juices and cold water. Delicious either hot or cold. *Makes about 1 quart.*

Cranberry Wassail Bowl

Delightful holiday punch—teen-agers will especially enjoy.

½ cup blanched almonds
1 cup seedless raisins
Rind of 1 orange
Rind of 1 lemon
1 teaspoon whole Cloves
¼ teaspoon Coriander Seed
6 whole Cardamom
2 3-inch pieces Cinnamon
½ teaspoon whole Allspice
1 quart water
2 quarts cranberry juice cocktail
2½ cups pineapple-grapefruit juice

Combine all ingredients except fruit juices in saucepan. Cover. Bring to a boil, then reduce heat and simmer 15 minutes. Cool. Chill fruit juices. If desired, strain spiced mixture; and just before serving, pour with chilled juices over a block of ice in large punch bowl. Or, you may serve hot in mugs, using Cinnamon Sticks as stirrers. *Makes about 1 gallon.*

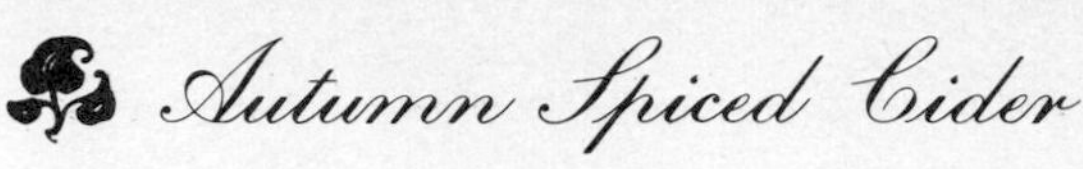

Autumn Spiced Cider

A marvelous drink for teen-age parties.

4 quarts apple cider
1 cup orange juice
½ cup sugar
2 teaspoons Orange Peel
1 teaspoon whole Allspice
½ teaspoon Mace
¼ teaspoon salt
1 teaspoon Coriander Seed
2 teaspoons whole Cloves
2 tablespoons Cinnamon Décors

Combine all ingredients in large saucepan. Cover. Bring to boiling point, then simmer 30 minutes. Strain. Delicious hot as a mulled drink, or you may serve it iced as a cold cider punch. *Makes 1 gallon.*

Island Fruit Punch

4 pieces whole Ginger
8 cups water
¼ cup Mint Flakes
1 tablespoon whole Allspice
1 tablespoon whole Cloves
5 cups sugar
2 quarts orange juice
2 cups lemon juice
2 46-ounce cans pineapple-grapefruit juice
2 cups guava juice, optional

Pound ginger root to bruise or cut into several pieces. Boil with 4 cups of the water 10 minutes or until a strong ginger flavor is obtained. Add mint flakes, allspice and whole cloves and steep until cool. Strain through a cloth. Boil sugar with the remaining 4 cups water to make a syrup. Cool. Combine with all other ingredients. Mix well. Chill and pour over ice ring made of frozen juice, using any one or a mixture of juices listed above. *Makes about 2 gallons.*

Spiced Tea

4 cups boiling water
4 Tea Bags
½ cup orange juice
¼ cup lemon juice
½ cup sugar
3 3-inch pieces Cinnamon
8 whole Cloves
Dash Nutmeg
7 slices lemon

Pour boiling water over tea bags in a heated teapot and steep 5 minutes. Remove tea bags and pour tea into a saucepan, preferably glass or stainless steel. Add orange juice, lemon juice, sugar, cinnamon, cloves and nutmeg. Keep hot, not simmering, for at least 30 minutes before serving, so that flavors may blend. Hold longer if desired. Serve hot with a paper-thin slice of lemon floating in each cup. *Makes about 7 servings.*

Apple Blossom Cooler

1 cup water
⅓ cup sugar
2 teaspoons Mint Flakes
1 3-inch piece Cinnamon
1 quart apple juice
½ cup lemon juice

Bring water, sugar, mint flakes and cinnamon to a boil; reduce heat and simmer 10 minutes. Cool. Combine apple juice and lemon juice. Strain syrup into juice mixture. Chill. *Makes about 5 cups.*

Mint Tea Hawaiian

4 cups boiling water
6 Tea Bags
½ teaspoon Mint Flakes
¼ cup sugar
⅓ cup lemon juice
¼ cup pineapple juice
Pineapple spears

Pour boiling water over tea bags and mint flakes in heated teapot. Cover and steep 5 minutes. Strain; combine with sugar, lemon juice and pineapple juice and mix well. Chill. Serve over ice cubes garnished with a spear of fresh or canned pineapple. *Makes 1 quart.*

Eggnog

3 eggs, separated
1 cup milk
1 teaspoon pure Vanilla Extract
1 teaspoon Rum Extract
1 teaspoon Brandy Extract
1 pint vanilla ice cream
Nutmeg

Beat egg yolks until light; mix in milk and extracts. Beat egg whites until stiff but not dry. Fold egg whites and softened ice cream into milk mixture. Sprinkle with nutmeg. *Makes 5 cups.*

Hot Cranberry Punch

4 pints cranberry juice cocktail
4 6-ounce cans frozen lemonade, undiluted
½ teaspoon salt
1 teaspoon ground Allspice
4 cups water
15 3-inch pieces Cinnamon

Combine all ingredients except cinnamon. Simmer 10 to 15 minutes; do not boil. Serve hot in mugs, using cinnamon sticks as stirrers.

Makes 15 1-cup servings.

Mexican Chocolate with Marshmallows

- 2 1-ounce squares unsweetened chocolate
- 2 tablespoons hot water
- ½ cup sugar
- ¼ teaspoon salt
- 2 teaspoons Cinnamon
- 2 cups hot strong coffee
- 3 cups hot milk
- 8 marshmallows
- 1½ teaspoons pure Vanilla Extract

Put chocolate and water in a 2-quart saucepan; melt over low heat, stirring. Combine sugar, salt and cinnamon and slowly stir into melted chocolate. Add coffee, stirring until smooth; cook a few minutes longer. Stir in milk; add marshmallows. Heat until marshmallows melt; add vanilla and beat until frothy. Serve hot. *Makes 8 servings.*

Cocoa with a Hint of Spice

- ¼ cup cocoa
- 3 tablespoons sugar
- ½ teaspoon ground Cinnamon
- Dash Cloves
- Dash Allspice
- Dash salt
- ¼ cup water
- 3 cups milk
- 4 3-inch pieces Cinnamon

Combine cocoa, sugar, ground cinnamon, cloves, allspice, salt and water; mix well. Cook over medium heat 2 minutes. Stir in milk and heat to just below boiling point but do not boil. Serve hot in cups using a stick of cinnamon as a stirrer. *Serves 4.*

Minted Mocha Float

- 2 1-ounce squares unsweetened chocolate
- 3 cups strong coffee
- ½ cup sugar
- Dash Cardamom
- 1 teaspoon pure Vanilla Extract
- 1 teaspoon Mint Flakes
- 2 cups milk
- 1 cup light cream
- 1 pint vanilla ice cream

Combine chocolate and ¼ cup of the coffee in saucepan. Cook over lowest heat, stirring, until chocolate is melted. Stir in sugar, cardamom and vanilla. Add mint flakes to milk and cream. Scald. Strain into chocolate mixture, stirring to mix well. Chill. Place a scoop of ice cream in each chilled glass and fill with chilled mocha drink. You may also serve hot omitting the ice cream. *Serves 6.*

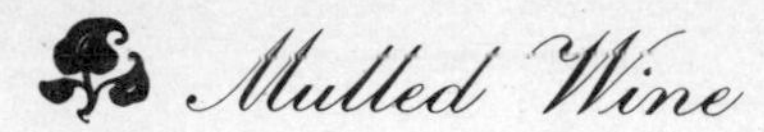

Mulled Wine

1 cup sugar
1 cup water
2 3-inch pieces Cinnamon
12 whole Allspice
12 whole Cloves
Dash Nutmeg
1 lemon
3 cups red wine

Combine sugar, water and spices in saucepan. Peel lemon and drop whole peel into sugar mixture. Stir to dissolve sugar. Simmer 5 minutes. Remove from heat and let stand 30 minutes. Strain. Add wine and heat slowly to just under boiling point. Serve hot. *Makes about 6 servings.*

French Hot Chocolate

4 1-ounce squares unsweetened chocolate
¼ cup water
1 quart milk
½ cup cream
½ cup sugar
¼ teaspoon salt
¼ teaspoon Mace
⅛ teaspoon Allspice
1 teaspoon pure Vanilla Extract
½ teaspoon Almond Extract
⅛ teaspoon Nutmeg
½ cup heavy cream, whipped

Place chocolate and water in saucepan; stir over low heat until melted and smooth. Slowly stir in milk, then add cream, sugar, salt, mace and allspice. Cook over medium heat, stirring occasionally, until milk is hot; stir in vanilla and almond extract. Carefully blend nutmeg into whipped cream. Top each cup of hot chocolate with a spoonful of the whipped cream.

Makes 6 servings.

VARIATION:

French Mint Chocolate—To the above recipe, add ½ teaspoon Mint or Mint and Peppermint Extract in place of almond extract.

Banana Frost

3 large ripe bananas
1 tablespoon lemon juice
1 tablespoon sugar
¼ teaspoon Cinnamon
⅛ teaspoon Cloves
⅛ teaspoon Mace
1 cup milk
1 cup soft vanilla ice cream

Peel and thoroughly mash bananas with fork. Sprinkle with lemon juice, then combine with remaining ingredients. Beat until smooth using rotary beater, electric mixer or blender. Pour into frosted glasses.

Makes 3 servings.

Lime-Mint Cooler

A teen-age favorite, cool and refreshing.

2 10-ounce bottles quinine water
½ cup lime juice
¼ teaspoon Mint Extract or Mint and Peppermint Extract
3 tablespoons sugar
Green Food Color
Ice cubes
Lime sherbet

Chill quinine water. Combine lime juice, extract and sugar, stirring to dissolve sugar. Tint to a delicate green with food color. Add quinine water and ice cubes. Mix well. Pour into tall glasses. Top each with a scoop of lime sherbet. Garnish with red maraschino cherry, sprig of mint or thin slice of lime. *Serves 4.*

Iced Viennese Coffee

A gay, delightful summer drink.

3 cups boiling water
2 tablespoons instant coffee
2 3-inch pieces Cinnamon
3 whole Cloves
5 whole Allspice
Whipped cream

Pour boiling water over coffee, cinnamon, cloves and allspice. Let stand one hour. Strain and pour over ice in tall glasses. Sweeten if desired. Top with whipped cream. *Serves 4.*

Ginger Peach Freeze

2 12-ounce packages frozen sliced peaches
1 pint vanilla ice cream
½ teaspoon Ginger
¼ teaspoon Allspice
¼ teaspoon Cinnamon
1 teaspoon Lemon Peel

Thaw peaches. Have ice cream soft enough to spoon easily. Mash peaches with a fork. Add spices and mix well. Add ice cream. Beat with rotary beater or an electric mixer until smooth. You will find this ideal to make in a blender. Serve in chilled glasses. *Makes 4 servings.*

1 cup cold milk
1 teaspoon pure Vanilla Extract
1 pint vanilla ice cream
¼ teaspoon Cinnamon
Dash Nutmeg

Mix all ingredients except nutmeg in a blender or beat with a mixer or rotary beater until light and fluffy. Pour into chilled glasses and top each with dash nutmeg. *Makes 2 milk shakes.*

L.C. Zippy Tomato Juice

2 cups tomato juice
¼ teaspoon Onion Powder
½ teaspoon Celery Salt
⅛ teaspoon dry Mustard
1 teaspoon lemon juice

Combine all ingredients and mix well. Chill at least two hours before serving to allow flavors to blend. Serve over ice cubes in glasses for a refreshing summer beverage. Wonderful pick-me-up at breakfast too.

Makes about 2 cups.

Traditional Wassail Bowl

Merrie Olde England's Christmas cup of cheer.

3 apples
1 cup water
1 cup sugar
½ teaspoon Nutmeg
1 piece whole Ginger, broken
1 3-inch piece Cinnamon
3 whole Cloves
3 whole Allspice
4 Coriander Seeds
2 whole Cardamom
½ teaspoon Mace
Rind of 1 lemon
⅘ quart sherry
3 12-ounce cans ale
3 eggs, separated

Wash apples; place in baking dish. Roast in 350°F. oven 45 minutes. Combine water, sugar, nutmeg, ginger, cinnamon, cloves, allspice, coriander seed, cardamom, mace and lemon rind. Bring to a boil; reduce heat and simmer 10 minutes. Pour sherry and ale into spice mixture. Heat to just under boiling point but do not boil. Strain. Beat egg whites until stiff. Beat yolks until thick; stir beaten whites into yolks. Slowly add spice mixture to eggs, beating constantly. Pour into silver or heatproof punch bowl. Float roasted apples on top. Serve hot. *Makes about 2 quarts.*

Holiday Cranberry Punch

¼ teaspoon ground Cinnamon
¼ teaspoon ground Nutmeg
¼ teaspoon ground Allspice
4 pints cranberry juice cocktail
1 6-ounce can frozen orange juice, reconstituted
6 12-ounce bottles ginger ale

Combine all ingredients except ginger ale. Mix well and bring to a boil. Strain through cheesecloth if desired. Chill. Add chilled ginger ale just before serving. *Makes about 5 quarts, or 42 4-ounce servings.*

Hot 'n' Spicy Punch

2 6-ounce cans frozen grape juice concentrate
1 6-ounce can frozen orange juice concentrate
7½ cups water
½ cup sugar
4 3-inch pieces Cinnamon
1 teaspoon whole Cloves
Juice of 2 lemons

Combine all ingredients except lemon juice; stir to dissolve sugar. Boil 5 minutes. Remove from heat; strain to remove spices and add lemon juice. Serve hot in punch cups or chill and serve over ice cubes.

Makes about 2 quarts.

SAUCES

Gourmet and Exotic Sauces

Beurre Noir 362

Caper Sauce 373

  Truffle Sauce 373

Hollandaise Sauce 371

Hot Exotic Curry Sauce 362

Parsley-Almond Sauce 372

Sauce Béarnaise 374

Sour Cream Mustard Sauce 360

Spiced Raisin Sauce 374

Sweet-Sour Mustard Sauce 372

Teriyaki Sauce 371

Tropical Barbecue Sauce 373

Flavored Butters

Curry Butter 374

Garlic Butter 367

Herb Butter 369

Honey Spice Butter 365

  Orange Butter 365

Onion Butter 365

Paprika Butter 366

Tangy Butter 365

Whipped Lemon Butter 369

Whipped Maple-Cinnamon Butter 369

Classic and Barbecue Sauces

Brown Sauce 366

  Herbed Giblet Sauce 366

  Onion Sauce 366

Creamy Curry Sauce 369

Classic and Barbecue Sauces (Cont.)

Creamy Lemon-Butter Sauce 370

Creamy Mustard Sauce 365

Dill Sauce 370

Hot Chinese Mustard 368

Mushroom Sauce 367

Quick 'n' Easy Barbecue Sauce 360

Red Cocktail Sauce 367

Sauce Piquant 368

Sauce Rémoulade 368

Sour Cream Topping 368

Spaghetti Sauce 364

  Pizza Sauce 364

Spicy Barbecue Sauce 372

Tartar Sauce 371

Tasty Cream Sauce 363

Tomato Sauce 361

White Sauce Supreme 360

Dessert and Pudding Sauces

Coconut Mace Sauce 361

Creamy Chocolate Sauce 363

Crème Anglaise 375

Holiday Nutmeg Sauce 361

Hot Chocolate Sauce 359

Mint Sauce for Desserts 364

Nutmeg Sauce 363

Pudding Sauce 363

Raspberry Sauce 370

Spiced Hard Sauce 375

Hot Chocolate Sauce

1 12-ounce package semisweet chocolate pieces
½ cup light corn syrup
¼ cup strong black coffee
1 teaspoon pure Vanilla Extract
⅛ teaspoon Rum, Brandy, Almond or Coconut Extract

Melt chocolate in top of double boiler over hot water. Stir in remaining ingredients. Serve hot over ice cream, or store in covered jar and reheat before serving. *Makes 1¾ cups.*

White Sauce Supreme

THIN SAUCE:

1 tablespoon butter
1 tablespoon flour
1 teaspoon Chicken Flavor Base
¼ teaspoon dry Mustard
⅛ teaspoon White Pepper
1 cup milk or cream

MEDIUM SAUCE:

In above recipe increase both butter and flour to 1½ to 2 tablespoons.

THICK SAUCE:

In above recipe increase both butter and flour to 3 to 4 tablespoons.

Melt butter in saucepan over low heat. Stir in flour, flavor base, dry mustard and pepper. Let mixture bubble 1 minute. Remove from heat. Stir in milk or cream, mixing well. Cook over medium heat, stirring constantly, until sauce thickens. *Makes 1 cup.*

Use thin sauce for creamed vegetables, creamed dried beef or as a base for thin creamed soups.

Use medium sauce for gravies, sauces for fish or egg dishes or creamed and scalloped dishes.

Use thick sauce for base for soufflés, croquettes and deviled crab.

Sour Cream Mustard Sauce

1 cup dairy sour cream
1 teaspoon dry Mustard
⅛ teaspoon White Pepper
½ teaspoon Onion Salt
¼ teaspoon salt
¼ teaspoon Turmeric

Combine all ingredients. Heat in top of double boiler or over very low heat, stirring several times. Serve on fish, corned beef, boiled beef, frankfurters, hamburgers or luncheon meats. This sauce is easy to make; use it as a dunk for meat balls, cocktail franks, shrimp, fried scallops or oysters.

Makes 1 cup.

Quick 'n' Easy Barbecue Sauce

1 cup ketchup
½ cup wine vinegar
1 teaspoon Worcestershire sauce
½ teaspoon Season-All
1 teaspoon Instant Minced Onion
¼ teaspoon Barbecue Spice
⅛ teaspoon Garlic Salt
⅛ teaspoon Black Pepper

Combine all ingredients and mix well. Use to baste grilled or broiled chicken, frankfurters, hamburgers as well as many other meats.

Makes 1½ cups.

Tomato Sauce

An excellent tangy sauce!

2 cups tomatoes
1 8-ounce can tomato sauce
1 tablespoon Instant Minced Onion
1 teaspoon Bell Pepper Flakes
⅛ teaspoon Black Pepper
¼ teaspoon Garlic Powder
⅛ teaspoon Thyme Leaves
1 teaspoon Parsley Flakes
1 Bay Leaf
Dash MSG
1 teaspoon Season-All or Bon Appétit
2 whole Cloves
2 tablespoons butter
1 teaspoon sugar

Cut tomatoes into small pieces. Combine all ingredients, mixing well. Bring to a boil and simmer 20 minutes. Serve on meat loaf, hamburgers, fish, frankfurters, boiled beef, veal or omelets. *Makes 3 cups.*

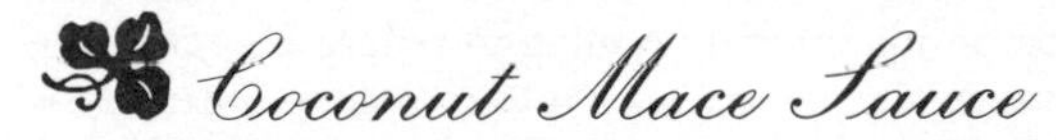

⅓ cup butter or margarine
1 cup shredded coconut
½ cup light brown sugar, packed
2 tablespoons corn syrup
¼ teaspoon Mace
Dash salt
¾ cup evaporated milk
½ teaspoon pure Vanilla Extract

Melt butter; add coconut and sauté until golden brown. Lift out coconut and set aside. To the butter in pan, add sugar, corn syrup, mace and salt. Cook over low heat, stirring constantly, until mixture boils vigorously. Stir in milk; simmer 1½ minutes. Remove from heat, then add vanilla and coconut. Serve warm or cold on ice cream, cakes, puddings or custards. *Makes about 1½ cups.*

Holiday Nutmeg Sauce

1 egg yolk
½ cup sugar
1 cup milk
1 teaspoon Nutmeg
1 teaspoon Arrowroot, optional

Beat together egg yolk, sugar and milk. Heat to the boiling point, stirring constantly. Remove from heat and add nutmeg. (Should you want a thicker sauce, make a thin, smooth paste by mixing together arrowroot with an equal amount of water. Stir into sauce and cook, stirring, until thickened.) Serve over apple pie, apple dumplings, steamed puddings, gingerbread or mincemeat pie. *Makes 1⅓ cups.*

Beurre Noir

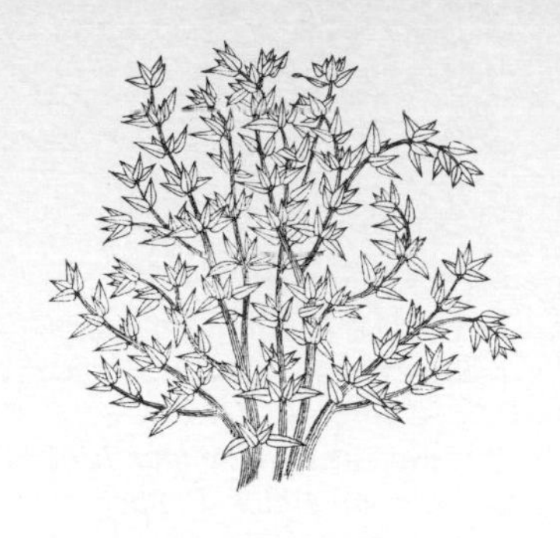

The classic French brown butter sauce.

¾ cup butter (1½ sticks)
1 teaspoon Parsley Flakes
⅛ teaspoon White Pepper
4 tablespoons fresh lemon juice
1 tablespoon dry white wine, optional

Melt butter in a heavy saucepan over medium to low heat. Skim off the foam and pour the clear yellow liquid into a small bowl. Be sure it is free of the milky residue at the bottom of the pan. (Strain if any particles of the milk solids should mix with the clear butter.) Wash and dry saucepan; return the clarified butter to it. Set over low to medium heat until butter turns deep golden brown; pour into a small heated bowl or saucepot. Stir in parsley flakes and pepper. Boil lemon juice to reduce to 1 tablespoon. (If wine is used, add to lemon juice before boiling to reduce volume.) Stir into butter. Keep butter sauce warm over hot, but not boiling, water until ready to serve. Serve over vegetables, fish, sautéed sweetbreads, shirred eggs, veal or chicken. *Makes about ½ cup.*

Hot Exotic Curry Sauce

This sauce is well worth your time and effort to prepare.

¼ cup Instant Minced Onion
⅛ teaspoon Garlic Powder
2 Bay Leaves
⅛ teaspoon ground Thyme or Thyme Leaves
¼ cup Celery Flakes
3 tablespoons Indian or Madras Curry Powder
1½ teaspoons Season-All
2 tablespoons butter
2 carrots, cut into slices
¼ cup grated coconut
1 tart apple, chopped
3 tablespoons chutney
2 tablespoons tomato paste or 1 fresh tomato, chopped
4 teaspoons Chicken Flavor Base
4 cups water
2 tablespoons Arrowroot

Combine all ingredients except arrowroot. Stir to mix well. Bring to a boil; reduce heat and simmer 2 hours. Strain through a sieve, pressing as much of the fruit and vegetables through as possible. Make a thin, smooth paste of arrowroot and an equal amount of water. Stir into sauce; cook over medium heat, stirring, until thickened. Serve over chicken, lamb, beef or rice; or add meats, chicken, shrimp, eggs or any leftover meat to sauce and serve over rice. *Makes about 3½ cups sauce.*

Creamy Chocolate Sauce

4 1-ounce squares unsweetened chocolate
2 cups sugar
1 tall can (14½ ounce) evaporated milk
1 teaspoon pure Vanilla Extract
Dash Mace

Melt chocolate over low heat, stirring. Add remaining ingredients; mix well. Cook over low heat, stirring constantly, until smooth and thickened. Serve warm over ice cream or cake. *Makes 2½ cups.*

Pudding Sauce

¼ cup butter or margarine
1 cup sugar
½ cup cream or evaporated milk
1½ teaspoons pure Vanilla Extract or Rum Extract
Dash Nutmeg

Combine butter, sugar and cream in saucepan. Cook over low heat, stirring occasionally, 10 minutes or until slightly thickened. Do not allow sauce to boil. Stir in extract and nutmeg. Serve hot or cold over ice cream, bread pudding, gingerbread, rice pudding, vanilla pudding, mincemeat pie or squares of warm cake. *Makes 1½ cups.*

Nutmeg Sauce

1 cup sugar
1 tablespoon Arrowroot
¼ teaspoon salt
1 cup boiling water
1 teaspoon butter
1 teaspoon Nutmeg

Mix sugar, arrowroot and salt; slowly add boiling water, stirring constantly. Add butter and cook 5 minutes. Remove from heat; add nutmeg. Serve hot on apple, date or other fruit puddings. *Makes 1⅓ cups.*

Tasty Cream Sauce

3 tablespoons butter
2 tablespoons flour
1½ teaspoons Instant Minced Onion
½ teaspoon Season-All
1 teaspoon Chicken Flavor Base
⅛ teaspoon White Pepper
1 cup milk or light cream

Melt butter. Add flour, onion, Season-All, flavor base and pepper. Stir until smooth and cook until bubbly but do not brown. Add milk, stirring constantly; cook until thickened. Serve over vegetables and top with toasted slivered almonds, or use as base for creamed dried beef, chicken, tuna or other creamed dishes. *Makes 1 cup.*

Spaghetti Sauce

3½ cups plum tomatoes (28-oz. can)
1 6-ounce can tomato paste
3 cups water
2 tablespoons Instant Minced Onion
½ teaspoon Garlic Powder
½ teaspoon Oregano Leaves
1 teaspoon Bon Appétit
1 Bay Leaf
1½ teaspoons salt
¼ teaspoon Black Pepper
1 teaspoon sugar
¼ teaspoon MSG
¼ teaspoon Crushed Red Pepper
2 tablespoons olive oil or salad oil
1 tablespoon Arrowroot, optional

Force tomatoes through a coarse sieve to purée and remove seed. Combine the tomato purée and remaining ingredients, except arrowroot, in glass or stainless steel saucepan. Bring to boil; reduce heat and simmer, uncovered, 1 hour. Remove bay leaf. For a thicker sauce, simmer 20 minutes longer; or thicken by making a thin, smooth paste of the arrowroot and an equal amount of water. Stir into sauce and cook, continuing to stir, until thickened. Serve over cooked spaghetti topped with grated Parmesan cheese. Meat balls, sautéed chicken livers, clams or calamari (very small whole squid) may be added to the sauce or served on the side.

Makes 5 cups sauce or enough for 1 pound spaghetti.

VARIATION:

Pizza Sauce—Make sauce following above recipe but simmer 1 hour and 30 minutes or until sauce is quite thick. Spread over pizza dough; top with grated Parmesan cheese, slices of Mozzarella cheese and any of the following: anchovies, sliced mushrooms, thin slices pepperoni or salami, or sliced olives. You may also sprinkle with Oregano Leaves. Bake; serve hot. *Makes enough for two 12-inch pizzas.*

Mint Sauce for Desserts

1 cup sugar
2 tablespoons Arrowroot
⅛ teaspoon salt
2 cups boiling water
¼ teaspoon Mint Extract or Mint and Peppermint Extract
2 drops Green Food Color

Combine sugar, arrowroot and salt in a saucepan. Gradually add boiling water, stirring constantly. Continue stirring and simmer over low heat 5 minutes or until clear and thickened. Remove from heat; mix in extract and food color. Serve hot. If a thicker sauce is desired, increase the arrowroot to 3 tablespoons. Delicious and colorful to serve over ice cream, vanilla pudding, plain cake, pound cake, angel food cake, chocolate brownies or chilled fruits. *Makes 2 cups.*

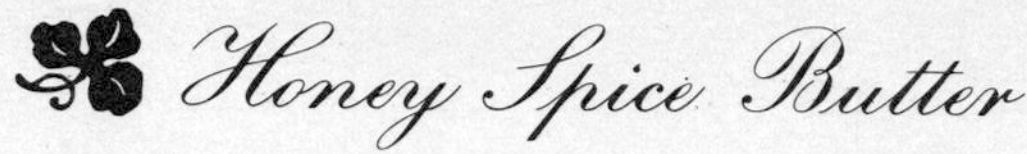

½ cup butter (1 stick)
2 teaspoons honey
½ teaspoon Cinnamon
⅛ teaspoon Nutmeg

Let butter soften at room temperature. Add remaining ingredients, mixing well. This makes an excellent spread for date nut bread, graham crackers, muffins, biscuits, banana bread, waffles, toast or pancakes. *Makes ½ cup.*

VARIATION:
Orange Butter—Add 2 teaspoons Orange Peel and dash Cloves in place of cinnamon and nutmeg in above recipe.

3 tablespoons butter or margarine
2 tablespoons flour
1 teaspoon dry Mustard
½ teaspoon salt
Dash White Pepper
1 egg yolk
1 cup milk
1 tablespoon lemon juice

Melt butter; stir in flour, dry mustard, salt and pepper. Mix well and cook until bubbly, about 1 minute. Remove from heat. Beat egg yolk; add milk and mix well. Stir into butter-flour mixture. Cook, stirring constantly, 3 minutes or until smooth and thickened. Remove from heat. Just before serving stir in lemon juice, mixing well. Serve hot over cauliflower, green beans or broccoli; or with fish, ham or boiled beef.

Makes about 1¼ cups sauce.

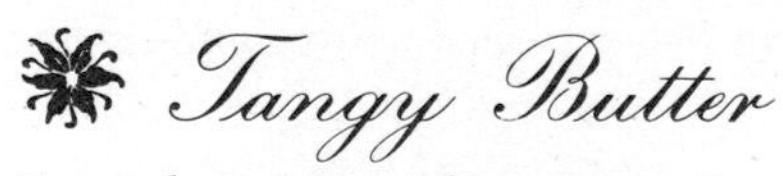

½ cup butter (1 stick)
1 teaspoon Herb Seasoning
3 dashes ground Red Pepper

Let butter soften at room temperature. Mix in remaining ingredients. You may like this hotter and more pungent; if so, increase the amount of red pepper. Serve on hamburgers, meat loaf, grilled meats, broiled or fried fish, baked or mashed potatoes, green beans or hot bread. *Makes ½ cup.*

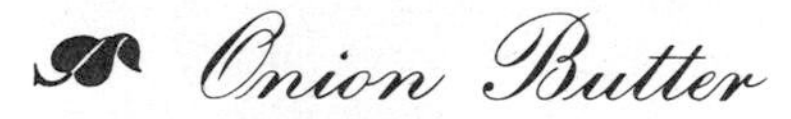

⅓ cup melted butter
1 teaspoon Instant Minced Onion
1 teaspoon lemon juice
⅛ teaspoon Herb Seasoning
Dash ground Red Pepper

Combine all ingredients and mix well. Excellent served over peas, green beans, boiled potatoes, carrots, chops, steaks, liver, sweetbreads, or baked or broiled fish. *Makes about ⅓ cup.*

Brown Sauce

A rich basic brown sauce, having many uses.

3 tablespoons butter
2 tablespoons flour
1 teaspoon Beef Flavor Base
⅛ teaspoon Onion Powder
⅛ teaspoon Black Pepper
⅛ teaspoon MSG
Dash Nutmeg
1 cup water

Heat butter in small heavy saucepan or skillet until browned. Stir in flour and blend well. Cook over low heat, stirring constantly, until flour is deep brown. Remove from heat; add beef flavor base, onion powder, pepper, MSG and nutmeg; mix well. Gradually stir in water. Return to heat and bring to a boil, stirring constantly. Boil 1 minute. Serve this sauce or its variations over rice, meat loaf, leftover meats, omelets, chops, steaks, tongue or hamburgers; or use as a base for many casserole dishes.

Makes about 1 cup.

VARIATIONS:

Onion Sauce—Sauté 1 to 2 tablespoons Chopped Instant Onions in 1 tablespoon butter until golden brown, watching carefully to prevent burning. Add to above recipe and let stand 10 to 15 minutes before serving to allow onions to soften.

Herbed Giblet Sauce—Stir ¼ teaspoon Poultry Seasoning and ¼ cup chopped cooked giblets into Brown Sauce (recipe above) and simmer 3 minutes longer.

Paprika Butter

½ cup soft butter (1 stick)
1 teaspoon Paprika
1 teaspoon lemon juice
¼ teaspoon salt
Dash Black Pepper or White Pepper

Combine all ingredients, mixing well with a fork. Let stand 30 minutes for flavors to blend. Spread over chicken, lobster, shrimp or fish before broiling. You will also find this excellent with steaks and chops. This is a must in seasoning vegetables such as cauliflower, onions or potatoes.

Makes ½ cup.

Mushroom Sauce

2 tablespoons butter
3 tablespoons flour
1 teaspoon Beef Flavor Base
⅛ teaspoon Black Pepper
Dash MSG
1 4-ounce can mushrooms
1 teaspoon Parsley Flakes
1 tablespoon Madeira

Melt butter; stir in flour. Cook, stirring constantly, until mixture is golden brown. Remove from heat; add beef flavor base, pepper and MSG, stirring well. Drain mushrooms and set aside; save liquid. Add enough water to liquid to make 1 cup. Stir into flour mixture and cook, stirring, over low heat until thickened. Add mushrooms and parsley flakes; cook until mushrooms are heated through. Just before serving, stir in Madeira. Serve over roast beef, filet mignon, sirloin steak, ham, chicken livers or omelets. *Makes about 1½ cups.*

Red Cocktail Sauce

1 cup ketchup
1 cup chili sauce
1½ teaspoons prepared horseradish
½ teaspoon Bon Appétit
¼ teaspoon MSG
2 tablespoons lemon juice
¼ cup finely minced celery
1 teaspoon capers, optional

Combine all ingredients, mixing well. Sauce improves in flavor if allowed to stand an hour or longer before using. Keeps well in refrigerator. Serve with shrimp, crab, oysters or any sea food. *Makes about 2 cups.*

Garlic Butter

½ cup soft butter (1 stick)
¼ teaspoon Garlic Powder
¼ teaspoon salt
Dash Black Pepper

Combine all ingredients, mixing well with a fork. Cover. Let stand 30 minutes for flavors to blend. Chill slightly if desired. Use to season green beans, stewed tomatoes, frogs' legs, steak, hamburgers, broiled fish, sautéed shrimp or lamb; or use as a spread for canapés. *Makes ½ cup.*

Sour Cream Topping

1 cup dairy sour cream
1½ teaspoons Bon Appétit
⅛ teaspoon Onion Powder
1 teaspoon Chives

Mix together all ingredients; allow to stand at least 1 hour for flavors to blend. Serve over baked potatoes, broccoli, green beans or boiled onions; or toss with water cress or cucumbers. *Makes 1 cup.*

Sauce Rémoulade

2 cups mayonnaise
6 tablespoons tomato paste
1 tablespoon prepared mustard
¼ teaspoon Celery Salt
⅛ teaspoon ground Red Pepper
4 anchovy fillets, washed and mashed
1 teaspoon Parsley Flakes
¼ teaspoon Tarragon Leaves
3 teaspoons Instant Minced Onion
1 tablespoon chopped capers
2 tablespoons minced sour pickles

Combine all ingredients; mix well. Let stand several hours to allow flavors to blend. Serve with cold shrimp, crab or lobster. You will find this makes an excellent topping for head lettuce, tossed salad or sliced avocado. Keeps well in refrigerator. *Makes 3 cups.*

Hot Chinese Mustard

¼ cup dry Mustard
2 tablespoons cold water

Put dry mustard in cup or small bowl. Gradually add cold water, stirring until thoroughly mixed. Make only the amount needed at a time, for it dries on standing. Serve with appetizers such as egg roll, sliced pork, shrimp or cubes of cheese and ham. Flat beer may be used in place of water. You will find this quite hot so use cautiously. *Makes about ¼ cup.*

Sauce Piquant

1 8-ounce package cream cheese
½ teaspoon salt
⅛ teaspoon White Pepper
¼ teaspoon dry Mustard
⅛ teaspoon ground Red Pepper
2 eggs
2 tablespoons lemon juice
½ cup dairy sour cream

Have cream cheese at room temperature. Add salt, pepper, dry mustard and red pepper. Cream thoroughly. Beat in eggs, one at a time, then add lemon juice and sour cream. Mix well. Set over simmering, but not boiling, water until heated thoroughly; stir often. Serve over asparagus, green beans, broccoli or poached or broiled fish; or serve with artichokes.

Makes 2 cups.

Whipped Maple-Cinnamon Butter

½ cup sweet butter, softened
1 teaspoon Maple Extract
1 teaspoon Cinnamon
2 tablespoons powdered sugar

Whip butter until very light and fluffy. Add remaining ingredients and continue whipping until thoroughly mixed. Serve on pancakes, coffee cake, French toast, waffles or breads. *Makes ½ cup.*

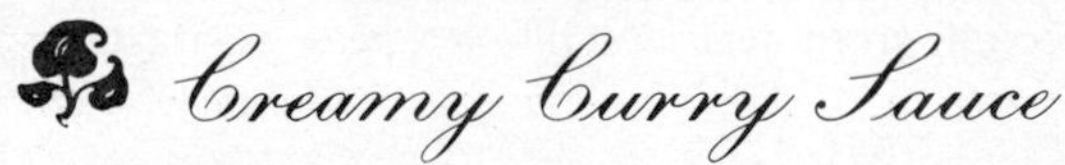

2 tablespoons butter or margarine
2 teaspoons Curry Powder
2 tablespoons all-purpose flour
¼ teaspoon salt
¼ teaspoon White Pepper
1¼ cups milk

Melt butter; stir in curry powder. (Curry powder may be decreased or increased according to individual taste.) Cook over low heat, stirring, 2 to 3 minutes. Add flour, salt and pepper, mixing until well blended and smooth. Cook until bubbly, stirring constantly. Remove from heat; stir in milk. Cook, continuing to stir, until thickened. To this sauce you will want to add cooked shrimp, chicken, lamb cubes or chopped hard-cooked eggs. Serve hot over rice. Curry is usually served with several condiments such as: slivered almonds, minced onion, chopped hard-cooked eggs, raisins, sliced Crystallized Ginger, chutney, mashed banana, grated coconut or crumbled crisp bacon. *Serves 4 to 6.*

½ cup butter
¼ teaspoon Tarragon Leaves
1 teaspoon Parsley Flakes
½ teaspoon Savory
⅛ teaspoon Thyme
Dash Black Pepper

Let butter soften at room temperature. Add remaining ingredients, mixing well. Use to season vegetables, fish or meats; or use as a spread for hot breads or sandwiches. *Makes ½ cup.*

Whipped Lemon Butter

½ cup soft butter (1 stick)
1 teaspoon dry Mustard
4 teaspoons lemon juice
Dash Paprika

Whip all ingredients with rotary beater or electric mixer until smooth. Use with vegetables, fish, meats or breads. *Makes ½ cup.*

Dill Sauce

2 tablespoons butter
1 tablespoon Arrowroot
1 teaspoon Bon Appétit
¼ teaspoon MSG
⅛ teaspoon White Pepper
1 teaspoon Chicken Flavor Base
½ cup water
1 cup dairy sour cream
1 tablespoon Dill Weed

Melt butter; blend in arrowroot, Bon Appétit, MSG, pepper, flavor base and water. Cook over low heat, stirring, until mixture thickens. Remove from heat. Stir in sour cream and dill weed. Heat but do not allow to boil. Serve over boiled potatoes, broccoli, green beans, cauliflower, peas, asparagus or carrots. *Makes 1½ cups.*

Raspberry Sauce

2 10-ounce packages frozen raspberries
3 tablespoons Arrowroot
½ cup sugar
¼ teaspoon salt
⅛ teaspoon Allspice
¼ teaspoon Mace
2 tablespoons butter

Thaw raspberries just enough to drain syrup. Measure syrup and add water to make 1½ cups. Mix arrowroot, sugar, salt, allspice and mace; stir into liquid. Cook, stirring, over medium heat until sauce thickens. Add drained raspberries and butter. (If you prefer a smoother sauce, press berries through fine sieve to remove seed and purée the fruit.) Simmer 3 minutes longer. Cool. Excellent topping for vanilla pudding, ice cream, ice cream pies, cheesecake or butter, angel food, pound or chiffon cake. *Makes 2½ cups.*

Creamy Lemon-Butter Sauce

¾ cup soft butter
¼ teaspoon salt
Dash ground Red Pepper
½ teaspoon Lemon Peel
1½ tablespoons lemon juice
3 egg yolks

Put butter in top of double boiler; before placing over hot water beat with rotary beater until creamy. Add salt, red pepper and lemon peel, mixing well. Gradually add lemon juice, beating constantly. Add egg yolks, one at a time, beating after addition of each. Continue beating until mixture is light and fluffy, then place sauce over hot water for a few minutes, beating constantly until glossy. Serve immediately. This is an excellent sauce over broccoli, asparagus, green beans, cauliflower or broiled or poached fish. *Makes 1⅓ cups.*

Tartar Sauce

¾ cup mayonnaise
3 tablespoons minced pickle
2 teaspoons Instant Minced Onion
1 tablespoon lemon juice
¼ teaspoon dry Mustard
¼ teaspoon Celery Salt
1 teaspoon capers, minced

Combine all ingredients and mix well. Refrigerate 1 hour, allowing flavors to blend. Serve with baked, broiled or fried fish and sea food or salmon or tuna croquettes. *Makes 1 cup.*

Hollandaise Sauce

1 cup butter
4 egg yolks
2 tablespoons lemon juice
¼ teaspoon salt
⅛ teaspoon ground Red Pepper
⅛ teaspoon White Pepper
¼ teaspoon dry Mustard

Divide butter into three equal parts. Put ⅓ of the butter, egg yolks and lemon juice in top of double boiler. (Never allow water in bottom of boiler to boil or to touch the bottom of top boiler.) Cook over hot water, stirring constantly, until butter melts. Add ⅓ of the butter; continue to stir until butter melts. Remove from heat and stir in remaining butter and seasonings. If sauce is not thick enough, continue cooking over hot water, stirring constantly. Should it start to separate, add 1 or 2 teaspoons boiling water; beat briskly until smooth. Serve warm over asparagus, broccoli or poached fish; or use in making Eggs Benedict. *Makes 1½ cups.*

Teriyaki Sauce

1 cup soy sauce
¼ cup brown sugar, packed
¼ teaspoon Garlic Powder
¼ teaspoon Onion Powder
2 tablespoons lemon juice
1 teaspoon ground Ginger or 10 to 12 pieces whole Ginger about size of shelled peanut

Combine all ingredients in jar. Shake to mix well and to dissolve sugar. For a marinade, let stand in sealed jar overnight. Pour over beef cubes, steak, pork chops or disjointed chicken and let marinate 2 hours or longer. Broil, brushing meat with marinade 2 or 3 times while cooking. For a sauce to be used in a side dish, simmer 10 minutes. Use for dunking shrimp, meat balls, bite-size pieces of meat or chicken, broiled pineapple cubes or French fried sweet potatoes; or serve over rice. Refrigerate extra sauce in a tightly sealed jar for future use. *Makes about 1 cup.*

Sweet-Sour Mustard Sauce

1 cup brown sugar, packed
¼ cup dry Mustard
2 teaspoons Arrowroot
¼ teaspoon salt
1 teaspoon Beef Flavor Base
½ cup hot water
½ cup vinegar
2 eggs, beaten

Mix together sugar, dry mustard, arrowroot and salt. Dissolve beef flavor base in hot water; add to sugar mixture. Stir in vinegar. Add beaten eggs, mixing well. Cook over low heat, stirring constantly, until it thickens. Cool. Serve in a sauce bowl. Excellent with ham, cold meats and fried shrimp.

Makes 2 cups.

Parsley-Almond Sauce

¼ cup butter or margarine
¼ cup slivered almonds
1 teaspoon Parsley Flakes
½ teaspoon Season-All
¼ teaspoon Black Pepper
3 tablespoons lemon juice

Melt butter. Add almonds and brown lightly, then add remaining ingredients. Serve hot over fish fillets, cauliflower, green beans or carrots.

Makes about ½ cup.

Spicy Barbecue Sauce

Do not let the long list of spices frighten you. You will probably have most of them on your shelf.

3 6-ounce cans tomato paste
3 cans water (2¼ cups)
¼ cup vinegar
3 tablespoons Worcestershire sauce
3 tablespoons butter
2 tablespoons Onion Flakes
2 tablespoons Celery Flakes
1 teaspoon Black Pepper
½ teaspoon Allspice
½ teaspoon Cinnamon
½ teaspoon Chili Powder
1 teaspoon Paprika
1 teaspoon dry Mustard
½ teaspoon Nutmeg
2 teaspoons Season-All
2 teaspoons Barbecue Spice
½ teaspoon Garlic Salt
Dash MSG
¼ teaspoon ground Red Pepper

Combine all ingredients in saucepan and mix well; cover. Slowly bring to a boil; reduce heat and simmer 1 hour or longer if time permits. Use to baste spareribs, pork chops, bologna roll or chicken.

Makes about 5 cups.

NOTE: This sauce will be one of your favorites and you will find it keeps weeks in the refrigerator and may also be frozen.

Caper Sauce

4 tablespoons butter
4 tablespoons flour
½ teaspoon Onion Powder
⅛ teaspoon MSG
3 teaspoons Chicken Flavor Base
⅛ teaspoon White Pepper
Dash Nutmeg
⅛ teaspoon Turmeric
1 teaspoon Parsley Flakes
4 whole Allspice
2 Bay Leaves
2 whole Cloves
Dash ground Red Pepper
1 cup water
1½ cups milk
½ cup heavy cream
2 tablespoons capers, chopped

Melt butter; stir in flour and cook over low heat, stirring, 2 minutes. Do not let it brown. Add seasonings; mix well, then stir in water and milk. Cook, stirring constantly, until sauce thickens. Reduce heat and simmer, uncovered, 20 minutes. Add cream and cook 5 minutes longer. Strain. Stir in capers. Delicious served hot with fish, broiled chicken, roast lamb, lobster, tongue, cauliflower or asparagus. *Makes 3 cups.*

VARIATION:

Truffle Sauce—Make sauce following recipe above except use ¼ cup thinly sliced truffles in place of capers. Superb on poached eggs and over sliced turkey on rice.

Tropical Barbecue Sauce

1 cup water
1 cup brown sugar, packed
3 tablespoons ketchup
1 tablespoon soy sauce
1 teaspoon dry Mustard
1 cup crushed pineapple
2 tablespoons Bell Pepper Flakes
1 tablespoon Arrowroot
¼ cup cold water

Mix together the 1 cup water and brown sugar. Add ketchup, soy sauce, dry mustard, pineapple and pepper flakes. Bring to a boil; simmer 10 minutes. Dissolve arrowroot in the ¼ cup water; add to sauce and cook, stirring, until sauce thickens. Serve hot with spareribs, pork, lamb, ham, shrimp or chicken; or serve as a dip for meat hors d'oeuvres. This sauce adds excellent flavor to oven roasted or broiled meats.

Makes 2½ cups.

Sauce Béarnaise

A renowned French sauce, superb with beef.

- *¼ cup white wine vinegar*
- *1 teaspoon Instant Minced Onion*
- *1½ teaspoons Tarragon Leaves*
- *1 teaspoon Parsley Flakes*
- *⅛ teaspoon Coarse Grind Black Pepper*
- *¼ teaspoon salt*
- *Dash ground Red Pepper*
- *3 egg yolks*
- *2 tablespoons cold butter*
- *½ cup melted butter*

Combine vinegar, onion, 1 teaspoon of the tarragon leaves, parsley flakes, pepper, salt and red pepper. Boil until mixture is reduced to 2 tablespoons; strain, if desired. Beat egg yolks in top of double boiler until thick. Add vinegar and 1 tablespoon of the cold butter. Cook over hot, not boiling, water until mixture is thickened, stirring constantly. Remove from heat and add the remaining tablespoon of cold butter; stir to blend. Slowly add melted butter, stirring constantly or use low speed on electric mixer. Add the remaining ½ teaspoon tarragon leaves. Serve warm with châteaubriand, filet mignon, sirloin steaks, roast leg of lamb or broiled or poached fish.

Makes about ¾ cup.

A quick way to add exciting new flavor to sandwiches, canapés and entrées.

- *½ cup soft butter (1 stick)*
- *1 teaspoon Indian or Madras Curry Powder*
- *¼ teaspoon salt*
- *Dash Black Pepper*

Combine all ingredients, mixing well with a fork. Let stand 30 minutes to 1 hour for flavors to blend. Use as a base for canapés, as a substitute for regular butter in making sandwiches; or serve on meats, fish, sea food, vegetables, noodles or rice.

Makes ½ cup.

Spiced Raisin Sauce

- *1 pound seedless raisins*
- *Water to cover*
- *½ cup vinegar*
- *¾ cup brown sugar, packed*
- *½ teaspoon Cinnamon*
- *½ teaspoon Ginger*
- *¼ teaspoon Allspice*
- *1 teaspoon Orange Peel*

Soak raisins in water 2 hours. Boil slowly until water is reduced to about one half. Add remaining ingredients and simmer until only a small amount of liquid is left and sauce is syrupy in appearance. Serve with baked ham, roast pork, leg of lamb, pork chops, duckling or tongue.

Makes about 3 cups.

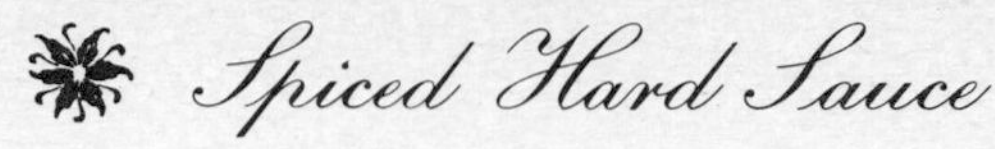

Spiced Hard Sauce

½ cup butter
2 cups powdered sugar
¼ teaspoon Mace
¼ teaspoon ground Cardamom
¾ teaspoon Cinnamon
¼ teaspoon Allspice

Cream butter until light and fluffy. Beat in sugar and spices. Chill. A must for plum pudding! Also good with fruit cobblers, mincemeat pie, bread puddings and other steamed puddings. *Makes about 1⅓ cups.*

Crème Anglaise

A delicate custard sauce.

1½ cups milk
4 egg yolks
Dash Mace
¼ cup sugar
¼ teaspoon salt
1 teaspoon pure Vanilla Extract
Dash Nutmeg

Scald milk in top of double boiler. In a small bowl beat together the egg yolks, mace, sugar and salt. Gradually stir in scalded milk. Return to double boiler. (Do not have the water in the bottom boiler touching the top boiler.) Cook, stirring constantly, until sauce thickens and forms a thin coating on a metal spoon. Remove from heat. Cool quickly. Stir in vanilla and chill thoroughly. Serve in dessert glasses topped with whipped cream; or use as a sauce over gingerbread, Floating Island Meringues (see recipe page 280) or other desserts. Top with dash of nutmeg.

Makes about 1½ cups.

CANNING

Chili Sauce and Vegetable Relishes

Chili Sauce 379

Chow-Chow 379

Corn Relish 380

Dixie Relish 380

Pickle Relish 381

Tomato Relish 381

Pickles

Bread and Butter Pickles 381

Cantaloupe Pickles 382

Crystal Pickles 382

Dill Pickles 383

Dilled Green Beans 383

Kosher Dill Pickles 383

Mixed Pickles 384

Mustard Pickles 384

Spiced Pickled Peaches 385

Sweet Cucumber Pickles 385

Pickles (Cont.)

Thousand Island Pickles 386

Watermelon Pickles 386

Chutneys and Mincemeat

Apple Chutney 387

Mango Chutney 387

Old-Time Mincemeat 388

Peach Chutney 389

Butters, Jellies, Preserves and Marmalade

Apple Butter 389

Basil-Apple Jelly 389

Cinnamon Peach Preserves 390

Mango Marmalade 390

Mint-Apple Jelly 390

Pear-Pineapple Butter 391

Spicy Peach Butter 391

NOTE: Directions for processing in boiling water-bath are on page 52 under Canning.

Chili Sauce

24 large red-ripe tomatoes
8 large onions, chopped
6 green peppers, chopped
2 cups vinegar
1 tablespoon salt
1 teaspoon Cinnamon
1 teaspoon Cloves
1 teaspoon Ginger
1 tablespoon Celery Seed
1 teaspoon Crushed Red Pepper
1 teaspoon dry Mustard
3 cups sugar

Peel, core and chop tomatoes; combine with remaining ingredients. Boil gently, uncovered, 4 hours or until thickened. Stir frequently to prevent sticking. Fill hot, sterilized canning jars, leaving ¼-inch head space. Close jars. Process 15 minutes in boiling water-bath. *Makes about 6½ pints.*

Chow-Chow

3 large heads of cabbage
12 large green peppers
3 bunches celery
18 large onions
12 large green tomatoes
10 large sweet cucumber pickles
5 tablespoons Celery Seed
4 tablespoons Turmeric
2 tablespoons ground Ginger
4 tablespoons Cinnamon
4 tablespoons salt
1 pound Mustard Seed
⅛ teaspoon ground Red Pepper
2 tablespoons Mace
1 tablespoon ground Allspice
2½ quarts vinegar
3 pounds brown sugar

Cover cabbage, peppers and celery with cold water and let stand 30 minutes to crisp. Drain. Chop all vegetables and pickles medium fine and include seeds of 2 of the green peppers. Place mixture in cheesecloth; squeeze out juice from vegetables, then discard juice. Add remaining ingredients to vegetables and bring to a rapid boil. Boil, uncovered, 10 minutes. Fill clean, hot canning jars, leaving ¼-inch head space. Close jars. Process 10 minutes in boiling water-bath. *Makes about 14 quarts.*

Corn Relish

1 cup chopped sweet red pepper
1½ cups chopped cabbage
1 cup chopped celery
1 cup chopped onion
1½ cups white vinegar
1 tablespoon salt
1 tablespoon Celery Seed
2 teaspoons dry Mustard
2 teaspoons Turmeric
1 cup sugar
2 16-ounce cans whole-kernel yellow corn, drained
2 tablespoons flour
¼ cup water

Wash and prepare vegetables; cut into ¼-inch cubes or pieces, then measure. Put in large saucepan and add vinegar and salt. Mix spices with sugar and stir into vegetable mixture. Boil, uncovered, 20 minutes. Add drained corn and cook 5 minutes longer, or until corn is thoroughly heated. Blend flour with water, then stir into relish. Cook 10 minutes or until slightly thickened. Fill clean, hot canning jars, leaving ½-inch head space. Close jars. Process 15 minutes in boiling water-bath. *Makes 3 pints.*

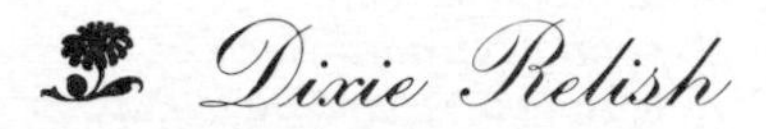

Dixie Relish

1 quart ground cabbage
1 pint ground white onions
1 pint ground sweet red peppers
½ cup salt
4 tablespoons Mustard Seed
3 tablespoons Celery Seed
1 quart cider vinegar
3 cups sugar
1 tablespoon salt
1 3-inch piece Cinnamon
1 tablespoon whole Cloves
1 tablespoon whole Allspice

Mix vegetables with the ½ cup salt and let stand 4 to 5 hours. Put mixture in cheesecloth and squeeze until free of juice. Put vegetables in large saucepan; add remaining ingredients, tying cinnamon, cloves and allspice in a cheesecloth bag for easy removal. Slowly bring to a boil, then simmer, uncovered, 10 minutes. Remove spice bag. Fill clean, hot, canning jars, leaving ½-inch head space. Close jars. Process 10 minutes in boiling water-bath.

Makes 5 pints.

Pickle Relish

24 medium to large cucumbers
10 medium-size onions
3 tablespoons salt
2 cups sugar
3 cups vinegar
1 tablespoon ground Turmeric
1 tablespoon Celery Seed
1 tablespoon Mustard Seed
1 tablespoon ground Ginger

Wash cucumbers and cover with ice water; let stand 3 hours. Drain. Slice cucumbers and onions paper thin and sprinkle with salt. Allow to stand 3 hours. Drain, reserving 1 cup of the juice. Combine this juice with remaining ingredients; add vegetables. Boil gently, uncovered, until vegetables are clear and transparent, about 40 minutes. Fill clean, hot canning jars, leaving ¼-inch head space. Close jars. Process 10 minutes in boiling water-bath.

Makes 5 pints.

Tomato Relish

24 large ripe tomatoes
7 medium-size onions
½ cup salt
1 teaspoon ground Red Pepper
2 teaspoons ground Allspice
2 teaspoons ground Cloves
2 teaspoons ground Ginger
2 teaspoons dry Mustard
1 quart vinegar
1 green pepper, cut fine
2 cups sugar
¼ pound (⅔ cup) Mustard Seed

Peel tomatoes and cut in half. Peel and slice onions. Sprinkle vegetables with salt and let stand overnight. Drain well and add red pepper, allspice, cloves, ginger, dry mustard, vinegar and green pepper. Simmer, uncovered, 2 hours. Add sugar and mustard seed; cook 10 minutes longer or until syrupy. Fill clean, hot canning jars, leaving ¼-inch head space. Close jars. Process 10 minutes in boiling water-bath.

Makes about 7 pints.

Bread and Butter Pickles

40 medium-size cucumbers
1 pound small white onions
1 green pepper
1 sweet red pepper
½ cup rock salt
3 quarts ice water
6 cups sugar
5 cups cider vinegar
2 tablespoons Mustard Seed
2 teaspoons Celery Seed
1 teaspoon ground Turmeric
½ teaspoon ground Cloves

Slice cucumbers and onions ⅛-inch thick. Cut peppers into ¼-inch strips. Dissolve salt in ice water; pour over vegetables and let stand 3 hours. Drain. Pack vegetables in clean, dry, canning jars. Combine remaining ingredients. Bring to a boil and boil, uncovered, 5 minutes. Pour over vegetables, leaving ¼-inch head space. Close jars. Process 15 minutes in boiling water-bath.

Makes 8 to 9 pints.

Cantaloupe Pickles

3 pints cantaloupe, cut into cubes
2 tablespoons coarse salt
Water
3 tablespoons powdered Alum
1 tablespoon ground Ginger
1½ cups white vinegar
3 cups light-brown sugar, packed
2 tablespoons Celery Seed
2 tablespoons Mustard Seed
1 3-inch piece Cinnamon
1 tablespoon whole Cloves

Peel cantaloupe, remove seed and cut into 1-inch cubes; measure. Put in stone crock or glass bowl and let stand 24 hours in a solution of coarse salt and 2 quarts of water. Wash and drain. Let stand 24 hours in a solution of alum and 1 quart of water. Wash and drain. Cover with water and let stand 24 hours. Drain. Add ginger to 1 quart of water and bring to a boil; add cantaloupe and boil, uncovered, 30 minutes. Drain. Make syrup of vinegar, brown sugar and the remaining spices tied in a cheesecloth bag. Add cantaloupe and cook 30 minutes, or until cantaloupe is clear and tender. Pack, hot, into clean, hot canning jars. Remove spice bag and pour the hot syrup into jars, leaving ¼-inch head space. Close jars. Process 10 minutes in boiling water-bath. *Makes 2 pints.*

Crystal Pickles

7 pounds cucumbers or green tomatoes
4 tablespoons slaked lime
2 gallons water
¾ cup powdered Alum
2 gallons water
½ cup ground ginger (1⅛ ounces)
2 gallons water
5 pounds sugar
2 quarts cider vinegar
1 teaspoon ground Cinnamon
1 teaspoon whole Cloves
1 teaspoon whole Allspice
1 teaspoon Celery Seed

Wash cucumbers or tomatoes and slice medium thin, then weigh. Place in stone crock or enamel container. Dissolve slaked lime in first 2 gallons water; pour over cucumbers. With glass plate, weight cucumbers so they are completely covered with brine at all times. Let stand 24 hours. Drain; wash well. Dissolve alum in second 2 gallons of water; pour over cucumbers. Let stand 24 hours. Drain; wash well. Stir ginger into third 2 gallons of water; pour over cucumbers. Let stand 6 hours. Drain and wash well. Make a syrup of sugar, vinegar and spices. Pour over cucumbers and let stand 4 hours. Bring to a boil and boil, uncovered, 5 minutes. Fill clean, hot canning jars with pickles. Add enough syrup to fill jars, leaving ½-inch head space. Close jars. Process in boiling water-bath 15 minutes. *Makes 10 to 12 pints.*

Dill Pickles

4 pounds cucumbers, about 4 inches long
1 cup Dill Seed
21 Peppercorns
3½ teaspoons Mustard Seed
3 cups white vinegar
3 cups water
6 tablespoons salt

Cut cucumbers in half lengthwise. Pack into clean, hot canning jars. To each jar, add about 2 tablespoons dill seed, 3 peppercorns and ½ teaspoon mustard seed. Bring the vinegar, water and salt to a boil. Pour, boiling hot, over cucumbers, leaving ¼-inch head space. Seal. Process 10 minutes in boiling water-bath. *Makes 7 pints.*

Dilled Green Beans

2 pounds green beans (young and tender)
1 teaspoon powdered Alum
1 gallon water
½ teaspoon Instant Minced Garlic
4 teaspoons Dill Seed
2 teaspoons Mustard Seed
1 teaspoon Crushed Red Pepper
2 cups water
2 cups vinegar
¼ cup salt

Wash beans and trim ends; place in stone crock or glass container. Dissolve alum in the 1 gallon of water; pour over beans and let stand 24 hours. Drain and wash. Pack beans, lengthwise, into 4 hot, pint-size canning jars. To each jar, add ⅛ teaspoon of the instant minced garlic, 1 teaspoon dill seed, ½ teaspoon mustard seed and ¼ teaspoon crushed red pepper. Combine remaining ingredients and bring to a boil. Pour over beans, leaving ¼-inch head space. Close jars. Process 25 minutes in boiling water-bath.

Makes 4 pints.

Kosher Dill Pickles

7 pounds medium-size cucumbers
4 tablespoons Dill Seed
¾ teaspoon Instant Minced Garlic
3 teaspoons Crushed Red Pepper
6 thick onion slices
1 quart vinegar
2 quarts water
½ cup salt

Wash cucumbers and pack into 6 clean, hot quart-size canning jars. To each jar, add 2 teaspoons dill seed, ⅛ teaspoon instant minced garlic, ½ teaspoon crushed red pepper and 1 slice of onion. For a stronger garlic flavor, use ¼ teaspoon instant minced garlic in each jar. Combine remaining ingredients and bring to a boil. Pour, boiling hot, over cucumbers, leaving ¼-inch head space. Close jars. Process 10 minutes in boiling water-bath.

Makes 6 quarts.

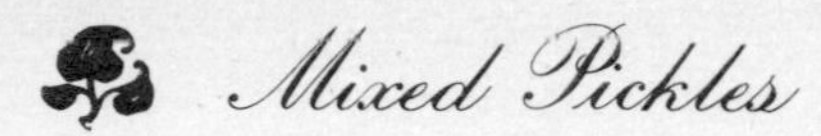

Mixed Pickles

4 cups cucumber pieces
2 cups carrot pieces
1 cauliflower
2 sweet red peppers
2 cups pickling onions
3 4-ounce cans mushroom crowns
1 cup salt
1 gallon water
2 cups sugar
2 quarts vinegar
4 tablespoons Mustard Seed
3 tablespoons Celery Seed
1 tablespoon Crushed Red Pepper
1 tablespoon Pickling Spice

Wash, rinse and drain vegetables. Before measuring, quarter cucumbers and cut into 1-inch lengths. Cut carrots into ½-inch pieces; measure. Break cauliflower into small flowerets. Seed and chop peppers. Peel onions. Drain mushrooms. Put all the vegetables in a stone crock. Dissolve salt in water and pour over vegetables. Let stand 18 hours; drain. Combine sugar, vinegar, mustard seed, celery seed, crushed red pepper and pickling spice and boil, uncovered, 3 minutes. Pack vegetables in clean, hot canning jars. Pour vinegar mixture over vegetables, leaving ¼-inch head space. Close jars and process 20 minutes in boiling water-bath. *Makes about 4 pints.*

Mustard Pickles

2 quarts medium-size cucumbers
1 quart green tomatoes
1 large cauliflower
2 sweet red peppers
1 quart pickling onions
1 cup salt
3 quarts water
6 tablespoons dry Mustard
1 tablespoon Turmeric
1 cup flour
¾ cup water
2 cups sugar
2 quarts cider vinegar
2 tablespoons Celery Seed
1 tablespoon Peppercorns

Wash and drain vegetables. Cut cucumbers into ½-inch cubes, tomatoes into wedges and cauliflower into small flowerets. Remove seed from peppers and cut peppers into small pieces. Peel onions and cut in half. Dissolve salt in the 3 quarts water and pour over vegetables. Let stand 12 hours. Rinse; drain 1 hour. Combine dry mustard, turmeric and flour. Gradually add the ¾ cup water, stirring until smooth. Add sugar, vinegar, celery seed and peppercorns. Cook over medium heat until sauce coats a metal spoon. Add vegetables and simmer 15 minutes. Pack, boiling hot, into clean, hot canning jars, leaving ¼-inch head space. Close jars. Process 10 minutes in boiling water-bath.

Makes 12 pints.

Spiced Pickled Peaches

10 pounds peaches
Whole Cloves
4 pounds brown sugar
1 pint cider vinegar
2 3-inch pieces Cinnamon

Peel peaches; stick 2 or 3 whole cloves in each. Cover peaches with brown sugar and let stand overnight. Drain off syrup and combine with vinegar and cinnamon; bring to boil. Drop peaches into boiling syrup, a few at a time, and cook 20 minutes or until tender. As peaches are cooked, pack into clean, hot canning jars. When all have been cooked, pour hot syrup over peaches in jars, leaving ¼-inch head space. Close jars. Process 10 minutes in boiling water-bath. You will find these excellent served with ham, roast poultry or game. *Makes 3 quarts.*

Sweet Cucumber Pickles

5 pounds small whole cucumbers
1 cup rock salt
2 quarts cold water
½ teaspoon powdered Alum
2 quarts boiling water
5 cups cider vinegar
2 tablespoons Pickling Spice
5 cups sugar

Wash cucumbers and place in stone crock or enamel container. If you cannot purchase small whole cucumbers, you may use 5 pounds large cucumbers, sliced; the yield may vary since slices pack more compactly than whole cucumbers. Mix salt with the 2 quarts cold water; pour over cucumbers. Let stand one week, weighting cucumbers with a glass plate so they are completely covered with brine at all times. Remove scum each day. At end of week, drain and rinse well. Mix alum with the 2 quarts boiling water; pour over cucumbers. Let stand 24 hours; drain. Combine vinegar, pickling spice and 3 cups of the sugar and bring to a boil; pour over pickles. Let stand 24 hours. Drain liquid into a saucepan; add ½ cup of the remaining sugar and bring to a boil. Pour over pickles. Let stand 24 hours. Repeat draining, adding ½ cup sugar and boiling each day for three more days. On the third and last day, pack pickles in clean, hot canning jars; cover with hot syrup, leaving ¼-inch head space. Close jars. Process 10 minutes in boiling water-bath. *Makes 6 to 7 pints.*

Thousand Island Pickles

4 quarts sliced cucumbers
4 medium-size onions, sliced
2 sweet red peppers, cut into strips
1 green pepper, cut into strips
3 cups sugar
3 cups vinegar
1 tablespoon dry Mustard
1 tablespoon Turmeric
¼ cup salt
2 tablespoons Mustard Seed

Divide cucumbers, onions, red pepper and green pepper evenly among 7 clean, hot, pint-size canning jars. Combine remaining ingredients. Heat, stirring, just until sugar is dissolved. Pour over vegetables, leaving ¼-inch head space. Close jars. Process 10 minutes in boiling water-bath.

Makes 7 pints.

Watermelon Pickles

4½ pounds peeled watermelon rind (about 4 quarts)
2 tablespoons rock salt
3 quarts water
2 tablespoons powdered Alum
1 quart white vinegar
9 cups sugar
¼ cup whole Cloves
2 3-inch pieces Cinnamon

Peel and cut rind into desired shapes; put in stone crock and let stand 24 hours in a solution of the salt and 2 quarts of the water. Drain thoroughly. Let stand 24 hours in a solution of alum and the remaining quart of water. Drain thoroughly. Add fresh water to cover and let stand 24 hours. Bring to a boil and cook until tender, about 30 minutes; drain. Make syrup of vinegar, sugar and spices tied in a cheesecloth bag. Add watermelon rind and cook, uncovered, until clear and tender, about 20 minutes. Remove rind from syrup and pack into clean, hot canning jars. Cook syrup 15 minutes longer; remove spice bag. Fill jars with hot syrup, leaving ¼-inch head space. Close jars. Process 10 minutes in boiling water-bath. *Makes 5 to 6 pints.*

Apple Chutney

8 cups chopped apples
2 cups chopped dried apricots
½ cup Chopped Instant Onions
1 pound brown sugar
1 pint vinegar
1 tablespoon ground Ginger
1 tablespoon Mint Flakes
2 teaspoons ground Allspice
2 teaspoons salt
1 tablespoon Mustard Seed
1 teaspoon ground Red Pepper
⅛ teaspoon Instant Minced Garlic

Peel and core apples. Coarsely chop apples and apricots, then measure. Combine with remaining ingredients. Simmer 1 hour, or until thickened. Fill clean, hot canning jars, leaving ¼-inch head space. Close jars. Process 15 minutes in boiling water-bath. Apple Chutney is delicious with lamb, pork, capon or duckling.

Makes about 2 pints.

Mango Chutney

The king of chutneys—highly prized as an accompaniment with curry.

1 pint cider vinegar
3½ cups brown sugar, firmly packed (1½ pounds)
2 medium-size onions, chopped
1 lemon, sliced thin
⅛ teaspoon Instant Minced Garlic
1½ cups seedless raisins or currants
¼ teaspoon ground Red Pepper
1½ teaspoons salt
1 tablespoon Mustard Seed
4 ounces Crystallized Ginger, thinly sliced
6 tomatoes, peeled and cut into eighths
1 green pepper, chopped
6 whole Cloves
¼ teaspoon Nutmeg
6 medium-size apples, peeled, cored and sliced
4 large mangoes, peeled and sliced

Combine all ingredients, except apples and mangoes, in a large kettle. Cook uncovered, 1 hour or until liquid is clear and syrupy. Add apples and mangoes; continue cooking until fruit is tender. Fill clean, hot canning jars, leaving ½-inch head space. Close jars. Process 10 minutes in boiling water-bath.

Makes about 5 pints.

Old-Time Mincemeat

- 1 3-pound rump roast
- 1 tablespoon salt
- 1 cup water
- 1 16-ounce can red, tart pitted cherries
- 1 pound brown sugar
- 1 pound dark seedless raisins
- 1 pound golden seedless raisins
- 1 11-ounce box currants
- 8 ounces candied citron, finely chopped
- 1½ cups chopped orange pulp
- ⅓ cup minced, fresh orange peel
- ¼ cup lemon juice
- 2 teaspoons grated lemon rind
- ½ pound ground suet
- 1 cup tart jelly
- 1 cup dark molasses
- 3 cups sweet cider
- 1 tablespoon Cinnamon
- 1 teaspoon Nutmeg
- 1 teaspoon Cloves
- 1 teaspoon Allspice
- 1 teaspoon Mace
- ½ teaspoon Ginger
- ½ teaspoon Black Pepper
- 3 quarts chopped, tart apples (about 4 pounds)
- 2 tablespoons Brandy Extract

Sprinkle beef with salt; add water and simmer, covered, 2 hours or until tender. Remove meat, reserving the liquid. When meat is cool, put through food grinder using fine blade; you should have 5 to 7 cups ground beef. Drain cherries, reserving juice. In a large saucepan or kettle, combine cherry juice, sugar, raisins, currants, citron, orange pulp and peel, lemon juice and rind, suet, jelly, molasses, cider and the spices. Mix well. Slowly bring to a boil, stirring occasionally. Then stir in ground beef, cherries, apples and brandy extract. Cook until mixture comes to a boil. Fill clean, hot canning jars, leaving ½-inch head space. Close jars. Process 30 minutes in boiling water-bath. *Caution:* Take care in filling to distribute as equally as possible the amount of liquid and solids.

Makes 6 quarts or enough for six 9-inch pies.

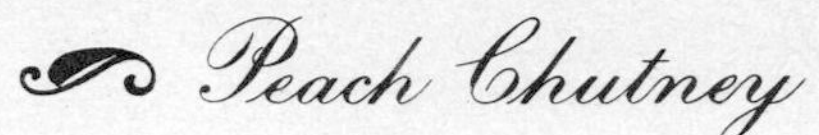

Peach Chutney

2 quarts peaches
4 tart apples
1 lemon
4 ounces Crystallized Ginger
1 cup raisins
1 pound brown sugar
1 pint vinegar
½ cup Chopped Instant Onions
⅛ teaspoon Instant Minced Garlic
1 teaspoon ground Ginger
2 teaspoons salt
2 tablespoons Mustard Seed
1 teaspoon ground Cloves
½ teaspoon ground Red Pepper
½ teaspoon ground Cinnamon

Peel and slice peaches. Peel apples and chop coarsely. Cut lemon into thin slices. Chop crystallized ginger. Combine all ingredients and simmer 1½ hours. Fill clean, hot canning jars, leaving ¼-inch head space. Close jars. Process 10 minutes in boiling water-bath. Excellent served as a condiment with curry; or serve with lamb, beef or duckling. Adds an interesting note to tuna or chicken salad. *Makes 5 pints.*

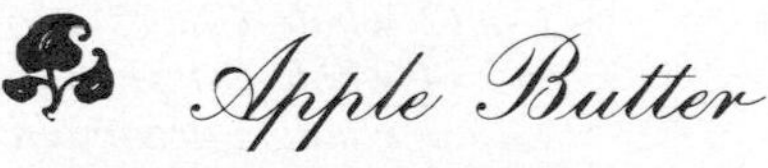

Apple Butter

15 medium-size apples
1½ quarts cider
1½ pounds (3 cups) sugar
1 teaspoon Cinnamon
1 teaspoon Allspice
1 teaspoon Cloves
¼ teaspoon Nutmeg

Select firm, tart cooking apples. Wash and slice; do not remove core, seed or peel. Add cider and boil 15 minutes or until apples are soft. Press through sieve. (You should have about 3 quarts pulp.) Gently boil the pulp 1 hour or until it begins to thicken, stirring occasionally. Stir in sugar and spices and continue cooking slowly 3 hours or until thickened, stirring frequently. Pour into clean, hot canning jars, leaving ¼-inch head space. Close jars. Process 10 minutes in boiling water-bath. *Makes about 3½ pints.*

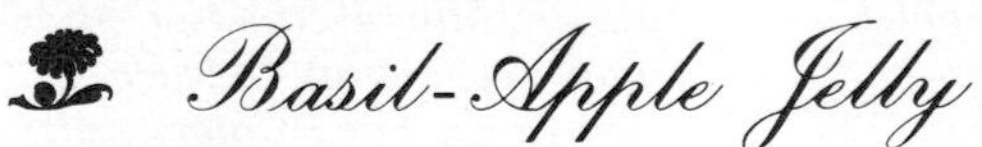

Basil-Apple Jelly

12 medium-size cooking apples
3 cups sugar
1 tablespoon Basil Leaves

Quarter apples, removing stem and blossom ends. Add just enough water to cover. Cook, covered, until apples are tender, about 20 minutes. Put apples, including juice, into jelly bag or 4 thicknesses of cheesecloth. Allow juice to drip from bag. (For clear jelly, do not squeeze bag.) Combine 4 cups of the juice with sugar. Tie basil leaves in cheesecloth bag and add to juice. Boil rapidly to jellying stage, 220°F. to 222°F., or until two drops of jelly will run together off side of spoon. Remove basil leaves. Pour into hot, sterilized jelly glasses or canning jars. Seal. *Makes about 4 half-pints.*

Cinnamon Peach Preserves

2 pounds quartered peaches (8 to 10)
3 cups sugar
1½ cups water
2 3-inch pieces Cinnamon

Peel, remove pit and quarter peaches; weigh. Make syrup of 1½ cups of the sugar, water and cinnamon. While boiling, add peaches and cook 15 minutes. Remove from heat and let peaches stand in syrup 1 hour. Add remaining 1½ cups sugar and bring to a boil. Cook rapidly to jelly stage, 220°F. to 222°F. Fill hot canning jars, leaving ¼-inch head space. Seal. Process 10 minutes in boiling water-bath.

Makes 1½ pints.

Mango Marmalade

½ large lemon
½ large orange
½ cup orange juice
5 cups diced, ripe mangoes
3 cups sugar
12 whole Cloves
4 whole Allspice
2 whole Cardamom

Slice lemon and orange into paper-thin slices; cut each slice in half. Combine with orange juice, diced mangoes and sugar in a large, heavy saucepan. Tie spices in a cheesecloth bag and add to mixture. Bring to a boil, stirring gently. Boil rapidly almost to, or to, the jellying point, 220°F. to 222°F., stirring often to prevent sticking. Remove spice bag. Pour boiling hot marmalade into hot, sterilized jars, leaving ¼-inch head space. Seal at once.

Makes about 2 pints.

Mint-Apple Jelly

12 medium-size cooking apples
3 cups sugar
1 teaspoon Mint Extract or Mint and Peppermint Extract
3 drops Green Food Color

Quarter apples; remove stem and blossom ends. Add just enough water to cover. Cook, covered, 20 minutes or until apples are tender. Put apples, including juice, into jelly bag or 4 thicknesses of cheesecloth. Allow juice to drip from bag. (For clear jelly, do not squeeze bag.) Combine 4 cups of the juice with sugar and boil rapidly to jellying point, 220°F. to 222°F., or until two drops of jelly will run together off side of spoon. Add extract and food color. Remove from heat. Pour into hot, sterilized jelly glasses or canning jars. Seal. You will find this to be excellent with lamb.

Makes about 4 half-pints.

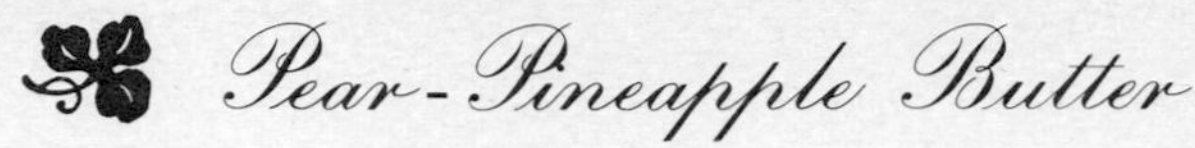

Pear-Pineapple Butter

4 cups grated pears (8 to 10 medium-size pears)
2 cups sugar
2 3-inch pieces Cinnamon
1 16-ounce can crushed pineapple

Combine pears, sugar and cinnamon in saucepan and boil 5 minutes, uncovered, stirring often. Add pineapple and boil 20 minutes longer, stirring occasionally. Fill clean, hot canning jars, leaving ¼-inch head space. Close jars. Process 15 minutes in boiling water-bath. *Makes 2½ pints.*

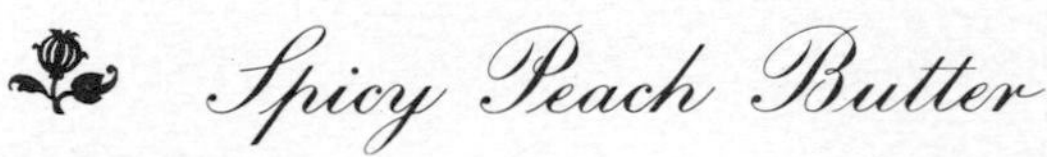

Spicy Peach Butter

26 medium-size ripe peaches
2 cups sugar
1¼ teaspoons Lemon Peel
½ teaspoon Cinnamon
¼ teaspoon ground Cardamom

Peel and slice peaches. Cook in small amount of water until peaches are soft. Mash and strain. Measure 4 cups pulp and combine with remaining ingredients. Cook, uncovered, until mixture thickens, about 45 minutes, stirring often. Fill clean, hot canning jars, leaving ¼-inch head space. Close jars. Process 10 minutes in boiling water-bath. *Makes 2 pints.*

Spice Index

Allspice, ground 13
Allspice Glaze 300
Apple Butter 389
Apple Chutney 387
Apple Cobbler 271
Apple Dumplings 282
Blackberry Jam Cake 291
Blueberry Pancakes 268
Broiled Bananas 213
Cardamom Butter Cookies 336
Cheesecake Elégante 274
Cherry Pie 311
Chicken Cacciatore 145
Choux Glacés à la Crème 278
Chow-Chow 379
Cinnamon Baked Apples 235
Cocoa with a Hint of Spice 351
Coffee Torte 275
Cornish Hens with Fruited Rice Stuffing 143
Cranberry Nut Bread 229
Czechoslovakian Cookies 330
Dark Fruit Cake 294
Date-Filled Squares 323
Date Roll 337
Deep Dish Peach Pie 310
Duckling à l'Orange 157
Easy Mincemeat Pie 318
English Plum Pudding 284
Excellent Prune Cake 292
Filled Fancies 326
French Hot Chocolate 352
French Mint Chocolate 352
Fruit Cake Cookies 327
Fun with Waffles 264
Ginger Peach Freeze 353
Holiday Confetti Bread 257
Holiday Cranberry Punch 355
Hot Cranberry Punch 350
Hot Cross Buns 257
Lamb Kebabs 125
Layered Orange Cranberry Mold 105
Lebkuchen 333
Old-Fashioned Spice Cake 293
Old-Time Mincemeat 388
Party Pink Fruit Salad 106
Party Punch 346
Pineapple Upside-Down Cake 297
Pumpkin Pie 308
Raisin Spice Cupcakes 296
Raspberry Sauce 370
Rhubarb Custard Pie 320
Rocks 329
Salted Spiced Walnuts 72
Sauerbraten Nibblers 63
Sesame Toffee Bars 341
Snappy Cheese-wiches 200
Sour Cream Dip for Fresh Fruit 63
Spice Chiffon Cake 295
Spiced Baked Ham Slice 128
Spiced Cranberry Juice Cocktail 64
Spiced Divinity 339
Spiced Graham Cracker Crust 319
Spiced Grape Punch 347
Spiced Hard Sauce 375
Spiced Mixed Nuts 330
Spiced Raisin Sauce 374
Spiced Sangria 345
Spicy Barbecue Sauce 372
Spicy Chocolate Frosting 302
Spicy Meringues 282
Spicy Oatmeal Cookies 334
Spicy Pastry 317
Steamed Date Pudding 278
Swedish Fruit Soup 86
Swedish Meat Balls 122
Sweet-Sour Red Cabbage 221
Tea House Punch 348
Tomato Relish 381
Wonderful Apple Pie 309
Allspice, whole 7
Autumn Spiced Cider 349
Beet Surprise Salad 100
Caper Sauce 373
Consommé Royale 92
Cranberry Wassail Bowl 348
Crystal Pickles 382
Dixie Relish 380
Fillet de Sole Véronique 171
Fish Poached in Court Bouillon 181
Iced Viennese Coffee 353
Island Fruit Punch 349
Mango Marmalade 390
Mulled Wine 352
Peaches Zanzibar 283
Piquant Tomato Aspic 101
Pot Roast aux Herbes 120
Rolled Rump Roast 240
Spice-Fruit Ring 346
Spiced Shrimp Maison 78
Spiced Tongue 135
Tomato Juice Cocktail 68
Traditional Wassail Bowl 354
Truffle Sauce 373
Alum, powdered
Cantaloupe Pickles 382
Crystal Pickles 382
Dilled Green Beans 383
Sweet Cucumber Pickles 385
Watermelon Pickles 386
Anise Seed 13-14
Anise Cookies 340
Dutch Apple Pie 305
Hungarian Goulash 118
Whole Wheat Salt Sticks 264
Apple Pie Spice
Deep Dish Apple Pie 308
Wonderful Apple Pie 309
Arrowroot
Apricot Duckling 142
Black Bottom Pie 311
Blackberry Cobbler 307
Cauliflower with Creamy Cheese Sauce 208
Celery and Carrots in Parsley Cream 222
Chicken Cantonese 150
Cinnamon-Nut Ice Cream 276
Corn Pudding 215
Creamed Clams 172
Dill Sauce 370
Eggs à la Goldenrod 186
Fish Poached in Court Bouillon 181
Fresh Corn Sauté 219
Harvard Beets 219
Holiday Nutmeg Sauce 361
Homemade Vanilla Ice Cream 276
Hot Exotic Curry Sauce 362
Lobster Cantonese 178
Mint Sauce for Desserts 364
Nutmeg Sauce 363
Pizza Sauce 364
Potatoes au Gratin 223
Pumpkin Pie 308
Raspberry Sauce 370
Sea Food Crêpes 175
Spaghetti Sauce 364
Spiced Coffee Ice Cream 276
Spiced Soufflé 279
Stewed Tomatoes with Oregano 210
Strawberry-Rhubarb Crisp 283
Sweet-Sour Mustard Sauce 372
Sweet-Sour Pork 130
Tropical Barbecue Sauce 373
Veal Paprika 134
Barbecue Spice
Baked Beans Bar-B-Q 242
Barbecued Baked Beans 209
Barbecued Bologna Roll 250
Barbecued Chicken 246
Barbecued Nibblers 69
Chuck Wagon Franks 240
Hot 'n' Tangy Burgers 249
Onion Rounds Delicious 251
Outdoor Chefs' Grillburgers 249
Party Biscuits 266
Patio Potatoes 247
Quick 'n' Easy Barbecue Sauce 360
Spicy Barbecue Sauce 372
Texas Barbecued Beef 195
Vegetable Kebabs 248
Basil Leaves 14
Baked Acorn Squash 217
Baked Stuffed Tomatoes 232
Basil-Apple Jelly 389
Brussels Sprouts with Chestnuts 211
Cabbage Rolls 190

Cannelloni 187
Carrot and Cauliflower Casserole 235
Chicken Paprika 150
Corn Chowder 83
Cornish Hens Stuffed with Wild Rice 156
Eggplant Florentine with Beef 188
Green Bean Salad 97
Herb French Dressing 110
Herb Pizza 201
Herb Seasoned Broccoli 220
Herbed Minute Steak 118
Hot Turkey Salad 234
Italian Pizza 201
Italian Spaghetti Sauce 185
Italian Style Peas 212
Lasagne 194
Lentil Soup 84
Manicotti 233
Marinated Mushrooms 78
Piquant Tomato Aspic 101
Pot Roast with Vegetables 230
Savory Salmon Loaf 180
Savory Stuffed Peppers 193
Shish Kebabs 245
Spaghetti with Superb Meat Sauce 197
Spiced Shrimp Maison 78
Stewed Tomatoes with Oregano 210
Swiss Steak 124
Turkey Pot Pie 141
Veal Marsala 115
Bay Leaves 14
Apricot Duckling 142
Arroz con Pollo 144
Beef Stew 229
Bouillabaisse 90
Brunswick Stew 186
Canard au Grand Marnier 158
Caper Sauce 373
Ceviche 71
Chicken Curry in Avocado 147
Chicken Curry in Papaya 147
Chicken Liver Spread 228
Chicken or Turkey Soup 85
Consommé Royale 92
Eggplant Parmigiana 209
Fillet de Sole Véronique 171
Fish Poached in Court Bouillon 181
French Onion Soup 84
Hot Exotic Curry Sauce 362
Indian Rice 194
Italian Spaghetti Sauce 185
Lobster Bisque Elégante 88
Manhattan Clam Chowder 89
New Orleans Shrimp Gumbo 86
Old-Fashioned Sauerbraten 120
Old-Fashioned Vegetable Soup 92
Oriental Spiced Shrimp 78
Oven Braised Short Ribs 122
Pâté de Foie en Aspic 67
Piquant Tomato Aspic 101
Pizza Sauce 364
Pot Roast aux Herbes 120
Ragout of Lamb Rosemary 127
Roast Goose Superb 159
Roast Pheasant 156
Rolled Rump Roast 240
Sauerbraten Nibblers 63
Savory Fresh Ham 230
Scallops and Mushrooms en Brochette 179
Scallops and Mushrooms in Sherry Sauce 169
Scotch Broth 93
Shrimp Creole 176
Spaghetti Sauce 364
Spaghetti with Superb Meat Sauce 197
Spiced Tongue 135
Tomato Juice Cocktail 68
Tomato Sauce 361
Tomato-Vegetable Soup 91
Truffle Sauce 373
Beef Flavor Base 15
Beef Stew 116
Brown Sauce 366
Chinese Stuffed Mushrooms 73
Country Style Venison Steak 136
Egg Drop Soup 91
French Onion Soup 84
Fried Rice 201
Green Beans with Dill 220
Hamburger De Luxe 117
Herb Roquefort Dip 66
Herbed Giblet Sauce 366
Kidneys in Sherry Sauce 137
Marjoram Meat Balls 70
Meat Loaf Baked in Sauce 119
Minestrone 87
Mushroom Sauce 367
Old-Fashioned Vegetable Soup 92
Onion Sauce 366
Osso Bucco 134
Oven Braised Short Ribs 122
Party Beef Casserole 191
Peppered Tenderloin 119
Pot Roast aux Herbes 120
Pot Roast with Vegetables 230
Ragout of Lamb Rosemary 127
Saltimbocca 133
Savory Fresh Ham 230
Savory Stuffed Peppers 193
Sesame Cheese Ball 68
Sesame Stuffing 165
Stuffed Breast of Veal 133
Swedish Meat Balls 122
Sweet-Sour Mustard Sauce 372
Toasted Onion Dip 75
Tomato-Vegetable Soup 91
Tuna and Tomato Mold 107
Veal Birds 132
Bell Pepper Flakes
Brunswick Stew 186
Chicken Cacciatore 145
Chicken en Casserole 144
Corn and Pepper Stroganoff 215
Manhattan Clam Chowder 89
Minestrone 87
New Orleans Shrimp Gumbo 86
Pepper Burgers 249
Sausage and Wild Rice Casserole 189
Spanish Rice 196
Tomato Sauce 361
Tropical Barbecue Sauce 373
Bon Appétit® 15
Baked Fish with Herb Stuffing 174
Barbecued Baked Beans 209
Barbecued Nibblers 69
Basic Bread Stuffing 162
Best Ever Stuffed Eggs 69
Bon Appétit Dip aux Herbes 70
Bouillabaisse 90
Broiled Clams 77
Broiled Fish Amandine 174
Broiled Salmon with Dill 171
Canard au Grand Marnier 158
Cannelloni 187
Ceviche 71
Cheese Soufflé 202
Chestnut Stuffing 162
Chicken Liver Spread 228
Chicken or Bacon Stuffed Eggs 69
Cold Cucumber Soup 228
Coleslaw Bon Appétit 104
Coquilles Saint-Jacques 76
Corn and Pepper Stroganoff 215
Cornish Hens Stuffed with Wild Rice 156
Country Captain 141
Country Kitchen Potato Salad 107
Crab Newburg 169
Crab Salad 99
Crab-Stuffed Mushrooms 80
Cream of Zucchini Soup 88
Creamed Onions 219
Creamed Spinach 211
Crown Roast of Lamb 126
Curried Sea Food Salad 99 (l.c.)
Curry Stuffed Eggs 69
Delectable Green Beans 221
Dill Sauce 370
Dilly of a Dip 70
Eggplant Florentine with Beef 188
Fillet Neapolitan 172
Fresh Corn Sauté 219
Frogs' Legs aux Fines Herbes 173
Frogs' Legs Provençale 173
Garden Vegetable Salad 100
Ginger Glazed Carrots 208
Gingered Crown Roast 126
Golden Cream of Carrot Soup 91
Green Bean Salad 97
Hamburger De Luxe 117
Herb Broiled Chicken 145
Herb Dumplings 151
Herb Stuffing 162
Herbed Minute Steaks 118
Hot Bleu Cheese Canapés 233
Kidneys in Sherry Sauce 137
Lima Bean Casserole 212
Liver Pâté Bon Appétit 73
Lobster Bisque Elégante 88
Lobster Cantonese 178
New England Clam Chowder 90
Old-Fashioned Baked Beans 209
Old-Fashioned Chicken and Dumplings 151
Outdoor Chefs' Grillburgers 249
Oven Braised Short Ribs 122
Oyster Stew 84
Oyster Stuffing 162

Oysters Rockefeller 76
Pan-Fried Fish 177
Party Beef Casserole 191
Pizza Sauce 364
Pork Mandarin 128
Pot Roast aux Herbes 120
Potato-Fennel Salad 107
Quiche Lorraine 66
Red Cocktail Sauce 367
Rice Pilaf 195
Roast Goose Superb 159
Roast Turkey Supreme 160
Roast Whole Tenderloin 123
Rolled Roast Rib Royale 123
Roquefort Dressing 111
Rye Herb Bread 267
Saltimbocca 133
Sautéed Frogs' Legs 173
Scalloped Potatoes with Cheese 207
Sea Food Crêpes 175
Shrimp and Lobster with Sauce Cavier 180
Shrimp Salad 98
Spaghetti Sauce 364
Spiced Shrimp Maison 78
Stuffed Celery Sticks 79
Stuffed Pork Chops 129
Toasted Onion Dip 75
Tomato Juice Cocktail 68
Tomato Sauce 361
Tomato Soup Oregano 85
Trout with Seasoned Butter 234
Truffled Chicken Breasts Elégante 154
Tuna Casserole with Batter Topping 198
Turkey Pot Pie 161
Veal Birds 132
Veal Orloff 115
Vegetable Kebabs 248
Vichyssoise 89
Wheat Pilaf 195

Caraway Seed 15-16

Cheese Dip Caraway 77
Easy Saffron Bread 267
Parsley Biscuits 268
Sauerkraut Caraway 210
Turkey Pot Pie 161
Veal Cutlets Viennese 132
Whole Wheat Salt Sticks 264

Cardamom, Ground 16-17

Baked Chicken Oriental 146
Barbecued Baked Beans 209
Blueberry Crumble 307
Cardamom Butter Cookies 336
Cardamom Cream Dressing 108
Cardamom Crescent 261
Cardamom Rice Pudding 276
Cardamom Ripple Cake 291
Champagne Salad 103
Choux Glacés à la Crème 278
Crown Roast of Lamb 126
Czechoslovakian Cookies 330
Danish Pastry 259
Deep Dish Peach Pie 310
Filled Cookies 325
Floating Island Meringues 280
Fluffy Snow Peak Frosting 299
Fresh Fruit Medley 104
Gingerbread 299
Gingered Crown Roast 126
Heavenly Hash 283
Herbed Crown Roast 126
Hot Cross Buns 257
Lane Cake 293
Lebkuchen 333
Minted Mocha Float 351
Old-Fashioned Baked Beans 209
Pfeffernüsse 331
Spice Muffins 265
Spiced Bavarian 284
Spiced Coconut Chiffon Pie 312
Spiced Graham Cracker Crust 319
Spiced Hard Sauce 375
Spicy Banana Nut Bread 265
Spicy Meringues 282
Spicy Pastry 317
Spicy Peach Butter 391
Strawberry-Rhubarb Crisp 283
Swedish Fruit Soup 86
Waldorf Salad 106
Whole Wheat Rolls 256

Cardamom, whole 16-17

Cranberry Wassail Bowl 348
Glögg 348
Indian Rice 194
Mango Marmalade 390
Manhattan Clam Chowder 89
Party Punch 346
Peaches Zanzibar 283
Pineapple-Grapefruit Delight 79
Scotch Broth 93
Spice-Fruit Ring 346
Spiced Cranberry Juice Cocktail 64
Spiced Shrimp Maison 78
Traditional Wassail Bowl 354
Tropical Delight 347

Cayenne (*See* Pepper, ground Red)

Celery Flakes 17

Chicken en Casserole 144
Chuck Wagon Franks 240
Glazed Boiled Beef 117
Hot Exotic Curry Sauce 362
Lentil Soup 84
Manhattan Clam Chowder 89
Minestrone 87
Old-Fashioned Chicken and Dumplings 151
Old-Fashioned Sauerbraten 120
Osso Bucco 134
Oysters Rockefeller 76
Piquant Tomato Aspic 101
Roast Goose Superb 159
Sauerbraten with Potato Dumplings 121
Scotch Broth 93
Sesame Stuffing 165
Spiced Tongue 135
Spicy Barbecue Sauce 372

Celery Salt 17

Asparagus Oriental 213
Brunswick Stew 186
Chicken Corn Soup 92
Crab Cakes 177
Crab Imperial 170
Dill Stuffed Eggs 69
Fish Poached in Court Bouillon 181
Flank Steak Western Style 251
Grilled Tomatoes 248
Herb Burgers 249
Lamb Shanks Divine 127
Manicotti 233
Mephisto Ham Dip 66
Mock Enchilada Casserole 188
Okra Southern Style 211
Old-Fashioned Vegetable Soup 92
Onion Rounds Delicious 251
Pâté de Foie en Aspic 67
Ragout of Lamb Rosemary 127
Ranch-Style Salad Dressing 97
Sauce Rémoulade 368
Savory Salmon Loaf 180
Savory Turkey Croquettes 155
South-of-the-Border Dressing 110
Spaghetti with Superb Meat Sauce 197
Superb Scalloped Oysters 178
Tartar Sauce 371
Vichyssoise 89
Zippy Tomato Juice 354

Celery Seed 17

Beef Stew 229
Bread and Butter Pickles 381
Cantaloupe Pickles 382
Celery Seed Dressing 108
Celery Seed Rolls 244
Chicken Liver Spread 228
Chili Suace 379
Chow-Chow 379
Coleslaw Bon Appétit 104
Corn Relish 380
Creamy Coleslaw 104
Crystal Pickles 382
Dixie Relish 380
Herbed Garlic and Cheese Bread 231
Mixed Pickles 384
Mustard Pickles 384
Oriental Spiced Shrimp 78
Pickle Relish 381
Stuffed Breast of Veal 133

Chicken Flavor Base 18

Apricot Duckling 142
Arroz con Pollo 144
Asparagus Oriental 213
Baked Chicken Oriental 146
Baked Stuffed Eggplant 214
Basic Bread Stuffing 162
Best Ever Stuffed Eggs 69
Bon Appétit Dip aux Herbes 70
Brussels Sprouts with Chestnuts 211
Buffet Turkey Loaf 98
Canard au Grand Marnier 158
Caper Sauce 373
Carrots Vichy 218
Cauliflower with Creamy Cheese Sauce 208
Celery and Carrots in Parsley Cream 222
Celery Victor 79
Chestnut Stuffing 162

Chicken Cantonese 150
Chicken Corn Soup 92
Chicken Curry in Avocado 147
Chicken Curry in Papaya 147
Chicken Liver Spread 228
Chicken or Turkey Soup 85
Chicken Paprika 150
Chicken-Vegetable Soup 231
Chinese Chicken Casserole 190
Chinese Stuffed Mushrooms 73
Clove-Studded Onions 213
Cold Cucumber Soup 228
Cornish Hens Stuffed with Wild Rice 156
Country Inn Pheasant 157
Cream of Zucchini Soup 88
Creamed Chicken Supreme 149
Dill Buttered Potatoes 210
Dill Sauce 370
Egg Drop Soup 91
Eggs à la Goldenrod 186
Fillet de Sole Véronique 171
Fish Poached in Court Bouillon 181
Ginger Glazed Carrots 208
Golden Cream of Carrot Soup 91
Herb Seasoned Broccoli 220
Herb Stuffing 162
Holiday Stuffing 164
Hot Exotic Curry Sauce 362
Indian Rice 194
Italian Style Peas 212
Liver Pâté Bon Appétit 73
Lobster Bisque Elégante 88
Lobster Cantonese 178
Macaroni and Cheese 199
Minted Peas 221
Mulligatawny 87
Mushroom-Rice Stuffing 162
New Orleans Shrimp Gumbo 86
Old South Corn Bread Stuffing 163
Oyster Stuffing 162
Paella 189
Parsley Buttered Potatoes 210
Pâté de Foie en Aspic 67
Potatoes au Gratin 223
Rice Pilaf 195
Sausage and Wild Rice Casserole 189
Sautéed Chicken Livers 152
Sautéed Chicken Livers Rosé 152
Savory Turkey Croquettes 155
Sea Food Crêpes 175
Spanish Rice 196
Spiced Chestnut Stuffing 165
Spinach Soup 83
Tasty Cream Sauce 363
Truffle Sauce 373
Tuna Casserole with Batter Topping 198
Turkey Pot Pie 161
Turkey Pot Pie with Vegetables 141
Turkey Rolls Delicious 155
Veal and Wild Rice in Casserole 192
Vichyssoise 89
Wheat Pilaf 195
White Sauce Supreme 360
Wild Rice Stuffing 163
Zucchini Parmesan 207

Chili Powder 18
Busy Day Casserole 203
Chili Broiled Chicken 145
Chili-Cheese Burgers 249
Chili Cheese Roll 68
Chili con Carne 190
Chunky Chili 231
Cucumbers in Sour Cream 102
Guacamole 65
Mexican Skillet Dinner 193
South-of-the-Border Dressing 110
Spicy Barbecue Sauce 372
Zesty Stuffed Frankfurters 137

Chives, Freeze-Dried, Chopped
Frogs' Legs aux Fines Herbes 173
Gazpacho 227
Green Goddess Dressing 109
Herb Dumplings 151
Hot Cheese Snacks 227
Italian Dressing 111
Old-Fashioned Chicken and Dumplings 151
Shrimp Sautéed in Herb Butter 177
Sour Cream Topping 368
Vichyssoise 89

Cinnamon, ground 18-19
Apple Butter 389
Apple Cider Squash 217
Apple Cobbler 271
Apple Dumplings 282
Applesauce Cake 298
Apricot Duckling 142
Apricot Pudding 285
Apricot Squares 340
Baked Apples 235, 280
Banana Fritters 280
Banana Frost 352
Bananas Flambé 272
Blackberry Cobbler 307
Blackberry Jam Cake 291
Broiled Bananas 213
Broiled Spiced Topping 302
Butterscotch Squares 324
Cardamom Butter Cookies 336
Chewy Popcorn Balls 342
Chili Sauce 379
Chocolate Carrot Cake 289
Chow-Chow 379
Cinnamon Chocolate Fudge 338
Cinnamon Frosting 301
Cinnamon Glaze 300
Cinnamon Ice Cream 279
Cinnamon Luncheon Cake 294
Cinnamon-Nut Ice Cream 276
Cinnamon-Pecan Biscuits 262
Cinnamon-Pineapple Buns 260
Cinnamon-Raisin Bread 256
Cinnamon Sandies 329
Cinnamon Sledges 336
Cinnamon-Vanilla Milk Shake 354
Cocoa with a Hint of Spice 351
Cool Lemon Soufflé 273
Cornish Hens Stuffed with Wild Rice 156
Cranberry Nut Bread 229
Crêpes Suzette 277
Crunchy Popcorn Balls 342
Crystal Pickles 382
Curried Nibblers 69
Dark Chocolate Frosting 289
Dark Fruit Cake 294
Date-Filled Squares 323
Date Roll 337
Date Sticks 333
Deep Dish Apple Pie 308
Devil's Food Cake 296
Doughnuts 266
Dutch Apple Pie 305
Easy Mincemeat Pie 318
English Plum Pudding 284
Excellent Prune Cake 292
Extra-Special Waffles 227
Filled Benne Lace Cookies 323
Filled Fancies 326
Fried Pies 316
Fruit Cake Cookies 327
Ginger Crêpes 277
Ginger Dessert Waffles 281
Ginger Peach Freeze 353
Gingerbread 299
Gingerbread Boys 332
Gingersnaps 328
Grilled Bananas 245
Holiday Cranberry Punch 355
Holiday Popcorn Balls 342
Honey Spice Butter 365
Honey Spice Dressing 110
Hot Cross Buns 257
Indian Rice 194
Lebkuchen 333
Mexican Chocolate with Marshmallows 351
Mincemeat Refrigerator Cookies 335
Old-Fashioned Spice Cake 293
Old-Time Mincemeat 388
Peach Chutney 389
Peach Cobbler Supreme 281
Pfeffernüsse 331
Philadelphia Sticky Buns 255
Pineapple Upside-Down Cake 297
Pineapple-Yam Kebabs 245
Prune-Filled Square 340
Pumpkin Pie 308
Raisin Spice Cupcakes 296
Raspberry Cloud Pie 310
Refrigerator Spice Cookies 328
Rocks 329
Rum Buns 260
Sesame Toffee Bars 341
Sour Cream Dip for Fresh Fruit 63
Southern Praline Cookies 330
Spice Chiffon Cake 295
Spice Muffins 265
Spiced Baked Ham Slice 128
Spiced Bread Pudding 275
Spiced Coconut Chiffon Pie 312
Spiced Coffee Ice Cream 276
Spiced Graham Cracker Crust 319
Spiced Grape Punch 347
Spiced Hard Sauce 375
Spiced Jelly Roll 290
Spiced Mixed Nuts 330
Spiced Raisin Sauce 374

Spiced Soufflé 279
Spicy Banana Nut Bread 265
Spicy Barbecue Sauce 372
Spicy Chocolate Frosting 302
Spicy Ice Cream Pie 306
Spicy Oatmeal Cookies 334
Spicy Peach Butter 391
Sugared Nuts 339
Tea House Punch 348
Welsh Pork Cake 298
Whipped Maple-Cinnamon Butter 369
Whole Wheat Rolls 256
Wonderful Apple Pie 309

Cinnamon, whole 18-19

Apple Blossom Cooler 350
Beef Surprise Salad 100
Café Diable 347
Cantaloupe Pickles 382
Cinnamon Peach Preserves 390
Cocoa with a Hint of Spice 351
Cranberry Wassail Bowl 348
Dixie Relish 380
Glögg 348
Hot Cranberry Punch 350
Hot 'n' Spicy Punch 355
Iced Viennese Coffee 353
Mulled Wine 352
Party Punch 346
Peach Preserves 390
Peaches Zanzibar 283
Pear-Pineapple Butter 391
Pineapple-Grapefruit Delight 79
Spice-Fruit Ring 346
Spiced Cranberry Juice Cocktail 64
Spiced Pickled Peaches 385
Spiced Sangria 345
Spiced Tea 349
Swedish Fruit Soup 86
Traditional Wassail Bowl 354
Tropical Delight 347
Watermelon Pickles 386

Cinnamon Sugar 18-19

Apple Dumplings 282
Cinnamon-Streusel Muffins 265
Deep Dish Apple Pie 308
Deep Dish Peach Pie 310
Fried Pies 316
Quick Cinnamon Twists 260
Raisin Spice Cupcakes 296
Strawberry-Rhubarb Crisp 283
Sugared Vanilla Wafers 332

Cloves, ground 19-20

Apple Butter 389
Apple Dumplings 282
Applesauce Cake 298
Apricot Squares 340
Banana Frost 352
Barbecued Baked Beans 209
Blackberry Jam Cake 291
Bread and Butter Pickles 381
Broiled Spiced Topping 302
Canadian Bacon on a Spit 246
Chili Sauce 379
Chinese Style Spareribs 241
Cocoa with a Hint of Spice 351
Crab Cakes 177
Dark Fruit Cake 294
Deep Dish Apple Pie 308
Fried Pies 316
Fruit Cake Cookies 327
Gingersnaps 328
Golden Clove Glazed Ham 131
Grilled Bananas 245
Harvard Beets 219
Honey Spice Dressing 110
Lebkuchen 333
Marinated Veal Steak 239
Mincemeat Refrigerator Cookies 335
Old-Fashioned Baked Beans 209
Old-Fashioned Spice Cake 293
Old-Time Mincemeat 388
Orange Butter 365
Party Pink Fruit Salad 106
Peach Chutney 389
Pfeffernüsse 331
Pineapple-Yam Kebabs 245
Prune-Filled Squares 340
Pumpkin Pie 308
Roast Pheasant 156
Rocks 329
Sauerbraten Nibblers 63
Spiced Chiffon Cake 295
Spiced Coffee Ice Cream 276
Spiced Cranberry Juice Cocktail 64
Spiced Graham Cracker Crust 319
Spiced Mixed Nuts 330
Spicy Pastry 317
Strawberry-Rhubarb Crisp 283
Sweet-Sour Red Cabbage 221
Tomato Relish 381
Welsh Pork Cake 298
Wonderful Apple Pie 309

Cloves, whole 19-20

Autumn Spiced Cider 349
Baked Fish with Herb Stuffing 174
Barbecued Bologna Roll 250
Beet Surprise Salad 100
Café Diable 347
Cantaloupe Pickles 382
Caper Sauce 373
Celery Victor 79
Chicken Curry in Avocado 147
Chicken Curry in Papaya 147
Chicken or Turkey Soup 85
Clove-Studded Broiled Ham 128
Clove-Studded Onions 213
Consommé Royale 92
Cranberry Wassail Bowl 348
Crystal Pickles 382
Curry Glazed Ham 131
Dixie Relish 380
Fish Poached in Court Bouillon 181
Glazed Boiled Beef 117
Glögg 348
Golden Clove Glazed Ham 131
Honey Glazed Ham 131
Hot 'n' Spicy Punch 355
Iced Viennese Coffee 353
Island Fruit Punch 349
Mango Chutney 387
Mango Marmalade 390
Manhattan Clam Chowder 89
Mulled Wine 352
Old-Fashioned Sauerbraten 120
Orange Glazed Ham 131
Party Punch 346
Peaches Zanzibar 283
Pineapple-Grapefruit Delight 79
Piquant Tomato Aspic 101
Pork Chops à l'Orange 129
Pork Mandarin 128
Rolled Rump Roast 240
Spice-Fruit Ring 346
Spiced Baked Ham Slice 128
Spiced Pickled Peaches 385
Spiced Tea 349
Spiced Tongue 135
Sweet-Sour Pork 130
Tomato Juice Cocktail 68
Tomato Sauce 361
Traditional Wassail Bowl 354
Truffle Sauce 373
Watermelon Pickles 386

Coriander Seed 20-21

Autumn Spiced Cider 349
Coriander Broiled Chicken 145
Cranberry Wassail Bowl 348
Fish Poached in Court Bouillon 181
Fried Pies 316
Indonesian Spareribs 129
Lobster Bisque Elégante 88
Mincemeat Refrigerator Cookies 335
Pineapple-Grapefruit Refresher 79
Roasted Dilly Corn 248
Scallops and Mushrooms en Brochette 179
Sole Epicurean 173
South-of-the-Border Dressing 110
Spiced Shrimp Maison 78
Traditional Wassail Bowl 354

Cream of Tartar

Black Bottom Pie 311
Blackberry Jam Cake 291
Broccoli Soufflé 214
Chocolate-Mace Cream Pie 314
Coffee Torte 275
Cranberry Chiffon Pie 312
Floating Island Meringues 280
Fondant 341
Fondant Tipped Almonds 341
Harvest Pumpkin Chiffon Pie 318
Lemon Angel Food Cake 292
Lemon Frosting 301
Mint Julep Frosting 299
Pink Perfection Frosting 300
Sesame Macaroons 332
Sour Cream Frosting 300
Spice Chiffon Cake 295
Spiced Coconut Chiffon Pie 312
Spiced Divinity 339
Spiced Soufflé 279
Spicy Meringues 282
Velvety Pumpkin Chiffon Pie 318

Cumin, ground 21

Brunswick Stew 186
Fiesta Egg Salad 102

Cumin Seed 21

Fiesta Egg Salad 102
Indonesian Spareribs 129

Curry Powder 21
Chicken Curry in Avocado 147
Chicken Curry in Papaya 147
Country Captain 141
Creamy Curry Sauce 369
Curried Chicken Balls 72
Curried Fruit Medley 281
Curried Lamb Chops Bengal 242
Curried Nibblers 69
Curried Sea Food Salad 99
Curried Turkey Amandine 154
Curry Butter 374
Curry Dip 80
Curry Glazed Ham 131
Curry Puffs 75
Curry Stuffed Eggs 69
East Indian Lamb Curry 126
Fried Chicken Curry 152
Herb French Dressing 110
Hot Exotic Curry Sauce 362
Mulligatawny 87
Oriental Spiced Shrimp 78
Party Biscuits 266
Pork Chops à l'Orange 129
Quick Curry Soup Indienne 85
Roast Turkey Supreme 160
Dill Seed 22-23
Dill Burgers 249
Dill Pickles 383
Dilled Green Beans 383
Green Beans with Dill 220
Kosher Dill Pickles 383
South-of-the-Border Dressing 110
Tomato-Vegetable Soup 91
Dill Weed 22-23
Baked Fish with Herb Stuffing 174
Broiled Salmon with Dill 171
Buttered Noodles with Dill 197
Cucumbers in Sour Cream 102
Dill Buttered Potatoes 210
Dill Flavored Potatoes 247
Dill Grilled Fish 244
Dill Macaroni Salad 103
Dill Ring 267
Dill Rolls 244
Dill Sauce 370
Dill Stuffed Eggs 69
Dilled Fish Fillets 243
Dilled Green Beans 383
Dilly of a Dip 70
Green Beans with Dill 220
Herb French Dressing 110
Hot Turkey Salad 234
Old-Fashioned Herb Bread 263
Oven Fried Chicken 153
Roasted Dilly Corn 248
Sole Meunière 172
Sweet-Sour Cucumbers with Onions 106
Veal Cutlets Viennese 132
Fennel Seed 23
Baked Fish with Herb Stuffing 174
Bouillabaisse 90
Grilled Fish Fennel 244
Herbed Fish Fillets 243
Oregano Batter Bread 258
Oysters Rockefeller 76
Potato-Fennel Salad 107
Sea Food Crêpes 175
Shrimp and Lobster with Sauce Caviar 180
Spiced Shrimp Maison 78
Garlic, Instant Minced 23-24
Apple Chutney 387
Arroz con Pollo 144
Bouillabaisse 90
Ceviche 71
Chicken Cacciatore 145
Cold Cucumber Soup 228
Dilled Green Beans 383
Kosher Dill Pickles 383
Mango Chutney 387
Minestrone 87
New Orleans Shrimp Gumbo 86
Noodles Romanoff 193
Peach Chutney 389
Ragout of Lamb Rosemary 127
Turkey Creole 160
Garlic Powder 23-25
American French Dressing 110
Barbecued Nibblers 69
Beef Teriyaki 71
Broiled Salmon Tarragon 171
Caesar Salad 101
Canneloni 187
Charcoal Grilled Steak 247
Chicken Curry in Avocado 147
Chicken Curry in Papaya 147
Chicken Italienne 146
Chicken Paprika 150
Chili Cheese Roll 68
Chili con Carne 190
Chinese Style Spareribs 241
Coq au Vin 149
Crab Meat Dunk 65
Dill Rolls 244
Eggplant Parmigiana 209
Fillet Neapolitan 172
Fish Poached in Court Bouillon 181
Frogs' Legs Provençale 173
Garden Vegetable Salad 100
Garlic Butter 367
Garlic Cheese Bread 262
Green Goddess Dressing 109
Grilled Garlic Bread 243
Herb Pizza 201
Herbed Garlic and Cheese Bread 231
Herbed Minute Steaks 118
Honey-Glazed Pork Shoulder 130
Hot Exotic Curry Sauce 362
Italian Dressing 111
Italian Pizza 201
Italian Spaghetti Sauce 185
Lamb in Gingered Cranberry Sauce 125
Lasagne 194
Lima-Sausage Casserole 191
Manhattan Clam Chowder 89
Meat Loaf Baked in Sauce 119
Oriental Spiced Shrimp 78
Osso Bucco 134
Oven Braised Short Ribs 122
Oysters Rockefeller 76
Paella 189
Party Beef Casserole 191
Pizza Sauce 364
Roast Leg of Lamb 124
Roast Whole Tenderloin 123
Rolled Rib Roast 251
Rolled Rib Roast Royale 123
Rosemary Roast 251
Rye Herb Bread 267
Scotch Broth 93
Shrimp Sautéed in Herb Butter 177
Spaghetti Sauce 364
Spaghetti with Superb Meat Sauce 197
Spanish Rice 196
Steak Teriyaki 367
Swiss Steak 124
Teriyaki Sauce 371
Thyme Roast 251
Tomato Sauce 361
Veal Parmigiana 131
Veal Scaloppine 135
Zucchini Sauté 212
Garlic Salt 23-25
Baked Eggs Florentine 185
Baked Stuffed Tomatoes 232
Barbecued Chicken 246
Chicken Rosemary 148
Chili-Cheese Burgers 249
Chunky Chili 231
Country Captain 141
Creamy Roquefort Dressing 108
Curried Lamb Chops Bengal 242
Dill Burgers 249
Gazpacho 227
Hamburgers 249
Herb Burgers 249
Herb Croutons 258
Herb Pizza 201
Hot 'n' Tangy Burgers 249
Italian Pizza 201
Lamb Shanks Divine 127
Manicotti 233
Marinated Artichoke Hearts 74
Marinated Veal Steak 239
Mephisto Ham Dip 66
Oriental Burgers 249
Outdoor Chefs' Grillburgers 249
Pepper Burgers 249
Peppered Steak 250
Peppered Tenderloin 119
Quick 'n' Easy Barbecue Sauce 360
Ranch-Style Salad Dressing 97
Red Hot Burgers 249
Salted Spiced Walnuts 72
Sauerbraten Nibblers 63
Sausage Stuffing 164
Sautéed Chicken Livers 152
Savory Burgers 249
Scallops and Mushrooms en Brochette 179
Scampi on a Skewer 243
Sesame Burgers 249
Sesame Steaks 123
Shish Kebabs 245
Spice Burgers 249
Spicy Barbecue Sauce 372
Swedish Meat Balls 122
Veal Marsala 115

Ginger, Crystalized 25
Creamy Curry Sauce 369
Festive Lime Pie 315
Ginger Cracker Crust 315
Ginger Crêpes 277
Harvest Pumpkin Chiffon Pie 318
Mango Chutney 387
Peach Chutney 389
Ginger, ground 25
Apple Chutney 387
Apple Cobbler 271
Apricot Squares 340
Asparagus Oriental 213
Baked Beans Bar-B-Q 242
Baked Chicken Oriental 146
Beef Teriyaki 71
Brunswick Stew 186
Cantaloupe Pickles 382
Champagne Salad 103
Chewy Popcorn Balls 342
Chicken Cantonese 150
Chicken Legs Waikiki 241
Chicken Paprika 150
Chili Sauce 379
Chinese Stuffed Mushrooms 73
Chinese Style Spareribs 241
Choux Glacés à la Crème 278
Chow-Chow 379
Cinnamon Baked Apples 235
Cornish Hens with Fruited Rice Stuffing 143
Crab Cakes 177
Crab Salad 99
Creamed Clams 172
Creamy Coleslaw 104
Crock Pot Beans 230
Crystal Pickles 382
Crunchy Popcorn Balls 342
Duckling à l'Orange 157
Easy Mincemeat Pie 318
Elegant Peach Pie 313
English Plum Pudding 284
Filled Fancies 326
Fresh Fruit Medley 104 (l.c.)
Frozen Bing Cherry Salad 105
Gingerbread 299
Gingerbread Boys 332
Ginger Cream Dressing 110
Ginger Dessert Waffles 281
Ginger Glazed Carrots 208
Ginger Peach Freeze 353
Ginger Peach Upside-Down-Cake 297
Gingered Crown Roast 126
Gingersnaps 328
Golden Cream of Carrot Soup 91
Grilled Bananas 245
Heavenly Hash 283
Holiday Chews 338
Holiday Confetti Bread 257
Holiday Popcorn Balls 342
Honey-Glazed Pork Shoulder 130
Honey Spice Dressing 110
Indonesian Spareribs 129
Lamb in Gingered Cranberry Sauce 125
Layered Orange-Cranberry Mold 105
Lemon Meringue Pie 305
Liver Pâté Bon Appétit 73
Mincemeat Refrigerator Cookies 335
Old-Time Mincemeat 388
Oriental Burgers 249
Party Punch 346
Peach Chutney 389
Philadelphia Sticky Buns 255
Pickle Relish 381
Pork Chops Luau 242
Pork Mandarin 128
Prune-Filled Squares 340
Pumpkin Pie 308
Roast Turkey Supreme 160
Rolled Rib Roast 251
Rosemary Roast 251
Rumaki 77
Salted Spiced Walnuts 72
Sauerbraten Nibblers 63
Sautéed Chicken Livers Rosé 152
Savory Fresh Ham 230
Scampi on a Skewer 243
Sesame Steaks 123
Sesame Stuffing 165
Spice Muffins 265
Spiced Bavarian 284
Spiced Bread Pudding 275
Spiced Coconut Chiffon Pie 312
Spiced Graham Cracker Crust 319
Spiced Jelly Roll 290
Spiced Mixed Nuts 330
Spiced Raisin Sauce 374
Spiced Shrimp Maison 78
Spiced Soufflé 279
Spicy Lemon Angel Pie 313
Steak Teriyaki 239
Stuffed Pork Chops 129
Stuffed Roast Capon 153
Sweet-Sour Pork 130
Teriyaki Sauce 371
Thyme Roast 251
Tomato Relish 381
Truffled Chicken Breast Elégante 154
Waldorf Salad 106
Zucchini Parmesan 207
Ginger, whole 25
Beef Teriyaki 71
Fish Poached in Court Bouillon 181
Glögg 348
Island Fruit Punch 349
Peaches Zanzibar 283
Pot Roast aux Herbes 120
Spice-Fruit Ring 346
Spiced Cranberry Juice Cocktail 64
Spiced Shrimp Maison 78
Traditional Wassail Bowl 354
Teriyaki Sauce 371
Herb Seasoning 25-26
Apricot Duckling 142
Baked Stuffed Eggplant 214
Gingered Crown Roast 126
Grilled Tomatoes 248
Herb-Broiled Sandwiches 200
Herb-Broiled Tomatoes 220
Herb Chicken 147
Herb Croutons 258
Herb Roquefort Dip 66
Herb Steak 117
Herb Waffles 264
Herbed Crown Roast 126
Herbed Potatoes 247
Onion Butter 365
Oven Braised Short Ribs 122
Party Biscuits 266
Roast Whole Tenderloin 123
Tangy Butter 365
Hickory Smoked Salt
Canadian Bacon on a Spit 246
Hickory Smoked Potatoes 247
Indonesian Spareribs 129
Outdoor Chefs' Grillburgers 249
Rolled Rump Roast 240
Smoky Chicken 145
Sour Cream Topping 368
Italian Seasoning
Chicken Cacciatore 145
Chicken Italienne 146
Fillet Neapolitan 172
Herb Broiled Chicken 145
Herb French Dressing 110
Herb Pizza 201
Manicotti 233
Minestrone 87
Mock Enchilada Casserole 188
Osso Bucco 134
Scampi on a Skewer 243
Swiss Steak 124
Veal Parmigiana 131
Lemon Peel 26-27
Apple Cobbler 271
Apple Dumplings 282
Apricot Duckling 142
Baked Apples 280
Baked Fish with Herb Stuffing 174
Banbury Tarts 319
Broiled Clams 77
Broiled Salmon Tarragon 171
Broiled Salmon with Dill 171
Brunswick Stew 186
Cardamom Crescent 261
Champagne Salad 103
Cheese and Caviar Croutelettes 67
Cherry Pie 311
Choux Glacés à la Crème 278
Clove-Studded Boiled Ham 128
Consommé Royale 92
Coquilles Saint-Jacques 76
Creamy Lemon-Butter Sauce 370
Date Sticks 333
Deviled Lobster Tails 170
Doughnuts 266
Elegant Peach Pie 313
English Plum Pudding 284
Filled Fancies 326
Floating Island Meringues 280
Fried Pies 316
Frozen Bing Cherry Salad 105
Fun with Waffles 264
Gay Tinted Glaze 300
Ginger Peach Freeze 353
Ginger Peach Upside-Down Cake 297
Holiday Confetti Bread 257

Honey Glazed Ham 131
Lebkuchen 333
Lemon Angel Food Cake 292
Lemon Butter Gems 331
Lemon Frosting 301
Lemon Glaze 300
Lemon Meringue Pie 305
Lemon Pastry 317
Lima Bean Casserole 212
Mincemeat Refrigerator Cookies 335
Oriental Burgers 249
Osso Bucco 134
Party Biscuits 266
Peach Cobbler Supreme 281
Pfeffernüsse 331
Quick Coffee Cake 263
Raspberry Cloud Pie 310
Savory Salmon Loaf 180
Spiced Soufflé 279
Spicy Lemon Angel Pie 313
Spicy Peach Butter 391
Steamed Date Pudding 278
Strawberry Filling 309
Strawberry Patch Pie 309
Strawberry-Rhubarb Crisp 283
Swedish Fruit Soup 86
Tuna and Tomato Mold 107
Tuna Casserole with Batter Topping 198
Waldorf Salad 106
Wonderful Apple Pie 309

Mace 27

Apple Cider Squash 217
Apricot Duckling 142
Autumn Spiced Cider 349
Banana Fritters 280
Banana Frost 352
Black Bottom Pie 311
Blueberry Crumble 307
Broiled Bananas 213
Broiled Clams 77
Champagne Salad 103
Chewy Popcorn Balls 342
Chicken or Turkey Soup 85
Chocolate Carrot Cake 289
Chocolate-Mace Cream Pie 314
Chocolate Mousse 274
Chocolate Nut Brownies 336
Choux Glacés à la Crème 278
Chow-Chow 379
Coconut Mace Sauce 361
Coffee Torte 275
Cool Lemon Soufflé 273
Creamed Chicken Supreme 149
Creamed Spinach 211
Creamy Chocolate Sauce 363
Cream Anglaise 375
Crêpes Suzette 277
Crunchy Popcorn Balls 342
Dark Fruit Cake 294
Filled Fancies 326
Fish Fillets in a Package 243
Floating Island Meringues 280
French Hot Chocolate 352
French Mint Chocolate 352
Fresh Fruit Medley 104
Frozen Bing Cherry Salad 105
Ginger Crêpes 277
Herb Roquefort Dip 66
Holiday Chews 338
Holiday Popcorn Balls 342
Lane Cake 293
Layered Orange-Cranberry Mold 105
Lebkuchen 333
Lemon Butter Gems 331
Lemon Meringue Pie 305
Mace-Blueberry Muffins 265
Mace Waffles 264
Marjoram Meat Balls 70
Meringue Cracker Crust 309
Mulligatawny 87
Old-Fashioned Spice Cake 293
Old-Time Mincemeat 388
Orange Butter Gems 331
Party Punch 346
Pfeffernüsse 331
Poppy Seed Cookies 334
Pork Chops Luau 242
Pound Cake 297
Raspberry Sauce 370
Roast Pheasant 156
Roast Whole Tenderloin 123
Sautéed Chicken Livers Rosé 152
Spiced Bavarian 284
Spiced Coconut Chiffon Pie 312
Spiced Divinity 339
Spiced Graham Cracker Crust 319
Spiced Hard Sauce 375
Spiced Soufflé 279
Spicy Banana Nut Bread 265
Spicy Chocolate Frosting 302
Spicy Custard Pie 315
Spicy Ice Cream Pie 306
Spicy Lemon Angel Pie 313
Spicy Meringues 282
Spicy Pastry 317
Steamed Date Pudding 278
Strawberries Romanoff 271
Strawberry Patch Pie 309
Sugared Nuts 339
Swedish Fruit Soup 86
Traditional Wassail Bowl 354
Tropical Delight 347
Turkey Rolls Delicious 155
Waldorf Salad 106
Whole Wheat Rolls 256

Marjoram, ground 27-28

Broiled Salmon Tarragon 171
Crown Roast of Lamb 126
French Onion Soup 84
Gingered Crown Roast 126
Herb Burgers 249
Herb Stuffing 162
Marjoram Meat Balls 70
Meat Loaf Baked in Sauce 119
Mushroom-Rice Stuffing 162
Turkey Creole 160

Marjoram Leaves 27-28

Baked Fish with Herb Stuffing 174
Beef Stew 116, 229
Bon Appétit Dip aux Herbes 70
Chicken Liver Spread 228
Gazpacho 227
Green Beans with Water Chestnuts 207
Herb French Dressing 110
Herb Pizza 201
Herb Seasoned Broccoli 220
Hot Bleu Cheese Canapés 233
Lentil Soup 84
Marinated Mushrooms 78
Old-Fashioned Herb Bread 263
Party Beef Casserole 191
Pot Roast aux Herbes 120
Potatoes with Marjoram 247
Ranch-Style Salad Dressing 97
Roast Goose Superb 159
Sausage and Wild Rice Casserole 189
Sautéed Chicken Livers 152
Scalloped Potatoes with Cheese 207
Shish Kebabs 245
Stuffed Breast of Veal 133
Trout with Seasoned Butter 234
Veal Marsala 115
Wild Rice Stuffing 163

Meat Tenderizer

Glazed Boiled Beef 117
Grilled Chuck Steak 250

Mint Flakes 28

Apple Blossom Cooler 350
Apple Chutney 387
Chicken Legs Waikiki 241
Island Fruit Punch 349
Mint Tea Hawaiian 350
Minted Mocha Float 351
Minted Peas 221
Pineapple-Grapefruit Refresher 79
Ragout of Lamb Rosemary 127
Tinted-Minted Pineapple 74

MSG (Monosodium Glutamate)

American French Dressing 110
Asparagus Oriental 213
Baked Beans Bar-B-Q 242
Baked Chicken Oriental 146
Baked Fish with Herb Stuffing 174
Baked Stuffed Eggplant 214
Barbecued Chicken 246
Beef and Noodle Casserole 192
Bologna Pinwheels 75
Broiled Chicken 145
Brown Sauce 366
Caesar Salad 101
Canneloni 187
Caper Sauce 373
Carrots Vichy 218
Cheese and Caviar Croutelettes 67
Cheese Soufflé 202
Chicken Corn Soup 92
Chicken en Casserole 144
Chicken Legs Waikiki 241
Chicken Salad 102
Chicken Tarragon 146
Chili Broiled Chicken 145
Chili con Carne 190
Chinese Stuffed Mushrooms 73
Chinese Style Spareribs 241
Coriander Broiled Chicken 145
Corn and Pepper Stroganoff 215

Cornish Hens with Fruited Rice Stuffing 143
Country Kitchen Potato Salad 107
Country Style Venison Steak 136
Crab Meat Dunk 65
Crab Salad 99
Cream of Zucchini Soup 88
Creamed Onions 219
Creamed Spinach 211
Creamy Roquefort Dressing 108
Crown Roast of Lamb 126
Curried Chicken Balls 72
Curry Dip 80
Dill Sauce 370
Dilled Fish Fillets 243
Dilly of a Dip 70
East Indian Lamb Curry 126
Egg Salad 102
Eggplant Florentine with Beef 188
Fiesta Egg Salad 102
French Dressing 110
Fried Chicken Curry 152
Garden Vegetable Salad 100
Gingered Crown Roast 126
Green Goddess Dressing 109
Herb Broiled Tomatoes 220
Herb French Dressing 110
Herb-Roasted Rack of Lamb 124
Herbed Crown Roast 126
Herbed Giblet Sauce 366
Herbed Minute Steaks 118
Herbed Potatoes 247
Honey-Glazed Pork Shoulder 130
Hot Canapés 72
Indonesian Spareribs 129
Kidneys in Sherry Sauce 137
Lamb in Gingered Cranberry Sauce 125
Lamb Kebabs 125
Lamb Shanks Divine 127
Lasagne 194
Lima-Sausage Casserole 191
Liver Pâté Bon Appétit 73
Manhattan Clam Chowder 89
Marjoram Meat Balls 70
Meat Loaf Baked in Sauce 119
Minted Peas 221
Mulligatawny 87
Mushroom Sauce 367
Okra Southern Style 211
Onion Sauce 366
Old-Fashioned Chicken and Dumplings 151
Old-Fashioned Sauerbraten 120
Old-Fashioned Vegetable Soup 92
Oyster Stew 84
Peppered Steak 250
Peppered Tenderloin 119
Pizza Sauce 364
Pork Chops à l'Orange 129
Pork Mandarin 128
Pot Roast aux Herbes 120
Potato-Fennel Salad 107
Quiche Lorraine 66
Ragout of Lamb Rosemary 127
Ranch-Style Salad Dressing 97
Red Cocktail Sauce 367
Ris de Veau à la Crème 136
Roast Goose Superb 159
Roast Turkey Supreme 160
Roasted Dilly Corn 248
Rolled Rump Roast 240
Roquefort Dressing 111
Saltimbocca 133
Sauerbraten with Potato Dumplings 121
Sautéed Mushrooms 216
Savory Onion Rounds 65
Scallops and Mushrooms en Brochette 179
Sea Food Crêpes 175
Sesame Steaks 123
Shish Kebabs 245
Shrimp and Lobster with Sauce Caviar 180
South-of-the-Border Dressing 110
Spaghetti Sauce 364
Spaghetti with Superb Meat Sauce 197
Spanish Rice 196
Spiced Tongue 135
Spicy Barbecue Sauce 372
Swiss Steak 124
Texas Barbecued Beef 195
Tomato Juice Cocktail 68
Tomato Sauce 361
Truffled Chicken Breasts Elégante 154
Truffle Sauce 373
Veal Birds 132
Veal Cutlets Viennese 132
Veal Parmigiana 131
Welsh Rabbit 203

Mustard, dry 29

American French Dressing 110
Asparagus Parmesan 222
Baked Beans Bar-B-Q 242
Baked Eggs Florentine 185
Baked Fish with Herb Stuffing 174
Barbecued Baked Beans 209
Barbecued Bologna Roll 250
Broiled Clams 77
Caesar Salad 101
Cardamom Cream Dressing 108
Cauliflower with Creamy Cheese Sauce 208
Celery Seed Dressing 108
Cheese and Caviar Croutelettes 67
Cheese Soufflé 202
Chicken Curry in Avocado 147
Chicken Curry in Papaya 147
Chicken Salad 102
Chili Sauce 379
Chinese Style Spareribs 241
Cocktail Meatballs in Red Wine 64
Coleslaw Bon Appétit 104
Coquilles Saint-Jacques 76
Corn Pudding 215
Corn Relish 380
Country Kitchen Potato Salad 107
Crab Cakes 177
Crab Imperial 170
Crab Salad 99
Creamed Clams 172
Creamed Onions 219
Creamy Coleslaw 104
Creamy Mustard Sauce 365
Creamy Roquefort Dressing 108
Crock Pot Beans 230
Crown Roast of Lamb 126
Deviled Crab 176
Deviled Lobster Tails 170
Dill Macaroni Salad 103
Duckling à l'Orange 157
East Indian Lamb Curry 126
Easter Egg Casserole 202
Egg Salad 102
Eggs à la Goldenrod 186
Fiesta Egg Salad 102
French Dressing 110
Garden Vegetable Salad 100
Gingered Crown Roast 126
Green Bean Salad 97
Ham Slice Delicious 241
Hamburger De Luxe 117
Herb French Dressing 110
Herb Roquefort Dip 66
Herbed Crown Roast 126
Herbed Garlic and Cheese Bread 231
Hollandaise Sauce 371
Honey Glazed Ham 131
Hot Canapés 72
Hot Cheese Snacks 227
Hot Chinese Mustard 368
Italian Dressing 111
Lamaze Dressing 109
Liver Pâté Bon Appétit 73
Macaroni and Cheese 199
Meat Loaf with Mushrooms 122
Mustard Pickles 384
Old Fashioned Baked Beans 209
Outdoor Chefs' Grillburgers 249
Pan-Fried Fish 177
Pâté de Foie en Aspic 67
Poppy Seed Dressing 109
Pork Chops Luau 242
Pork Mandarin 128
Pot Roast aux Herbes 120
Potato-Fennel Salad 107
Potatoes au Gratin 223
Roast Goose Superb 159
Roast Turkey Supreme 160
Roasted Fiesta Corn 248
Rolled Rib Roast 251
Rolled Rib Roast Royale 123
Roquefort Dressing 111
Rosemary Roast 251
Rye Herb Bread 267
Sauce Piquant 368
Sauerkraut Caraway 210
Sautéed Chicken Livers Rosé 152
Savory Onions Rounds 65
Savory Salmon Loaf 180
Sea Food Crêpes 175
Sesame Cheese Ball 68
Shrimp and Lobster with Sauce Caviar 180
Shrimp Sautéed in Herb Butter 177
Sole Meunière 172
Sour Cream Mustard Sauce 360
South-of-the-Border Dressing 110

Special Turkey Sandwich on Waffles 232
Spice Burgers 249
Spiced Baked Ham Slice 128
Spiced Shrimp Maison 78
Spicy Barbecue Sauce 372
Steak Teriyaki 239
Stuffed Celery Sticks 79
Stuffed Pork Chops 129
Sweet-Sour Mustard Sauce 372
Swiss Steak 124
Tarragon Tuna Salad 99
Tartar Sauce 371
Texas Barbecued Beef 195
Thousand Island Pickles 386
Thyme Roast 251
Tomato Relish 381
Tomato-Vegetable Soup 91
Tropical Barbecue Sauce 373
Truffled Chicken Breasts Elégante 154
Tuna and Tomato Mold 107
Tuna Croquettes 179
Turkey Pot Pie 161
Veal Birds 132
Waldorf Salad 106
Welsh Rabbit 203
Whipped Lemon Butter 369
White Sauce Supreme 360
Zesty Stuffed Frankfurters 137
Zippy Tomato Juice 354

Mustard Seed 29
Apple Chutney 387
Bread and Butter Pickles 381
Cantaloupe Pickles 382
Chow-Chow 379
Dill Pickles 383
Dilled Green Beans 383
Dixie Relish 380
Mango Chutney 387
Marinated Mushrooms 78
Mixed Pickles 384
Old-Fashioned Sauerbraten 120
Peach Chutney 389
Pickle Relish 381
Thousand Island Pickles 386
Tomato Relish 381

Nutmeg, ground 29-30
Apple Butter 389
Apple Cobbler 271
Apple Dumplings 282
Applesauce Cake 298
Apricot Duckling 142
Apricot Pudding 285
Apricot Squares 340
Bananas Flambé 272
Banbury Tarts 319
Beef Stroganoff 116
Blackberry Jam Cake 291
Broccoli Soufflé 214
Broiled Fish Amandine 174
Broiled Spiced Topping 302
Brown Sauce 366
Brussels Sprouts with Chestnuts 211
Caper Sauce 373
Cardamon Rice Pudding 276
Cherry Pie 311
Chicken Cantonese 150
Chicken en Casserole 144
Chicken or Turkey Soup 85
Chicken Paprika 150
Chicken Salad 102
Chocolate Carrot Cake 289
Cinnamon-Pineapple Buns 260
Cinnamon-Vanilla Milk Shake 354
Cool Lemon Soufflé 273
Coq au Vin 149
Country Inn Pheasant 157
Country Style Venison Steak 136
Creamed Chicken Supreme 149
Creamy Rice Pudding 276
Crème Anglaise 375
Dark Fruit Cake 294
Date Roll 337
Date Sticks 333
Deep Dish Apple Pie 308
Deep Dish Peach Pie 310
Devil's Food Cake 296
Doughnuts 266
Dutch Apple Pie 305
East Indian Lamb Curry 126
Easy Mincemeat Pie 318
Eggnog 350
Eggs à la Goldenrod 186
English Plum Pudding 284
Excellent Prune Cake 292
Extra-Special Waffles 227
Festive Lime Pie 315
Floating Island Meringues 280
Fluffy Snow Peak Frosting 299
French Hot Chocolate 352
French Mint Chocolate 352
Fried Pies 316
Frosted Nutmeg Logs 335
Fruit Cake Cookies 327
Ginger Cracker Crust 315
Ginger Glazed Carrots 208
Grilled Bananas 245
Hamburger De Luxe 117
Herb Roquefort Dip 66
Herb Seasoned Broccoli 220
Herbed Giblet Sauce 366
Herbed Minute Steaks 118
Holiday Cranberry Punch 355
Holiday Nutmeg Sauce 361
Honey Spice Butter 365
Hot Canapés 72
Individual Chili Meat Loaves 234
Layered Orange-Cranberry Mold 105
Liver Pâté Bon Appétit 73
Macaroni and Cheese 199
Mango Chutney 387
Meat Loaf Baked in Sauce 119
Mincemeat Refrigerator Cookies 335
Mulled Wine 352
Nutmeg Glaze 300
Nutmeg Sauce 363
Old-Fashioned Spice Cake 293
Old-Fashioned Tea Cakes 327
Old-Time Mincemeat 388
Onion Sauce 366
Pan-Fried Fish 177
Party Pink Fruit Salad 106
Peach Cobbler Supreme 281
Pecan Cookie Balls 329
Pineapple-Yam Kebabs 245
Pfeffernüsse 331
Philadelphia Sticky Buns 255
Potatoes au Gratin 223
Prune-Filled Squares 340
Pudding Sauce 363
Pumpkin Pie 308
Quiche Lorraine 66
Raisin Spice Cupcakes 296
Refrigerator Spice Cookies 328
Rhubarb Custard Pie 320
Roast Goose Superb 159
Roast Leg of Lamb 124
Roast Turkey Supreme 160
Roasted Dilly Corn 248
Rocks 329
Sautéed Cabbage and Apples 216
Sautéed Chicken Livers 152
Sea Food Crêpes 175
Sesame Toffee Bars 341
Shrimp and Lobster with Sauce Caviar 180
Snappy Cheese-wiches 200
Sour Cream Dip for Fresh Fruit 63
Spaghetti with Superb Meat Sauce 197
Spice Burgers 249
Spice Chiffon Cake 295
Spice Muffins 265
Spiced Baked Ham Slice 128
Spiced Bread Pudding 275
Spiced Chestnut Stuffing 165
Spiced Coffee Ice Cream 276
Spiced Graham Cracker Crust 319
Spiced Grape Punch 347
Spiced Jelly Roll 290
Spiced Mixed Nuts 330
Spiced Tea 349
Spicy Barbecue Sauce 372
Spicy Custard Pie 315
Spicy Ice Cream Pie 306
Spicy Oatmeal Cookies 334
Spicy Pastry 317
Spinach Soup 83
Strawberry-Rhubarb Crisp 283
Stuffed Roast Capon 153
Swedish Fruit Soup 86
Tea House Punch 348
Traditional Wassail Bowl 354
Truffled Chicken Breasts Elégante 154
Truffle Sauce 373
Vanilla-Rum Frosting 335
Veal Orloff 115
Veal Scaloppine 135
Vegetable Kebabs 248
Welsh Pork Cake 298
Wiener Schnitzel 135
Wonderful Apple Pie 309

Onion, Instant Minced 30-32
Baked Chicken Oriental 146
Baked Eggs Florentine 185
Baked Fish with Herb Stuffing 174
Baked Stuffed Tomatoes 232
Barbecued Baked Beans 209
Barbecued Chicken 246

Beef and Noodle Casserole 192
Beef Stew 229
Beef Stroganoff 116
Bon Appétit Dip aux Herbes 70
Broccoli Soufflé 214
Busy Day Casserole 203
Cabbage Rolls 190
Cannelloni 187
Celery Victor 79
Cheese Dip Caraway 77
Chicken Cacciatore 145
Chicken Curry in Avocado 147
Chicken Curry in Papaya 147
Chicken en Casserole 144
Chicken Liver Spread 228
Chicken Tarragon 146
Chicken-Vegetable Soup 231
Chili-Cheese Burgers 249
Chuck Wagon Franks 240
Cocktail Meatballs in Red Wine 64
Cold Cucumber Soup 228
Coquilles Saint-Jacques 76
Corn Pudding 215
Cornish Hens Stuffed with Wild Rice 156
Country-Good Baked Squash 217
Country Kitchen Potato Salad 107
Crab Meat Dunk 65
Crab Newburg 169
Crab Stuffed Mushrooms 80
Cream of Zucchini Soup 88
Crock Pot Beans 230
Cucumbers in Sour Cream 102
Curried Lamb Chops Bengal 242
Curried Turkey Amandine 154
Delectable Green Beans 221
Deviled Crab 176
Deviled Lobster Tails 170
Dill Burgers 249
Dill Macaroni Salad 103
Easter Egg Casserole 202
Easy Saffron Bread 267
Eggplant Florentine with Beef 188
Fish Poached in Court Bouillon 181
Fresh Corn Sauté 219
Fried Rice 201
Garden Vegetable Salad 100
Gazpacho 227
Hamburgers 249
Herb Burgers 249
Herb Chicken 147
Herbed Garlic and Cheese Bread 231
Holiday Stuffing 164
Hot Canapés 72
Hot Exotic Curry Sauce 362
Hot 'n' Tangy Burgers 249
Hot Turkey Salad 234
Indian Rice 194
Individual Chili Meatloaves 234
Indonesian Spareribs 129
Italian Dressing 111
Italian Style Peas 212
Kidneys in Sherry Sauce 137
Lamb Kebabs 125
Lamb Shanks Divine 127
Lasagne 194
Lima Bean Casserole 212
Lima-Sausage Casserole 191
Liver Pâté Bon Appétit 73
Lobster Cantonese 178
Manicotti 233
Meat Loaf Baked in Sauce 119
Meat Loaf with Mushrooms 122
Mephisto Ham Dip 66
Mock Enchilada Casserole 188
Mulligatawny 87
Mushroom-Rice Stuffing 162
New England Clam Chowder 90
New Orleans Shrimp Gumbo 86
Noodles Romanoff 193
Old-Fashioned Baked Beans 209
Onion Butter 365
Oriental Burgers 249
Outdoor Chefs' Grillburgers 249
Oven Braised Short Ribs 122
Oysters Rockefeller 76
Pâté de Foie en Aspic 67
Peach Chutney 389
Pepper Burgers 249
Pizza Sauce 364
Potato-Fennel Salad 107
Princess Omelet 200
Quick 'n' Easy Barbecue Sauce 360
Red Hot Burgers 249
Rice Gourmet 195
Rice Pilaf 195
Rolled Rump Roast 240
Saffron Rice 196
Sauce Rémoulade 368
Sauerbraten Nibblers 63
Sauerkraut Caraway 210
Sausage and Wild Rice Casserole 189
Sausage Stuffing 164
Savory Burgers 249
Savory Fresh Ham 230
Savory Salmon Loaf 180
Savory Turkey Croquettes 155
Scallops and Mushrooms in Sherry Sauce 169
Scotch Broth 93
Sesame Burgers 249
Sesame Cheese Ball 68
Shrimp Creole 176
Spaghetti Sauce 364
Spice Burgers 249
Spiced Chestnut Stuffing 165
Spinach Soup 83
Stuffed Breast of Veal 133
Stuffed Pork Chops 129
Swedish Meat Balls 122
Swiss Steak 124
Tarragon Tuna Salad 99
Tartar Sauce 371
Tasty Cream Sauce 363
Tomato Juice Cocktail 68
Tomato Sauce 361
Veal and Wild Rice Casserole 192
Veal Birds 132
Veal Orloff 115
Veal Scaloppine 135
Wheat Pilaf 195
Zesty Stuffed Frankfurters 137
Zucchini Parmesan 207
Zucchini Sauté 212

Onion Flakes 30-32
Chili con Carne 190
Country Captain 141
Country Inn Pheasant 157
Green Bean Salad 97
Lobster Bisque Elégante 88
Old-Fashioned Chicken and Dumplings 151
Piquant Tomato Aspic 101
Spicy Barbecue Sauce 372

Onion Powder 30-32
Asparagus Parmesan 222
Baked Beans Bar-B-Q 242
Best Ever Stuffed Eggs 69
Broiled Chicken 145
Broiled Clams 77
Broiled Fish Amandine 174
Broiled Salmon with Dill 171
Brown Sauce 366
Buffet Turkey Loaf 98
Canard au Grand Marnier 158
Caper Sauce 373
Carrot and Cauliflower Casserole 235
Carrots Vichy 218
Cauliflower with Creamy Cheese Sauce 208
Chicken Kiev 148
Chicken Legs Waikiki 241
Chinese Style Spareribs 241
Coriander Broiled Chicken 145
Curried Chicken Balls 72
Dilly of a Dip 70
Egg Salad 102
Fiesta Egg Salad 102
Fillet de Sole Véronique 171
Flank Steak Western Style 251
Fried Chicken Curry 152
Frogs' Legs aux Fines Herbes 173
Frogs' Legs Provençale 173
Golden Cream of Carrot Soup 91
Green Goddess Dressing 109
Hamburger De Luxe 117
Herb Pizza 201
Herb-Roasted Rack of Lamb 124
Herb Seasoned Broccoli 220
Herbed Giblet Sauce 366
Herbed Minute Steaks 118
Italian Pizza 201
Macaroni and Cheese 199
Marjoram Meat Balls 70
Okra Southern Style 211
Onion Sauce 366
Oriental Spiced Shrimp 78
Oven Fried Chicken 153
Pan-Fried Fish 177
Poppy Seed Dressing 109
Ris de Veau à la Crème 136
Roast Goose Superb 159
Roast Leg of Lamb 124
Roast Turkey Supreme 160
Sautéed Chicken Livers 152
Sautéed Frogs' Legs 173
Sea Food Crêpes 175
Sesame Steaks 123
Sour Cream Topping 368

Spaghetti with Superb Meat Sauce 197
Special Turkey Sandwich on Waffles 232
Superb Scalloped Oysters 178
Sweet-Sour Pork 130
Teriyaki Sauce 371
Tomato Soup Oregano 85
Truffle Sauce 373
Veal Cutlets Viennese 132
Vichyssoise 89
Welsh Rabbit 203
Zesty Stuffed Frankfurters 137
Zippy Tomato Juice 354
Onion Salt 30-32
Beef Teriyaki 71
Bonfire Green Beans 246
Celery Seed Dressing 108
Charcoal Grilled Steak 247
Cheese and Caviar Croutelettes 67
Creamed Clams 172
Creamed Spinach 211
Coleslaw Bon Appétit 104
Curried Nibblers 69
Fish Fillets in a Package 243
Guacamole 65
Marinated Mushrooms 78
Oregano Rolls 244
Potatoes with Marjoram 247
Ranch-Style Salad Dressing 97
Rolled Rib Roast 251
Rolled Rib Roast Royale 123
Rosemary Roast 251
Sauerbraten with Potato Dumplings 121
Shish Kebabs 245
Shrimp and Lobster with Sauce Caviar 180
Snappy Cheese-wiches 200
Sole Meunière 172
Sour Cream Mustard Sauce 360
Thyme Roast 251
Tuna Croquettes 179
Turkey Pot Pie 141
Turkey Rolls Delicious 155
Veal Marsala 115
Onions, Chopped Instant 30-32
Apple Chutney 387
Arroz con Pollo 144
Baked Stuffed Eggplant 214
Basic Bread Stuffing 162
Bouillabaisse 90
Brunswick Stew 186
Canard au Grand Marnier 158
Celery and Carrots in Parsley Cream 222
Ceviche 71
Chestnut Stuffing 162
Chicken Cantonese 150
Chicken or Turkey Soup 85
Chunky Chili 231
Corn Chowder 83
Country Inn Pheasant 157
Country Style Venison Steak 136
East Indian Lamb Curry 126
Fillet Neapolitan 172
French Onion Soup 84
Herb Stuffing 162
Hungarian Goulash 118
Lamb in Gingered Cranberry Sauce 125
Lentil Soup 84
Manhattan Clam Chowder 89
Mexican Skillet Dinner 193
Minestrone 87
Old-Fashioned Sauerbraten 120
Old-Fashioned Vegetable Soup 92
Old South Corn Bread Stuffing 163
Onion Sauce 366
Oyster Stuffing 162
Paella 189
Party Beef Casserole 191
Peach Chutney 389
Pot Roast with Vegetables 230
Quick 'n' Easy Stuffing 161
Ragout of Lamb Rosemary 127
Salmon Luncheon Pie 199
Sauerbraten with Potato Dumplings 121
Sautéed Cabbage and Apples 216
Savory Stuffed Peppers 193
Savory Stuffing 163
Sesame Stuffing 165
Spanish Rice 196
Spiced Tongue 135
Stewed Tomatoes with Oregano 210
Sweet-Sour Red Cabbage 221
Texas Barbecued Beef 195
Toasted Onion Dip 75
Turkey Pot Pie 161
Veal Paprika 134
Wild Rice Stuffing 163
Orange Peel 26-27
Apricot Squares 340
Autumn Spiced Cider 349
Blueberry Crumble 307
Bouillabaisse 90
Broiled Spiced Topping 302
Canard au Grand Marnier 158
Candied Sweet Potatoes 218
Candied Sweet Potatoes and Apples 218
Cinnamon-Pecan Biscuits 262
Coconut Crust 317
Cranberry Chiffon Pie 312
Cranberry Nut Bread 229
Crêpes Suzette 277
Crown Roast of Lamb 126
Danish Pastry 259
Date Roll 337
Duckling à l'Orange 157
English Plum Pudding 284
Fried Pies 316
Ginger Dessert Waffles 281
Gingered Crown Roast 126
Glögg 348
Ham Slice Delicious 241
Harvard Beets 219
Heavenly Hash 283
Herbed Crown Roast 126
Holiday Chews 338
Lane Cake 293
Lebkuchen 333
Orange Bread Custard 285
Orange Butter 365
Orange Butter Gems 331
Orange Glaze 300
Orange Glazed Ham 131
Orange Muffins 265
Orange Whipped Cream Topping 301
Party Biscuits 266
Party Pink Fruit Salad 106
Pork Chops à l'Orange 129
Pork Mandarin 128
Prune-Filled Squares 340
Rhubarb Custard Pie 320
Spice Chiffon Cake 295
Spiced Mixed Nuts 330
Spiced Raisin Sauce 374
Steamed Date Pudding 278
Stuffed Breast of Veal 133
Sugared Nuts 339
Sweet Potato-Pineapple Rings 218
Welsh Pork Cake 298
Oregano, ground 32
Broiled Salmon with Dill 171
Cannelloni 187
Eggplant Florentine with Beef 188
Grilled Tomatoes 248
Herb Pizza 201
Italian Pizza 201
Lamb in Gingered Cranberry Sauce 125
Meat Loaf Baked in Sauce 119
Tomato Soup Oregano 85
Tuna and Tomato Mold 107
Zucchini Sauté 212
Oregano Leaves 32
Cannelloni 187
Chunky Chili 231
Herb Broiled Tomatoes 220
Herb French Dressing 110
Herb Pizza 201
Herbed Garlic and Cheese Bread 231
Herbed Minute Steaks 118
Italian Dressing 111
Italian Pizza 201
Italian Spaghetti Sauce 185
Lamb Kebabs 125
Lamb Shank Divine 127
Lasagne 194
Marinated Artichoke Hearts 74
Marinated Veal Steak 239
Oregano Batter Bread 258
Oregano Rolls 244
Oriental Spiced Shrimp 78
Pizza Sauce 364
Pot Roast aux Herbes 120
Pot Roast with Vegetables 230
Spaghetti Sauce 364
Spaghetti with Superb Meat Sauce 197
Stewed Tomatoes with Oregano 210
Tomato-Vegetable Soup 91
Veal Parmigiana 131
Wild Rice Stuffing 163
Paprika 32-33
American French Dressing 110
Best Ever Stuffed Eggs 69
Broiled Fish Amandine 174

Broiled Salmon with Dill 171
Buffet Turkey Loaf 98
Cauliflower with Creamy Cheese Sauce 208
Celery Seed Dressing 108
Chicken Paprika 150
Chicken Salad 102
Chicken Tarragon 146
Clove-Studded Onions 213
Coleslaw Bon Appétit 104
Coq au Vin 149
Country Inn Pheasant 157
Crab Imperial 170
Crab Salad 99
Cream of Zucchini Soup 88
Creamy Coleslaw 104
Deviled Lobster Tails 170
Easter Egg Casserole 202
Eggs à la Goldenrod 186
Fillet de Sole Véronique 171
Fish Poached in Court Bouillon 181
Ham Slice Delicious 241
Herb Broiled Chicken 145
Herb Chicken 147
Herbed Minute Steaks 118
Hungarian Goulash 118
Lamaze Dressing 109
Macaroni and Cheese 199
Mock Enchilada Casserole 188
Oregano Rolls 244
Oven Fried Chicken 153
Oyster Stew 84
Paella 189
Pan-Fried Fish 177
Paprika Butter 366
Party Beef Casserole 191
Pork Chops à l'Orange 129
Potatoes au Gratin 223
Potatoes with Marjoram 247
Roast Turkey Supreme 160
Roquefort Dressing 111
Sautéed Chicken Livers 152
Savory Stuffed Peppers 193
Shrimp and Lobster with Sauce Caviar 180
Smoky Chicken 145
Sole Epicurean 173
Sole Meunière 172
South-of-the-Border Dressing 110
Spicy Barbecue Sauce 372
Stuffed Celery Sticks 79
Surprise Cheese Puffs 74
Trout with Seasoned Butter 234
Veal and Wild Rice in Casserole 192
Veal Paprika 134
Veal Scaloppine 135
Viennese Noodles au Gratin 198
Welsh Rabbit 203
Whipped Lemon Butter 369

Parsley Flakes 33

Arroz con Pollo 144
Baked Eggs Florentine 185
Baked Fish with Herb Stuffing 174
Baked Stuffed Tomatoes 232
Basic Bread Stuffing 162
Beef Stew 116
Best Ever Stuffed Eggs 69
Beurre Noir 362
Bouillabaisse 90
Broiled Fish Amandine 174
Brunswick Stew 186
Canard au Grand Marnier 158
Caper Sauce 373
Carrot and Cauliflower Casserole 235
Carrots Vichy 218
Celery and Carrots in Parsley Cream 222
Celery Victor 79
Cheese Omelet aux Herbes 196
Chestnut Stuffing 162
Chicken Corn Soup 92
Coq au Vin 149
Cornish Hens Stuffed with Wild Rice 156
Cornish Hens with Fruited Rice Stuffing 143
Country-Good Baked Squash 217
Crab Cakes 177
Cream of Zucchini Soup 88
Curried Sea Food Salad 99
Eggplant Parmigiana 209
Fillet Neapolitan 172
Frogs' Legs aux Fines Herbes 173
Frogs' Legs Provençale 173
Gazpacho 227
Ginger Glazed Carrots 208
Green Goddess Dressing 109
Herb Burgers 249
Herb Butter 369
Herb Chicken 147
Herb French Dressing 110
Herb Stuffing 162
Herb Waffles 264
Italian Dressing 111
Italian Style Peas 212
Lima-Sausage Casserole 191
Liver Pâté Bon Appétit 73
Manicotti 233
Mephisto Ham Dip 66
Minestrone 87
Mulligatawny 87
Mushroom-Rice Stuffing 162
Mushroom Sauce 367
Old South Corn Bread Stuffing 163
Oriental Spiced Shrimp 78
Osso Bucco 134
Oyster Stuffing 162
Oysters Rockefeller 76
Paella 189
Parsley-Almond Sauce 372
Parsley Biscuits 268
Parsley Buttered Potatoes 210
Pâté de Foie en Aspic 67
Quick 'n' Easy Stuffing 161
Ranch-Style Salad Dressing 97
Rice Gourmet 195
Roast Goose Superb 159
Rye Herb Bread 267
Salmon Luncheon Pie 199
Sauce Rémoulade 368
Savory Salmon Loaf 180
Savory Turkey Croquettes 155
Scallops and Mushrooms in Sherry Sauce 169
Shrimp Creole 176
Shrimp Sautéed in Herb Butter 177
Spaghetti with Superb Meat Sauce 197
Spiced Chestnut Stuffing 165
Superb Scalloped Oysters 178
Tarragon Tuna Salad 99
Tomato Sauce 361
Truffle Sauce 373
Veal Birds 132
Veal Paprika 134
Wiener Schnitzel 135
Zucchini Sauté 212

Pepper, Coarse Grind Black 33-35

Arroz con Pollo 144
Cornish Hens Stuffed with Wild Rice 156
Flank Steak Western Style 251
Glazed Boiled Beef 117
Green Bean Salad 97
Grilled Chuck Steak 250
Herb Dumplings 151
Herb Pizza 201
Hungarian Goulash 118
Indian Rice 194
Italian Pizza 201
Lamb Kebabs 125
Lentil Soup 84
Manhattan Clam Chowder 89
Minestrone 87
Old-Fashioned Chicken Dumplings 151
Onion Rounds Delicious 251
Osso Bucco 134
Peppered Steak 250
Peppered Tenderloin 119
Roast Whole Tenderloin 123
Rolled Rib Roast 251
Rosemary Roast 251
Sauce Béarnaise 374
Steak Teriyaki 239
Superb Scalloped Oysters 178
Thyme Roast 251
Turkey Creole 160
Turkey Pot Pie 161

Pepper, Cracked Black 33-35

Chef's Salad Bowl 98
Cucumbers in Sour Cream 102
Flank Steak Western Style 251
Hickory Smoked Potatoes 247
Peppered Steak 250
Pot Roast aux Herbes 120
Sweet-Sour Cucumbers with Onions 106

Pepper, Ground Black 33-35

Apple Cider Squash 217
Arroz con Pollo 144
Asparagus Parmesan 222
Baked Acorn Squash 217
Baked Beans Bar-B-Q 242
Baked Chicken Oriental 146
Baked Eggs Florentine 185
Baked Stuffed Eggplant 214
Baked Stuffed Tomatoes 232
Basic Bread Stuffing 162

Barbecued Baked Beans 209
Barbecued Chicken 246
Beef and Noodle Casserole 192
Beef Stew 116, 229
Bouillabaisse 90
Broccoli Soufflé 214
Broiled Fish Amandine 174
Brown Sauce 366
Brunswick Stew 186
Brussels Sprouts with Chestnuts 211
Busy Day Casserole 203
Cabbage Rolls 190
Canard au Grand Marnier 158
Cannelloni 187
Carrot and Cauliflower Casserole 235
Celery and Carrots in Parsley Cream 222
Charcoal Grilled Steak 247
Cheese Omelet aux Herbes 196
Chestnut Stuffing 162
Chicken Cacciatore 145
Chicken Corn Soup 92
Chicken en Casserole 144
Chicken Italienne 146
Chicken Kiev 148
Chicken Legs Waikiki 241
Chicken Liver Spread 228
Chicken Paprika 150
Chicken Rosemary 148
Chicken Tarragon 146
Chicken-Vegetable Soup 231
Chili-Cheese Burgers 249
Chuck Wagon Franks 240
Cocktail Meatballs in Red Wine 64
Coq au Vin 149
Country Captain 141
Country-Good Baked Squash 217
Country Style Venison Steak 136
Crab Cakes 177
Crab Imperial 170
Crock Pot Beans 230
Crown Roast of Lamb 126
Curried Lamb Chops Bengal 242
Curried Turkey Amandine 154
Curry Butter 374
Delectable Green Beans 221
Dill Burgers 249
Dill Flavored Potatoes 247
Dilled Fish Fillets 243
Duckling à l'Orange 157
Easter Egg Casserole 202
Eggplant Florentine with Beef 188
Eggplant Parmigiana 209
Fillet Neapolitan 172
French Onion Soup 84
Fried Chicken Curry 152
Fried Rice 201
Garlic Butter 367
Gingered Crown Roast 126
Green Beans with Water Chestnuts 207
Guacamole 65
Hamburger De Luxe 117
Hamburgers 249
Herb Burgers 249
Herb Butter 369
Herb Chicken 147
Herb Stuffing 162
Herb-Roasted Rack of Lamb 124
Herbed Crown Roast 126
Herbed Fish Fillets 243
Herbed Giblet Sauce 366
Herbed Minute Steaks 118
Holiday Stuffing 164
Honey-Glazed Pork Shoulder 130
Hot Bleu Cheese Canapés 233
Hot Canapés 72
Hot 'n' Tangy Burgers 249
Hot Turkey Salad 234
Individual Chili Meatloaves 234
Indonesian Spareribs 129
Italian Spaghetti Sauce 185
Italian Style Peas 212
Kidneys in Sherry Sauce 137
Lamaze Dressing 109
Lamb in Gingered Cranberry Sauce 125
Lamb Shanks Divine 127
Lima Bean Casserole 212
Lobster Cantonese 178
Manicotti 233
Marnated Veal Steak 239
Marjoram Meat Balls 70
Meat Loaf Baked in Sauce 119
Mephisto Ham Dip 66
Mock Enchilada Casserole 188
Mulligatawny 87
Mushroom Rice Stuffing 162
Mushroom Sauce 367
Okra Southern Style 211
Old-Fashioned Baked Beans 209
Old-Fashioned Chicken and Dumplings 151
Old-Fashioned Sauerbraten 120
Old-Fashioned Vegetable Soup 92
Old South Corn Bread Stuffing 163
Old-Time Mincemeat 388
Onion Sauce 366
Oriental Burgers 249
Outdoor Chefs, Grillburgers 249
Oven Braised Short Ribs 122
Oven Fried Chicken 153
Oyster Stew 84
Oyster Stuffing 162
Paella 189
Pan-Fried Fish 177
Paprika Butter 366
Parsley-Almond Sauce 372
Party Beef Casserole 191
Pepper Burgers 249
Pfeffernüsse 331
Pizza Sauce 364
Pork Chops à l'Orange 129
Potatoes with Marjoram 247
Quick 'n' Easy Stuffing 161
Quik 'n' Easy Barbecue Sauce 360
Ranch-Style Salad Dressing 97
Red Hot Burgers 249
Rice Gourmet 195
Roast Goose Superb 159
Roast Leg of Lamb 124
Roast Pheasant 156
Rolled Rib Roast Royale 123
Roquefort Dressing 111
Rumaki 77
Rye Herb Bread 267
Saffron Rice 196
Salmon Luncheon Pie 199
Saltimbocca 133
Sauerbraten with Potato Dumplings 121
Sausage Stuffing 164
Sautéed Chicken Livers 152
Sautéed Mushrooms 216
Savory Burgers 249
Savory Fresh Ham 230
Savory Salmon Loaf 180
Savory Stuffing 163
Savory Turkey Croquettes 155
Scallops and Mushrooms en Brochette 179
Scallops and Mushrooms in Sherry Sauce 169
Sea Food Crêpes 175
Sesame Burgers 249
Sesame Steaks 123
Sesame Stuffing 165
Shish Kebabs 245
Shrimp and Lobster with Sauce Caviar 180
Spaghetti Sauce 364
Spahetti with Superb Meat Sauce 197
Spanish Rice 196
Spice Burgers 249
Spiced Chestnut Stuffing 165
Spicy Barbecue Sauce 372
Stewed Tomatoes with Oregano 210
Stuffed Pork Chops 129
Stuffed Roast Capon 153
Swedish Meat Balls 122
Sweet-Sour Red Cabbage 221
Swiss Steak 124
Tomato Juice Cocktail 68
Tomato Sauce 361
Tomato Vegetable Soup 91
Truffled Chicken Breasts Elégante 154
Tuna Croquettes 179
Turkey Pot Pie with Vegetables 141
Veal Birds 132
Veal Cutlets Viennese 132
Veal Marsala 115
Veal Orloff 115
Veal Paprika 134
Veal Parmigiana 131
Veal Scaloppine 135
Vegetable Kebabs 248
Wiener Schnitzel 135
Wild Rice Stuffing 163
Zucchini Sauté 212
Pepper, White 33-35
American French Dressing 110
Apricot Duckling 142
Asparagus Oriental 213
Baked Eggs Florentine 185
Best Ever Stuffed Eggs 69
Beurre Noir 362
Bologna Pinwheels 75
Broiled Salmon with Dill 171
Caper Sauce 373

Cardamom Cream Dressing 108
Cauliflower with Creamy Cheese Sauce 208
Ceviche 71
Cheese and Caviar Croutelettes 67
Chicken Salad 102
Corn Chowder 83
Corn Pudding 215
Country Kitchen Potato Salad 107
Crab Newburg 169
Crab Salad 99
Cream of Zucchini Soup 88
Creamed Chicken Supreme 149
Creamed Onions 219
Creamy Coleslaw 104
Creamy Curry Sauce 369
Creamy Mustard Sauce 365
Creamy Roquefort Dessing 108
Deviled Lobster Tails 170
Dill Macaroni Salad 103
Dill Sauce 370
Egg Salad 102
Eggs à la Goldenrod 186
Fiesta Egg Salad 102
Fillet de Sole Véronique 171
Fish Poached in Court Bouillon 181
French Dressing 110
Fresh Corn Sauté 219
Frogs' Legs aux Fines Herbes 173
Frogs' Legs Provençale 173
Garden Vegetable Salad 100
Herb French Dressing 110
Hollandaise Sauce 371
Italian Dressing 111
Macaroni and Cheese 199
Mock Enchilada Casserole 188
New England Clam Chowder 90
Oyster Stew 84
Paprika Butter 366
Potato-Fennel Salad 107
Potatoes au Gratin 223
Rice Gourmet 195
Ris de Veau à la Creme 136
Roast Turkey Supreme 160
Salmon Luncheon Pie 199
Sauce Piquant 368
Sauerbraten with Potato Dumplings 121
Sautéed Frogs' Legs 173
Scalloped Potatoes with Cheese 207
Sea Food Crêpes 175
Shrimp and Lobster with Sauce Caviar 180
Shrimp Salad 98
Sole Epicurean 173
Sole Meunière 172
Sour Cream Mustard Sauce 360
South-of-the-Border Dressing 110
Spinach Soup 83
Tarragon Tuna Salad 99
Tasty Cream Sauce 363
Trout with Seasoned Butter 234
Truffle Sauce 373
Tuna Casserole with Batter Topping 198
Veal Orloff 115
Vichyssoise 89
White Sauce Supreme 360
Zucchini Sauté 212

Peppercorn (whole Black Pepper) 33-35

Caesar Salad 101
Celery Victor 79
Chicken or Turkey Soup 85
Consomé Royale 92
Dill Pickles 383
Lobster Bisque Elégante 88
Mustard Pickles 384
Old-Fashioned Sauerbraten 120
Oriental Spiced Shrimp 78
Piquant Tomato Aspic 101
Rolled Rump Roast 240
Sauerbraten Nibblers 63
Scotch Broth 93
Spiced Cranberry Juice Cocktail 64
Spiced Tongue 135

Pepper, Crushed Red 35

Beef Stew 229
Ceviche 71
Chicken Cacciatore 145
Chili Sauce 379
Dilled Green Beans 383
Herb Pizza 201
Hot Turkey Salad 234
Italian Pizza 201
Kosher Dill Pickles 383
Minestrone 87
Mixed Pickles 384
Pizza Sauce 364
Princess Omelet 200
Red Hot Burgers 249
Spaghetti Sauce 364
Spaghetti with Superb Meat Sauce 197
Spiced Shrimp 78
Spiced Tongue 135

Pepper, ground Red 35

Apple Chutney 387
Arroz con Pollo 144
Broiled Salmon Tarragon 171
Broccoli Soufflé 214
Brunswick Stew 186
Cannelloni 187
Caper Sauce 373
Cheese Soufflé 202
Chicken Liver Spread 228
Chinese Stuffed Mushrooms 73
Chow-Chow 379
Chuck Wagon Franks 240
Coleslaw Bon Appétit 104
Corn Pudding 215
Crab Cakes 177
Crab Imperial 170
Crab Meat Dunk 65
Crab Newburg 169
Crab Salad 99
Crab Stuffed Mushrooms 80
Creamed Clams 172
Creamy Lemon-Butter Sauce 370
Cucumbers in Sour Cream 102
Curried Nibblers 69
Curry Dip 80
Deviled Crab 176
Deviled Lobster Tails 170
Dill Macaroni Salad 103
Dill Stuffed Eggs 69
Eggs à la Goldenrod 186
Herbed Potatoes 247
Hollandaise Sauce 371
Hungarian Goulash 118
Italian Dressing 111
Macaroni and Cheese 199
Mango Chutney 387
Noodles Romanoff 193
Onion Butter 365
Oysters Rockefeller 76
Peach Chutney 389
Quiche Lorraine 66
Roquefort Dressing 111
Sauce Béarnaise 374
Sauce Piquant 368
Sauce Rémoulade 368
Sautéed Cabbage and Apples 216
Sea Food Crêpes 175
Shrimp Creole 176
Shrimp Salad 98
Shrimp Sautéed in Herb Butter 177
Snappy Cheese-wiches 200
Spicy Barbecue Sauce 372
Surprise Cheese Puffs 74
Sweet-Sour Cucumbers with Onions 106
Tangy Butter 365
Tomato Relish 381
Truffle Sauce 373
Tuna Croquettes 179
Turkey Creole 160
Turkey Rolls Delicious 155
Welsh Rabbit 203

Pickling Spice 35-36

Mixed Pickles 384
Sauerbraten with Potato Dumplings 121
Spiced Shrimp 78
Sweet Cucumber Pickles 385

Poppy Seed 36

Apricot Squares 340
Buttered Noodles with Poppy Seed 197
Danish Pastry 259
Dill Ring 267
Filled Fancies 326
Golden Saffron Cake 291
Hot Bleu Cheese Canapes 233
Old-Fashioned Herb Bread 263
Parsley Biscuits 268
Poppy Seed Cake 295
Poppy Seed Dressing 109
Poppy Seed Goodies 334
Poppy Seed Pastry 317
Prune-Filled Squares 340
Veal Cutlets Viennese 132
Viennese Noodles au Gratin 198

Poultry Seasoning 37

Apricot Duckling 142
Basic Bread Stuffing 162
Chestnut Stuffing 162
Cornish Hens with Fruited Rice Stuffing 143
Creamed Chicken Supreme 149
Herb Stuffing 162
Herbed Giblet Sauce 366

Holiday Stuffing 164
Old South Corn Bread Stuffing 163
Oyster Stuffing 162
Quick 'n' Easy Stuffing 161
Roast Turkey Supreme 160
Sausage Stuffing 164
Savory Stuffing 163
Sesame Stuffing 165
Stuffed Pork Chops 129
Stuffed Roast Capon 153
Truffled Chicken Breasts Elégante 154
Turkey Pot Pie 161
Turkey Rolls Delicious 155
Veal Birds 132
Pumpkin Pie Spice 37
Candied Sweet Potatoes 218
Candied Sweet Potatoes and Apples 218
Coconut Crust 317
Date Nut Cookies 328
Harvest Pumpkin Chiffon Pie 318
Holiday Chews 338
Pumpkin Pie 308
Quick Coffee Cake 263
Spice Muffins 265
Spiced Coconut Chiffon Pie 312
Spiced Whipped Cream Topping 301
Sticky Spice Buns 262
Sweet Potato-Pecan Pie 314
Sweet Potato Pudding 216
Sweet Potatoes-Pineapple Rings 218
Velvety Pumpkin Chiffon Pie 318
Rosemary Leaves 37-38
Cannelloni 187
Celery and Carrots in Parsley Cream 222
Chicken Legs Waikiki 241
Chicken Rosemary 148
Coq au Vin 149
Corn Sticks Rosemary 258
Gingered Crown Roast 126
Herb Pizza 201
Herbed Crown Roast 126
Herbed Fish Filets 243
Italian Pizza 201
Lasagne 194
Lima-Sausage Casserole 191
Old-Fashioned Herb Bread 263
Pâté de Foie en Aspic 67
Ragout of Lamb Rosemary 127
Rosemary Roast 251
Rye Herb Bread 267
Spaghetti with Superb Meat Sauce 197
Spiced Chestnut Stuffing 165
Spiced Shrimp Maison 78
Saffron 38
Arroz con Pollo 144
Bouillabaisse 90
Chicken Corn Soup 92
Easter Egg Casserole 202
Easy Saffron Bread 267
Golden Saffron Cake 291
Indian Rice 194
Paella 189
Saffron Rice 196
Sage, rubbed or ground 39
Apricot Duckling 142
Baked Fish with Herb Stuffing 174
Canard au Grand Marnier 158
Herb Stuffing 162
Minestrone 87
Roast Turkey Supreme 160
Rye Herb Bread 267
Sage Waffles 264
Saltimbocca 133
Savory Stuffed Peppers 193
Savory Stuffing 163
Savory Turkey Croquettes 155
Spiced Chestnut Stuffing 165
Turkey Pot Pie with Vegetables 141
Veal Birds 132
Sage Leaves 39
Lamb Shanks Divine 127
Salad Herbs
Chef's Salad Bowl 98
Herb French Dressing 110
Savory 39-40
Baked Fish with Herb Stuffing 174
Best Ever Stuffed Eggs 69
Brussels Sprouts with Chestnuts 211
Chicken Kiev 148
Cornish Hens with Fruited Rice Stuffing 143
Delectable Green Beans 221
Herb Butter 369
Old-Fashioned Vegetable Soup 92
Ranch-Style Salad Dressing 97
Roast Turkey Supreme 160
Savory Burgers 249
Savory Onion Rounds 65
Veal and Wild Rice in Casserole 192
Season-All® 40
Arroz con Pollo 144
Asparagus Oriental 213
Asparagus Parmesan 222
Baked Acorn Squash 217
Baked Chicken Oriental 146
Baked Stuffed Tomatoes 232
Barbecued Chicken 246
Beef and Noodle Casserole 192
Beef Stew 229
Beef Stroganoff 116
Bologna Pinwheels 75
Broiled Chicken 145
Broiled Salmon Tarragon 171
Brunswick Stew 186
Brussels Sprouts with Chestnuts 211
Buffet Turkey Loaf 98
Busy Day Casserole 203
Cabbage Rolls 190
Caesar Salad 101
Camper's Green Beans 246
Cannelloni 187
Carrot and Cauliflower Casserole 235
Celery Seed Rolls 244
Celery Victor 79
Charcoal Grilled Steak 247
Cheese Dip Caraway 77
Cheese Omelet Aux Herbes 196
Chicken Cacciatore 145
Chicken Curry in Avocado 147
Chicken Curry in Papaya 147
Chicken Italienne 146
Chicken Kiev 148
Chicken Legs Waikiki 241
Chicken Paprika 150
Chicken Rosemary 148
Chicken Salad 102
Chicken Tarragon 146
Chuck Wagon Franks 240
Chunky Chili 231
Clove-Studded Onions 213
Cocktail Meatballs in Red Wine 64
Coq au Vin 149
Coriander Broiled Chicken 145
Corn Chowder 83
Corn Pudding 215
Cornish Hens with Fruited Rice Stuffing 143
Country Inn Pheasant 157
Country Style Venison Steak 136
Crab Imperial 170
Cream of Zucchini Soup 88
Creamed Chicken Supreme 149
Creamy Coleslaw 104
Curried Chicken Balls 72
Curried Lamb Chops Bengal 242
Curried Turkey Amandine 154
Curry Puffs 75
Deviled Lobster Tails 170
Dill Buttered Potatoes 210
Dill Macaroni Salad 103
Egg Salad 102
Egglant Parmigiana 209
Fiesta Egg Salad 102
Fish Fillets in a Package 243
Fish Poached in Court Bouillon 181
Flank Steak Western Style 251
Frogs' Legs aux Fines Herbes 173
Frogs' Legs Provençale 173
Gingered Crown Roast 126
Glazed Boiled Beef 117
Grilled Tomatoes 248
Herb Broiled Tomatoes 220
Herb Chicken 147
Herb Croutons 258
Herb-Roasted Rack of Lamb 124
Herb Steak 117
Herbed Crown Roast 126
Holiday Stuffing 164
Honey-Glazed Pork Shoulder 130
Hot Exotic Curry Sauce 362
Hot 'n' Tangy Burgers 249
Hot Turkey Salad 234
Hungarian Goulash 118
Individual Chili Meatloaves 234
Italian Dressing 111
Italian Spaghetti Sauce 185
Lamaze Dressing 109
Lamb in Gingered Cranberry Sauce 125
Lamb Kebabs 125

Lamb Shanks Divine 127
Macaroni and Cheese 199
Manhattan Clam Chowder 89
Marjoram Meat Balls 70
Meat Loaf Baked in Sauce 119
Meat Loaf with Mushrooms 122
Mexican Skillet Dinner 193
Noodles Romanoff 193
Okra Southern Style 211
Old-Fashioned Chicken and Dumplings 151
Old-Fashioned Vegetable Soup 92
Old South Corn Bread Stuffing 163
Onion Rounds Delicious 251
Osso Bucco 134
Oven Fried Chicken 153
Paella 189
Parsley-Almond Sauce 372
Parsley Buttered Potatoes 210
Party Beef Casserole 191
Piquant Tomato Aspic 101
Pork Chops à l'Orange 129
Pot Roast with Vegetables 230
Potatoes au Gratin 223
Quiche Lorraine 66
Quick 'n' Easy Barbecue Sauce 360
Ragout of Lamb Rosemary 127
Rice Gourmet 195
Roast Goose Superb 159
Roast Leg of Lamb 124
Roast Pheasant 156
Roast Turkey Supreme 160
Roasted Fiesta Corn 248
Rolled Dumplings 151
Rolled Rib Roast 251
Rolled Rump Roast 240
Rosemary Roast 251
Rumaki 77
Salmon Luncheon Pie 199
Salted Spiced Walnuts 72
Sausage Stuffing 164
Sautéed Cabbage and Apples 216
Sautéed Chicken Livers Rosé 152
Sautéed Frogs' Legs 173
Sautéed Mushrooms 216
Savory Onion Rounds 65
Savory Stuffed Peppers 193
Scallops and Mushrooms en Brochette 179
Scotch Broth 93
Shish Kebabs 245
Shrimp Creole 176
Shrimp Sautéed in Herb Butter 177
Sole Epicurean 173
Sole Meunière 172
Spaghetti with Superb Meat Sauce 197
Spanish Rice 196
Special Turkey Sandwich on Waffles 232
Spiced Shrimp 78
Spicy Barbecue Sauce 372
Stuffed Breast of Veal 133
Stuffed Pork Chops 129
Stuffed Roast Capon 153
Superb Scalloped Oysters 178
Swedish Meat Balls 122
Swiss Steak 124
Tarragon Tuna Salad 99
Tasty Cream Sauce 363
Thyme Roast 251
Tomato Sauce 361
Tomato-Vegetable Soup 91
Turkey Creole 160
Turkey Pot Pie with Vegetables 141
Veal and Wild Rice in Casserole 192
Veal Cutlets Viennese 132
Veal Paprika 134
Veal Parmigiana 131
Veal Scaloppine 135
Wiener Schnitzel 135
Wild Rice Stuffing 163
Zucchini Parmesan 207
Zucchini Sauté 212

Sesame Seed 40-41
Barbecued Nibblers 69
Chinese Stuffed Mushrooms 73
Parsley Biscuits 268
Sesame Burgers 249
Sesame Cheese Ball 68
Sesame Macaroons 332
Sesame Pecan Pie 320
Sesame Pralines 337
Sesame Ring 257
Sesame Seed Pastry 317
Sesame Steaks 123
Sesame Stuffing 165
Sesame Toffee Bars 341
Sesame Wafers 339
Sesame Waffles 264
Trout with Seasoned Butter 234
Veal Cutlets Viennese 132

Tarragon Leaves 41-42
Baked Fish with Herb Stuffing 174
Beef Stew 116
Bon Appétit dip aux Herbes 70
Broiled Salmon Tarragon 171
Chicken Tarragon 146
Country-Good Baked Squash 217
Eggs à la Goldenrod 186
Frogs' Legs aux Fines Herbes 173
Green Bean Salad 97
Green Beans with Water Chestnuts 207
Green Goddess Dressing 109
Grilled Tarragon Fish 244
Herb Butter 369
Herb French Dressing 110
Herbed Fish Fillets 243
Marinated Artichoke Hearts 74
Oysters Rockefeller 76
Rye Herb Bread 267
Sauce Béarnaise 374
Sauce Rémoulade 368
Savory Fresh Ham 230
Shrimp Salad 98
Shrimp Sautéed in Herb Butter 177
Sole Epicurean 173
Spiced Shrimp Maison 78
Tarragon Tuna Salad 99
Tuna Casserole with Batter Topping 198

Thyme, ground 42
Busy Day Casserole 203
Canard au Grand Marnier 158
Crock Pot Beans 230
Gingered Crown Roast 126
Grilled Tomatoes 248
Herb Burgers 249
Herb Butter 369
Herb-Roasted Rack of Lamb 124
Herb Stuffing 162
Herbed Crown Roast 126
Hot Exotic Curry Roast 362
Marjoram Meat Balls 70
Minestrone 87
Mushroom-Rice Stuffing 162
Oven Braised Short Ribs 122
Pork Mandarin 128
Pot Roast with Vegetables 230
Quick 'n' Easy Stuffing 161
Roast Leg of Lamb 124
Roast Turkey Supreme 160
Rye Herb Bread 267
Veal and Wild Rice in Casserole 192

Thyme Leaves 42
Beef and Noodle Casserole 192
Beef Stew 229
Bouillabaisse 90
Cannelloni 187
Chicken-Vegetable Soup 231
Coq au Vin 149
Country Captain 141
Gingered Crown Roast 126
Grilled Fish with Thyme 244
Herb Chicken 147
Herb Pizza 201
Herbed Crown Roast 126
Hot Exotic Curry Sauce 362
Italian Spaghetti Sauce 185
Lamb Kebabs 125
Lima-Sausage Casserole 191
Manhattan Clam Chowder 89
New Orleans Shrimp Gumbo 86
Old-Fashioned Herb Bread 263
Old-Fashioned Sauerbraten 120
Old-Fashioned Vegetable Soup 92
Party Beef Casserole 191
Pâté de Foie en Aspic 67
Sauerbraten Nibblers 63
Sausage and Wild Rice Casserole 189
Sautéed Chicken Livers 152
Savory Fresh Ham 230
Scalloped Potatoes with Cheese 207
Scallops and Mushrooms in Sherry Sauce 169
Scotch Broth 93
Shish Kebabs 245
Spiced Shrimp Maison 78
Thyme Roast 251
Tomato Sauce 361
Tomato-Vegetable Soup 91
Wild Rice Stuffing 163

Turmeric 42-43
Best Ever Stuffed Eggs 69
Bread and Butter Pickles 381

Caper Sauce 373
Chow-Chow 379
Corn Relish 380
Lamaze Dressing 109
Mulligatawny 87
Mustard Pickles 384
Pickle Relish 381
Sour Cream Mustard Sauce 360
Thousand Island Pickles 386
Truffle Sauce 373
Vegetable Flakes
Canard au Grand Marnier 158
Chicken or Turkey Soup 85
Lobster Bisque Elégante 88
Mulligatawny 87
Tomato-Vegetable Soup 91

Extracts, Décors, Food Colors and Tea

EXTRACTS
Almond Extract
Cherry Pie 311
Chewy Popcorn Balls 342
Coffee Torte 275
Cool Lemon Souflé 273
Crunchy Popcorn Balls 342
Danish Pastry 259
Dark Chocolate Frosting 289
Elegant Peach pie 313
Filled Fancies 326
French Hot Chocolate 352
Holiday Popcorn Balls 342
Hot Chocolate Sauce 359
Lebkuchen 333
Lemon Angel Food Cake 292
Pound Cake 297
Sesame Macaroons 332
Sesame Wafers 339
Imitation Brandy Extract
Chicken Tarragon 146
Dark Fruit Cake 294
Deep Dish Apple Pie 308
Devil's Food Cake 296
Easy Mincemeat Pie 318
Eggnog 350
Hot Chocolate Sauce 359
Old-Time Mincemeat 388
Pfeffernüsse 331
Cherry Extract
Pink Perfection Frosting 300
Imitation Coconut Extract
Hot Chocolate Sauce 359
Lemon Extract
Gay Tinted Glaze 300
Hot Cross Buns 257
Lemon Angel Food Cake 292
Lemon Butter Gems 331
Lemon Glaze 300
Pound Cake 297
Maple Extract/Imitation Maple Flavor
Whipped Maple Cinnamon Butter 369
Mint or Mint and Peppermint Extract
Fondant Tipped Almond 341
French Mint Chocolate 352
Lime-Mint Cooler 353
Mint-Apple Jelly 390
Mint Julep Frosting 299
Mint Sauce for Desserts 364
Orange Extract
Orange Butter Gems 331
Orange Glaze 300
Orange Muffins 265
Imitation Rum Extract
Bananas Flambé 272
Black Bottom Pie 311
Cheesecake Elégante 274
Eggnog 350
English Plum Pudding 284
Filled Fancies 326
Frosted Nutmeg Logs 335
Hot Chocolate Sauce 359
Pfeffernüsse 331
Pudding Sauce 363
Rum Buns 260
Sour Cream Dip for Fresh Fruit 63
Vanilla-Rum Frosting 335
Sherry Extract
Baked Beans Bar-B-Q 242
Kidneys in Sherry Sauce 137
Imitation Strawberry Extract
Pink Perfection Frosting 300
Vanilla Extract 43-44
Anise Cookies 340
Banana Fritters 280
Black Bottom Pie 311
Blackberry Cobbler 307
Blackberry Jam Cake 291
Blueberry Crumble 307
Blueberry Pancakes 268
Broiled Spiced Topping 302
Butterscotch Squares 324
Cardamom Butter Cookies 336
Cardamom Rice Pudding 276
Cardamom Ripple Cake 291
Cheesecake Elégante 274
Chocolate Carrot Cake 289
Chocolate-Mace Cream Pie 314
Chocolate Mousse 274
Chocolate Nut Brownies 336
Chewy Popcorn Balls 342
Cinnamon Chocolate Fudge 338
Cinnamon Sandies 329
Cinnamon-Nut Ice Cream 276
Cinnamon-Streusel Muffins 265
Cinnamon-Vanilla Milk Shake 354
Coconut Mace Sauce 361
Cool Lemon Soufflé 273
Creamy Chocolate Sauce 363
Creamy Rice Pudding 276
Crème Anglaise 375
Crunchy Popcorn Balls 342
Czechoslovakian Cookies 330
Dark Chocolate Frosting 289
Dark Fruit Cake 294
Date-Filled Squares 323
Date Nut Cookies 328
Date Roll 337
Date Sticks 333
English Plum Pudding 284
Eggnog 350
Extra-Special Waffles 227
Fancy Decorated Cookies 325
Filled Cookies 325
Filled Fancies 326
Floating Island Meringues 280
Fluffy Snow Peak Frosting 299
French Hot Chocolate 352
French Mint Chocolate 352
Frosted Nutmeg Logs 335
Frozen Bing Cherry Salad 105
Fun with Waffles 264
Ginger Dessert Waffles 281
Ginger Peach Upside-Down Cake 297
Golden Saffron Cake 291
Holiday Chews 338
Holiday Popcorn Balls 342
Homemade Vanilla Ice Cream 276
Hot Chocolate Sauce 359
Lane Cake 293
Lemon Angel Food Cake 292
Lemon Frosting 301
Lemon Meringue Pie 305
Mace-Blueberry Muffins 265
Meringue Cracker Crust 309
Mexican Chocolate with Marshmallows 351
Mincemeat Refrigerator Cookies 335
Minted Mocha Float 351
Muffins 265
Old-Fashioned Tea Cakes 327
Orange Bread Custard 285
Orange Muffins 265
Orange Whipped Cream Topping 301
Pecan Cookie Balls 329
Pineapple Upside-Down Cake 297
Pink Perfection Frosting 300
Poppy Seed Goodies 334
Pound Cake 297
Pudding Sauce 363
Raisin Spice Cupcakes 296
Raspberry Cloud Pie 310
Refrigerator Spice Cookies 328
Sesame Pecan Pie 320
Sesame Toffee Bars 341
Sour Cream Dip for Fresh Fruit 63
Sour Cream Frosting 300
Southern Praline Cookies 330

Spice Muffins 265
Spiced Bavarian 284
Spiced Bread Pudding 275
Spiced Coconut Chiffon Pie 312
Spiced Coffee Ice Cream 276
Spiced Divinity 339
Spiced Jelly Roll 290
Spiced Soufflé 279
Spiced Whipped Cream Topping 301
Spicy Banana Nut Bread 265
Spicy Chocolate Frosting 302
Spicy Custard Pie 315
Spicy Meringues 282
Spicy Oatmeal Cookies 334
Strawberry Patch Pie 309
Sugared Nuts 339
Sugared Vanilla Wafers 332
Vanilla-Rum Frosting 335

DECORS

Autumn Spiced Cider 349
Black Bottom Pie 311
Devil's Food Cake 296
Fancy Decorated Cookies 325
Golden Saffron Cake 291

FOOD COLORS

Baked Apples 280
Cardamom Ripple Cake 291
Champagne Salad 103
Cheese and Caviar Croutelettes 67
Cranberry Chiffon Pie 312
Fancy Decorated Cookies 325
Festive Lime Pie 315
Fondant 341
Fondant Tipped Almonds 341
Frozen Bing Cherry Salad 105
Gay Tinted Glaze 300
Lemon Frosting 301
Lime Chiffon Filling 315
Lime-Mint Cooler 353
Mint-Apple Jelly 390
Mint Julep Frosting 299
Mint Sauce for Desserts 364
Party Pink Fruit Salad 106
Pink Perfection Frosting 300
Tinted-Minted Pineapple 74
Strawberry-Rhubarb Crisp 283

TEA

Mint Tea Hawaiian 350
Spiced Tea 349
Tea House Punch 348

General Index

[*NOTE:* Low-calorie recipes are designated by the abbreviation "l.c." after the folio.]

Abbreviations commonly used 56
Allspice 13
  Glaze 300
Almond(s):
  Broiled Fish Amandine 174
  Country Captain (chicken curry) 141
  Curried Turkey Amandine 154
  Fondant Tipped 341
  Parsley-Almond Sauce 372
American French Dressing 110
Angel Food Cake, Lemon 292
Anise Cookies 340
Anise 13-14
Appetizers:
  Artichoke Hearts, Marinated 74
  Barbecued Nibblers 69
    Curried Nibblers 69
  Beef Teriyaki 71
  Bologna Pinwheels 75
  Canapés, Hot 72
  Celery Sticks, Stuffed 79
  Celery Victor 79
  Ceviche (lime-marinated fish bits) 71
  Cheese Ball, Sesame 68
  Cheese & Cavier Croutelettes 67
  Cheese Puffs, Surprise 74
  Cheese Roll, Chili 68
  Chicken Balls, Curried 72
  Chicken Liver Spread 228
  Clams, Broiled 77
  Cocktail Meatballs in Red Wine 64
  Coquilles Saint-Jacques 76
  Curry Puffs 75
  Dips and Dunks (*see* Dips and Dunks)
  Eggs, Best Ever Stuffed 69
    Chicken or Bacon Stuffed 69
    Curry Stuffed 69
    Dill Stuffed 69
  Hot Bleu Cheese Canapés 233
  Hot Cheese Snacks 227
  Liver Pâté Bon Appétit 73
  Meat Balls, marjoram 70
  Mushrooms, Crab-Stuffed 80
  Mushrooms, Chinese Stuffed 73
  Mushrooms, Marinated 78
  Onion Rounds, Savory 65
  Oysters Rockefeller 76
  Pâté de Foie en Aspic 67
  Pineapple-Grapefruit Delight 79
    Grapefruit Refresher 79
  Pineapple, Tinted-Minted 74
  Quiche Lorraine 66
  Rumaki 77
  Sauerbraten Nibblers 63
  Scampi on a Skewer 243 (l.c.)
  Shrimp, Spiced 78 (l.c.)
Appetizers (*cont.*)
    Oriental Spiced Shrimp 78 (l.c.)
    Shrimp Maison, Spiced 78 (l.c.)
  Sour Cream Dip for Fresh Fruit 63
  Spiced Cranberry Juice Cocktail 64
  Tomato Juice Cocktail 68 (l.c.)
  Walnuts, Salted Spiced 72
Apple Cider:
  Autumn Spiced 349
  Squash 217
Apple(s):
  Apple Blossom Cooler 350
  Applesauce Cake 298
  Baked 280
  Butter 389
  and Cabbage Sautéed 216
  and Candied Sweet Potatoes 218
  Chutney 387
  Cinnamon Baked 235
  Cobbler 271
  Dumplings 282
  Dutch Apple Pie 305
  Filling 316
  Jelly, Apple-Basil 389
  Jelly, Apple and Mint 390
  Pie, Deep Dish Apple 308
  Pie, Wonderful Apple 309
  Waldorf Salad 106
Applesauce Cake 298
Apricot(s):
  Apple Chutney 387
  Apricot Duckling 142
  Cornish Hens with Fruited Rice Stuffing 143
  Filling for Danish Pastry 259
  Filling for Filled Fancies 326
  Filling for Fried Pies 316
  Pudding 285
  Squares (cookies) 340
Arrowroot 48
Arroz con Pollo (chicken and rice) 144
Artichoke Hearts, Marinated 74
Asparagus Oriental 213
Asparagus Parmesan 222
Aspic:
  Pâté de Foie en 67
  Piquant Tomato 101 (l.c.)
Autumn Spiced Cider 349
Avocado:
  Chicken Curry in Avocado 147
  Guacamole (dip) 65

Bacon:
  Canadian Bacon on a Spit 246
  Hot Cheese Snacks 227
  Special Turkey Sandwich on Waffles 232
Bacon (*cont.*)
  Stuffed Eggs 69
Baked Acorn Squash 217
Baked Apples 235, 280
Baked Beans:
  Bar-B-Q 242
  Barbecued 209
  Old-Fashioned 209
Baked Chicken Oriental 146
Baked Eggs Florentine 185
Baked Fish with Herb Stuffing 174
Baked Stuffed Eggplant 214
Banana(s):
  Bread, Spicy Banana Nut Bread 265
  Broiled 213
  Flambé 272
  Fritters 280
  Frost 352
  Grilled 245
Banbury Tarts 319
Barbecue Recipes:
  Bananas, Grilled 245
  Baked Beans 209
  Baked Beans, Bar-B-Q 242
  Beef, Texas Barbecued 195
  Bologna Roll 250
  Bread, Grilled Garlic 243
  Canadian Bacon on a Spit 246
  Chicken 246
  Chicken Legs Waikiki 241
  Corn, Roasted Dilly 248
    Roasted Fiesta 248
  Fish Fillets in a Package 243
    Dilled 243
    Herbed 243
  Fish Fennel, Grilled 244
    Dill Grilled Fish 244
    Grilled Fish with Thyme 244
    Grilled Tarragon Fish 244
  Franks, Chuck wagon 240
  Green Beans, Bonfire 246
    Camper's Green Beans 246
  Grillburgers, Outdoor Chefs' 249
  Hamburgers 249
    Chili-Cheese 249
    Dill 249
    Herb 249
    Hot 'n' Tangy 249
    Oriental 249
    Pepper 249
    Red Hot 249
    Savory 249
    Sesame 249
    Spice 249
  Ham Slice Delicious 241
  Kebabs, Pineapple-Yam 245
  Kebabs, Vegetable 248
  Lamb Chops Bengal, Curried 242

Barbecue Recipes (*cont.*)
Marinated Veal Steak 239
Onion Rounds Delicious 251
Pork Chops Luau 242
Potatoes, Patio 247
Dill Flavored 247
Herbed 247
Hickory Smoked 247
with Marjoram 247
Roast (s):
Rib, Rolled 251 (l.c.)
Rosemary 251 (l.c.)
Thyme 251 (l.c.)
Rump, Rolled 240 (l.c.)
Rolls, Celery Seed 244
Dill Rolls 244
Oregano Rolls 244
Sauces:
Quick 'n' Easy Barbecue 360
Spicy Barbecue 372
Tropical Barbecue 373
Scampi on a Skewer 243
Shish Kebabs 245
Spareribs, Chinese Style 241
Steak(s):
Charcoal Grilled 247
Chuck, Grilled 250
Flank Steak, Western Style 251
Peppered 250 (l.c.)
Teriyaki 239 (l.c.)
Tomatoes, Grilled 248
Barbecued Baked Beans 209
Barbecued Bologna Roll 250
Barbecued Chicken 246
Barbecued Nibblers 69
Basic Bread Stuffing 162
Basil 14
Basil-Apple Jelly 389
Bavarian, Spiced 284
Bay Leaves 14
Beans:
Baked Bar-B-Q 242
Baked, Old-Fashioned 209
Barbecued Baked 209
Crock Pot Beans 230
Green Beans
Bonfire 246
Camper's 246
Delectable 221
Dilled 383
with Dill 220 (l.c.)
Salad 97
Suggested seasonings 10
with Water Chestnuts 207
Lima Bean Casserole 212
Lima-Sausage Casserole 191
Béarnaise Sauce 374
Beef:
Boiled Beef, Glazed 117
Busy Day Casserole 203
Cabbage Rolls 190
Canapés, Hot 72
Chili con Carne 190
Chunky Chili 231
Beef (*cont.*)
Cocktail Meatballs in Red Wine 64
Eggplant Florentine 188
Grillburgers, Outdoor Chefs' 249
Hamburgers 249
Chili-Cheese 249
De Luxe 117
Dill 249
Herb 249
Hot 'n' Tangy 249
Oriental 249
Pepper 249
Red Hot 249
Savory 249
Sesame 249
Spice 249
Hungarian Goulash 118
Individual Chili Meatloaves 234
Italian Spaghetti Sauce 185
Lasagne 194
Meat Balls, Marjoram 70
Meat Balls, Swedish 122
Meat Loaf Baked in Sauce 119
Meat Loaf with Mushrooms 122
Mincemeat, Old-Time 388
and Noodle Casserole 192
Party Beef Casserole 191
Peppers, Savory Stuffed 193
Pot Roast aux Herbes 120
Pot Roast with Vegetables 230
Roasting Chart 53
Roast(s):
Rib Roast Royale, Rolled 123 (l.c.)
Rib Roast, Rolled 251 (l.c.)
Rosemary 251 (l.c.)
Thyme 251 (l.c.)
Rump Roast, Rolled 240 (l.c.)
Tenderloin, Whole 123 (l.c.)
Sauerbraten Nibblers 63
Sauerbraten with Potato Dumplings 121
Sauerbraten, Old-Fashioned 120
Short Ribs, Oven Braised 122
Spaghetti with Superb Meat Sauce 197
Steak(s):
Charcoal Grilled 247 (l.c.)
Chuck, Grilled 250 (l.c.)
Flank Steak Western Style 251
Herb 117
Minute, Herbed 118
Peppered 250 (l.c.)
Sesame 123
Swiss 124
Teriyaki 239
Stew 116, 229
Stroganoff 116
Suggested seasonings 9
Tenderloin, Peppered 119 (l.c.)
Teriyaki 71, 239 (l.c.)
Texas Barbecued 195
Tongue, Spiced 135
Beef Flavor Base 15
Beet Surprise Salad 100
Beets, Harvard 219
Best Ever Stuffed Eggs 69
Beurre Noir (brown butter sauce) 362
Beverages:
Apple Blossom Cooler 350
Banana Frost 352
Café Diable 347
Cider, Autumn Spiced 349
Chocolate, French Hot 352
Chocolate, French Mint 352
Chocolate with Marshmallows, Mexican 351
Cocoa with a Hint of Spice 351
Coffee, Iced Viennese 353
Float, Minted Mocha 351
Ginger Peach Freeze 353
Lime-Mint Cooler 353
Milk Shake, Cinnamon-Vanilla 354
Mint Tea Hawaiian 350
Pineapple-Grapefruit Delight 79
Pineapple-Grapefruit Refresher 79
Punch(es):
Cranberry Wassail Bowl 348
Cranberry, Holiday 355
Cranberry, Hot 350
Eggnog 350
Glögg 348
Grape, Spiced 347
Hot 'n' Spicy 355
Island Fruit 349
Party 346
Spice-Fruit Ring 346
Tea House 348
Tropical Delight 347
Wassail Bowl, Traditional 354
Spiced Cranberry Juice Cocktail 64
Spiced Sangria 345
Tea, Spiced 349
Tomato Juice Cocktail 68 (l.c.)
Tomato Juice Zippy 354 (l.c.)
Wine, Mulled 352
Biscuits: (*see* Breads and Rolls)
Black Bottom Pie 311
Blackberry:
Cobbler 307
Jam Cake 291
Blend, definition 8
Blueberry:
Crumble 307
Mace-Blueberry Muffins 265
Pancakes 268
Bologna:
Barbecued Roll 250
Pinwheels 75
Bon Appétit 15
Dip aux Herbes 70
Bonfire Green Beans 246
Bouillabaisse 90
Bread and Butter Pickles 381
Bread Pudding:
Orange Custard 285
Spiced 275
Breads and Rolls:
Biscuits:
Cinnamon-Pecan 262

Breads and Rolls (*cont.*)
Parsley 268
Party 266
Bread(s):
Banana Nut, Spicy 265
Batter, Oregano 258
Cinnamon-Raisin Bread 256
Cranberry Nut Bread 229
Garlic Cheese 262
Garlic, Grilled 243
Herb, Old-Fashioned 263
Herbed Garlic and Cheese 231
Holiday Confetti 257
Rye Herb 267
Saffron, Easy 267
Buns
Cinnamon-Pineapple 260
Hot Cross 257
Philadelphia Sticky Buns 255
Rum 260
Sticky Spice 262
Crescent, Cardamom 261
Cinnamon Twists, Quick 260
Coffee Cake, Quick 263
Corn Sticks Rosemary 258
Croutons, Herb 258
Danish Pastry 259
Dill Ring 267
Doughnuts 266
Muffins 265
Cinnamon-Streusel 265
Mace-Blueberry 265
Orange 265
Spice 265
Pancakes, Blueberry 268
Rolls, Celery Seed 244
Dill Rolls 244
Oregano Rolls 244
Whole Wheat Rolls 256
Sesame Ring 257
Stuffing (*see* Stuffings)
Waffles, Fun with 264
Herb 264
Mace 264
Sage 264
Sesame 264
Suggested Seasonings 12
Whole Wheat Salt Sticks 264
Broccoli:
Herb Seasoned 220 (l.c.)
Soufflé 214
Broiled:
Bananas 213
Chicken 145
Chili Broiled 114 (l.c.)
Coriander Broiled 145 (l.c.)
Herb Broiled 145 (l.c.)
Smoky Broiled 145 (l.c.)
Clams 77
Fish Amandine 174
Salmon Tarragon 171
Salmon with Dill 171
Spiced Topping 302 (l.c.)
Brown Sauce 366
Brownies, Chocolate Nut 336
Brunswick Stew 186
Brussels Sprouts with Chestnuts 211
Buffet Turkey Loaf 98
Buns: (*see* Breads and Rolls)
Busy Day Casserole 203
Buttered Noodles with Dill 197
With Poppy Seed 197
Butter(s):
Apple 389
Cinnamon Peach Preserves 390
Curry 374
Garlic 367
Herb 369
Honey Spice 365
Orange 365
Lemon Whipped 369
Maple-Cinnamon, Whipped 369
Onion 365
Paprika 366
Peach, Spicy 391
Pear-Pineapple 391
Tangy 365
Butterscotch Squares 324

Cabbage:
and Apples Sautéed 216
Chow-Chow 379
Coleslaw, Creamy 104
Coleslaw Bon Appétit 104
Corn Relish 380
Dixie Relish 380
Rolls 190
Sweet-Sour Red 221
Caesar Salad 101
Café Diable 347
Cake(s):
Angel Food, Lemon 292
Applesauce 298
Blackberry Jam 291
Cardamom Ripple 291
Chocolate Carrot Cake 289
Cinnamon Luncheon 294
Chiffon, Spice 295
Cupcakes, Raisin Spice 296
Devil's Food 296
Fruit, Dark 294
Gingerbread 299
Lane 293
Peach Upside-Down, Ginger 297
Pineapple Upside-Down 297
Poppy Seed 295
Pound 297
Prune, Excellent 292
Saffron, Golden 291
Spice, Old-Fashioned 293
Spiced Jelly Roll 290
Welsh Pork 298
Camper's Green Beans 246
Candian Bacon on a Spit 246
Canapés, Hot 72
(*see also* Appetizers)
Canard au Grand Marnier 158
Candied Sweet Potatoes 218
and Apples 218
Candy:
Date Roll 337
Divinity, Spiced 339
Fondant 341
Tipped Almonds 341
Fudge, Cinnamon Chocolate 338
Candy (*cont.*)
Pralines, Sesame 337
Test for Candy Making 51
Cannelloni 187
Canning:
Butters
Apple 389
Pear-Pineapple 391
Spicy Peach 391
Chili Sauce 379
Chow-Chow 379
Chutneys
Apple 387
Mango 387
Peach 389
Cinnamon Peach Preserves 390
Directions for processing in boiling-water bath 52
Jellies
Basil-Apple 389
Mint-Apple 390
Mango Marmalade 390
Mincemeat, Old-Time 388
Pickles
Bread and Butter 381
Cantaloupe 382
Crystal 382
Dill 383
Dilled Green Beans 383
Kosher Dill 383
Mixed 384
Mustard 384
Spiced Pickled Peaches 385
Sweet Cucumber 385
Thousand Island 386
Watermelon 386
Relishes:
Corn 380
Dixie 380
Pickle 381
Tomato 381
Suggestions for successful 52
Cantaloupe Pickles 382
Caper Sauce 373
Capon, Stuffed Roast 153
Caraway Biscuit Crust 161
Caraway Seed 15-16
Cardamom 16-17
Cardamom Butter Cookies 336
Cardamom Crescent 261
Fruit Filling 261
Glaze 261
Cardamom Dressing, Cream 108
Cardamom Rice Pudding 276
Cardamom Ripple Cake 291
Carrots:
and Cauliflower Casserole 235
and Celery in Parsley Cream 222
Chocolate Carrot Cake 289
Ginger Glazed 208
Golden Cream of Carrot Soup 91
Mixed Pickles 384
Suggested seasonings 11
Vichy 218 (l.c.)
Casserole(s):
Baked Eggs Florentine 185
Beef, Party 191
Beef and Noodle 192

Casserole(s) (*cont.*)
Busy Day 203
Carrot and Cauliflower 235
Chicken en 144
Chicken, Chinese 190
Egg, Easter 202
Eggplant Florentine with Beef 188
Enchilada, Mock 188
Italian Spaghetti Sauce 185
Lasagne 194
Lima Bean 212
Lima-Sausage 191
Mexican Skillet Dinner 193
Paella 189
Sausage and Wild Rice 189
Tuna Casserole with Batter Topping 198
Veal and Wild Rice in 192
Cauliflower:
Carrot and Cauliflower Casserole 235
With Creamy Cheese Sauce 208
Mixed Pickles 384
Mustard Pickles 384
Caviar:
and Cream Cheese Croutelettes 67
Sauce for Lobster and Shrimp 180
Celery 17
Celery and Carrots in Parsley Cream 222
Celery Sticks, Stuffed 79
Celery Victor 79 (l.c.)
Celery Seed Dressing 108
Celery Seed Rolls 244
Ceviche (lime-marinated fish bits) 71 (l.c.)
Champagne Salad 103
Charcoal Grilled Steak 247
Cheese:
Asparagus Parmesan 222
Baked Eggs Florentine 185
Baked Stuffed Tomatoes 232
Bread, Garlic Cheese 262
Carrot and Cauliflower Casserole 235
Cauliflower with Creamy Cheese Sauce 208
and Caviar Croutelettes 67
Cheesecake Elégante 274
Chili-Cheese Burgers 249
Cream:
Celery Sticks, Stuffed 79
Chili-Cheese Roll 68
Dips (*see* Dips and Dunks)
Eggplant Parmigiana 209
Herbed Garlic and Cheese Bread 231
Hot Bleu Cheese Canapés 233
Hot Cheese Snacks 227
Lasagne 194
Macaroni and 199
Manicotti 233
Noodles au Gratin, Viennese 198
Noodles Romanoff 193
Omelet aux Herbes 196
Cheese (*cont.*)
Puffs, Surprise 74
Potatoes au Gratin 223
Roquefort;
Dip, Herb 66
Dressing 111
Dressing, Creamy 108
Scalloped Potatoes with Cheese 207
Sesame Cheese Ball 68
Snappy Cheese-wiches 200
Soufflé 202
Special Turkey Sandwich on Waffles 232
Veal Orloff 115
Welsh Rabbit 203
Cheesecake Elégante 274
Chef's Salad Bowl 98
Cherry:
Frozen Bing Cherry Salad 105
Pie 311
Chestnut(s):
Brussels Sprouts with 211
Spiced Chestnut Stuffing 165
Stuffing 162
Chewy Popcorn Balls 342
Chicken:
Arroz con Pollo 144
Baked Chicken Oriental 146
Barbecued 246
Broiled 145 (l.c.)
Chili 145 (l.c.)
Coriander 145 (l.c.)
Herb 145 (l.c.)
Smoky 145 (l.c.)
Brunswick Stew 186
Cacciatore 145
Cannelloni 187
Cantonese 150
Capon, Stuffed Roast 153
en Casserole 144
Casserole, Chinese 190
Chicken Breasts Elégante, Truffled 154
Coq au Vin 149
Corn Soup 92
Cornish Hens Stuffed with Wild Rice 156
Country Captain (curry) 141
Creamed Chicken Supreme 149
Curried Chicken Balls 72
Curry, Fried Chicken 152
Curry in Papaya 147
Curry in Avocado 147
and Dumplings, Old-Fashioned 151
Herb 147
Italienne 146
Kiev 148
Legs Waikiki 241
Livers:
Pâté Bon Appétit 73
Pâté de Foie en Aspic 67
Rumaki 77
Sautéed 152
Sautéed Rosé 152
Spread 228
Mulligatawny Soup 87
Chicken (*cont.*)
Oven Fried 153
Paella 189
Paprika 150
Roasting Chart 53
Rosemary 148
Salad 102
Soup, Chicken or Turkey 85
Stuffed Eggs 69
Suggested seasonings 9
Tarragon 146
-Vegetable Soup 231
Chicken Flavor Base 18
Chiffon Cake, Spice 295
Chili:
Broiled Chicken 145
Cheese Burgers 249
Cheese Roll 68
Chunk 231
con Carne 190
Individual Chili Meatloaves 234
Powder 18
Sauce 379
Chinese Chicken Casserole 190
Chinese Stuffed Mushrooms 73
Chinese Style Spareribs 241
Chocolate:
Black Bottom Pie 311
Brownies, Chocolate Nut 336
Carrot Cake 289
Chocolate with Marshmallows, Mexican 351
Cocoa with a Hint of Spice 351
Cream Pie, Chocolate-Mace 314
Dark Chocolate Frosting 289
Devil's Food Cake 296
Filled Benne Lace Cookies 323
French Hot 352
French Mint 352
Float, Minted Mocha 351
Frosting, Spicy Chocolate 302
Fudge, Cinnamon Chocolate 338
Hot Chocolate Sauce 359
Mousse 274
Sauce, Creamy Chocolate 363
Toffee Bars, Sesame 341
Choux Glacés à la Crème 278
Spiced Cream Filling 278
Chow-Chow 379
Chowder (*see* Soups and Chowders)
Chuck Wagon Franks 240
Chutney:
Apple 387
Mango 387
Peach 389
Cider (*see* Apple Cider)
Cilantro 20
Cinnamon 18-19
Cinnamon Chocolate Fudge 338
Cinnamon Frosting 301
Cinnamon Glaze 300
Cinnamon Ice Cream 279
Cinnamon Luncheon Cake 294
Cinnamon-Nut Ice Cream 276
Cinnamon Peach Preserves 390
Cinnamon-Pecan Biscuits 262
Cinnamon-Pineapple Buns 260

Cinnamon-Raisin Bread 256
Cinnamon Sandies 329
Cinnamon Sledges 336
Cinnamon-Streusel Muffins 265
Cinnamon-Vanilla Milk Shake 354
Clams:
  Broiled 77
  Chowder, Manhattan 89
  Chowder, New England 90
  Creamed 172
Clove-Studded Broiled Ham 128
Clove-Studded Onions 213
Cloves 19-20
Cobbler:
  Apple 271
  Blackberry 307
  Peach Cobbler Supreme 281
Cocoa with a Hint of Spice 351
Cocktail Meatballs in Red Wine 64
Coconut:
  Broiled Spiced Topping 302
  Chiffon Pie, Spiced 312
  Crust 317
  Holiday Chews 338
  Mace Sauce 361
Coffee:
  Café Diable 347
  Float, Minted Mocha 351
  Ice Cream, Spiced Coffee 276
  Iced Viennese 353
  Torte 275
Coffee Cake, Quick 263
  Streusel Topping 263
Coleslaw, Creamy 104
  Coleslaw Bon Appétit 104
Condiment, definition 8
Confections:
  Nuts, Spiced Mixed 330
  Nuts, Sugared 339
  Popcorn Balls, Chewy 342
    Crunchy Popcorn Balls 342
    Holiday Popcorn Balls 342
  (*See also* Candy; Cookies)
Consomme Royale 92
Cookies:
  Anise 340
  Brownies, Chocolate Nut 336
  Butter, Cardamom 336
  Butterscotch Squares 324
  Cinnamon Sandies 329
  Cinnamon Sledges 336
  Czechoslovakian 330
  Date-Filled Squares 323
  Date Nut 328
  Date Sticks 333
  Decorated, Fancy 325
  Filled 325
  Filled Benne Lace Cookies 323
  Filled Fancies 326
    Apricot 326
    Fig 326
    Poppy Seed-Cheese 326
  Fruit Cake 327
  Gingerbread Boys 332
  Gingersnaps 328
  Hints for successful baking 50
  Holiday Chews 338
  Lebkuchen 333
Cookies (*cont.*)
  Macaroons, Sesame 332
  Mincemeat Refrigerator 335
  Nutmeg Logs, Frosted 335
  Oatmeal, Spicy 334
  Orange Butter Gems 331
    Lemon Butter Gems 331
  Pecan Cookie Balls 329
  Pfeffernüsse 331
  Poppy Seed Goodies 334
  Praline, Southern 330
  Prune-Filled Squares 340
    Apricot Squares 340
  Refrigerator:
    Mincemeat 335
    Spice 328
  Rocks 329
  Tea Cakes, Old-Fashioned 327
  Toffee Bars, Sesame 341
  Vanilla Wafers, Sugared 332
  Wafers, Sesame 339
Cooking Hints 48-50
Cool Lemon Soufflé 273
Coq au Vin 149
Coquilles Saint-Jacques 76
Coriander 20-21
Coriander Broiled Chicken 145
Corn:
  Chowder 83
  Fresh Corn Sauté 219
  and Pepper Stroganoff 215
  Pudding 215
  Relish 380
  Roasted Dilly 248
    Roasted Fiesta 248
  Soup Chicken Corn 92
  Suggested seasonings 10
Corn Bread Stuffing 163
Corn Sticks Rosemary 258
Cornish Hens Stuffed with Wild
    Rice 156
Cornish Hens with Fruited Rice
    Stuffing 143
Country-Good Baked Squash 217
Country Inn Pheasant 157
Country Kitchen Potato Salad 107
Country Style Venison Steak 136
Crab (Meat):
  Cakes 177
  Deviled 176
  Dunk 65
  Imperial 170
  Mushrooms, Crab-Stuffed 80
  Newburg 169
  Salad 99
  Suggested Seasonings 10
Cranberry:
  Chiffon Pie 312
  Lamb in Gingered Cranberry
    Sauce 125
  Nut Bread 229
  Orange-Cranberry Mold,
    Layered 105
  Punch, Holiday 355
  Punch, Hot 350
  Spiced Cranberry Juice Cocktail
    64
  Wassail Bowl 348
Cream (*see* Whipped Cream)
Cream Cheese (*see* Cheese)
Cream of Zucchini Soup 88
Cream Pies (*see* Pies)
Cream Puffs (Choux Glacés à la
    Crème) 278
Creamed Chicken Supreme 149
Creamed Clams 172
Creamed Onions 219
Creamed Spinach 211
Creamy Chocolate Sauce 363
Creamy Coleslaw 104
Creamy Curry Sauce 369
Creamy Lemon-Butter Sauce
    370
Creamy Mustard Sauce 365
Creamy Rice Pudding 276
Creamy Roquefort Dressing 108
Crème Anglaise 375
Crêpes:
  Ginger 277
  Sea Food 175
  Suzette 277
Crock Pot Beans 230
Croquettes:
  Tuna 179
  Turkey, Savory 155
Croutons, Herb 258
Crown Roast of Lamb 126
Crunchy Popcorn Balls 342
Crystal Pickles 382
Cucumbers:
  Bread and Butter Pickles 381
  Cold Cucumber Soup 228
  Crystal Pickles 382
  Dill Pickles 383
  Kosher Dill Pickles 383
  Mixed Pickles 384
  Mustard Pickles 384
  Pickle Relish 381
  in Sour Cream 102
  Sweet Pickles 385
  Sweet-Sour Cucumbers with
    Onions 106 (l.c.)
  Thousand Island Pickles 386
Cumin 21
Cupcakes, Raisin Spice 296
Curried Dishes:
  Butter 374
  Chicken Balls 72
  Chicken Curry in Papaya 147
  Chicken Curry in Avocado 147
  Country Captain (chicken) 141
  Dip 80
  Fried Chicken Curry 152
  Fruit Medley 281
  Ham, Glazed 131
  Lamb, East Indian 126
  Lamb Chops Bengal 242
  Nibblers 69
  Puffs 75
  Sauce, Creamy 369
  Sauce, Hot Exotic 362
  Sea Food Salad 99
  Soup Indienne, Quick 85
  Stuffed Eggs 69
  Turkey Amandine 154
Curry Powder 21-22

Custard Sauce (Crème Anglaise) 375
Custard:
Orange Bread 285
Pie, Rhubarb Custard 320
Pie, Spicy Custard 315
Czechoslovakian Cookies 330

Danish Pastry 259
Apricot Filling 259
Poppy Seed Filling 259
Raspberry Filling 259
Dark Fruit Cake 294
Date(s):
Date-Filled Squares 323
Nut Cookies 328
Pudding, Steamed Date 278
Roll 337
Sticks 333
Deep Dish:
Apple Pie 308
Peach Pie 310
Delectable Green Beans 221
Dessert Sauces (*see* Sauces, Dessert)
Desserts:
Apple Cobbler 271
Apple Dumplings 282
Apples, Baked 280
Apples, Cinnamon Baked 235
Banana Fritters 280
Bananas Flambé 272
Bavarian, Spiced 284
Blueberry Crumble 307
Bread Pudding, Spiced 275
Cheesecake Elégante 274
Chocolate Mousse 274
Cobbler, Blackberry 307
Cobbler Supreme, Peach 281
Cool Lemon Soufflé 273
Cream Puffs (Choux Glacés à la Crème) 278
Crêpes Suzette 277
Ginger Crêpes 277
Custard, Orange Bread 285
Date Pudding, Steamed 278
Fruit Medley, Curried 281
Heavenly Hash 283
Ice Cream:
Cinnamon 279
Cinnamon-Nut 276
Spiced Coffee 276
Spicy Ice Cream Pie 306
Vanilla, Homemade 276
Meringues, Floating Island 280
Meringues, Spicy 282
Peaches Zanzibar 283
Plum Pudding, English 284
Pudding, Apricot 285
Rice Pudding, Creamy 276
Cardamom 276
Soufflé, Spiced 279
Strawberries Romanoff 271
Strawberry-Rhubarb Crisp 283
Torte, Coffee 275
Waffles, Ginger Desert 281
(*See also* Cakes; Pies; and Puddings)
Deviled Crab 176
Deviled Lobster Tails 170
Devil's Food Cake 296
Dill 22-23
Dill Burgers 249
Dill Buttered Potatoes 210
Dill Flavored Potatoes 247
Dill Grilled Fish 244
Dill Macaroni Salad 103
Dill Pickles 383
Dill Ring 267
Dill Rolls 244
Dill Sauce 370
Dill Stuffed Eggs 69
Dilled Fish Fillets 243
Dilled Green Beans 383
Dilly of a Dip 70
Dips and Dunks:
Bon Appétit Dip aux Herbes 70
Cheese Dip Caraway 77
Crab Meat Dunk 65
Curry Dip 80
Dilly of a Dip 70
Guacamole (Avocado) 65
Herb Roquefort Dip 66
Hot Chinese Mustard 368
Mephisto Ham Dip 66
Sour Cream Dip for Fresh Fruit 63
Sour Cream Mustard Sauce 360
Teriyaki Sauce 371
Toasted Onion Dip 75
Tropical Barbecue Sauce 373
(*See also* Appetizers)
Divinity, Spiced 339
Dixie Relish 380
Doughnuts 266
Drinks (*see* Beverages)
Duckling à l'Orange 157
Ducks:
Apricot Duckling 142
Canard au Grand Marnier 158
Duckling à l'Orange 157
Roasting Chart 53
Dumplings:
Apple 282
Herb 151
Potato 121
Rolled 151
Suggested seasonings 12
Dutch Apple Pie 305

East Indian Lamb Curry 126
Easter Egg Casserole 202
Easy Mincemeat Pie 318
Easy Saffron Bread 267
Egg Drop Soup 91
Eggnog 350
Eggplant:
Baked Stuffed 214
Florentine with Beef 188
Parmigiana 209
Suggested seasonings 11
Egg(s):
à la Goldenrod 186
Baked Eggs Florentine 185
Best Ever Stuffed 69
Chicken or Bacon 69
Egg(s) (*cont.*)
Curry 69
Dill 69
Easter Egg Casserole 202
Eggnog 350
Omelet aux Herbes, Cheese 196
Omelet Princess 200
Salad 102
Fiesta Egg 102
Soufflé
Broccoli 214
Cheese 202
Cool Lemon Soufflé 273
Spiced 279
Elegant Peach Pie 313
English Plum Pudding 284
Equivalents
Common Food 54-55
Measures 55
Excellent Prune Cake 292

Fancy Decorated Cookies 325
Fennel Seed 23
Festive Lime Pie 315
Fiesta Egg Salad 102
Fig Filling for Filled Fancies 326
Filled Benne Lace Cookies 323
Filled Cookies 325
Filled Fancies 326
Apricot Filling 326
Fig Filling 326
Poppy Seed-Cheese Filling 326
Fillet of Sole:
Fillet Neapolitan 172
Sole Epicurean 173
Sole Meunière 172
Véronique 171
Fillet Neapolitan 172
Fillings:
Apple, for Fried Pies 316
Apricot:
for Apricot-Filled Squares 340
for Danish Pasry 259
for Filled Fancies 326
for Fried Pies 316
for Cannelloni 187
Currant Jelly 290
Fig, for Filled Fancies 326
Fruit, Cardamom 261
Lane Cake 293
Lime Chiffon 315
Poppy Seed, for Danish Pastry 259
Poppy Seed-Cheese, for Filled Fancies 326
Prune, for Prune-Filled Squares 340
Raspberry, for Danish Pastry 259
Sea Food 175
Spiced Cream 278
for Spiced Jelly Roll 290
Strawberry 309
Fish and Sea-Food:
Baked Fish with Herb Stuffing 174
Bouillabaisse 90

Fish and Sea-Food (*cont.*)
Broiled Fish Amandine 174
Ceviche (lime-marinated fish bits) 71
Clams:
Broiled 77
Chowder, Manhattan 89
Chowder, New England 90
Creamed 172
Coquilles Saint-Jacques 76
Crab Cakes 177
Crab, Deviled 176
Crab Imperial 170
Crab Newburg 169
Crab Salad 99
Dilled Fish Fillets 243
Fillet de Sole Véronique 171
Fillet Neapolitan 172
Fillets, Herbed Fish 243 (l.c.)
Fillets in a Package 243 (l.c.)
Fish Poached in Court Bouillon 181
Grilled Fish Fennel 244
Dill Grilled Fish 244
Grilled Tarragon Fish 244
Grilled Fish with Thyme 244
Lobster Bisque Elégante 88
Lobster Cantonese 178
Lobster Tails, Deviled 170
Oyster Stew 84
Oysters Rockefeller 76
Oysters, Superb Scalloped 178
Pan-Fried Fish 177
Salmon Loaf, Savory 180
Salmon Luncheon Pie 199
Salmon Tarragon, Broiled 171
Salmon with Dill, Broiled 171
Scallops and Mushrooms en Brochette 179 (l.c.)
Scallops and Mushrooms in Sherry Sauce 169
Scampi on a Skewer 243 (l.c.)
Sea Food Crêpes 175
Sea Food Salad, Curried 99
Shrimp and Lobster with Sauce Caviar 180
Shrimp Creole 176
Shrimp Gumbo, New Orleans 86
Shrimp Salad 98
Shrimp Sautéed in Herb Butter 177
Shrimp, Spiced 78
Oriental Spiced Shrimp 78 (l.c.)
Spiced Shrimp Maison 78 (l.c.)
Sole Epicurean 173
Sole Meunière 172
Suggested seasonings 10
Suggestions for cooking 51-52
Trout with Seasoned Butter 234
Tuna Casserole with Batter Topping 198
Tuna Croquettes 179
Tuna Salad, Tarragon 99
Tuna and Tomato Mold 107
(*See also* under names of Fish or Shellfish)
Flank Steak Western Style 251
Floating Island Meringues 280
Fluffy Snow Peak Frosting 299
Fondant 341
Tipped Almonds 341
Food Processors 226
Chicken Liver Spread 228
Cold Cucumber Soup 229
Cranberry Nut Bread 229
Extra-Special Waffles 227
Gazpacho 227
Hot Cheese Snacks 227
Frankfurters:
Chuck Wagon Franks 240
Zesty Stuffed 137
French Dressing 110
American 110
Herb 110
South-of-the-Border 110
French Hot Chocolate 352
French Mint Chocolate 352
French Onion Soup 84
Fresh Corn Sauté 219
Fresh Fruit Medley 104
Fried Chicken Curry 152
Fried Pies 316
Apple Filling 316
Apricot Filling 316
Fried Rice 201
Fritters, Banana 280
Frogs' Legs, Sautéed 173
aux Fines Herbes 173
Provençale 173
Frosted Nutmeg Logs 335
Frosting(s):
Broiled Spiced Topping 302
Chocolate, Spicy 302
Cinnamon 301
Dark Chocolate Frosting 289
Fluffy Snow Peak 299
Glaze, Lemon 300
Allspice 300
Cinnamon 300
Gay Tinted 300
Nutmeg 300
Orange 300
Lemon 301
Mint Julep 299
Sour Cream 300
Pink Perfection 300
Spiced Topping, Broiled 302
Vanilla-Rum 335
Whipped Cream Topping, Spiced 301
Orange Whipped Cream Topping 301
(*See also* Toppings)
Frozen Bing Cherry Salad 105
Fruit Cake, Dark 294
Fruit Cake Cookies 327
Fruit(s):
Apples, Baked 235, 280
Bananas, Broiled 213
Bananas, Grilled 245
Cornish Hens with Fruited Rice Stuffing 143
Curried Fruit Medley 281
Heavenly Hash 283
Peaches Zanzibar 283
Pies (*see* Pies)
Fruit(s) (*cont.*)
Punch, Island Fruit 349
Salad:
Bing Cherry, Frozen 105
Champagne 103
Fruit Medley, Fresh 104
Fruit, Party Pink 106
Orange-Cranberry Mold, Layered 105
Suggested Seasonings 12
Waldorf 106
Spice-Fruit Ring 346
Soup, Swedish Fruit 86
Sour Cream Dip for Fresh Fruit 63
Strawberry-Rhubarb Crisp 283
(*See also* names of Fruits)
Fudge, Cinnamon Chocolate 338
Fun with Waffles 264

Game:
Goose Superb, Roast 159
Pheasant, Country Inn 157
Pheasant, Roast 156
Venison Steak, Country Style 136
Garden Vegetable Salad 100
Garlic 23-25
Garlic Butter 367
Garlic Cheese Bread 262
Gay Tinted Glaze 300
Gazpacho 227
Giblets, Herbed Sauce 366
Ginger 25
Ginger Cracker Crust 315
Ginger Cream Dressing 110
Ginger Crêpes 277
Ginger Dessert Waffles 281
Ginger Glazed Carrots 208
Ginger Peach Freeze 353
Ginger Peach Upside-Down Cake 297
Gingerbread 299
Gingerbread Boys 332
Gingered Crown Roast of Lamb 126
Gingersnaps 328
Glazed Boiled Beef 117
Glazes (*see* Frostings)
Glögg (Swedish Christmas Drink) 348
Glossary of food and cooking terms 56-59
Golden Clove Glazed Ham 131
Golden Cream of Carrot Soup 91
Golden Saffron Cake 291
Goose:
Roast Goose Superb 159
Roasting Chart 53
Graham Crackers:
Ginger Cracker Crust 315
Spiced Graham Cracker Crust 319
Grand Marnier:
Apricot Duckling 142
Canard au 158
Cool Lemon Soufflé 273
Ginger Crêpes 277

Grand Marnier (*cont.*)
Soufflé Sauce 279
Grapefruit:
Pineapple-Grapefruit Delight 79
Pineapple-Grapefruit Refresher 79
Grape Punch, Spiced 347
Green Beans (*see* Beans)
Green Goddess Dressing 109
Green Peppers:
Chow-chow 379
Savory Stuffed 193
Thousand Island Pickles 386
Grilled Bananas 245
Grilled Chuck Steak 250
Grilled Fish Fennel 244
Grilled Fish with Thyme 244
Grilled Garlic Bread 243
Grilled Tarragon Fish 244
Grilled Tomatoes 248
Guacamole (Avocado Dip) 65

Ham:
Baked Eggs Florentine 185
Clove Glazed, Golden 131
Curry Glazed 131
Honey Glazed 131
Orange Glazed 131
Clove-Studded Broiled 128
Dip, Mephisto Ham 66
Roasting Chart 53
Savory Fresh Ham 230
Slice Delicious 241
Spiced Baked Ham Slice 128
Hamburgers (*see* Beef)
Hard Sauce, Spiced 375
Harvard Beets 219
Harvest Pumpkin Chiffon Pie 318
Heavenly Hash 283
Herb Broiled Chicken 145
Herb-Broiled Sandwiches 200
Herb Broiled Tomatoes 220
Herb Burgers 249
Herb Butter 369
Herb Chicken 147
Herb Croutons 258
Herb Dumplings 151
Herb French Dressing 110
Herb Pizza 201
Herb-Roasted Rack of Lamb 124
Herb Roquefort Dip 66
Herb Seasoned Broccoli 220 (l.c.)
Herb Seasoning 25-26
Herb Steak 117
Herb Stuffing 162
Herb Waffles 264
Herbed Crown Roast of Lamb 126
Herbed Fish Fillets 243
Herbed Garlic and Cheese Bread 231
Herbed Giblet Sauce 366
Herbed Minute Steaks 118
Herbed Potatoes 247
Herbs, definition facing page 8
Hickory Smoked Potatoes 247
Holiday Chews 338
Holiday Confetti Bread 257
Holiday Cranberry Punch 355
Holiday Nutmeg Sauce 361
Holiday Popcorn Balls 342
Holiday Stuffing 164
Hollandaise Sauce 371
Homemade Vanilla Ice Cream 276
Honey:
Apricot Duckling 142
Glazed Ham 131
-Glazed Pork Shoulder 130
Lebkuchen 333
Spice Butter 365
Spice Dressing 110
Hors d'Oeuvres (*see* Appetizers)
Hot Bleu Cheese Canapés 233
Hot Canapés 72
Hot Chinese Mustard 368
Hot Cranberry Punch 350
Hot Cross Buns 257
Hot Exotic Curry Sauce 362
Hot 'n' Spicy Punch 355
Hot 'n' Tangy Burgers 249
Hungarian Goulash 118

Ice Cream:
Cinnamon 279
Homemade Vanilla 276
Cinnamon-Nut 276
Spiced Coffee 276
Spicy Ice Cream Pie 306
Iced Viennese Coffee 353
Indian Rice 194
Indonesian Spareribs 129
Island Fruit Punch 349
Italian Dressing 111
Italian Pizza 201
Italian Spaghetti Sauce 185
Italian Style Peas 212

Jellies:
Basil-Apple 389
Cinnamon Peach Preserves 390
Mango Marmalade 390
Mint-Apple 390
(*See also* Preserves)
Jelly Roll, Spiced 290
Juices (*see* Beverages)

Kebabs:
Lamb 125
Pineapple-Yam 245
Shish 245 (l.c.)
Vegetable 248
Kidneys in Sherry Sauce 137
Kosher Dill Pickles 383

Lamaze Dressing 109
Lamb:
Crown Roast of 126
Gingered 126
Herbed 126
Curried Lamb Chops Bengal 242
Curry, East Indian 126
Curry Puffs 75
in Gingered Cranberry Sauce 125
Kebabs 125
Kidneys in Sherry Sauce 137
Lamb (*cont.*)
Rack of Lamb, Herb-Roasted 124
Ragout of Lamb Rosemary 127
Roast Leg of 124 (l.c.)
Roasting Chart 53
Scotch Broth 93
Shanks Divine 127
Shish Kebabs 245 (l.c.)
Suggested Seasonings 10
Lane Cake 293
Lasagne 194
Layered Orange-Cranberry Mold 105
Lebkuchen 333
Lemon:
Angel Food Cake 292
Butter Gems 331
Butter, Whipped Lemon 369
Candied Lemon Shreds 273
Cool Lemon Soufflé 273
Frosting 301
Glaze 300
Lemon Meringue Pie 305
Pastry 317
Pie, Spicy Lemon Angel 313
Sauce, Creamy Lemon-Butter 370
Lemon Peel 26-27
Lentil Soup 84
Lima Bean:
Casserole 212
-Sausage Casserole 191
Lime:
-Mint Cooler 353
Pie, Festive Lime 315
Livers(s), Chicken:
Chicken Liver Spread 228
Pâté Bon Appétit, Liver 73
Pâté de Foie en Aspic 67
Rumaki 77
Sautéed 152
Sautéed Rosé 152
Lobster:
Bisque Elégante 88
Cantonese 178
Tails, Deviled 170
and Shrimp with Sauce Caviar 180
Low Calorie Recipes (l.c.):
Beverages:
Tomato Juice Cocktail 68
Zippy Tomato Juice 354
Fish:
Ceviche 71
Fish Fillets in a Package 243
Scallops and Mushrooms en Brochette 179
Scampi on a Skewer 243
Spiced Shrimp 78
Fruit:
Fresh Fruit Medley 104
Meat:
Beef Teriyaki 71
Broiled Chicken, 145
Grilled Flank Steak 250
Herb-Roasted Rack of Lamb 124

Meat (*cont.*)
Peppered Steak 250
Roast Leg of Lamb 124
Roast Turkey 160
Roast Whole Tenderloin 123
Rolled Rib Roast 123, 251
Rolled Rump Roast 240
Shish Kebabs 245
Spiced Tongue 135
Vegetables:
Carrots Vichy 218
Celery Victor 79
Chef's Salad Bowl 98
Green Beans with Dill 220
Herb Seasoned Broccoli 220
Marinated Mushrooms 78
Piquant Tomato Aspic 101
Sauerkraut Caraway 210
Sweet-Sour Cucumbers with Onions 106

Macaroni Salad, Dill 103
Hot Turkey Salad 234
Suggested Seasonings 12
Macaroons, Sesame 332
Mace 27
Mace-Blueberry Muffins 265
Mace Waffles 264
Mango:
Chutney 387
Marmalade 390
Manhattan Clam Chowder 89
Manicotti 233
Maple-Cinnamon Butter, Whipped 369
Marinated Artichoke Hearts 74
Marinated Mushrooms 78
Marinated Veal Steak 239
Marjoram 27-28
Marjoram Meat Balls 70
Marmalade, Mango 390
Mayonnaise (*see* Salad Dressings)
Measures and Measuring 53-54
Meat, Roasting Chart 53
Meat Balls, Swedish 122
Meat Loaf Baked in Sauce 119
Meat Loaf with Mushrooms 122
Meatballs in Red Wine, Cocktail 64
Meatloaves, Individual Chili 234
Meats:
Roasting Chart 53
Suggested seasonings 9
(*See also* Beef; Lamb; Pork; Poultry; Veal)
Mephisto Ham Dip 66
Meringues:
Cracker Crust 309
Floating Island 280
Lemon Meringue Pie 305
Spicy 282
Mexican Chocolate with Marshmallows 351
Mexican Skillet Dinner 193
Microwave Ovens 226
Carrot and Cauliflower Casserole 235
Cinnamon Baked Apples 235
Hot Turkey Salad 234
Microwave Ovens (*cont.*)
Individual Chili Meatloaves 234
Manicotti 233
Trout with Seasoned Butter 234
Milk Shake, Cinnamon-Vanilla 354
Mincemeat:
Cookies, Refrigerator 335
Old-Time 388
Pie, Easy 318
Minestrone 87
Mint 28
Mint-Apple Jelly 390
Mint Julep Frosting 299
Mint Sauce for Desserts 364
Mint Tea Hawaiian 350
Minted Mocha Float 351
Minted Peas 221
Mixed Pickles 384
Mock Enchilada Casserole 188
Mousse, Chocolate 274
Muffins (*see* Breads and Rolls)
Mulled Wine 352
Mulligatawny 87
Mushroom(s):
Chinese Stuffed 73
Crab-Stuffed 80
Marinated 78
-Rice Stuffing 162
Sauce 367
Sautéed 216
Scallops and Mushrooms en Brochette 179
and Scallops in Sherry Sauce 169
Mustard 29
Mustard:
Hot Chinese 368
Pickles 384
Sauce, Creamy 365
Sauce, Sour Cream 360
Sauce, Sweet-Sour 372

New England Clam Chowder 90
New Orleans Shrimp Gumbo 86
Noodles (*see* Pastas)
Nutmeg 29-30
Nutmeg Glaze 300
Nutmeg Logs, Frosted 335
Nutmeg Sauce 363
Nuts:
Almonds, Fondant Tipped 341
Mixed, Spiced 330
Sugared 339
Walnuts, Salted Spiced 72

Oatmeal Cookies, Spicy 334
Okra Southern Style 211
Old-Fashioned Baked Beans 209
Barbecued Baked Beans 209
Old-Fashioned Chicken and Dumplings 151
Old-Fashioned Herb Bread 263
Old-Fashioned Sauerbraten 120
Old-Fashioned Spice Cake 293
Old-Fashioned Tea Cakes 327
Old-Fashioned Vegetable Soup 92
Old South Corn Bread Stuffing 163
Old-Time Mincemeat 388
Omelets:
Cheese Omelet aux Herbes 196
Princess 200
Onions 30-32
Butter 365
Chow-Chow 379
Clove-Studded 213
Creamed 219
Dip, Toasted 75
Rounds Delicious 251
Rounds, Savory 65
Sauce 366
Soup, French 84
Suggested seasonings 11
Orange:
Bread Custard 285
Butter 365
Butter Gems 331
Glaze 300
Muffins 265
Whipped Cream Topping 301
Orange Peel 26-27
Oregano 32
Oregano Batter Bread 258
Oregano Rolls 244
Oriental Burgers 249
Oriental Spiced Shrimp 78
Osso Bucco (braised veal shanks) 134
Outdoor Chefs' Grillburgers 249
Outdoor Cooking 50
Baked Beans Bar-B-Q 242
Barbecued Chicken 246
Bonfire Green Beans 246
Celery Seed Rolls 244
Charcoal Grilled Steak 247
Chicken Legs Waikiki 241
Chili-Cheese Burgers 249
Chinese Style Spareribs 241
Chuck Wagon Franks 240
Curried Lamb Chops Bengal 242
Dill Burgers 249
Dill Flavored Potatoes 247
Dill Rolls 244
Fish and Sea Food:
Dill Grilled Fish 244
Dilled Fish Fillets 243
Fish Fillets in a Package 243
Grilled Fish Fennel 244
Grilled Fish with Thyme 244
Grilled Tarragon Fish 243
Herbed Fish Fillets 243
Scampi on a Skewer (l.c.) 243
Flank Steak Western Style 251
Grilled Bananas 245
Grilled Chuck Steak (l.c.) 250
Grilled Garlic Bread 243
Grilled Tomatoes 248
Ham Slice Delicious 241
Hamburgers 249
Herb Burgers 249
Herbed Potatoes 247
Hickory Smoked Potatoes 247
Hot 'n' Tangy Burgers 249
Marinated Veal Steak 239
Onion Rounds Delicious 251
Oregano Rolls 244
Oriental Burgers 249

Outdoor Cooking (*cont.*)
Outdoor Chefs' Grillburgers 249
Patio Potatoes 247
Pepper Burgers 249
Peppered Steak 250 (l.c.)
Pineapple-Yam Kebabs 245
Pork Chops Luau 242
Potatoes with Marjoram 247
Red Hot Burgers 249
Roasted Dilly Corn 248
Roasted Fiesta Corn 248
Savory Burgers 249
Sesame Burgers 249
Shish Kebabs 245 (l.c.)
Spice Burgers 249
Spit Barbecuing
Barbecued Bologna Roll 250
Canadian Bacon on a Spit 246
Rolled Rib Roast 251 (l.c.)
Rolled Rump Roast 240 (l.c.)
Rosemary Roast 251 (l.c.)
Thyme Roast 251 (l.c.)
Steak Teriyaki 239
Vegetable Kebabs 248
(*See also* Barbecue Recipes)
Oven Braised Short Ribs 122
Oven Fried Chicken 153
Oyster(s):
Rockefeller 76
Scalloped, Superb 178
Stew 84
Stuffing 162

Paella 189
Pancakes (*see* Waffles and Pancakes)
Pan-Fried Fish 177
Papaya, Chicken Curry in 147
Paprika 32-33
Paprika Butter 366
Parsley 33
Parsley-Almond Sauce 372
Parsley Biscuits 268
Parsley Buttered Potatoes 210
Party Beef Casserole 191
Party Biscuits 266
Party Pink Fruit Salad 106
Party Punch 346
Pastas:
Cannelloni 187
Italian Spaghetti Sauce 185
Lasagne 194
Macaroni and Cheese 199
Macaroni Salad, Dill 103
Manicotti 233
Noodle Casserole, Beef and 192
Noodles with Dill, Buttered 197
with Poppy Seed 197
Noodles au Gratin, Viennese 198
Noodles Romanoff 193
Spaghetti with Superb Meat Sauce 197
Wheat Pilaf 195
Pastry and Pie Crusts:
Caraway Biscuit Crust 161
Chocolate Wafers 306
Coconut Crust 317
Ginger Cracker Crust 315
Pastry and Pie Crusts (*cont.*)
Graham Cracker Crust, Spiced 319
Meringue Cracker Crust 309
Pizza Crust 201
Plain Pastry 317
Lemon 317
Poppy Seed 317
Sesame Seed 317
Spicy 317
Pâté:
Liver Pâté Bon Appétit 73
de Foie en Aspic 67
Patio Potatoes 247
Peach(es)
Butter, Spicy Peach 391
Cake, Ginger Peach Upside-Down 297
Cinnamon Peach Preserves 390
Chutney 389
Cobbler Supreme 281
Ginger Peach Freeze 353
Pie, Deep Dish Peach 310
Pie, Elegant Peach 313
Spiced Pickled 385
Zanzibar 283
Pear-Pineapple Butter 391
Peas:
Italian Style 212
Minted 221
Suggested seasonings 11
Turkey Pot Pie with Vegetables 141
Pecan(s):
Butterscotch Squares 324
Cinnamon-Pecan Biscuits 262
Cookies, Southern Praline 330
Cookie Balls 329
Cranberry Nut Bread 229
Date-Filled Squares 323
Date Nut Cookies 328
Pie, Sesame 320
Pie, Sweet Potato-Pecan 314
Pralines, Sesame 337
Spiced Mixed Nuts 330
Pepper 33-35
Pepper, Red 35
Pepper Burgers 249
Peppered Steak 250 (l.c.)
Peppered Tenderloin 119 (l.c.)
Peppers, Green (*see* Green Peppers)
Pfeffernüsse (German Christmas cookie) 331
Pheasant:
Country Inn 157
Roast 156
Philadelphia Sticky Buns 255
Pickle Relish 381
Pickles (*see* Relishes and Pickles)
Pickling Spice 35-36
Pie Crusts (*see* Pastry and Pie Crusts)
Pie(s):
Apple: Deep Dish 308
Dutch 305
Wonderful 309
Banbury Tarts 319
Pie(s) (*cont.*)
Cherry 311
Chiffon:
Black Bottom 311
Coconut, Spiced 312
Cranberry 312
Lemon Angel Pie, Spicy 313
Lime, Festive 315
Pumpkin, Velvety 318
Harvest Pumpkin 318
Raspberry Cloud 310
Cream, Chocolate-Mace 314
Custard:
Rhubarb 320
Spicy 315
Fried 316
Apple Filling 316
Apricot Filling 316
Lemon Meringue Pie 305
Mincemeat, Easy 318
Peach, Deep Dish 310
Peach, Elegant 313
Pecan, Sesame 320
Pumpkin 308
Spicy Ice Cream Pie 306
Strawberry Patch 309
Sweet Potato-Pecan 314
Turkey Pot Pie 161
Pilaf, Wheat 195
Rice Pilaf 195
Pineapple:
Cinnamon-Pineapple Buns 260
Cornish Hens with Fruited Rice Stuffing 143
-Grapefruit Delight 79
-Grapefruit Refresher 79
Pear-Pineapple Butter 391
Sweet Potatoes-Pineapple Rings 218
Tinted-Minted 74
Upside-Down Cake 297
-Yam Kebabs 245
Pink Perfection Frosting 300
Piquant Tomato Aspic 101 (l.c.)
Pizza:
Italian 201
Herb 201
Sauce 364
Plain Pastry 317
Plum Pudding, English 284
Popcorn Balls, Chewy 342
Crunchy Popcorn Balls 342
Holiday Popcorn Balls 342
Poppy Seed 36
Poppy Seed Cake 295
Poppy Seed Dressing 109
Poppy Seed Filling for Danish Pastry 259
Poppy Seed Filling for Filled Fancies 326
Poppy Seed Goodies 334
Poppy Seed Pastry 317
Pork:
Canadian Bacon on a Spit 246
Chops à l'Orange 129
Chops Luau 242
Chops, Stuffed 129
Ham (*see* Ham)

Pork (*cont.*)
Loin Roast (Pork Mandarin) 128
Mandarin 128
Roasting Chart 53
Savory Fresh Ham 230
Shoulder, Honey-Glazed 130
Spareribs, Chinese Style 241
Spareribs, Indonesian 129
Suggested seasonings 9
Sweet-Sour 130
Welsh Pork Cake 298
Pot Roast aux Herbes 120
Potato(es):
Dumplings 121
au Gratin 223
Parsley Buttered 210
Dill Buttered 210
Patio 247
Dill Flavored 247
Herbed 247
Hickory Smoked 247
with Marjoram 247
Salad, Country Kitchen 107
Salad, Potato-Fennel 107
Scalloped Potatoes 207
Suggested Seasonings 11
Vichyssoise 89
Poultry:
Roasting Chart 53
Stuffings (*see* Stuffings)
(*See also* Chicken; Cornish Hens; Duck; Turkey; Game)
Poultry Seasoning 37
Pound Cake 297
Pralines:
Sesame 337
Southern Praline Cookies 330
Preserves, Cinnamon Peach 390
(*See also* Butters and Marmalade)
Princess Omelet 200
Prune:
Cake, Excellent 292
Filled Squares 340
Filling 340
Pudding(s)
Apple Cobbler 271
Apricot 285
Bread, Spiced 275
Corn 215
Plum, English 284
Rice, Cardamom 276
Rice, Creamy 276
Sauce, Pudding 363
Steamed Date 278
Sweet Potato 216
Pumpkin:
Chiffon Pie, Velvety 318
Harvest Pumpkin Pie 318
Pie 308
Pie Spice 37
Punch (*see* Beverages)

Quiche Lorraine 66
Quick Cinnamon Twists 260
Quick Coffee Cake 263
Quick Curry Soup Indienne 85
Quick 'n' Easy Barbecue Sauce 360
Quick 'n' Easy Stuffing 161

Ragout of Lamb Rosemary 127
Raisin Bread, Cinnamon 256
Raisin Cookies (Rocks) 329
Raisin Spice Cupcakes 296
Raisin Sauce, Spiced 374
Ranch-Style Salad Dressing 97
Raspberry:
Cloud Pie 310
Filling for Danish Pastry 259
Sauce 370
Red Cabbage, Sweet-Sour 221
Red Cocktail Sauce 367
Red Hot Burgers 249
Red Pepper 35
Refrigerator Spice Cookies 328
Relishes and Pickles:
Chili Sauce 379
Chow-Chow 379
Chutney:
Apple 387
Mango 387
Peach 389
Cucumbers in Sour Cream 102
Green Beans, Dilled 383
Peaches, Spiced Pickled 385
Pickles:
Bread and Butter 381
Cantaloupe 382
Crystal 382
Dill 383
Kosher Dill 383
Mixed 384
Mustard 384
Sweet Cucumber 385
Thousand Island 386
Watermelon 386
Relish:
Corn 380
Dixie 380
Pickle 381
Tomato 381
Rhubarb:
Custard Pie 320
Strawberry-Rhubarb Crisp 283
Rice:
Arroz con Pollo (Saffron rice and Chicken) 144
Casserole, Sausage and Wild Rice 189
Casserole, Veal and Wild Rice in 192
Cornish Hens Stuffed with Wild Rice 156
Cornish Hens with Fruited Rice Stuffing 143
Fried 201
Gourmet 195
Indian 194
Paella 189
Pilaf 195
Pudding, Creamy 276
Cardamom 276
Saffron 196
Rice (*cont.*)
Spanish 196
Stuffing, Mushroom-Rice 162
Stuffing, Wild Rice 163
Ris de Veau à la Crème 136
Roasted Dilly Corn 248
Fiesta Corn 248
Roasting Chart, Meat and Poultry 53
Roast(s):
Beef:
Pot Roast aux Herbes 120
Rolled Rib Roast 251 (l.c.)
Rosemary Roast 251 (l.c.)
Thyme Roast 251 (l.c.)
Rolled Rib Roast Royale 123
Rolled Rump Roast 240
Whole Tenderloin 123 (l.c.)
Goose Superb 159
Lamb:
Crown Roast of 126
Gingered Crown Roast 126
Herbed Crown Roast 126
Herb-Roasted Rack of 124
Leg of 124
Pheasant 156
Pheasant, Country Inn 157
Pork:
Mandarin 128
Shoulder, Honey-Glazed 130
(*See also* Ham)
Poultry:
Capon, Stuffed Roast 153
Turkey Supreme 160
Roasting Chart 53
Veal, Stuffed Breast of 133
Rocks (Raisin cookies) 329
Rolled Dumplings 151
Rolled Rib Roast 123, 251 (l.c.)
Rosemary Roast 251 (l.c.)
Thyme Roast 251 (l.c.)
Rolled Rib Roast Royale 123 (l.c.)
Rolled Rump Roast 240 (l.c.)
Roquefort Cheese (see Cheese)
Roquefort Dressing 111
Rosemary 37-38
Rum Buns 260
Rumaki 77
Rye Herb Bread 267

Saffron 38
Saffron Bread, Easy 267
Saffron Cake, Golden 291
Saffron Rice 196
Sage 39
Sage Waffles 264
Salad Dressing(s):
Cardamom Cream 108
Celery Seed 108
French 110
American 110
Herb 110
South-of-the-Border 110
Ginger Cream 110
Green Goddess 109
Honey Spice 110
Italian 111
Lamaze 109

Salad Dressing(s) (*cont.*)
Poppy Seed 109
Ranch-Style 97
Roquefort 111
Roquefort, Creamy 108
Sauce Rémoulade 368
Suggested seasonings 11
Salad(s):
Beet Surprise 100
Caesar 101
Chef's Salad Bowl 98 (l.c.)
Chicken 102
Coleslaw, Creamy 104
Bon Appétit 104
Crab 99
Cucumbers in Sour Cream 102
Cucumbers with Onions, Sweet-Sour 106 (l.c.)
Egg 102
Fiesta Egg 102
Fruit:
Bing Cherry, Frozen 105
Champagne 103
Fruit Medley, Fresh 104
Party Pink 106
Orange-Cranberry Mold, Layered 105
Waldorf Salad 106
Green Beans 97
Hot Turkey 234
Macaroni, Dill 103
Potato, Country Kitchen 107
Potato-Fennel 107
Sea Food, Curried 99
Shrimp 98
Suggested seasonings 12
Tomato Aspic, Piquant 101 (l.c.)
Tuna and Tomato Mold 107
Tuna, Tarragon 99
Turkey Loaf, Buffet 98
Vegetable, Garden 100
Salmon:
Broiled Salmon Tarragon 171
with Dill 171
Loaf, Savory 180
Pie, Luncheon 199
Salt Sticks, Whole Wheat 264
Salted Spiced Walnuts 72
Saltimbocca 133
Sandwiches:
Herb-Broiled 200
Snappy Cheese-wiches 200
Special Turkey Sandwich on Waffles 232
Sangria Spiced 345
Sauce(s):
Barbecue:
Quick 'n' Easy 360
Spicy 372
Tropical 373
Béarnaise 374
Beurre Noir (brown butter) 362
Brown 366
Herbed Giblet 366
Onion 366
for Canard au Grand Marnier 158
Sauce(s) (*cont.*)
for Cannelloni 187
Caper 373
Truffle 373
Caviar, for Lobster and Shrimp 180
Chili Sauce 379
Cream, Tasty 363
Curry:
Butter 374
Creamy 369
Hot Exotic 362
Dessert and Pudding:
Chocolate, Creamy 363
Coconut Mace 361
Custard (Creme Anglaise) 375
Hard, Spiced 375
Hot Chocolate 359
Mint 364
Nutmeg 363
Nutmeg, Holiday 361
Pudding 363
Raspberry 370
Soufflé Grand Marnier 279
Suzette 277
Dill 370
Hollandaise 371
Italian Spaghetti 185
Lemon-Butter, Creamy 370
Mushroom 367
Mustard:
Creamy 365
Hot Chinese 368
Sour Cream 360
Sweet-Sour 372
Parsley-Almond 372
Parsley Cream 222
Piquant 368
Pizza 201
Raisin, Spiced 374
Red Cocktail 367
Rémoulade 368
Sherry, for Scallops and Mushrooms 169
Sour Cream Topping 368
Spaghetti 364
Italian 185
Pizza 364
Tartar 371
Teriyaki 371
Tomato 361
for Individual Chili Meatloaves 234
for Manicotti 233
Tomato, Zesty 119
White Sauce Supreme 360
Medium 360
Thick 360
Thin 360
(*See also* Butters)
Sauerbraten Nibblers 63
Sauerbraten with Potato Dumplings 121
Sauerbraten, Old-Fashioned 120
Sauerkraut Caraway 210 (l.c.)
Sausage:
Casserole, Lima-Sausage 191
Sausage (*cont.*)
Casserole, Sausage and Wild Rice 189
Manicotti 233
Stuffing 164
Sautéed Cabbage and Apples 216
Sautéed Chicken Livers 152
Rosé 152
Sautéed Frogs' Legs 173
Sautéed Mushrooms 216
Savory 39-40
Savory Burgers 249
Savory Fresh Ham 230
Savory Onion Rounds 65
Savory Salmon Loaf 180
Savory Stuffed Peppers 193
Savory Stuffing 163
Savory Turkey Croquettes 155
Scaloppine, Veal 135
Scalloped Potatoes with Cheese 207
Scallops:
and Mushrooms en Brochette 179 (l.c.)
and Mushrooms in Sherry Sauce 169
Suggested seasonings 10
Scampi on a Skewer 243 (l.c.)
Scotch Broth 93
Sea Food (*see* Fish and Sea Food)
Sea Food Crêpes 175
Season-All 40
Seeds, definition facing page 8
Sesame Burgers 249
Sesame Cheese Ball 68
Sesame Macaroons 332
Sesame Pastry 317
Sesame Pecan Pie 320
Sesame Pralines 337
Sesame Seed 40-41
Sesame Ring (Hot Roll) 257
Sesame Steaks 123
Sesame Stuffing 165
Sesame Toffee Bars 341
Sesame Wafers 339
Sesame Waffles 264
Shish Kebabs 245
Short Ribs, Oven Braised 122
Shrimp:
Creole 176
Gumbo, New Orleans 86
and Lobster with Sauce Caviar 180
Salad 98
Sautéed in Herb Butter 177
Scampi on a Skewer 243 (l.c.)
Spiced 78 (l.c.)
Oriental Spiced 78 (l.c.)
Spiced Shrimp Maison 78 (l.c.)
Suggested seasonings 10
Slow Cookers 226
Beef Stew 229
Chicken-Vegetable Soup 231
Chunky Chili 231
Crock Pot Beans 230
Pot Roast with Vegetables 230
Savory Fresh Ham 230

Smokey Chicken 145
Snappy Cheese-wiches 200
Sole Epicurean 173
Sole Meunière 172
(*See also* Fillet of Sole)
Soufflés: (see Eggs)
Soup(s) and Chowder(s):
Bouillabaisse 90
Brunswick Stew 186
Carrot Soup, Golden Cream of 91
Chicken Corn Soup 92
Chicken or Turkey Soup 85
Chicken-Vegetable 231
Clam Chowder, Manhattan 89
Clam Chowder, New England 90
Cold Cucumber 228
Consommé Royale 92
Corn Chowder 83
Curry Soup Indienne, Quick 85
Egg Drop Soup 91
Fruit Soup, Swedish 86
Gazpacho 227
Lentil Soup 84
Lobster Bisque Elégante 88
Minestrone 87
Mulligatawny 87
Onion Soup, French 84
Oyster Stew 84
Scotch Broth 93
Shrimp Gumbo, New Orleans 86
Spinach 83
Tomato Soup Oregano 85
Tomato-Vegetable Soup 91
Vegetable Soup, Old-Fashioned 92
Vichyssoise 89
Zucchini, Cream of 88
Sour Cream:
Cold Cucumber Soup 228
Dip for Fresh Fruit 63
Frosting 300
Pink Perfection Frosting 300
Mustard Sauce 360
Topping 368
South-of-the-Border Dressing 110
Southern Praline Cookies 330
Spaghetti Sauce 364
Pizza Sauce 364
Spaghetti with Superb Meat Sauce 197
Spanish Rice 196
Spareribs, Chinese Style 241
Spareribs, Indonesian 129
Special Appliance Cooking 226
Food Processors (*see* Food Processors)
Microwave Oven (*see* Microwave Oven)
Pottery-lined Slow Cookers (*see* Slow Cookers)
Toaster Ovens (*see* Toaster Ovens)
Spice Burgers 249
Spice Chiffon Cake 295
Spice-Fruit Ring (to chill punch) 346
Spice Muffins 265
Spiced Baked Ham Slice 128
Spiced Bavarian 284
Spiced Bread Pudding 275
Spiced Chestnut Stuffing 165
Spiced Coconut Chiffon Pie 312
Spiced Coffee Ice Cream 276
Spiced Cranberry Juice Cocktail 64
Spiced Cream Filling 278
Spiced Divinity 339
Spiced Graham Cracker Crust 319
Spiced Grape Punch 347
Spiced Hard Sauce 375
Spiced Jelly Roll 290
Spiced Mixed Nuts 330
Spiced Pickled Peaches 385
Spiced Raisin Sauce 374
Spiced Sangria 345
Spiced Shrimp 78 (l.c.)
Spiced Shrimp Maison 78 (l.c.)
Spiced Soufflé 279
Spiced Tea 349
Spiced Tongue 135
Spiced Whipped Cream Topping 301
Spices 1-46
Definition facing page 8
Guide to Creative Seasoning 9-12
Historical background 1-6
How to use 8-46
Seasoning of Foods 8
Spice Index
Use in restricted diets 45
(*See also* names of Spices)
Spicy Banana Nut Bread 265
Spicy Barbecue Sauce 372
Spicy Chocolate Frosting 302
Spicy Custard Pie 315
Spicy Lemon Angel Pie 313
Spicy Meringues 282
Spicy Oatmeal Cookies 334
Spicy Pastry 317
Spicy Peach Butter 391
Spinach:
Baked Eggs Florentine 185
Creamed 211
Soup 83
Suggested seasonings 11
Veal Orloff 115
Squash:
Apple Cider 217
Baked Acorn 217
Country-Good Baked 217
Steak(s):
Charcoal Grilled 247
Chuck, Grilled 250
Flank, Western Style 251
Herb 117
Minute, Herbed 118
Peppered 250
Sesame 123
Swiss 124
Tenderloin, Peppered 119
Teriyaki 239
Venison, Country Style 136
Steamed Date Pudding 278
Stewed Tomatoes with Oregano 210
Stew(s):
Beef 116, 229
Brunswick 186
Hungarian Goulash 118
Ragout of Lamb Rosemary 127
Oyster 84
Sticky Spice Buns 262
Strawberry:
Patch Pie 309
-Rhubarb Crisp 283
Romanoff 271
Streusel Topping 263
Stroganoff, Beef 116
Stroganoff, Corn and Pepper 215
Stuffed Breast of Veal 133
Stuffed Celery Sticks 79
Stuffed Eggs 202
Stuffed Peppers, Savory 193
Stuffed Pork Chops 129
Stuffed Roast Capon 153
Stuffing(s):
Bread, Basic 162
Chestnut 162
Herb 162
Oyster 162
Chestnut, Spiced 165
Corn Bread, Old South 163
Fruited Rice 143
Holiday 164
Mushroom-Rice 162
Quick 'n' Easy 161
Sausage 164
Savory 163
Sesame 165
for Veal Birds 132
Wild Rice 163
Substitutions of Ingredients 53-54
Sugared Nuts 339
Sugared Vanilla Wafers 332
Superb Scalloped Oysters 178
Surprise Cheese Puffs 74
Swedish Fruit Soup 86
Swedish Meat Balls 122
Sweetbreads (Ris de Veau à la Crème) 136
Sweet Cucumber Pickles 385
Sweet Potato(es):
Candied 218
and Apples 218
Pecan Pie 314
Pineapple Rings 218
Pineapple-Yam Kebabs 245
Pudding 216
Sweet-Sour Cucumbers with Onions 106 (l.c.)
Sweet-Sour Mustard Sauce 372
Sweet-Sour Pork 130
Sweet-Sour Red Cabbage 221
Swiss Steak 124

Tangy Butter 365
Tarragon 41-42
Tarragon Tuna Salad 99
Tartar Sauce 371
Tarts, Banbury 319
Tasty Cream Sauce 363
Tea:
Mint, Hawaiian 350

Tea (*cont.*)
Punch, Tea House 348
Spiced 349
Teriyaki Sauce 371
Texas Barbecued Beef 195
Thousand Island Pickles 386
Thyme 42
Tinted-Minted Pineapple 74
Toaster Ovens 226
Baked Stuffed Tomatoes 232
Herbed Garlic and Cheese Bread 231
Hot Bleu Cheese Canapés 233
Special Turkey Sandwich on Waffles 232
Tomato(es):
Aspic, Piquant 101 (l.c.)
Baked Stuffed 232
Chili Sauce 379
Gazpacho 227
Green:
Crystal Pickles 382
Grilled 248
Herb Broiled 220
Italian Spaghetti Sauce 185
Juice Cocktail 68 (l.c.)
Juice, Zippy 354 (l.c.)
Relish 381
Sauce 361
Sauce, Zesty 119
Soup, Oregano 85
Soup, Tomato-Vegetable 91
Stewed with Oregano 210
Suggested seasonings 10
Tuna and Tomato Mold 107
Tongue, Spiced 135
Toppings:
Batter Topping for Tuna Casserole 198
Broiled Spiced 302
Pecan 314
Sour Cream 368
Spiced Whipped Cream 301
Orange 301
Streusel 263
(*See also* Frosting)
Torte, Coffee 275
Traditional Wassail Bowl 354
Tropical Barbecue Sauce 373
Tropical Delight (fruit punch) 347
Trout with Seasoned Butter 234
Truffle Sauce 373
Truffled Chicken Breasts Elégante 154
Tuna (Fish):
Casserole with Batter Topping 198
Croquettes 179
Salad, Tarragon 99
and Tomato Mold 107
Turkey:
Creole 160
Croquettes, Savory 155
Curried Amandine 154
Hot Turkey Salad 234
Loaf, Buffet 98
Pot Pie 161
Pot Pie with Vegetables 141
Turkey (*cont.*)
Roast Supreme 160
Roasting Chart 53
Rolls Delicious 155
Soup 85
Special Turkey Sandwich on Waffles 232
Turmeric 42-43

Vanilla 43-44
Vanilla-Rum Frosting 335
Veal:
Birds 132
Breast of, Stuffed 133
Cutlets Viennese 132
Marinated Veal Steak 239
Marsala 115
Orloff 115
Osso Bucco (braised shanks) 134
Paprika 134
Parmigiana 131
Roasting Chart 53
Saltimbocca 133
Scaloppine 135
Wiener Schnitzel 135
and Wild Rice in Casserole 192
Vegetables:
Artichoke Hearts, Marinated 74
Asparagus:
Oriental 213
Parmesan 222
Bananas, Broiled 213
Beans(s):
Baked, Old-Fashioned 209
Barbecued Baked 209
Green, Bonfire 246
Camper's 246
Green with Dill 220
Green, Delectable 221
Lima Casserole 212
Beets, Harvard 219
Beet Surprise Salad 100
Broccoli:
Herb Seasoned 220 (l.c.)
Soufflé 214
Brussels Sprouts with Chestnuts 211
Cabbage:
and Apples, Sautéed 216
Red, Sweet-Sour 221
Rolls 190
Carrot(s):
Celery and Carrots in Parsley Cream 222
Ginger Glazed 208
Soup, Golden Cream of 91
Vichy 218 (l.c.)
Cauliflower with Creamy Cheese Sauce 208
Celery and Carrots in Parsley Cream 222
Celery Victor 79 (l.c.)
Chicken-Vegetable Soup 231
Corn (*see* Corn)
Cucumbers in Sour Cream 102
Cucumbers with Onions, Sweet-Sour 106 (l.c.)
Vegetables (*cont.*)
Eggplant:
Baked Stuffed 214
Florentine with Beef 188
Parmigiana 209
Green Beans:
Bonfire 246
Camper's 246
Delectable 221
with Dill 220 (l.c.)
with Water Chestnuts 207
Mushrooms, Marinated 78 (l.c.)
Mushrooms, Sautéed 216
Okra, Southern Style 211
Onion(s):
Creamed 219
Clove-Studded 213
Rounds Delicious 251
Peas, Italian Style 212
Peas, Minted 221
Peppers, Savory Stuffed 193
Potatoes (*see* Potatoes)
Salad, Garden Vegetable 100
Sauerkraut Caraway 210 (l.c.)
Soup, Old-Fashioned 92
Spinach, Creamed 211
Squash:
Apple Cider 217
Baked Acorn 217
Country-Good Baked 217
Suggested seasonings 10-11
Sweet Potatoes, Candied 218
and Apples 218
Sweet Potato Pudding 216
Sweet Potatoes-Pineapple Rings 218
Tomato-Vegetable Soup 91
(*See also* Tomatoes)
Turkey Pot Pie with 141
Vegetable Kebabs 248
Zucchini Parmesan 207
Zucchini Sauté 212
Zucchini Soup, Cream of 88
Velvety Pumpkin Chiffon Pie 318
Venison Steak, Country Style 136
Vichyssoise 89
Viennese Noodles au Gratin 198

Waffles and Pancakes:
Blueberry Pancakes 268
Cannelloni (Pancakes for) 187
Dessert Waffles, Ginger 281
Extra-Special Waffles 227
Fun with Waffles 264
Herb 264
Mace 264
Sage 264
Sesame 264
Special Turkey Sandwich on Waffles 232
Suggested seasoning 12
Waldorf Salad 106
Walnuts:
Salted Spiced 72
Spiced Mixed Nuts 330
Wassail Bowl:
Cranberry 348
Traditional 354

Water Chestnuts with Green Beans 207
Watermelon Pickles 386
Welsh Pork Cake 298
Welsh Rabbit 203
Wheat Pilaf 195
Whipped Cream:
  Flavorful 273
  Spiced Whipped Cream Topping 301
  Orange 301
Whipped Lemon Butter 369
Whipped Maple-Cinnamon Butter 369
White Sauce Supreme 360
Whole Wheat Rolls 256
Whole Wheat Salt Sticks 264
Wiener Schnitzel 135
Wild Rice Stuffing 163
Wine:
  Glögg 348
  Mulled 352
Wine (*cont.*)
  Spiced Sangria 345
Wonderful Apple Pie 309
Yams (*see* Sweet Potatoes)
Zesty Stuffed Frankfurters 137
Zippy Tomato Juice 354 (l.c.)
Zucchini:
  Parmesan 207
  Sauté 212
  Soup, Cream of 88

Notes

Notes

Notes

Notes

Notes